Public Policy's Role in Achieving Sustainable Development Goals

Mahani Hamdan
Universiti Brunei Darussalam, Brunei

Muhammad Anshari
Universiti Brunei Darussalam, Brunei

Norainie Ahmad
Universiti Brunei Darussalam, Brunei

Emil Ali
Universiti Brunei Darussalam, Brunei

A volume in the Advances in Public Policy and Administration (APPA) Book Series

IGI Global
PUBLISHER of TIMELY KNOWLEDGE

Published in the United States of America by
IGI Global
Information Science Reference (an imprint of IGI Global)
701 E. Chocolate Avenue
Hershey PA, USA 17033
Tel: 717-533-8845
Fax: 717-533-8661
E-mail: cust@igi-global.com
Web site: http://www.igi-global.com

Library of Congress Cataloging-in-Publication Data

Names: Hamdan, Mahani, 1979- editor. | Anshari, Muhammad, 1977- editor. | Ahmad, Norainie, 1980- editor. | Ali, Emil, 1983- editor.
Title: Public policy's role in achieving sustainable development goals / edited by: Mahani Hamdan, Muhammad Anshari, Norainie Ahmad, and Emil Ali.
Description: Hershey PA : Information Science Reference, [2023] | Includes bibliographical references. | Summary: "Public Policy's Role in Achieving Sustainable Development Goals is authored by various esteemed researchers, policymakers, and academics from a multidisciplinary perspective and emphasizes quality research-based studies that contribute to theory, lessons learned, best practices, critical understanding, and policy implications or formulation on the Sustainable Development Goals (SDGs) in any country. It supports the acceleration required to implement the SDGs by mobilizing the academic community, policymakers, industry, and civil society to discuss experiences focusing on the SDGs and their implementation in the context of public policy, administration, and governance deemed most important for world regions"-- Provided by publisher.
Identifiers: LCCN 2023021225 (print) | LCCN 2023021226 (ebook) | ISBN 9781668489031 (hardcover) | ISBN 9781668489079 (paperback) | ISBN 9781668489048 (ebook)
Subjects: LCSH: Sustainable development--Government policy. | Sustainable Development Goals.
Classification: LCC HC79.E5 P834 2023 (print) | LCC HC79.E5 (ebook) | DDC 338.9/27--dc23/eng/20230602
LC record available at https://lccn.loc.gov/2023021225
LC ebook record available at https://lccn.loc.gov/2023021226

This book is published in the IGI Global book series Advances in Public Policy and Administration (APPA) (ISSN: 2475-6644; eISSN: 2475-6652)

British Cataloguing in Publication Data
A Cataloguing in Publication record for this book is available from the British Library.

For electronic access to this publication, please contact: eresources@igi-global.com.

Advances in Public Policy and Administration (APPA) Book Series

ISSN:2475-6644
EISSN:2475-6652

Mission

Proper management of the public sphere is necessary in order to maintain order in modern society. Research developments in the field of public policy and administration can assist in uncovering the latest tools, practices, and methodologies for governing societies around the world.

The **Advances in Public Policy and Administration (APPA) Book Series** aims to publish scholarly publications focused on topics pertaining to the governance of the public domain. APPA's focus on timely topics relating to government, public funding, politics, public safety, policy, and law enforcement is particularly relevant to academicians, government officials, and upper-level students seeking the most up-to-date research in their field.

Coverage

- Government
- Law Enforcement
- Political Economy
- Politics
- Public Administration
- Public Funding
- Public Policy
- Resource Allocation
- Urban Planning

IGI Global is currently accepting manuscripts for publication within this series. To submit a proposal for a volume in this series, please contact our Acquisition Editors at Acquisitions@igi-global.com or visit: http://www.igi-global.com/publish/.

The Advances in Public Policy and Administration (APPA) Book Series (ISSN 2475-6644) is published by IGI Global, 701 E. Chocolate Avenue, Hershey, PA 17033-1240, USA, www.igi-global.com. This series is composed of titles available for purchase individually; each title is edited to be contextually exclusive from any other title within the series. For pricing and ordering information please visit http://www.igi-global.com/book-series/advances-public-policy-administration/97862. Postmaster: Send all address changes to above address.

Titles in this Series

For a list of additional titles in this series, please visit: www.igi-global.com/book-series/advances-public-policy-administration/97862

Global Perspectives on the Emerging Trends in Public Diplomacy
Samet Kavoğlu (Marmara University, Turkey) and Ergün Köksoy (Marmara University, Turkey)
Information Science Reference • © 2023 • 282pp • H/C (ISBN: 9781668491614) • US $240.00

Insights and Explorations in Democracy, Political Unrest, and Propaganda in Elections
Opeyemi Idowu Aluko (Ajayi Crowther University, Nigeria) and Lalekan Bolu Oluwadele (Walden University, USA)
Information Science Reference • © 2023 • 377pp • H/C (ISBN: 9781668486290) • US $215.00

Historical and Political Analysis on Power Balances and Deglobalization
Emily Brynn Stacey (Rose State College, USA)
Information Science Reference • © 2023 • 300pp • H/C (ISBN: 9781668456330) • US $205.00

Integrating Principles of Success in Planning Denial and Deception Missions
Eugenie de Silva (Booz Allen Hamilton, USA)
Information Science Reference • © 2024 • 330pp • H/C (ISBN: 9781668468401) • US $215.00

Governmental Power Market-Ing in the VU-CHAOS World
Kittisak Jermsittiparsert (University of City Island, Cyprus) Srirath Gohwong (Universitas Muhammadiyah Sidenreng Rappang, Indonesia) Shayut Pavapanunkul (Universitas Muhammadiyah Sidenreng Rappang, Indonesia) and Nasaran Mahittichatkul (Universitas Muhammadiyah Sidenreng Rappang, Indonesia)
Information Science Reference • © 2024 • 360pp • H/C (ISBN: 9781668472804) • US $205.00

Reimagining Systems Thinking in a Post-Pandemic World
M. Elizabeth Azukas (East Stroudsburg University of Pennsylvania, USA) and Minkyoung Kim (University of West Florida, USA)
Information Science Reference • © 2023 • 325pp • H/C (ISBN: 9781668472859) • US $215.00

Taking on Climate Change Through Green Taxation
Ana Arromba Dinis (Research Centre on Accounting and Taxation, Polytechnic Institute of Cávado and Ave, Portugal) Fátima David (Research Centre on Accounting and Taxation, Polytechnic Institute of Cávado and Ave, Portugal) Liliana Pereira (Research Centre on Accounting and Taxation, Polytechnic Institute of Cávado and Ave, Portugal) and Sara Luís Dias (Polytechnic Institute of Cávado and Ave, Portugal)
Information Science Reference • © 2023 • 320pp • H/C (ISBN: 9781668485927) • US $215.00

IGI Global
PUBLISHER of TIMELY KNOWLEDGE

701 East Chocolate Avenue, Hershey, PA 17033, USA
Tel: 717-533-8845 x100 • Fax: 717-533-8661
E-Mail: cust@igi-global.com • www.igi-global.com

Table of Contents

Detailed Table of Contents

As sites of economic, political, and social convergence, cities absorb the earliest effects of global crises. These dynamics are observable also in environmental crises and resilience – longer-running challenges to legacy models of urban governance. Shifting epistemic and practical contexts invite scholarship to more thoroughly examine the dynamics of urban policy with regard to the 'localization' of the Sustainable Development Goals (SDGs) and the contribution of city governments to global environmental policy. This chapter examines urban sustainability as an ontologically complex or 'wicked' policy problem, a framing concept with a history in the urban planning and policy literatures but deserving fresh revisitation. The argument is that a 'complexity science' approach that avoids narrative capture is needed to better understand global environmental crisis and its manifestation in cities. This approach seeks to challenge the predominance of linear, atomistic, and reductionist perspectives that remain embedded in policy thinking.

Non-profits and NGOs serve communities through programs, which are often complex to execute. Board members demand accountability for the execution of such programs, and as a result, these organizations adopt monitoring and evaluation practices to determine the success of failure based on a set of performance criteria. This study focuses on defining the program monitoring and evaluation process and exploring in depth its benefits, functions, and stages. Moreover, an examination of the stakeholders involved in the process is performed, and a set of currencies and power and influence criteria are explored.

Is EU law conducive to successful implementation of SDG 15? This chapter assesses the effectiveness of the legal representation of sustainability in EU biodiversity law and the foundation it establishes for ensuring biodiversity protection. It identifies the policy anchors that foster the human self-entitlement and the various forms of interest involved in the legal representation of the principle of sustainable development, and which impede the effectiveness of EU law intended to protect biodiversity. Advocacy is made to review the accurate transposition of the Brundtland report into legal principles and to incorporate the newly acknowledged human right to a clean environment in EU law, as a footing to facilitate effective biodiversity protection.

This chapter analyzes China's Belt and Road Initiative (BRI) and its potential to help accomplish the Sustainable Development Goals (SDGs) set by the United Nations. It examines how the BRI has affected public policy, international collaboration, and the Sustainable Development Goals. This chapter provides a comprehensive analysis of BRI's plans and projects, as well as their compatibility with the 17 SDGs. This chapter examines the development of China's public policy, the lessons learned, and the potential barriers to achieving the SDGs. Finally, it provides policy recommendations, stressing the significance of grasping the nexus between government action, international initiatives, and long-term sustainability.

Public policy scholars have warned that the conventional public policy (CPP) framework is not effective enough to address the post-pandemic problems as it has blatantly failed the litmus test of time. The CPP framework has been criticised on various grounds and blamed for the problems of unsustainability and overarching poverty that plague humanity. The objective of this chapter is to explain a quadric public policy framework (PPI) that has recently been proposed as an efficient alternative public policy framework. The explanation is limited to only one out of the four components of the framework, called the Maqasid al-Shariah component, also known as public interest theory. The findings show that the PPI framework can link policymakers from different sectors and provide a platform for a whole-of-government approach to achieving the SDGs, especially poverty alleviation and eradication.

Brunei Darussalam is committed to the Sustainable Development Goals. This study focuses on future sustainability of Kampong Ayer, largely a settlement as a consequence of land-based development. Many that remain are in the low-income group due to the lack of economic opportunities. They have become dependent on government welfare programmes. The cost of frequent home repairs due to environmental factors has become a burden in the modern world. Although the people have a close relationship with the estuary, and are highly adaptive, climate change is a slow and imperceptible process and will therefore catch the people off-guard. This study argues that intervention is needed. A policy based on SDGs 1, 11, and 13 would be most appropriate, as they address the most pressing issues in KA: poverty, sustainable cities and communities, and climate adaption.

The purpose of this chapter is to discuss the implications of the 2023 fuel subsidy removal in Nigeria. Using the discourse analysis methodology, the authors offer some insight into the macroeconomic and microeconomic implications of the 2023 fuel subsidy removal in Nigeria. The positive implications are that fuel subsidy removal would free up financial resources for other sectors of the economy, incentivize domestic refineries to produce more petroleum products, reduce Nigeria's dependence on imported fuel, increase employment, channel funds for the development of critical public infrastructure, reduce the budget deficit and generate a budget surplus in the near future, reduce government borrowing, curb corruption associated with fuel subsidy payments, increase competition, reinvigorate domestic refineries, and reduce pressure on the exchange rate.

The welfare of a country is related to how equitably its national income is distributed, rather than its wealth. The increase in income inequalities between individuals or social classes causes the deterioration of social peace and stability and a slowdown in economic development and growth. In this study, the effect of more than one socio-economic factor on income inequalities was examined in 35 developing countries. The 2019 data compiled for the selected countries were analyzed with the ARAS method. From the findings of the ARAS method, which was carried out using the aforementioned weighting method, it was determined that the countries with the best performance in terms of income justice were Chechia, Estonia, Slovakia, Thailand, and Hungary. The results of the analysis showed that Colombia, Brazil, Mexico, Bolivia, and Bangladesh were the countries with the highest income inequality. The ARAS findings used in the study are theoretically and expectedly satisfactory.

The development banks (DBs) contribute to a broader aspect of the financial system, rather than private banks that serve more specific areas in retail, wholesale, and investment needs. In this chapter, the author discusses how DBs work to support the implementation of the United Nations Sustainable Development Goals (SDGs) by providing financing for sustainable infrastructure, renewable energy, climate change

ill-effects of corruption. Moreover, effective and engaged civil society is key to the realization of the United Nations 2030 Agenda for sustainable development SDGs. The conclusions drawn from this chapter will generate valuable insights into the issues of anti-corruption and civil society involvement in sustainable development in Algeria and other countries of similar social and cultural settings. Also, the chapter attempts to draw the attention of researchers, policy-makers, and anti-corruption professionals to the significant role of civil society in the collective efforts of combating corruption and strengthening institutional accountability in the country.

Preface

As editors of this esteemed reference book, it is with great pleasure that we present *Public Policy's Role in Achieving Sustainable Development Goals*. In 2015, the United Nations launched a monumental initiative, comprising 17 global Sustainable Development Goals (SDGs), aimed at eradicating poverty, safeguarding the environment, and fostering prosperity for all. The SDGs represent a shared commitment to creating a more equitable and sustainable world, and their achievement relies on the collective efforts of academia, policymakers, industry leaders, and civil society.

With a multidisciplinary perspective, this edited book brings together a diverse group of researchers, policymakers, and academics to shed light on the crucial role of public policy in advancing the SDGs. We seek to provide a platform for quality research-based studies that contribute not only to theoretical understanding but also to practical lessons, best practices, and policy implications surrounding the SDGs in various countries.

We are proud to present a collection of chapters that cover a wide array of topics, including government strategies supporting SDG implementation, global and regional policy directions for promoting health and well-being, the interplay between digital government, industry, and innovation in the context of SDGs, and the challenges and best practices for integrating SDGs into policy formulation and implementation.

Furthermore, the book delves into specific regions, exploring the implementation of SDGs in the Asia Pacific, European, American, and Africa and Middle East regions, while recognizing the unique contexts and nuances that characterize each area. By addressing the SDGs through a regional lens, we hope to foster a more nuanced and comprehensive understanding of the challenges and opportunities for sustainable development across the globe.

The target audience for this book is vast, encompassing academia and researchers from various fields, including social sciences, arts and humanities, sociology, politics, business, and economics. Additionally, we envision this volume becoming an indispensable resource for policymakers, corporations, NGOs, research centers, think tanks, and university libraries worldwide seeking credible references on SDG implementation, particularly within the realms of policy and administration.

We extend our heartfelt gratitude to all the contributors who have made this endeavor possible. Their dedication to advancing knowledge and their invaluable insights have enriched the contents of this book, making it a comprehensive and authoritative resource on the critical role of public policy in achieving the SDGs.

Lastly, we express our sincere appreciation to the publisher for their support throughout the editorial process. The rigorous refereeing and editorial standards employed in shaping this book have ensured its academic rigor and relevance.

We hope that *Public Policy's Role in Achieving Sustainable Development Goals* will inspire and empower readers to actively contribute to global efforts toward a sustainable and prosperous future. May the knowledge shared within these pages serve as a catalyst for positive change and meaningful action.

CHAPTER OVERVIEW

Chapter 1: Complexity and Uncertainty in Late-Stage Technocracy: The Case of Urban Sustainability

In this thought-provoking chapter, Kris Hartley from City University of Hong Kong and Ola G. Ek-Taliwai from the University of Twente delve into the intricate dynamics of urban sustainability within the context of global crises. They emphasize that cities often serve as the first line of defense in absorbing the impacts of economic, political, and social disruptions, including environmental crises and resilience challenges.

The authors contend that urban sustainability presents itself as a complex and 'wicked' policy problem, demanding fresh examination despite its history in the urban planning and policy literature. To shed light on the 'localization' of the Sustainable Development Goals (SDGs) and the role of city governments in shaping global environmental policy, they advocate for an innovative 'complexity science' approach.

This approach strives to break away from linear, atomistic, and reductionist perspectives that have long influenced policy thinking. By avoiding narrative capture, the authors seek to provide a more comprehensive understanding of the global environmental crisis and how it manifests in cities. This chapter calls for a paradigm shift in the way we approach urban sustainability, emphasizing the importance of embracing complexity and uncertainty as we tackle the challenges that lie ahead.

Chapter 2: Program Monitoring and Evaluation of Sustainable Development Goals for Non-Profits and NGOs: Benefits, Functions, Stages, and Stakeholders

Authored by Simon Cleveland from Purdue University Global and Marisa Cleveland from Northeastern University, this chapter delves into the vital role of non-profit organizations and NGOs in serving communities through complex programs. As these organizations strive to execute their programs effectively, they face increasing demands for accountability from their board members.

To address this need for accountability and to gauge the success of their initiatives, non-profits and NGOs adopt monitoring and evaluation practices. The chapter focuses on defining the program monitoring and evaluation process, shedding light on its various benefits, functions, and stages. This comprehensive exploration aims to equip practitioners with the knowledge and tools needed to assess program success based on a set of performance criteria.

Moreover, the authors undertake an examination of the diverse stakeholders involved in the monitoring and evaluation process. Understanding the perspectives, interests, and influence of these stakeholders becomes crucial in shaping effective program evaluation strategies. To this end, the chapter explores a range of currencies, power dynamics, and influence criteria that play a pivotal role in the monitoring and evaluation landscape.

By providing insights into the program monitoring and evaluation practices employed by non-profits and NGOs, this chapter contributes to the broader understanding of how these organizations can align their efforts with the Sustainable Development Goals (SDGs) more effectively. The information presented in this chapter serves as a valuable resource for organizations seeking to improve their impact, enhance accountability, and better serve the communities they aim to assist.

Chapter 3: Is EU Law Conducive to the SDG 15? Interests Reflected in the Legal Representation of the Sustainability Principle in the EU

Authored by Antje Ilberg, an independent researcher from Germany, this chapter critically examines the alignment of EU law with the successful implementation of SDG 15, which focuses on biodiversity conservation. The chapter seeks to evaluate the effectiveness of legal representations of sustainability within EU biodiversity law and their potential to ensure the protection of biodiversity.

Through a thorough analysis, the chapter identifies the policy anchors that shape human self-entitlement and explores the diverse forms of interest that influence the legal representation of the principle of sustainable development. These interests, in turn, may hinder the full effectiveness of EU law in safeguarding biodiversity. By shedding light on these complexities, the chapter highlights the need for careful consideration and introspection in EU policy-making to ensure that sustainable development goals are adequately integrated and prioritized.

The author advocates for a review of the accurate transposition of the Brundtland report into legal principles. The Brundtland report, also known as "Our Common Future," played a seminal role in shaping the concept of sustainable development. By reassessing how this report's principles have been translated into legal frameworks, the chapter seeks to strengthen the foundation for biodiversity protection within the EU.

Furthermore, the chapter emphasizes the importance of incorporating the newly acknowledged human right to a clean environment into EU law. Recognizing this right can serve as a crucial footing to facilitate more effective biodiversity protection, empowering individuals and communities to engage in environmental preservation.

By examining the interplay between EU law, sustainability principles, and biodiversity protection, this chapter provides valuable insights into the challenges and opportunities in achieving SDG 15 within the European context. It calls for a comprehensive and thoughtful approach to policymaking, aiming to foster a legal framework that truly supports biodiversity conservation and sustainable development in the region.

Chapter 4: China's Belt and Road Initiative (BRI) and Its Implications for Sustainable Development Goals: A Public Policy Perspective

In this illuminating chapter, Mohamad Zreik, a scholar from Sun Yat-sen University in China, conducts a comprehensive analysis of China's Belt and Road Initiative (BRI) and its potential impact on achieving the Sustainable Development Goals (SDGs) established by the United Nations. With a focus on public policy, international collaboration, and sustainable development, this chapter sheds light on the intricate relationship between the BRI and the SDGs.

The author meticulously examines the extensive plans and projects encompassed within the Belt and Road Initiative, exploring their alignment with the 17 SDGs. By doing so, the chapter aims to unveil the opportunities and challenges presented by the BRI in contributing to sustainable development on a global scale.

Furthermore, the chapter delves into the development of China's public policy, drawing valuable lessons from the implementation of the BRI and its implications for sustainable development. The author emphasizes the significance of understanding the complex interplay between government action, international initiatives, and long-term sustainability, recognizing that the success of the BRI in supporting the SDGs hinges on effective public policy measures.

By critically analyzing the BRI's compatibility with the SDGs, the chapter highlights potential barriers that might hinder the achievement of sustainable development goals in the context of this ambitious initiative. With a keen eye on policy recommendations, the chapter offers insights into how governments and stakeholders can capitalize on the BRI's potential to foster sustainable development effectively.

As the Belt and Road Initiative continues to shape the global landscape, this chapter serves as an essential resource for policymakers, researchers, and practitioners seeking a deeper understanding of the initiative's implications for achieving the SDGs. By providing a public policy perspective on this complex undertaking, the chapter contributes valuable knowledge to the ongoing discourse on sustainable development and international collaboration.

Chapter 5: Application of Maqasid al-Shariah-based Public Policy Framework in SDGs Policies: Poverty Eradication (SDG 1) As a Case Study

Authored by Ahmad Labeeb Tajudeen from the Islamic University of Minnesota, Brunei Darussalam, and Manzoor Apenna Lawal from Sikiru Adetona College of Education, Science, and Technology, Nigeria, this chapter introduces an innovative quadric public policy framework (PPI-TMSI) proposed as an efficient alternative to the conventional public policy framework (CPP). The authors argue that the CPP has proven inadequate in addressing post-pandemic problems and has been unsuccessful in combating persistent poverty and promoting sustainability.

In this chapter, the authors focus on one key component of the quadric public policy framework, namely the Maqasid al-Shariah component, which is also known as the Theory of public interest. Maqasid al-Shariah is a fundamental concept in Islamic jurisprudence, emphasizing the overarching objectives and principles that underpin Islamic law. The authors elucidate on how this component can serve as a powerful tool in public policy, particularly in achieving the Sustainable Development Goals (SDGs), with a specific focus on poverty eradication (SDG 1).

The framework's application demonstrates its ability to link different sectors and foster a whole-of-government approach in realizing the SDGs, particularly in the context of poverty eradication. By aligning policy decisions with the core principles of Maqasid al-Shariah, this framework aims to promote a more sustainable and equitable approach to public policy, transcending conventional paradigms.

The chapter presents the Maqasid al-Shariah-based public policy framework as a promising alternative that holds the potential to address the challenges posed by the CPP. As the world seeks effective solutions to complex problems, this chapter offers valuable insights into how an Islamic perspective can contribute to more inclusive and sustainable public policy practices, particularly in the pursuit of poverty eradication and other SDGs.

Chapter 6: Climate Change and Sustainable Development of Kampong Ayer: Its History, People, and Environment

Authored by Noor Hasharina Pg Hj Hassan and Gabriel Y. V. Yong from Universiti Brunei Darussalam, this chapter delves into the critical issue of sustainable development in Kampong Ayer, a historic water village settlement in Brunei Darussalam. As a nation committed to the Sustainable Development Goals (SDGs), Brunei aims to address the challenges faced by Kampong Ayer in the context of climate change and evolving socio-economic factors.

The chapter provides a comprehensive examination of Kampong Ayer's historical development and the impact of land-based development, which has shaped the settlement's present condition. As a result, many residents find themselves in the low-income group due to limited economic opportunities, leading to a dependence on government welfare programs.

The study highlights the growing burden of frequent home repairs due to environmental factors in the modern world, posing significant challenges to the community's well-being and sustainability. While the people of Kampong Ayer have a close relationship with the estuary and demonstrate high adaptability, the slow and imperceptible process of climate change threatens to catch them off-guard.

The authors advocate for intervention to address these pressing issues. They propose a policy approach based on the principles of SDG 1 (No Poverty), SDG 11 (Sustainable Cities and Communities), and SDG 13 (Climate Action). These goals are seen as particularly relevant in the context of Kampong Ayer, as they target poverty alleviation, the creation of sustainable communities, and climate adaptation, which are critical for the village's future sustainability.

By shedding light on the specific challenges faced by Kampong Ayer and proposing targeted policy recommendations, this chapter contributes valuable insights to the broader discussion on sustainable development in the face of climate change. It emphasizes the importance of integrating the SDGs into local policy frameworks and calls for collective efforts to secure a sustainable and resilient future for Kampong Ayer and its people.

Chapter 7: Implications of Fuel Subsidy Removal on the Nigerian Economy

Authored by Peterson K. Ozili and Kingsley Obiora from the Central Bank of Nigeria, this paper delves into a critical policy decision in Nigeria—the 2023 fuel subsidy removal—and its implications on the economy. Using discourse analysis as the methodology, the authors present a comprehensive assessment of the macroeconomic and microeconomic consequences of this significant policy change.

The paper highlights the positive implications of fuel subsidy removal, emphasizing how it can free up financial resources that were previously allocated to subsidies for other vital sectors of the economy. This reallocation of funds can serve as an incentive for domestic refineries to increase their production of petroleum products, ultimately reducing Nigeria's reliance on imported fuel and promoting self-sufficiency.

Furthermore, the authors argue that the removal of fuel subsidies can have far-reaching effects on employment, generating opportunities for job creation and promoting economic growth. The freed-up funds can also be directed towards the development of critical public infrastructure, addressing long-standing deficits in the country's infrastructure.

From a fiscal perspective, the removal of fuel subsidies has the potential to reduce the budget deficit and even generate a budget surplus in the near future. This surplus can be instrumental in reducing government borrowing, alleviating fiscal pressures, and fostering sustainable economic growth.

In addition to the financial benefits, the paper highlights the positive impact on curbing corruption associated with fuel subsidy payments. By eliminating this avenue for potential graft, the government can improve transparency and enhance public trust.

Moreover, the removal of fuel subsidies is expected to stimulate competition in the petroleum sector, revitalizing domestic refineries, and encouraging innovation in the industry.

Finally, the paper notes that the fuel subsidy removal can potentially reduce pressure on the exchange rate, contributing to a more stable economic environment.

In conclusion, this chapter offers valuable insights into the implications of fuel subsidy removal on the Nigerian economy. By critically examining the potential benefits, the authors provide important considerations for policymakers as they navigate this significant policy change and its potential impact on Nigeria's economic trajectory.

Chapter 8: Income Inequalities in Developing Countries: A Performance Analysis

Authored by Betül İnam from Bilecik Seyh Edebali University and Dilek Murat from Bursa Uludag University in Turkey, this study examines the crucial relationship between income distribution and a country's welfare in the context of developing countries. The authors highlight that equitable distribution of national income, rather than overall wealth, plays a significant role in fostering social peace, stability, and sustainable economic development and growth.

The study focuses on income inequalities in thirty-five developing countries and analyzes the impact of multiple socio-economic factors on these disparities. The researchers utilized the ARAS method, which involves analyzing 2019 data compiled for the selected countries to assess their performance in terms of income justice.

The findings derived from the ARAS method, employing the aforementioned weighting technique, revealed the countries with the best performance in terms of income justice, including Chechia, Estonia, Slovakia, Thailand, and Hungary. These nations demonstrated more equitable income distribution, which can contribute to greater social cohesion and economic progress.

Conversely, the analysis identified Colombia, Brazil, Mexico, Bolivia, and Bangladesh as countries with the highest income inequality. High levels of income disparities in these nations may lead to social tensions and hinder economic advancement.

The ARAS method used in this study is considered theoretically and practically satisfactory in evaluating income inequalities in the selected developing countries. By shedding light on the countries with both better and worse income distribution performance, this chapter provides valuable insights for policymakers and researchers seeking to address income inequality challenges in the developing world.

Through the lens of performance analysis, this chapter underscores the significance of promoting income justice as a critical component of sustainable development and inclusive growth in developing countries. The findings of this study contribute to the broader understanding of income inequalities and can serve as a foundation for designing policies aimed at fostering more equitable and prosperous societies.

Chapter 9: The Role of Development Banks in Green Finance and Sustainability

Authored by Hazik Mohamed from Stellar Consulting Group in Singapore, this paper delves into the pivotal role of development banks (DBs) in advancing sustainability and supporting the implementation of the United Nations Sustainable Development Goals (SDGs). Unlike private banks that primarily focus on specific financial services, development banks contribute to a broader aspect of the financial system, providing financing for sustainable infrastructure, renewable energy, climate change adaptation and mitigation, and biodiversity conservation.

The chapter highlights how development banks play a critical role in supporting sustainable economic development across the world, with a particular emphasis on advanced and developed economies, which often bear significant responsibility as major polluters. By investing in green and sustainable finance initiatives, these banks contribute significantly to achieving public policy objectives related to environmental conservation and sustainability.

The paper discusses the essential functions of development banks in promoting sustainability, including their role in providing financing for projects and initiatives that align with the SDGs. They help countries build resilience against the impacts of climate change and environmental degradation, fostering a more sustainable and climate-conscious approach to development.

Throughout the chapter, the authors underscore the importance of supporting sustainable economic development, particularly in light of the urgent need to address environmental challenges and reduce global carbon emissions. By channeling resources towards green and sustainable projects, development banks play a key role in the global effort to combat climate change and protect natural resources.

The chapter concludes with thoughtful reflections on existing regulations, programs, and incentives that support sustainable finance initiatives and calls for further recommendations to strengthen and expand the impact of development banks in shaping a more sustainable future.

In summary, this chapter sheds light on the indispensable role of development banks in advancing sustainability and supporting the implementation of the SDGs. By leveraging their financial resources and expertise, development banks become crucial actors in driving green finance and contributing to a more sustainable and resilient global economy.

Chapter 10: Constructing an Integrated Sustainable Halal Policy (ISHP) in Brunei Darussalam: Refiguring the Domains of Conventional Policy Multiverses

Authored by Izni Azrein Noor Azalie from Universiti Brunei Darussalam, this chapter takes a novel approach in reevaluating the domains of public, industrial, and economic policies and proposes a new integrated and synchronized framework. The chapter draws on the experiences of the Brunei halal industry as a case study, aiming to break down silos and explore how these three domains can work together more effectively.

The timing of this chapter is especially pertinent as Brunei aims to diversify its economy and achieve its development goals outlined in the Brunei Vision 2035. The food industry is one of the key sectors targeted for development, aligning with the principles of the Sustainable Development Goals (SDGs). By examining the experiences of Brunei's food industry players, the chapter emphasizes the importance of integrating the principles of Islamic Governance into the development of an Integrated Sustainable Halal Policy (ISHP).

The proposed ISHP framework holds significant promise in addressing multiple SDGs, including poverty alleviation (SDG 1), the development of sustainable cities and communities (SDG 8), and promoting responsible production and consumption (SDG 12). Furthermore, it supports the promotion of decent work and economic growth (SDG 11). By connecting these goals within an integrated halal policy, the chapter showcases the potential for a holistic and synergetic approach to sustainable development.

The chapter highlights the interdependence of policies and their impact on different aspects of sustainable development. It also underlines the relevance of Islamic principles in shaping policy frameworks that consider both economic and societal dimensions.

In conclusion, this chapter offers a thought-provoking exploration of how an Integrated Sustainable Halal Policy can contribute to achieving multiple SDGs and foster sustainable economic and social development. By providing valuable insights into the Brunei halal industry's experiences, the chapter offers inspiration and guidance for policymakers seeking to build more integrated and effective policy frameworks for sustainable development.

Chapter 11: Education Reform to Attain SDG4: A Broad Overview

Authored by Hamizah Haidi and Jainatul Halida Jaidin from Universiti Brunei Darussalam, this paper delves into Brunei's efforts to achieve the fourth United Nations Sustainable Development Goal (SDG4), which focuses on providing inclusive, equitable, and high-quality education for all. The chapter sheds light on the policies and strategies implemented by Brunei to accomplish SDG4 targets, offering a thematic analysis of educational policies and their alignment with all SDG4 targets.

The study's findings indicate that Brunei has made substantial progress in providing high-quality education, demonstrating steady strides toward achieving SDG4. Despite the challenges posed by the Covid-19 outbreak, Brunei's commitment to equitable access to education is evident, as the country implemented policies to ensure inclusivity and continuity during the pandemic.

The authors highlight the significance of high-quality education as the foundation of sustainable development and better living conditions. By systematically examining the policies in place and mapping them to SDG4 targets, the chapter provides valuable insights into Brunei's approach to education reform.

Furthermore, the chapter emphasizes the Ministry of Education's ongoing initiatives and partnerships to methodically and comprehensively meet SDG4 targets by 2030. The collaborative efforts of policymakers and educational stakeholders play a crucial role in identifying and implementing policies that can effectively close gaps and address challenges in attaining SDG4.

In conclusion, this chapter contributes a comprehensive overview of Brunei's education reform journey and its progress toward SDG4. It highlights the importance of high-quality education in driving sustainable development and underscores the need for continued commitment and collaboration to achieve education-related targets by 2030.

By examining Brunei's experiences and approaches to education reform, this paper provides valuable insights that can inform policymakers worldwide in their pursuit of achieving SDG4 and ensuring inclusive, equitable, and quality education for all.

Chapter 12: Equity and Excellence in Education: SDG 4 of the 2030 Agenda in the Italian Context - Public Education Policies and Their Impact

Authored by Valerio Ferrero from the University of Torino, Italy, this chapter delves into the policy commitment outlined in the 2030 Agenda concerning the crucial role of schooling in promoting social justice and equity as essential aspects of educational action. The chapter embarks on a reflective journey through three key steps, aimed at understanding and enhancing the pursuit of equity and excellence in education:

1. Theoretical-Conceptual Framework on Social Justice and Equity: The chapter constructs a theoretical and conceptual framework, exploring the concepts of social justice and equity, with an emphasis on classical and non-traditional factors contributing to inequality in education.
2. Analysis of Equity in the 2030 Agenda: The chapter analyzes the idea of equity as promoted by the 2030 Agenda, particularly focusing on Goal 4, which aims to ensure inclusive and quality education. The relationship of Goal 4 with Goals 5 (Gender Equality), 10 (Reduced Inequalities), and 16 (Peace, Justice, and Strong Institutions) is also explored to understand the interconnectedness of these goals in promoting equity in education.
3. Focus on the Italian Context: The chapter conducts a thematic analysis of public education policies implemented in Italy to achieve Goal 4 of the 2030 Agenda. Additionally, it reviews relevant literature to assess the impact of these policies on equity in the Italian school system. The chapter concludes with ameliorative proposals to further enhance equity in education in Italy.

By examining the strategic approach of the 2030 Agenda towards equity in education, the chapter provides valuable insights into promoting social justice and quality education globally. The focus on the Italian context allows for a deeper understanding of policies, practices, and challenges faced by a specific school system, providing valuable lessons for other school systems with similar characteristics and issues.

Overall, this chapter contributes to the broader discussion on equity and excellence in education, providing a comprehensive exploration of the theoretical foundations, international commitments, and national policy efforts in achieving SDG 4. The chapter's proposals for enhancing equity in the Italian education system offer valuable recommendations for policymakers and educators striving to create inclusive and high-quality educational environments worldwide.

Chapter 13: Impact of Audio-visual Resources on Student Performance in Higher Education in Support of SDG 4

Authored by Mohamed Mohi El-Din Ahmed from Universiti Brunei Darussalam, this research chapter explores the significance of integrating audiovisual resources in higher education to support the achievement of Sustainable Development Goal (SDG) 4, which emphasizes the importance of quality education for all.

The chapter highlights the role of technological advancements, particularly the use of audiovisual resources, in enhancing the learning experience for students in higher institutions. Embracing these resources aligns with SDG 4's objectives of providing inclusive, equitable, and lifelong learning opportunities.

The research focuses on examining the impact of audiovisual resources on student achievement, specifically in teaching Arabic language skills to non-native speakers at Universiti Brunei Darussalam. Mobile technologies have become widely adopted by students in higher education, creating an opportunity to leverage these technologies for educational purposes.

The study adopts a semi-experimental approach, with a randomly selected sample of Arabic language students participating in the research. By employing this method, the chapter aims to evaluate the effectiveness of audiovisual resources in enhancing learning outcomes and supporting the attainment of SDG 4.

Overall, the chapter contributes to the growing body of research on innovative educational practices that can positively impact student performance and contribute to the advancement of SDG 4. By exploring the potential benefits of audiovisual resources in teaching Arabic language skills, the research provides valuable insights for educators and policymakers seeking to foster inclusive and high-quality education in higher institutions.

The findings of this study can serve as a valuable reference for educators and institutions interested in integrating audiovisual resources and mobile technologies into their teaching methodologies, ultimately contributing to the global effort to achieve quality education for all, as envisioned by SDG 4.

Chapter 14: Public Policy and Sustainable Waste Management: The Concept of Waste in Islam in Relation to Sustainability

Authored by Fathin Awang Mat Japar, Emil Ali, and Hamizah Haidi from Universiti Brunei Darussalam, this chapter delves into the intersection of public policy and sustainable waste management, particularly within the context of Islamic principles. The focus lies on understanding the concept of waste in Islam, derived from the Qur'ān and Sunnah (Prophetic traditions), and how it relates to sustainability and waste management practices.

The chapter highlights that public policy plays a pivotal role in various aspects of the public domain, including waste management, which is an integral part of Sustainable Development Goal 12 (SDG12): sustainable consumption and production. To comprehend the concept of waste management in Islam, the authors begin with an exploration of the broader notion of waste itself, drawing insights from Islamic teachings.

Through this examination, the chapter uncovers that the concept of waste in Islam adopts an interdisciplinary approach, taking into account various dimensions and principles within Islamic teachings. The understanding of waste management in Islam incorporates sustainability elements and emphasizes the integration of multiple dimensions, making it a holistic and comprehensive approach to address waste-related issues.

By examining the Islamic perspective on waste and waste management, the chapter provides valuable insights for policymakers, practitioners, and researchers seeking to develop sustainable waste management policies and practices. The incorporation of Islamic principles into waste management strategies can contribute to achieving SDG12's objectives of promoting sustainable consumption and production patterns.

Overall, this chapter contributes to the ongoing discourse on sustainable waste management and offers a unique perspective grounded in Islamic teachings. The interdisciplinary approach to waste management in Islam serves as a valuable reference for fostering sustainable waste practices that align with broader sustainability goals, demonstrating the potential of integrating religious and cultural perspectives into environmental policymaking and actions.

Chapter 15: Radiological Detector Aircraft for Marine Life's Sustainability in Supporting Sustainable Development Goals (SDGs)

Authored by Aldi Alauddin Pattiroei, Muhammad Anshari, Mahani Hamdan, and Emil Ali from Universiti Brunei Darussalam, this article focuses on the role of Radiological Detector Aircraft (RDA) in supporting the Sustainable Development Goals (SDGs), particularly those related to marine life's sustainability.

The SDGs encompass various targets aimed at protecting oceans and ensuring their sustainable use, including the preservation of marine and coastal habitats, the reduction of marine pollution, and the mitigation of ocean acidification. To promote the implementation of these goals, the article evaluates Indonesia's marine patrols, considering the country's status as the World Maritime Axis.

The study explores the capability of Indonesia's marine patrols in addressing issues related to the use of nuclear energy as an alternative source of energy for maritime patrol. Data for the research were gathered through qualitative methods, involving nuclear specialists and maritime patrol officers. The Ishikawa Model was employed to depict the stakeholder analysis structure.

The research findings highlight the significance of Indonesia's capacity to identify nuclear material, particularly in the context of the World Maritime Axis. Understanding and addressing the risks associated with nuclear energy use in marine patrols is crucial for marine life's resilience and the success of SDG implementation.

The article offers valuable insights into how nuclear energy can be leveraged to enhance maritime patrol capabilities, contributing to the body of knowledge in sustainable development and marine conservation. By exploring the potential of Radiological Detector Aircraft in supporting SDGs, the research sheds light on innovative approaches to safeguarding marine environments and addressing challenges in marine pollution and environmental resilience.

Overall, this chapter serves as an important contribution to the ongoing efforts to achieve SDGs, particularly in the context of marine life's sustainability. The exploration of nuclear energy as an alternative source for maritime patrol highlights the potential benefits and risks associated with this approach, providing policymakers and researchers with valuable information to make informed decisions about sustainable and effective marine conservation strategies.

Chapter 16: The Use of Benefits Management in e-Government Projects

Authored by Teresa Matos Fernandes from the Portuguese Administration, Jorge Vareda Gomes from Universidade Lusófona, and Mario Romão from Universidade de Lisboa, Portugal, this article delves into the significance of Benefits Management (BM) in Information Systems and Information Technology (IS/IT) investment projects, particularly within the context of e-Government initiatives.

The expenses associated with IS/IT investments represent a significant portion of organizations' budgets. However, despite these investments, IS/IT projects continue to face challenges and show reduced success rates. Benefits Management has emerged as a crucial approach not only to understand the reasons behind these failures but also to enhance the success of IS/IT investments.

The primary objective of this article is to explore how Benefits Management can be effectively applied in IS/IT investments within the Public Administration (PA) context, with a focus on e-Government projects. The authors conducted a case study, using a specific e-Government project in the Portuguese Public Administration, to demonstrate the application of BM and its potential to leverage the benefits of such investments.

The study highlights the importance of a Benefits Management approach in this environment, shedding light on the challenges that must be considered during implementation. By adopting BM, the researchers identified and evaluated several unanticipated benefits that arose from the e-Government project. This evaluation provided valuable insights into the true contribution of IS/IT investments in enhancing citizen services and improving public organizations' performance.

Overall, this chapter offers a valuable contribution to the field of e-Government and IS/IT investment management. The insights from the case study provide practical guidance for public administrations seeking to enhance the success and impact of their IS/IT investments. By employing a Benefits

Management approach, organizations can better understand and quantify the benefits of their projects, ensuring that these investments deliver the intended outcomes and drive positive results for citizens and public organizations alike.

Chapter 17: Rethinking Anti-Corruption Efforts in Algeria: The Role of Civil Society

Authored by Abderrahmane Benlahcene, Awang Hapni, and Nurul Izaah Mohamed Ghozali from Universiti Utara Malaysia, this chapter critically examines the role of civil society in curbing corruption in Algeria. The central argument is that active engagement of civil society actors in the fight against corruption is essential for achieving a better balance between prevention and enforcement measures in addressing the adverse impacts of corruption.

The chapter emphasizes that an effective and engaged civil society plays a key role in realizing the United Nations' 2030 Agenda for sustainable development and the Sustainable Development Goals (SDGs). The involvement of civil society in anti-corruption efforts can contribute significantly to promoting transparency, accountability, and good governance, all of which are crucial components of sustainable development.

Through its analysis of the role of civil society in Algeria's fight against corruption, this chapter aims to provide valuable insights into the interplay between anti-corruption initiatives and civil society engagement in the context of sustainable development. The findings and conclusions drawn from this study can be relevant not only to Algeria but also to other countries with similar social and cultural settings, highlighting the universal importance of civil society involvement in combating corruption and strengthening institutional accountability.

Moreover, the chapter seeks to draw attention to the significant role of civil society in collective efforts to combat corruption and promote good governance. By bringing the perspectives of researchers, policymakers, and anti-corruption professionals into focus, the chapter aims to foster a greater understanding of the vital role civil society plays in the overall fight against corruption and its impact on the broader goals of sustainable development.

Overall, this chapter provides a comprehensive and insightful analysis of the role of civil society in anti-corruption efforts in Algeria. By highlighting the importance of civil society engagement in curbing corruption, it contributes to the ongoing discussions and efforts to promote transparency, accountability, and sustainable development in the country and beyond.

In Summary

As editors of this edited reference book on Public Policy's Role in Achieving Sustainable Development Goals, we are pleased to present a comprehensive compilation of scholarly works that explore the intricate relationship between public policy and the pursuit of sustainable development goals. Our aim was to mobilize the academic community, policymakers, industry, and civil society to engage in a global discussion while addressing the unique challenges faced by each region.

The contributions from esteemed researchers, policymakers, and academics have shed light on various dimensions of sustainable development, spanning from environmental preservation and climate action to equitable education, poverty eradication, and good governance. Through quality research-based studies, critical understanding, and policy implications, this book offers valuable insights into the multifaceted nature of sustainable development.

Each chapter contributes to the collective effort of supporting the acceleration required to achieve the 17 global Sustainable Development Goals (SDGs) agreed upon by UN member states in 2015. By examining policy directions, best practices, and challenges, this book provides a roadmap for policymakers, corporations, NGOs, and governments to navigate the complex terrain of sustainable development.

From examining urban sustainability as a wicked policy problem to evaluating the implications of fuel subsidy removal on the Nigerian economy, the chapters in this book present a diverse range of topics that are essential for addressing the pressing issues of our time. The integration of various academic fields, including social sciences, politics, economics, and Islamic studies, underscores the interdisciplinary nature of sustainable development and its relevance to global progress.

Notably, several chapters also shed light on the role of civil society, which proves instrumental in fostering transparency, accountability, and good governance. The active engagement of civil society in anti-corruption efforts, waste management, and e-Government projects has been highlighted as a vital component in achieving sustainable development goals.

We believe that this edited reference book will serve as a valuable resource for academia, researchers, policymakers, and institutions worldwide. The insights and recommendations presented here offer a nuanced understanding of the challenges and opportunities that lie ahead on the journey towards sustainable development.

As editors, we express our gratitude to all the contributors for their invaluable efforts in enriching this book with their knowledge and expertise. We hope that this collective endeavor will contribute to the realization of a more sustainable and equitable world, where the principles of the 2030 Agenda are embraced and implemented by all nations and stakeholders.

May this book inspire continued dialogue, research, and action towards achieving the Sustainable Development Goals and fostering a brighter and more sustainable future for generations to come.

Sincerely,

Acknowledgment

We express our gratitude for the invaluable professional support provided by IGI Publishers, which has played a vital role in ensuring the success and quality of our project.

Our sincere thanks are extended to the Institute of Policy Studies at Universiti Brunei for the research grant on Public Policy and Sustainable Development Goals.

Additionally, we extend our heartfelt appreciation to the esteemed international researchers and authors for their exceptional research papers on sustainability and public policy. Your unwavering efforts and remarkable insights are highly valued.

Last but not least, we would like to convey our appreciation to the dedicated reviewers listed below. Their professional insights and thorough evaluations have significantly contributed to upholding the quality of the research chapters:

Abderahman Rejeb
Abderrahmane Benlahcene
Abdul Fatah Tsalis
Abdul Malik Omar
Antje Ilberg
Balamuralithara Balakrishnan
Dwi Kartikasari
Egi Firmansyah
Hapini Awang
Hazik Mohamed
Kris Hartley
Mia Fithriyah
Mohamad Zreik
Mohammad Yazid Surieshtino-Dino
Muhammad Iqbal
Nabilah Sani Mohammed
Pang Li Li
Parimal Roy
Simon Cleveland
Valerio Ferrero

Chapter 1
Complexity and Uncertainty in Late-Stage Technocracy:
The Case of Urban Sustainability

Kris Hartley
City University of Hong Kong, Hong Kong

Ola G. El-Taliawi
University of Twente, The Netherlands

ABSTRACT

As sites of economic, political, and social convergence, cities absorb the earliest effects of global crises. These dynamics are observable also in environmental crises and resilience – longer-running challenges to legacy models of urban governance. Shifting epistemic and practical contexts invite scholarship to more thoroughly examine the dynamics of urban policy with regard to the 'localization' of the Sustainable Development Goals (SDGs) and the contribution of city governments to global environmental policy. This chapter examines urban sustainability as an ontologically complex or 'wicked' policy problem, a framing concept with a history in the urban planning and policy literatures but deserving fresh revisitation. The argument is that a 'complexity science' approach that avoids narrative capture is needed to better understand global environmental crisis and its manifestation in cities. This approach seeks to challenge the predominance of linear, atomistic, and reductionist perspectives that remain embedded in policy thinking.

1. INTRODUCTION

Urban policymaking is characterized by the increasing convergence of complex problems. These include not only local challenges like housing affordability and traffic management but also the localized impacts of global crises like pandemics, climate change, investment and capital flow dynamics, and others. This chapter explores how urban problems and the localization of global problems can be understood and addressed through the perspective of complexity science. This conceptual orientation is one way to

DOI: 10.4018/978-1-6684-8903-1.ch001

unseat the predominance of linear, atomistic, and reductionist approaches to managing urban crises that engage only what is measured, focus on optimization of decontextualized metrics, and fail to recognize systemic interconnectedness.

This chapter outlines policymaking approaches regarding complex problems in an urban context, explores the application of complexity science to crisis response, and applies the complexity science approach to urban policy through soft systems methodology. The analysis illustrates how a crisis can be explored thoroughly for its complexity and used to draw practical insights. The chapter begins with a review of the mechanics of urban management in the current era, focusing on two salient issues: technology (e.g., 'civic technology' and Fourth Industrial Revolution technologies) and external engagement by government parties (e.g., bilateral and multilateral global urban networks). These issues are selected because they play the greatest role, according to the current urban sustainability discourse, in helping cities fortify themselves against climate threats and meet certain SDG targets (e.g., through adoption of SDGs in urban plans – or, 'SDG localization'). The chapter then examines the theoretical dimensions and applicability of a 'complexity mindset' as a crisis response frame for urban sustainability and crisis management. Examples of complexity mindset applications are outlined, including leadership, collaborative policymaking, and systems-thinking tools. The conclusion brings these ideas together under the broader political theme of public trust in expertise and technocracy, populist 'pushback' against science and technology, and the implications for new ways of thinking about urban resilience, smart cities, and the 'wickedness' of the global sustainability crisis.

2. MECHANICS OF URBAN GOVERNANCE IN THE MODERN ERA

2.1 Technology

The evolving role of technology in daily life, urban planning, and policy practice has substantial implications for SDG localization efforts. Technology's contribution to urban policy (particularly monitoring and forecasting) and to sustainability efforts more generally is evident in the near ubiquitous use of data and its integration into decisionmaking processes. At the same time, the potential for technology to advance SDG localization goes beyond data. AI is already transforming how information is gathered and processed. In the realm of industry – where much of the sustainability crisis originated – the advent of the so-called 'fourth industrial revolution' (hereafter, '4IR') presents some opportunities for technology to reduce the impact of production on the environment (e.g., through better monitoring and analysis and efficiency gains; for further discussion, see Herweijer et al., 2018). It is clear that the narrative concerning the role of technology in urban sustainability is largely sanguine. For example, at a UN Industrial Development Organization (UNIDO) conference in 2019,[1] the director of Adapt, a South Africa-based organization focused on sustainable development, stated that "this digital revolution, like the industrial revolutions before it, promises jobs, increased livings standards, and better health for more people." A 2017 PwC report[2] describes ten types of emerging 4IR technologies (p. 2) and recommends several policy interventions including robust governance structures and safeguards, policy development support to individual countries, and additional research.

The potential of 4IR to transform industrial platforms and the future of work enjoys an already copious body of research (Ślusarczyk, 2018; Hattingh, 2018), and most discussion focuses on application in industry and the private sector. However, there is growing anticipation that 4IR and other emerging technologies can play a role in urban policy and SDG localization, including in environmental projects (e.g., smart urban grids for transport and electricity, and risk-sensitive infrastructure management) and social projects (time-sensitive communication between individual health monitoring systems and nearby care providers). Indeed, the panoply of emerging technologies is vast: artificial intelligence (AI), robotics, and machine learning; blockchain, distributed ledgers, and fintech; Internet of things (IoT); cloud computing; and autonomous systems for transport and energy. Given that 4IR is conceptually built on the autonomous interconnection among technological systems and between those systems and non-technological ones, the applied potential is anticipated for gains not only in data collection and monitoring (see Chicago's Array of Things (AoT) project as an example[3]) but also in efficiency of public service delivery, policy responsiveness, and iterative alignment of urban management systems with evolving environmental, economic, and social conditions.

Another applied example of the role of technology in urban management and sustainability is civic technology (hereafter, 'civic tech'), which likewise has high potential for attracting interest in supporting SDG localization. According to Hartley (2019), civic tech is "the technology-enabled engagement of civil society in urban governance...encompassing systems across governance tasks (policy design, implementation, and evaluation, etc.) and operational areas (transport, safety, waste management, land use, economic development, etc.)" (p. 3). One example of the application of civic tech is government-sponsored virtual platforms on which social entrepreneurs host smartphone applications (e.g., for transportation, safety, political engagement, and health). Such platforms function like a commons, as in a virtual public park, in which the government has little or no jurisdiction over functionality and content (beyond regulating legality) but supplies the infrastructure as a service to enable the emergence of third-party innovators for whom hosting platforms can be prohibitively expensive. As such, civic tech addresses the public welfare while potentially enabling initiatives that relate to sustainability. It also provides a portal for the participation of civil society in local social and collective action on the SDGs.

2.2 Local and Global Engagement

While infrastructure and technology are recognized as means by which cities can make progress on SDG localization, softer aspects of social engagement and institutional design are also crucial. Such initiatives can be understood through the perspective of collaborative governance and reflect on-the-ground conditions that impact the political legitimacy of SDG policies. This subsection discusses three such avenues: collaborations with community groups, community development organizations (CDOs), and non-government organizations (NGOs); engagement of educational institutions; and contributions from the private sector and industry associations.

First, community groups and NGOs, as 'knowledge agents,' represent a crucial link between the perceptions of policymakers and the experiences of residents. As such, these groups have been seen as instrumental not only for understanding and monitoring conditions but also for seeking qualitative input, building support for program implementation, and establishing knowledge feedback loops as programs progress and mature. NGOs and CDOs are especially crucial for strengthening empowerment in traditionally marginalized communities that struggle against SDG-related issues such as poverty, education, public health, and environmental degradation. This approach not only generates urban and local engagement across most SDGs but also directly addresses #16 (peace, justice and strong institutions). Moreover, engaging such organizations in policymaking requires political will at high levels and must be promoted institutionally through participatory processes. These are often lacking in cities around the world. According to a working paper[4] published by the Instituto de Desarrollo Sostenible y Relaciones Internacionales, "emerging forms of collaboration between NGOs are a way to operationalize the integrated and universal nature of the SDGs. However, these collaborations will remain fragile if governments and the UN do not follow the example to overcome silos, and if some types of NGOs are not sufficiently included in national and international processes" (p. 1).

Second, cities typically have a wealth of capacity in educational institutions. Engagement of primary and secondary school students has been pursued through integration of SDG principles across curricular realms (Zguir et al., 2021). There is strong potential for such engagement as children are often climate-aware and may be able to relate such issues to their daily experiences, including growing food, conserving water, and walking or cycling to school. The SDGs have also been used to provide a unifying narrative for class discussions. An example is the institutional effort in South Africa's primary and secondary schools to address social and environmental justice, democracy, and inclusivity (McKay, 2018). Students are also availed of the opportunity to participate in extra-curricular activities related to SDG implementation, including through educational visits and programs organized by community organizations (e.g., environmental clean-ups, management of urban gardens, and other activities integrating education, participation, and feedback). Interest among young people should not be underestimated; the rise in global visibility of student climate activist Greta Thunberg and the school strike for climate[5] are recent examples. Regarding tertiary institutions, the value of universities is evident in their research capacity and global engagement. Additionally, the student bodies of universities are a source for participants in ideation and outreach activities, as authors and researchers for monitoring reports, and as ambassadors for student-based delegations at international network events. For example, Los Angeles has integrated the work and feedback of university students in the development of that city's SDG Voluntary Local Review (VLR).

For local governments, open and institutionalized channels of communication have been instrumental in facilitating collaboration among public servants, the private sector, and the general public. One supporting strategy is to distil complex sustainability concepts into digestible and compelling imagery that can be used to educate shareholders and the public. Indeed, structures for collaboration and communication already exist but city leaders must consider how they can be used to advance SDG implementation; examples are SDG-related working groups and co-sponsorship of monitoring and reporting about progress within both public and private organizations. In summarizing the value of engaging all stakeholders in SDG localization, Anthony Pipa[6] argues that "The SDGs offer a platform for new models of city governance, to enable coordination, partnerships, and new ways of working among multiple community stakeholders, including local businesses, civil society, and universities. This requires a shift in mindset and a collaborative spirit and can prove useful in overcoming the inherent fragmentation among different sectors within the city" (p. 4).

Cities are taking an increasingly globalized and collaborative approach to SDG localization, presenting an opportunity to strengthen existing global networks and forge new ones (for a useful overview of global urban networks, see Acuto and Rayner (2016) and Acuto (2013); for the same in the context of sustainability, see Gordon and Johnson (2018) and Keiner and Kim (2007)). According to a Brookings report,[7] "Integrating the SDGs into the city-to-city networks in which they participate will, by sharing best practices and innovations, help to leverage needed capabilities. It will also provide a platform for elevating their voice in debates about the SDGs." Evidence indicates, however, that the topical focus (as aligned with individual SDGs) of urban networks varies. For example, a study by Tjandradewi and Marcotullio (2009) found that among Asian cities participating in such networks, leaders felt issues pertaining to environment, health, education, and infrastructure were more applicable to urban policy than were issues pertaining to gender empowerment, poverty, housing, finance, and economic development.

Urban networks have coalesced around specific issues. An example is the portfolio of targets related to the Intergovernmental Panel on Climate Change's (IPCC) report "Global Warming of 1.5°C," for which "city-networks are operating at the interstices of urban and global governance, building bridges across national borders between city governments and a variety of other actors, and aiming to engender coordinated actions that produce meaningful collective effects" (Gordon and Johnson, 2018; p. 39). Likewise, motives behind the creation of urban networks vary by city type. For example, Mocca (2017) finds in a European study that cities with relatively advanced economies (e.g., those that transitioned away from hard industry and towards knowledge and innovation-based economies) and those with relatively high administrative autonomy are more likely to participate in sustainability-based urban networks, using those networks to build their own regional economic and political profiles. According to the study, cities with center-left governments are more likely to join networks focused on sustainability, raising the prospect of political alignment as a determinant for network-based action. The challenge for policy at the global level is to ensure that urban networks for SDG localization do not resemble a club for the privileged few.

3. CRISIS POLICYMAKING AND COMPLEXITY

The policy tools and institutional structures that enable urban action on the SDGs, while varying by context, provide a useful lens for examining urban resilience. At the same time, this perspective looks at the 'supply side' of urban environmental policy; that is, how policies evolve and are implemented. Of equal importance is the 'demand side;' that is, the nature of urban policy problems themselves, the study of which can help illuminate whether and how policy interventions match the characteristics of the problems they seek to solve. As such, a consideration of the nature of urban policy problems is essential when examining how cities respond to the sustainability imperative. Much literature has examined how policy problems are measured, highlighting the relevance of technology and associated monitoring systems. At the same time, a deeper perspective focuses more 'up-stream' – eschewing the assumption that problems exist in the way that they are currently understood in mainstream policymaking and instead reconsidering how problems are conceptualized. This analytical approach reveals pathways for alternative epistemological understandings to influence how urban policy problems are theorized and managed in practical settings. This section describes one such epistemological approach, complexity science, and how urban environmental policymaking can be structured or improved based on complexity science.

3.1 Understanding Complexity Science

Efforts to understand environmental crises as a localized phenomenon (something to be addressed by individual local governments) have, over time, ceded to the growing realization that such crises have global dimensions and should be addressed as such. At the same time, global governance efforts in the wake of crises (e.g., the Covid-19 pandemic) often expose weaknesses, inconsistencies, and rifts in global coordination mechanisms. In this way, such crises also illuminate opportunities for practical improvement and theoretical advancement. Amidst and in the wake of crisis, policy learning in its manifold forms is undertaken to avoid a repeat of whatever mistakes were made. Problem-diagnostic and analytical tools are tweaked and re-deployed to understand how the crisis materialized. For many crises, the imperative to learn is increasingly urgent given rapidly unfolding technological, social, and environmental change. Rationalist and instrumentalist policy epistemics of the 20th century are now often regarded to be outmatched by highly complex and interconnected problems (Hartley et al., 2019). The sustainability crisis, as experienced at local levels, illustrates the need for a more robust complexity mindset, including a transboundary and collaborative perspective in crisis preparation and a more holistic view of problem definition.

Literature about complexity theory in the context of public policy is growing and increasingly contextually diverse (Eppel and Rhodes, 2018; Guntzburger and Pauchant, 2014; Morçöl, 2013; Cairney, 2012; Geyer and Rihani, 2010; Manson, 2001). Nevertheless, complexity science is variously defined and suffers conceptually and methodologically from its treatment as a pseudo-science (Phelan, 2001). According to Coveney and Highfield (1995), "complexity is a watchword for a new way of thinking about the collective behaviour of many basic but interacting units" (p. 7). Complexity science thus represents a revolution in the way policy problems are conceptualized. Homer-Dixon (2011) describes complexity as constitutive of multiple interconnected components, characterized by non-linearity (small changes having large effects, and large changes small effects), and reflective of the concept of emergence (novel properties that defy existing understandings). Because complex systems can be found in many areas of human society, complexity science is applicable to a number of fields across the social sciences; this interdisciplinary nature also makes it a useful theoretical orientation for the field of public policy. Concepts like self-adaptation and emergence reflect the environment in which public policy operates – including crises and systemic disruption.

Complexity science focuses not only on the parts that contribute to the whole but also on how each part interacts with others in the emergence of new realities. As complexity science is seen to adopt a more comprehensive understanding of systems with multiple and often unpredictable components, Turner and Baker (2019) argue that causal research is difficult. According to Turner and Baker, novel theoretical models that reflect 'real-life complexity' are needed, including the use of complex adaptive systems (CAS) as an analytical framework. The remainder of this section justifies the complexity-based and CAS approaches to understanding policy dynamics in crisis situations.

Crises and other wicked policy problems are often aberrations; their complexities are illegible to existing epistemic vocabularies, methods, and general understandings. A mindset based on complexity science is one alternative for making enough sense of unstructured and unpredictable situations to establish a coherent reactive policy posture. As such, there is a need to adopt a complexity mindset in policymaking and analysis. One way for policy interventions to follow suit is to move away from linear, atomistic, and discrete interventions and towards more holistic and evolving programs of work. Corollary perspectives recognize that complexity characterizes not only the environment in which problems are defined and solutions designed but also the varied settings in which policies are developed and take effect; for example, Butler and Allen (2008) view implementation as an adaptive, interpreted, and self-organizing process that precludes reduction to 'best practices' approaches. Policymakers must understand how complexity defines not only the crisis but also the response to the crisis.

From a practical perspective, complex and adaptive-systems approaches have implications for both qualitative and quantitative analytical methods. Examples of how this epistemological approach is translated into methodological innovations useful to practice include stock and flow and causal loop diagrams, participatory system mapping, and group model building. These and other tools have been used by governments to improve the complexity and nuance of understandings about policy problems. For example, the Singapore government introduced a mix of policy approaches to support its 'whole of government approach' (Low, 2016) for addressing wicked problems, including a matrix approach to help departments better share information, work horizontally, and utilize computer-assisted modeling and scenario-building tools to address the mitigation of systemic risks (Stockdale-Otárola, 2017).

3.2 Crisis Policymaking in Response to Sustainability Challenges

Crises are crucial moments in which all the capacities of the state are tested in concurrent and often unpredictable ways. Quality of leadership is defined in large measure by crisis response (Farazmand, 2007). For example, American President George W. Bush was credited for responding quickly to the September 11 events, with a public speech generating a 'rally' effect in the time immediately following the attacks (Schubert et al., 2002). Nevertheless, Bush's legacy was significantly tarnished by the two wars that followed and by what many critics considered to be an insufficient crisis response to the Hurricane Katrina disaster in 2005 (Boin et al., 2010; Malhotra and Kuo, 2008; Sylves, 2006). American President Donald Trump's tenure saw two major opportunities for crisis leadership largely mishandled. The first was the administration's lagging response to the Covid-19 crisis (Lipton et al., 2020). The second, occurring in the shadow of the first, was the administration's response to protests against the murder of a Black man by a police officer (Edmondson, 2020). Trump and his staff, in one widely panned episode, withdrew into a bunker below the White House before having protesters forcibly cleared to enable a photo opportunity in front of a church (Shear and Rogers, 2020).

Whether local, national, or global in scale, crisis policymaking differs substantially from policymaking in normal situations, since there are often no shelf-ready or proven solutions (Hartley et al., 2019; Wenzelburger et al., 2019). During such times, three principal challenges face policymakers. The first is information management. Amidst or immediately following a crisis, policymakers and analysts can experience information overload, where data that is meant to produce evidence-based decisions increases ambiguity about causes and possible solutions (Zahariadis, 2007; Grossman, 2019). Leaders often respond in this situation by using hasty instinct and heuristics, depending on leadership style. These are moments when ideology and political survival can take precedence over rational deliberation.

The translation of information into policies is dependent in part on the cognitive characteristics and processes of policymakers and political leaders. This translation occurs now in environments of increasing epistemic uncertainty, political tension, and problem wickedness, adding further stress on cognitive functioning (Head, 2019; Rittel and Webber, 1973). Consequently, policymakers may be confronted not only by uncertainty about information and knowledge but also by diverging interpretations of the policy problem itself – potentially impacting political will to act on certain dimensions of crisis (Hermann and Dayton, 2009). High degrees of uncertainty confound problem definition, projections of outcomes, and normative orientations (Wenzelburger et al., 2019). Furthermore, the rapid materialization of negative impacts can engender panic and press policymakers to embrace quick solutions. Policymakers may also face credibility traps that undermine the legitimacy of policy interventions in the eyes of the media and public; an example is the emergence of 'post-truth' and 'anti-science' movements (Fischer, 2021; 2020) and a general skepticism of expertise and intellectualism (Peters and Pierre, 2019; Hermann and Dayton, 2009).

The second key challenge is stakeholder management. According to scholars, crises can involve 'contraction of authority' that concentrates decision making power in the hands of leaders and close advisers, with the consequence that decisions do not reflect bureaucratic compromise or societal preferences (Boin et al., 2016; Hermann, 2001; 1963; 't Hart, 1997; Hermann and Dayton, 2009). Further, transboundary issues like global sustainability and pandemics can cause sudden growth in the number and diversity of affected stakeholders with potentially divergent interests, differing understandings about the nature or cause of problems, and lower levels of inter-group political and social capital. According to Ansell et al. (2010), this increase in stakeholder diversity can impact collective efforts to manage the crisis.

The multi-stakeholder scenario reflects the long-running tension between the policy influence of expertise and that of lay wisdom. That is, if particular challenges call for expert knowledge, the optioning and decision-making stages of policy development may appear less democratic. One policy arena in which this dynamic is particularly evident is smart cities, for which technical knowledge shapes the logic by which problems are defined and solutions are proposed. Under such circumstances, the credibility of technical knowledge and influence of commercial interests can shape the policy agenda (Kuecker and Hartley, 2020a; Raco and Savini, 2019). A similar dynamic is revealed during the Covid-19 pandemic. Throughout the early months of the United States' struggle to contain the virus, political tensions were stoked by populist commentators about whether a chief health advisor, Dr. Anthony Fauci, was ideologically compromised in his contradictions of President Donald Trump's off-handed and unscientific medical claims (Amir Singh, 2020; Kahn, 2020). In a politically charged environment, stakeholder engagement can be used as a strategy to signal political responsiveness. Politicians are sensitive to their constituencies, while experts are beholden to professional expectations about impartiality and scientific rigour. Decisions about scientifically and technically complex policy issues often reflect a compromise between the two.

The third key challenge facing policymakers is time management. Amidst quickly evolving crises, information uncertainty and the element of surprise combine to increase the urgency for expedient intervention (Boin et al., 2005; Hermann and Dayton, 2009). In such cases, rapid policy response must proceed without a full understanding about the nature of the problem. Policymakers rely on lessons from experience with similar situations (Chung et al., 2011), but this approach becomes more difficult for unprecedented crises. For example, Hong Kong relied on some knowledge learned from the 2003 SARS crisis to manage the Covid-19 crisis (Law et al., 2020). However, for a crisis like climate change, there are no experiences with an analogous event. When policymakers are stressed for response time, efforts to temper instinctual policy decisions with sober scientific expertise – when political pressure for immediate and conclusive action is high (Schneider, 1995) – can be a fraught endeavor. One criticism of the Donald Trump administration's response to the Covid-19 crisis is that the government acted too slowly (Lipton et al., 2020). It is evident, in retrospect, that the administration's slow action was unlikely the result of a cautious approach in waiting for additional scientific evidence to be gathered; rather, the delay is largely thought to be the result of an attempt to downplay the severity of the outbreak in order to maintain economic stability (Leonhardt, 2020). Regarding the speed of response, a widely circulated independent projection showed that mandatory distancing imposed even two weeks sooner would have saved 83 percent of lives lost (Pei et al., 2020). Clearly, time management is crucial in crisis response, with determining factors including understandings about the severity of the crisis, the need to collect more information, and consideration for tangential impacts on society, politics, and economy.

In the context of urban policy for sustainability, timeframes are not uniform across all related problems. The long-unfolding phenomenon of climate change is unlikely to be experienced in any single event, in which the future observers look back to a specific date when 'pre' became 'post.' At the same time, climate change is observable in a multitude of individual events that indeed present themselves as immediate and acute crises; examples are wildfires (e.g., in Australia in 2019-2020 and Canada in 2023) and erratic weather events (e.g., more intense heat waves, floods and droughts, and typhoons and hurricanes). Policymakers must fortify society against immediate crises in the short-run while also waging a policy battle for stability in the face of long-term climate change. Management of information, time, and stakeholder engagement are key focus areas that can help governments maintain crisis-response capacity for multi-faceted policy crises that have both short-run and long-run manifestations. Furthermore, a more receptive epistemic orientation in problem definition can help policymakers and analysts recognize complexity and advocate for a resilient policy posture.

4. LEADERSHIP AND COMPLEXITY IN THE SUSTAINABILITY CRISIS

In the clutches of crisis, policymakers must consider a mix of factors that define available options and determine the effects of chosen interventions; these include policy interactions and spillover effects (how one policy affects another), unintended consequences, durability of interventions, and policy buffers and safeguards, among others (Hynes, 2017). According to Ramos (2017), policies are designed often within the narrow epistemological confines of a particular issue. That is, the prevailing or mainstream (collective) understanding of a policy issue tends to be the one that defines it, whether in a technocratically or politically oriented setting. When crises emerge, circumstantial imperatives force policymakers to mobilize on multiple fronts; each policy may have been designed effectively for a particular issue but could fail to cohere with other policies in the context of systemic crisis-based mobilization. The harmonization of multiple policies in parallel domains requires both leadership and policy design with a broad view of crisis complexity. This approach reflects a type of systems-thinking that eschews silo-based approaches to problem conceptualization and policy development and implementation (Sucha, 2017). Policymakers in such cases must strive for integrated solutions and consider policy problems from a macro and holistic perspective. Based on a complexity mindset, the following recommendations for managing the emerging urban sustainability crisis are elaborated in the remainder of this section: adopting complexity leadership, collaborative policymaking, and use of systems-thinking tools.

4.1 Complexity Leadership

The notion of complexity leadership draws on the idea that multiple elements of policy mixes must be brought together and applied in a complementary way. Uhl-Bien et al. (2007) argue that the leadership needed for this action prioritizes learning, innovation, and adaptability. According to Baltaci and Balcı (2017), complexity leadership has three types: traditional leadership shaped by Weberian-style administrative hierarchy, adaptive and creative leadership responsive to evolving conditions, and acutely reactive leadership that mobilizes quickly in urgent situations. First, it is appropriate to consider that governance systems and leadership styles are often embedded and thus slow to change. The endurance of organizational systems and cultures acts to preserve legacy policies and institutional elements that existed as organizations first developed. In many cases, organizations and their cultures emerged at a time in history when hierarchical and top-down management models were common. These traditional or 'sticky' organizational elements remain to this day a contextual reality that must be mediated and managed amidst emergent ideas and unprecedented policy challenges. This tension underscores the need for effective, open-minded, and credible leadership.

The second dimension of complexity leadership pertains to systems-based thinking (e.g., the spirit of learning, innovation, and adaptability). This leadership perspective accords with the concepts of emergence and systemic disruption that characterize many modern understandings of crisis and complexity. It also treats complexity not as an affront to order and rationality but as a reality that cannot be ignored or conveniently wished away. Systems-based complexity leadership recognizes that policy crises must be thoroughly understood (learning within and beyond traditional epistemic boundaries), leading to novel insights (innovations) that aid in the ability of society to endure unanticipated disruptions (adaptability).

The final dimension of Baltaci and Balcı's (2017) complexity leadership is acutely reactive leadership. This leadership property can be seen as a form of policy triage that immediately assesses crisis situations on the basis of limited information and mobilizes resources for response on the basis of this incomplete understanding. This leadership process is not characterized by deliberation or the types of decisionmaking processes that necessarily constitute democratic or participatory policymaking; rather, it is an instinctive or broadly heuristic response to mitigate the early severity of an emerging crisis. Given that crises are often unpredictable and have uniquely complicated characteristics, there are few opportunities to apply lessons learned from institutional memory. Policy responses often must be based on the judicious and creative adaptation of knowledge developed through broadly but not perfectly similar experiences, while aiming not to exacerbate the situation, compound the causes, or obstruct additional policy efforts that materialize around new understandings of the problem.

4.2 Collaborative Policymaking

Crises are typically multifaceted in that they impact multiple policy arenas. As such, interventions must consider the input of numerous constituencies (Boyd and Martin, 2020). Collaborative and democratic mechanisms are common ways to facilitate such feedback and have been applied in both immediate response situations and in efforts to establish longer-term resilience (e.g., for urban sustainability). The public administration literature has developed a thorough and detailed body of knowledge pertaining to collaborative governance (Weber and Khademian, 2008; Huxham and Vangen, 2005; Vigoda, 2002) and has also examined collaborative governance and networks specifically in crisis situations (Kapucu et al., 2010; Moynihan, 2009; Waugh and Streib, 2006).

Crucial elements driving collaborative policymaking for crisis response and preparation include information-sourcing and expert analysis, participation and democratic legitimacy, and shared understandings about the nature and dimensions of policy problems. Hannah and Baekkeskov (2020) argue that the method by which ideas are framed and engaged can promote collaboration and coalition-building. In their ambiguity, according to the authors, 'polysemic' ideas (e.g., broad concepts like sustainability and social inclusion) can bring opposing groups together under high-level framings even amidst disagreement over interests and idea specificities. For an issue as broad as urban sustainability – relating not only to environmental health but also to the function of social, economic, and political systems – polysemic ideas offer one pathway to bridge problem complexity and political sensitivity.

At a higher theoretical level, emphasis on collaboration is one vehicle for dissolving epistemic hegemony. The framing of public policy problems has a history deeply rooted in the logic of positivism and instrumental rationalism; these epistemics shape and are shaped by technocratic administrative processes that regard only what their logic can process while marginalizing the rest. This legacy approach comes at substantial peril for efforts to develop policies that are effective, flexible, durable, and politically legitimate. Crisis response governance risks perpetuating epistemic lock-in and existing narratives by strategically refashioning them for modern problems (Kuecker and Hartley, 2020b); in this process, ways of understanding problems are merely repackaged for emerging crises without being fundamentally altered to break the epistemic path-dependence that may have contributed to crises. In matters pertaining to resilience, so-called folk, local, and indigenous wisdoms are examples of 'other knowledges' that can be crucial in filling gaps ignored by technocratic ways of framing problems and solutions. Collaborative processes can precipitate a transformation in epistemic framing by diversifying input sources and enlarging the visionary scope of policymaking.

4.3 Systems-Thinking Tools

The interpretation of threats to urban sustainability and other crises as complex policy problems invites a systems-based perspective that has implications for how policy ideas are gathered, synthesized, and actualized. Leischow et al. (2008) argue that systems-thinking brings a valuable perspective to policymaking and that related research should be 'transdisciplinary' and 'translational.' The implication is that governments play an important role in facilitating the connection between knowledge and practice, particularly for a policy field that comprises a "complex, adaptive federation of systems" (Leischow et al., 2008; p. S201). Given that a systems approach is useful in simplifying a universe that is "confusing, complex, and sometimes opaque to our queries of it" (Waltner-Toews et al., 2008; p. ix), the applied setting of urban sustainability and other types of multifaceted crises seems well suited for such a perspective.

From a practical perspective, systems-thinking can go hand-in-hand with 'soft systems methodology,' which Carey et al. (2015) argue has applicability for multi-faceted issues like public health. Soft systems methodology is an approach for modeling almost any human activity (Platt and Warwick, 1995) and can be applied to "tackling problematical, messy situations of all kinds" (Checkland and Poulter, 2010; p. 191). According to Checkland (1989), soft systems methodology uses "models of purposeful activity systems to set up a debate about change"; these changes "would be both (systematically) desirable and (culturally) feasible" (p. 273). Soft systems methodology is based on seven stages that broadly involve the delineation of a problem, identification of its root causes, and a reversion of the conclusions back to real-world terms that precipitate the desired outcome. The methodology is a fundamentally social and collaborative exercise that focuses on insights and learning; as such, it is relevant to the study of crisis situations with high degrees of complexity, definitional ambiguity, and interpretive latitude.

5. CONCLUSION

Efforts by local governments to integrate the SDGs into urban planning and management – and more broadly to address the sustainability crisis – are dependent not only on technology but also the diverse wisdom that comes from multi-stakeholder engagement. Further, such efforts may also benefit from a broader epistemic scope, recognizing that the way policy problems are often named and framed is a vestige of legacy governance styles that originated in eras having different problems and different types of problems. Alternative understandings about policy crisis have more opportunity to emerge in settings that embrace the idea of complexity, emergence, adaptation, and empirical ambiguity. This approach is not necessarily idealistic; contestation about the definition of policy problems (including which ones deserve intervention) is a political reality facing many governments in the current era of populist turbulence.

Facilitating a productive policy conversation across the current era's yawning political gap, does, however, necessitate a common understanding about the terms of debate. This understanding includes agreement about the validity of information, whether from scientists, technical experts, or the community. Validity, however, need not imply preeminence; many valid points of view may exist but there is no space to privilege all at once. At the same time, the notion of 'politicizing' the policy process has moved up-stream. Experts and policymakers once outlined a set of options around which the political debate could then proceed; the facts and assumptions had largely consensus legitimacy. However, the notion of 'upstream' suggests that political debate is inserting itself into the fact- and information-collection stage. Debates about the nature of data inputs are increasingly salient given the growing level of distrust of not only policy institutions but also knowledge institutions. Examples of this dynamic are observable in right-wing distrust of universities and transnational governance organizations like the United Nations and World Bank.

At a practical level, the development and implementation of urban policies addressing sustainability are increasingly shaped by the global policy narrative. Numerous conduits for the sharing of knowledge and 'best practices,' including global urban networks and the influence of global development and finance institutions, have enabled the sustainability narrative to spread around the world, in a process that policy scholars often label policy transfer, policy learning, or policy diffusion. At the same time, differing fiscal and policy capacities across countries and cities impact which SDGs receive attention – particularly in settings where limited resources prevent action on all SDGs at once. In a study comparing progress on SDGs at the national level, Allen et al. (2018) find the greatest types of implementation gaps (low percentage of countries reporting progress) to be policy evaluation and assessment of interlinkages among SDG targets (both below 10%). By contrast, the most widespread progress was made on establishing coordination mechanisms, stakeholder consultation processes, and mapping and aligning the SDGs against national strategies and plans (all above 90% of countries). In time, scholars and analysts will be able to take a more longitudinal perspective on implementation progress, allowing them to isolate the effects of particular governance variables and compare their effects across cities and developmental contexts.

In acting upon these practical imperatives, a complexity thinking approach can help to account for interrelated challenges and policy domains and to prepare governance systems for future crises. According to Peters (2017), "the nature of wicked, and/or complex, problems is that there is no magic bullet to solve problems, but a better understanding can help facilitate what may be only limited answers" (p. 395). As public policy and administration practice and scholarship advocated for 'modernization' of governance systems throughout the 20th century, the notion that a problem is too complex to fully measure and an ideal solution too elusive to ponder is somewhat epistemically disruptive. This chapter has used SDG localization and the urban sustainability agenda to discuss the complex, interrelated, and multijurisdictional dimensions of crises and consider how theoretical understandings and practical policy strategies can be improved through the adoption of a complexity mindset.

In closing, it is fruitful to reflect more broadly on the epistemic dimensions of emerging crises. Two of the 21st century's most pressing global crises so far – climate change and pandemics – concern issues that have substantial scientific dimensions. The role of science in developing informed understandings is crucial for the function and effectiveness of policy responses. The Covid-19 pandemic is a useful comparison to the sustainability crisis; both are scientific and technical in nature, and both have generated political contestation. Throughout the pandemic in the United States, some scientists and experts appeared in the public eye through daily briefings. The pronouncements of Dr. Anthony Fauci and other medical staff, however, came into contradiction with a political narrative promoted by the presidential administration. The former cautioned against taking the crisis too lightly or failing to fully understand it, while the latter sought to downplay its severity in the interest of maintaining economic activity. The politicization of science was on display when right-wing political commentators reflected openly about whether the scientists were part of a more organized effort to discredit the presidential administration politically (Alba and Frenkel, 2020). This division exemplifies the type of complexities characterizing acute and complex crises. Not only are they inherently multifaceted, but efforts to understand and address them are also shaped by social systems that are not always prepared to deal collectively with disruption to existing understandings or epistemics.

Whether populist pushback against science is blunt political rhetoric or a shrewd and tactically designed revolution against the positivist claims of scientific rationality, there appears to be a growing crisis of epistemic legitimacy that casts science as elitist and populist pushback as heroism. The current era may indeed be characterized by 'late-stage technocracy,' in which the credibility of experts is compromised and claiming possession of the only legitimate policy information is a profitable political strategy. According to Hartley et al. (2020), "in countries with democratic systems and even in some autocracies, disaffection and distrust…is leading to populist agitation, challenging the legitimacy and logic of legacy governance models now relied on to address complex issues" (p. 270). This political-epistemic dynamic was evident during the pandemic and showed signs of eventual emergence even at times over decades of discussions about climate change. It is tempting to view pushback against received or mainstream policy narratives as an effort to dismantle epistemic hegemony and thus borne of social constructivism. Accordingly, Fischer (2020) argues that no amount of fact, however copious or well verified, can overcome fact-denialism or the political forces driving it. Epistemic instability is a political reality in the 21st century, coming at a time when evidence and science are more at the center of the policy debate than ever before. This turbulent era is an opportunity to revisit and strengthen scholarly understandings about complexity for urban sustainability research and practice.

REFERENCES

Acuto, M. (2018). *Engaging with global urban governance. In Doing Global Urban Research.* Sage.

Acuto, M., & Rayner, S. (2016). City networks: Breaking gridlocks or forging (new) lock-ins? *International Affairs*, *92*(5), 1147–1166. doi:10.1111/1468-2346.12700

Alba, D., & Frenkel, S. (2020). Medical Expert Who Corrects Trump Is Now a Target of the Far Right. *The New York Times*. https://www.nytimes.com/2020/03/28/technology/coronavirus-fauci-trump-conspiracy-target.html

Allen, C., Metternicht, G., & Wiedmann, T. (2018). Initial progress in implementing the Sustainable Development Goals (SDGs): A review of evidence from countries. *Sustainability Science*, *13*(5), 1453–1467. doi:10.100711625-018-0572-3

Amir Singh, J. (2020). COVID-19: Science and global health governance under attack. *SAMJ: South African Medical Journal*, *110*(6), 1–2. PMID:32880545

Ansell, C., Boin, A., & Keller, A. (2010). Managing transboundary crises: Identifying the building blocks of an effective response system. *Journal of Contingencies and Crisis Management*, *18*(4), 195–207. doi:10.1111/j.1468-5973.2010.00620.x

Baltaci, A., & Balcı, A. (2017). Complexity leadership: A theorical perspective. *International Journal of Educational Leadership and Management*, *5*(1), 30–58. doi:10.17583/ijelm.2017.2435

Boin, A., Hart, P., Stern, E., & Sundelius, B. (2005). *The politics of crisis management: Understanding public leadership when it matters most*. Academic Press.

Boin, A. (2009). The new world of crises and crisis management: Implications for policymaking and research. *The Review of Policy Research*, *26*(4), 367–377. doi:10.1111/j.1541-1338.2009.00389.x

Boin, A., Hart, P. T., McConnell, A., & Preston, T. (2010). Leadership style, crisis response and blame management: The case of Hurricane Katrina. *Public Administration*, *88*(3), 706–723. doi:10.1111/j.1467-9299.2010.01836.x

Boin, A., Stern, E., & Sundelius, B. (2016). *The politics of crisis management: Public leadership under pressure*. Cambridge University Press. doi:10.1017/9781316339756

Boyd, N. M., & Martin, E. C. (2020). Sense of community responsibility at the forefront of crisis management. *Administrative Theory & Praxis*, 1–13.

Butler, M. J., & Allen, P. M. (2008). Understanding policy implementation processes as self-organizing systems. *Public Management Review*, *10*(3), 421–440. doi:10.1080/14719030802002923

Cairney, P. (2012). Complexity theory in political science and public policy. *Political Studies Review*, *10*(3), 346–358. doi:10.1111/j.1478-9302.2012.00270.x

Carey, G., Malbon, E., Carey, N., Joyce, A., Crammond, B., & Carey, A. (2015). Systems science and systems thinking for public health: A systematic review of the field. *BMJ Open*, *5*(12), e009002. doi:10.1136/bmjopen-2015-009002 PMID:26719314

Checkland, P., & Poulter, J. (2010). Soft systems methodology. In *Systems approaches to managing change: A practical guide* (pp. 191–242). Springer. doi:10.1007/978-1-84882-809-4_5

Checkland, P. B. (1989). Soft systems methodology. *Human Systems Management*, *8*(4), 273–289. doi:10.3233/HSM-1989-8405

Chung, H., & Thewissen, S. (2011). Falling back on old habits? A comparison of the social and unemployment crisis reactive policy strategies in Germany, the UK and Sweden. *Social Policy and Administration*, *45*(4), 354–370. doi:10.1111/j.1467-9515.2011.00779.x

Coveney, P., & Highfield, R. (1995). *Frontiers of complexity: The search for order in a chaotic world*. Fawcett Columbine.

Edmondson, C. (2020). Trump's Response to Protests Draws Bipartisan Rebuke in Congress. *The New York Times*. https://www.nytimes.com/2020/06/02/us/politics/trump-congress-protesters-tear-gas.html

Eppel, E. A., & Rhodes, M. L. (2018). Complexity theory and public management: A 'becoming' field. *Public Management Review*, *20*(7), 949–959. doi:10.1080/14719037.2017.1364414

Farazmand, A. (2007). Learning from the Katrina crisis: A global and international perspective with implications for future crisis management. *Public Administration Review*, *67*, 149–159. doi:10.1111/j.1540-6210.2007.00824.x

Fischer, F. (2020). Post-truth politics and climate denial: Further reflections. *Critical Policy Studies, 14*(1), 124–130. doi:10.1080/19460171.2020.1734846

Fischer, F. (2021). *Truth and Post-Truth in Public Policy*. Cambridge University Press. doi:10.1017/9781108854344

Geyer, R., & Rihani, S. (2010). *Complexity and public policy: a new approach to twenty-first century politics, policy and society*. Routledge Press.

Gordon, D. J., & Johnson, C. A. (2018). City-networks, global climate governance, and the road to 1.5 C. *Current Opinion in Environmental Sustainability, 30*, 35–41. doi:10.1016/j.cosust.2018.02.011

Grossman, P. Z. (2019). Utilizing Ostrom's institutional analysis and development framework toward an understanding of crisis-driven policy. *Policy Sciences, 52*(1), 3–20. doi:10.100711077-018-9331-7

Guntzburger, Y., & Pauchant, T. C. (2014). Complexity and ethical crisis management: A systemic analysis of the Fukushima Daiichi nuclear disaster. *Journal of Organizational Effectiveness: People and Performance, 1*(4), 378–401. doi:10.1108/JOEPP-09-2014-0060

Hannah, A., & Baekkeskov, E. (2020). The promises and pitfalls of polysemic ideas: 'One Health' and antimicrobial resistance policy in Australia and the UK. *Policy Sciences, 53*(3), 437–452. doi:10.100711077-020-09390-3 PMID:32836405

Hartley, K. (2015). *Can Government Think? Flexible economic opportunism and the pursuit of global competitiveness*. Routledge Press. doi:10.4324/9781315744674

Hartley, K., & Bales, S. (2020). COVID-19 response in Vietnam: Coordination and capacity in the new developmentalist paradigm. *Policy Design and Practice*.

Hartley, K., Kuecker, G., & Woo, J. J. (2019). Practicing public policy in an age of disruption. *Policy Design and Practice, 2*(2), 163–181. doi:10.1080/25741292.2019.1622276

Hartley, K., Leischow, G., Waschak, M., Woo, J. J., & Phua, C. (2020). Conclusion: The future of Asian cities in an age of disruption. In K. Hartley, G. Kuecker, M. Waschak, J. J. Woo, & C. C. R. Phua (Eds.), *Governing cities: Asia's urban transformation* (pp. 270–275). Routledge. doi:10.4324/9780429439940-20

Hattingh, S. (2018). Preparing the workforce for the Fourth Industrial Revolution. *Skills at Work: Theory and Practice Journal, 9*(1), 6–18.

Head, B. W. (2019). Forty years of wicked problems literature: Forging closer links to policy studies. *Policy and Society, 38*(2), 180–197. doi:10.1080/14494035.2018.1488797

Hermann, C. F. (1963). Some consequences of crisis which limit the viability of organizations. *Administrative Science Quarterly, 8*(1), 61–82. doi:10.2307/2390887

Hermann, M. G. (2001). How decision units shape foreign policy: A theoretical framework. *International Studies Review, 3*(2), 47–81. doi:10.1111/1521-9488.00234

Hermann, M. G., & Dayton, B. W. (2009). Transboundary crises through the eyes of policymakers: Sense making and crisis management. *Journal of Contingencies and Crisis Management, 17*(4), 233–241. doi:10.1111/j.1468-5973.2009.00590.x

Herweijer, C., Combes, B., Johnson, L., McCargow, R., Bhardwaj, S., Jackson, B., & Ramchandani, P. (2018). *Enabling a sustainable Fourth Industrial Revolution: How G20 countries can create the conditions for emerging technologies to benefit people and the planet (No. 2018-32)*. Economics Discussion Papers.

Homer-Dixon, T. (2011). Complexity science. *Oxford Leadership Journal*, *2*(1), 1–15.

Huxham, C., & Vangen, S. (2013). *Managing to collaborate: The theory and practice of collaborative advantage*. Routledge Press. doi:10.4324/9780203010167

Hynes, W. (2017). Introduction: a complexity approach to economic challenges. In *Debate the Issues: Complexity and policy making. OECD Insights*. OECD Publishing. doi:10.1787/9789264271531-

Kahn, L. H. (2020). *Who's In charge? Leadership during epidemics, bioterror attacks, and other public health crises*. ABC-CLIO.

Kapucu, N., Arslan, T., & Collins, M. L. (2010). Examining intergovernmental and interorganizational response to catastrophic disasters: Toward a network-centered approach. *Administration & Society*, *42*(2), 222–247. doi:10.1177/0095399710362517

Keiner, M., & Kim, A. (2007). Transnational city networks for sustainability. *European Planning Studies*, *15*(10), 1369–1395. doi:10.1080/09654310701550843

Kuecker, G. D., & Hartley, K. (2020a). How smart cities became the urban norm: Power and knowledge in New Songdo City. *Annals of the American Association of Geographers*, *110*(2), 516–524. doi:10.1080/24694452.2019.1617102

Kuecker, G. D., & Hartley, K. (2020b Forthcoming). Disaster risk reduction and the development narrative: towards a new public policy epistemic. In A. Brik & L. Pal (Eds.), *The Future of the Policy Sciences*. Edward Elgar Publishing.

Law, S., Leung, A. W., & Xu, C. (2020). Severe acute respiratory syndrome (SARS) and coronavirus disease-2019 (COVID-19): From causes to preventions in Hong Kong. *International Journal of Infectious Diseases*, *94*, 156–163. doi:10.1016/j.ijid.2020.03.059 PMID:32251790

Leischow, S. J., Best, A., Trochim, W. M., Clark, P. I., Gallagher, R. S., Marcus, S. E., & Matthews, E. (2008). Systems thinking to improve the public's health. *American Journal of Preventive Medicine*, *35*(2), S196–S203. doi:10.1016/j.amepre.2008.05.014 PMID:18619400

Leonhardt, D. (2020). A Complete List of Trump's Attempts to Play Down Coronavirus. *The New York Times*. https://www.nytimes.com/2020/03/15/opinion/trump-coronavirus.html

Lipton, E., Sanger, D., Haberman, M., Shear, M., Mazzetti, M., & Barnes, J. (2020). He Could Have Seen What Was Coming: Behind Trump's Failure on the Virus. *The New York Times*. https://www.nytimes.com/2020/04/11/us/politics/coronavirus-trump-response.html

Low, J. (2016). Singapore's Whole-of-Government Approach in Crisis Management. *Ethos (Berkeley, Calif.)*, 16.

Malhotra, N., & Kuo, A. G. (2008). Attributing blame: The public's response to Hurricane Katrina. *The Journal of Politics*, *70*(1), 120–135. doi:10.1017/S0022381607080097

Manson, S. M. (2001). Simplifying complexity: A review of complexity theory. *Geoforum*, *32*(3), 405–414. doi:10.1016/S0016-7185(00)00035-X

McKay, V. (2018). Introducing a parallel curriculum to enhance social and environmental awareness in South African school workbooks. Balancing individualism and collectivism: Social and environmental justice, 97-122. doi:10.1007/978-3-319-58014-2_5

Mocca, E. (2017). City networks for sustainability in Europe: An urban-level analysis. *Journal of Urban Affairs*, *39*(5), 691–710. doi:10.1080/07352166.2017.1282769

Morçöl, G. (2013). *A complexity theory for public policy*. Routledge Press. doi:10.4324/9780203112694

Moynihan, D. P. (2009). The network governance of crisis response: Case studies of incident command systems. *Journal of Public Administration: Research and Theory*, *19*(4), 895–915. doi:10.1093/jopart/mun033

PeiS.KandulaS.ShamanJ. 2020. Differential Effects of Intervention Timing on COVID-19 Spread in the United States. medRxiv.

Peters, B. G. (2017). What is so wicked about wicked problems? A conceptual analysis and a research program. *Policy and Society*, *36*(3), 385–396. doi:10.1080/14494035.2017.1361633

Peters, B. G., & Pierre, J. (2019). Populism and public administration: Confronting the administrative state. *Administration & Society*, *51*(10), 1521–1545. doi:10.1177/0095399719874749

Phelan, S.E. (2001). What is complexity science, really? *Emergence, A Journal of Complexity Issues in Organizations and Management,* *3*(1), 120-136.

Platt, A., & Warwick, S. (1995). Review of soft systems methodology. *Industrial Management & Data Systems*, *95*(4), 19–21. doi:10.1108/02635579510086698

Raco, M., & Savini, F. (Eds.). (2019). *Planning and knowledge: How new forms of technocracy are shaping contemporary cities*. Policy Press.

Ramos, G. (2017). It's not just the economy: Society is a complex system too. In *Debate the Issues: Complexity and policy making. OECD Insights*. OECD Publishing. doi:10.1787/9789264271531-

Rittel, H. W., & Webber, M. M. (1973). Dilemmas in a general theory of planning. *Policy Sciences*, *4*(2), 155–169. doi:10.1007/BF01405730

Sabatier, P. (2007). *Theories of the Policy Process*. Taylor & Francis.

Schneider, S. K. (1995). *Flirting with disaster: Public management in crisis situations*. ME Sharpe.

Schubert, J. N., Stewart, P. A., & Curran, M. A. (2002). A defining presidential moment: 9/11 and the rally effect. *Political Psychology*, *23*(3), 559–583. doi:10.1111/0162-895X.00298

Shear, M., & Rogers, K. (2020). Trump and Aides Try to Change the Narrative of the White House Protests. *The New York Times*.https://www.nytimes.com/2020/06/03/us/politics/trump-protests.html>

Ślusarczyk, B. (2018). Industry 4.0: Are we ready? *Polish Journal of Management Studies*, 17.

Stockdale-Otárola, J. (2017). Navigating wicked problems. In *Debate the Issues: Complexity and policy making. OECD Insights*. OECD Publishing. doi:10.1787/9789264271531-

Sucha, V. (2017). A new role for science in policy formation in the age of complexity? In *Debate the Issues: Complexity and policy making. OECD Insights*. OECD Publishing. doi:10.1787/9789264271531-

Sylves, R. T. (2006). President Bush and Hurricane Katrina: A presidential leadership study. *The Annals of the American Academy of Political and Social Science, 604*(1), 26–56. doi:10.1177/0002716205286066

't Hart, P. (1997). Preparing policy makers for crisis management: The role of simulations. *Journal of Contingencies and Crisis Management, 5*(4), 207–215. doi:10.1111/1468-5973.00058

Turner, J. R., & Baker, R. M. (2019). Complexity theory: An overview with potential applications for the social sciences. *Systems, 7*(1), 4. doi:10.3390ystems7010004

Uhl-Bien, M., Marion, R., & McKelvey, B. (2007). Complexity leadership theory: Shifting leadership from the industrial age to the knowledge era. *The Leadership Quarterly, 18*(4), 298–318. doi:10.1016/j.leaqua.2007.04.002

Versluis, E., van Asselt, M., & Kim, J. (2019). The multilevel regulation of complex policy problems: Uncertainty and the swine flu pandemic. *European Policy Analysis, 5*(1), 80–98. doi:10.1002/epa2.1064 PMID:34616904

Vigoda, E. (2002). From responsiveness to collaboration: Governance, citizens, and the next generation of public administration. *Public Administration Review, 62*(5), 527–540. doi:10.1111/1540-6210.00235

Waltner-Toews, D., Kay, J., Kay, J. J., & Lister, N. M. E. (Eds.). (2008). *The ecosystem approach: complexity, uncertainty, and managing for sustainability*. Columbia University Press.

Waugh, W. L., & Streib, G. (2006). Collaboration and leadership for effective emergency management. *Public Administration Review, 66*(s1), 131–140. doi:10.1111/j.1540-6210.2006.00673.x

Weber, E., & Khademian, A. M. (2008). Managing collaborative processes: Common practices, uncommon circumstances. *Administration & Society, 40*(5), 431–464. doi:10.1177/0095399708320181

Wenzelburger, G., König, P. D., & Wolf, F. (2019). Policy theories in hard times? Assessing the explanatory power of policy theories in the context of crisis. *Public Organization Review, 19*(1), 97–118. doi:10.100711115-017-0387-1

Zahariadis, N. (2007). The multiple streams framework: Structure, limitations, prospects. In P. A. Sabatier (Ed.), *Theories of the policy process*. Westview Press.

Zguir, M. F., Dubis, S., & Koç, M. (2021). Embedding Education for Sustainable Development (ESD) and SDGs values in curriculum: A comparative review on Qatar, Singapore and New Zealand. *Journal of Cleaner Production, 319*, 128534. doi:10.1016/j.jclepro.2021.128534

ENDNOTES

1 https://www.unido.org/news/boosting-dialogue-fourth-industrial-revolution-11th-africa-energy-indaba
2 https://www.pwc.co.uk/sustainability-climate-change/assets/enabling-a-sustainable-fourth-industrial-revolution.pdf
3 https://arrayofthings.github.io/
4 https://www.iddri.org/sites/default/files/import/publications/working-paper-sdgs-and-ngos_eh-dd.pdf
5 https://www.nytimes.com/2019/03/14/world/europe/climate-action-strikes-youth.html
6 https://www.brookings.edu/wp-content/uploads/2019/06/City-leadership-on-the-SDGs.pdf
7 https://www.brookings.edu/blog/future-development/2019/06/18/cities-the-labs-for-sustainable-development-goal-innovation/

Chapter 2
Program Monitoring and Evaluation of Sustainable Development Goals for Non-Profits and NGOs:
Benefits, Functions, Stages, and Stakeholders

Simon Cleveland
https://orcid.org/0000-0001-9293-3905
Purdue University Global, USA

Marisa Cleveland
Northeastern University, USA

ABSTRACT

Non-profits and NGOs serve communities through programs, which are often complex to execute. Board members demand accountability for the execution of such programs, and as a result, these organizations adopt monitoring and evaluation practices to determine the success of failure based on a set of performance criteria. This study focuses on defining the program monitoring and evaluation process and exploring in depth its benefits, functions, and stages. Moreover, an examination of the stakeholders involved in the process is performed, and a set of currencies and power and influence criteria are explored.

INTRODUCTION

Non-profit organizations and nongovernmental organizations (NGOs) exist to provide assistance to various individuals or groups, which is not available through government supported programs (Lee, 2008). The role of an NGO is to create an engagement and dialogue among stakeholders with a particular area

DOI: 10.4018/978-1-6684-8903-1.ch002

(Legutko, 2018). Moreover, this engagement should not take place in isolation, but by encouraging participation of all parties who would benefits directly and indirectly from the deliverables by the NGO's work (Mayya, 2015).

In 2015, the United Nations Member States adopted a 2030 Agenda for Sustainable Development, which identified a roadmap to allow the member states to advance toward prosperity and improvement of health, economic development, decrease in inequality and increase in health (United Nations, n.d.).

To deliver on their sustainable development goals (SDG), non-profits and NGOs, who pursue the United Nations 2030 Agenda, need to launch programs which require continuous monitoring and evaluation to determine whether they have accomplished their strategic intent. While the literature is abundant on the subjects of project and program management, there is a gap in the areas addressing the complexity around the program monitoring and evaluation process, including its benefits, functions, stages and stakeholders. As a result, the research question for this study is: What are the benefits, functions, stages and stakeholders of the program monitoring and evaluation process for NGOs and non-profit organizations?

This rest of the paper is organized as follows. First, an overview of program monitoring and evaluation process is provided. Next, a detailed examination of the monitoring and evaluation benefits, functions and stages is proposed. This is followed by an overview of the monitoring and evaluation stakeholders, including identification of several currencies, which could be used by program managers when dealing with difficult stakeholders. The paper concludes with methods to characterize the stakeholders' power and influence on monitoring and evaluation projects as well as recommendations for future research.

PROGRAM MONITORING AND EVALUATION

According to Markiewicz and Patrick (2016), program monitoring and evaluation, referred to as monitoring and evaluation (M&E) throughout this study is a process that provides "… routine monitoring and periodic evaluation that will take place over the life of a program or initiative. Typically, these parameters include a focus on evaluation domains, particularly those of appropriateness, effectiveness, efficiency, impact, and sustainability." (p.1). The goal of M&E is to establish connections between the past, present and future results, in order to derive information that can be leveraged to re-align new and existing programs.

Program managers spend a lot of their time having to communicate the status of the program to stakeholders and consistent communication is essential to ensure cross-program and program collaboration (Zulch, 2014). Any significant changes to the programs need to be shared across the organization so that quick and relevant decisions are made to correct any deviations in order to prevent any rework, delays or additional scope and cost to programs. To accomplish this, program managers collect consistently data related to the status of the program. This includes the use of specific indicators of metrics (Curlee & Gordon, 2013).

According to UNDP (2009), program monitoring is an ongoing process that serves various stakeholders to get feedback on the progress made by a program towards accomplishing its SDGs. The key here is that monitoring involves progress reviews against specific SDGs to determine whether these SDGs are achieved. Monitoring involves the tracking of projects, programs, strategies and actions taken by an NGOs or non-profits' stakeholders in order to determine next steps toward improved results (Paul, 2021). Furthermore, monitoring involves real-time information required by management and often creates questions that need to be addressed by the evaluation process. The lessons learned from the monitoring process are examined periodically for the purposes of making decisions and taking actions.

Program evaluation "is the systematic examination of a specific government program to provide information on the full range of the program's short and long –term effects." (Asfaw, 2011, p. 9). The evaluation process involves an independent assessment of completed or ongoing tasks to derive the level which objectives are achieved (UNDP, 2009). This process can be applied to projects and programs, but should be conducted independently so that an objective review can give management an idea whether the said program is accomplishing its SDGs. The evaluation process consists of rigorous steps, procedures and methods that incorporate detailed analysis. Evaluations rely on the data collected through the monitoring process of a project or a program.

MONITORING AND EVALUATION BENEFITS

According to Kariuki and Reddy (2017) M&E improves the development of policy and improves financial management. Furthermore, it enables organizations to align their priorities. M&E also assists management in conducting better governance, accountability and enhances services delivery. POPT (n.d.) provided additional benefits of the M&E process. These include: quantification of the attainment of program SDGs and sub- SDGs such as whether the actions were implemented as planned for the program, whether assumptions made during identification of the problem and its context were correct; whether the actions have resulted in risk reductions; and whether new information has emerged that requires a strengthening and/or modification to the risk management plan.

Moreover, M&E addresses the questions that funders and other stakeholders of NGOs and non-profits have – mainly whether a program has spent its money appropriately and desired outcomes have been achieved. M&E provides answers to questions such as: Has the program worked? How have resources been spent? Should the program continue? What are the program's strengths and weaknesses? What are the implementation problems? Why have things worked, or not? What are the good practice issues?

Magagula (2019) argued that M&E provides the following set of benefits: 1) Management decision-making - M&E fosters effective managerial processes and decision-making; 2) Organizational learning – M&E provides information on what interventions, programs and projects will address the problems of society and the outcomes of M&E lead to organizational learning; 3) Accountability – M&E delivers structured and formalized information that promotes analysis of activities at all levels; 4) Soliciting support for programs – M&E results help management make decisions about budgetary allocations for a specific programs and projects; 5) Supporting advocacy – M&E results help management identify issues that can assist in the decision to either continue, adjust or terminate programs; 6) Promoting transparency – M&E results help promote transparency in the organization.

Chimwendo (2004) argued that M&E delivers to management and stakeholders frequent data on the progress of programs, which promotes: 1) Accountability: Showcases to various donors, taxpayers and beneficiaries that expenses, actions and results are as expected; 2) Operational management and implementation: Delivery of data needed for the coordination of financial, physical and human resources allocated to programs and projects; 3) Strategic management: Delivery of data to promote the establishment or modification of strategies and/or objectives; 4) Capacity building: Where stakeholders build confidence and self-reliance to create and deliver various initiatives.

Additionally, Chimwendo (2004) provided a set of M&E benefits at both the sector and project levels. Sector level benefits include program design improvements through feedback provided from comparisons to the baseline, midterm, terminal and ex-post evaluations; consensus building between stakeholders by providing evidence of the program results. Project level benefits include: 1) Regular feedback on project performance and show any need for 'mid-course' corrections; 2) Identification of problems early with proposed solutions; 3) Monitoring of access to project services and outcomes by the target population; 4) Evaluation of achievement of project objectives; and 5) Incorporating stakeholder views and promoting participation, ownership and accountability.

MONITORING AND EVALUATION FUNCTIONS

Asfaw (2011) argued there is a distinction between the functions of the monitoring and evaluation process. The monitoring process is implementation oriented. It tracks results to assess intermediate status and focuses on timeliness. The emphasis here is on multi-level results, it informs budgeting, strengthens accountability for managing results and can use disaggregated data. In contrast to monitoring, the evaluation process is policy oriented, explains results, assesses attributes, focuses on rigor, emphasis is on final results. The evaluation process informs broad resources allocation, strengthens accountability for results. It is essential for strategy development and may require aggregated data.

Farrell (2009) argued that the monitoring function is a form of formative evaluation. It is used to connect inputs and activities to anticipated results. Its approach is to provide information about the present status of programs, their use of resources and their ability to achieve short-term results. Moreover, the monitoring function is to generate data that empowers management to make adjustments during the implementation phase of the program's cycle. Finally, the function of the monitoring process is to deliver data for stakeholder reports as it relates to the program progress and any needs for changes, which create transparency.

As for evaluation, Farrell (2009) argued that is a form of summative evaluation, whose function is to deliver data about the accomplishment of intermediate and long-term results, program efficiency and post-intervention sustainability. Moreover, the function of the evaluation process is to explore unintended results, generate evidence about causality as to why results were, or were not, achieved. The evaluation process also provides information for synthesizing lessons learned about learning for strategy development.

Paru (2019) proposed that NGOs and non-profits should use monitoring and evaluation-specific department in order to: 1) Prepare guidelines to facilitate the application of the monitoring and evaluation framework; 2) Develop and promote standards for monitoring and evaluation and quality assurance; 3) Promote knowledge management and organizational learning; 4) Oversee the application of the policy framework and identify bottlenecks in the organizations.

Chibonore (2016) argued that there are three functions of the M&E processes for organizations. These include: 1) Institutional function – where the assessment of project outcomes is performed to determine whether organizational standards are achieved. The need to maintain standards helps organizations attract additional resource from donors and to obtain help from volunteers and other stakeholders. This is due to the fact that these stakeholders are able to determine through the M&E process whether the organization has achieved a set of standards which are often indicators for progress and success; 2) Managerial function – which is concerned with the measurement of data for better decision making in order to adjust specific activities to meet certain standards; to identify potential issues and problems that take corrective actions; and 3) Technical function – determine the extent to which the programs provide effective and efficient delivery of their products or services. The goal is to ensure that stakeholders are happy with products and services delivered. This particular function ensures that programs have good governance of the NGOs and non-profits which provides openness, transparency and accountability.

MONITORING AND EVALUATION STAGES

According to Gosling and Edwards (2003) the monitoring stage includes: 1) Definition of the aim of the monitoring -where it is decided who and what needs to be monitored as well as setting the objectives of the monitoring process; 2) Selection of relevant information - where it is decided what are the existing systems, what are the key indicators and what models and frameworks will be used for the monitoring process; 3) Data collection and analysis - where the methods of data collection are decided, the type of training and support needed for the resources involved in the data collection and the analysis of data; 4) Results presentation - where it is decided the type of feedback and the findings are discussed. Also, the results for the planning procedures, institutional learning are used as basis for the evaluation. 5) Organization - where it is decided who would be involved in the monitoring, whether any people would participate from outside the program, how the monitoring of the work with another organization would be performed and how the monitoring process will be maintained including resources, training, support and supervision.

Gosling and Edwards (2003) argued that the evaluation stages consist of: 1) Definition of the purpose - where it is decided why thee valuation is necessary; 2) Determination of stakeholders - where it is decided who will use the results; 3) Identification of objectives and key questions - where it is decided what are the objectives of the evaluation and the specific questions that should be addressed; 4) Collection and analysis of the information - where it is decided what information is necessary to answer specific questions, where the information will come from, what indicators will be used to measure the impact of the work and how the information will be collected, analyzed and presented; 5) Presentation of the results - where it is decided what would be the conclusions and recommendations, how the findings will be recorded and presented to various stakeholders, the type of feedback will be delivered about the findings and the people and processes involved in the work; and, 6) Organization- where it is decided who should be involved including their tasks and responsibilities, the timescale and type of resources required.

MONITORING AND EVALUATION STAKEHOLDERS

What are stakeholders? Cleland (1998) defined stakeholders as parties that have "legitimate claims against the substantive aspects of the project. What is a stake? A stake is an interest or share or claim in a project; it can range from informal interest in the undertaking, at one extreme, to a legal claim of ownership at the other extreme."

In the paper by Winch (2004), stakeholders are represented as a diverse group and classified them as internal and external. The internal stakeholders typically have a contract with the client and as a result are positively inclined toward program's success, while external stakeholders do not have a direct influence on whether a program is initiated or not.

Preskill and Jones (2009) proposed additional types of stakeholders. These include:

1. Program/initiative staff – staff, leadership
2. Organizational leadership – executives, board of directors, advisory boards
3. Grantees
4. Program/initiative beneficiaries – participants, clients, patients
5. Program/Initiative researchers and evaluators
6. Volunteers
7. Contributors – founders, donors, other funders and co-funders, collaborating organizations
8. Community groups and leaders – Community-based organizations, community leaders, religious leaders, law enforcement, community service groups, business leaders
9. Experts – expert consultants, evaluators of similar programs/initiatives, researchers, academics
10. Policy groups – policy makers (local, state, federal), advocacy organizations, government agencies
11. Other – staff from similar programs/initiatives, professional associations, media

According to the CDC (2012), stakeholders are capable of either helping, or have negative impact during the M&E process. Moreover, "Stakeholders are much more likely to support the evaluation and act on the results and recommendations if they are involved in the evaluation process. Conversely, without stakeholder support, your evaluation may be ignored, criticized, resisted, or even sabotaged." (CDC, 2012).

In his study, Winch (2004) proposed several processes for stakeholder management. These include: 1) Identifying stakeholders who have a claim in the program; 2) Categorizing each stakeholder's claim; 3) Assessing stakeholder's capacity to pursue such claims; 4) Managing the handling of any claims.

Furthermore, CDC (2012) proposed that you should focus on stakeholders who 'increase the credibility' of the M&E process, who are involved in the daily 'implementation of the activities' of the program, who will 'advocate for or authorize changes to the program', and who have control and will providing funding for the program. Think of it as if stakeholders have two distinct perspectives in the M&E process. These include the M&E team perspective and the stakeholders' perspective.

Table 1 identifies the common questions, which emerge from each perspective.

Table 1. Common questions

M&E Team's Perspective	Stakeholders' Perspective
Whose cooperation will we need?	What differences exist between the team and those on whom the team will depend?
Whose agreement or approval will we need?	How do the stakeholders view the project?
Whose opposition would keep us from accomplishing the project?	What is the status of our relationships with the stakeholders?
	What sources of influence does the team have relative to the stakeholders?

Weiss (1993) argued that the M&E process is impacted by the stakeholders because in various organizations, the process occurs in a 'political context.' As a result, program managers engaged in the M&E should take into account three key factors that influence stakeholders perceptions: 1) The programs were "proposed, defined, debated, enacted, and funded" as a result of political decisions (p. 93). As a result, stakeholders would exhibit both supportive and aggressive perceptions toward the program; 2) Programs compete for resources with other programs. Therefore, certain stakeholders would be more sympathetic, while others unsympathetic to the M&E process since the "outcomes has to compete for attention with other factors that carry weight in the political process."; 3) The outcomes of the M&E process would reveal 'problematic nature of some programs.' As a result, certain stakeholders may feel more intimidated than others if the results question the 'legitimacy of program goals and program strategies.'

Stakeholder Currencies

There is an intricate network of stakeholders in the M&E process who have various degrees of influence. Each stakeholder possesses various degrees of currency influence. Here, cooperative relationships are built on the exchange of organizational "currencies" (favors).

Larson and Gray (2017) propose various types of organizational currencies that program managers can leverage to ensure successful completion of the M&E process. First, we have task-related currencies. For example, you can use Resources as currency. This involves the lending or giving money, budget increases, personnel, etc. With Assistance, you can help with existing projects or undertaking unwanted tasks. There is Cooperation, where you Give task support, provide quicker response time, or aide implementation. Finally, you can use Information to provide organizational as well as technical knowledge.

Next, we have Position-related currencies. Most common currencies here include Advancement – giving a task or assignment that can result in promotion. Also, there is Recognition – acknowledging effort, accomplishments, or abilities. There is Visibility, or Providing a chance to be known by higher-ups or significant others in the organization. Finally, Network - providing opportunities for linking with others.

There are also inspiration-related currencies. Here, you can use Vision - being involved in a task that has larger significance for the unit, organization, customer, or society. You can also use Excellence - having a chance to do important things really well. Finally, you can have Ethical correctness -doing what is "right" by a higher standard than efficiency.

Another type of currencies are Relationship-related. There is Acceptance -providing closeness and friendship; Personal support- giving personal and emotional backing; and Understanding -listening to others' concerns and issues.

The last type of currencies are the personal-related currencies. You can use Challenge/learning - sharing tasks that increase skills and abilities. You can use Ownership/involvement - letting others have ownership and influence. Finally, you can use Gratitude -expressing appreciation.

Stakeholders Power and Influence

During the M&E process, program managers engage in identification and analysis of the stakeholders. Varvasovszky and Brugha (2000) argued that the analysis process leads to an overall understanding of the stakeholders' behaviors, intentions, interests and the 'influence and resources they bring to bear on decision-making' (p. 338). The researchers proposed three preliminary questions to consider prior to the stakeholder analysis. These include:

1. What is the purpose and time frame of the analysis – this question will help program managers determine the scope (breadth, complexity, role of stakeholders) and duration (short or long-term);
2. What is the context of the analysis – this question will help with the approach to dealing with specific stakeholders (managerial, administrative, political);

3. What is the level of the analysis – this question helps with identifying the depth of analysis such as local, national, international.

The analysis of stakeholders includes mapping of the participants in a tool called stakeholder register. Here, you will create maps and group stakeholders within clusters of either proponents or opponents and then try to relate them to the objectives of the program, and any specific problems and solutions that can occur in the M&E process. You can use a power/interest matrix for the adoption of a strategy to manage the identified stakeholders. The matrix can consist of two dimensions - power of the stakeholder's influence and the level of interest that the stakeholder. Based on the identification of each stakeholder against the power/interest matrix, you may classify your stakeholders as:

Requiring minimal effort – stakeholders that are client's customers, or local and national government that require general information: 1) Be kept informed - local residents, conservationists, or environmentalists; 2) Be kept satisfied - regulatory bodies and the supply-side stakeholders; 3) Are key players – central clients and sponsors who need to be managed closely.

Finally, Winch proposed four main sources of relevant stakeholder power. These include: 1) Positional power – Relevant to a stakeholder's position in the organizational hierarchy; 2) Resource power – Relevant to a stakeholder's ability to provide resources for the project (such as capital); 3) Expert power – Relevant to a stakeholder's expertise and competence in a field directly relevant to the program; 4) Personal power – Relevant to a stakeholder's charisma to direct individuals' opinions.

CONCLUSION

The 2030 Agenda for Sustainable Development adopted by the United Nations Member States, which calls for all member states to advance toward prosperity and improvement of health, economic development, decrease in inequality and increase in health, depends not only on government institutions, but also on non-profits and NGOs to deliver on the Agenda's sustainable development goals through programs requiring continuous monitoring and evaluation.

This study sought to address the following research question: What are the benefits, functions, stages and stakeholders of the program monitoring and evaluation process for NGOs and non-profit organizations?

For this purpose, the study defined the program monitoring and evaluation process and then proposed a set of relevant benefits for such organizations. Next, the study explored the extant literature on monitoring and evaluation functions and stages and concluded with exploration of the stakeholders involved in the M&E process. This study advances the body of knowledge on the M&E process for non-profits and NGOs and adds practical value for existing or novice program managers who seek to qualify the factors, which could create complexity during program execution.

Further research should focus on specific case studies to examine the applicability of the proposed M&E factors and to align the explore whether the interests of the identified stakeholders can be aligned against the proposed power and influence dimensions. Furthermore, future research should attempt to develop a framework to the M&E process in order to catalog the proposed factors.

REFERENCES

Asfaw, A. (2011). *Assessment of the monitoring and evaluation processes and challenges: the case of integrated family service organization, sustainable development for children project* [Doctoral dissertation]. St. Mary's University.

CDC. (2012). *Program Evaluation for Public Health Programs: A Self-Study Guide.* Retrieved from https://www.cdc.gov/eval/guide/step1/

Chibonore, W. C. (2016). *Monitoring and evaluation practices in selected non governmental organisations* [Doctoral dissertation].

Chimwendo. (2004). *Designing Monitoring and Evaluation Systems for NEPAD Projects.* UNECA.

Cleland, D. I. (1998). Stakeholder management. In J. Pinto (Ed.), *Project management handbook.* Jossey-Bass.

Curlee, W., & Gordon, R. L. (2013). *Successful program management: Complexity theory, communication, and leadership.* CRC Press. doi:10.1201/b15925

Farrell, G. M. (2009). *Results-based monitoring and evaluation at the Commonwealth of Learning. Commonwealth of Learning.* COL.

Gosling, L., & Edwards, M. (2003). *Toolkits: A practical guide to planning, monitoring, evaluation and impact assessment.* Save the Children UK.

Kariuki, P., & Reddy, P. (2017). Operationalising an effective monitoring and evaluation system for local government: Considerations for best practice. *African Evaluation Journal, 5*(2), 1–8. doi:10.4102/aej.v5i2.240

Larson, E. W., & Gray, C. F. (2017). *Project Management: The Managerial Process* (7th ed.). McGraw-Hill Education.

Lee, M. (2008). Government Influence on the Formation of Nonprofits: A dual relationship between local government and local nonprofits. *International Review of Public Administration, 13*(2), 97–115. doi:10.1080/12294659.2008.10805124

Legutko, A. J. (2018). NGO in the Modern State. *Institutionalist Perspectives on Development: A Multidisciplinary Approach*, 59-74.

Magagula, B. S. (2019). *An evaluation of the implementation of monitoring and evaluation systems in the office of the Premier, Free State provincial government* [Doctoral dissertation]. Central University of Technology, Free State.

Markiewicz, A., & Patrick, I. (2016). *Developing monitoring and evaluation frameworks (No. BOOK).* Sage Publications. doi:10.4135/9781071878774

Mayya, S. (2015). Role of Non Governmental Organisation in Rural Development: A Study in Dakshina Kannada District. *Sumedha Journal of Management, 4*(4), 27–38.

Paru, B. (2019). *The role of monitoring and evaluation system in promoting performance of Non-Governmental Organizations in Juba County.*

Paul, K. A. (2021). Collaborative Evaluation for Program Monitoring. In Total School Cluster Grouping & Differentiation (pp. 87-96). Routledge. doi:10.4324/9781003239239-7

POPT. (n.d.). *Benefits of Monitoring and Evaluation.* Retrieved from http://www.popstoolkit.com/riskmanagement/module/step5/benefits.aspx

Preskill, H., & Jones, N. (2009). *A practical guide for engaging stakeholders in developing evaluation questions.* Academic Press.

United Nations. (n.d.). *The 17 Goals.* Department of Economic and Social Affairs Sustainable Development. Retrieved from https://sdgs.un.org/goals

Varvasovszky, Z., & Brugha, R. (2000). A stakeholder analysis. *Health Policy and Planning, 15*(3), 338–345. doi:10.1093/heapol/15.3.338 PMID:11012410

Weiss, C. H. (1993). Where politics and evaluation research meet. *Evaluation Practice, 14*(1), 93–106. doi:10.1177/109821409301400119

Winch, G. M. (2007). *Managing project stakeholders. The Wiley Guide to Project, Program, and Portfolio Management.* Wiley.

Zulch, B. (2014). Leadership communication in project management. *Procedia: Social and Behavioral Sciences, 119*, 172–181. doi:10.1016/j.sbspro.2014.03.021

Chapter 3
Is EU Law Conducive to the SDG 15?
Interests Reflected in the Legal Representation of the Sustainability Principle in the EU

Antje Ilberg
https://orcid.org/0000-0003-3865-0976
Independent Researcher, Germany

ABSTRACT

Is EU law conducive to successful implementation of SDG 15? This chapter assesses the effectiveness of the legal representation of sustainability in EU biodiversity law and the foundation it establishes for ensuring biodiversity protection. It identifies the policy anchors that foster the human self-entitlement and the various forms of interest involved in the legal representation of the principle of sustainable development, and which impede the effectiveness of EU law intended to protect biodiversity. Advocacy is made to review the accurate transposition of the Brundtland report into legal principles and to incorporate the newly acknowledged human right to a clean environment in EU law, as a footing to facilitate effective biodiversity protection.

INTRODUCTION

Sustainable Development Goal (SDG) 15 calls to "Protect, restore and promote sustainable use of terrestrial ecosystems, sustainably manage forests, combat desertification, and halt and reverse land degradation and halt biodiversity loss," (UN, n.d.). This chapter discusses the implementation of SDG 15 on biodiversity protection through EU environmental law. As part of this, it is assessed how the sustainability principle as carried forward by the SDGs, is transposed in EU environmental law.

The recent monitoring of the SDG implementation by the EU noted "continued and strong declines in biodiversity and species abundance, and continued land degradation," (2022). The UN reports that

DOI: 10.4018/978-1-6684-8903-1.ch003

"the risk of species extinction is increasing at a rate unprecedented in human history," (2022). The Global Assessment Report on Biodiversity and Ecosystem Services attests that the "negative trends in biodiversity and ecosystem services are expected to hinder progress towards the Agenda 2030 and its SDG targets," (EU, n.d). The following analysis seeks to identify the starting point of the barriers to effective biodiversity protection in the EU. It calls for a fundamental correction of the anthropocentric misinterpretation of the sustainability principle in EU environmental law. It is argued that the Rio Declaration on Environment and Development 1992 - the starting point of bundling global sustainability commitments into sets of goals, first the MDGs, which were succeeded by the SDGs - does not actually fully capture the spirit of its foundational source, the Brundtland Report, (UN, 1987). It is suggested to readjust the representation of the originally clearly divergent morale of sustainability, as multiple legal documents refer to the declaration and it shapes modern policy and law.

The questions raised rank around the effectiveness of the EU legal framework to protect biodiversity. EU statute law represents a series of interests and rights in the legal transposition of the sustainability principle. Based on it, environmental exploitation can take place in the name of development. As long as considerations of environmental protection will remain subordinated to economic interests with the support of law, it will not be effective in fulfilling its purpose. The references that legal documents make to the sustainability principle, which is captured in the first principle of the Rio Declaration on Environment and Development in 1992 and has become customary, epitomize the critical subject. Priorities must shift away from humans' self-entitlement in the interest of humankind. The Chapter examines the exhibition of 'interest' in EU law, including interest that may override a legal provision. To support effective implementation of the SDG 15 and other important international commitments that aim at biodiversity protection, it is strongly suggested to review and revise the legal references to the sustainability principle and to the Rio Summit, and correct the anthropocentric interpretation that EU legislation has adopted in conjunction with the sustainability principle in general and with biodiversity protection specifically. The Chapter further advocates to timely accommodate the newly acknowledged human right to a clean and healthy environment in law. Effective biodiversity protection must be backed by effective law, and governance must reflect the uncompromised willingness to prioritise the safeguarding of biodiversity.

SUSTAINABLE DEVELOPMENT

The Rio Declaration was grounded in the landmark report of the Brundtland commission 'Our Common Future' ('Brundtland Report') from 1987, which was endorsed by the UN General Assembly in Resolution 42/187 (Figure 1). Through the Brundtland Report, the commonly applied definition of 'sustainable development' was born: 'Sustainable development is development that meets the needs of the present without compromising the ability of future generations to meet their own needs," (UN, 1987). The Rio Declaration, which took up this definition is not legally binding, but handed over a significant foundation for EU environmental law.

Through its very first principle, however, the Rio Declaration has enshrined an anthropocentric approach to the apprehension of sustainable development in international environmental law. It reads: 'Human beings are at the centre of concerns for sustainable development. They are entitled to a healthy and productive life in harmony with nature.' While generally appearing positive, the statement sets an inhibition by entitling humans as the centre point of a balancing of interests. This is cause of concern for the success prospects of biodiversity protection. In the phraseology of the Rio Declaration, 'neither

Figure 1. Important milestones on the road to the Agenda 2030
Source: EU (2022)[1]

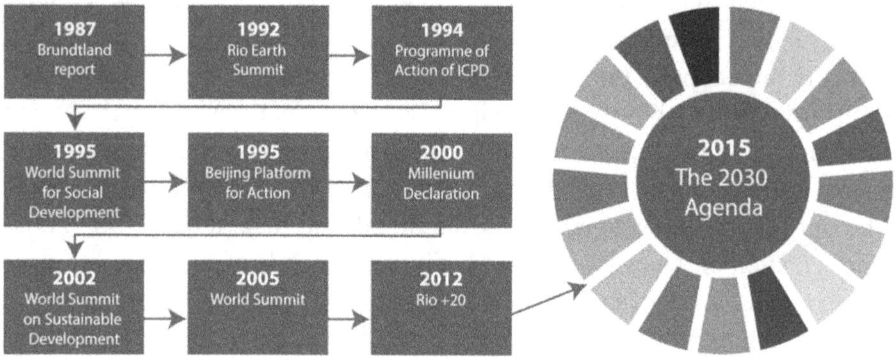

environmental protection nor human rights trump the right to economic development," (Birnie, Boyle, Redgwell, 2009).

Principle 2 of the declaration allows states to 'exploit their own resources pursuant to their own environmental and development policies." (The Laywers and Jurists, n.d). By leaving the scope of environmental legislation up for interpretation by the individual country, the statement could also impede a principled implementation of biodiversity protection. Besides, it limits the requirement 'to not damage environment' to 'areas beyond the limits of national jurisdiction', which enshrines the 'no harm' ethics but practically excludes environment within a country's borders.

Principle 3 embodies the sustainability principle and means to shape development in conjunction with an intra- and intergenerational responsibility; 'The right to development must be fulfilled so as to equitably meet developmental and environmental needs of present and future generations.' The comprised reference to developmental needs of present generations, however leads to some ambiguity. The 'right to development', which 'must be fulfilled' could genuinely be misinterpreted as a human entitlement, while any limitation that should frame 'development' despite being a right, remains unexplicit, contrary to the core message of the Brundtland Report, (UN, n.d.).

Besides promoting human entitlement, the first principle, in conjunction with Principle 11, could also entitle governments of developed countries to continue business as usual, while merely just acknowledging differences of economic power:

States shall enact effective environmental legislation, Environmental standards, management objectives, and priorities should reflect the environmental and developmental context to which they apply. Standards applied by some countries may be inappropriate and of unwarranted economic and social cost to other countries, in particular developing countries. (UN General Assembly, 1992)

The Brundtland Report had urged that no aspect can be treated in isolation. Principle 4 is transposing the thought up to the term 'process': 'In order to achieve sustainable development, environmental protection shall constitute an integral part of the development process and cannot be considered in isolation from it.' But whether or not environment may (as well) be 'considered in isolation' should not form part of the argument. The modified substance could impede the strengthening of current environmental law.

Principle 11 cited before introduces room for economic interests to outweigh environmental aspects. An interpretation of how the environmental and development context should be reflected, is possible in any way. 'Environmental standards' can never be 'unwarranted' in view of economic or social cost, and are instead critical in the macro-economic and public interest, and including social interest.

In 2010, a UN report had remarked that 'the notion of sustainable development has lost traction since the Brundtland report and Rio Summit because of the dominance of the economic growth agenda,' (Drexhage, Murphy, 2010). The shift toward an economic growth agenda was taken note of. The original argumentation by the Brundtland Commission did not contain any foundation for interpretation in an anthropocentric sense, and the Rio Declaration misrepresents the key message of 'Our Common Future'. This is relevant, as the Rio Earth Summit 1992 serves as a reference for other international agreements, including the 2030 Agenda for Sustainable Development connected to publication of the SDGs. The 2030 Agenda later presents sustainable development as a balance of the environmental, economic and social dimensions, (UN, n.d) which 'Our Common Future' did not. The principal pledge of Brundtland was for the necessity to limit economic growth to such level, that is in the common interest of human survival. It details that 'sustainable development requires the conservation of plant and animal species (UN, n.d) and does not spur any compromise of this target. In terms of human-centered regards, the Brundtland Report only takes up egality, inclusiveness and support for the underprivileged but no economic dimension. It may be argued, that the Rio Declaration has laid the foundation for a biased interpretation of the sustainability principle, in misalignment with the key intention. This notion became further enshrined though later Conventions and legal documents that reference the Rio Summit, and disseminated through communication and non–legal documents, with EU law further altering the original spirit of sustainability.

FRAMEWORK FOR BIODIVERSITY PROTECTION IN EU LAW AND REVIEW OF EFFECTIVENESS

Through Article 38 (1c) of the Statute of the International Court of Justice, 'general principles of law recognized by civilized nations' and international custom become sources of international law,' (European Environment Agency, 2012). This way, the key environmental principles recognized by international conventions receive a role in international, European and national law, (Beyerlin, Marauhn, 2011). Among the 27 principles that were laid out by the Rio Declaration in 1992, there are concepts with normative quality that have become customary international law and build the foundation for international and EU environmental law, (Beyerlin, Marauhn, 2011). The concepts recognised to represent the elemental 'ethics of solidarity and justice' (Beyerlin, Stoutenburg, 2010) are 'no harm', 'polluter pays', 'precautionary action', 'common but differentiated responsibilities', 'intergenerational equity' and 'sustainable development', (Beyerlin, Marauhn, 2011) whereby sustainable development as originating in the Brundtland Report encompasses intergenerational equity.

Passage of the principles to EU law is also through Article 37 of the Charter of Fundamental Rights of the EU, environmental protection, through reference "to the principle of sustainable development'. The Consolidated Version of the Treaty on European Union (TEU) refers to the principle of sustainable development in its preamble, thus transmitting it into a statutory position for the EU. Similar to the Charter of Fundamental Rights, TEU in Article 3 (ex. Article 2 TEU), calls for a 'high level of protection of the environment'. There, it is treated in conjunction with economic growth and objectives of 'full employment and social progress'. The sustainability concept that is legally supported by the TEU, thus mirrors an abandonment of the original concept once elaborated by the Brundtland Commission and adopted through UN resolution. The intent of preserving the environment is not further pronounced elsewhere in the TEU, and reference is predominantly made to economic growth and 'competitive social market economy' but also to respect for human rights (Article 3 ex. 2 TEU). The TEU itself does not necessarily provoke interpretation of 'sustainable development' as an act of balancing between environmental, economic and social intents, or even weighing of priorities - it may however be a starting point of the wide practice in EU environmental law. A shift of the interpretation of the sustainability definition - from the safeguarding of resources with the aim of inter-generational and intra-generational justice, to an understanding of interest-responsive weighing between economic, social, and environmental priorities – can be noted in EU law. Principles 1 and 11 of the Rio Declaration may have set a foundation for this.

In December 2022, 188 countries have agreed on 23 biodiversity protection targets chronicled in the Kunming-Montreal Global Biodiversity Framework ('Kunming-Montreal Framework'), UNEP (2022) which understands itself as a "contribution to the achievement of the 2030 Agenda for SustainableDevelopment," UNEP (2022). A key outcome is the commitment to the global conservation of a quantified land and marine area fixing spatial, area-based target. This quantification represents a breakthrough as a foundation for new accountability on biodiversity protection. It was pledged to conserve and manage 'at least 30 per cent of terrestrial, inland water, and of coastal and marine areas, especially areas of particular importance for biodiversity and ecosystem functions and services' by 2030, UNEP (2022). The framework 'aims to catalyse, enable and galvanize urgent and transformative action by Governments, subnational and local governments, and with the involvement of all of society to halt and reverse biodiversity loss,' UNEP (2022). The Kunming-Montreal Framework makes linkages to the 'right to development' in Article 13, and to the 'principles of the Rio Declaration' in Article 18, UNEP (2022). Article 18 of the framework subjects its implementation and the intended halt and reversal of biodiversity loss to the principles of the Rio Declaration on Environment and Development. The connection made to the anthropocentric understanding of the Rio Declaration could be detrimental to its power in regard to biodiversity protection, as biodiversity loss can only be halted and reversed if it is commonly accepted that humans form a dependent part of the ecosystems they live in.

The EU highlighted its pole position to start its implementation, (European Commission, 2022). with the help of the already published EU Biodiversity Strategy for 2030, which calls to protect 'at least 30% of the land and 30% of the sea' in the EU, and of which a third shall be strictly protected, (European Commission, 2021). Therein promoted is European Territorial Cooperation and a Trans-European Nature Network to increase the area and achieve more coherence of the protected areas, (European Commission, 2021). Significantly, the strategy makes a pledge to 'ensure that environmentrelated legislation with an impact on biodiversity is better implemented, enforced and – where necessary – reviewed and revised,' (European Commission, 2021).

Effectiveness of EU Legislation on Biodiversity Protection

The Charter of Fundamental Rights of the EU on environmental protection in Article 37 requires the integration of 'a high level of environmental protection and the improvement of the quality of the environment' into EU policies, to be 'ensured in accordance with the principle of sustainable development.' The framework outlining EUs functioning, the Treaty on the Functioning of the European Union (TFEU), (Consolidated Version of the Treaty on the Functioning of the European Union, 2012) clarifies the principles for environmental protection in the EU in Article 191. Article 191(1) calls for 'preserving, protecting and improving the quality of the environment', the 'prudent and rational utilisation of natural resources', and international advocacy. In transferring the responsibility for identifying the means to achieve this to the member countries and citizens, it adopts a modern, goal–oriented legislative model.

The effectiveness of the main legal instruments that embody the biodiversity protection framework and protection of habitat in the EU was reviewed by the EC in 2016, specifically the Birds and the Habitats Directives, (European Commission, 2016). The EC found that across the EU, 'only 16% of the habitat assessments at biogeographical level are favourable,' (European Commission, 2016). 'For terrestrial ecosystems, the most frequently reported pressures and threats were 'agriculture' and 'human-induced modifications of natural conditions,' (European Commission, 2016). Out of the Sites of Community Importance (SCIs), one third had not yet been designated by the member states by the deadline set by the Directives (European Commission, 2016) and progress in securing 'a fully functional network of sites' was falling behind the targets, (European Commission, 2016). The review pronounced that the monitoring framework is inadequate to allow for evaluations, and the Directives are deficient in regard to contributing 'to the maintenance and restoration of habitats as well as the management of features of the landscape outside of the [Natura 2000] network,' (European Commission, 2016). A new Proposal for a Regulation on Nature Restoration ((COD) Proposal for a Regulation of the European Parliament and of the Council on Nature Restoration, 2022) therefore seeks to address the compromised effectiveness of the Habitat Directive (Council Directive, 1992) and the Birds Directive, (2009) and to facilitate implementation of the EU Biodiversity Strategy by establishing quantifiable spatial and time-bound requirements for nature restoration measures,((COD) Proposal for a Regulation of the European Parliament and of the Council on Nature Restoration, 2022).

Effectiveness of EU Biodiversity Protection Targets

The EU Biodiversity Strategy aims to strictly protect 'at least one third of protected areas – representing 10% of EU land and 10% of EU sea,' (European Commission, n.d). Currently, 3% of land and 1% of sea area are strictly protected, (European Commission, 2022) with unevenly distributed contributions to Natura 2000 sites by the member countries resulting in the EU average, with up to 38% contribution, (European Commission, 2022). The EC notes in a working document that the meaning of 'legal protection' is not defined in the Natura 2000 strategy but reminds that 'strictly protected areas need to be *legally* protected,' (European Commission, 2022). According to the note, means of legal protection may range from a formal legal designation, to an administrative act or contractual agreement, depending on national practices and on each case itself, (European Commission, 2022) including a zoning of strictly protected areas within wider environmental management areas, (European Commission, 2022). As part of the legal reviews and explaining the meaning of 'protection of land and sea areas', the EC has advised to improve the protection measures that have 'temporary nature', (European Commission, 2022) but proposed to account for seasonal protection, and for urban and peri-urban green areas, (European Commission, 2022). This provides the impression that the primary concern is the reporting score, rather than the most meaningful approach to nature protection that will effectively sustain biodiversity.

The importance of a spatial planning component in biodiversity protection at EU level is raised by the EU Biodiversity Strategy, which promotes European Territorial Cooperation and a Trans-European Nature Network. Currently, the implementation of the network takes a patchwork approach without spatial planning, whereby member countries are to 'classify [ ] the most suitable territories in number and size as special protection areas,' (Birds Directive, 2009) and submit lists of sites that fulfil few overall criteria.

Yet, the Directive highlights species protection as a 'trans-frontier environment problem entailing common responsibilities' (Birds Directive, 2009). Among site selection criteria proposed by the ECs note is a requirement for 'scientific evidence that leads to their selection for designation' (Birds Directive, 2009). Aspects of connectivity, size and geographical location that would require transboundary planning and coordination, are so far not enforced as part of such evidence. The guidance document formulates that:

As for protected areas in general, the contributions of individual Member States towards the strategy targets have to be proportionate to the natural values they host that would benefit from strict protection in accordance with the strategy, and to the potential they have for restoration of those same natural values. (European Commission, n.d.)

To achieve a coordinated approach and fulfil the pledge for spatial coherence and for 'functionally meaningful' (European Commission, n.d) sites, overarching, trans-governmental spatial planning is needed, with indicators that account for coherent nature reserves. Building on the integrated assessment undertaken by the European Environmental Agency (EEA) and its European Topic Centre on Urban, Land and Soil Systems (European Commission, n.d) on the status of the Trans- European Nature Network, a joint spatial planning and scientific identification effort could be most effective and meaningful, consume less time, and be easier to enforce and to monitor, instead of requiring each EU member country individually to submit lists of sites proposed for protection under the EU framework. An opportunity to discuss the overarching planning efforts is offered in the TFEU, which promotes opportunity for Inter-parliamentary Cooperation, (European Commission, n.d.).

SUSTAINABLE DEVELOPMENT AND THE OVERLAP WITH 'INTERESTS'

While the law does not anywhere clearly prioritize environmental concerns over others, it is found that it does not even insist in an actual balance between environmental, economic and social concerns, where it promotes such balancing, similar to the Agenda 2030. The current frameworks are instead instrumental in enabling acceptance of *imbalances* to the disadvantage of biodiversity protection if in competition with other interests.

The shift from a concept of inter-generational responsibility to the *weighing* between economic, environmental and social aspects as part of development occurred with the legal space that was introduced to facilitate consideration of "interest". A foundation for this can be seen in the anthropocentrism that was supported by the first principle of the Rio Declaration. The connection made in the Brundtland Report between the economy and the environment clearly differs from the implementation of the sustainability principle in EU law.

Already at the time, the Brundtland Report had alerted that 'environmental degradation is eroding the potential for development,' (UN, n.d). In congruence with the report and the inter-generational principle that it represents, David Pearce in 1989 advocated for an interpretation of 'sustainable development' whereby the 'total environmental capital is not decreased from generation to generation' (Niland, 1991) because for one, many environmental assets cannot be compensated for, two, environmental implications cannot be fully projected, and three, environmental damage is irreversible, (Niland, 1991). These same three aspects are neglected in EU law – that is – knowingly. Indeed, their circumvention forms the underlying legal concepts of EU environmental law by;

First, allowing for compensation and offsetting of biodiversity loss caused by development projects;
Second, exercising impact assessments which contribute information to decision-making processes but do not even represent deciding matter when environmental damage is projected; and
Third, accepting the option for retrospective action on environmental damage, for example through theories of carbon or biodiversity credit trading, and also essentially by the internationally renowned concept of the polluter-pays principle.

The TFEU, one of the principal documents defining governance in the EU, acknowledges the objective of 'sustainable development' in Article 11; 'Environmental protection requirements must be integrated into the definition and implementation of the Union's policies and activities, in particular with a view to promoting sustainable development,' (2022). The article initiates the mainstreaming of environmental concerns in EU policy and in development to anchor an inter-generational commitment. It does not promote environmental protection requirements as a distinct priority, assuming an approach of weighing-in environmental concerns in development. To that point, it reflects a neutral understanding of the problematic of environmental protection in the best case; it could however also lead to the neglect of the subject, depending on the interpretation and implementation of 'sustainable development', which is prone to being interest-driven. In conclusion, the provision lacks regulatory quality for it to be clearly supportive of environmental protection, but it may serve as a legal reference for the intent if needed. Article 37 of the Charter of Fundamental Rights of the EU, which addresses environmental protection, opens room to weigh in other interests and priorities, when deciding on the eventual 'level' of environmental protection. The Habitat Directive is the first specific example of statute law, where provisions regarding environmental conservation are presented in a context of taking 'account of economic, social and cultural requirements and regional and local characteristics,' (Habitat Directive, n.d). Even though common communication practice is often found to adopt a substitution of sustainability by calling for a social, environmental and economic balance, analysis has shown that it was not originally enshrined in policy as such. The Habitat Directive thus opened up an even wider space for interpretation and possibly compromising biodiversity protection efforts for other interests. The Birds Directive, the purpose of which is to protect all wild bird species that occur in the EU and which lays out the rules of profiteering, (Birds Directive, 2009) also refers to 'sustainable development' in its preamble. Article 2 of the Birds Directive sets as objective 'to maintain the population' of the concerned species 'while taking account of economic and recreational requirements', discerning that recreational requirements mostly have economic, and some social aspects. Similar to the Article 2 of the Habitat Directive, it introduces an option of weighing in species protection with other economic and business interests. As the scope for interpretation leads to some uncertainty, the ECJ ruled in C-57/89 Commission v Germany ('Leybucht Dykes') that economic requirements must not be considered 'general interest superior to the general interest represented by the ecological objective of the [Birds] Directive', (European Commission, 2006) a ruling which sets strong limitations to interpretation. But as also elaborated in the case, Article 7 of the Habitat Directive requires the application of Article 6(4) to the areas classified under Article 4(1) and 4(2) of the Birds Directive, and justification of 'encroachment upon SPAs by expressly including therein reasons of a social or economic nature,' (European Commission, 2006), Article 9 of the Birds Directive, like Article 6 of the Habitat Directive does for priority habitat, eases protection requirements for reasons of public health and safety; the Birds Directive also does so in the interest of farming and livestock keeping. While these are all anthropocentric interests, public health should also be regarded in conjunction with environmental health, whereby one is dependent on the other and not meant to compete.

The Water Framework Directive (WFD) (2000) the purpose of which is the safeguarding and sustainable use of water resources, allows for instigating a declining quality of water bodies for the purpose of development in Article 7. It regulates that 'failure to prevent deterioration from high status to good status of a body of surface water [as] the result of new sustainable human development activities' is lawful. In this case, interpretation of 'sustainable' is clearly based on its – however nowhere legally anchored – substitution through a concept of weighing between economic, environmental and social interests; it does not fulfil its pledge according to the original definition in the sense of inter-generational justice. The WFD allows for sustainable development to outweigh the environmental objectives that are set by itself, when considered as 'overriding public interest,' (2000). It is one of the statutory examples that assumes a substitution for the original definition of 'sustainable development', pursuing its incorrect interpretation.

Reverting to Brundtland

As has been discussed, the weighing of economic, environmental and social considerations should be recognized as a misrepresentation of the sustainability definition. The Brundtland Report had called for a principled form of development that will always consider environmental concerns and that will make compromises on the level of economic gains, rather than compromising environmental protection. It had urged for moderation and for the setting of limits to development and economic growth to at least such degree as necessary to enable the perseverance of a good state of environment. The focus of Brundtland was on *the difference* to the type of growth that may otherwise be illimited, but is unsustainable. The transposition of the ideas is wrong in supporting limitations to biodiversity protection to enable development and growth, instead of setting limitations to economic gains.

Legal provisions suggesting to 'balance' the three aspects, are further distorted, as to permitting unequal treatment and preference setting, and not in fact balanced consideration of the three. The representation of the concept of 'sustainable development' in EU law is evidently promoting such anthropocentric interests, that are mainly economic individual rather than communal. The report of origin did nowhere provide an argumentative basis that would entitle humankind to exploit biodiversity. Yet, legislation reflects the assumption that nature is to serve a purpose for humans, even in furthering the environmental targets. Where discussing the targets of nature restoration, the Biodiversity Strategy proposes to select 'in particular those [areas] with the *most potential* to capture and store carbon and to prevent and reduce the impact of natural disasters,' (European Commission, n.d). It maintains thus an assumption of utility that environment shall fulfil, whereas Brundtland clearly puts 'utility aside, there are also moral, ethical, cultural, aesthetic, and purely scientific reasons for conserving wild beings,' (UN, n.d). The examples from EU law show how it enables, and in parts even favours non-communal interests and prioritization of economic interests, with a simultaneous unspecified referral to social interests, also in the context of economic growth. Legislative ambiguities allow room for proceedings in particular interests. No explanation is found, why the pursual of environmental interest is not instead at least also equally bridged through a reasoning of social interest. One may suspect an intended support for the interests of far fewer beneficiaries, rather than the interests that would be more commonly shared by the whole community.

There is no clear definition, as to what 'social interest' actually is in EU biodiversity law. The Brundtland Report discusses social considerations contextual to the specific objectives of 'social development, particularly to improve the position of women in society, to protect vulnerable groups, and to promote local participation in decision making,' (UN, n.d). The range of argumentation in the social interest could be broader and more inclusive; But for further application it can be asked, why the actual legal opportunity, which referrals to social considerations would open up, remains unused throughout the analysed statutory texts. This reconfirms that legal interpretation leans toward prioritization of the economic aspect among the three interests that policy requests to balance in sustainable development. Environmental considerations are compromised even in some of the statutes themselves. Social considerations are not further explained, except for a few singled-out priorities for example by the Habitat Directive, (Council Directive, 1992) when prioritizing human health and public safety but neglecting inclusivity and equality.

The newly acknowledged human right could influence future interpretation of law to this end: in mid-2022, a UN resolution recognised the right to a clean, healthy, and sustainable environment as a Human Right, (UN, 2021) (ILO, 2022). Human health considerations should amplify the weight of environmental protection and not compete. The new human right should be responded to by amending EU environmental law accordingly. The amendments should include improved guidance to the weighing of interest in legal interpretation to reflect the added human right, which could possibly give more weight to environmental considerations in future acts of balancing interest. A reference to this new universal right in legal interpretation should cause a significant shift when interpreting and implementing 'sustainable development', and lift environmental preservation to becoming a stronger component among the central, then even anthropocentric matters. With human rights already enshrined, and possibly revised interpretation of 'sustainable' due to the newly added human right, a powerful tool has been availed that shall disable future diminishment of environmental concerns in the equation. These are low hanging fruit that could initiate more weight to be given to biodiversity protection in the interpretation of biodiversity law.

Interests Linked to Societal and Economic Norms Reflected in EU Biodiversity Law

The following section looks at the representation of various forms of 'interest' in EU biodiversity law by isolating them. It interprets the legal reflections of interests of the public and assesses the enabling elements found in law that maintain pursual of interests other than uncompromised biodiversity protection.

The Brundtland Commission in 1987 had urged to examine the established decision-making that gives preference to economic aspects: 'To successfully advance in solving global problems, we need to develop new methods of thinking, to elaborate new moral and value criteria, and, no doubt, new patterns of behaviour. (UN, n.d.)

The upheld failure to live up to this strong advocacy for change is illustrated by the legal support that interests other than environmental protection receive in environmental law, and that are not representing the interest of the 'world community,' (UN, n.d.). Brundtland was clear in highlighting that maintaining *business as usual* will not be sustainable:

We call for a common endeavour and for new norms of behaviour at all levels and in the interests of all. The changes in attitudes, in social values, and in aspirations that the report urges will depend on vast campaigns of education, debate and public participation. (UN, n.d.)

At the time, need for political will and the legal support for effective implementation were not also targeted by the statement. These will be foundational aspects to successful behavioural change, before even calling out the responsibility of civil society. An assessment of the EU Biodiversity Strategy for 2030 proves strong intentions to correct misinterpretation of the sustainability principle by aiming "to ensure that environmental and social interests are fully embedded into business strategies" (European Commission, n.d.).

Public Interest and Overriding Public Interest

The referrals made to 'interest' by the legal framework and by future legislative proposals are explored, including interest that has been assigned the power to override a legal provision along with references to factors of sustainable development as they link to 'interest'.

EU law, like other legal systems, makes room for the concept of public interest,[2] whereby public interest however remains undefined in most documents. The use of 'public interest' often has a drafting effect of withdrawing clarity from the legislation, particularly observed in environmental law. Because of its ambiguity and the openness for interpretation by the judicial system, Wyatt (2020) questions 'the utility of the public interest as a legal concept'.[3] He also probes the appropriateness of assuming a 'legal public interest in the EU in general', arguing that it may not be an established content in the current legal and political system.[4] Regarding the degree of representativeness of 'public interest' across the EU, it may be asked whether the available options for public participation are sufficiently capable to determine the actual public interest on a case-by-case basis. To what degree does the Council of the EU really represent the public when taking decisions in the public interest? The public consultations site of the EC shows participation in the range of 1,000 respondents per subject.[5] Opinion polls do not seem to serve the purpose, if not larger efforts are made to enhance public awareness.

EU statute law relevant to biodiversity protection allows 'reasons relating to the public interest' to 'override' other factors that were to be balanced in decision-making. The concept of 'overriding interest' itself is traced to an English legal concept in the land sector, dating 1925.[6] It stands for 'interests that are not protected' and yet binding.[7] The Habitat Directive allows for compromising the protection of habitat sites for social and economic reasons - environmental concerns may be outweighed in the balancing exercise that is meant to achieve sustainable development, by 'imperative reasons of overriding public interest' (IROPI).[8] Article 6(4) makes room for a plan or project to 'be carried out for imperative reasons of overriding public interest, including those of a social or economic nature' that potentially negatively affect such areas protected under the *Natura 2000* network and accepts compensatory acts. Article 16 allows to make derogations to species protection for IROPI. Möckel (2017) leads this back to 'the European Principle of Proportionality pursuant to Article 5(4) of the TEU'[9] and 'the aims of sustainable development within the meaning of Article 11 of the TFEU'.[10] An EC working commission notes that the effectiveness of the Habitat Directive when allowing 'to offset loss of or damage to Natura 2000 sites has not yet been fully assessed.'[11]

EU statute law is complemented by case law, which adds to its effectiveness. The EC has also issued guidance on Article 6(4) of the Habitat Directive for decisions regarding the designation of SCIs that make part of *Natura 2000*.[12] The guidance offers explanation of IROPI, since it recognizes that the concept 'is not defined in the Directive'[13] and the ECJ has not 'given clear indications for the interpretation of this specific concept'.[14] The note therefore expounds that 'not every kind of public interest' is overriding and that it should be a 'long-term interest'.[15] In including this, it recognises a legislative gap that remains. Nevertheless, Möckel (2017) found that the derogation is not widely used in practice, but its application became standard practice in some member countries and particularly in Germany. [16] Where land is concerned, the conflicts of interests involve by default its conservation in competition with physical development and infrastructure projects. Infrastructure projects, even if in the name of the public, primarily facilitate trade and support private and macro-economic, sectoral state interests. The interest in an approved project is not necessarily commonly shared, when IROPI is evoked. It comes down to the conclusion by the competent national authorities, whether site integrity is affected and whether there are alternative solutions considered viable.[17] The example of Germany demonstrates that a weakening of Natura 2000 is possible when adopting an interest-driven interpretation of the Habitat Directive and the Directive is insufficiently protective.

In the judgment of the ECJ of 11 July 1996, Regina v Secretary of State for the Environment, ex parte: Royal Society for the Protection of Bird,[18] it was clarified that, while it is possible to reduce the area of an SPA under Article 6 of the Habitat Directive in the public interest, it is not possible to *not first* designate identified sites for the same reason of public interest.[19] Holder (1997) identifies this ruling as powerful in securing 'the dismantling of economic arguments against conservation', resolving that "economic considerations can play no part in the decision".[20] The court clarified that presumptions of possible overriding of legal requirements in the future cannot justify their disobeying in the present. Notwithstanding, the future application of Article 6 may already be speculated on at the time of fulfilling it. In general, case law strengthens the obligatory sequential treatment of the scrutiny requirements that are inbuilt in the Habitat Directive. Yet, establishment of IROPI may lead to acceptance of projects with an adverse impact on biodiversity.[21] An assessment of EEB of the effectiveness of ECJ rulings in preventing and further disincentivising development that is adversely impacting habitat has demonstrated not only limited follow up on the rulings, but also limited compliance where follow up has taken place.[22] Compensation approaches have almost become mainstream but require correction. What they do is to sustain business as usual. Neither naturally grown environments nor animals or organisms are replaceable. As Dasgupta states, the 'ignorance of the economic worth of natural capital remains the greatest barrier to an understanding of economic development.'[23]

The Proposal for a Regulation on Nature Restoration[24] means to initiate 'more decisive action…to achieve the EU climate and biodiversity objectives' and to set binding targets to be monitored. Yet, it also leaves room for ('unavoidable') habitat transformations 'as a result of a plan or project of overriding public interest for which no less damaging alternative solutions are available'.[25] The new proposal with corrections meant to achieve higher legal efficiency in the implementation of the Habitats and Birds Directives, further maintains the space for projects of overriding public interest within and outside *Natura 2000*.[26] Articles 4(8) and 5(8) also waive the restoration objectives outside *Natura 2000* areas for projects of overriding public interest. It must be argued that there is always a less damaging solution and no habitat transformation due to a plan or project is indeed 'unavoidable'.

The Industrial Emissions Directive[27] ('IED') is complementary to biodiversity protection efforts. It is one of few legal documents, which contains a definition for 'the public' and for 'the public concerned'.[28] According to the definitions, even one 'natural or legal person' can stand for 'the public', in which case public interest would reflect the interest of one legal person. The definition of 'the public concerned' encompasses registered NGOs 'promoting environmental protection' based on the recognition of their 'interest'. This provides rights to participation,[29] rights to access information,[30] and the right to legally challenge an environmental permit,[31] except if 'impairment' is established. With this, the IED secures options available to civil society to enforce accountability. For other disputants, 'sufficient interest' must first be proven, and the details for this process depend on each member country.[32] For an 'overriding need for energy supplies',[33] the IED waives the legal requirement to prevent pollution, which mirrors interests other than to sustain the environment in a clean and healthy state. Considering enactment was in 2010, the IED would now stand in need for an amendment to incorporate a legal reflection of the newly added human right to a clean environment as well as new available technologies for renewable energy generation, which would provide cause to remove the waiver.

Remedying environmental pollution is also a subject of liability. Biodiversity is regarded insofar as pollution negatively impacts on habitat and species. The Environmental Liability Directive[34] ('ELD') implements the Polluter-Pays principle that is anchored in EU law.[35] There are examples of successful litigation to remedy pollution.[36] Article 3 extends liability to defaults on habitat and species protection. Notwithstanding the impossibility to factually remedy biodiversity loss, the ELD even accepts for remediation measures to be waived, if these are considered too expensive by the competent authority with costs considered 'disproportionate to the environmental benefits'.[37] Phelps (2021) suggests that liability litigation may also help safeguarding biodiversity[38] and the body of respective cases should be grown to gradually raise the prospects for successful litigation. Enforcing remedies cannot safeguard biodiversity but it could be a way of reducing purposive damages by providing reverse incentives. It should be noted that the ELD deliberately excludes liability for biodiversity loss that may be caused by a series of specified 'occupational activities', except when the operator has been at fault or negligent.[39] The occupational activities, which are excluded from liability, comprise permitted releases of pollutants into the environment and resource extraction activities - all set to negatively impact biodiversity. The current Directive thus protects an operator from legal claims of being at fault or negligent when fulfilling the regulatory and permitting requirements; but technically, the operator is at fault when undertaking the derogated activity.

The interpretation of policies and law relevant to biodiversity protection has shown that it allows the validation of economic interests to override it, despite the alert by the Brundtland Commission that 'economics and ecology must be completely integrated in decision making and lawmaking processes'.[40] The Commission's insistence that 'long term sustainable growth will require far-reaching changes to produce trade, capital, and technology flows that are more equitable and better synchronized to environmental imperatives'[41] is not given respect in legal transposition. The report had called for the setting of limitations to growth about 35 years ago as an imperative necessity in the market-based economic context, to support action in the common interest. Setting such limitations must imperatively receive the legal backup to become the prior concern in sustainable development. Dasgupta, who prepared 'The Economics of Biodiversity: The Dasgupta Review'[42] for the UN about 34 years after Brundtland upholds to remind of the 'devastating cost' that human's prosperity has on ecosystems.[43] Essentially, his assessment is a conclusion that the sustainability principle, as it was defined through the Brundtland Report, is not respected, by stating: 'We have degraded the biosphere to the point where the demands we make of its goods and services far exceed its ability to meet them on a sustainable basis.'[44] Therefore, the Dasgupta Review theorises to value nature in terms of an economic asset when assessing economic progress and inclusive wealth[45] and undertaking macro-economic modelling,[46] to integrate with the anthropocentric approach to biodiversity protection.

Community Interest

Concepts around 'interest' in EU biodiversity law also include reference to 'community interest'. It stands for interest of the EU community and its member countries, and is used in the Habitat Directive.

The term serves to clarify that measures that are linked to implementing 'community interest' are 'a common responsibility of all Member States'.

The Directive's scope relates to such habitats and species listed by it and referred to as 'natural habitats and species of Community interest'.[47] The objective of maintaining or restoring the listed habitat and species 'at favourable conservation status'[48] is to be pursued by taking 'account of economic, social and cultural requirements and regional and local characteristics'.[49] This mirrors the weighing approach again, whereby habitat and species' conservation is weighed against other aspects. The Directive introduces weighing of the level of protection, even though protection of the listed habitat and species itself was declared 'community interest'.[50] This means that the 'economic, social and cultural requirements' can be assigned such weight that it may exceed the weight of 'community interest'.

Common Interest

'Common interest' is used in the TFEU[51] and may be interchanged to express a 'common European interest' of EU member states, as to implement EU law.[52] TFEU also extends this tool specifically to the EUs interest in physical projects by referring to 'projects of common interest'.[53] Such projects require approval by the member state where its location is proposed. Seemingly inconsistent, this is despite the concerned member state is per default a representative of the 'common interest'. This demonstrates that 'common interest' is not assumed to always be unilaterally and inclusively representing the interest of all members states. At the same time, it reflects the general dilemma of declaring an interest - public, common, or overriding – it may not represent the interest of a specific party that is however part of the interest group.

It is not clear in what way 'common interest' and 'community interest' are used differently, or why there is no consistent terminology adopted throughout EU statute law. Both 'community interest' or 'common interest' refer to groups of people in a known spatial delineation, that is the EU. In policy documents, 'common interest' may otherwise refer to an interest shared by a particular group of people.[54]

General Interest and 'Services of General Economic Interest'

The TFEU explains 'general interest' in Article 285, whereby 'general interest' is the EUs general interest. Protocol No. 26 in the TFEU introduces 'services of general interest', which according to Article 1 are most particularly services of general economic interest.[55] Article 2 proceeds by permitting for member states to also undertake non-economic services of general interest, this way clearly distinguishing the two. This legal anchor might explain why in EU law, economic interest can outweigh the other interests of a non-economic nature. Article 14 legitimates state aid for private companies as a service of 'general economic interest' on a selective basis, particularly for infrastructure services.

The Habitat Directive employs the term 'general interest' in part II of the preamble. It states that the 'preservation, protection and improvement of the quality of the environment, including the conservation of natural habitats and of wild fauna and flora' are 'an essential objective of general interest', therewith linking to the anchor for non-economic services in TFEU Article 2.

A Proposal on the making available on the Union market as well as export from the Union of certain commodities and products associated with deforestation and forest degradation and repealing Regulation (EU) No 995/2010[56] applies the term 'general interest when building a foundation for defending interests of environmental protection against the range of fundamental rights as laid out by the Charter of

Fundamental rights of the EU[57] and implementing the European Convention on Human Rights (ECHR)[58] as it is part of the recognised interests in the context of solidarity.[59]

Ensuring a high level of environmental protection and the improvement of the quality of the environment constitutes, in particular, an objective of general interest recognised by the Charter which might justify limitations to other fundamental rights.[60]

If the Charter and the Convention would be amended to accommodate the newly acknowledged human right to a clean and healthy environment, the above proposal will maintain its validity, but would no longer be necessitated. The most recent amendments to the Convention[61] date before the recognition of the new human right, however, no reform process involving the expansion of human rights in the ECHR and include the right to a healthy environment is so far identifiable.

RIGHTS TO NATURE RESOURCES AND SPATIAL PLANNING AS REFLECTED IN EU BIODIVERSITY LAW

This section explores 'rights' in their sense of representing interests, and particularly rights to environmental resources, as a continuation of discussing the recognition of interests within law.

Land Rights and Land Use Planning and Management

'About three-quarters of the Earth's land surface has been altered by humans' over the last one thousand years.[62] About one third of land use has been changed within only the last sixty years.[63] The rapid transformation and fragmentation of land cover cause biodiversity loss, land and environmental degradation, water quality decline, extinction of wildlife[64] (Figure 2).

EU environmental law allows assigning portions of territory to purposes of protecting biodiversity, associated with different rights to activities which may be undertaken therein. Such 'biodiversity-sensitive areas' include the *Natura 2000* network of protected areas, UNESCO World Heritage sites and Key Biodiversity Areas, as well as other protected areas referred to in Appendix D of Annex II of Commission Delegated Regulation (EU) 2021/213912.[65] The *Natura 2000* network is protected under the Birds and Habitats Directives and comprises sites of habitat and species protection in accordance with their listings by the Directives. The Emerald Network under the Bern Convention[66] is compatible with *Natura 2000* and typifies the second of the two most important European site protection networks.[67] In 1999, the ESDP European Spatial Development Perspective[68] has discussed the role of territorial land use planning in habitat protection. At the time, the document sounded apologetic, explaining that 'even though strict protection measures are *sometimes justified*, it is often more sensible to integrate protection and management of the endangered areas into spatial development strategies for larger areas.' The Proposal for a Regulation on the making available on the Union market as well as export from the Union of certain commodities and products associated with deforestation and forest degradation and repealing Regulation (EU) No 995/2010[69] also includes a clause of justification for site protection, to excuse a possible perception as an infringement of rights, because of the benefit to all constituting an objective of 'general interest'.[70] Article 17 of the Charter of Fundamental Rights of the EU on *Right to property* established that 'the use of property may be regulated by law in so far as is necessary for the general interest'.[71] These provisions are contextual to the content and action of spatial planning, which regulates and may restrict the use of land and nature resources; their change including restrictions have been postulated in policy processes with a connotation of not being democratic and to deprive of rights.[72] However, the other side of the picture in biodiversity protection policy is the need for coordination to successfully implement policies beyond local decision-making levels. To successfully protect biodiversity and life on Earth and implement the agreed targets of the Kunming-Montreal Framework, an updated accord must be found on land use planning and enforcement mandates. It must be asked whether there is not any need for a degree or an aspect of global land use planning; whether there is no need for an evidence-based and balanced land use planning, that supports the globally shared interest of biodiversity protection at a supra-national scale, and how this may be possible while acknowledging the importance of local public participation in planning.

Regional planning, that risks being looked at as dictating, may be one reason why policies that are meant to protect nature end up dismantling their own authority. For example, the EC publication Natura 2000 and spatial planning (2017) backtracks the conservation mandate to finding 'a way that both economic development and *Natura 2000* policy objectives are taken into consideration'.[73] As a matter of fact, Niland has predicted in 1991, that debates on the balance between 'the interests of the environment and the interests of the economy'[74] would be subject of discourses for one or more decades, and he has remained right about it.

The Guidelines on Wilderness in Natura 2000, prescribe for wild nature reserves to be managed in a way to support the 'general objective to ensure a favourable conservation status of the species and habitats for which the sites have been designated'.[75] Therein reflected is again the assumption of a human entitlement to intervene into ecosystems - in this case even ecosystems that are adjudged to be 'wilderness' - and a privilege to decide, which species and habitat has more right to exist over another. Supported as the elemental motivation in the decision-making is *usefulness* of the species and habitat for humans.[76] Even on sites that are designated to nature protection, a range of (human) choices for their use remain in competition.[77] Biodiversity management objectives are subject to interpretation and require choices that designate environment either as a 'non-intervention environment', or deploy it as an 'agro-ecosystem'.[78] The human-made choice of type of environment promoted under the management concept will impact on the resulting prevalence of species and habitat. The EC even felt the need to clarify that the guidelines are not 'aiming to turn all Natura 2000 sites into wilderness areas'.[79]

The Habitat Directive builds a legal foundation for the *Natura 2000* network. *Natura 2000* is not actually a network characterised by spatial connectivity yet *(Figure 2)*. [80] Article 21 of the Directive determines the procedure for the network's establishment. No actual land use planning process is entailed but an overarching spatial planning approach would be a precondition to achieve spatial coherence and connectivity. Implementation of the Directive concerned with protecting types of habitats and endangered, vulnerable, rare or endemic species listed in its Annex,[81] is put into effect by compiling lists of proposed sites from the member countries.[82] The framework ignores the importance of indicators that would prescribe land area, spatial coherence, and ecosystem reinstatement where applicable, to achieve a type of planning that aims at land area conservation, ensures presence of undeveloped land area and wildlife corridors, and includes reflection of wildlife migratory patterns. Similarly, effective implementation of the EIA Directive[83] would require linkage to an EU wide spatial planning and monitoring component, but it does not include the means to effectively achieve and enforce the limitations to 'land take' for physical projects that is it trying to achieve:

Figure 2. Landscape fragmentation in NUTS-X regions in 2009
Source: EEA Report No. 5 (2012)

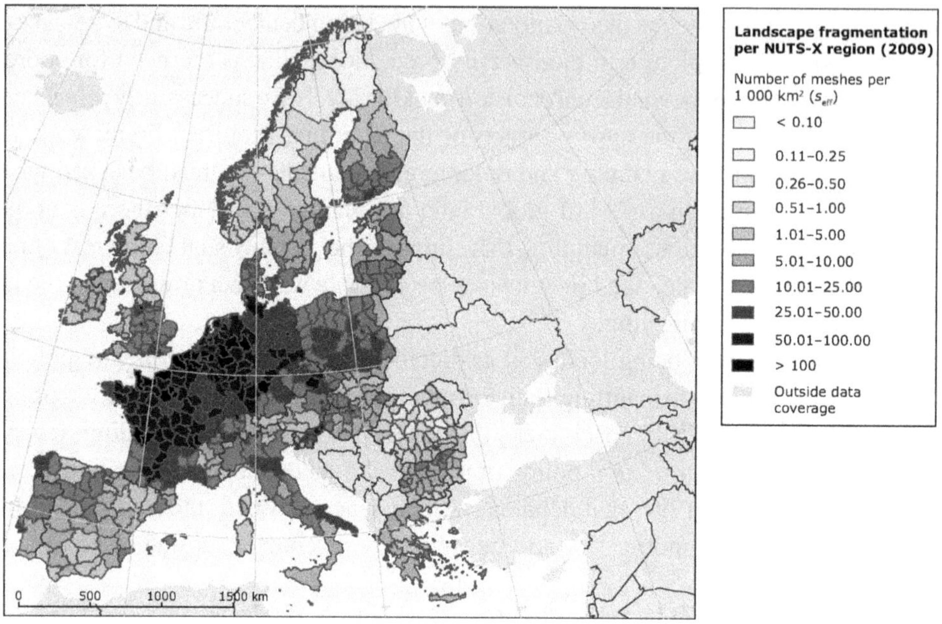

Their impact on land, particularly as regards land take, and on soil, including as regards organic matter, erosion, compaction and sealing; appropriate land use plans and policies at national, regional and local level are also relevant in this regard.[84]

The provisions in its Annexes III and IV, which require regard to 'the use of natural resources, in particular land, soil, water and biodiversity' and consideration to 'the sustainable availability of these resources', does equally call for a spatial planning and quantification method to ensure compliance.

Community and Indigenous Land Management

In contrast to individual property rights in a market economy, management of land functioning based on community land rights[85] and customs of land-based societies allows people to live from the land, while respecting it as a shared resource. The population is sustained by the use of land instead of 'off-farm industry and urban employment'.[86] With the promotion of industrialisation and urbanisation, this form of coexistence and co-management of resources shrank. Policy that also promoted the adjudication of individual land titles in formerly indigenous systems have oriented use of land toward its economic exploitation, and to the abrogation of natural resource management in the communal interest. The shift away from a farming economy across Europe had begun in the 19th century, when society started subordinating to an 'individualist mercantile logic' and a system based on private property rights that was enforced by the state. This process coincided with the creation of municipalities and urbanization.[87] Serrano Alvarez (2014) notes in connection with this observation, that 'the non-recognition of the capacity of local communities [by the state] to manage their commons ended in a significant imbalance'.[88] He highlights that the 'established obligations of solidarity' were the strengths of communal resource management: 'Community rules and regulations, although they did not prevent unequal use of common property, did have a strong egalitarian nature and imposed the same obligations [ ] and established obligations of solidarity'. Even if the system does 'not prevent unequal use' of the property, it yet prevents overexploitation for the good of the community as a whole, with the community being the managers and beneficiaries of the resources. Serrano Alvarez (2014) agrees with Elinor Ostrom that any administrative and legal intervention in established common resource management has a negative impact. Subsistence farming is to this day still found even in Europe. While in some rural areas, common land management may persist, it is however difficult to coexist in a context of global trade, if the resources are not protected against entering into commercial markets; even the managers of common land not seldom take personal advantage of the parallel land market.[89] The securing of land rights through a formal registration was a general recommendation given by the World Bank already in 1993 as a measure of preparing preconditions for a free-market economy in reform contexts.[90] The registration of ownership rights to an asset, along with a right to trade with it, including nature resources, set it to be exploited for maximum economic gain if no or little restrictions are attached. With the difficulty to protect nature resources from the effects of the globally prevailing property system, worldwide examples show that the effects lead to the collapse of ecosystems, which indigenous populations were living on from responsible subsistence farming and fishing. A recent example is the collapse of the ecosystem around the *Yukong salmon* that sustained the indigenous population.[91] The Kunming-Montreal Framework gave a voice to nature-based communities and recognised their indigenous knowledge on natural resource management in its document of global outreach.[92] The framework did not go as far as to pledge for the general protection of the indigenous nature resources from the effects of market economic forces, or even debate the feasibility of a partial adoption of sustainable, indigenous resource management at a global scale.

Niland (1991) has pointed out that competing with the market– and property- based understanding of regulation is the understanding that environment needs protection to a higher standard 'than that implied in the idea of property rights to be traded'.[93] He did not discuss making use of public property rights or land trusts, as a tool to deliberately keep out immovable property from the market for their strict protection. Effecting changes to pre-existing rights to property, however, requires either expropriation in the public interest, or site designation at the time of land adjudication, which can usually only be undertaken during a reform process. Points in time with an opportunity for land reform prior to private land adjudication have, however, passed in most parts of the world.

Dasgupta (2021) concluded on the necessity of including nature into economic accounting, to be accounted for as part of economic stock.[94] In conjunction with private ownership concepts, unlimited exploitation does otherwise spiral downward into environmental destruction along with the individualisation of society. The idea of trust funds breaks through this principle, a concept the economics of which was assessed by Elinor Ostrom.[95] Elinor Ostrom highlights that successful collective action and management of shared resources depends on the strength of the institutional arrangement under which the collective resource management are organised,[96] and as long as the resource receives collective protection from overexploitation.

Rights of Habitat and Species

The dilemma, which interest-prone frameworks and market-based systems entail, have led to an exploration of theories testing an ''ecocentric' view [on] environmental rights'.[97] The approaches include advocacy work for rights other than humans, with initiatives to adjudicate property rights to wildlife to protect them from habitat destruction,[98] [99] and attribute natural legal personalities to natural features or animals.[100] 'Environmental personhood has been studied as a way of protecting nature since at least the 1970s'[101] when it was proposed by Christopher D. Stone.[102] The rights, where legally acknowledged, can be claimed in trials with the help of advocates representing the natural feature or animal. In 2017 for example, the *New Zealand Whanganui River* received legal personality[103] through legal settlement that was signed into law.[104] While such initiatives attempt breaking the common anthropocentric views, the inclusion of personhood into a legal system entails new problems. Where a river receives personhood, it may also be sued,[105] for example for destroying people's livelihood when flooding their homes. Yet, the cause for the harm done to the residents or to farmers is likely an effect induced by human activities causing climate change, or a result of projects that intervene in natural ecosystems. To allow for the type of litigations will trigger a cascade of trials. Nonetheless, both the theory and its practical implications contribute to raising the awareness about the imperative of biodiversity protection as the unconditional goal of the legal theoretic attempts, and to a 'collective understanding and desire for a better environment'.[106]

Conservation Enforcement and Democracy

Besides an overarching planning approach, biodiversity protection also depends on public regulation, including setting of incentives such as subsidisation or disincentives such as taxation.[107] This demands the full alignment of all policy and regulatory measures with each other. In the EU Biodiversity Strategy, the EC sets the objective to 'put in place a new European biodiversity governance framework'.[108] The commission projects that it will 'consider whether a legally binding approach to governance is needed'.[109] This analysis supports that binding and clear law is required to ensure compliance with EU biodiversity policy and strategies, which is otherwise compromised for other interests. In Article 16, the new proposal for nature restoration regulations,[110] is inducted to equip civil society organisations with a right to challenge actions undertaken by competent authorities to enforce proper implementation of the law, and to enable a review of authority decisions at low or no cost.[111] Such measures will help empower the actual representatives of the public interest to demand accountability on biodiversity protection, and will be an essential, powerful component to enforcement. In the same line of review of the currently available tools by the EC, the Environmental Crime Directive (ECD) 2008 proposed for amendment 2021,[112] includes provisions to improve the effectiveness of investigations, prosecution and adjudication of environmental criminal offences[113] for an enhanced enforcement.

CONCLUSION: AN ADVOCACY TO ABANDON ANTHROPOCENTRISM IN LEGISLATION FOR AN EFFECTIVE BIODIVERSITY PROTECTION

The Chapter concludes with an advocacy to abandon the anthropocentrism in law as the precondition for "sustainable use of terrestrial ecosystems", "halt and reverse land degradation and halt biodiversity loss"[114] and the successful implementation of SDG 15.

Policy and legal attempts over the last four decades to harness imbalanced decision-making that compromises the state of nature and biodiversity started out with the introduction of the sustainability principle. The original concept of 'sustainable development' is, however, not adequately supported by effective EU environmental law, and is diluted by other justifiable interests making it subject to circumvention. The law even introduces provisions that elude its own content. Its ethics is curbed by the principles of governance determined by a market economy, and effective biodiversity protection is threatened by exemptions to the rule, that benefit few and erode a common understanding of the public good.

Various legal treatments of 'interest' provide the evidence for this. Part of the cornerstones is the fundamental property concept that enables individuals to benefit from resources that the safeguarding biodiversity relies on. The human self-entitlement found represented in EU biodiversity law initiates imbalances in favour of interests that are in fact *not* 'common'. The newly acknowledged human right to a clean and healthy environment would help correct the present disadvantage that environmental considerations receive in decision-making, if transposed into law.

Theoretical proposals attempted finding solutions to the systemic and legal shortcomings that constrain biodiversity protection. One is an advocacy to respect natural features as assets in a wider economic context, which should be accounted for as an actual composite among the anthropocentric interests. This builds on the established economic system. Further, an ecocentric - as opposed to anthropocentric – theory is still also an extension to the established legal and administrative system. It is grounded in admittance of rights and legal personalities to nature and animals, to defend their interests and allow breaking through human self-entitlement. These principal propositions mean to re-introduce a connotation of nature and environment being something tangible in need to be respected, while law has failed to fulfil this role, in being an outlet of anthropocentrism and individualism that is not accountable to humankind. In nature-based societies, concepts of registered property and written law were inexistent. In the modern global economy, the resources, their circularity, and unity with nature have lost legal protection, despite the re-acknowledgement of indigenous rights as part of later adjustment processes. A long-term coexistence of the two principally different systems seems impossible, as the mere act of delineating and registering natural features assimilate them within a system that sustains itself through their exploitation.

It is understood that commerce with natural resources, even if registered, must be capped in a market economy, while humankind depends on what nature provides. If the full right of existence will be universally acknowledged for nature and biodiversity, law must be fully deployed to achieve this outcome. Their unbiased and uncompromised protection must be the actual role of environmental law; any other models look for fixes to the fundamental shortcoming but cannot succeed as long as law is taking an adverse position from the outset. After commonly agreeing that biodiversity is essential and in need of protection – as recorded in Montreal in December 2022[115] – justification through financial modelling should not be required; justifications will remain prone to be flawed if biased toward interests and gains. Uncompromised effective law must be treated as the fundamental precondition to protect nature resources, without any need for justification in competition with other interests. The question remains, how this will be practically possible while human survival depends on the consumption of resources that nature provides.

Consumption cannot effectively be regulated, controlled or even dictated. The dilemma in an open market economy as adopted by the EU member states,[116] lies in the requirement for individuals and private entities to financially sustain themselves. The only way to reduce the demand for, and the consumption of natural resources is by excluding large amounts from trade without any compromise, while portions must remain part of the same. The Kunming-Montreal Convention achieved a strong yet modest agreement in this line, and it must be paired with the required legal support. Once biodiversity law is unambiguous, it must be expanded to aspects of biodiversity decline that remain unregulated so far. The EU Biodiversity Strategy for 2030 makes effort to pave the way and address each subject area holistically, including pollution prevention and animal protection. Fulfilling the pledge of the Biodiversity Strategy to cause improvement to legal effectiveness will be key to successful biodiversity protection.

The legal strengths and effectiveness that is advocated for, finally, needs complementation by supranational spatial planning support. The combination of law and spatial planning, and an uncompromised legal effectiveness form the seemingly only path for successful biodiversity preservation, and it must be paired with high transparency, accountability and public participation. It is time to set priorities other than humans' self-entitlement, and make biodiversity and ecosystem protection the only overriding interest. The achievement of SDG 15 and effective biodiversity protection must start by raising its weight in law. The first and most significant measures to result in a more effective legal framework do not entail much drafting effort, but the willingness for coherent policy implementation in the interest of humankind.

REFERENCES

Alden Wily, L. (2011). *Customary Land Tenure in the Modern World Rights to Resources in Crisis: Reviewing the Fate of Customary Tenure in Africa.* Brief #1 of 5. https://dlc.dlib.indiana.edu/dlc/bitstream/handle/10535/7713/customary%20land%20tenure%20in%20the%20modern%20world.pdf?sequence=1

All Answers Ltd. (2022). Right to Environment of Human Right. *Lawteacher.net.* https://www.lawteacher.net/free-law-essays/human-rights/right-to-environment-of-human-right.php?vref=1

Ankersmit, L. (2012). The diversion of the Acheloos river under EU environmental law. *European Law Blog.* https://europeanlawblog.eu/2012/09/26/the-diversion-of-the-acheloos-river-under-eu-environmental-law/

Bendana, C. (2022). Uganda takes to the courts to stop land grabs and protect forests. *farmlandgrab.org.* https://www.farmlandgrab.org/post/view/31319

Beyerlin, U., & Grote Stoutenburg, J. (2010). *Environment, International Protection.* Max Planck Encyclopedia of Public International Law.

Beyerlin, U., & Marauhn, T. (2011). *International Environmental Law.* Hart Publishing. doi:10.5771/9783845265582

Birnie, P., Boyle, A., & Redgwell, C. (2009). *International Law and the Environment.* Oxford University Press.

Buck, S. J. (1992). Governing the Commons: The Evolution of Institutions for Collective Action by Elinor Ostrom. *Natural Resources Journal, 32*(2), 415–417. https://www.jstor.org/stable/24884388

Burkart, K. (2022). Indigenous land rights take center stage in a new global framework for biodiversity conservation (commentary). *Mongabay.* https://news.mongabay.com/2022/03/indigenous-land-rights-take-center-stage-in-a-new-global-framework-for-biodiversity-conservation/

Client Earth. (2020). *Enforcing the Habitats Directive in national courts.* https://www.clientearth.org/media/pb5g0lpe/webinar-8-enforcing-the-habitats-directive-in-national-courts.pdf

Council of the European Unition (2022). *Proposal for a Directive of the European Parliament and the Council on the protection of the environment through criminal law*. Author.

Crown. (2021). *The Economics of Biodiversity: The Dasgupta Review*. https://assets.publishing.service.gov.uk/government/uploads/system/uploads/attachment_data/file/962785/The_Economics_of_Biodiversity_The_Dasgupta_Review_Full_Report.pdf

Dotinga, H. (2022). *Overriding Public Interest' to speed up permitting procedures for RES and grids? A legal perspective on the application of 'Imperative Reasons of overriding Public Interest' (IROPI) – and related risks under the EU Nature Directive*. RGI. https://renewables-grid.eu/fileadmin/user_upload/Files_RGI/Event_material/RGI_IROPI_Webinar_120522_HD_text_and_maps_only.pdf

Drexhage, J., & Murphy, D. (2010). *Sustainable Development: From Brundtland to Rio 2012*. UN.

Elliott, L., & Carrington, D. (2021, February 2). Economics' failure over destruction of nature presents 'extreme risks'. *The Guardian*. https://www.theguardian.com/environment/2021/feb/02/economics-failure-over-destruction-of-nature-presents-extreme-risk

Equality and Human Rights Commission. (2021). *What is the Charter of Fundamental Rights of the European Union?* https://www.equalityhumanrights.com/en/what-are-human-rights/how-are-your-rights-protected/what-charter-fundamental-rights-european-union

European Commission. (1990). *ESDP European Spatial Development Perspective*. Towards Balanced and Sustainable Development of the Territory of the European Union.

European Commission. (2006). *Nature and Biodiversity Cases Ruling of the European Court of Justice*. Author.

European Commission. (2007). *Guidance document on Article 6(4) of the 'Habitats Directive' 92/43/EEC*. Author.

European Commission. (2013). *Guidelines on Wilderness in Natura 2000*. Author.

European Commission. (2017). *Natura 2000 and spatial planning*. Author.

European Commission. (2019). *Air Quality and Noise Legislation, Module 4: Principles for Directives 2008/50/EC and 2002/49/EC*. https://ec.europa.eu/environment/legal/law/5/e_learning/module_4_7.htm

European Commission. (2022). *Commission Staff Working Document Criteria and guidance for protected areas designations*. https://environment.ec.europa.eu/system/files/2022-01/SWD_guidance_protected_areas.pdf

European Commission. (2022). *Proposal for a Regulation of the European Parliament and of the Council on nature restoration*. Author.

European Commission. (2022). *Statement by President von der Leyen on the Kunming-Montreal biodiversity agreement.* https://ec.europa.eu/commission/presscorner/detail/en/statement_22_7827

European Commission. (n.d.). *Public consultations and other consultation activities.* https://ec.europa.eu/social/main.jsp?catId=333&langId=en

European Commission (2016). Commission Staff Working Document Fitness Check of the EU Nature Legislation (Birds and Habitats Directives) Directive 2009/147/EC of the European Parliament and of the Council of 30 November 2009 on the conservation of wild birds and Council Directive 92/43/EEC of 21 May 1992 on the conservation of natural habitats and of wild fauna and flora.

European Commission (2021). EU Biodiversity Strategy for 2020. Bringing Nature Back into our lives. *Communication from the Commission to the European Parliament, the Council, the European Economic and Social Committee and the Committee of the Regions.*

European Commission (2016). Fitness Check of the EU Nature Legislation (Birds and Habitats Directives) Directive 2009/147/EC of the European Parliament and of the Council of 30 November 2009 on the conservation of wild birds and Council Directive 92/43/EEC of 21 May 1992 on the conservation of natural habitats and of wild fauna and flora. *Commission Staff Working Document.*

European Environment Agency. (2012). *Protected areas in Europe — an overview.* Author.

European Environment Agency. (2012). *Workshop on EU legislation, Principles of EU Environmental Law, the Polluter Pays Principle.* Author.

European Environment Agency. (2020a). *An introduction to Europe's Protected Areas 2020.* Author.

European Environment Agency. (2020b). *Building a coherent Trans European Nature Network.* Author.

European Environment Agency. (2022). *EU27 - Birds and Habitats Directives.* https://www.eea.europa.eu/data-and-maps/figures/natura-2000-birds-and-habitat-directives-12/eu27-birds-and-habitats-directives

European Parliament. (2013). *Semi-Subsistence Farming: Value and Directions of Development.* Author.

European Union. (2022). *Sustainable development in the European Union, Monitoring report on progress towards the SDGs in an EU context, 2022 edition.* Author.

Evans, K. (2020, March 20). In 2017, New Zealand granted legal personhood to the Whanganui River. Since then, other nations have followed suit in an effort to protect the environment. *BBC.*

Fraser, B. (2022, January 24). Is a river a person? Advocates for the legal rights of nature say yes. *Earthbeat.*

GOV.UK. (2021). *European Convention on Human Rights protocol comes into force.* https://www.gov.uk/government/news/european-convention-on-human-rights-protocol-comes-into-force

Hamlett, C. (2021, October 18). Could Property Law Help Achieve 'Rights of Nature' for Wild Animals? *The Revelator.*

Hildt, L. (2019). *Implementation of rulings for nature conservation Court of Justice of the European Union case studies*. EEB.

Holder, J. (1997). Case C-44/95, R. v. Secretary of State for the Environment, ex parte Royal Society for the Protection of Birds, Judgment of the Court of Justice 11 July 1996, [1996] ECR I-3805. *Common Market Law Review*, *34*(6), 1469–1480. doi:10.54648/148721

Hutchison, A. (2014). The Whanganui River as a Legal Person. *Alternative Law Journal*, *39*(3), 179–182. doi:10.1177/1037969X1403900309

ILO. (2022, September 29). *UN General Assembly recognizes human right to a clean, healthy, and sustainable environment*. https://www.ilo.org/global/about-the-ilo/newsroom/news/WCMS_857164/lang--en/index.htm#:~:text=This%20reality%20was%20recognized%20by,been%20a%20long%20time%20coming

Jabareen, Y. (2011). Teaching Sustainability: A Multidisciplinary Approach. *Scientific Research*, *2*(4), 388–392.

Law Insider. (2023). *Overriding reasons relating to the public interest definition*. https://www.lawinsider.com/dictionary/overriding-reasons-relating-to-the-public-interest

May, C. (2020). Should rivers have legal rights? *Melbourne Law School*. https://law.unimelb.edu.au/news/MLS/should-rivers-have-legal-rights

McKean, M., & Ostrom, E. (n.d.). *Common property regimes in the forest: Just a relic from the past?* Academic Press.

Möckel, S. (2017). The European ecological network "Natura 2000" and its derogation procedure to ensure compatibility with competing public interests. *Nature Conservation*, *23*, 87–116.

Niland, J. (1991). *The Appropriate Role of Property Rights in Environmental Protection*. doi:10.1177/103530469100200108

NOAA. (2022, August 23). *What's Behind Chinook and Chum Salmon Declines in Alaska?* https://www.fisheries.noaa.gov/feature-story/whats-behind-chinook-and-chum-salmon-declines-alaska

Pearce, D., & Turner, R. K. (1990). *Economics of natural resources and the environment*. Johns Hopkins University Press.

Phelps, J. (2021). *Environmental liability litigation could remedy biodiversity loss*. Wiley. doi:10.1111/conl.12821

Practical Law. (2023). *Overriding interests*. https://uk.practicallaw.thomsonreuters.com/5-107-6954?transitionType=Default&contextData=(sc.Default)&firstPage=true

Reichert, G., Schwind, S., De Petris, A., Jousseaume, M. (2020, May 20). EU Communication, Biodiversity Strategy 2030. *cepPolicyBrief*.

SER. (2021). *Scientists in Support for an Ambitious EU Nature Restoration Law*. SER.

Serrano Alvarez, J. A. (2014). When the enemy is the state: Common lands management in northwest Spain (1850–1936). *The International Journal of the Commons*, *8*(1), 107–133. doi:10.18352/ijc.389

Strona, G., & Bradshaw, C. J. A. (2022, December 16). Coextinctions dominate future vertebrate losses from climate and land use change. *Science Advances*, *8*(50), eabn4345. doi:10.1126ciadv.abn4345 PMID:36525487

The Lawyers and Jurists. (n.d.). *The Principle of Sustainable Development Means an Integration of Development and Environmental Imperatives*. https://www.lawyersnjurists.com/article/the-principle-of-sustainable-development-means-an-integration-of-development-and-environmental-imperatives/

The World Bank. (1993). *Housing Enabling Markets to Work*. World Bank Books.

Umweltbundesamt. (2019). *BD-R-2: Protected areas*. https://www.umweltbundesamt.de/en/topics/climate-energy/climate-impacts-adaptation/impacts-of-climate-change/monitoring-report-2019/indicators-of-climate-change-impacts-adaptation/cluster-biodiversity/bd-r-2-protected-areas#bd-r-2-protected-areas

UN. (1987). *Our Common Future*. Report of the World Commission on Environment and Development.

UN. (1987). 42/187 Report of the World Commission on Environment and Development. *General Assembly 42nd session.*

UN. (2007). *Framing Sustainable Development The Brundtland Report – 20 Years On*. Sustainable Development in Action.

UN. (2020). *Sustainable Development: From Brundtland to Rio 2012*. http://www.surdurulebilirkalkinma.gov.tr/wp-content/uploads/2016/06/Background_on_Sustainable_Development.pdf

UN. (2021). *The right to a healthy environment: 6 things you need to know*. UN News. https://news.un.org/en/story/2021/10/1103082

UN. (2022). *The Sustainable Development Goals Report 2022*. UN.

UN. (n.d.). *Transforming our world: the 2030 Agenda for Sustainable Development*. https://sdgs.un.org/2030agenda

UN General Assembly. (1992). *Rio Declaration on Environment and Development*. Author.

UNEP. (2022). *Convention on Biological Diversity, Kunming-Montreal Global biodiversity framework, Draft decision submitted by the President*. https://www.cbd.int/doc/c/e6d3/cd1d/daf663719a03902a9b116c34/cop-15-l-25-en.pdf?appLinkHandling=true

UNEP. (2022). *COP15 ends with landmark biodiversity agreement.* https://www.unep.org/news-and-stories/story/cop15-ends-landmark-biodiversity-agreement

Winkler, K., Fuchs, R., Rounsevell, M., & Herold, M. (2022, May). Global land use changes are four times greater than previously estimated. *Nature Communications.* https://www.nature.com/articles/s41467-021-22702-2

Wyatt, D. (2020). *The Anaemic Existence of the Overriding Public Interest in Disclosure in the EU's Access to Documents Regime.* Cambridge University Press.

ENDNOTES

2 Wyatt, D. (2020). The Anaemic Existence of the Overriding Public Interest in Disclosure in the EU's Access to Documents Regime. *Cambridge University Press. p. 690.*

3 Wyatt (n77) p.691.

4 Ibid.

5 European Commission (n.d.). Public consultations and other consultation activities. https://ec.europa.eu/social/main.jsp?catId=333&langId=en

6 Practical Law (2023). Overriding interests. https://uk.practicallaw.thomsonreuters.com/5-107-6954?transitionType=Default&contextData=(sc.Default)&firstPage=true

7 Ibid.

8 Habitat Directive [6].

9 Möckel, S. (2017). The European ecological network "Natura 2000" and its derogation procedure to ensure compatibility with competing public interests. *Nature Conservation 23, p. 88.*

10 Möckel (n85), p. 91.

11 European Commission (n31) p. 34.

12 European Commission (2007). Guidance document on Article 6(4) of the 'Habitats Directive' 92/43/EEC.

13 European Commission (n88) 7.

14 European Commission (n88) 7.

15 European Commission (n88) 8.

16 Möckel (n85), p. 113.

17 Habitat Directive [6(3)], [6(4)].

18 Holder, J. (1997). Case C-44/95, R. v. Secretary of State for the Environment, ex parte Royal Society for the Protection of Birds, Judgment of the Court of Justice 11 July 1996, [1996] ECR I-3805. *Common Market Law Review, Volume 34, Issue 6, pp. 1469–1480* https://doi.org/10.54648/148721

19 European Commission (n64) 67.

20 Holder (n94).

21 Client Earth (2020). Enforcing the Habitats Directive in national courts. https://www.clientearth.org/media/pb5g0lpe/webinar-8-enforcing-the-habitats-directive-in-national-courts.pdf

22 Hildt, L. (2019). Implementation of rulings for nature conservation Court of Justice of the European Union case studies. *EEB.* https://eeb.org/wp-content/uploads/2020/09/Implementation-of-rulings-for-nature-conservation2.pdf

23 Crown (2021). The Economics of Biodiversity: The Dasgupta Review. https://assets.publishing.service.gov.uk/government/uploads/system/uploads/attachment_data/file/962785/The_Economics_of_Biodiversity_The_Dasgupta_Review_Full_Report.pdf, pp. 352f.

24 2022/0195 (COD) Proposal for a Regulation of the European Parliament and of the Council on Nature Restoration.

25 Ibid [35].

26 Ibid [35].

27 Directive 2010/75/EU of the European Parliament and of the Council of 24 November 2010 on industrial emissions (integrated pollution prevention and control).

28 Industrial Emissions Directive [1] (16, 17).

29 Industrial Emissions Directive [24].

30 Industrial Emissions Directive [19].

31 Industrial Emissions Directive [25].

32 Industrial Emissions Directive [25].

33 Industrial Emissions Directive [30], [37].

34 Directive 2004/35/EC of the European Parliament and of the Council of 21 April 2004 on environmental liability with regard to the prevention and remedying of environmental damage (Environmental Liability Directive)

35 Environmental Liability Directive [2].

36 Phelps, J. et. Al (2021). Environmental liability litigation could remedy biodiversity loss. *Wiley. DOI: 10.1111/conl.12821, p. 2.*

37 Environmental Liability Directive s1.3.3.

38 Phelps (n112).

39 Environmental Liability Directive [3.1a], in conjunction with Annex III.

40 UN (n6) [42].

41 Ibid. [52].

42 Crown (n99).

43 Elliott, L., Carrington, D. (2021, February 2). Economics' failure over destruction of nature presents 'extreme risks. *The Guardian*

44 Crown (n99) 5.

45 Ibid.

46 Crown (n99) 338.

47 In Habitat Directive [1] and part II.

48 Habitat Directive [2].

49 Ibid.

50 Habitat Directive, *preamble.*

51 E.g. in TFEU [88].

52 TFEU [197].

53 E.g. TFEU [172].

54 As in UN (n6) [18], 39.

55 TFEU [1].

56 2021/0366 (COD) Proposal for a Regulation of the European Parliament and of the Council on the making available on the Union market as well as export from the Union of certain commodities and products associated with deforestation and forest degradation and repealing Regulation (EU) No 995/2010

57 2021/0366 (COD), 10.

58 Equality and Human Rights Commission (2021). What is the Charter of Fundamental Rights of the European Union? https://www.equalityhumanrights.com/en/what-are-human-rights /how-are-your-rights-protected/what-charter-fundamental-righ ts-european-union

59 Charter of Fundamental Rights of the EU [37].

60 2021/0366 (COD), 10.

61 GOV.UK (2021). European Convention on Human Rights protocol comes into force. https://www.gov.uk/government/news/european-convention-on-hu man-rights-protocol-comes-into-force

62 Winkler, K., Fuchs, R., Rounsevell, M., Herold, M. (2022). Global land use changes are four times greater than previously estimated. *Nature communications.* https://www.nature.com/articles/s41467-021-22702-2, p. 2.

63 Ibid.

64 Ibid.

65 Corrigendum to Commission Delegated Regulation (EU) 2022/1288 of 6 April 2022 supplementing Regulation (EU) 2019/2088 of the European Parliament and of the Council with regard to regulatory technical standards specifying the details of the content and presentation of the information in relation to the principle of 'do no significant harm', specifying the content, methodologies and presentation of information in relation to sustainability indicators and adverse sustainability impacts, and the content and presentation of the information in relation to the promotion of environmental or social characteristics and sustainable investment objectives in pre-contractual documents, on websites and in periodic reports, ANNEX I Template principal adverse sustainability impacts statement, (EU, 2022) [19].

66 European Environment Agency (n.d.). An introduction to Europe's Protected Areas 2020. https://www.eea.europa.eu/themes/biodiversity/europe-protect ed-areas

67 European Environment Agency (n142).

68 European Commission (1990). ESDP European Spatial Development Perspective, Towards Balanced and Sustainable Development of the Territory of the European Union. *p. 30.*

69 2021/0366 (COD).

70 2021/0366 (COD) 10.

71 Charter of Fundamental Rights of the EU [17].

72 See for example in the UK, when regional town and country planning was abolished in conjunction with the Localism Act 2011.

73 European Commission (2017). Natura 2000 and spatial planning. *p. 57.*

74 Niland (n57) 134.

75 European Commission (2013). Guidelines on Wilderness in Natura 2000. https://ec.europa.eu/environment/nature/natura2000/wilderness/pdf/WildernessGuidelines.pdf, p. 66.

76 European Commission (n149) 66.

77 E.g. European Commission (n151) 6

78 European Commission (n149) 54f.

79 European Commission (n149) 6.

80 See also: European Environment Agency (2022). EU27 - Birds and Habitats Directives. https://www.eea.europa.eu/data-and-maps/figures/natura-2000-birds-and-habitat-directives-12/eu27-birds-and-habitats-directives

81 Habitat Directive [1].

82 Habitat Directive [3].

83 Directive 2014/52/EU of the European Parliament and of the Council of 16 April 2014 amending Directive 2011/92/EU on the assessment of the effects of certain public and private projects on the environment (EIA Directive).

84 EIA Directive, preamble (9).

85 Burkart, K. (2022). Indigenous land rights take center stage in a new global framework for biodiversity conservation (commentary). *Mongabay.* https://news.mongabay.com/2022/03/indigenous-land-rights-take-center-stage-in-a-new-global-framework-for-biodiversity-conservation/

86 Alden Wily, L. (2011). Customary Land Tenure in the Modern World Rights to Resources in Crisis: Reviewing the Fate of Customary Tenure in Africa - Brief #1 of 5. https://dlc.dlib.indiana.edu/dlc/bitstream/handle/10535/7713/customary%20land%20tenure%20in%20the%20modern%20world.pdf?sequence=1, p. 2.

87 Serrano Alvarez, J.A. (2014). When the enemy is the state: common lands management in northwest Spain (1850–1936). *International Journal of the Commons, 8(1), pp. 107–133.* https://www.thecommonsjournal.org/article/10.18352/ijc.389/ accessed 8 Jan 2023.

88 Serrano Alvarez (n163).

89 One of many examples reported here: Bendana, C. (2022). Uganda takes to the courts to stop land grabs and protect forests. farmlandgrab..org https://www.farmlandgrab.org/post/view/31319

90 The World Bank (1993). Enabling Housing Markets to Work. *World Bank Books.*

91 NOAA (2022). What's Behind Chinook and Chum Salmon Declines in Alaska? https://www.fisheries.noaa.gov/feature-story/whats-behind-chinook-and-chum-salmon-declines-alaska

92 Kunming-Montreal Global biodiversity framework, Target 3.

93 Niland (n57) 133.

94 Crown (n99) 113.

95 Buck, S.J. (1992). Governing the Commons: The Evolution of Institutions for Collective Action by Elinor Ostrom. *Natural Resources Journal Vol. 32, No. 2, Spring* https://www.jstor.org/stable/24884388

96 Buck (n171).

97 All Answers ltd, (2022, July). Right to Environment of Human Right. *Lawteacher.net* https://www.lawteacher.net/free-law-essays/human-rights/right-to-environment-of-human-right.php?vref=1

98 Hamlett, C. (2021). Could Property Law Help Achieve 'Rights of Nature' for Wild Animals? *The Revelator.* https://therevelator.org/wildlife-property-law/

99 Hamlett (n174).

100 Fraser, B. (2022). Is a river a person? Advocates for the legal rights of nature say yes. *Earthbeat.* https://www.ncronline.org/news/earthbeat/river-person-advocates-legal-rights-nature-say-yes

101 Evans, K. (2020). In 2017, New Zealand granted legal personhood to the Whanganui River. Since then, other nations have followed suit in an effort to protect the environment. *BBC.* https://www.bbc.com/travel/article/20200319-the-new-zealand-river-that-became-a-legal-person

102 May, C. (2020). Should rivers have legal rights? *Melbourne Law School* https://law.unimelb.edu.au/news/MLS/should-rivers-have-legal-rights

103 Evans (n177).

104 Hutchison, A. (2014). The Whanganui River as a Legal Person. Alternative Law Journal, 39(3), 179–182. https://doi.org/10.1177/1037969X1403900309

105 May (n178).

106 May (n178).

107 Reichert, G., Schwind, S., De Petris, A., Jousseaume, M. (2020). EU Communication, Biodiversity Strategy 2030. *cepPolicyBrief*

108 European Commission (n27) 14.

109 European Commission (n27) 14.

110 2022/0195 (COD) Proposal for a Regulation of the European Parliament and of the Council on Nature Restoration.

111 2022/0195 (COD) Proposal for a Regulation of the European Parliament and of the Council on Nature Restoration [16].

112 Council of the European Unition: Proposal for a Directive of the European Parliament and the Council on the protection of the environment through criminal law (2022).

113 Council of the European Unition (n188).

114 UN (n1).

115 UNEP (n22).

116 TEU [4].

APPENDIX

Abbreviations:

BD Birds Directive
CJEU Court of Justice of the European Union (=ECJ)
EC European Commission
ECD Environmental Crime Directive
ECJ European Court of Justice (=CJEU)
ECHR European Charter of Human Rights
EEA European Environment Agency
EEC European Economic Community
EIA Environmental Impact Assessment
ELD Environmental Liability Directive
ESDP European Spatial Development Perspective
ETC/ULS European Topic Centre on Urban, Land and Soil Systems
EU European Union
GDP Gross Domestic Product
HD Habitats Directive
IED Industrial Emissions Directive
IROPI Imperative reasons of overriding public interest
KBA Key Biodiversity Area
MDG Millennium Development Goal
NGO Non-Governmental Organisation
No. Number
NUTS Nomenclature des unités territoriales statistiques
p. Page
SCI Site of Community Importance
SDG Sustainable Development Goal
SPA Special Protection Area
TEU Treaty of the European Union
TFEU Treaty on the Functioning of the European Union
UN United Nations
UNESCO United Nations Educational, Scientific and Cultural Organization
WFD Water Framework Directive

Table of Statutes

Charter of Fundamental Rights of the European Union, 2012/C 326/02.

Council Directive 92/43/EEC of 21 May 1992 on the conservation of natural habitats and of wild fauna and flora ('Habitat Directive').

Consolidated Version of the Treaty on European Union, C 326/13 ('TEU').

Consolidated Version of the Treaty on the Functioning of the European Union, C 326/15, 2012.

Corrigendum to Commission Delegated Regulation (EU) 2022/1288 of 6 April 2022 supplementing Regulation (EU) 2019/2088 of the European Parliament and of the Council with regard to regulatory technical standards specifying the details of the content and presentation of the information in relation to the principle of 'do no significant harm', specifying the content, methodologies and presentation of information in relation to sustainability indicators and adverse sustainability impacts, and the content and presentation of the information in relation to the promotion of environmental or social characteristics and sustainable investment objectives in pre-contractual documents, on websites and in periodic reports.

Directive 2014/52/EU of the European Parliament and of the Council of 16 April 2014 amending Directive 2011/92/EU on the assessment of the effects of certain public and private projects on the environment (EIA Directive).

Directive 2000/60/EC of the European Parliament and of the Council of 23 October 2000 establishing a framework for Community action in the field of water policy ('Water Framework Directive').

Directive 2009/147/EC of the European Parliament and of the Council of 30 November 2009 on the conservation of wild birds ('Birds Directive').

Directive 2004/35/EC of the European Parliament and of the Council of 21 April 2004 on environmental liability with regard to the prevention and remedying of environmental damage (Environmental Liability Directive).

Directive 2010/75/EU of the European Parliament and of the Council of 24 November 2010 on industrial emissions (integrated pollution prevention and control) ('Industrial Emissions Directive').

Council of Europe, 'Convention for the Protection of Human Rights and Fundamental Freedoms', (Council of Europe Treaty Series 005, 1950) ('European Convention on Human Rights').

Directive (EU) 2018/2001 of the European Parliament and of the Council of 11 December 2018 on the promotion of the use of energy from renewable sources (recast) ('Renewable Energy Directive').

Statute of the International Court of Justice.

Statutes in Policy Process

2022/0195 (COD) Proposal for a Regulation of the European Parliament and of the Council on Nature Restoration.

2021/0366 (COD) Proposal for a Regulation of the European Parliament and of the Council on the making available on the Union market as well as export from the Union of certain commodities and products associated with deforestation and forest degradation and repealing Regulation (EU) No 995/2010.

2021/0422 (COD) Proposal for a Directive of the European Parliament and the Council on the protection of the environment through criminal law and replacing Directive 2008/99/EC.

Table of Cases

Commission of the European Communities v Federal Republic of Germany, C-57/89 [1991] ('Leybucht Dykes').

R. v. Secretary of State for the Environment, ex parte Royal Society for the Protection of Birds, C-44/95 [1996].

Chapter 4
China's Belt and Road Initiative (BRI) and Its Implications for Sustainable Development Goals:
A Public Policy Perspective

Mohamad Zreik
https://orcid.org/0000-0002-6812-6529
Independent Researcher, Lebanon

ABSTRACT

This chapter analyzes China's Belt and Road Initiative (BRI) and its potential to help accomplish the Sustainable Development Goals (SDGs) set by the United Nations. It examines how the BRI has affected public policy, international collaboration, and the Sustainable Development Goals. This chapter provides a comprehensive analysis of BRI's plans and projects, as well as their compatibility with the 17 SDGs. This chapter examines the development of China's public policy, the lessons learned, and the potential barriers to achieving the SDGs. Finally, it provides policy recommendations, stressing the significance of grasping the nexus between government action, international initiatives, and long-term sustainability.

1. INTRODUCTION

Chinese President Xi Jinping first announced the Belt and Road Initiative (BRI) in 2013. It is a global development strategy with lofty goals. This initiative establishes connections between Asia, Africa, and Europe, the initiative hopes to promote economic growth, regional cooperation, and infrastructure development (Zreik, 2021a). To date, close to 138 countries, or around two-thirds of the world's population, have joined the initiative (Shakib et al., 2022). Thus, the BRI is an essential element in the development of international economies and infrastructures.

At the same time, nations around the world are trying to accomplish the United Nations' Sustainable Development Goals (SDGs), a series of 17 interconnected global objectives created in 2015 (Stead, 2019). By 2030, these objectives hope to have made progress on a wide range of pressing global problems,

DOI: 10.4018/978-1-6684-8903-1.ch004

including as poverty and inequality and climate change and environmental degradation. The SDGs are the world's consensus on what a sustainable, egalitarian, and prosperous future should look like. They offer a guide for countries to implement significant change and act as a global rallying cry for cooperation (Leal Filho et al., 2019).

With its immense scale and influence, the BRI might play a significant role in achieving the SDGs in this context. This connection, however, is far from simple, as it depends on a nuanced balancing act between public policy, international economic strategy, and sustainable development concerns. The purpose of this chapter is to investigate and shed light on this connection. This chapter seeks to determine how the goals of a major international economic cooperation project might match with and support sustainable development goals through a thorough analysis of the BRI and its implications for the SDGs.

This chapter begins a deep dive into the connections between China's BRI and the SDGs set forth by the United Nations. The focus is on the BRI and how public policy, global economic strategy, and sustainable development all interact with one another. The major goal is to identify ways in which the BRI may contribute to the UN's Sustainable Development Goals, which are a collection of goals spanning economic development, environmental protection, and other areas of concern.

The chapter opens with a comprehensive summary of the BRI, discussing its background, goals, core initiatives, and major projects. The seventeen SDGs and their relationship to the BRI are then discussed in detail. After that, the chapter get into the BRI's and SDGs' complex relationship to one another. The chapter details the potential benefits and drawbacks of the BRI in terms of achieving the SDGs, particularly in regards to the promotion of clean energy, infrastructure, innovation, and industry.

Later in the chapter, China's public policy is analyzed critically in light of the BRI and the SDGs. This research investigates the link between policymaking and the achievement of the Millennium Development Goals. In the parts that follow, we'll look at how the BRI contributes to global sustainable development by highlighting the initiative's potential to facilitate knowledge sharing and technological innovation while also posing some unique obstacles, especially for the developing countries involved.

To ensure the greatest possible impact of the BRI on global SDG initiatives, this chapter finishes with a set of policy recommendations. Public policy, global projects like the BRI, and sustainable development all interact in complex ways, and this chapter highlights that fact. Therefore, the goal of this chapter is to serve as a resource for a wide range of audiences, including policymakers, corporations, NGOs, and academics.

2. BELT AND ROAD INITIATIVE (BRI) OVERVIEW

2.1. Origin and Objectives

To increase regional connectivity and stimulate economic growth, Chinese President Xi Jinping announced the Belt and Road Initiative in 2013. The initiative gets its name and concept from the ancient trading route known as the Silk Road, which served as a conduit for the free flow of products, ideas, and information between East and West (Rippa, 2020).

The BRI is an ambitious plan to re-route traffic between Asia, Africa, and Europe via a system of land and sea links. The "Belt" is the Silk Road Economic Belt, through which the initiative plans to build a land corridor from China via Central Asia and Eastern Europe to the western part of Europe. The "Road," in contrast to the common usage of the name, alludes to the 21st century Maritime Silk

Road, which would be a maritime route from the southern coast of China to the eastern coast of Africa and eventually to Europe (Bitabarova, 2018).

The BRI aims to do several different things. Its primary objective is to promote regional economic growth in the Belt and Road countries by increasing trade and investment. Secondly, it hopes to improve policy coordination, financial integration, unrestricted trade, infrastructural connectivity, and ties between people in the participating nations. The initiative's final goal is to promote cultural exchanges and mutual learning among the Belt and Road countries (Yin, 2019).

The BRI has the scope and geographical reach to dramatically impact economic landscapes and development patterns around the world. Studying the initiative's congruence with global objectives like the SDGs is important since it will help with navigating the initiative's intricacies and potential pitfalls.

2.2. Strategies and Key Projects

The basic goals of the BRI are to improve policy coordination, provide infrastructure connectivity, allow for freer trade and financial integration, and strengthen ties between the people of the participating nations.

The central objective is policy coordination, which seeks to encourage policy interchange and conversation among the nations in order to create a unified and conducive setting for the creation and execution of BRI projects. Improve policy transparency and predictability for project implementation while coordinating economic development plans, planning, and standards (Rana & Ji, 2020).

As the BRI's physical backbone, infrastructural connectivity is the focus of the second approach. Building a well-connected system of land, sea, and air channels requires the construction of transportation infrastructure like railroads, motorways, air routes, telecommunications, oil and gas pipelines, ports, and logistics nodes.

Moreover, the BRI seeks to reduce administrative burdens and open up new markets for companies operating in BRI member states. There has to be better customs cooperation, lower trade costs, and easier trade facilitation for this to happen (Zreik, Iqbal, & Rahman, 2022).

One of the most important strategies is financial integration, which calls for increased cooperation in the financial sector, more bilateral currency swap agreements, and the use of local currencies in trade and investment across BRI member states (Zhang et al., 2017). A stable, sustainable, and risk-controllable financial system in Asia is also a part of this strategy.

The sixth tactic is to foster connections between people. Education, science, culture, sports, tourism, health, and other areas of collaboration, as well as the promotion of exchanges and mutual learning among the people of the participating countries, are all emphasized (Zreik, 2021b).

Numerous types of initiatives are important to the BRI. The China-Pakistan Economic Corridor (CPEC) stands out among them; it is a $62 billion initiative that includes the development of transportation infrastructure, energy infrastructure, and business zones (Khetran & Khalid, 2019). The China-Laos railway is another massive undertaking, costing an estimated $6 billion to build from Boten on the China-Laos border to Vientiane, the capital of Laos (Kuik, 2021). The strategic importance of marine routes is reflected in the BRI's emphasis on large-scale port developments like the ones at Piraeus, Greece, and Gwadar, Pakistan (Lee & Shen, 2020).

3. SUSTAINABLE DEVELOPMENT GOALS (SDGS) OVERVIEW

3.1. Definition and Purpose of SDGs

The United Nations' Sustainable Development Goals are a set of 17 global objectives meant to serve as a "blueprint to achieve a better and more sustainable future for all" (Im, 2020). The SDGs were formulated by the United Nations in 2015 as part of the 2030 Agenda for Sustainable Development. They are an expansion on the Millennium Development Goals (MDGs) and address issues such as climate change, economic inequality, innovation, sustainable consumption, peace and justice, and more (Wiktor-Mach, 2020).

A comprehensive set of 169 targets has been established to serve as benchmarks for measuring success across all SDGs. SMART goals, characterized by being specific, measurable, attainable, relevant, and time-bound, are instrumental in guiding, implementing, and evaluating policies (Caiado et al., 2018).

The SDGs serve a wide variety of functions. They work on ending extreme poverty, which represents both the largest global problem and a necessary condition for sustainable development. The goals aim to increase prosperity while also protecting the planet; they stress the importance of addressing social needs like education, health care, and job creation, as well as combating climate change and protecting the environment.

To put it simply, the SDGs advocate for a comprehensive approach to sustainable development that takes into account the interconnectedness of issues such as reducing poverty, increasing economic growth, meeting a wide variety of social needs, and combating climate change. The SDGs are universal because they acknowledge that problems on a global scale are intertwined and that their solutions must look beyond the borders of individual nations (Schleicher, Schaafsma, & Vira, 2018). Given this, the potential of global projects like the BRI to contribute to the SDGs' realization becomes all the more essential.

3.2. The 17 Goals

All UN Member States approved the 17 Sustainable Development Goals in 2015 as an urgent call to action to make the world a better, more sustainable place by 2030. They address many different aspects of economic and social growth and are meant to work together, so that one area's success doesn't have to be at the expense of another.

1. *No Poverty:* Efforts to provide social safety systems, provide equal access to economic resources, and strengthen community resilience in the face of natural, economic, and social disasters are all part of this global effort to eradicate poverty.
2. *Zero Hunger:* Efforts to end hunger, ensure access to sufficient, nutritious food, and encourage environmentally responsible farming methods.
3. *Good Health and Well-being:* Efforts are made to ensure people of all ages have access to high-quality medical care, pharmaceuticals, and immunizations, and to reduce serious threats to world health.
4. *Quality Education:* Goals include expanding access to high-quality education for all students and encouraging people of all ages to keep learning.
5. *Gender Equality:* Promotes the rights of women and girls and seeks to eliminate the barriers they face, such as violence and discrimination.

6. *Clean Water and Sanitation:* It hopes to make water and sanitation accessible to everyone and manage them effectively for the long term.
7. *Affordable and Clean Energy:* Efforts to guarantee that everyone can afford to use clean, contemporary energy that won't deplete the planet's resources.
8. *Decent Work and Economic Growth:* Efforts to ensure that everyone has access to full and productive employment and good working conditions are encouraged.
9. *Industry, Innovation, and Infrastructure:* It seeks to strengthen institutions, advance equitable and environmentally sound industrialization, and encourage creative problem solving.
10. *Reduced Inequalities:* Efforts to promote the social, economic, and political inclusion of all members of society and the reduction of inequality both within and across nations.
11. *Sustainable Cities and Communities:* Aims to ensure that all people may feel safe and secure in their communities and that human settlements can withstand natural disasters and other stresses.
12. *Responsible Consumption and Production:* Promotes efficient use of resources and energy, as well as environmentally friendly building practices, to guarantee a sustainable way of life for future generations.
13. *Climate Action:* Efforts to mitigate and adapt to the adverse effects of climate change are prioritized.
14. *Life Below Water:* Efforts to preserve and wisely put maritime resources to use for long-term progress.
15. *Life on Land:* Goals include preventing and reversing land degradation and biodiversity loss, as well as protecting and restoring terrestrial ecosystems and promoting their sustainable use.
16. *Peace, Justice, and Strong Institutions:* Efforts are made to ensure that everyone has access to justice and that institutions at all levels are strong, transparent, and democratic.
17. *Partnerships for the Goals:* Goals include bolstering sustainable development's implementation tools and reviving international cooperation on the issue.

These objectives define the course of global progress over the next decade and indicate a consensus on how to achieve a more just and prosperous world. Initiatives like China's BRI can play a vital role within this context since they highlight the importance of cooperation between states, industry, and civil society.

4. INTERPLAY BETWEEN BRI AND SDGS

4.1. Mapping BRI Onto SDGs

Given the scope of the BRI and its emphasis on economic growth and regional integration, the SDGs will be profoundly affected by it. To see how the BRI contributes to the SDGs, it is helpful to map the initiative's many parts onto the 17 goals.

The goals of the BRI are consistent with several of the SDGs on a fundamental level. The BRI's goals of generating economic growth and promoting regional integration are very congruent with SDG 8, which aspires to promote inclusive and sustainable economic growth, full and productive employment, and decent work for all.

Building robust infrastructure, encouraging innovation, and supporting sustainable industrialization are all goals of SDG 9, which have direct parallels with the BRI's emphasis on infrastructure development. Connectivity improvements and increased industrial output are two potential outcomes of infrastructure projects including motorways, railways, ports, and telecommunications networks, all of which are relevant to achieving SDG 9.

Furthermore, SDG 17, which aims to strengthen the means of implementation and revitalize the global partnership for sustainable development, is in line with the BRI's emphasis on policy coordination and financial integration (Marzuki et al., 2023). Attaining SDG 17 requires the kind of policy discourse and cooperation, financial system connectivity, and mutual learning that the BRI promotes.

The BRI might have positive and negative effects on the SDGs. For instance, SDGs 13 on climate action, SDG 14 on life below water, and SDG 15 on life on land may be threatened by the focus on infrastructural development and industrial growth (Yin, 2019). Without proper forethought and management, large-scale infrastructure projects can have detrimental effects on the environment and speed up global warming.

The complicated connection between a global economic cooperation project and SDGs is illustrated by this mapping of BRI onto SDGs. In doing so, it emphasizes the need for rigorous planning, policy creation, and execution to prevent any negative impacts while also highlighting the BRI's potential to advance the SDGs. To guarantee the BRI positively contributes to the global effort of achieving the SDGs, a balanced, educated, and policy-driven approach is required.

4.2. Potential Advances and Hindrances

The BRI has the scope and ambition to make considerable progress toward a number of the SDGs. Potential advantages must be balanced against obstacles and negative effects on desired outcomes.

SDGs 9 (Industry, Innovation, and Infrastructure) and 11 (Sustainable Cities and Communities) stand to benefit greatly from the BRI's investments in infrastructure development, like as transportation and communication networks. Such progress has the potential to boost urban and rural living standards, spur innovation, and increase regional connectedness.

To further contribute to SDGs 1 (No Poverty) and 8 (Decent Work and Economic Growth), the BRI aims to increase trade and investment and promote regional economic integration (Li & Zhu, 2019). To achieve sustainable development, a collective and integrated approach is needed, and the initiative's focus on policy discussion, financial integration, and people-to-people ties is in line with SDG 17 (Partnerships for the Goals).

There could be obstacles and difficulties, though. Challenges to SDGs 13 (Climate Action), 14 (Life Below Water), and 15 (Life on Land) relating to environmental sustainability are posed by the scale of infrastructure development under the BRI if it is not managed responsibly. Carbon emissions could rise as a result of increased industrial activity and transportation, exacerbating the negative effects on the environment (Zhuang et al., 2022).

Concerns have also been raised about the BRI's potential to deepen existing economic and social divides. Inequalities could widen and progress toward SDG 10 (Reduced Inequalities) could be slowed if large-scale investment and development programs favored economically viable regions and groups.

Some BRI projects, especially those in underdeveloped nations, have also been criticized for their high levels of debt (Mouritz, 2020). Both SDG 1 (No Poverty) and SDG 8 (Decent Work and Economic Growth) can be undermined by excessive debt.

4.3. Case Studies: Specific Emphasis on Sectors (Clean Energy, Infrastructure, Innovation, and Industry)

The BRI has achieved substantial progress toward achieving the SDGs in many different fields, including clean energy, infrastructure, innovation, and industry. Here are a few examples to help illustrate the point:

Clean Energy (SDG 7): Several renewable energy projects have been made possible because to the BRI, which is helping to achieve SDG 7 (Affordable and renewable Energy). The Quaid-e-Azam Solar Park in Pakistan is a good illustration; it is one of the largest solar farms in the world and was funded in large part by the Chinese government. This project helps reduce carbon emissions while increasing Pakistan's energy capability (Irfan et al., 2019). A larger emphasis on renewable energy projects is required, as the BRI's engagement in coal-fired power plants in some nations raises environmental sustainability concerns despite delivering much-needed energy (Bogojević & Zou, 2021).

Infrastructure (SDGs 9 and 11): The BRI is centered on the construction of new infrastructure, which helps achieve Sustainable Development Goals 9 (Industry, Innovation, and Infrastructure) and 11 (Sustainable Cities and Communities). Such a revolutionary project is the China-Laos railway, which aims to increase accessibility, boost economic growth, and promote regional cohesion (Ly, 2020).

Innovation (SDG 9): A part of the BRI, "the Digital Silk Road" plans to improve things like digital infrastructure, e-commerce, and smart city initiatives. Huawei's Smart City Solutions are one such example, having been put into action in Duisburg, Germany (Hoffman, 2022). By encouraging cutting-edge research and development, these projects contribute to SDG 9. However, there is a serious need for reflection on data privacy and cybersecurity.

Industry (SDGs 9 and 8): The China-Egypt Suez Economic and Trade Cooperation Zone is a prime example of the BRI's impact on manufacturing (Ye et al., 2020). SDGs 9 (Decent Work) and 8 (Economic Growth) are supported by the presence of numerous Chinese businesses in this industrial park. To ensure that industrial innovations positively contribute to sustainable development, fair labor practices and the equal sharing of economic advantages are essential.

These examples demonstrate how BRI projects can contribute to achieving specific SDGs. On the other hand, they highlight the importance of more sustainable, equitable, and inclusive approaches to guarantee that these initiatives contribute to the SDGs as a whole.

5. ANALYSIS OF CHINA'S PUBLIC POLICY IN RELATION TO BRI AND SDGS

5.1. Policy Formulation and Implementation

Understanding how the BRI's potential for sustainable development is being exploited and what hurdles remain may be gained by analyzing China's public policy in regard to the BRI and the SDGs.

Policy Formulation: The BRI's potential to foster mutually beneficial economic relationships has been repeatedly touted by the Chinese leadership (Williams, Robinson, & Bouzarovski, 2020). SDG-aligned ideas like green development, people-centered development, and high-quality development have been tied by Chinese leaders to the BRI in policy documents and speeches (Bridges & Eubank, 2020). These policy documents provide evidence that an effort was made to coordinate the BRI with international sustainability targets.

While the SDGs are intended to be included into and promoted by BRI projects, a closer study reveals a lack of concrete regulations or recommendations on how to do so (Yin, 2019). While sustainable, green, and people-centered development are praised in theory, there are few real policy measures or structures in place to ensure that SDGs are taken into account in BRI projects. The BRI's capacity to contribute to the SDGs may be hampered by this lack of policy formulation.

Policy Implementation: There is some good news and some bad news on the BRI projects. There is evidence that certain projects are helping to achieve the SDGs, especially in the fields of sustainable energy and digital infrastructure. Projects involving the development of digital infrastructure, for instance, contribute to SDG 9 (Industry, Innovation, and Infrastructure), which is in line with SDG 7 (Affordable and Clean Energy) (Lewis et al., 2021).

On the other hand, BRI projects have sometimes been criticized for not being financially, socially, or environmentally sustainable. SDGs relating to environmental sustainability and economic growth could be hampered by, for instance, environmental degradation linked to infrastructure projects and worries over debt sustainability in some partner nations (Mouritz, 2020).

These problems indicate that public policy on the BRI and the SDGs is not being fully implemented. To guarantee that BRI projects positively contribute to the SDGs, stronger procedures for policy enforcement, project oversight, and stakeholder engagement are required.

5.2. Impact Assessment

Assessing the BRI's impact in light of the SDGs requires looking at both the immediate results and the long-term consequences of BRI initiatives.

Economic Impact: Economic growth in BRI countries has been substantial, helping to advance SDG 8 (Good Jobs and Economic Growth). Local economies have benefited from infrastructure developments in several ways, including the addition of new jobs and improved communication between neighboring areas. Concerns regarding long-term debt and economic inequality, on the other hand, argue that the BRI's economic gains should be dispersed more fairly if they are to ensure sustainable progress toward SDGs.

Social Impact: Increased access to services made possible by better infrastructure is one example of how the BRI may contribute to achieving SDGs such as SDG 3 (Peace, Justice, and Strong Institutions) and SDG 4 (Quality Education). The necessity for improved social impact management in BRI projects has been highlighted by social concerns such as the relocation of local residents in the course of infrastructure development.

Environmental Impact: The environmental effects of the BRI are difficult to predict. One way in which the BRI can aid Sustainable Development Goal 7 (Affordable and Clean Energy) and SDG 13 (Climate Action) is by funding clean energy projects. However, SDGs 14 (Life Below Water) and 15 (Life on Land) might be negatively impacted if infrastructure development is not managed sustainably. That's why BRI projects need stricter environmental rules and sustainability measures (Renwick, Gu, & Gong, 2018).

Governance Impact: The BRI has advanced SDG 17 (Partnerships for the Goals) by increasing the amount of time spent on policy discourse and international cooperation. However, in order to maximize the initiative's contribution to the SDGs, problems with openness, accountability, and stakeholder involvement in BRI projects should be fixed.

Based on the results of the impact assessment, the BRI has the potential to make significant progress toward the SDGs. It also highlights the importance of thorough project planning, administration, and oversight in realizing this promise and meeting the accompanying challenges.

6. THE ROLE OF THE BRI IN GLOBAL SUSTAINABLE DEVELOPMENT

6.1. Sharing of Best Practices and Technology Transfer

Sharing best practices and transferring technology across participating nations is one of the major ways the BRI may aid in the achievement of the SDGs.

Best practices are being shared across industries. As an example, other developing countries can learn from China's success in reducing poverty, which has helped hundreds of millions of people escape poverty in a short period of time (Liu et al., 2021). Similarly, other BRI countries wanting to utilize digital technology for growth and contribute to SDG 9 (Industry, Innovation, and Infrastructure) might learn from China's initiatives in digital transformation, smart city development, and e-commerce (Ullah et al., 2021).

In addition, the BRI makes it easier to exchange technological know-how, a key factor in progress toward multiple SDGs. To contribute to SDG 7 (Affordable and Clean Energy), China might teach other BRI countries how to use its solar and wind power technologies, for instance, to create more sustainable energy infrastructure. Similarly, some SDGs, such as SDG 9 (Adequate and equitable education) and SDG 11 (Sustainable cities and communities), can be supported through the transfer of technologies linked to high-speed rail, telecommunications, and digital infrastructure to participating nations.

However, cooperation in this area must be founded on learning from one another and respecting the different stages of development in each country. All nations, especially the less developed ones, should be able to reap the benefits of the BRI, so the process must be fair and open. In addition, capacity building initiatives should accompany technology transfer to guarantee that the receiving countries can make full use of and adapt the technologies.

6.2. Challenges for Developing Countries

Opportunities to speed up progress towards the SDGs exist within the BRI, but the initiative also brings significant problems that must be carefully considered and managed.

Debt Sustainability: The inability to pay off the debt is a huge worry. There is a higher chance of unmanageable debt levels in developing countries that take part in large-scale infrastructure projects backed by loans (Lai, Lin, & Sidaway, 2020). Progress towards SDGs such as SDG 1 (No Poverty), SDG 3 (Good Health and Well-being), and SDG 4 (Quality Education) may be hampered by high debt burdens if governments are unable to invest in other vital sectors such as health, education, and social welfare.

Environmental Impact: The maintenance of a healthy environment is another pressing problem. If the BRI's infrastructure projects aren't handled in a sustainable manner, they could have a major impact on the environment. This may have an effect on SDGs 13 (Climate Action), 14 (Life Below Water), and 15 (Life on Land), all of which are concerned with environmental sustainability.

Social Impact: Displacement of local populations and a possible worsening of social inequality are two examples of the social repercussions that give rise to concern. Goal 10 (Reduced Inequalities) and Goal 11 (Sustainable Cities and Communities) could be hampered if these problems aren't handled effectively.

Capacity and Governance: Developing nations may have trouble with capability and governance (Beet et al., 2020). To guarantee project success, financial management, and environmental and social safeguards throughout implementation of large-scale projects, solid institutional capabilities and strong governance structures are required. The potential advantages of BRI projects may be reduced or even negatively affected by deficiencies in these areas.

It will take teamwork to overcome these obstacles. Establishing good financial arrangements, enforcing sustainability norms, enhancing capability, and strengthening governance processes require collaboration between the Chinese government, recipient nations, and international organizations. By taking these steps, the BRI will be able to help poor nations achieve the SDGs.

7. POLICY RECOMMENDATIONS

7.1. Ensuring Positive BRI Contribution to SDGs

There needs to be cooperation on multiple fronts for the BRI to successfully impact the SDGs. Policymakers and project managers alike should be clear about how the SDGs relate to BRI initiatives. It is imperative to establish and enforce transparent policy standards and procedures for incorporating SDGs into the design, execution, and assessment of BRI projects. To achieve the SDGs, concrete action must be taken beyond the broad concepts of sustainable development.

Strong systems for monitoring projects and involving relevant parties are required. Stakeholder engagement may promote openness, inclusion, and accountability in project implementation, while effective project oversight can ensure that BRI projects conform to environmental, social, and financial sustainability requirements. Involvement from all relevant parties—governments, local communities, civil society organizations, and the corporate sector—is essential for striking a fair balance between competing interests and mitigating any negative effects that may arise from BRI projects.

In addition, making an attempt to expand capacity need to be a top priority. Institutional capacity and technical competence are typically lacking in BRI-participating developing nations, making it difficult to effectively implement and manage large-scale projects (Ram & Zhang, 2020). Increased capacity to plan, manage, and oversee BRI projects can help these countries reap the long-term benefits of the initiative.

It is crucial to deal with the issues of debt sustainability. This includes supporting prudent borrowing and lending practices, securing stable financing for BRI projects, and providing technical assistance to help debtor countries manage its debts.

By acting in this way, the BRI can help the international community reach the SDGs and create a more just, sustainable, and affluent world. But to do this, all relevant parties must pool their resources and efforts toward a common goal of sustainable progress.

7.2. Overcoming Identified Challenges

Addressing the problems that have been discovered in relation to the contribution of the BRI to the SDGs calls for a comprehensive strategy.

China, as the world's largest creditor, is in a unique position to pioneer more responsible and open approaches to financing debt relief (Zreik, 2023). Among these measures include implementing loan conditions that are flexible and take into account the economic realities of borrowing countries. Helping recipient countries improve their debt management capacities and negotiate equitable loan terms is another key role that international financial institutions should play.

Improved environmental standards enforcement in BRI projects is one way to address environmental sustainability challenges. The environmental impact of BRI projects can be reduced through the use of sustainable building methods, the completion of thorough environmental impact assessments, and the incorporation of climate resilience into project design (Li, 2021). Furthermore, China might use its expertise in green technologies to support BRI projects that are good for the environment.

Stronger community engagement should be encouraged during all phases of BRI projects to lessen negative social effects. So that their wants and concerns are taken into account, local communities should be involved in the project's design, execution, and monitoring. In addition, local community capacity building and job creation can help spread project benefits more widely.

Addressing issues of capacity and governance requires donor countries to improve their institutional capacities and governance systems. These nations can be helped to better manage and oversee BRI projects through the provision of technical support and capacity building. Risks of corruption and mismanagement can be mitigated if project implementation is conducted in an open and accountable manner.

It is crucial to work toward a closer integration between the BRI and the SDGs. To this end, it is necessary to establish unambiguous policy guidelines and procedures for incorporating the SDGs into the design, execution, and assessment of BRI projects. It is possible to keep BRI projects on track to contribute to the SDGs through regular monitoring and evaluation.

It won't be simple to overcome these obstacles. Governments, non-governmental groups, citizens, and businesses must all work together to achieve this goal. However, a shared dedication to sustainable development is imperative in order to overcome these challenges and ensure that the BRI makes a positive and meaningful impact towards the global pursuit of the SDGs.

8. CONCLUSION

As we wrap up this chapter, it becomes clear that China's BRI, one of the world's most ambitious global development initiatives, has the potential to make a sizable contribution to the SDGs set forth by the United Nations. However, this potential cannot be reached without a deep comprehension of the connections between global economic cooperation, public policymaking, and long-term growth and prosperity.

We have explained the rationale behind the BRI and provided an overview of its key strategy and completed initiatives. To set the stage for the investigation of the complex connection between the BRI and the SDGs, we have also looked into the SDGs, their purpose, and their specific targets. We have explored the possibility of the BRI helping or hurting the 17 SDGs by mapping them onto the BRI.

By analyzing China's public policy in regards to the BRI and SDGs, we have shown the potential and the difficulties of incorporating sustainable development principles into BRI initiatives. Clean energy, infrastructure, innovation, and industry are only a few examples of sectors where BRI has been successful, proving that its ability to contribute to sustainable development is not purely theoretical. But we have also highlighted the significant difficulties, especially for developing nations engaging in the BRI, pertaining to concerns like debt sustainability, environmental effect, social ramifications, and governance.

In the future, it will be critical to execute policy recommendations that will assist guarantee the BRI positively contributes to the SDGs. It is crucial that the SDGs be incorporated into the development and execution of BRI projects with clear policy guidelines. In order to strike a balance between different interests, deal with potential negative repercussions, and encourage openness and accountability in project implementation, it is necessary to set up strong oversight structures and stakeholder engagement processes. The debt sustainability issues encountered by developing countries can only be overcome by placing a premium on capacity building and implementing responsible lending policies. Similarly, protecting the planet's health for future generations depends on making sure initiatives are carried out in an eco-friendly manner.

Collective effort between public agencies, private businesses, non-profits, and educational institutions is essential. To be successful, this partnership must be based on trust, communication, and a commitment to creating a more just, sustainable, and prosperous society for all parties involved. By working together, we can tap into the game-changing potential of initiatives like the BRI, translating global strategy into local benefits and accelerating progress toward the SDGs.

The BRI represents an exciting but challenging new frontier in international development at a time when the world is still struggling with enormous developmental issues. The first step is to grasp its significance for the SDGs. The true challenge is realizing the BRI's promise to improve the lives of billions of people around the world. We can make the BRI a potent tool in the quest of global sustainable development through diligent work, well-defined policy directions, and international cooperation. This is an opportunity and a responsibility we can't afford to ignore. The path ahead is convoluted and challenging, but the destination is worth it.

REFERENCES

Beer, A., McKenzie, F., Blažek, J., Sotarauta, M., & Ayres, S. (2020). *Every place matters: towards effective place-based policy*. Routledge. doi:10.4324/9781003110118

Bitabarova, A. G. (2018). Unpacking Sino-Central Asian engagement along the new silk road: A case study of Kazakhstan. *Journal of Contemporary East Asia Studies*, *7*(2), 149–173. doi:10.1080/24761028.2018.1553226

Bogojević, S., & Zou, M. (2021). Making Infrastructure 'Visible'in Environmental Law: The Belt and Road Initiative and Climate Change Friction. *Transnational Environmental Law*, *10*(1), 35–56. doi:10.1017/S2047102520000278

Bridges, T., & Eubank, D. (2020). *Leading Sustainably: The Path to Sustainable Business and how the SDGs Changed Everything*. Routledge. doi:10.4324/9780367855468

Caiado, R. G. G., Leal Filho, W., Quelhas, O. L. G., de Mattos Nascimento, D. L., & Ávila, L. V. (2018). A literature-based review on potentials and constraints in the implementation of the sustainable development goals. *Journal of Cleaner Production*, *198*, 1276–1288. doi:10.1016/j.jclepro.2018.07.102

Hoffman, S. (2022). China's Tech-Enhanced Authoritarianism. *Journal of Democracy*, *33*(2), 76–89. doi:10.1353/jod.2022.0019

Im, J. (2020). Earth observations and geographic information science for sustainable development goals. *GIScience & Remote Sensing*, *57*(5), 591–592. doi:10.1080/15481603.2020.1763041

Irfan, M., Zhao, Z. Y., Ahmad, M., & Mukeshimana, M. C. (2019). Solar energy development in Pakistan: Barriers and policy recommendations. *Sustainability (Basel)*, *11*(4), 1206. doi:10.3390u11041206

Khetran, M. S. B., & Khalid, M. H. (2019). The China-Pakistan Economic Corridor: Gateway to Central Asia. *China Quarterly of International Strategic Studies*, *5*(03), 455–469. doi:10.1142/S2377740019500179

Kuik, C. C. (2021). Laos's Enthusiastic Embrace of China's Belt and Road Initiative. *Asian Perspective*, *45*(4), 735–759. doi:10.1353/apr.2021.0042

Lai, K. P., Lin, S., & Sidaway, J. D. (2020). Financing the Belt and Road Initiative (BRI): Research agendas beyond the "debt-trap" discourse. *Eurasian Geography and Economics*, *61*(2), 109–124. doi:10.1080/15387216.2020.1726787

Leal Filho, W., Tripathi, S. K., Andrade Guerra, J. B. S. O. D., Giné-Garriga, R., Orlovic Lovren, V., & Willats, J. (2019). Using the sustainable development goals towards a better understanding of sustainability challenges. *International Journal of Sustainable Development and World Ecology*, *26*(2), 179–190. doi:10.1080/13504509.2018.1505674

Lee, H. L., & Shen, Z. J. M. (2020). Supply chain and logistics innovations with the Belt and Road Initiative. *Journal of Management Science and Engineering*, *5*(2), 77 86. doi:10.1016/j.jmse.2020.05.001

Lewis, D. J., Yang, X., Moise, D., & Roddy, S. J. (2021). Dynamic synergies between China's belt and road initiative and the UN's sustainable development goals. *Journal of International Business Policy*, *4*(1), 58–79. doi:10.105742214-020-00082-6

Li, L. (2021). Integrating climate change impact in new building design process: A review of building life cycle carbon emission assessment methodologies. *Cleaner Engineering and Technology*, *5*, 100286. doi:10.1016/j.clet.2021.100286

Li, Y., & Zhu, X. (2019). The 2030 agenda for sustainable development and China's belt and road initiative in Latin America and the Caribbean. *Sustainability (Basel)*, *11*(8), 2297. doi:10.3390u11082297

Liu, F., Li, L., Zhang, Y., Ngo, Q. T., & Iqbal, W. (2021). Role of education in poverty reduction: Macroeconomic and social determinants form developing economies. *Environmental Science and Pollution Research International*, *28*(44), 63163–63177. doi:10.100711356-021-15252-z PMID:34226999

Ly, B. (2020). Challenge and perspective for digital Silk road. *Cogent Business & Management*, *7*(1), 1804180. doi:10.1080/23311975.2020.1804180

Marzuki, S. Z., Zreik, M., Buyong, S. Z., Goyipnazarov, S., Mirzaliev, S., & Bakhramovna, I. A. (2023). An Importance Satisfaction Analysis of Hosting Events in Hangzhou, China: A Pilot Study. *Advances in Social Sciences Research Journal*, *10*(6.2), 107–117. doi:10.14738/assrj.106.2.14996

Mouritz, F. (2020). Implications of the COVID-19 pandemic on China's Belt and Road Initiative. *Connections*, *19*(2), 115–124. doi:10.11610/Connections.19.2.09

Ram, J., & Zhang, Z. (2020). Belt and road initiative (BRI) supply chain risks: Propositions and model development. *International Journal of Logistics Management, 31*(4), 777–799. doi:10.1108/IJLM-12-2019-0366

Rana, P. B., & Ji, X. (2020). *China's Belt and Road Initiative*. Springer Singapore. doi:10.1007/978-981-15-5171-0

Renwick, N., Gu, J., & Gong, S. (2018). *The impact of BRI investment in infrastructure on achieving the Sustainable Development Goals. In K4D emerging issues report*. Institute of Development Studies.

Rippa, A. (2020). Mapping the margins of China's global ambitions: Economic corridors, Silk Roads, and the end of proximity in the borderlands. *Eurasian Geography and Economics, 61*(1), 55–76. doi:10.1080/15387216.2020.1717363

Schleicher, J., Schaafsma, M., & Vira, B. (2018). Will the Sustainable Development Goals address the links between poverty and the natural environment? *Current Opinion in Environmental Sustainability, 34*, 43–47. doi:10.1016/j.cosust.2018.09.004

Shakib, M., Yumei, H., Rauf, A., Alam, M., Murshed, M., & Mahmood, H. (2022). Revisiting the energy-economy-environment relationships for attaining environmental sustainability: Evidence from Belt and Road Initiative countries. *Environmental Science and Pollution Research International, 29*(3), 3808–3825. doi:10.100711356-021-15860-9 PMID:34402005

Stead, S. M. (2019). Using systems thinking and open innovation to strengthen aquaculture policy for the United Nations Sustainable Development Goals. *Journal of Fish Biology, 94*(6), 837–844. doi:10.1111/jfb.13970 PMID:30887512

Ullah, A., Pinglu, C., Ullah, S., Abbas, H. S. M., & Khan, S. (2021). The role of e-governance in combating COVID-19 and promoting sustainable development: A comparative study of China and Pakistan. *Chinese Political Science Review, 6*(1), 86–118. doi:10.100741111-020-00167-w

Wiktor-Mach, D. (2020). What role for culture in the age of sustainable development? UNESCO's advocacy in the 2030 Agenda negotiations. *International Journal of Cultural Policy, 26*(3), 312–327. doi:10.1080/10286632.2018.1534841

Williams, J., Robinson, C., & Bouzarovski, S. (2020). China's Belt and Road Initiative and the emerging geographies of global urbanisation. *The Geographical Journal, 186*(1), 128–140. doi:10.1111/geoj.12332

Ye, C., Li, S., Zhuang, L., & Zhu, X. (2020). A comparison and case analysis between domestic and overseas industrial parks of China since the Belt and Road Initiative. *Journal of Geographical Sciences, 30*(8), 1266–1282. doi:10.100711442-020-1781-0

Yin, W. (2019). Integrating sustainable development goals into the belt and road initiative: Would it be a new model for green and sustainable investment? *Sustainability (Basel), 11*(24), 6991. doi:10.3390u11246991

Zhang, F., Yu, M., Yu, J., & Jin, Y. (2017). The effect of RMB internationalization on belt and road initiative: Evidence from bilateral swap agreements. *Emerging Markets Finance & Trade, 53*(12), 2845–2857. doi:10.1080/1540496X.2017.1382346

Zhuang, Y., Yang, S., Razzaq, A., & Khan, Z. (2022). Environmental impact of infrastructure-led Chinese outward FDI, tourism development and technology innovation: A regional country analysis. *Journal of Environmental Planning and Management*, *66*(2), 367–399. doi:10.1080/09640568.2021.1989672

Zreik, M. (2021a). The Potential of a Sino-Lebanese Partnership through the Belt and Road Initiative (BRI). *Contemporary Arab Affairs*, *14*(3), 125–145. doi:10.1525/caa.2021.14.3.125

Zreik, M. (2021b). Academic Exchange Programs between China and the Arab Region: A Means of Cultural Harmony or Indirect Chinese Influence? *Arab Studies Quarterly*, *43*(2). Advance online publication. doi:10.13169/arabstudquar.43.2.0172

Zreik, M. (2023). Analytical study on Foreign Direct Investment Divestment Inflows and Outflows in Developing Economies: Evidence of China. *Chinese Economy*, 1–16. doi:10.1080/10971475.2023.2193118

Zreik, M., Iqbal, B. A., & Rahman, M. N. (2022). Outward FDI: Determinants and Flows in Emerging Economies: Evidence from China. *China and WTO Review*, *8*(2), 385–402. doi:10.14330/cwr.2022.8.2.07

Chapter 5
Application of Maqasid al-Shariah-Based Public Policy Framework in SDGs Policies:
Poverty Eradication (SDG 1) as a Case Study

Ahmad Labeeb Tajudeen
Islamic University of Minnesota, USA

Manzoor Apenna Lawal
Sikiru Adetona College of Education Science and Technology, Omu-Ajose, Nigeria

ABSTRACT

Public policy scholars have warned that the conventional public policy (CPP) framework is not effective enough to address the post-pandemic problems as it has blatantly failed the litmus test of time. The CPP framework has been criticised on various grounds and blamed for the problems of unsustainability and overarching poverty that plague humanity. The objective of this chapter is to explain a quadric public policy framework (PPI) that has recently been proposed as an efficient alternative public policy framework. The explanation is limited to only one out of the four components of the framework, called the Maqasid al-Shariah component, also known as public interest theory. The findings show that the PPI framework can link policymakers from different sectors and provide a platform for a whole-of-government approach to achieving the SDGs, especially poverty alleviation and eradication.

INTRODUCTION

The Sustainable Development Goals (SDGs) or Global Goals are a set of 17 interconnected and interdependent goals adopted by the United Nations in 2015, to end poverty, protect the planet, and ensure prosperity for all. According to Sachs, et al. (2019), these goals focus on time-bound targets for the five Ps: prosperity, people, planet, peace, and partnership. A closer look at the Sustainable Development

DOI: 10.4018/978-1-6684-8903-1.ch005

Goals reveals that most of the goals are social security parameters that are *condiciones sine quibus non* in the public policy of any country. Although governments, inter-governmental organizations (IGOs), non-governmental organizations (NGOs), faith-based organizations (FBOs) and relevant humanitarian agencies have recognized social security as a fundamental human right, countries around the world still face challenges in designing effective policies that guarantee the social security for their citizens. This is evident in the recent report of the International Labor Organization (ILO) for the period 2020-2022, which laments that about 4.1 billion people around the world are still wholly unprotected by any form of social security (Batchabi, 2022). Unfortunately, the Coronavirus outbreak in late year 2019 aggravated and exacerbated the hitherto reeling social security measures and posed more daunting challenges to policymakers. According to the World Bank Group development report, the COVID-19 pandemic has triggered the most encompassing economic crisis in almost a century, poverty rates have soared, public debt has reached unprecedented levels, and inequality has widened both across and within countries. The socio-economic effect of the COVID-19 pandemic, the report continues, has been rated to be more devastating than the two world wars, the Great Depression of the 1930s, the emerging economy debt crises of the 1980s, and the 2007–09 global financial crisis (World Bank, 2022). Consequently, the COVID-19 pandemic has made the actualization of SDGs more challenging, and the pressing need for a 'saviour policy' can never be overemphasized.

The Knowledge Gap

Although there is a pressing need for effective policy, conventional policymakers have very few useful levers to deal with the post-pandemic recession, as many of their tried-and-true approaches have clearly failed the litmus test of time (Jacobs, 2020). Scholars of public policy have warned that the conventional public policy framework (CPP) cannot solve the post-pandemic problems (Abdelgafar, 2021; Johal, et al, 2022; Nicklin, 2019; Sewerin, et al, 2022). They criticize and accuse the CPP of inefficiency and blame its ideological foundation for the woes of unsustainability and overarching poverty that plague humanity (Abdelgafar, 2021). Hence, they call for an alternative public policy framework that is more efficient and inclusive (Abdelgafar, 2021; Johal, et al, 2022; Sewerin, et al, 2022).

For instance, Basma Abdelgafar, a professor of public policy at the International Peace College, in South Africa, criticized the conventional public policy framework as being propelled by a deep neoliberal ideology (Abdelgafar, 2021) which is anathema to equal sustainability (Langridge, 2013). Therefore, "sustainable development and improving quality of life demands a wholly new approach to understanding, formulating and implementing public policy. Policies that are unjust, serving only particular interests must be dismantled not marginally softened" (Abdelgafar, 2021; p. 10). She warns that "if nothing serious is done to reform global policy regimes that reproduce inequalities, the pandemic like other crises, will represent nothing more than a massive transfer of global wealth to big business including pharmaceuticals, technology and food retail giants, as Naomi Klein has argued was the case in past crises" (Abdelgafar, 2021; p. 4).

A recent report coordinated by Johal Anthony, a professor of public policy at the University of Toronto, posits that "policy tools and processes that delivered results in the 1950s and 1960s are no longer fit for purpose in the face of changing public expectations, ever more complex and interconnected challenges, and the advent of new technologies" (Johal, et al, 2022). This is in total agreement with the Organisation for Economic Co-operation and Development (OECD)'s report that asserts that "many of the policies which have been implemented across the OECD, not just over the last decade but over the last forty years or so, appear no longer able to improve economic and social outcomes in the ways they once promised" (Jacobs, 2020). Johal, et al, (2022)'s report called on policymakers to consider, experiment with, and adopt new approaches to policy development, implementation, and service delivery to ensure policy frameworks are flexible and robust enough for an increasingly unpredictable world (Johal, et al, 2022).

The above submissions are in congruence with the critical viewpoint of Sewerin et al. (2022) that "to tackle the manifold crises of our times, most strikingly the plethora of environmental crises we face, ambitious policy action is urgently needed to achieve the necessary radical transformation of our industrialized societies. In other words, paradigmatic policy change is needed to achieve transformative societal change". What is key in all the submissions is the pressing need for an alternative public policy framework or paradigm shift, and that the use of the conventional public policy framework to solve the current problems is a confirmed futile exercise.

Since the late seventies, Islam as both a religion and system of governance has been explored to offer solace to many economic problems and has proven its effectiveness. The Islamic solutions in the banking and finance sectors have been tested, trusted and attested and have been widely adopted in many Western countries including the UK (for review see: Ahyani, et al., 2021; Bello, et al, 2018). In the same vein, there have been attempts to beam light on Islamic public policy (e.g., Abdelgafar, 2018, 2021; Behdad, 2006; Heyneman, 2004; Mahyudi, 2015).

This paper aims to provide some insights regarding the recently proposed Islamic public policy (PPI-TMSI) framework with emphasis on the theory of *the Maqasid al-Shari'ah* component. Here we discuss, albeit briefly, and demonstrate how the theory fills one of the existing gaps in public policy and how it can be applied in the policy-making process, especially to actualize the SDGs taking SDG1 (poverty eradication) as a case study.

While the title of this chapter sounds 'Islamic', the intended audience is by no way limited to the Muslim folks, it seeks its audience among researchers and readers who are enthusiast of development and alternative solutions in the field of Social sciences, especially in the managerial and policy studies.

The Theory of Maqasid al-Sharı'ah: A Synopsis

The *Maqasid al-Sharı'ah* is a two-word Arabic phrase: *Maqasid and al-Sharı'ah*, where *Maqasid* (singular *Maqsid*) means goal, and *Shariah* broadly refers to the way of life dictated by the Creator of the universe, Allah (Surah Al-Ma'idah:48).

Maqasid al-Sharı'ah can simply be described as a framework that articulates all the sub-systems in the Islamic system of governance and is regarded as the epicentre of any discussion concerning Islam (Majdey, 2020). It is sometimes referred to as the rules for public interest (Auda, 2008). Since public policy determines the scope, limits, and forms of social actions, the theory of *Maqasid al-Sharı'ah* provides a set of five cardinal goals (each denoted by M in this paper) that serve as guiding and regulatory principles and determines and legitimises the purpose, limits, and forms of social actions. These five goals provide the principles for solving socioeconomic problems and are conceptually complex enough for specialists to deconstruct and formulate pathways to address the intricacies and sensitivities of public administration (Aziz, 2019).

It is noteworthy that the *Maqasid al-Sharı'ah* is not merely a declaration of "empty" goals that can be achieved by any means, regardless of the nature of the means. Rather, the *Maqasid al-Sharı'ah* is a theory of purpose that summarises the goals of the various principles that apply in all social systems. In other words, the principles embedded in each of the goal guide the means to achieve other similar ends. Therefore, each *Maqsad* is a calibration tool to sanction or not any human intellectual effort in matters of jurisprudence or policy that falls within the scope of the established principles under each *Maqsad*. Consequently, the set of principles that each cardinal objective contains provides a repository of prototypical solutions or strategies to social problems that a policy maker could use to develop efficient solutions to social problems in an analogical deduction manner. In the following sections, we discuss the five cardinal goals in the public policy parlance:

M1: Hifzud-Deen (means to preserve and promote faith): This refers to the set of rules and principles that guide policy in religious matters. It also contains laws that aim to instill discipline in matters of faith, uphold religious rights and act proactively against apostasy and heresy. This cardinal goal aims to religious harmony both within Islamic fold and in the human society at large. As for within, it aims to protect an ideal Islamic society from treachery that could threaten the security and harmony of the members of the society and, by extension, create social crisis. An ideal Islamic society is characterised by the strongest fabric of brotherhood (Surah Al-Hujurat: 10), where safety and security are at their greatest, as evidenced through the greetings between two or more Muslims assuring each other of peace, safety and mercy whenever they meet. It is a society where races, skin colours, social status and tribal differences are totally condemned (Surah Al-Hujurat: 13). However, this society has a semi-permeable border that grants absolute freedom of choice when entering from the outside but not for exits. This deters hypocritical enemies who want to exploit the strong bond of brotherhood to enter and gather important confidential information to attack those who belong to Islam after leaving (Surah Al-Munafiqun: 1-4). It also prevents gullible members of Islamic society from being misled by any means to leave the strongest bond of brotherhood (Surah Al-Baqarah:105; 109; Surah Al-Anfal:36). Moreover, it protects against the rash entry of unthinking persons who change faith for whatever reason and make religion a matter of frivolity (Surah Al-A'raf: 51; Surah An-Nisa': 137). Just as every country in the world today has its immigration, citizenship and exit laws to protect its sovereignty, and which anyone who chooses to stay in the country must strictly abide by, this cardinal objective can also be seen as a representation of the laws of Islam's sovereignty that anyone who wishes to enter the Islamic community must abide by.

In addition, this cardinal goal also contains principles that guarantee the rights of non-Muslims and guide the relations between a Muslim and a non-Muslim in all matters, including marriage, common defence and security. This cardinal goal (M1) is applied in formulating policies that promote the peaceful coexistence of people of different faiths in society.

M2: Hifzun-Nafs (to preserve and promote human life): This objective refers to the set of rules and principles established in Islam to protect life and promote the procreation of the human race. The protection of life encompasses three main areas: the maintenance of good health, including reproductive health; the physical security and safety of the life of the individual; and the security of the environment, which may be immediately or indirectly related to protection of human life. There are many principles under this cardinal goal. One of the principles is the principle of the sanctity and supremacy of the human being (Surah Al-Isra': 70), which guides policy on blood donation and organ transplantation, abortion, cloning of human cells, use of the human body for experimentation, etc. Another example of principles under this cardinal goal is the principle of collective safety of human life (Surah al-Maidah: 32-34), which states that "no one is safe until everyone is safe". This principle is applied in the punishment of murder and terrorism.

M3: Hifzun-Nasl (protection of progeny to prevent corruption of the family and to promote the sanctity of the family institution). This cardinal goal refers to a set of laws and principles that aim to uphold social justice in matters of relations between men and women. It includes principles that govern many aspects of family life, such as the rights and custody of children, the legitimacy of and rights in marital relations (marriage and divorce), rules on defamation (*qadhf*), the rights of parents, inheritance, the right to privacy, etc.

M4: Hifzul-Aql (promotion and protection of the human mind): This objective addresses principles aimed at promoting mental health and intellectual development, as well as principles put in place to prevent mental dysfunction. Education policies, hard drug control policies, public and social media policies, etc., all fall into this category.

M5: Hifzul-Mal (promote wealth creation and protect property). This is the goal that contains all the principles that guide economic and financial laws and principles. It is the goal that embodies policies on economic empowerment, wealth creation and distribution, rules on theft and protection of individual and public property. As will be explained in more detail later, the principles for eradicating poverty belong to this category.

These five *Maqasid* (goals) serve as a guide to what a genuine purpose of policy in each of these public sectors should be, as well as the purpose that must not be contradicted when making policies. In the Islamic context, policies and strategic objectives must be aligned with these five *Maqasid*. Moreover, these goals can be operationalised as interventions to achieve strategic goals, including the seventeen Sustainable Development Goals (SDGs). It is noteworthy that all public policies can be traced back to one or more of these five cardinal goals. In summary, the theory of the *Maqasid al-Sharı'ah* provides the epistemological basis for public policy, as it can be used to justify or otherwise account for the purpose of any public policy.

Practical implications of the Theory of the Maqasid al-Sharı'ah

Here we will discuss the uniqueness of a public policy framework that is founded on the *Maqasid al-Sharı'ah*. In doing so, we will highlight some of the key practical implications associated with the application of the *Maqasid al-Sharı'ah* in the policy-making process and the role it would play in that process.

A key feature of a *Maqasid al-Sharı'ah*-based public policy (MPP) is that the five M1-M5 are mutually dependent, with each *Maqsad* (cardinal goal) depending on and requiring the contributions of the other *Maqasid*. This provides a framework that promotes the effective involvement of different stakeholders in the policy-making process. As will be discussed shortly, the MPP enables the various stakeholders to contribute to the policy of a sector that is not primarily within their purview. Research has shown that the effective involvement of diverse stakeholders in the policy-making process creates what Spillane (1999) called a "zone of enactment" that helps in achieving policy objectives (Lemke, & Harris-Wai, 2015; Yaro, et al., 2017).

In public policy, the MPP would systematically insist that other strategic objectives are taken into account in policy formulation by preventing any policy stakeholder, actor and influencer from focusing only on their core business and neglecting others. The MPP provides opportunities for mutual support and coalition building between different stakeholders, not only between governmental organisations, but also between non-governmental organisations, civil society and all members of society. This creates opportunities for all members of society to work towards common goals (Aziz, 2019). Although there are efforts to design a comprehensive policy framework that links and ranks the seventeen SDGs (e.g. Guerrero & Castañeda 2020; Ike et al, 2019; Kumar, et al, 2018; Sommer, et al, 2021; Swain & Ranganathan 2021; Sachs, et al, 2019; Yang, et al, 2020), the linkage and ranking are usually arbitrary and lack epistemological foundation. The MPP framework solves this problem by using the theory of the

Maqasid al-Shari'ah as its epistemology. In this way, the MPP framework corrects the errors of narrow-mindedness and exclusion, and addresses the problem of selfishness, nepotism, favouritism, etc. It is a framework that guarantees transparency and takes a whole-of-government approach to policy-making.

Another uniqueness of the MPP framework is that it specifies how different policies can be prioritised and ranked when competing for scarce resources. Islamic scholars agree that these goals are not equal on the preference scale, and there is near consensus on the M1-M5 order for all or most cardinal goals[1]. For example, abortion is in the M2 category (protection of life and procreation), which is higher than wealth creation in M5. For this reason, poverty cannot be used as a justification for abortion or population reduction in accordance with theory of *Maqasid al-Shari'ah*. In Islam, population is considered an asset rather than a liability, and therefore policies should be developed for its overall benefit rather than for reducing the number of births[2].

While there are situations where the M1-M5 order is broken, even this disorder is guided by principles that are also detailed and well-considered (for an overview see: al-Kabeesy, 2006). In policymaking, the MPP can determine the technical magnitude of a solution to a social problem, indicating the extent to which it is important to solve this problem, its limitations and the share it should take in the national budget and financing. It also shows how the problem should be ranked in comparison to other social problems that might also be urgent. This would prevent focusing too much on one problem and neglecting other, more important problems.

Another practical aspect of the MPP is that it provides some ready-made prototypes of solutions that can be used to develop new policies. As will be shown later, Islam has a wealth of principles and schemes for solving various social problems that policy makers can contextualise to develop intervention programmes within the framework of available resources and socio-economic variables.

SDG 1 (Poverty Eradication): A Case Study

In general, the Islamic mechanism for alleviating or eliminating poverty is based on two main principles: Eliminating/preventing the root causes of poverty and creating an enabling economic environment guided by social responsibility. In eliminating the real causes of poverty, Islam promotes risk sharing with the less privileged people instead of further burgeoning them with interest on loans and accumulated debts. Islam fights against laziness, unproductivity and the culture of welfare dependency, and encourages personal responsibility, calculated risk-taking and the circulation of wealth. On the other hand, Islam promotes the creation of a competitive and open economic environment that creates opportunities to close the gaps between the haves and have-nots, and prohibits market monopolies, hoarding, exploitation, excessive consumption and waste. Furthermore, Islam promotes effective use of resources, equitable wealth distribution and sharing, knowledge empowerment and development of human resources through skilling and upskilling of all the citizenry, to mention but a few.

Policies to eradicate poverty are multi-faceted and involve different spheres of government. The best way to tackle poverty is therefore to address it with a cross-governmental approach. This can be achieved through the MPP framework. The conventional policy framework (CPP) has always tackled the poverty problem without addressing the multidimensional nature and root cause of poverty. The solution offered has always focused only on the economic dimension, which is also not comprehensive. In many cases, most interventions do not address the root cause of poverty but take the form of palliatives which sometimes do more harm than good to the economy, such as stagflation, large fiscal deficits due to higher government spending, high taxes to cover the deficit, unstable balance of payments and low growth rates, etc. (Khan, 1990). MPP solves this problem by providing a platform that coordinates various sectors to contribute policies to eradicate poverty. While a detailed discussion of the methodology for the inclusion of various stakeholders and coordination of their interaction goes beyond the scope of this paper, the theoretical framework for such inclusion of stakeholders is presented in a mathematical expression as follows:

P(SDG1) = Σf(SDG1, Mi).. (i)

Here, Σ denotes the summation sign, f represents the function, SDG1 represents the first Sustainable Development Goal which is poverty eradication, and Mi represents the individual factors (principles of *Maqasid al-Shariah*) M1, M2, M3, M4, and M5 that influence SDG1.

In this notation, the formula indicates that P(SDG1) is the sum of the function 'f' evaluated for SDG1 and each of the individual factors M1, M2, M3, M4, and M5.

For practical application, this formula can be further simplified in the following way:

P(SDG1) = *f*(SDG1, M1, M2, M3, M4, M5)........................... (ii)

This simplified mathematical expression indicates that the design of public policies for poverty alleviation should involve a careful study of the relationship between SDG1 (poverty eradication) and the various factors that are informed by the five *Maqasid shariah* which are represented by M1, M2, M3, M4, and M5. This would involve analyzing the forward and backward relationships between poverty and religious injunctions, data on poverty levels and health outcomes, family structures, education system, and economic principles, to better understand how these factors are related to poverty and how they might be addressed through public policy interventions.

The function *f* represents the specific relationship between the variables and usually takes the form of a forward and backward relationship. For example, the forward relationship between SDG1 and M1 examines the effect of poverty on religious beliefs, while the backward relationship investigates the effects of religious beliefs on poverty. This opens a wide range of anthropological research that would dig deep into the root of poverty in society. It will also open the door to possible religious solutions that could be tapped to devise policies to eradicate poverty.

The mathematical expression also suggests that a careful study of these relationships is necessary to design effective public policies for poverty alleviation. By understanding how the various factors represented by M1, M2, M3, M4, and M5 are related to poverty and each other, policymakers can develop interventions that are more likely to be effective and that address the underlying causes of poverty rather than just the symptoms. Below is a simple illustration of the formula derived from the MPP framework to design poverty eradication/alleviation policies.

SDG1*M1 = Poverty eradication and preservation of religious injunctions: This is applied in the public policy-making process by answering questions on the effects of religious principles on poverty alleviation. The likely questions that may be thrown to enhance brainstorming concerning poverty eradication include but are not limited to the followings: How is poverty defined and its levels determined in Islam? How can *the faqir-miskin* dichotomy be operationalized in policymaking? Why does Islam link poverty and *kufr* (infidelity), and what does the link mean in policymaking? Were there poverty eradication programs or principles that have proven effective in the history of Islam? How can those principles be modernized and transformed into policies in the contemporary world? etc.

One of the benefits of including Islamic studies experts in the policy-making process is that they widen policy experts' thinking faculty and expose them to existing prototype solutions enshrined in Islam. By this, policy experts do not start from zero and would think outside the box. Another benefit of such inclusion is that it would give room for conveying the lived experience at the grassroots to the policy-making team, as religious leaders such as Imams are some of the closest personnel to people at the grassroots and are custodians of peoples' confidential welfare information. By so doing, religious leaders can also serve as conveyors of policy outcomes to the public through their religious messages which are very effective in conviction, especially in Muslim-dominated countries and communities. This would enhance a whole-of-nation approach to public policy.

In Islam, poverty (*faqr*) is likened to *kufr* (infidelity), and both are believed to go together in a *Pari-passu* manner. Islam, therefore, frowns at poverty and enjoin Muslims to seek refuge from Allah against poverty. It is therefore evident that designing efficient policies and mechanisms that alleviate poverty in an Islamic country is ranked to be at the level of M1 which is for the preservation and promotion of faith. SDG1*M1 reveals that poverty eradication is not just at the level of M5 which is for wealth creation and protection in general and must be accorded the importance of highest order.

SDG1*M2 = Poverty eradication and Preservation of Life: This is concerned with the health, security, and environmental perspectives on poverty eradication. Here, policymakers would seek answers to questions such as: What should be the boundary and limits between poverty eradication policy and health policy, security policy, and environmental protection policy? What are the major health hindrances that are facing majorly the poor population and affecting their productivity? What are the health issues that are draining the hard-earned income of the citizenry? How could situations in those areas be ameliorated? What are the specific areas in health services that create opportunities and enhance poverty eradication? What is the current correlation between reproductive health and poverty? How could environmental protection programs be designed to provide opportunities for poverty eradication and enhancement of green and blue economies? What are the impending environmental problems and how could there be solutions that can be tailored to provide opportunities for poverty eradication? etc.

Research has shown that improving public health can accelerate progress toward complex development goals such as SDGs (McArthur & Rasmussen, 2018). Some health sub-sectors have a direct impact on poverty and drain incomes. For instance, the estimated global direct health expenditure on diabetes in 2019 is USD 760 billion and is expected to grow to a projected USD 825 billion by 2030 (Williams, et al, 2020). According to a study published in the Lancet Diabetes & Endocrinology in 2021, it was estimated that diabetes was responsible for 4.2 million deaths worldwide in 2019 alone and that the number of deaths attributable to diabetes had increased by 38% from 2000 to 2019. This would have a direct impact on the manpower available to propel production and economic growth.

It is evident here that health and environmental experts as well as community leaders at the grassroots levels must be members of the policy-making team on poverty eradication.

SDG1*M3 = Poverty eradication and Procreation and Preservation of Progeny: The main aim here is to shed light on the forward and backward relationships between poverty eradication and family institution. Questions for policymaking include: How can family institutions be improved to support wealth creation and human efficiency? How can policy be made to instrument the growing population as an asset for economic growth and empowerment, not a liability? How does gender role in the family affect the family income and expenses? How does marital status contribute to poverty eradication? What are the contributions of divorce to the poverty problem in society? etc. Qualitative answers to these questions and first-hand information can be obtained from different stakeholders, especially the leaders of the community at the grassroots level such as heads of villages, local government councils, etc. Quantitative answers and data can also be gathered through surveys and from the National Bureau of Statistics.

There is a strong relationship between poverty and family factors, and any poverty eradication program that ignores the relationship is bound to fail. Poverty disrupts family functioning, and results in a reduction of stability, security, quality time together as well as access to resources. It may result in risky behaviours. A United Nations report laments the sheer negligence of the family role in poverty eradication programs positing: "Despite negative effects on family functioning, most anti-poverty programs have focused on the individual rather than a family as a unit, or typically focus on women and children... Primarily, it is vital to create sound policy frameworks at the national, regional, and international levels, based on pro-poor and gender-sensitive development strategies. Policies targeting families in social protection provision and access to basic services have had the largest impact on family poverty reduction" (UN, 2017, p.2). It concludes thus: "Families themselves and family-oriented policies can contribute to the achievement of several SDG targets. In particular, families play an essential role in achieving SDG targets in poverty and hunger, health, education as well as gender equality" (ibid, p. 32).

Therefore, finding solutions to poverty in family institutions should not be regarded as a potentially futile exercise. Research has proven that quality marriage has a significant role in strengthening the health system (Koball, et al, 2010; Trief, et al, 2002; Whisman, et al, 2014) to the extent that individuals who remained married, despite having a significantly increased weight, were significantly less likely to develop diabetes than their divorced counterparts (de Oliveira, et al. 2020). It is therefore evident that quality marriage contributes to solving a health problem that is regarded by WHO as the seventh leading cause of death globally, and a major contributor to morbidity and mortality from cardiovascular disease, kidney failure, and other complications. When we take the estimated direct health expenditure on diabetes into account which is projected to reach USD 825 billion by 2030 the role of strengthening marriage in preventing poverty can never be over-emphasized.

SDG1*M4 = Poverty eradication and Intellectual enhancement and preservation: This has to do with education, training, and skills. Questions that would be answered here by education and curriculum experts include the following: What aspect/component of the education system has the greatest effect on poverty eradication? How can learners be skilled and upskilled to enhance their employability and economic independence? What are the current skills and vocations that are efficient in providing meaningful incomes for the poor population? How can educational programmes be reformed and redesigned to ensure economic independence and job creation rather than produce job seekers? etc.

As earlier mentioned, poverty eradication in Islam is not only centred on offering assistance and palliatives or *sadaqah* (charity), but also includes activation of the labour potential of people. In doing so, the curriculum must constantly be examined and reformed. John Taylor Gatto an award-winning American educationist provides some insights in this regard in his book titled "Weapons of Mass Instruction: A Schoolteacher's Journey through the Dark World of Compulsory Schooling". Gatto presents a critical analysis of the modern education system, questioning its effectiveness and exploring alternative approaches to education. He argued that the schooling system contributes to the high rise of unemployment, as the prevailing education system primarily prepares students for traditional employment rather than encouraging entrepreneurship or self-employment. He believed that by not fostering an entrepreneurial mindset or providing practical business education, the system limits opportunities for individuals to create jobs and contribute to the economy. Gatto further argued that the education system often fails to equip students with the necessary skills and practical knowledge required for the workforce. He believed that the system does not pay adequate attention to the development of critical thinking, problem-solving abilities, creativity, individuality, and practical skills that are in demand in the job market.

SDG1*M5 = Poverty eradication and Wealth creation and preservation: This has to do with questions that economists along with Islamists would answer to proffer economic solutions on the subject matter. At this point, all the inputs gathered from discussions on M1-M4 are interpreted in economic terms. The major question here is how the answers and data gathered from SDG*M1-M4 be used to design effective policies that could eradicate poverty. Another question is how could some of the established Islamic principles of wealth creation and distribution (such as *zakat, waqf, Mudarabah, Musharakah* and *murabaha* financing, zero-interest financing...etc) be instrumented to design programs and products to eradicate poverty?

For instance, when there are graduates or skilled hands population with no jobs, the principles of *mudarabah* and *Musharakah* in Islam can be used to establish Public Private Partnership (PPP) policy that is based on a planned self-liquidating scheme which would spiral economic activities through innovations, enhance production and create more jobs. The same principles can be instrumented to design policies that empower the semi-skilled and unskilled population through apprentice-to-partnership schemes which can all be financed through *zakat* (alms giving) and endowment funds. For instance, in Kazakhstan, the Government enhanced the targeting of social protection measures by implementing a cash transfer programme among low-income citizens based on 'mutual obligation', through the development of private farming in the form of a diminishing *Musharakah*. For farmers' empowerment, Islam has a special loan for them called *Baiy'-salam*[1] which can be used to design a government loan policy that is based on PPP[1], or based on loan-for-farm-produce which could be organized through governments' dedicated agencies or institutions to directly purchase farm produce from farmers, providing them with an assured market, thereby enforce quality standards and maintain strategic reserves.

The Universality of MPP Framework

There is no gainsaying that the *Maqasid al-Shariah* is the default managerial reference for a Muslim country, organization, or community. However, there is a need to answer a pressing question that bothers on the applicability of *Maqasid al-Shariah*-based public policy MPP framework in non-Muslim countries and organizations: Can a non-Muslim country or organization apply *Maqasid al-Shariah* principles in its governance?

First, it should be reiterated here that the *Maqasid al-Shariah* is a body of principles that are universal (Abdelgafar, 2021) and are conceptually complex enough for policy specialist to deconstruct and formulate pathways to address the intricacies and sensitivities of public administration (Aziz, 2019). Studies have shown that the *Maqasid al-Shariah* principles can be operationalized to construct a public policy framework that enhances justice, equity, transparency, accountability, and participatory decision-making in managerial practices (Dusuki, 2009; Hasan, *et al.*, 2018; Laldin, & Furqani, 2013; Sarif, *et al.*, 2017). With its claim of universality, it provides leeway to the current conventional framework and presents an experimental candidate for an unbiased policy scientist who anticipates and supports reforms in public policy science. Such an alternative framework with these arguable qualities is desirable at a time humanity is in dire need of more efficient public policy frameworks and should not be viewed as an Islamic occidental enterprise. Therefore, the principles of the *Maqasid al-Shariah*-based public policy framework can be studied with a full sense of objectivity and 'juiced' for its benefit, regardless of the faith or religious inclination of the policy scientist.

Second, it is glaring that the *Maqasid al-Shariah*-based public policy (MPP) framework has some Islamic basis, but the Islamic elements in it are not proselytization instruments. This is evident in the fact that some of the *Maqasid al-Shariah* principles are already being accepted, adopted and applied by some non-Muslim countries, organizations and individuals, to different degrees (see: Djafri, *et al.*, 2021; Hasan, *et al.*, 2022; Laldin&Furqani, 2013; Mathew, 2014; Sarker, *et al.*, 2020). For instance, the growing global orthorexia nervosa has further driven many non-Muslims to adopt *Halal* consumption which is a principle under the cardinal goal of *Hifzun-Nafs* (M2 i.e. Preservation of life). This is evident in studies that confirm non-Muslims' preference for halal food (e.g.: Damit, *et al.*, 2019; Mathew, 2014; Wibowo & Ahmad 2016; Wilkins, et al. 2019). In addition, there is a wide acceptance of some Islamic principles under the cardinal goal of *Hifzul-Mal* (M5 i.e.Wealth creation and protection) among many non-Muslim countries and individuals (Biancone &Shakhatreh, 2015; Djafri, *et al.*, 2021; Ezeh & Nkamnebe 2022; Hassan *et al.*, 2021; Nurhayati, *et al.*, 2021; Shabbir, *et al.*, 2016; Soud, &Sayılır, 2017). These are a few testimonies that the *Maqasid al-Shariah* principles can be applied by non-Muslims.

Thus, future research should focus on disseminating in-depth knowledge about *Maqasid al-Shariah* by demystifying and expatiating its various principles and elucidating the methodologies to operationalize those principles in modern ways.

CONCLUSION

The *Maqasid al-Shariah*-based MPP framework for public policy provides a platform that enables the inclusion of various stakeholders in the policy-making process. In this way, it fills the gap left by the conventional public policy framework. MPP is also a proactive approach to public policy making that better explores the root causes of social problems and fills the gap of superficiality in public policy. It also contains some ready-made prototype solutions to many social problems, so that policymakers do not have to start from scratch.

In the MPP, policy experts interact with other stakeholders and learn from each other. There is a need for further research whose aim would be detailing the various principles involved in each *Maqsid*. This paper also recommends exploring the forward and backward relationships between all SDGs 1 to 17 and each *Maqasid al-Shariah* (SDG1-17*M1-M5), focusing on contextual applications.

While the MPP provides a theoretical framework for engaging different stakeholders in the policy-making process, there is a need for a research methodology that could be used to achieve it. Such a research methodology would do away with the quantitative-qualitative dichotomy, beyond the prevailing 'concoction' of research methodologies or triangulation of methods referred to as mixed methods. Islamic epistemology contradicts both quantitative and qualitative epistemologies that are popular today (Tajudeen, 2017), but Islamic epistemology has a unique way of combining qualitative and quantitative methodologies. It should be noted here that MPP as discussed in this paper is only a fragment of a comprehensive alternative framework PPI-TMSI recently proposed by Basma Abdelgafar, a professor of public policy. It is recommended here that a detailed and comprehensive study of the framework be conducted and found a way to integrate it with the Islamic Governance Matrix proposed by Amin Abdul Aziz, a professor of Islamic governance. In this way, the Sustainable Development Goals (SDGs) would chart a new course towards their realisation.

REFERENCES

Abdelgafar, B. I. (2018). *Public policy: Beyond traditional jurisprudence: A Maqasid approach.* International Institute of Islamic Thought (IIIT).

Ahyani, H., Slamet, M., &Mutmainah, N. (2021). The Contribution of the Western World to the Islamic Economy in Indonesia. *Al-Amwal: Jurnal Ekonomi dan PerbankanSyari'ah, 13*(2), 153-170.

Akanle, O., & Omobowale, A. O. (2022). Contemporary Issues in Public Policy. In *Public Policy and Research in Africa* (pp. 123–158). Springer International Publishing.

Al-Amidi, A.M (d. 631/1233). Al-Ihkam fi Usul al-Ahkam. Dar Al-kitab AL-Araby.

Al-Ghazali, M. (d.505 AH/1111 CE). Al-Mustasfa

Al-Kabeesy, B. M.L. (2006). Al-Maqasid al-Shar'iyyahwakayfiyyatut-Ta'mulma'hah 'indat-ta'arud. *Journal of kuliyyah al-Imam al-A'zam,* 1.

Al-Shatibi,I. (d. 790 AH/1388 CE) al-Muwafaqat fi Usul al-Shariʿah al-Islamiyyah.

Auda, J. (2008). Maqasid al-Shariah: An introductory guide. Herndon: International Institute of Islamic Thought.

Aziz, A. (2019). Islamic governance and the articulation of Maqasid al-Shariah in Brunei Darussalam. In *Maqasid al-Shari'ah in the Brunei Civil Service: Civil Servants' Perspectives.* Bandar Seri Begawan: QasrunNafis Publishing House. Available online also at: https://www. academia. edu/41888816/MAQ% C4

Batchabi, D. (2022). *World social protection report 2020-22.* Regional companion report for Africa.

Behdad, S., & Nomani, F. (Eds.). (2006). *Islam and the everyday world: Public policy dilemmas.* Routledge. doi:10.4324/9780203028032

Bello, H. S., Ahmad, N., & Galadima, I. S. (2018). Islamic economy as an alternative solution to managing economic crisis: Some fashionable case studies of Iran, Malaysia Saudi Arabia. Academic Press.

Biancone, P. P., &Shakhatreh, M. Z. (2015). Using Islamic Finance for infrastructure Projects in non-Muslim countries. *European Journal of Islamic Finance*, (2).

Brown, J. D., & Brown, J. D. (2019). Ideologies, worldviews, and personalities. Reflective Practice of Counseling and Psychotherapy in a Diverse Society, 33-52.

Burrows, T., Goldman, S., Pursey, K., & Lim, R. (2017). Is there an association between dietary intake and academic achievement: A systematic review. *Journal of Human Nutrition and Dietetics, 30*(2), 117–140. doi:10.1111/jhn.12407 PMID:27599886

Chapra, M. U. (2011). *The Economic Problem: Can Islam Play an Effective Role in Solving it Efficiently as well as Equitably?* Working Papers 2011-1, The Islamic Research and Teaching Institute (IRTI).

Damit, D. H. D. A., Harun, A., Martin, D., Othman, B., & Ahmad, H. (2019). What makes a non-Muslim purchase halal food in a Muslim country? An application of theory of planned behaviour. *Management Science Letters, 9*(12), 2029–2038. doi:10.5267/j.msl.2019.7.003

de Oliveira, C. M., Viater Tureck, L., Alvares, D., Liu, C., Horimoto, A. R. V. R., Balcells, M., de Oliveira Alvim, R., Krieger, J. E., & Pereira, A. C. (2020). Relationship between marital status and incidence of type 2 diabetes mellitus in a Brazilian rural population: The Baependi Heart Study. *PLoS One*, *15*(8), e0236869. doi:10.1371/journal.pone.0236869 PMID:32745127

Djafri, F., Laldin, M. A., & Laallam, A. (2021). The global perspective of Islamic finance and the potential for China to tap into the Islamic finance market. *Journal of Islamic Business and Management*, *11*(1), 14–28.

Dusuki, A. W. (2009). *Challenges of Realizing Maqasid Al-shari'ah (objectives of Shari'ah) in the Islamic Capital Market: Special Focus on Equaty-based Sukuk Structures*. International Shari'ah Research Acedemy for Islamic Finance (ISRA).

Ezeh, P. C., & Nkamnebe, A. D. (2022). Determinants of Islamic banking adoption among non-Muslim customers in a Muslim zone. *Journal of Islamic Accounting and Business Research*, *13*(4), 666–683. doi:10.1108/JIABR-10-2021-0280

Folke, O., & Rickne, J. (2020). All the single ladies: Job promotions and the durability of marriage. *American Economic Journal. Applied Economics*, *12*(1), 260–287. doi:10.1257/app.20180435

Fuller, R., Landrigan, P. J., Balakrishnan, K., Bathan, G., Bose-O'Reilly, S., Brauer, M., Caravanos, J., Chiles, T., Cohen, A., Corra, L., Cropper, M., Ferraro, G., Hanna, J., Hanrahan, D., Hu, H., Hunter, D., Janata, G., Kupka, R., Lanphear, B., ... Yan, C. (2022). Pollution and health: A progress update. *The Lancet. Planetary Health*, *6*(6), e535–e547. doi:10.1016/S2542-5196(22)00090-0 PMID:35594895

Guerrero, O. A., & Castañeda, G. (2020). Policy priority inference: A computational framework to analyze the allocation of resources for the sustainable development goals. *Data & Policy*, *2*, e17. doi:10.1017/dap.2020.18

Hasan, N. N. B. A., Noor, K. B. M., Malik, A. A., & Ghani, Z. A. (2018). *The proposed model of the integration of the principle of Maqasid Al-Shariah in managerial decision-making process in shariah-compliant securities. Journal of Islamic, Social, Economics and Development.*

Hassan, M. K., Saraç, M., & Khan, A. (2021). *Islamic finance and sustainable development*. Springer International Publishing. doi:10.1007/978-3-030-76016-8

Heikkilä, J., & Laukkanen, I. (2022). Gender-specific call of duty: A note on the neglect of conscription in gender equality indices. *Defence and Peace Economics*, *33*(5), 603–615. doi:10.1080/10242694.2020.1844400

Heyneman, S. P. (Ed.). (2004). *Islam and social policy*. Vanderbilt University Press. doi:10.2307/j.ctv17vf6q5

Hillix, W. A., & L'Abate, L. (2011). The role of paradigms in science and theory construction. In *Paradigms in theory construction* (pp. 3–17). Springer New York.

Homei, A. (2016). The science of population and birth control in post-war Japan. *Science, technology, and medicine in the modern Japanese empire*.

Ike, M., Donovan, J. D., Topple, C., & Masli, E. K. (2019). The process of selecting and prioritising corporate sustainability issues: Insights for achieving the Sustainable Development Goals. *Journal of Cleaner Production*, *236*, 117661. doi:10.1016/j.jclepro.2019.117661

Jackson, A. P., & Meyers, J. (2016). The role of social support in reducing psychological distress among African American single mothers. *Journal of Family Issues*, *37*(10), 1428–1452.

Jacobs, M. (2020). *Beyond growth: towards a new economic approach*. OECD Publishing.

Johal, S., Anthony, L., Dragicevic, N., Thirgood, J., & Dockree, T. (2022). *Navigating Complexity: Policy Making for an Evolving World*. Canadian Standards Association.

Judiasih, S. D., Sudini, L. P., Rubiati, B., Yuanitasari, D., Kusmayanti, H., & Salim, E. F. (2019). Sustainable Development Goals and Elimination of Children's Marriage Practice in Indonesia. *JurnalNotariil*, *4*(1), 1–12.

Karan, A., Negandhi, H., Hussain, S., Zapata, T., Mairembam, D., De Graeve, H., Buchan, J., & Zodpey, S. (2021). Size, composition and distribution of health workforce in India: Why, and where to invest? *Human Resources for Health*, *19*(1), 1–14. doi:10.118612960-021-00575-2 PMID:33752675

Karraker, A., Latham, K., & Segrin, C. (2019). Divorce and health: Current trends and future directions. *Journal of Marriage and Family*, *81*(4), 835–851.

Khan, M. A. (1990). Elimination of poverty in the Islamic economic framework. *Islamic Studies*, *29*(2), 143–162.

Kilonzo, S. M., & Ojebode, A. (2022). Research Methods for Public Policy. In *Public Policy and Research in Africa* (pp. 63–85). Springer International Publishing.

Koball, H. L., Moiduddin, E., Henderson, J., Goesling, B., & Besculides, M. (2010). What Do We Know About the Link Between Marriage and Health? *Journal of Family Issues*, *31*(8), 1019–1040. doi:10.1177/0192513X10365834

Kumar, P., Ahmed, F., Singh, R. K., & Sinha, P. (2018). Determination of hierarchical relationships among sustainable development goals using interpretive structural modeling. *Environment, Development and Sustainability*, *20*(5), 2119–2137. doi:10.100710668-017-9981-1

Laldin, M. A., & Furqani, H. (2013). Developing Islamic finance in the framework of maqasid al-Shari'ah: Understanding the ends (maqasid) and the means (wasa'il). *International Journal of Islamic and Middle Eastern Finance and Management*, *6*(4), 278–289. doi:10.1108/IMEFM-05-2013-0057

Langridge, C. (2013). *Liberalism: Another Tool of Western Hegemony*. E-International Relations.

Lemke, A. A., & Harris-Wai, J. N. (2015). Stakeholder engagement in policy development: Challenges and opportunities for human genomics. *Genetics in Medicine*, *17*(12), 949–957. doi:10.1038/gim.2015.8 PMID:25764215

Li, G., Fang, C., Wang, S., & Sun, S. (2016). The effect of economic growth, urbanization, and industrialization on fine particulate matter (PM2. 5) concentrations in China. *Environmental Science & Technology*, *50*(21), 11452–11459. doi:10.1021/acs.est.6b02562 PMID:27709931

Liu, H., & Reczek, C. (2015). Cohabitation and US adult mortality: An examination by gender and race. *Journal of Health and Social Behavior, 56*(3), 405–422.

Lodhi, I. (2021). Globalisation and public policy: Bridging the disciplinary and epistemological boundaries. *Policy and Society, 40*(4), 522–544. doi:10.1080/14494035.2021.1987137

Mahyudi, M. (2015). Reviving the Islamic economic system through shariah-based public policy. *Humanomics, 31*(4), 415–429. doi:10.1108/H-06-2015-0037

Mathew, V. N., Abdullah, A. M. R. A., & Ismail, S. N. M. (2014). Acceptance on halal food among non-Muslim consumers. *Procedia: Social and Behavioral Sciences, 121*, 262–271. doi:10.1016/j.sbspro.2014.01.1127

McArthur, J. W., & Rasmussen, K. (2018). Change of pace: Accelerations and advances during the Millennium Development Goal era. *World Development, 105*, 132–143. doi:10.1016/j.worlddev.2017.12.030

Meirison, M. (2017). The development of Islamic economics in various parts of the world. *JEBI (Jurnal Ekonomi dan Bisnis Islam), 2*(2), 197-206.

Nicklin, G. (2019). Dynamic narrative: A new framework for policy success. *International Review of Public Policy, 1*(2), 173-193.

Nurhayati, L., Mandey, S. L., Taroreh, R. N., Trang, I., & Djamali, R. (2021). Why Non-Muslims Become Customers of Islamic Banking? *Estudios de Economía Aplicada, 39*(12). Advance online publication. doi:10.25115/eea.v39i12.6336

Page, E. C. (2016). What's methodology got to do with it? Public policy evaluations, observational analysis and RCTs. In *Handbook of Research Methods and Applications in Political Science* (pp. 483–496). Edward Elgar Publishing. doi:10.4337/9781784710828.00042

Purtell, K. M., & Gershoff, E. T. (2015). Fast food consumption and academic growth in late childhood. *Clinical Pediatrics, 54*(9), 871–877. doi:10.1177/0009922814561742 PMID:25480321

Rahman, M. M., Rana, R., & Khanam, R. (2022). Determinants of life expectancy in most polluted countries: Exploring the effect of environmental degradation. *PLoS One, 17*(1), e0262802. doi:10.1371/journal.pone.0262802 PMID:35061838

Sachs, J. D., Schmidt-Traub, G., Mazzucato, M., Messner, D., Nakicenovic, N., & Rockström, J. (2019). Six transformations to achieve the sustainable development goals. *Nature Sustainability, 2*(9), 805–814. doi:10.103841893-019-0352-9

Sandström, G., & Stanfors, M. (2022). Socio-economic status and the rise of divorce in Sweden: The case of the 1880–1954 marriage cohorts in Västerbotten. *Population Studies*, 1–19. PMID:36603598

Sarif, S. M., Ismail, Y., & Azlan, Z. (2017). Effects of Maqasid Al-Shariah for ethical decision making among social entrepreneurs. *Journal of Islamic Management Studies, 1*(1), 1–14.

Sewerin, S., Cashore, B., & Howlett, M. (2022). New pathways to paradigm change in public policy: Combining insights from policy design, mix and feedback. *Policy and Politics, 50*(3), 442–459. doi:10.1332/030557321X16528864819376

Sheying, C. (2003). General Public Policy and Development Strategy. The Chinese state in perspective. *China perspectives, 2003*(48).

Sommer, M., Torondel, B., Hennegan, J., Phillips-Howard, P. A., Mahon, T., Motivans, A., Zulaika, G., Gruer, C., Haver, J., & Caruso, B. A.Monitoring Menstrual Health and Hygiene Group. (2021). How addressing menstrual health and hygiene may enable progress across the Sustainable Development Goals. *Global Health Action, 14*(1), 1920315. doi:10.1080/16549716.2021.1920315 PMID:34190034

Soud, N. S., & Sayılır, Ö. (2017). Perceptions of Islamic banking among Muslim and Non-Muslim citizens in Tanzania. *International Journal of Islamic Economics and Finance Studies*, *3*(3), 15–29.

Spillane, J. P. (1999). External reform initiatives and teachers' efforts to reconstruct their practice: The mediating role of teachers' zones of enactment. *Journal of Curriculum Studies*, *31*(2), 143–175. doi:10.1080/002202799183205

Swain, R. B., & Ranganathan, S. (2021). Modeling interlinkages between sustainable development goals using network analysis. *World Development, 138*, 105136. doi:10.1016/j.worlddev.2020.105136

Swinkels, M. (2020). How ideas matter in public policy: a review of concepts, mechanisms, and methods. *International Review of Public Policy, 2*(3), 281-316.

Tajudeen, A. L.(2017). *Deficiencies and incompatibility of neither Qualitative nor Quantitative research paradigms with Islamic research: How could Grounded Theory methodology help*? An unpublished workshop presentation as part of mini-conference SPARC organized by Sultan Hassanal Bolkiah Institute of education, University of Brunei Darussalam.

Trief, P. M., Wade, M. J., Britton, K. D., & Weinstock, R. S. (2002). A prospective analysis of marital relationship factors and quality of life in diabetes. *Diabetes Care*, *25*(7), 1154–1158. doi:10.2337/diacare.25.7.1154 PMID:12087013

Tsuya, N. O., Choe, M. K., & Wang, F. (2019). *Convergence to very low fertility in East Asia: Processes, causes, and implications*. Springer Japan. doi:10.1007/978-4-431-55781-4

United Nations Department of Economic and Social Affairs. (2017). *2016 Family Expert Group Meeting*. Accessed from https://www.un.org/esa/socdev/family/docs/egm16/summary.pdf

Wada, K. (2015). *The Economic Impact of Population Decline and Aging in Japan: The Post-demographic Transition Phase*. Springer.

Wan Ahmad, W. M., Hisham Hanifa, M., & Hyo, K. C. (2019). Are non-Muslims willing to patronize Islamic financial services? *Journal of Islamic Marketing, 10*(3), 743–758. doi:10.1108/JIMA-01-2017-0007

Whisman, M. A., Li, A., Sbarra, D. A., & Raison, C. L. (2014). Marital quality and diabetes: Results from the Health and Retirement Study. *Health Psychology*, *33*(8), 832–840. doi:10.1037/hea0000064 PMID:25068454

Wibowo, M. W., & Ahmad, F. S. (2016). Non-Muslim consumers' halal food product acceptance model. *Procedia Economics and Finance*, *37*, 276–283. doi:10.1016/S2212-5671(16)30125-3

Wilkins, S., Butt, M. M., Shams, F., & Pérez, A. (2019). The acceptance of halal food in non-Muslim countries: Effects of religious identity, national identification, consumer ethnocentrism and consumer cosmopolitanism. *Journal of Islamic Marketing*, *10*(4), 1308–1331. doi:10.1108/JIMA-11-2017-0132

Williams, R., Karuranga, S., Malanda, B., Saeedi, P., Basit, A., Besançon, S., Bommer, C., Esteghamati, A., Ogurtsova, K., Zhang, P., & Colagiuri, S. (2020). Global and regional estimates and projections of diabetes-related health expenditure: Results from the International Diabetes Federation Diabetes Atlas. *Diabetes Research and Clinical Practice*, *162*, 108072. doi:10.1016/j.diabres.2020.108072 PMID:32061820

World Bank. (2022). *World Development Report 2022: Finance for an equitable recovery*. The World Bank.

Yang, S., Zhao, W., Liu, Y., Cherubini, F., Fu, B., & Pereira, P. (2020). Prioritizing sustainable development goals and linking them to ecosystem services: A global expert's knowledge evaluation. *Geography and Sustainability*, *1*(4), 321–330. doi:10.1016/j.geosus.2020.09.004

Yaro, I., Arshad, R., & Salleh, D. (2017). Relevance of stakeholders in policy implementation. *Journal of Public Management Research*, *3*(1), 25–2. doi:10.5296/jpmr.v3i1.10632

KEY TERMS AND DEFINITIONS

Bayi' Salam: Is a form of forward contract whereby the price of an Agric/farm product is paid upfront at the time of the contract for the product to be delivered later, with the objective of helping farmer's business activities and in exchange for a lower price.

Diminshing Musharakah: Is a form of Musharakah partnership that occurs when Mudarabh and Musharakah are combined. It is done by dividing the share of the financier of joint venture into a number of units, and the other partner (s) will purchase the units of the share of the financier periodically according to the agreement, thus increasing his (their) own share till all the units of the financier are purchased by him (them) and become the sole owner of the joint venture.

Epistemology: Is a branch of philosophy that investigates knowledge creation and justification. It is about how we justify that a particular information is knowledge and true. In policy making parlance, epistemology refers to the set of beliefs espoused by policymakers regarding the nature of a valid and reliable policy, sources of policy, etc.

Mudarabah: Is a kind of partnership in business where one partner gives money to another for investing it in a commercial enterprise. The investment comes from one partner and the expertise and management come from the other partner. They share profits based on agreed upon percentages/ratio.

Murabahah: Is where an asset/product is delivered immediately for the price to be paid on deferred basis based on agreed profit ratio.

Musharakah: Is a kind of partnership in business in which both investment and management of the joint venture come from all the partners. They share profits based on agreed upon percentages/ratio. There are situations where a manager may also invest some of his money into the business in a Mudarabah joint venture. In such a case, Musharakah and Mudarabah are combined.

Surah: It literarily refers to a chapter in the holy Qur'an, the Holy book of Islam. There are 114 chapters in the Qur'an, and each chapter contains verses, the minimum number of verses that could be found in a Surah is three (3) verses and the maximum number of verses is 286 verses.

ENDNOTES

1 The Islamic Jurists unanimously agreed that these *Maqasid* (cardinal goals) are not of the same weight and degree, some of them are more important than others. However, many early scholars of the *Maqasid* did not pay much attention to the arrangement of the *Maqasid* according to their priorities and degrees. For instance, Imam Al-Shatibi (d. 790 AH/1388 CE) did not adhere to a single arrangement of the *Maqasid* in his book, in some places he put the protection of progeny before the intellect and wealth, and in another, he placed the mind/intellect before the progeny and wealth. In the works of Abu Hamid al-Ghazali (d.505 AH/1111 CE) and Al-'Izz bin Abdus-Salam (d.660 AH/1209 CE), there are discussions about the arrangement and priorities of the *Maqasid*, but without a convincing evidence. The work of Al-Amidi (d. 631/1233) in his book Al-Ihkam, (Vol.4, p.289) is perhaps the most detailed analysis of the arrangement of *Maqasid* as follows: preservation of faith, life, progeny, intellect, and wealth. This is the arrangement we adopted in this research paper.

2 We take Japan as an example here. Shortly after the end of World War II, Japan introduced policies which directly and indirectly reduce the childbirth rate to checkmate a perceived population problem (Homei, 2016). Consequently, Japan's population began to shrink noticeably and has been projected to have adverse socio-economic effects in the coming years, not only in Japan but on the global economy (Bloom, et al., 2015; Tsuya et al, 2019; Wada, 2015). Japan's neighbours are equally staring down the same problem. South Korea's population would begin to shrink soon, and China's working-age population has already peaked. China has an additional problem which is that it will become old before it becomes rich. China has recently reversed its one-child policy, but averting the looming demographic consequences is perhaps impossible. Proactively, countries like Russia, Kazakhstan and Belarus are designing policies to encourage fertility, such as Maternal Capital Programme in Russia and Family Capital Programme in Belarus.

3 Check for meanings of these technical terms at the end of this chapter.

4 One example of such a policy is the Agricultural Credit Guarantee Scheme Fund (ACGSF) designed by the Nigerian government: The policy purpose is to provide loan guarantees to farmers through collaboration between the government, financial institutions, and farmers. Under the ACGS, banks provide loans to farmers, and the government guarantees a portion of the loan, reducing the risk for lenders. This collaboration between the government and financial institutions encourages banks to provide more loans to farmers, stimulating agricultural growth.

Chapter 6
Climate Change and Sustainable Development of Kampong Ayer:
Its History, People, and Environment

Noor Hasharina Hassan
https://orcid.org/0000-0002-5104-9897
Universiti Brunei Darussalam, Brunei

Gabriel Y. V. Yong
Universiti Brunei Darussalam, Brunei

ABSTRACT

Brunei Darussalam is committed to the Sustainable Development Goals. This study focuses on future sustainability of Kampong Ayer, largely a settlement as a consequence of land-based development. Many that remain are in the low-income group due to the lack of economic opportunities. They have become dependent on government welfare programmes. The cost of frequent home repairs due to environmental factors has become a burden in the modern world. Although the people have a close relationship with the estuary, and are highly adaptive, climate change is a slow and imperceptible process and will therefore catch the people off-guard. This study argues that intervention is needed. A policy based on SDGs 1, 11, and 13 would be most appropriate, as they address the most pressing issues in KA: poverty, sustainable cities and communities, and climate adaption.

1. INTRODUCTION: BRIEF CHAPTER STRUCTURE

At the Earth Summit in Rio de Janeiro in 1992, the United Nations Framework Convention on Climate Change (UNFCCC) was opened for signatures. It entered into force in 1994, establishing a framework for international cooperation on climate change, a platform for countries to negotiate and develop strategies to reduce greenhouse gas emissions and adapt to the impacts of climate change. The convention also established a governing body, the Conference of the Parties (COP) to drive and monitor international efforts to stabilise anthropogenic greenhouse gas concentrations in the atmosphere via the Kyoto Protocol

DOI: 10.4018/978-1-6684-8903-1.ch006

in 1997 and the Paris Agreement in 2015. The latter, adopted in COP 21 aims to hold global average temperature from rising to 2°C above 'pre-industrial' (1850-1900) levels. Participating country's efforts are tracked through 'nationally determined contributions' (NDCs), which comprised of (i) "mitigation" (reducing greenhouse gas, primarily CO2, emissions) and (ii) "adaptation" measures (building resilience to climate impacts).

Prior to COP 21, the United Nations (UN) adopted the 2030 Agenda for Sustainable Development on 25 September 2015. It is an outcome of Rio + 20 on the "Future We Want"[1]. This shared blueprint for "peace and prosperity for people and the planet"[2] is guided by 17 interconnected Sustainable Development Goals (SDG). The Paris Agreement and SDG goals are complementary and mutually reinforcing frameworks that address different aspects of sustainable development and climate change, which is addressed specifically in SDG 13[3]. Brunei Darussalam (for brevity, "Brunei") is a signatory of Agenda 21 at the Earth Summit, and together with ASEAN adopted a number of agreements and programmes on various aspects of sustainable development. In 2007, Brunei embarked on a long-term plan, *Wawasan* ('Vision') 2035[4] to achieve a highly educated citizenry (Goal 1), high quality of life and sustainable environment (Goal 2), and a vibrant and stable economy (Goal 3). In 2010, it established a national council on climate change, and a national secretariat in 2018. It has adopted a 'whole nation' approach to combating climate change[5].

Against this background, the Chapter will examine the evolution of Kampong Ayer (KA) and its resiliency to climate change. KA was once the primary city of the Brunei Sultanate. The arrival of the British, Second World War, modernisation, discovery of oil and gas, and migration of people and economy to land, reduced it to merely another settlement, quite bereft of economy. KA is a mix-mesh of built structure, where modern housing projects are juxtaposed with dilapidated old wooden dwellings and interspersed with houses and business premises refurbished with the latest building materials. In terms of style, the built environment has retained an eclectic mix of traditional and modern facades that is uniquely Bruneian. KA was a city, and due to its densely-packed and clustered organisation of dwellings, wards (*Kampong*) and 'blocks' (*mukim*), it is essentially an urban area, and one that is facing a number of sustainability concerns. SDG 11 on making cities and human settlements inclusive, safe, resilient and sustainable will therefore be used in the analysis of KA with respect to sustainable development and climate resiliency.

Since 2018, the authors and collaborators have been conducting research on KA, its history, people, culture, and evolution. This Chapter draws from earlier findings and examines sustainability concerns in the foreseeable future against a warming climate and rising sea. Published works include studies on cultural traits (Noor Hasharina Hassan and Yong, 2019a; Yong, 2021), housing and migration to land (Noor Hasharina Hassan and Yong, 2019b; Nurul Hazirah Zainuddin, 2021; Noor Hasharina Hassan, 2023), heritage industry and conservation (Izni Azrein Noor Azrein & Yong, 2022), trade and riverine lifelines (Yong, Izni Azrein Noor Azalie & Noor Hasharina Hassan, forthcoming), evolution of the physical environment (Yong and Noor Hasharina Hassan, 2022), as well as poverty in KA (Noor Hasharina Hassan et al., 2022). A number of papers are in preparation or under review at the time of writing.

In this chapter we will describe the characteristics of Brunei's climate and explain how it is changing and would affect KA. It will then elaborate on the people and culture, their close relationship with the environment, and how modernisation has caused people, culture, economy and built environment to change over time. The vulnerability of pockets of people in KA is then elucidated, as well as the resiliency of the people in general. The Chapter then discusses the exposure of KA to anticipated climate and consequences on the community. Finally, the Chapter discusses policy directions in relation to SDG 1, 11 and 13, as a means of climate adaptation. Figure 1 shows the location and environment of the study area.

Figure 1. Location of Kampong Ayer in Brunei Darussalam. Inset shows houses in Kampong Ayer and location of the two rejuvenation projects at Lorong Sikuna (LS) and Bolkiah (B). Main image is a satellite image showing urbanised areas in pink and vegetated areas in green.

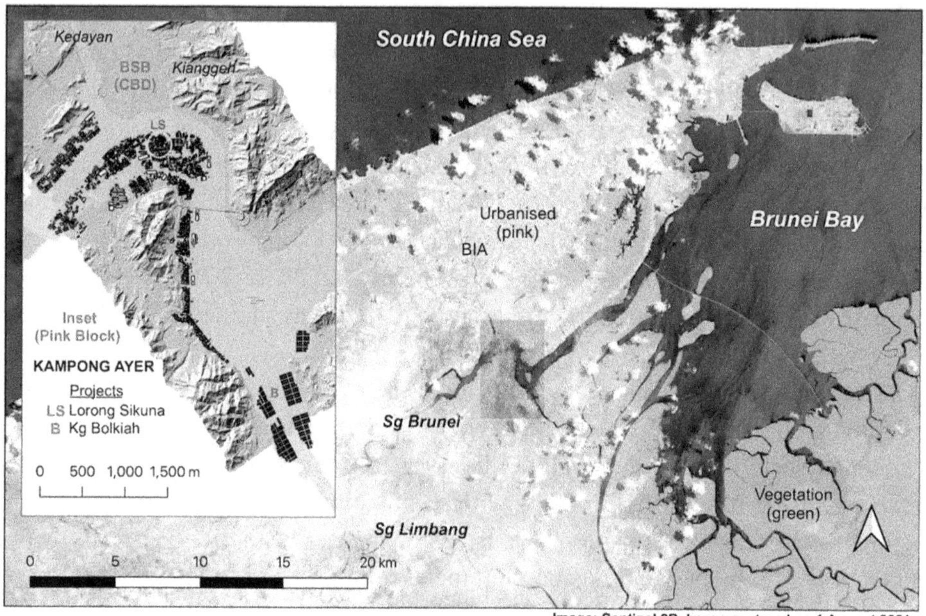

Image: Sentinel 2B, Image captured on 1 August 2021

Climate, Climate Change, and Its Impacts

Climate Change (CC) is often erroneously associated with natural disasters. Indeed, most people's knowledge (and misunderstanding) of CC are based on simplified narratives disseminated by media, climate agencies, teachers and academics, celebrities, and interested individuals. It is important to know how climate is defined, observed and described before assessing if it has changed. Climate is the typical pattern of weather over a year from 1st January to 31st December based on long-term records[6]. Weather refers to the state of the atmosphere or air around us. Climate Change is only observable if the period of observation is long enough to determine if its characteristics have indeed changed. Climate differs across the surface of the planet due to: the shape and tilt of the Earth; the planet's revolution around the Sun and distance from it; solar activity; spatial relation of land and ocean; landform and land cover; as well as environmental flows and processes. Development and land use could therefore alter climate because it alters the topography and material composition of the land, thereby disrupting the hydro-meteorological patterns that have been established over millennia. Urbanisation and development are the leading cause of environmental change, the degree of which commensurate with scale and intensity.

(a) Brunei's Climate

Brunei is located 5° N of the equator in the region referred to as "Humid Tropical Rainforest"[7]. The main controlling factors are its proximity to (a) the equator and (b) the South China Sea (SCS). This is a region of maximum solar intensity and therefore intense weather activity characterised by high levels of evaporation, humidity, cloudiness, lightning activity, precipitation and thunderstorms. The climate is however moderated by the maritime effects of the SCS, chiefly through the diurnal land-sea breeze cycles. Due to its location, seasonality is controlled mainly by the migration of the Inter-Tropical Convergence Zone (ITCZ) to the north and south of Brunei in summer and winter respectively over each year. This exposes Brunei to different regional winds[8], resulting in the Southwest Monsoon (SWM) and Northeast Monsoon (NEM) seasons. The latter brings more moisture and rainfall from winds blowing across the SCS between November to January. During the NEM, the coastal climate is characterised by the greater occurrence of high-energy destructive waves and storm tides. Meanwhile, during the SWM, rainfall is generally lower because part of its moisture has precipitated as the wind crosses the central highlands of Borneo between May and September. Typhoon, which passes the region north-northeast of Brunei between May and November, do not affect Brunei directly, but could generate unsettled squally weather (Cooper, 1992).

In between the two monsoons, the daily sea-land breeze cycles become more prominent. Light-gentle breeze blows inland during the day and towards the sea at night until dawn. Intense heating during the day generates conventional thunderstorms in the evenings. In general, air temperature rises to the maximum from around noon to early afternoon, and is coolest in the few hours before sunrise. However, the average monthly temperature is fairly constant throughout the year, rising slightly during summer. Humidity is high, with Relative Humidity (RF) generally over 80 due to high evaporation and evapotranspiration rates. RF could dip as low as 50, if the sun is shining (causing warm air to rise) between 10:00 am and 5 p.m.

The atmosphere and ocean form a coupled system with continuous exchanges of energy and moisture that give raise to hydro-meteorological processes, which drive circulation in the lower atmosphere and surface layer of the ocean. The effects of atmospheric-ocean exchanges in one region on seemingly unconnected regions further away is known as 'teleconnections'[9]. Brunei's climate is affected by regional circulations, notably, the El Nino Southern Oscillation (ENSO) in the Equatorial Pacific Ocean. El Nino events, which recur in 2-5 years are associated with less moisture (rainfall) arriving in Brunei due to a weakening of the Walker Circulation. La Nina events are the opposite. The two occurs as anomalies in between 'normal' conditions. They add to the natural variability of Brunei's rainfall, as is evident in its standard deviation and range, which is evident in Table 1.

(b) Climate Change

Climate data recorded at the Brunei International Airport (BIA) by the Brunei Darussalam Meteorological Department (BDMD) is the only available dataset. However, as it covers 56 years, it is sufficiently long to examine if the climate (in the BIA area) has indeed changed. It must be noted that the station is located in an area that has undergone rapid urbanisation over the past 30-40 years. Referring to Table 1, the 1996-1995 and 1992-2021 columns show that the mean and variability of rainfall have increased over the two 30-year periods, indicating that the climate here has become wetter since the 1990s. The Mean Monthly and Annual rainfall have increased by just over 10%, while the standard deviation for monthly and annual rainfall has risen by 10% and 16% respectively. However, while this suggests that

Table 1. Rainfall pattern, Brunei International Airport, 1966-2021

Statistics	1966-1995	1992-2021	1966-2021
Mean (Monthly)	235.5	260.6	249.8
Std. Dev. (Monthly)	135.8	149.1	143.9
Minimum (Monthly)	0.6	3.1	0.6
Maximum (Monthly)	715.6	977.0	977.0
Mean (Annual)	2,817.9	3,118.4	2,989.2
Std. Dev. (Annual)	428.8	496.4	490.4
Minimum (Annual)	2,153.0	2,135.7	2,135.7
Maximum (Annual)	3,707.1	4,443.1	4,443.1
Total Rainfall (30 years)	84,537	93,553	167,398

Source: BDMD.

climate in terms of rainfall has changed, it cannot be confirmed with further studies because the change observed could be due to teleconnections.

Figure 2 shows a rising trend in Mean Temperature with R^2 of 0.76. The mean temperature in 1979 was around 26.7°C. In 2020, it has risen to 28°C. This suggests that mean temperature could be close to 29°C by 2050, if this trend persists. There is however variability in mean temperature based on the scatter of data points and the 3-year moving average (green dotted line). The mean temperature in 2022, for example, was lower than the trend by 0.5°C. While the temperature data supports the climate change theory, it could be attributed to urbanisation rather than CO2 emission alone due to the fact the urban environment, which displaced the natural rainforest, would absorb sunlight but emit heat (as well as CO2), contributing to a higher level of heat energy in the air. In contrast, forests absorb sunlight for photosynthesis and therefore lowers sensible heat in the air. Forests also intercept rainfall and return moisture to the air through evapotranspiration, a diurnal hydro-meteorological pump that keeps the climate cool(er) and moist. In contrast, urbanisation would make the climate hotter, which is associated with more thunderstorms and potential for flash floods.

(c) Sea Level Rise

A global sea level rise (SLR) resulting from melting land ice is anticipated due to rising global temperatures and CO2 concentration. SLR is however notoriously difficult to measure. Tidal or sea level gauges are used to record continuous changes in sea level, but only in specific locations. Although there are some measurements of sea levels in Brunei, they are ad hoc, project-based, of short duration, and not accessible. Measurements of SLR and associated processes are therefore derived from agencies such as the National Ocean and Atmospheric Administration (NOAA) of the US Government[10]. SLR measurements are based on a combination of satellite altimetry and tidal gauge records. According to NOAA, since the turn of the century, SLR has increased to over 3 mm/yr., in contrast to 1.4 mm/yr. for much of the 20th Century. A study of sea level anomaly (SLA) in the SCS by Fu et al. (2019) suggests that the rate of SLR is closer to 4 mm/yr. They also found a high degree of variability ('anomalies') in sea level, and that sea level are generally lower during the NE Monsoon and El Nino periods but higher during the SW Monsoon and La Nina events. Taking an SLR rate of 4.2 mm/yr. (Fu et al., 2019), sea

Figure 2. Temperature trend, 1979-2021, measured at Brunei International Airport
Source: BDMB.

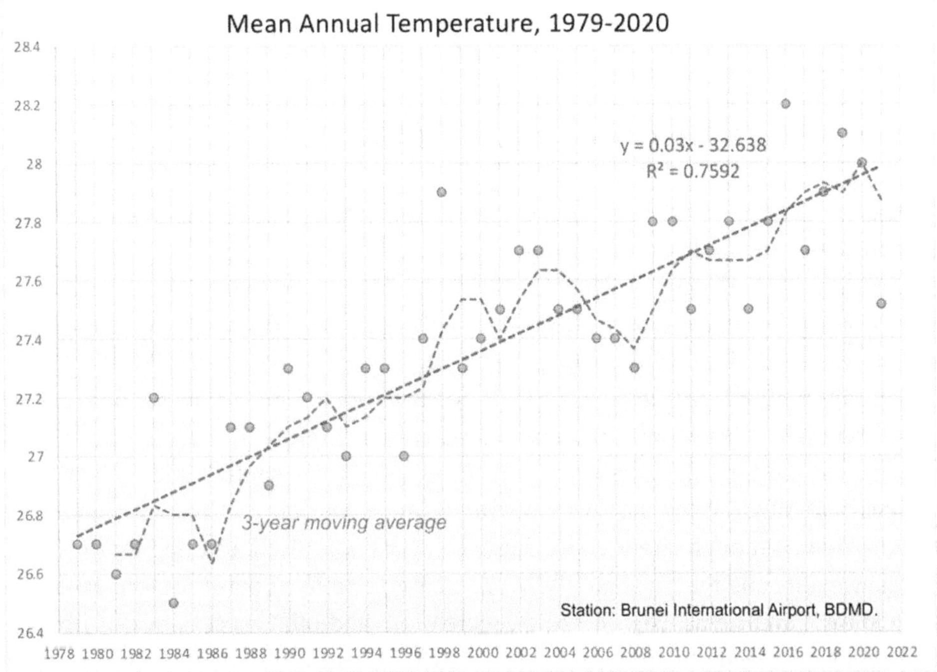

level along the coast of Brunei would be higher by 11-12 cm by the year 2050, and about 33 cm by the end of the century.

Although the expected SLR appears to be quite small, its effects would be quite significant in KA. This is because tidal levels are amplified in narrow estuaries, such as Sg Brunei. Presently, Brunei's maximum tidal range is about 1.5 m along the coast but has been recorded at 2.7 m in the Brunei estuary (Yong, 2010). A modest 12-cm rise in mean sea level could therefore raise high spring tidal level above 3 m, which could enter some of the older houses with lower stilts more frequently. By the end of the century, all of the older houses would be affected by tidal flooding on a regular basis. The newer sections of Kg Ayer under renewal/improvement projects, are not likely to suffer from tidal floods.

(d) Impact on Kampong Ayer

The degree of deleterious impacts due to climate change is proportional to the vulnerability of the population at risk, which is directly related to the quality of the built environment. Furthermore, they occur at specific locations, where higher magnitude hazards intersect with the area occupied by the vulnerable population. Vulnerability is largely a consequence of circumstances, such as: low/no income; no/limited means of accessing resources and assistance to improve living standards; inadequate infrastructure to cope with natural hazards; or lack of climate change adaptation programmes. In KA, a sizeable proportion of people live under these conditions, making do and staying poor (Noor Hasharina Hassan et al., 2022). In general, the dwellings and built environment in KA, which provides people with shelter and means of survival, are not durable, as they are susceptible to biodegradation by isopods, tiny crustaceans known locally as '*kapang*' (Nurul Hazirah Zainudddin, 2021). The stability of support structures (stilts) is also continually being undermined by tidal and storm discharge currents, which is a feature of estuarine environments. Climate Change is likely to exacerbate these problems, thereby compromising the low level of resiliency further. Without appropriate preparation, CC would increase the vulnerability of KA.

2. HISTORY, ENVIRONMENT, AND VULNERABILITY

Historically, KA has existed in various locations along the Brunei estuary since probably the 15th century. The sheltered location and plentiful supply from the hinterland provided a degree of protection, resources and livelihoods to support a sizeable population. The settlement complex, boats, implements and household wares were made largely from materials harvested from the immediate surroundings (Noor Hasharina Hassan & Rigg, forthcoming; Noor Hasharina Hassan et. al, 2022). KA, despite being a cluster of dwellings built on stilts in an estuary, is however not a fishing village. While many engaged in fishing, and employed a variety of artisanal methods of catching fish, shellfish, shrimps, crabs, and such, other processed food, produced a variety of dried, salted, fermented, and cooked food from the aquatic resources harvested. Wood has been an important material, and the surrounding mangroves were the main provider, although larger, more durable variety was also harvested for the construction of structures for the wealthy and the royal family. Wood is used to make boats (dug-out canoes), fish traps, jetties, as well as toys, and items used in sports, recreation, and other necessities of life. The location of KA at the interface between the hinterland and the SCS makes it an important point of connection between the interior and the wider region and beyond for trade. It is, therefore, a centre of exchange and industry, and was prosperous.

(a) Natural Environment

The natural environment is an estuary, i.e., a semi-enclosed body of brackish water that is connected to the sea at one end and freshwater sources at the other. The physical landform could be described as a tidal inlet, created when the sea level rose as the Earth warmed during the current Holocene Epoch and inundated the Sg Brunei valley to the present level some 5,000 years ago. An estuary is the most productive of ecosystems, as its position at the interface of rivers and ocean makes it a natural repository of deposits from land, which contains nutrients, and organisms from the vast marine ecosystem. Food and materials are therefore abundant in estuaries, which is why they are often sites of settlements, cities and ports. Sg Brunei is a micro-meso tidal estuary, where its typical tidal range is around 2 m. It is partially mixed at KA but more stratified to the east and south, which receives high freshwater discharge from the Sg Limbang basin. Ebb tidal currents are stronger than flood flows, and they tend to undermine structures, such as stilts of houses and jetties. The ecosystem however also contributes to the degradation of settlements built in the estuary. Tiny crustaceans, known locally as *kapang* (sometimes as KA 'termites') actively chew away at wooden stilt structures (Nurul Hazirah Haji Zainuddin, 2021). This will be elaborated in the section on vulnerability. Modernisation accelerated the siltation and infilling of the estuary and introduced pollutants, invasive species and modification of the physical environment to serve industrial and developmental needs.

(b) Transition and Transformation of KA

Traditionally, the roofs of dwellings in KA were made from woven palm leaves (*kajang*), while the floors were fashioned from trunks of the *nibung* palms (Oncosperma tigillarium) and stilts made from bamboo poles tied together with rattan (Adanan Abdul Latiff, 2016; Nurul Hazirah Zainuddin, 2011; Hassan et al., 2022). These light building materials were derived from the surrounding. They were lightweight, relatively easy to harvest and work, and provided simple shelter. However, they were also not durable and readily eaten up by insects (e.g., termites) and *kapang*. Moreover, they are flammable, which means that whole villages could quickly be destroyed whether in an attack or by accident. Following the Second World War, and the discovery of offshore oil and gas fields, the transition to land gained momentum. The resettlement program which was initiated during the British Residency period before the War similarly accelerated under a national housing program (Noor Hasharina Hassan and Yong 2019b), with concomitant changes and transformation in the economy, settlement, cultural activities and political system under national development programs and integration/assimilation of foreign ideas, products, education-trade and political systems.

In KA, houses were modernised in the 1950s and 1960s. Traditional *kajang* roofs were replaced with zinc and wooden foundations, including stilts, with concrete. Modern infrastructure was installed in the late 1960s, connecting KA by wooden walkways and with water and electricity supply. The main means of getting around, which was the simple dug-out canoe (*gubang*) gave way to more modern boat powered by outboard motors. Modernisation and development altered KA drastically, and in the process, transformed its population, settlement pattern, culture and the relationship between people and the environment in KA. The people are less dependent on the environment as a resource base, but instead, buy imported goods and materials from suppliers on land, increasing the cost of living considerably for many. Over time, despite the use of modern materials, the built environment continues to suffer from deterioration with more rapid and grave consequences than the settlement on the land. Many collapsed into the estuary after a certain period, as stilts gave way due to instability caused by water currents and or decay by *kapang*. Additionally, they were also susceptible to fires, which gutted parts of or whole villages on many occasions, leaving behind areas of concrete stilts and tiled bathroom units.

In 1993, the *Yayasan* ('Foundation') Sultan Hassanal Bolkiah introduced modern subsidised housing in the Kg. Bolkiah A and B project. Each house was built at a safe distance from one another to minimise the spread of fire. The houses had the necessary modern facilities and infrastructure for a safe, hygienic and comfortable living experience. Applicants were given two options; Type A houses with two bedrooms and Type B houses with 4 bedrooms, both with a monthly repayment of BN $138 and BN$162[11] over 20 years. In 2012, a revitalisation project built modern housing at Kg. Lorong Sikuna, which had been ravaged by fire. The houses have higher concrete stilts and vacuum sewer system[12]. They have a mezzanine level where it functions as a storage area (see **Figure 3**). In the old Bandar Seri Begawan (BSB) area, formerly Brunei Town, a section of KA destroyed by fire was reclaimed and now supports a modern building complex, which includes the Foundation Sultan Hassanal Bolkiah, and more recently, the Taman Makhota Jubli Emas. It is interesting to note that the height of stilts has increased with each redevelopment or revitalisation project. This suggests rising sea levels as modern projects always began with technical surveys of the environment.

(c) Vulnerability

The vulnerability of KA to climate change could be traced to the resettlement scheme initiated by the British Resident in 1906, which shifted the focus of the country, its development and its economy to land, leaving KA neglected and cut off. In 1911, the British Resident issued an order to halt the construction of new houses and the rebuilding of collapsed houses in its previous location in KA (Noor Hasharina Hassan et al. 2022). Although a British-appointed health ofðcer remarked that "Bruneians were naturally 'riverine dweller[s]' and any effort to relocate them inland would be misguided" (Leake 1989, p. 42 cited in Hamdi et al. 2023, p. 176) a decade later. This policy of preventing rebuilding a home that has been damaged beyond repair or demolishing houses that are vacated due to relocation to land has however been practiced on and off. Together with the national housing and temporary resettlement (e.g., due to fire or house collapse) schemes, KA has been depopulating after peaking in the 1980s, at the height of rapid urbanisation powered by high oil price. In 2015, the population was about 13,000 people (Bakar, 2021), accounting for only 2.3% of Brunei's population, and almost half of its population just over a decade earlier[13].

KA has become a marginalised settlement. Noor Hasharina Hassan et al. (2022) highlighted that, despite its physical proximity to the Central Business District (CBD), it operates largely quite independently from the core economy of BSB. This isolation is accentuated by its location in the estuary, which could only be reached by water taxi from the CBD. This marginalisation is both structural, which limits local employment opportunities, and spatial, where the population comprises of disproportionately larger lower income group and a high level of unemployment[14]. KA also draws a significant number of low-wage migrant workers due to its relative isolation and lower cost of living. With a GDP per capita of BND 51,645.9[15] (Department of Statistics, 2023), Brunei is generally regarded as a wealthy state, not afflicted by poverty. However, Saadiah Tamit (2009) stated that over 2,700 were living in relative poverty in KA. The Government of Brunei has three agencies mandated to provide assistance to those living in poverty, or more accurately, a state of deprivation. They are the Department of Community Development (JAPEM[16]), the Brunei Islamic Religious Council (MUIB[17]) and the District Office, which has a division on KA and another on community welfare and wellbeing[18].

Most of the lower income individuals receive monthly allowances (*Bantuan Kebajikan Bulanan)* and other forms of monthly aid including education aid from the government or the Brunei Darussalam Islamic Religious Council (MUIB). In 2021, the Minister of Home Affairs noted that the cost of building a house is higher in KA than on land and said that building subsidies for KA were being considered, particularly when the majority of residents in KA earn below BND $1,000 (Bakar, 2021)[19]. The majority of the lower income (in 'relative poverty') in KA comprises a combination of (i) the elderly, who have a strong sense of attachment to KA and thus are less willing to move, (ii) those engaged in place-based livelihoods, such as water taxi operators, fishermen, and boat makers, and (iii) those that found living on land costly and inconvenient (Noor Hasharina Hassan et al., 2022). The study showed that the three characteristics, which do overlap with one another, shape the next generation to a large extent, keeping some households poor, with low education attainment, and some in poor health. For some of the younger generation in KA, the lack of employment opportunities is a push factor to move to land in search of an improved quality of life.

In addition, these older houses are lower in height compared to the newer, modern, or renovated houses and walkways. The difference in height is obvious between the old houses with those of the government-provided houses in Lorong Sikuna (see Image). Respondents in a study conducted by Noor Hasharina

Figure 3. Lorong Sikuna Project, 2012 (L), and Kg Peramu (R). Stilts of the modern houses is 1.6 to 2m taller than stilts of the old houses, built in 1970s. The walkways are at the same level as the old houses.
Source: Photo by author, 12 June 2023.

Hassan et al. (2022) recalled how water would come into their houses, flooding the floorboards of their old run-down houses in particular the veranda area.

With respect to the built environment, although the assimilation of foreign modern technologies and imported materials have improved durability, environmental processes continue to degrade built structures, but only at a slower rate. Built structures in KA are exposed to conditions that are more deleterious than on land. Water currents from a combination of tides and storm discharge, undermines the stability of stilts that hold up homes, walkways and other buildings, by scouring away the sediments around them. This occurs even though modern concrete stilts are much larger in diameter (30-40cm) and have a large concrete anchor connecting the stilt to sets of 12 *bakau* (Rhizopora mangrove) poles hammered 4 m into the mudflat (Nurul Hazirah Zainuddin, 2021). Concrete stilts, introduced in the 1970s-1980s, greatly limit the damaging effects of *kapang* infestation. However, termites also eat into timber walls, flooring, ceiling and supporting beams. Meanwhile, cracks eventually form in many concrete stilts, but a collapse due to failure is rare. It must be noted that the concrete stilts do not strictly follow engineering standards. This is because they are made by self-styled KA contractors who combined knowledge gained directly or indirectly through involvement as a site worker with the public works department, with available tools (such as a 2-handle hammer used to pound the poles into the ground, and custom-made metal-sheet mould for stilt making) and materials, as well as cost, and environmental controls (stilts are only installed during low tides). The concrete mix is therefore not tested in physical labs but in the field while on the job. Concrete piles cost BND 150-200 each, and the average house require 6-12 stilts.

KA residents are continually confronted with the need to repair something, and sometimes, the cost is higher than usual. While the District Office is tasked to administer KA, JAPEM and MUIB in collaboration with the District Office offers home repair financial aid in response to requests by residents living in relative poverty. The common repairs and installations requests by residents are the roofs, toilets, kitchen and stilts. If the house is deemed unsafe to live in, the applicant will be offered a resettlement scheme by offering social or public housing on the land. Noor Hasharina Hassan's (2022) study found that all their recipients applied for house repair aids or financing to purchase a house in KA, however, the process takes a while but the repairs on their current house needed are urgent to avoid further damage to the house. They end up using their monthly welfare assistance to pay for the pressing home repairs required by hiring a local contractor in KA while also needing to pay for their groceries and utility bills including water and electricity. A local contractor interviewed in the study described the house he was repairing, whose owner is a recipient of monthly welfare and had also applied for home repairs funding, as "expired" or "unfit to live in", with the owners only inhabiting the lower floor of the house as the top floor was deemed unsafe to live in due to leaks in the roof and weakening structure of the house (Noor Hasharina Hassan et al., 2022: 138). Another recipient recalled how they would hurriedly use buckets and bowls to catch the leaks every time is rains they cannot afford to repair the roof yet. However, she was thankful to receive help from the government for the repairs of her house toilet and stilts.

Fire remains a major concern for the government and people in KA with six significant fires occurring between 2013- 2021 due to leaving cooking unattended, poor or loose wiring, and children playing with fire[20]. The government also provides aid in the form of re-housing or resettling them on land due to the higher cost of building and repairing houses on the water. An officer at the District Office shared that building a house in KA would be equivalent to about six houses under the national housing scheme on land. Those who wish to remain in KA to repair or rebuild their homes affected by the fire would be given some financial assistance. In addition, some of those who were resettled to the newer areas of KA to modern houses such as in Kg Bolkiah A and B due to fire have abandoned their houses to move onto land after their children received houses from the national housing scheme on land due to the convenience and work opportunities on land.

3. ADAPTIVE AND RESILIENT: A KAMPONG AYER TRAIT

KA is the product of interaction between a group of people and the environment since the 15th century, manifesting a culture that has adapted to life in a dynamic tropical estuarine environment (Noor Hasharina Hassan & Yong, 2019a: 49). This is evident in the cultural landscape and characteristics of built structures (Noor Hasharina Hassan, 2023; Nurul Hazirah Zainuddin, 2021; Yong, 2021). Here, the gamut of social-cultural activity, including religious events, work, industry, food production, and recreation, is played out in confined spaces within the settlement complex raised above the estuary on stilts. In pre-modern times, most of the materials used in creating the built environment were derived from the surrounding, sometimes extending further into the forest beyond the riparian zone of mangrove swamps.

As described earlier (section 3), built structures made from wood and plant-based products lack durability and are readily biodegraded and destroyed by fire. Meanwhile, support structures are constantly being undermined by tidal and storm discharge currents, which topple them after some time. Yet, KA has remained. The capacity to adapt to a highly dynamic environment appears to be a trait of the people of KA that has allowed them to thrive in this location for more than 650 years. This trait is elaborated in four examples: (i) a culture of recycling, (ii) maintaining structural stability, and (iii) new economic opportunities; (iv) social-cultural ecosystem.

(i) A Culture of Recycling

In KA, when a house collapsed into the estuary, it will be quickly cannibalised over a few days by others, who needed materials and parts to shore up their own homes. This active recycling of materials is characteristic of the natural ecosystem (Yong, 2021). A sustainable system is one where the ecological loops are interconnected, such that there is no real 'waste' in the system. The culture of cannibalising collapsed and abandoned homes is undoubtedly an outcome of the close interconnection between people and the environment. The lower income dwellers in KA often opt to purchase these cheaper second-hand or recycled materials sold by those who cannabalise and gather housing materials. Another aspect of this is the disposal of materials to the surrounding, where waste wood from traditional wood working (*meramu*), food preparation and other cultural activities are discarded into the surrounding, adding to food and sediments (Noor Hasharina Hassan and Yong, 2019a). In the modern day, however, this characteristic has given rise to trash pollution because much of the waste generated is not biodegradable.

(ii) Maintaining Structural Stability

Stilts are critical features of KA because they hold the built complex and people above water. The stability of the stilts is therefore of paramount importance. Typically, dwellings have a high density of stilts to counter the strong currents that could undermine them. In KA, when sets of stilts begin to tilt, residents add timber or logs on the downward side to prop up the building, which they refer to as *menungkat* ('adding a cane or crutch'). This is a reactive but adaptive strategy of countering potential failure due to forces that are acting to undermine the support structure of their homes. Biodegradation by *kapang* was another common way of undermining the stability of stilts, which would be eaten up at the intertidal level over time. The people would try to shore up the weakened sections by nailing wooden planks around them, wrapping a concrete cast around the damaged area, or proactively adding a PVC tube during installation to prolong the durability of the stilt (Nurul Hazirah Zainuddin, 2021). Replacing the use of timber with concrete as stilt material is itself a result of maintaining structural stability that people learn from interacting with the changing environment. In this case, some members of the community were exposed to modern materials, technologies, and methods whilst employed by the Public Works Department. They then adapted the knowledge to the KA environment and started concrete stilt enterprise to cater to the needs of the locals (Nurul Hazirah Zainuddin, 2021: 99)

(iii) New Economic Opportunities

Modern-day KA is largely a settlement area with low economic opportunity and activity. However, given its historical and heritage value, KA is promoted as a tourism destination. Through the initiatives of the Tourism Department, a number of enterprises have spawned. They included homestays, travel services, traditional craft and food-processing workshops, and a number of eateries. Most of the latter, however, cater to the local residents. The present modern realities also gave rise to services that meet basic needs, such as: boat engine sales and repairs, building contractors, silt makers and installation, and waste collectors. As people adapt to change, some found new ways and means to make a living. Noor Hasharina Hassan et al.'s (2022) study also found that people in KA benefit from micro-economies of scale for selling and buying necessities to get by in KA such as selling individual home-cooked meals or baking a few extra cakes to market informally to the people in their ward. Living in KA also created an economy of trust where people especially the relatively poor or lower income can and are willing to pay in instalments for services and goods while waiting for their monthly benefits to be deposited into their accounts (ibid, 2022).

(iv) Social-Cultural Ecosystem

Social capital in the form of collectivism and strong community support is a common practice in KA. Living near family and relatives within the same ward or village is their social blanket. There strong connection between the elderly and their younger relatives improves their survival potential, and therefore resilience from external shocks. The community resembles a tight-knit ecosystem, allowing the most vulnerable to cope in KA but not elsewhere in Brunei (Noor Hasharina Hassan et al., 2022). Foreign nationals and itinerant merchants are also part of the ecosystem, as are government social workers and officers in charge of various aspects of urban governance. Although dependence on this ecosystem becomes inherited liabilities (Hassan et al., 2022: 135), it has allowed the most vulnerable to survive.

Moreover, aside from the monthly aid provided by MUIB and JAPEM, the provision of universal welfare provided by the welfarist state or government helps Bruneians and in particular the lower-income Bruneians get by and support their adaptive capabilities (see also Gweshengwe and Hassan, 2019; Gweshengwe et al., 2020; Noor Hasharina Hassan and Yong, 2019b; Noor Hasharina Hassan et al. 2022; Noor Hasharina Hassan, 2023). This includes subsidised education and health care as well as necessary food items.

4. ADAPTING TO CLIMATE CHANGE, BUILDING RESILIENCY

The people in KA are highly adaptable, and therefore, resilient, based on history and evolution. The effects of climate change on KA have been examined in section 2. However, a crucial point to understand is that the process occurs at an imperceptible rate, making it difficult to prepare without referring to scientific observation and data analysis. For example, the water level is rising at rates of 3-4 mm/year, or about 0.01 mm per day. This cannot be observed, particularly when tidal fluctuation is typically between 1.5 to 2 m each day. Consequently, over decades, as one generation gives way to the next, the height of walkways and houses above the estuary will gradually appear to become increasingly lower, until water enters through the floor and wash over walkways with increasing frequency. This would occur, firstly, during high spring tides or as a consequence of storm surges that originate in the South China Sea, perhaps due to storm events driven by more energetic atmospheric circulation in the region. Oftentimes, such events would be associated with strong currents, either tidal or combination of tide, storm surges, and or storm discharges from land. Residents will be caught off-guard and could be at risk of damage to property, injury, and even, death. The need to repair and modify structures in the home and surrounding would become more frequent, resulting in a higher cost of living.

If the sea level were to rise faster than currently observed, then the timeline would be compressed, with the population experiencing the above sooner rather than later. Furthermore, if the sea level continues to rise, eventually, the estuarine water will inundate sections of the older walkways and homes that have lower stilts regularly or permanently. Even if it were only a few centimetres deep, residents would have to make more drastic decisions, including abandoning their homes. However, for the many KA residents that are not well off, this is not likely to be an option. As is their nature, people will try to adapt to the new environment, such as building floors or parts of it that are higher, so as to stay above the highest tide. They could adapt and survive, but at greater expenses and risk. This would drag the most vulnerable into poverty and precarious living condition. Vulnerable communities within KA would therefore be impacted in terms of quality of life, the potential for advancement or prosperity, and health and well-being. They would also be at risk of diseases and wild animals, notably, crocodiles that are present in the natural environment. The weather would be warmer, with higher rainfall, more frequent storms, and lightning activity, but also more variable. This would amplify the difficulties faced by many in having to constantly repair damages to their homes due to weathering and biodegradation (Noor Hasharina Hassam et al., 2022). This will further increase the cost of living, with a corresponding decline in quality of life, and heighten the potential to slide into poverty.

Intervention is therefore needed, because residents of KA, as well as authorities in general, would not be aware of the changing environment due to its imperceptible nature. The impacts of climate change are however real and will therefore creep up on the unsuspecting population, particularly the lower income, less educated and less connected people. A viable strategy would be to align with two of the SDGs as they are within the framework of Brunei's *Wawasan* (Vision) 2035 and commitment to achieving the UN SDG goals and the Paris Agreement. The two SDG goals, which are interconnected, complementary, and mutually reinforcing, are: SDG 11 on Sustainable City, Housing and Community and SDG 1 on poverty eradication in all forms.

SDG 11: Sustainable City, Housing, and Community

SDG 11 focuses on making cities and human settlements inclusive, safe, resilient, and sustainable. This means redeveloping the infrastructure and built environment to be durable enough to withstand more intense, warmer, humid and wetter weather and higher sea level, and which could accommodate every individual across the gamut of social-economic strata, where every individual or household have access to basic services. This would include communal spaces and amenities that could absorb the shocks to community life due to hydro-meteorological hazards. A sustainable approach would however entail adopting an integrated policy and plan that promotes a compact and connected urban structure that uses sustainable materials and systems to provide the necessary services. KA is already a dense, compact and well-connected urban complex. Its main problem is the low durability of the material used. A sustainable design therefore would need to focus more attention on the design and construction material. A biomimetic approach (e.g., Yong, 2022) would be a good way to achieve this.

Protecting cultural and natural heritage is also a part of SDG 11. This encompasses historic sites, landmarks, and ecosystems within cities, as well as promoting the sustainable management of urban areas to protect and enhance their cultural and natural values. KA is the cultural hearth of Brunei. It is therefore a historic site and contains intangible heritage in its history and the numerous stories, memorabilia and heirlooms of individuals, families and clans, as well as traditional arts and crafts. Izni Azrein Azalie and Yong (2022) proposed the establishment of a heritage industry as a means of conserving this cultural heritage that is rapidly fading or being eroded by modernity and regional-global cultural, economic and developmental processes. They posit that industrial networks and supply chains for arts and crafts, which were once part of the old city prior to the modern era, must be restored and reinvented to suit modern-day realities and that of a heritage-based industry. This could revitalise the economy of KA and facilitate community development, continuous improvement of the built environment and urban amenities, and conserve the fading intangible heritage.

A prerequisite of this strategy however would be to declare KA a historic site, for which there is provision under the 1967 (amended 1984) Antiquity and Treasure Troves Act (article 17, p.14). The development and management of the site would then be under the authority in charge of heritage instead of Ministry of Home Affairs. In practice, all sustainable cities require integrated planning and governance, and involve the participation of the community, civil society and the private sector. Enhancing urban resilience would involve the deliberate design and installation of structures and systems to safeguard against natural and man-made hazards, including climate-related ones. An adequately capable team that involves multiple public and private agencies is critical to climate change adaptation, a core interest of the Brunei Darussalam Climate Change Council.

SDG 1: Eradicating Poverty in All Its Forms

Addressing inequality, particularly in terms of income, access to services, and means of personal development and prosperity, is one of the core pillars of the sustainable development concept and principle as defined by the World Commission for Environment and Development (1987). Twenty years on from the Earth Summit, it has taken on greater urgency, and is identified as the primary SDG. At national levels, this is often addressed through a combination of social protection and economic empowerment programmes, community / regional development, women empowerment, improving access services, environmental protection and sustainable development projects, as well as collaborative programmes with civil society, private sector and international partners. There are often challenges presented by households that are deeply entrenched in circumstances of deprivation and the associated vicious circle of the inability of rising above them and making choices that keep them in it or exacerbate the circumstances. Climate Change adds to the challenges of SDG 1 in KA, as explained above.

A study of deprivation/poverty in KA (Noor Hasharina Hassan et al., 2022; Gweshengwe and Hassan, 2019; Gweshengwe et al., 2020a; 2020b) found that a portion of the population lives in a precarious existence, making do and depending on aid. The Brunei government currently provides aid through a number of agencies: JAPEM, MUIB and the District Office. A paper on these services and the challenges faced is presently under review. Aids for low-income individuals and households are in the form of the Monthly Welfare Assistance (*Bantuan Kebajikan Bulanan).* Other monthly provisions received by the lower income groups in KA include housing rental payment distribution school or education distribution or allowances, old age pension, and persons with disabilities (Noor Hasharina Hassan et al., 2022). There are also programmes for skills training and business development. However, the training programmes are not well-developed, well-funded, or adequately staffed, and mainly ad hoc in nature. Consequently, they have largely not been effective. The most sought-after aids are disbursements to help with home repairs, school fees, and living expenses. While social protection and welfare schemes are available, they are inefficiently disbursed, causing many recipients much anxiety in meeting daily and unforeseen needs. In the medium to long-term, they are inadequate to address the impacts of climate change and therefore address SDG 1.

There is however a close connection between eradicating poverty, sustainable development and sustainable urban design, and particularly, in combating climate change. This is acknowledged in the UN 2030 Sustainable Development agenda and adoption of SDG goals, i.e., the complex, interconnected and mutually affecting and reinforcing nature of the goals and their 'solutions'. The root of poverty is lack of opportunity to participate in the economy. KA is bereft of economic activity, a consequence of migration to land and transition to a modern, oil-based economy. The present low-level economic activity is due largely to the country's tourism drive, which promotes KA as a destination due to its historical and heritage importance. This has given rise to spots of touristic development in the form of homestays, exhibitions, eateries and traditional activities, which benefits only a small group modestly. Integrating SDG 1 with SDG 11 through the development of a heritage-based industry and improvement of the urban infrastructure, design, material and social-commercial spaces and services, would provide a major boost to the SDG 1 programme. This would address the two main causes of deprivation in KA: (i) the high cost of maintaining the home and surrounding physical structure, which makes up a significant part of their meagre income; and (ii) the amount of income they could earn, which is currently low and comprised mainly of aids. Achievement of SDG 11 could provide low-income earners to draw larger income and offer them a wider range of employment options in the vicinity.

5. CONCLUSION

KA is naturally resilient and has adapted to its dynamic estuarine environment and political, economic and physical changes through its 600-year history. Climate Change is however a slow and imperceptible process, which would sneak up on the people, catching them off-guard, with deleterious impacts anticipated. The lower income, who are just getting by with government support, will be the most vulnerable. However, a proactive approach to climate change would be to turn the threat into an opportunity for installing new structures and systems so that KA can adapt to the effects of climate change, notably rising sea level. Policy intervention founded on SDGs 1, 11 and 13 would address the two most vulnerable aspects identified: poverty or 'lack' (SDG 1) and homes and built environment that are susceptible to environmental decay (SD11). These two sustainable development agendas would be mutually supportive and affective, and when implemented together with SDG 13 on combating climate change, would build resiliency, one of the two NDCs of Brunei's commitment under the Paris Agreement. Integrating industry into the development programme would further strengthen resilience by making KA self-sustaining, and conserving this national heritage.

REFERENCES

Adanan Abdul Latiff. (2016). Corak dan Seni Bina Rumah Melayu Brunei Tinjauan Ringkas. Dewan Bahasa dan Pustaka, Bandar Seri Begawan.

Bakar, R. H. A. (2021). Gov't studying viability of new public housing in Kampong Ayer. *The Scoop*. https://thescoop.co/2021/03/20/ moha-reconsiders-building-new-public-housing-in-kg-ayer/

Brunei Darussalam Climate Change Secretariat. (2023). *About Brunei Climate Change Secretariat*. http://www.climatechange.gov.bn/SitePages/Pages/about-bccs.aspx

Cooper, R. (1992). Forecasting and Understanding Local Weather in Brunei Darussalam. *Brunei Museum Journal*, *7*(4), 88–98.

Department of Statistics. (2023). *National Accounts*. Bandar Seri Begawan: Department of Economic Planning and Statistics. Ministry of Finance and Economy, Brunei Darussalam. https://deps.mofe.gov.bn/SitePages/National%20Accounts.aspx

Fu, Y., Zhou, X., Zhou, D., Sun, W., & Jiang, C. (2019). Sea Level Trend and Variability in the South China Sea. *ISPRS Annals of the Photogrammetry, Remote Sensing and Spatial Information Sciences*, *IV-2*(W5), 589–593. doi:10.5194/isprs-annals-IV-2-W5-589-2019

Gweshengwe, B. & Hassan, N.H. (2019). Knowledge to Policy: Understanding Poverty to Create Policies that Facilitate Zero Poverty in Brunei Darussalam. Southeast Asia: A Multidisciplinary Journal, 19, 95-104.

Gweshengwe, B., Hassan, N. H., & Ali Maricar, H. (2020). Perceptions of the Language and Meaning of Poverty in Brunei Darussalam. *Journal of Asian and African Studies*, *55*(7), 929–946. doi:10.1177/0021909619900218

Gweshengwe, B., & Hassan, N.H. (2020). Defining the characteristics of poverty and their implications for poverty analysis. *Cogent Soc. Sci.*, *6*(1). https://www.tandfonline.com/doi/epub/10.1080/23311886.2020.1768669?needAccess=true

Hamdi, M. F. Z., Abdullah, N., Diyana, H., & Carnegie, P. J. (2023). Belonging and unbelonging in Kampong Ayer, Brunei Darussalam. In *(Re)presenting Brunei Darussalam: A Sociology of the Everyday*. Springer Nature Singapore. . doi:10.1007/978-981-19-6059-8

Hassan, N. H., Rigg, J., Azalie, I. A., Yong, G. Y. V., Nurul, H. H. Z., & Shamsul, M. A. S. M. (2022). Making do and staying poor: The poverty context of Urban Brunei. *Geoforum*, *136*, 132–141. doi:10.1016/j.geoforum.2022.09.012

Izni Azrein Noor Azalie & Yong, G.Y.V. (2022). Heritage Industry as Conservation Strategy for Kampong Ayer (Brunei Darussalam). *The Brunei Museums J.*

NOAA. (2008). *National Weather Services. Climate Prediction Centre*. https://www.cpc.ncep.noaa.gov/data/teledoc/teleintro.shtml

Noor Hasharina Hassan, & Rigg, J. (forthcoming). Borneo, Livelihoods and The Meantime: Learning from Brunei's Kampong Ayer. In Within Borneo, Beyond Borneo: Issues and Perspectives. Springer Nature Singapore.

Noor Hasharina Hassan, & Yong, G.Y.V. (2019b). A Vision in Which Every Family Has Basic Shelter. In Sustainable Development Goals in Southeast Asia and ASEAN: National and Regional Approaches. Brill.

Nurul Hazirah Haji Zainuddin. (2021). Evolution of Stilts in Kampong Ayer. *Brunei Museum J.*

Permata, M. (2017). *Usaha Pelihara Kg. Ayer*. https://mediapermata.com.bn/usaha-pelihara-kg-ayer/.

Saadiah, D.D.W.W., & Haji, T. (2009). Kampong Ayer Brunei Darussalam: Meniti arus pembangunan. *Borneo Res. J.*, *3*, 209–219.

Noor Hasharina Hassan, (2023). The Sociocultural Significance of Homeownership in Brunei Darussalam. In (Re)presenting Brunei Darussalam: A Sociology of the Everyday. Springer Nature Singapore. doi:10.1007/978-981-19-6059-8

UN Department of Economic and Social Affairs. (n.d.a). *Sustainable Development. The 17 Goals.* https://sdgs.un.org/goals

UN Department of Economic and Social Affairs. (n.d.b). *Sustainable Development. Goals 13. Take urgent action to combat climate change and its impacts.* https://sdgs.un.org/goals/goal13

United Nations (UN) Environment Programme. (n.d.). *Rio+20 outcome document "The Future We Want".* https://www.unep.org/resources/report/rio20-outcome-document-future-we-want

Wawasan Brunei. (2019). *Wawasan Brunei 2035.* https://www.wawasanbrunei.gov.bn/en/SitePages/wawasan-brunei-2035.aspx

World Commission for Environment and Development. (1987). *Our Common Future.* Oxford University Press.

Yong, G. Y. V. (2010). Brunei (Negara Brunei Darussalam). In E. C. F. Bird (Ed.), *Encyclopedia of the World's Coastal Landforms* (pp. 1141–1144). Springer. doi:10.1007/978-1-4020 8639-7_211

Noor Hasharina Hassan, & Yong, G.Y.V. (2019). The Cultural Value of Bakuts in Kampong Ayer, Brunei Darussalam. *Southeast Asia: A Multidisciplinary J.*, *19*, 47–63.

Noor Hasharina Hassan, & Yong, G.Y.V. (2019a). The Cultural Value of Bakuts in Kampong Ayer, Brunei- Darussalam. Southeast Asia: A Multidisciplinary Journal,19, 47–63.

Yong, G. Y. V. (2021). Identifying Cultural Traits of the Historic Kampong Ayer of Brunei Darussalam using Biomimetic Analysis. *International Journal of Environment, Architecture, and Societies*, *1*(2), 83–94. doi:10.26418/ijeas.2021.1.02.83-94

Yong, G. Y. V. (2022). Climate-Resilient Urban Design from Biomimicry-Arcology Perspective. *International Journal of Environment, Architecture, and Societies*, *2*(1), 1–15. doi:10.26418/ijeas.2022.2.01.1-15

ENDNOTES

1. https://www.unep.org/resources/report/rio20-outcome-document-future-we-want
2. https://sdgs.un.org/goals
3. https://sdgs.un.org/goals/goal13
4. https://www.wawasanbrunei.gov.bn/en/SitePages/wawasan-brunei-2035.aspx
5. http://www.climatechange.gov.bn/SitePages/Pages/about-bccs.aspx

6 At least 30 years, https://public.wmo.int/en/our-mandate/climate

7 Koppen classification of climate and ecozone on the Earth surface.

8 These are Northeast and Southeast Trade Winds, which converged at the ITCZ.

9 https://www.cpc.ncep.noaa.gov/data/teledoc/teleintro.shtml

10 https://www.climate.gov/climatedashboard

11 In 1991, majority of people in KA earned less than BN $1500 a month. Repayment for the foundation housing will be about 10%. (1991 Census).

12 Human and kitchen waste is discharged directly into the estuary in the older parts of KA.

13 In in 1980 the population of KA was about 28,000 and in 2006, the population was around 19,978.

14 Information found in Noor Hasharina Hassan et al. (2022).

15 https://deps.mofe.gov.bn/SitePages/National%20Accounts.aspx

16 Name in Malay, Jabatan Pembangunan Masyarakat.

17 Name in Malay, Majlis Ugama Islam Brunei.

18 Name in Malay, Unit Kebajikan dan Kesejahteraan Masyarakat

19 https://thescoop.co/2021/03/20/moha-reconsiders-building-new-public-housing-in-kg-ayer/

20 https://mediapermata.com.bn/usaha-pelihara-kg-ayer/

Chapter 7
Implications of Fuel Subsidy Removal on the Nigerian Economy

Peterson K. Ozili
https://orcid.org/0000-0001-6292-1161
Central Bank of Nigeria, Nigeria

Kingsley Obiora
Central Bank of Nigeria, Nigeria

ABSTRACT

The purpose of this chapter is to discuss the implications of the 2023 fuel subsidy removal in Nigeria. Using the discourse analysis methodology, the authors offer some insight into the macroeconomic and microeconomic implications of the 2023 fuel subsidy removal in Nigeria. The positive implications are that fuel subsidy removal would free up financial resources for other sectors of the economy, incentivize domestic refineries to produce more petroleum products, reduce Nigeria's dependence on imported fuel, increase employment, channel funds for the development of critical public infrastructure, reduce the budget deficit and generate a budget surplus in the near future, reduce government borrowing, curb corruption associated with fuel subsidy payments, increase competition, reinvigorate domestic refineries, and reduce pressure on the exchange rate.

1. INTRODUCTION

Fuel subsidy is a government discount on the market price of fossil fuel to make consumers pay less than the prevailing market price of fuel (Ovaga and Okechukwu, 2022). When subsidies are in place, consumers would pay below the market price per litre of the petroleum product. Globally, there are debates about fuel subsidy because of its huge amount and its effect on citizens welfare and the fiscal health of a nation.

DOI: 10.4018/978-1-6684-8903-1.ch007

The size of global fossil fuel subsidy is large and is estimated at $1 trillion in 2022 from $325 billion in 2018, according to the International Energy Agency. This amount is significantly higher than the value of global aid which was estimated at $204 billion in 2022 and larger than the combined government revenue of developing countries. This has led to calls for the removal of global fossil fuel subsidy so that the saved funds can be channelled to assist the poor and vulnerable in need of humanitarian assistance in developing countries (Couharde and Mouhoud, 2020; Ozili and Ozen, 2021). However, the removal of fossil fuel subsidy is contentious because there is the argument that fossil fuel subsidy is a form of aid because it makes fuel more affordable for the poor. Despite this favourable argument, a large literature documents the negative consequences of fuel subsidy which include increasing air pollution and green-house gas emissions (Sweeney, 2020), road congestion (McCulloch, Moerenhout and Yang, 2021), road accidents and premature deaths (Parry, Black and Vernon, 2021), foregone tax revenue (Sweeney, 2020) and it increases inequality between the poor and the rich (McCulloch, Moerenhout and Yang, 2021). However, policymakers in many countries are reluctant to remove fuel subsidy and to implement fuel subsidy reforms because such reforms may result in a significant increase in fuel or electricity prices which could lead to economic hardship for low-income and poor citizens, and might lead to massive protest and increase the risk of a revolution or the overthrow of the incumbent government.

In Nigeria, fuel subsidies were first introduced in the 1970s as a response to the oil price shock in 1973. Fuel subsidies were partially removed in 1986. Since then, the fuel subsidies have been in place. In 2012, the government abruptly removed fuel subsidy. The removal led to massive protests which was intended for the government to reinstate the fuel subsidy it had removed. The government subsequently reinstated fuel subsidy in 2012 due to the massive protests. Since then, fuel subsidy payment in Nigeria has grown enormously. In 2022, fuel subsidy reached ₦4 trillion (US$6.088 billion) which amounted to 23 percent of the national budget of ₦17.126 trillion (US$25.87 billion) in 2022. As a result, Nigeria could no longer sustain fuel subsidy in 2023, and the government announced that fuel subsidy would be removed in June 2023.

Recent evidence in the Nigerian literature shows mixed effect of fuel subsidy. Some studies identify some benefits of fuel subsidy and call for transparency in the administration of fuel subsidy while other studies highlight the negative consequences of fuel subsidy and advocate for its removal. For example, Omitogun et al (2021) show that the removal of fuel subsidy might reduce the amount of carbon emission in the Nigerian economy. Similarly, Adekunle and Oseni (2021) argue that fuel subsidy removal could reduce the growth in carbon emissions through low energy consumption channels even though it could lead to higher energy prices. Asare et al (2020) argue in support of fuel subsidy removal and that the revenue gained from removing fuel subsidy could provide additional resources for the government to respond with immediate interventions to address the COVID-19 crisis and enable the government to shift resources into more productive spending for long-run post-COVID recovery and resilience (Ozili and Arun, 2023). Other studies highlight the consequence of fuel subsidy removal. Umeji and Eleanya (2021) argue that Nigerian oil wealth has not translated to improved standard of living despite the introduction of fuel subsidy, and that fuel subsidy removal could have severe consequences which can be mitigated by transparency on the part of government in spending the funds saved from fuel subsidy removal for infrastructural development. Also, Ovaga and Okechukwu (2022) argue that fuel subsidy breeds corruption in Nigeria because a group of corrupt people have been working against the functioning of existing refineries and they undermine efforts to build new refineries in Nigeria so that fuel importation would be sustained and fuel subsidy would be retained for the purpose of satisfying their selfish desires. Omotosho (2020) points out that fuel subsidy removal could lead to higher macroeconomic instability through rising energy prices and inflation in Nigeria. Furthermore, McCulloch, Moerenhout and Yang (2021) show that many Nigerian citizens oppose fuel subsidy removal or reforms because they believe the government is corrupt and lacks the capability to undertake transparent reforms.

Despite these evidence in the literature, there is little or no discussion about the impact of the recent fuel removal in Nigeria in 2023. The way the fuel subsidy was removed, without first providing some palliatives, led to controversy about how the fuel subsidy removal would affect the Nigerian economy and Nigerians. Therefore, there is a need to identify and understand the macroeconomic implications and the microeconomic implications of the 2023 fuel subsidy removal in Nigeria. This paper provides a rigorous assessment of the macroeconomic and macroeconomic implications of the recent fuel subsidy removal in Africa's largest economy – Nigeria.

This study contributes to the literature that examine the beneficial and harmful effects of fuel subsidy (see, for example, Omitogun et al, 2021; Adekunle and Oseni, 2021; Asare et al, 2020; Umeji and Eleanya, 2021; Ovaga and Okechukwu, 2022; Omotosho, 2020; McCulloch, Moerenhout and Yang, 2021). The study also contributes to the literature that examine the contribution of fossil fuels to climate change. The study further contributes to on-going debates about the negative consequences of fuel subsidy for climate change mitigation and adaption.

This rest of the paper is structured as follows. Section 2 presents the review of related literature. Section 3 presents the macroeconomic implications of fuel subsidy removal in Nigeria. Section 4 presents the microeconomic implications of fuel subsidy removal in Nigeria. Section 5 presents other implications. Section 6 presents the concluding section.

2. RELATED LITERATURE

Nigeria is not the only country to remove fuel subsidy. In 1997, Indonesia removed fuel subsidy after the Asian financial crisis. The removal of fuel subsidy increased the domestic price of fuel and suddenly ignited protests and violent riots which occurred for weeks and forced the incumbent government to resign in 1998 (Chelminski, 2018). Dartanto (2013) examined the relationship between existing fuel subsidies and fiscal balance in Indonesia between 1998 and 2013 and found that removing 25 percent of fuel subsidies increased poverty by 0.259 percentage points while 100 percent removal of fuel subsidies and the reallocation of 50 percent of them to government spending decreased poverty by 0.277 percentage points. Fathurrahman et al. (2017) showed that the reallocation of subsidy payments to low-income households could slow down economic development but improve social welfare. However, removing fuel subsidy usually comes with the promise of using the money saved from subsidy to undertake targeted reform. But in Indonesia, citizens find promises to replace fuel subsidies with targeted spending less credible and would resist the reform if they believe the government is corrupt (Kyle, 2018).

Other international studies have also analysed the effect of fuel subsidy removal. Harring et al. (2023) analysed cross-country attitudes towards fossil fuel subsidy removal and found that the public would have positive attitudes towards subsidy removal if there were optimal use of the saved fiscal revenues. In Malaysia, Chatri (2014) assessed the economy-wide effects of gas subsidy removal in the power sector and found that gas subsidy reductions lead to increases in the price of electricity followed by a decline in demand for electricity by other economic sectors and a decrease in gross domestic product. Antimiani et al. (2023) showed that fossil fuels are still highly subsidised in EU countries, and there are deliberations to remove fossil fuel subsidies and reuse the revenues to foster the technological transition to a sustainable and decarbonised EU economy. Sampedro et al. (2017) also argued that fossil fuel subsidy is a barrier to tackling climate change in the EU because it diverts investment away from clean energy sources, and fossil fuel subsidies amounted to US$233 billion in 2014 which is four times the amount of subsidies allocated to promote renewable energy. However, they showed that fuel subsidy removal would give rise to only a small reduction in CO2 because people would switch from fuel to coal and gas. Nowag et al. (2021) suggest the use of state aid to phase out fossil fuel subsidies in the EU. Erickson et al. (2017) showed that the removal of tax incentives and other fossil fuel support policies could hasten the attainment of the G20 climate commitments. Lin and Li (2012) examined the case of China and showed that fuel subsidy removal would generate negative externalities in China but would generate positive externalities to other world regions without subsidy removal. In a related study, Ouyang and Lin (2014) showed that the economic benefits of renewable energy subsidies were lower than the economic benefits of fossil fuel subsidies in China.

3. MACROECONOMIC IMPLICATIONS OF FUEL SUBSIDY REMOVAL

3.1. The Positive Macroeconomic Implications

3.1.1. The Saved Funds From Fuel Subsidy Removal Would Be Channelled to Develop Critical Public Infrastructure

A positive macroeconomic implication of the removal of fuel subsidy in Nigeria is that the funds that would have been used for fuel subsidy payment could be channelled to the development of critical public infrastructure in Nigeria. There is a consensus among academic economists that the funds used for subsidy payments can be channelled to public infrastructure spending (Bazilian and Onyeji, 2012; Majekodunmi, 2013). Prior to the removal of fuel subsidy, Nigeria did not have sufficient money to fund the development of critical public infrastructure (see figure 1). The lack of sufficient funds led the government to incur huge debts to finance the budget. However, with the removal of fuel subsidy in 2023, the government could use these funds and channel them appropriately for the purpose of developing critical public infrastructure in Nigeria. This outcome can only occur if the government is transparent, honest and is held to account, to ensure that the saved funds from fuel subsidy removal are channelled to the development of critical public infrastructure.

3.1.2. Financial Resources Are Freed Up for the Development of Other Sectors

Other studies suggest that the savings from fuel subsidy removal could be channelled for the development of other sectors of the economy (Gidigbi and Bello, 2020; Ogunode, Ahmed and Olugbenga, 2023). In addition to developing Nigeria's critical public infrastructure, the removal of fuel subsidy can free up financial resources for the development of other sectors that require significant government intervention and funding. The funds that would have been used for fuel subsidy payment could be channelled to sectors such as agriculture, healthcare, tourism, education and to fund the implementation of the Student Loan Act. Prior to the removal of fuel subsidy, many sectors of the economy did not perform optimally due to weak private sector investment and an abysmal level of public expenditure into those sectors due to insufficient government revenue as shown in Figure 1. With the removal of fuel subsidy, it is hoped that the Federal Government would channel the freed-up resources into other sectors that need government funding.

Figure 1. Nigeria government revenues
Source: Central Bank of Nigeria

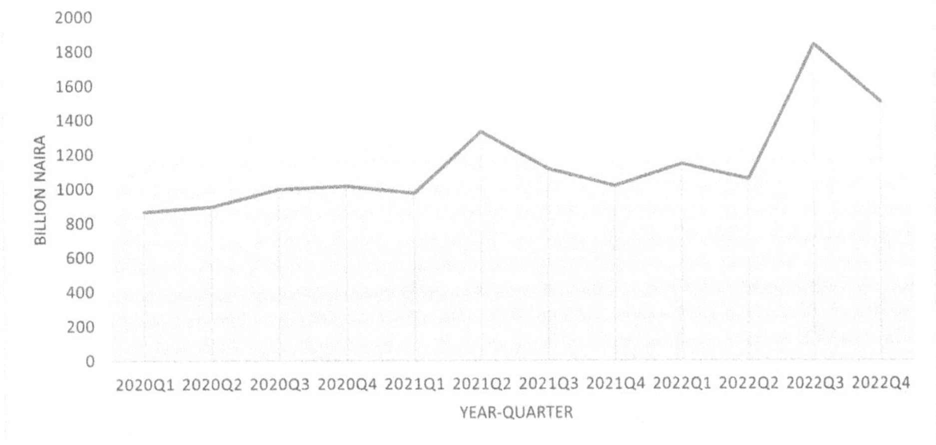

3.1.3. Fuel Subsidy Removal Will Reduce the Budget Deficit and Could Generate a Budget Surplus in the Near Future

Another positive macroeconomic implication of the removal of fuel subsidy is that the funds would be used to fund the current budget deficit. Existing studies show that fuel subsidy contributes to Nigeria's rising fiscal deficit and call for the need to remove fuel subsidy (Harun et al, 2018; Adagunodo, 2022). Historically, Nigeria has had a budget deficit in the last 10 years. Figure 2 shows that Nigeria's budget to GDP ratio has remained in negative territory for over a decade. More recently, the petrol subsidy was billed to consume ₦4 trillion in 2022 and a whooping ₦17 trillion in 2023 (see Figure 3), meanwhile the approved 2023 budget was only ₦21.83 trillion. This implies that the fuel subsidy would consume about 77% of the budget which already puts Nigeria in a chronic budget deficit and would drive Nigeria towards bankruptcy. In addition to that, 90% of Nigeria's revenue is used to service its external debt which further complicated Nigeria's financial situation during the fuel subsidy regime. The recent removal of fuel subsidy is indeed a positive development for Nigeria's finances because it would reduce Nigeria's current budget deficit as the ₦17 trillion would be used to augment the national budget. And over time, Nigeria could have a budget surplus.

3.1.4. Reduced Government Borrowing

There have been debates about the adverse effect of fuel subsidy payments on government borrowing (Okongwu and Imoisi, 2022). Since the start of the fuel subsidy regime, the Nigerian government has been borrowing, and the borrowing worsened during the 2016 recession and the 2020 COVID-19 pandemic (Ozili, 2022). Recently, in 2022, the government constantly borrowed from the Central Bank of

Figure 2. Budget deficit to GDP ratio
Source: Central Bank of Nigeria (CBN)

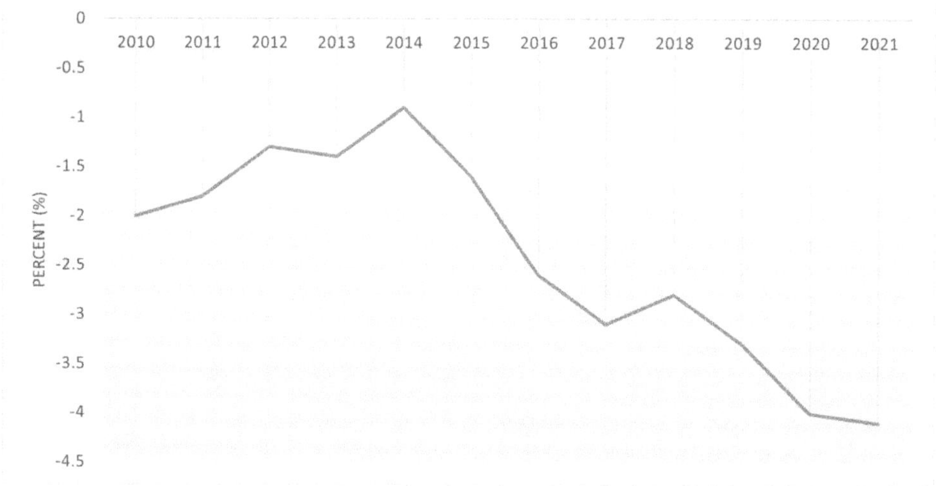

Nigeria (CBN) through the ways and means provision for debt repayment and subsidy payment. The government had no choice but to increase borrowing from the Central bank. The government owed the Central Bank ₦22.7 trillion which was recently securitized by the FG with the approval of the national assembly in 2023. The recent removal of fuel subsidy implies that government borrowing from the Central Bank would stop, as the saved funds from fuel subsidy removal will become available for the government to use to meet its public expenditures.

3.1.5. Increase in Employment

Another positive macroeconomic implication of the fuel subsidy removal is that it would create jobs. The total deregulation of the downstream sector will allow more companies to import fuel at competitive

Figure 3. Fuel subsidy amount in the budget
Source: CBN & NNPC

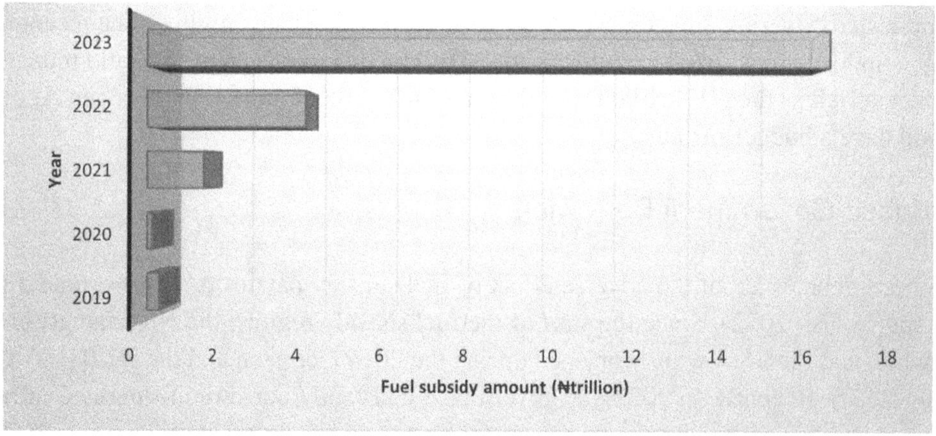

rates (Olujobi, 2021). These companies will hire workers, thereby creating jobs. Also, the reinvigoration of domestic refineries in Nigeria will lead to job creation. Furthermore, when the Dangote refinery starts producing, it could create more than 10,000 direct jobs in Lagos alone and over 30,000 indirect jobs across Nigeria, thereby increasing the level of employment.

3.1.6. Strengthen the Exchange Rate or Reduce Pressure on the Exchange Rate

Following the removal of fuel subsidy, the government should allow domestic refineries to produce more crude oil and other petroleum products. This will reduce the importation of petroleum products and increase the exportation of locally produced petroleum products (Akinola, 2018). This, in turn, will conserve foreign exchange from imported petrol and increase foreign exchange accretion from exported petrol. The foreign exchange accretion will boost foreign exchange supply in the foreign exchange market and strengthen the Naira against the U.S. Dollar. This, in turn, will lead to the appreciation of the Naira and an improved exchange rate. For example, the Dangote Refinery which has a refining capacity of 650,000 barrels per day, can meet Nigeria's domestic demand for refined petroleum products, reduce petrol importation and generate a surplus for export. As a result, the government could save billions of dollars spent on petroleum imports, and such savings could be used to ease the pressure on the exchange rate and improve trade balances.

3.1.7. Reduce Nigeria's Dependence on Imported Petrol

If the removal of fuel subsidy is followed by the reinvigoration of Nigeria's domestic refineries, it could incentivize domestic refineries to produce more petroleum products and reduce Nigeria's dependence on imported fuel (Akinola, 2018). Consider the newly created Dangote Refinery. It has a massive refining capacity of 650,000 barrels per day, which is sufficient to meet Nigeria's domestic demand for refined petroleum products, generate a surplus for export, and reduce petrol importation significantly. In addition to the Dangote Refinery, other local refineries with their differing refining capacity levels will further enhance Nigeria's refining capabilities and Nigeria's dependence on imported petrol.

3.1.8. Low Carbon Emission Through Fuel Subsidy Removal

The presence of fuel subsidy in the last decade encouraged fossil fuel-based economic activities that increase air pollution and carbon emission in Nigeria. The CO2 damage in Nigeria, which is partly attributed to fuel subsidy, rose from US$1.5bn in 1998 to US$5.23bn in 2021 (see Figure 4). The removal of fuel subsidy in Nigeria would support ongoing climate change mitigation efforts and reduce Nigeria's contribution to global greenhouse gas emissions by 2030. Fuel subsidy removal in Nigeria would also decrease both the demand and supply of fossil fuels, thereby reducing carbon emission in Nigeria (Omitogun et al, 2021).

Figure 4. Carbon dioxide damage in Nigeria from 1998 to 2021
Source: World Development Indicators (World Bank)

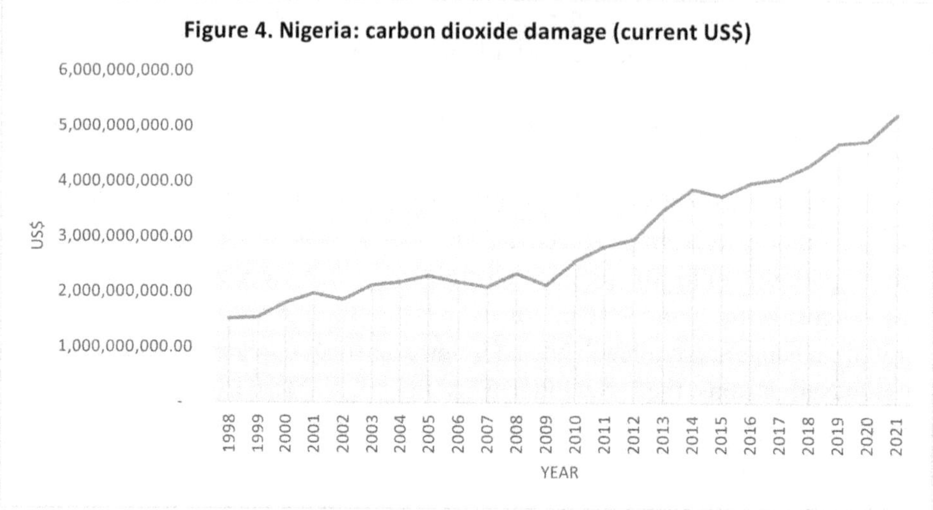

3.2. Negative Macroeconomic Implications

3.2.1. Decrease in Economic Growth in the Short-Term

One negative macroeconomic implication of the removal of fuel subsidy is that the rate of economic growth could decrease (Houeland, 2020). The fuel subsidy removal would lead to increase in price of essential goods and services. As a result, there would be fewer disposable income in the hands of individuals and small businesses due to rising prices, stagnant wages, and a fixed national minimum wage. This will lead to a reduction in consumption expenditure and would act as a drag on aggregate demand. The reduction in consumption would translate to weak consumer demand for the goods and services produced by firms. This, in turn, could decrease economic output and gross domestic product, and slow the rate of economic growth.

3.2.2. High Inflation and Reduced Purchasing Power

Another negative macroeconomic implication of the removal of fuel subsidy is that the inflation rate would increase (Mohammed, Ahmed and Adedeji, 2020). The removal of fuel subsidy led to a rise in the price of petrol from a subsidized price of ₦190 in May 2023 to an unsubsidized price of ₦537 in June 2023 and ₦617 in July 2023 in Abuja. Meanwhile, the price of petrol could rise above ₦600 in the far North such as in Borno State due to high transportation cost. The implication is that the price of most consumer and industrial goods, which are produced or transported with petrol, will increase sharply. The cost of bread will increase, and the cost of local transportation will also increase, making it expensive to afford for poor individuals and low-income earners. The effect will also be felt by both the rich and the poor, but as always, the poor will suffer the most, through a significant reduction in their purchasing power. The inflation effect could be further worsened by the late rollout of palliatives by the Federal

Government to support the poor and households who are affected by the rise in the price of essential goods and services immediately after fuel subsidy removal.

4. MICROECONOMIC IMPLICATIONS

4.1. Positive Microeconomic Implications

4.1.1. There Will Be Market-Determined Pricing

One positive microeconomic implication of the removal of fuel subsidy is that price of petrol, or Premium Motor Spirit (PMS) will be determined by the forces of demand and supply (Su et al, 2020), rather than being determined by government regulation or through subsidy. This will prevent the under-pricing of petrol and would curb corruption arising from inflating the quantity of imported PMS under the fuel subsidy regime. The removal of fuel subsidy will also lead to accurate pricing that reflects actual conditions in the international market for crude oil.

4.1.2. It Will Curb Systemic Corruption Associated With Fuel Subsidy Payments

Another positive microeconomic implication of the removal of fuel subsidy is that the removal of fuel subsidy could bring an end to corruption in fuel subsidy payments. There is the perception that the fuel subsidy is a ploy to continue to siphon Nigeria's hard earned foreign exchange into private accounts abroad (Itumo and Onyejiuba, 2019; Sheyin, 2018). Recent data show that the international price of oil crude has not gone up substantially, but Nigeria's crude oil output has risen, and generated around two million barrels per day. Yet, Nigeria's external reserves have continuously been reported declining. What could have been responsible for this? It is plain corruption. For example, an oil marketer imports only fifteen metric tons of petrol and will go to the Petroleum Products Pricing Regulatory Agency (PPPRA) in Abuja to report that he imported seventy-five metric tons of petrol. The importers will collude with some officials of the PPPRA so that they will get their own share of the inflated sixty metric tons. This has been the major corruption that has been taking place during the fuel subsidy regime. But with the removal of fuel subsidy, this type of corruption will stop completely. Now, the importers will only get paid for the actual petrol they import into the country.

4.1.3. Increased Competition

Another positive microeconomic implication of the removal of fuel subsidy is that the removal of fuel subsidy will usher in a market-determined price and could, over time, result in reduced product prices due to healthy competition (Bagirov and Mateus, 2019). The total deregulation of the oil sector will foster market competition, and lead to enhanced efficiency in the downstream sector. The deregulation also allows for flexible pricing mechanisms that are driven solely by market forces. The removal of fuel subsidy will allow new entrants and investors to enter the downstream sector and would aid competition and eliminate the monopoly of the Nigerian National Petroleum Corporation (NNPC) in the importation of petrol into Nigeria. When competition comes in, the market will determine the price of petrol and there would be a downward fall in the price of petrol as competition becomes intense.

4.1.4. Revitalise Domestic Refineries to Work

Another positive microeconomic implication of the removal of fuel subsidy is that it could lead to the reinvigoration of the domestic refineries. Nigeria's domestic refineries have been in a bad state since the fuel subsidy regime started (Okongwu and Imoisi, 2022). The presence of subsidy has not led to the revitalization of domestic refineries due to endemic corruption associated with fuel subsidy. Following the removal of fuel subsidy, if the government introduce reforms to revive Nigeria's domestic refineries, such reforms could revive domestic oil producing firms and increase domestic production of crude oil in Nigeria.

4.2. Negative Microeconomic Implications

4.2.1. Increase in Poverty and Vulnerability

A negative microeconomic implication of the removal of fuel subsidy is that it will increase poverty in the short term (Raji, 2018). It will lead to immediate pain and hunger for families. At the individual level, the removal of fuel subsidy, and without any palliatives, could lead to fewer disposable income, fewer food in the land, fewer medicine for sick people, and inability to afford basic education in several parts of the country especially in the Northern region of Nigeria. More families will go hungry, more children will cry in hunger and more parents will cry at their children's despair. The poor and middle-class consumers will witness a fall in their purchasing power, and small businesses will find their profit margins squeezed because they will face higher costs and reduced sales volumes. And if they attempt to pass on the cost to consumers, consumers might refuse to buy or reduce the quantity purchased, thereby leading to low business patronage. Furthermore, the fuel subsidy removal could affect poor vulnerable groups disproportionately if there are no economic safety nets or social assistance programmes that can alleviate the economic hardship caused by the fuel subsidy removal.

4.2.2. Social Unrest and Protest

Another negative microeconomic implication of the removal of fuel subsidy is that it could lead to protests and social unrest (Houeland, 2020). The rise in the price of petroleum products could trigger protests. If the prices continue to go up, poor households will be pushed to the wall and will be left with no option but to engage in protest and social unrest to get the government to reverse the fuel subsidy removal.

4.2.3. Rise in Fuel Smuggling

Another negative microeconomic implication of the removal of fuel subsidy is the potential for fuel smuggling. The increase in the price of petrol following the removal of fuel subsidy could increase the smuggling of cheaper fuel into Nigeria from neighbouring countries, as opposed to the case when people smuggled Nigeria's cheap fuel to Niger Republic when the fuel subsidy was still in place (Idrisu, 2020). With the removal of fuel subsidy, there is likely to be an increase in the smuggling of cheaper fuel to the rural areas in Nigeria as many people in the rural areas cannot afford to buy fuel at the cost of ₦537.

4.2.4. Rise in Crime

Another negative microeconomic implication of the removal of fuel subsidy is the potential for crime to increase (Shagali and Yusuf, 2022). The increase in the price of petrol following the removal of fuel subsidy might lead to other forms of crime such as theft of petrol from refinery warehouses, people's cars, residential houses and from people's electric generator. The crime rate could worsen as more Nigerians struggle to make ends meet.

4.2.5. Increase in the Prices of Petroleum Products

The removal of fuel subsidy has led to the rise in the prices of petroleum products. This has led to low demand for petrol, and a reduction in the quantity of petrol purchased. The declining demand will narrow the profit of small businesses that rely on petrol. Everyone will feel the effect, but as always, the poor will suffer the most. Although there is the argument that the fuel subsidy removal in 2023 will bring competition among petrol marketers and the competition would drive prices downwards, this expectation is purely academic, and is unlikely to occur in the near future, because the price of crude oil in the international market will largely determine the prices of petroleum products in Nigeria. The implication is that the current soaring prices of petroleum will remain this way for a long time (Raji, 2018).

4.2.6. Loss of Job in the Informal Sector

The removal of fuel subsidy will lead to job loss in the informal sector that rely mostly on PMS or petrol (Houeland, 2022). The formal sector uses mostly diesel for their activities while the informal sector relies mostly on petrol. The rise in petrol prices would lead to the shutdown of small businesses that cannot afford the rising cost of petrol and whose profit margins have been completely eroded by fuel subsidy removal in the formal sector.

5. OTHER IMPLICATIONS

5.1. Environmental Implication of Fuel Subsidy Removal

Given the global push for climate change mitigation, the recent removal of fuel subsidy could help to mitigate climate change in Nigeria. On the positive side, the fuel subsidy removal presents an opportunity for environmentalists to advocate for a transition to clean energy, increased investment in renewable energy sources and the formulation of policies to stimulate the green economy. Nigeria needs a comprehensive strategy to ensure that the fuel subsidy removal benefits the environment. However, fuel subsidy removal could create some environmental challenges if higher fuel prices discourage individuals from utilising private vehicles and lead to a shift to public transportation vehicles that release substantial amounts of pollutants into the environment than private cars. Such pollutants could harm air quality and public health. Furthermore, the public transportation infrastructure in Nigeria is inefficient and there are no sustainable alternatives. Therefore, the Nigerian government should ensure that a part of the saved funds from fuel subsidy removal is used to upgrade the public transportation infrastructure and to support the use of public transport vehicles that contribute little to climate change in order to protect the environment.

5.2. Social and Cultural Implications

The fuel subsidy removal also has social and cultural implications. Historically, Nigerian households have a culture of coping with pain, and this is evident in the little number of protests that have taken place in the last 10 years. Therefore, it is expected that Nigerian households would cope with the adverse price effect of the fuel subsidy removal, and their coping culture could manifest through the immediate change in consumption and spending behaviour. It could lead to a reduction in transportation expenses as many people would avoid unnecessary movements and travels. Households would avoid impulse purchases as a coping strategy, while some would avoid luxury purchases and unnecessary social gatherings that require the spending of money. These cultural practices and societal norms could influence people's reactions to the policy change.

5.3. Economic Diversification and Development Opportunities

The removal of fuel subsidy and the associated rise in petrol should stimulate discussions about how the funds saved from fuel subsidy removal, can be strategically allocated to promote sectors with high growth and job creation potentials, such as renewable energy, technology, agriculture, and manufacturing. Furthermore, certain sectors of the Nigerian economy require little government policy support. Little policy support from the government would position such sectors for high growth e.g., the entertainment, sport betting, financial services, and tourism. These are the sectors which the government needs to focus on for economic diversification, while other sectors that require huge government support should be supported with enabling government policies and investment from private investors.

5.4. Other Socioeconomic Impact

The removal of fuel subsidies might impact different regions in Nigeria. Certain regions would be more vulnerable to the negative consequences of fuel subsidy removal than other regions. The differential regional impact is due to inequality in regional development in the country, as some regions are more developed and have a low poverty rate compared to other regions with a high poverty rate. Therefore, policymakers should consider how regional disparities or inequalities could affect the policies designed to cushion the effect of fuel subsidy removal across all regions in Nigeria. Also, political economy and governance challenges could arise when oligopolists (i.e., the few major marketers) emerge and control the supply or importation of petrol in their favour. The selling price of the oligopolists may be influenced by vested interests. There could also be political dynamics, and other challenges that could affect the success of the fuel subsidy removal regime.

6. CONCLUSION

This paper presents a discussion about the implications of the 2023 fuel subsidy removal in Nigeria with a focus on the macroeconomic and microeconomic implications. The paper uses discourse analysis methodology and offers some insight into the implications of fuel subsidy removal in Nigeria. Fuel subsidy removal has been a highly debated topic in Nigeria, with many economists and analysts calling for its removal, while others think fuel subsidy should remain until a more affordable alternative source of energy is available. Despite these differing views, the fuel subsidy removal has some positive macroeconomic implications such as helping to free up financial resources for the development of other sectors of the economy so that the government can increase spending on education, healthcare, and infrastructure development. The removal of fuel subsidy could also incentivize domestic refineries to produce more petroleum products, reduce Nigeria's dependence on imported fuel and increase employment. The financial resources saved from fuel subsidy removal can also be channelled to the development of critical public infrastructure, reducing the budget deficit, and generating a budget surplus in the near future, reducing government borrowing and reducing pressure on the exchange rate. In contrast, fuel subsidy removal in Nigeria has some negative macroeconomic implications which includes decreasing economic growth and increasing inflation. Fuel subsidy removal also has some positive microeconomic implications which includes the introduction of market-determined pricing mechanisms, curbing corruption associated with fuel subsidy payments, increasing competition, and reinvigorating domestic refineries. In contrast, fuel subsidy removal in Nigeria has some negative microeconomic implications which includes increase in poverty, social unrest, and protest, rise in fuel smuggling, rise in crime, increase in the prices of petroleum products and loss of job in the informal sector.

The conclusion from the discussion in this paper is that the government should carefully consider the impact of removing fuel subsidy on citizens and provide palliatives and other welfare-enhancing initiatives to cushion the effect on individuals, households, and firms. The government could consider increasing the national wage, increasing the salary of civil servants, and introducing monetary palliatives to help the poor cope with the effect of fuel subsidy removal. Other social protection measures and social safety nets, such as unemployment benefits and cash transfers, can be adopted too. The government may also need to dialogue with labour unions to find a middle ground solution that meets the government's need and the needs of the people. It is also important to introduce economic reforms that lead to a more inclusive society. In the end, the success of the fuel subsidy removal will depend on how the government uses the saved funds from the removal of fuel subsidy and what they have achieved with it.

REFERENCES

Adagunodo, M. (2022). The Effect of Oil Receipts and Fuel Subsidy Payment on the Current Account Deficit in Nigeria and Venezuela. Annals of Spiru Haret University. *Economic Series*, *22*(1), 137–152.

Adekunle, I. A., & Oseni, I. O. (2021). Fuel subsidies and carbon emission: Evidence from asymmetric modelling. *Environmental Science and Pollution Research International*, *28*(18), 22729–22741. doi:10.100711356-021-12384-0 PMID:33423202

Akinola, A. O. (2018). Oil subsidy administration in Nigeria. *Globalization, Democracy and Oil Sector Reform in Nigeria*, 231-265.

Antimiani, A., Costantini, V., & Paglialunga, E. (2023). Fossil fuels subsidy removal and the EU carbon neutrality policy. *Energy Economics*, *119*, 106524. doi:10.1016/j.eneco.2023.106524

Asare, J., Reguant, M., Saab, M., & Sacchetto, C. (2020). Low oil prices during COVID-19 and the case for removing fuel subsidies. *Internation Growth Centre*, (August), 1–15.

Bagirov, M., & Mateus, C. (2019). Oil prices, stock markets and firm performance: Evidence from Europe. *International Review of Economics & Finance*, *61*, 270–288. doi:10.1016/j.iref.2019.02.007

Bazilian, M., & Onyeji, I. (2012). Fossil fuel subsidy removal and inadequate public power supply: Implications for businesses. *Energy Policy*, *45*, 1–5. doi:10.1016/j.enpol.2012.02.057

Chatri, F. (2014). Economy-Wide Effects of Fuel Subsidy Removals in Malaysia. *Proceedings of the 9th Malaysian National Economic Conference.*

Chelminski, K. (2018). Fossil fuel subsidy reform in Indonesia. *The politics of fossil fuel subsidies and their reform*, 193-211.

Couharde, C., & Mouhoud, S. (2020). Fossil fuel subsidies, income inequality, and poverty: Evidence from developing countries. *Journal of Economic Surveys*, *34*(5), 981–1006. doi:10.1111/joes.12384

Dartanto, T. (2013). Reducing fuel subsidies and the implication on fiscal balance and poverty in Indonesia: A simulation analysis. *Energy Policy*, *58*, 117–134. doi:10.1016/j.enpol.2013.02.040

Erickson, P., Down, A., Lazarus, M., & Koplow, D. (2017). Effect of subsidies to fossil fuel companies on United States crude oil production. *Nature Energy*, *2*(11), 891–898. doi:10.103841560-017-0009-8

Fathurrahman, F., Kat, B., & Soytaş, U. (2017). Simulating Indonesian fuel subsidy reform: A social accounting matrix analysis. *Annals of Operations Research*, *255*(1-2), 591–615. doi:10.100710479-015-1954-x

Gidigbi, M. O., & Bello, K. M. (2020). Petroleum Subsidy Reduction and Poverty in Nigeria: A Choice between Maintaining the Subsidy or Providing Infrastructural Services Equivalent to the Deadweight Loss. *Asian Development Perspectives*, *11*(1), 70–81.

Harring, N., Jönsson, E., Matti, S., Mundaca, G., & Jagers, S. C. (2023). Cross-national analysis of attitudes towards fossil fuel subsidy removal. *Nature Climate Change*, *13*(3), 244–249. doi:10.103841558-023-01597-5

Harun, M., Mat, S. H. C., Fadzim, W. R., Khan, S. J. M., & Noor, M. S. Z. (2018). The effects of fuel subsidy removal on input costs of productions: Leontief input-output price model. *International Journal of Supply Chain Management*, *7*(5), 529–534.

Houeland, C. (2020). Contentious and institutional politics in a petro-state: Nigeria's 2012 fuel subsidy protests. *The Extractive Industries and Society*, *7*(4), 1230–1237. doi:10.1016/j.exis.2020.05.010

Houeland, C. (2022). The social contract and industrial citizenship: Nigerian trade unions' role in the recurring fuel subsidy protests. *Africa*, *92*(5), 860–879. doi:10.1017/S0001972022000523

Idrisu, B. (2020). *Fossil fuel subsidy reform for sustainable development in Nigeria: the role of renewable energy diffusion*. University of Delaware.

Itumo, A., & Onyejiuba, E. I. (2019). Oil Subsidy And Development Of Local Refineries In Nigeria: A Critical Analysis. *African Journal of Politics and Administrative Studies*, *12*, 1.

Kyle, J. (2018). Local corruption and popular support for fuel subsidy reform in Indonesia. *Comparative Political Studies*, *51*(11), 1472–1503. doi:10.1177/0010414018758755

Lin, B., & Li, A. (2012). Impacts of removing fossil fuel subsidies on China: How large and how to mitigate? *Energy*, *44*(1), 741–749. doi:10.1016/j.energy.2012.05.018

Majekodunmi, A. (2013). The political economy of fuel subsidy removal in Nigeria. *International Journal of Management and Social Sciences Research*, *2*(7), 76–81.

McCulloch, N., Moerenhout, T., & Yang, J. (2021). Fuel subsidy reform and the social contract in Nigeria: A micro-economic analysis. *Energy Policy*, *156*, 112336. doi:10.1016/j.enpol.2021.112336 PMID:34483438

Mohammed, A. B., Ahmed, F. F., & Adedeji, A. N. (2020). Assessment of Impact of Fuel Subsidy Removal on Socio-economic Characteristics: A Survey of Households in Maiduguri, Borno State, Nigeria. *Journal of Business and Economic Development*, *5*(1), 10. doi:10.11648/j.jbed.20200501.12

Nowag, J., Mundaca, L., & Åhman, M. (2021). Phasing out fossil fuel subsidies in the EU? Exploring the role of state aid rules. *Climate Policy*, *21*(8), 1037–1052. doi:10.1080/14693062.2021.1965523

Ogunode, N. J., Ahmed, I., & Olugbenga, A. V. (2023). Application of Petrol Subsidy Funds to Address the Problems of Universal Basic Education for Sustainable Development in Nigeria. Web of Scholars. *Multidimensional Research Journal*, *2*(1), 1–9.

Okongwu, C. J., & Imoisi, S. E. (2022). Removal of Petrol Subsidy: Legal Implications for the Nigerian Economy. *Nnamdi Azikiwe University Journal of International Law and Jurisprudence*, *13*(2), 135–139.

Olujobi, O. J. (2021). Deregulation of the downstream petroleum industry: An overview of the legal quandaries and proposal for improvement in Nigeria. *Heliyon*, *7*(4), e06848. doi:10.1016/j.heliyon.2021.e06848 PMID:33997390

Omitogun, O., Longe, A. E., Muhammad, S., & Adekomi, I. J. (2021). Environmental Impact of Economic Growth and Fuel Subsidy in Nigeria. *Economic Insights - Trends and Challenges*, *2021*(1), 1. doi:10.51865/EITC.2021.01.03

Omotosho, B. S. (2020). Oil price shocks, fuel subsidies and macroeconomic (in) stability in Nigeria. *Fuel Subsidies and Macroeconomic (In) stability in Nigeria.*

Ouyang, X., & Lin, B. (2014). Impacts of increasing renewable energy subsidies and phasing out fossil fuel subsidies in China. *Renewable & Sustainable Energy Reviews*, *37*, 933–942. doi:10.1016/j.rser.2014.05.013

Ovaga, O. H., & Okechukwu, M. E. (2022). Subsidy in the downstream oil sector and the fate of the masses in Nigeria. *Kuwait Chapter of Arabian Journal of Business and Management Review*, *1*(6), 1–20.

Ozili, P. (2022). COVID-19 in Africa: Socio-economic impact, policy response and opportunities. *The International Journal of Sociology and Social Policy*, *42*(3/4), 177–200. doi:10.1108/IJSSP-05-2020-0171

Ozili, P. K., & Arun, T. (2023). Spillover of COVID-19: impact on the Global Economy. In *Managing inflation and supply chain disruptions in the global economy* (pp. 41–61). IGI Global.

Ozili, P. K., & Ozen, E. (2021). Global energy crisis: impact on the global economy. In *Proceedings of IAC in Budapest 2021* (Vol. 1, pp. 85-89). Czech Institute of Academic Education.

Parry, I., Black, M. S., & Vernon, N. (2021). *Still not getting energy prices right: a global and country update of fossil fuel subsidies*. International Monetary Fund.

Raji, A. (2018). *Fuel subsidy removal and the lives of rural dwellers in Nigeria* [Doctoral dissertation]. Department of Sociology, Faculty of Social Sciences, University of Ilorin, Ilorin, Nigeria.

Sampedro, J., Arto, I., & González-Eguino, M. (2017). Implications of switching fossil fuel subsidies to solar: A case study for the European Union. *Sustainability, 10*(1), 50.

Shagali, A. A., & Yusuf, R. (2022). Political economy of fuel subsidy removal in Nigeria: Issues, challenges and the way forward. *Zamfara Journal of Politics and Development*, *3*(3), 12–12.

Sheyin, A. O. (2018). The Effects of Subsidy Removal on the Escalation of Political Corruption in Nigeria. *KIU Journal of Social Sciences*, *4*(3), 157–168.

Su, C. W., Qin, M., Tao, R., Moldovan, N. C., & Lobonţ, O. R. (2020). Factors driving oil price—From the perspective of United States. *Energy*, *197*, 117219. doi:10.1016/j.energy.2020.117219

Sweeney, S. (2020, January). Weaponizing the Numbers: The Hidden Agenda Behind Fossil-Fuel Subsidy Reform. *New Labor Forum*, *29*(1), 87–92. doi:10.1177/1095796019893317

Umeji, G., & Eleanya, E. (2021). *Assessing the Impact of Fuel Subsidy Removal in Nigeria on the Poor in the COVID-19 Era*. SERBD-International Journal of Multidisciplinary Sciences.

Chapter 8
Income Inequalities in Developing Countries:
A Performance Analysis

Betül İnam
Bilecik Seyh Edebali University, Turkey

Dilek Murat
Bursa Uludag University, Turkey

ABSTRACT

The welfare of a country is related to how equitably its national income is distributed, rather than its wealth. The increase in income inequalities between individuals or social classes causes the deterioration of social peace and stability and a slowdown in economic development and growth. In this study, the effect of more than one socio-economic factor on income inequalities was examined in 35 developing countries. The 2019 data compiled for the selected countries were analyzed with the ARAS method. From the findings of the ARAS method, which was carried out using the aforementioned weighting method, it was determined that the countries with the best performance in terms of income justice were Chechia, Estonia, Slovakia, Thailand, and Hungary. The results of the analysis showed that Colombia, Brazil, Mexico, Bolivia, and Bangladesh were the countries with the highest income inequality. The ARAS findings used in the study are theoretically and expectedly satisfactory.

INTRODUCTION

Income inequality is a multifaceted problem with deep roots. It is not possible to say that the inequalities in income distribution in the world show a regular tendency. The history of inequality is shaped by strong social changes as well as economic events. Income and wealth differences between different income groups in the society can be the cause or result of the changes. Economies with high income inequalities become unstable and unsustainable in the long run. The deepening of income differences between individuals or social groups causes an increase in social conflicts and deterioration of social

DOI: 10.4018/978-1-6684-8903-1.ch008

peace and stability (Stiglitz, 2015: 146). Despite the increasing material wealth around the world, the gap between the rich and the poor is increasing day by day. The richest 10% earn 40% of global income, while the poorest 10% have share between 2-7% of global income. Rising income inequality threatens social cohesion, slows economic growth and frustrates efforts to eradicate poverty (EU, 2017: 197). Global income among individuals have two basic features: inequality among different nations and regions and inequality within the particular country itself. In the contemporary global economy, these two constituents of disparity are considerable. Inequality between different nations of the world is very striking today although the emerging economies have been catching up to developed world over the past four decades. If all countries in the world have a rapid rise in income inequality like the USA since 1980, the richest 1% of the world will have a 28% share of the global income in 2050, while the poorest 50% of the global will receive a 6% share of the global income. In cases where income inequality is relatively low, as in European countries, it is estimated that the share of the richest 1% in global income will decrease to 19% in 2050, and the share of the poorest 50% in global income will rise to 13% (Alvaredo et.al, 2018: 250). Recent studies show that inequalities are increasing rapidly around the world during the Covid 19 pandemic. Between 2021 and 2019, the wealth of the top grew by 0.001%, while average global wealth is estimated to have risen by just 1%. On top of that, global billionaire wealth increased by more than 50% between 2019 and 2021 (Chancel et.al, 2022: 46). Decreasing inequalities and ensuring no one is left behind are crucial steps to be taken toward achieving the Sustainable Development Goals. The effects of the COVID-19 pandemic seem to overturn any positive evolution of narrowing income inequality. The pandemic has also thicken the structural and systematic discrimination up and eventually emerging markets and developing economies have experienced slow recoveries against disparities in income. The number of refugees and migrant deaths worldwide reached at the highest level in 2021. Meanwhile, the war in Ukraine has turned nasty, forcing millions of people away from their homes and creating one of the largest refugee crises in recent history.

The factors affecting income inequalities have been the subject of many studies in the literature. However, studies generally focus on the relationship between a single factor and income inequalities. In a small number of studies, the effect of more than one factor on income inequalities has been examined for various country groups.

In this study, the performance of developing countries on income justice using multiple economic and social variables are analyzed. In this context, first, the related literature is reviewed in the background section and the focal point of our investigation is presented. In the the chapter of income inequalities in the world and developing countries, the information about the general view of income inequalities in the world and especially in developing economies is given from past to present. In the data and methodology section, the data employed in the analysis and methodology is elaborated in a detailed form. There commendations for future studies are provided in the part of the future directions for research. After the analytical findings are presented in the empirical findings section, the conclusion section includes comments and evaluations related to our case study.

BACKGROUND

Distribution of personal income is based on neo-classical theory and is revealed by the application of income tax. (Karacan, 2014: 40). What is important in personal income distribution is the amount of income, not solely its source and component. The differences (degree of inequality) between the highest and lowest income groups and the mechanisms that lead to this unequal distribution are examined. In the distribution of personal income, the amount of income earned by individuals and consumer units in a certain period is taken into account, and the total income per capita shows the level of economic development. Personal income distribution is used to measure income inequalities in a country and allows international comparisons (Öztürk, 2009: 15). Personal income distribution is effective in the interpretation of income inequalities and thus in shaping the legislation in areas such as taxation and social security. Many measurement methods have been developed to qualify income inequality. In today's studies, some criteria are used more frequently than others. These criteria allow comparisons between countries and are sensitive to transfers, changes and movements in income. The Gini Coefficient is one of the most used methods to measure inequalities in income distribution. The level of inequality is measured by a single coefficient between 0 and 1. The closer the coefficient is to 1, the greater the inequality is, and the closer to zero, the less inequity. In practical use, a gini coefficient below 0.20 indicates low inequality, between 0.20 and 0.50 represents moderate inequality, and above 0.50 depicts high inequality. Such a grouping provides the advantage of being relatively insensitive to the presence of abnormal values above or below the distribution (Haidich and Ioannidis, 2004: 342).

Although there are many studies in the literature on the factors affecting income inequalities, a complex theory covering all the factors affecting this situation has not yet been found. Studies on income inequalities focus either on a single factor or on several factors (Kaasa, 2005: 5). The study of Simon Kuznets in 1955 was the first to measure social inequalities empirically. For this calculation, Kuznets used the federal income tax returns of the USA between 1913-1948 and the US national income estimates (Piketty, 2014: 13). Kuznets argued that income inequality generally increases in the early stages of economic development and then decreases spontaneously in later periods. This inverse U relationship between inequality and development is known as the Kuznets Curve. In the advanced stages of development, inequality in income distribution will begin to decrease automatically with the increase in income (Deutsch and Silber, 2004: 110). After this study, many studies have been conducted examining the relationship between per capita income and income inequalities. While some of them reached similar conclusions with Kuznets (Dawson (1997), List and Gallet (1999), Tsakloglou (1988), Barro (2000), Dağdeviren and Topuz (2020)), some of them obtained results rejecting the Kuznets hypothesis (Ravallion and Chen (2022), Wu and Yao (2015), Cook and Uchida (2008)).

Gupta, et al. (2002) focused on the relationship between corruption and income inequalities. They determined that a decrease of 2.52 points in a country's corruption index caused an increase of approximately 4.4 points in the Gini coefficient. There are many studies that found similar results between corruption and income inequalities (Li et al. (2000), Gyimah-Brempong (2002), Dinçer et al (2012), Policardo et.al(2019), Inam et.al) (2019)). However, there are also others who find different results for corruption and income inequalities. In a study conducted for Latin American countries, it was concluded that low corruption rates increase income inequalities, and it was emphasized that the reason for this might be the misdirection of institutional reform policies (Andres and Dobson, 2011).

Thalossinos, et al. (2012) examined the relationship between income inequalities and inflation for thirteen EU countries and found that inflation had a drastic effect on income inequalities. They also stated that all control variables, except GDP, increase income inequalities. Narob (2015) examined the relationship between inflation and income inequalities for 46 developing countries. It has been understood that inflation has a positive and significant impact on income inequalities. Namini and Hudson (2019), in their study for two groups of developed and developing countries, found that there was no bidirectional Granger causality relationship between inflation and income inequalities in the short run, but also they detected a Granger causality relationship for both groups in the long run. They concluded that monetary policy can be effective in reducing income inequalities. Deyshappriya (2017), in his study of 33 Asian countries, concluded that while education and labor force participation reduce inequality, high inflation, political risk, terms of trade and unemployment rate increase it dramatically. Güder (2019) examined the factors affecting income distribution in high-income countries and found that inflation, economic growth, unemployment, and public income variables increase income inequalities. In the same study, he concluded that economic globalization contributed to the improvement of income distribution in these countries. Zandi et al. (2022) examined the dynamic role of corruption, inflation and unemployment on income inequality in 12 Asian countries and found that these variables were positively related to income inequalities. Engel et al. (1999) examined the relationship between taxes and income inequalities in Chile. They found that there was no significant change in pre- and post-tax income inequalities. They concluded that focusing on public expenditures would yield better results in eliminating imbalances in income distribution in developing countries. Joumard et al. (2012) stated that taxes and transfers reduce inequalities in disposable income in OECD countries and emphasized that the redistributive effect of taxes and transfers varies in countries according to size, mix and progressivity. Binder and Haup (2022) compared the USA and Germany in their study examining the relationship between tax systems and income inequalities. They concluded that increasing inequality was prevented by using progressive income tax and credit facilities provided to low-income groups in the USA. Malla and Pathranarakul (2022) focused on the impact of fiscal policies on income inequalities for developed and developing countries. They emphasized that income tax can reduce income inequalities in developing countries, and they revealed that public expenditures are negatively related to income inequalities only in developed countries. Duncan and Peter (2016) found that the negative impact of the progressivity of the personnel income tax (PIT) structure on income inequalities is stronger, especially in countries with developed democratic institutions. Larch (2012) found that income inequalities make fiscal discipline difficult, and the link between income distribution and financial performance is affected by political factors. Bartak, et al. (2022), examined the relationship between income inequalities and public debt and found that sudden increases in public expenditures increase income inequalities and public debt together. Lee and Lee (2018) investigated the impact of country risks, including economic, financial and political risks on income inequality in their study using data from 110 countries. They found that higher economic and political risks often lead to higher inequality. Lee and Lee also emphasized that it is important for policy makers to reduce country risk and maintain political and economic stability in order to improve income distribution. Wu et al. (2022) investigated the impact of country risks and geopolitical risks on income inequalities for 19 emerging market economies. They determined that all risks are positively related to income inequalities and found that all risks increase income inequalities.

MAIN FOCUS OF THE CHAPTER

The focus of this study is to determine the performance of selected developing countries on income justice. For this purpose, a dataset was created by using the factors affecting income inequalities in various aspects and the ARAS method, which is a Multi Criteria Decision Making method, was applied to these data. Today this method is used in many fields, but its use in the field of economy is newer than other fields. This method is used in solving decision problems, ranking countries and businesses, and

Table 1. Income inequality in selected regions 1820-2000

Years	Western Europe	Eastern Europe	Western Offshoots	Latin America Caribbean	East Asia	South-Southeast Asia	MENA Countries	Sub-Sahran Africa
1820	54	51	51		45	35	-	53
1850	45	49	42	37	34	38	46	46
1870	50	48	51	48	41	42	52	50
1890	41	36	45	41	32	34	35	36
1910	46	39	50	45	40	35	40	42
1929	48	40	52	55	44	36	48	48
1950	42	35	39	47	33	39	43	43
1960	40	30	37	54	32	39	49	53
1970	38	26	36	53	29	40	47	49
1980	36	27	37	52	31	35	47	46
1990	38	27	39	52	34	41	46	47
2000	40	36	44	54	43	48	46	49

Source: van Zanden, J. L. et al. (eds.) How was life? Global Well-Being Since 1820, OECD Publishing
Notes: The so-called "Western Offshoots" include the United States, Canada, and Australia.

evaluating the performance of countries on the relevant subject by including many economic and social criteria of varying importance in the analysis.

INCOME INEQUALITIES IN WORLD AND DEVELOPING COUNTRIES

Although the pursuit of equality in every society reflects an ideal situation, achieving absolute equality was not possible in the past, nor does it seem possible in the future. It is not easy to say that the inequalities in income distribution in the world show a regular trend. The history of inequality is shaped by strong social changes as well as economic events. Income and wealth differences between different income groups in society continue to be the cause or result of the changes. Today, the gap between the life standards of people living in rich and poor economies is unpredictable compared to the period before the 1800s. While in the pre-industrial period the income difference between the societies with the best economic conditions and the worst ones was 3-4 times, this difference has increased to 40 to 1 in the modern world (Clark, 2013: 213). The table below shows the estimated Gini coefficients for selected regions between 1820-2000.

As can be seen from Table 1, Latin America and the Caribbean was the region with the highest rates of intra-country inequality in the twentieth century. While it had the lowest level of inequality with Asian countries in the nineteenth century, unfortunately, this situation was completely reversed in the later periods. It can be said that economic growth leads to the widening of inequalities within the country in both geographies (van Zanden et al. 2014, 209). In the 1950-1990 period, it is striking that inequalities in eastern Europe were considerably lower than in other regions. However, with the collapse of the Soviet Union in 1990, it is clear that there was a rapid expansion in inequalities. In Western Europe, from the 1820s to the 1980s, inequalities in income distribution declined rapidly. After the 1980s, there was a slight increase. In the USA, Canada and Australia, which are called the European extension, a similar trend to Western Europe was observed until the 1980s, but a rapid increase in income inequalities was observed after 1990. Although there is a decrease in income inequalities from time to time in the Middle East, North Africa and Sub-Saharan Africa, it can be said that high income inequalities have been dominant throughout history.

Income inequality has increased rapidly in North America and Asia since 1980, while it has followed a relatively moderate course in Europe. In the Middle East, Sub-Saharan Africa and Brazil, it has stabilized at extremely high levels. In this process, income growth for individuals between the poorest 50% and the richest 1% of the global population has been stagnant or even zero. This includes low- and middle-income groups in North America and Europe. On a global basis, the wealthiest 1% took a 16% share of global income in 1980, while this ratio rose to 22% in 2000 and then declined to 20%. The reason for the decrease in the rate after 2000 is the decline in the average income inequality in the countries (Alverado et al., 2018: 40). Figure 1 shows the shares of different income groups from national income in various regions of the world in 2021.

Figure 1. The poorest half lags behind: Bottom 50%, middle 40% and top 10% income shares across the world in 2021
Source: Chancel et al. (2022), World Inequality Report (2022), World Inequality Lab wir2022.wid.world

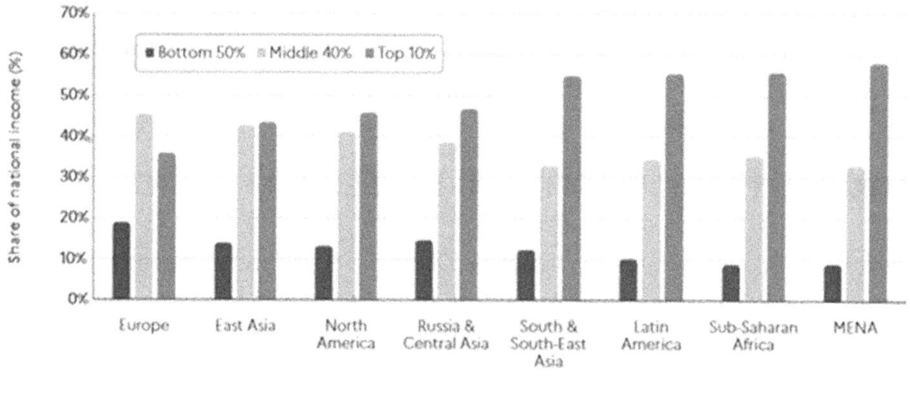

As seen in Figure 1, the place where the poorest 50% receives the highest share of national income is European countries, where the rate is approximately 20%. It is observed that the countries where the poorest 50% have the lowest share of national income are Sub-Saharan Africa and MENA countries. When we look at the shares of the richest 10%, it is clear that the highest ratios are MENA, Sub-Saharan Africa, Latin America and South & South-East Asia, in contrast to the Bottom 50%. It would not be wrong to say that the share of income groups in national income in the developed countries group called North America is more unfair compared to Europe. In these countries, the share of the richest 10% is higher than in Europe and East Asia. In the Bottom 50% group, it is observed that they have a worse rate than Europe, East Asia, Russia and Central Asia.

Income inequalities are higher in developing countries than in developed economies. In most major developing economies, income inequality has increased over the past three decades. Income inequalities in China, Russia, South Africa and India, which are members of the G-20, are higher than in the past

(Derviş and Qureshi, 2016, 2). In the process that started with the collapse of the Union of Societies, the share of the poorest 50% in Russia decreased rapidly and decreased to about 15% today. Similar to Russia, the share of the poorest 50% has declined rapidly in India and China over the last three decades. This is also true for North America. In the Middle East and Brazil, unlike the others, the share of the poorest 50% in national income has been increasing in recent years (Alverado et al., 2018, 45). While an unequal distribution of income negatively affects growth in developing countries, it also prevents the formation of economic and political institutions necessary for growth and investment. In countries with multi-ethnic structures, income distribution disorders have a negative effect on civil and social life (Birdsall, 2007, 3). Income transfers made in favor of low-income social groups from high-income social groups in order to ensure fair income distribution have an effect on increasing social benefit and welfare. The social cost of these transfers is low, but the social benefit is high. In addition, although justice in income distribution increases equality of opportunity among individuals, it also helps to realize important functions such as maintaining price stability in the economy and performing full work (Türk, 1979, 259). Gini Indexes of selected developing countries are given in Figure 2.

Figure 2. Gini Index (2019) in selected developing countries
Source: Compiled from World Bank data.

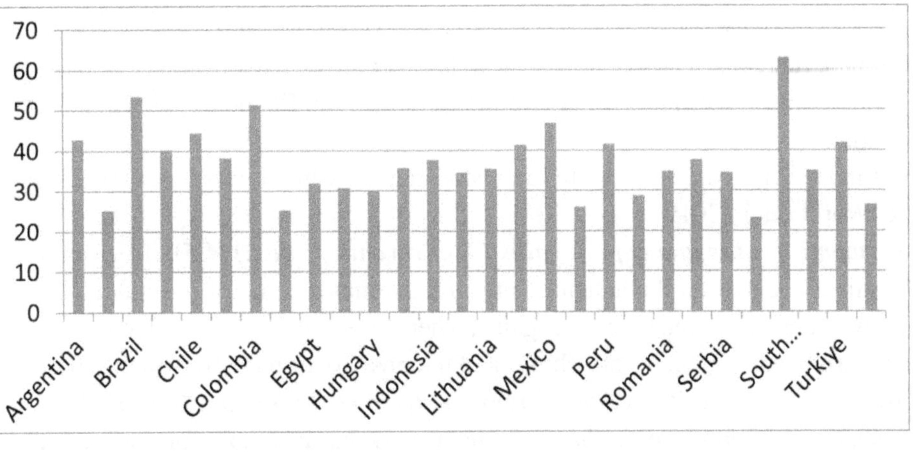

As can be seen from Figure 2, income inequalities are high in most of the developing countries. In countries such as Argentina, Brazil, South Africa, Turkey and Mexico, the Gini Index is above 40 points. On the other hand, relatively lower Gini index values are observed in developing European countries, countries that left the former Soviet Union, or countries that were ruled by a communist regime before the 1990s.

DATASET AND METHODOLOGY

Data compiled for some developing countries selected in the study were used to analyze income inequality performance. A total of thirty-five developing countries, including Albania, Argentina, Bangladesh, Belarus, Bolivia, Brazil, Bulgaria, Chile, China, Colombia, Czechia, Dominican Republic, Egypt, Estonia, Hungary, India, Indonesia, Kazakhstan, Latvia, Lithuania, Malaysia, Mexico, Moldova, Pakistan, Philippines, Poland, Romania, Russia, Serbia, Slovakia, South Africa, Thailand, Tunisia and Turkey have been involved in the study. Most of the data for 2019, which is the most recent year available for these countries, has been compiled from the World Bank data base. Gini index, inflation rate, Corruption Perception Index (CPI), Rule of Law (RL), taxes on income, profits and capital gains (tax), unemployment rate, GDP per capita, social assistance expenditure (soc_ass), bottom_50% income share refers to the decision criteria to be used in performance analysis. Detailed explanations for these variables are given below.

Gini index (min.) (C1): Gini index measures the extent to which the distribution of income (or, in some cases, consumption expenditure) among individuals or households within an economy deviates from a perfectly equal distribution. Gini index of 0 represents perfect equality, while an index of 100 implies perfect inequality. (World Bank, 2019).

Inflation rate consumer prices (annual %)(min.) (C2): Inflation as measured by the consumer price index reflects the annual percentage change in the cost to the average consumer of acquiring a basket of goods and services that may be fixed or changed at specified intervals, such as yearly (World Bank, 2019).

Corruption Perception Index (CPI) (max.) (C3): Refers to an index that scores countries on the perceived levels of government corruption by country. Scores range from zero to 100, with zero indicating high levels of corruption and 100 indicating low levels. (https://www.transparency.org/en/cpi/2019)

Rule of Law (RL) (max.) (C4): The RL variable is a sub-index of the Political Risk Index that expresses the legal regulations. The Political Risk Index accounts for the overall risk of a country and the methodology of the index considers the risk attached to turmoil, financial transfers, direct investments, and export markets.

The higher index values are attached to low risk countries while lower index values represent higher political risk (World Bank, 2019).

Taxes on income, profits and capital gains (% of revenue) (max.) (C5): Taxes on income, profits, and capital gains are levied on the actual or presumptive net income of individuals, on the profits of corporations and enterprises, and on capital gains, whether realized or not, on land, securities, and other assets. Intragovernmental payments are eliminated in consolidation (World Bank, 2019).

Unemployment, total (% of total labor force) (modeled ILO estimate) (min.) (C6): Unemployment refers to the share of the labor force that is without work but available for and seeking employment (World Bank 2019).

GDP per capita (current US$) (max.) (C7): GDP per capita is gross domestic product divided by mid-year population. GDP is the sum of gross value added by all resident producers in the economy plus any product taxes and minus any subsidies not included in the value of the products.

Social assistance expenditure (%GDP) (max.) (C8): Social assistance (SA) expenditure refers to spending on benefits and administrative costs. Annual social assistance (SA) expenditure is calculated by aggregating program-level social assistance data for the most recent available year between the period of 2015-2021. Expenditure is aggregated into standardized social assistance categories, which are then aggregated to calculate overall social assistance expenditure. Total social assistance expenditure is divided by country GDP (current values) to calculate the indicator.

Bottom %50 income share (max.) (C9): Nüfusun en yoksul yüzde %50'sinin milli gelirden aldığı yüzdelik payı ifade etmektedir.

ARAS Method

The ARAS method, which is adopted as a new approach in solving MCDM problems, was introduced by Zavadskas and Turskis (2010). This method aims to rank the decision alternatives according to the utility function value under various criteria. In this approach, a utility function value determines the relative efficiency of one decision alternative with respect to the other decision alternative. While the ARAS method evaluates the performance of decision alternatives, it reveals the proportional similarity of each decision alternative to the ideal decision alternative (Özbek, 2017: 69). The difference of this method from other methods is the comparison of the utility function values of the decision alternatives with the utility function value of the optimal alternative added to the decision problem by the decision maker. The ARAS method is seen as one of the most suitable for the purpose of proportional rating among other MCDM methods (Ayçin, 2019: 52).

The ARAS method can be summarized in the following five steps (Zavadskas and Turskis, 2010: 163-165; Zavadskas et al., 2010: 126-129; Sliogerience et al., 2013: 14-15):

Step 1: The decision matrix is created for m alternative (i=0,1,2,…,m) and n criterion (j=1,2,…,n)

$$X = \begin{bmatrix} x_{01} & x_{02} & \cdots & x_{0n} \\ x_{11} & x_{12} & \cdots & x_{1n} \\ \cdots & \cdots & \cdots & \cdots \\ x_{m1} & x_{m2} & \cdots & x_{mn} \end{bmatrix} \quad (1)$$

In this method, unlike other MCDM methods, a line consisting of optimal values for each criterion is included. In cases where this value is not known, if the criterion is benefit (maximization) oriented, $x_{0j} = \underset{i}{maks}\ \mathrm{x}_{\mathrm{ij}}$ equation is used for the calculation and when it is cost (minimization) oriented, $x_{0j} = \underset{i}{\min}\ \mathrm{x}_{\mathrm{ij}}$ equation is conducted.

Step 2: Decision matrix is normalized considering Equations 2 and 3. In this process, if the criterion is benefit (maximization) oriented,

$$\overline{x}_{\mathrm{ij}} = \frac{x_{ij}}{\underset{\mathrm{i}}{\max}\ (x_{ij})} \quad (2)$$

$$\overline{x}_{\mathrm{ij}} = \frac{\underset{\mathrm{i}}{\min}\ (x_{ij})}{x_{ij}} \quad (3)$$

equations are used and as a result, normalize decision matrix in Equation 4 is created ((i=0,1,2,…,m) and (j=1,2,…,n)).

$$\bar{X} = \begin{bmatrix} \bar{x}_{01} & \bar{x}_{02} & \cdots & \bar{x}_{0n} \\ \bar{x}_{11} & \bar{x}_{12} & \cdots & \bar{x}_{1n} \\ \cdots & \cdots & \cdots & \cdots \\ \bar{x}_{m1} & \bar{x}_{m2} & \cdots & \bar{x}_{mn} \end{bmatrix} \tag{4}$$

Step 3: A weighted normalized decision matrix is created using w_j weights with $0<w_j<1$ feature. Here, condition $\sum_{j=1}^{n} w_j = 1$ must also be satisfied. The normalized decision matrix, $\hat{x}_{ij} = \bar{x}_{ij} w_j$ and (i=0,1,2,…,m) (j=1,2,…,n), is calculated as in Equation 5.

$$\hat{X} = \begin{bmatrix} \hat{x}_{01} & \hat{x}_{02} & \cdots & \hat{x}_{0n} \\ \hat{x}_{11} & \hat{x}_{12} & \cdots & \hat{x}_{1n} \\ \cdots & \cdots & \cdots & \cdots \\ \hat{x}_{m1} & \hat{x}_{m2} & \cdots & \hat{x}_{mn} \end{bmatrix} \tag{5}$$

Step 4: At this stage, the optimality function value for each decision alternative is calculated with the help of Equation 6 by using the weighted normalized decision matrix.

$$S_i = \sum_{j=1}^{n} \hat{x}_{ij} \; (i=0,1,2,\ldots,m) \tag{6}$$

S_i value is the optimality value of i. decision alternative. The largest calculated S_i value is considered the best, and the smallest S_i value is considered the worst. Considering the calculation process, the value of S_i is directly related to x_{ij} and w_j, which have an effect on the final result. Therefore, S_i is considered a more efficient alternative with a higher optimality function value.

Step 5: By proportioning the optimality function value S_i of a decision alternative to the optimality function value S_0 of the best alternative, the benefit degree K_i is calculated with the help of Equation 7.

$$K_i = \frac{S_i}{S_0} \; (i=0,1,2,\ldots,m) \tag{7}$$

The relative efficiency of the alternatives is determined by ordering the K_i values calculated in the range of [0, 1], and as a result, the evaluation of the alternatives is made.

EMPIRICAL FINDINGS

In this study, the performances of some selected developing countries, including Turkey, on the fairness of income distribution were analyzed. In this research, in which thirty-five countries and nine criteria were taken into account, the data of 2019 were examined with the help of the ARAS method. Gini index, inflation rate, corruption perception index, Rule of Law index, taxes on income, profits and capital gains, unemployment rate, GDP per capita, social assistance expenditures, bottom_50% income share variables, which are thought to affect income distribution, were included as decision criteria for the research. The Decision matrix, which constitutes the first step of the study, is given in Table 2.

The variables defined as criteria for analysis can be seen in Table 2. When the Gini values given in the table are examined, it is seen that the countries with the fairest income distribution are Slovakia, Belarus, Czechia, Moldova and Kazakhstan. South Africa, Brazil and Colombia, on the other hand, are countries with high income inequalities. Turkey ranked 8th from the last on the list in terms of income justice. The countries with the highest inflation rates were Argentina, Turkey, Pakistan, Egypt and Tunisia, while the countries with the lowest values were Thailand, Malaysia and Albania. Countries with the lowest CPI scores are Bangladesh, Russia, Dominican Republic, Mexico and Bolivia, while the countries with the highest CPI are Estonia, Chili and Lithuania. Turkey is among the countries with a medium CPI score. The countries with the highest Rule of Law values are Chechia, Latvia and Tunisia, while the countries with the lowest values in this variable are Mexico, South Africa and Colombia.

Thailand, Chechia and Philippines have the lowest unemployment rates, while South Africa, Tunisia and Turkey have the highest unemployment rates. Chechia, Estonia and Lithuania have the highest GDP per capita, while Pakistan, India and Bangladesh have the lowest. In terms of this criterion, Turkey has an average per capita income among thirty-five countries. In terms of the bottom 50% income share criterion, the countries with the highest rate are Chechia, Slovakia and Belarus. Countries such as South Africa, Mexico and Chile, where the lowest levels of this criterion are observed, stand out as the countries with the highest income inequalities.

As in all MCDM methods, weighting of the criteria is an important step in the application of the ARAS method. Various methods are used for this purpose. The weights given with the help of the subjective weighting method preferred in this study are presented in Table 3. Existing literature and theoretical expectations were taken into account while giving these weights.

When the subjective results given in Table 3 are examined, it can be seen that the criteria with the highest weight are Gini index, bottom 50% income share, corruption perception index(CPI) and GDP per capita. These criteria are governed by the Rule of Law index, inflation rate, taxes, unemployment rate, social assistance expenditure monitors the variables. The findings of the ARAS method applied using the aforementioned subjective weights are as in Table 4.

According to the findings presented in Table 4, the best performing countries in terms of fair income distribution are Chechia, Estonia, Slovakia, Thailand and Hungary, respectively. Similarly, Colombia, Brazil and Mexico are the countries with the highest income inequality. In other words, it can be said that they are the worst performing countries in terms of fair income distribution.

Table 2. Decision matrix

Country/Criteria	C1	C2	C3	C4	C5	C6	C7	C8	C9
Albania	30.1	1.4	35	0.5	18.4	11.5	5.396	1.87	0.18
Argentina	42.9	53.5	45	0.33	8.4	9.8	9.963	3.26	0.13
Bangladesh	32.4	5.6	26	0.33	25.4	4.4	2.122	0.77	0.17
Belarus	25.3	5.6	45	0.58	3	4.2	6.837	2.38	0.22
Bolivia	41.6	1.8	31	0.42	14	3.7	3.472	1.9	0.1
Brazil	53.5	3.7	35	0.42	24.9	12.1	8.845	1.28	0.1
Bulgaria	40.3	3.1	43	0.5	15.7	4.2	9.879	1.09	0.16
Chile	44.4	2.6	67	0.67	38	7.3	14.631	3.53	0.06
China	38.2	2.9	41	0.58	18.9	4.6	10.143	1.05	0.13
Colombia	51.3	3.5	37	0.33	21.8	10	6.438	3.44	0.08
Czechia	25.3	2.8	56	0.83	16.8	2	23.664	0.79	0.25
Dominican Rep.	41.9	1.8	28	0.5	27.2	6.2	8.173	1.31	0.12
Egypt	31.9	9.2	35	0.5	24.1	7.9	2.869	2.92	0.15
Estonia	30.8	2.3	74	0.67	19.8	4.5	23.424	2.25	0.16
Hungary	30	3.3	44	0.67	16.1	3.4	16.783	1.83	0.22
India	35.7	3.7	41	0.75	45.6	6.5	2.047	1.43	0.13
Indonesia	37.6	3	40	0.42	39.4	3.6	4.151	0.55	0.12
Kazakhstan	27.8	5.2	34	0.58	30.9	4.8	9.812	1.62	0.16
Latvia	34.5	2.8	56	0.83	4.7	6.3	17.945	1.02	0.17
Lithuania	35.3	2.3	60	0.67	29.1	6.3	19.595	0.43	0.07
Malaysia	41.2	0.7	53	0.67	46.6	3.3	11.132	0.57	0.17
Mexico	46.7	3.6	29	0.25	36.4	3.5	10.145	1.62	0.06
Moldova	26	4.8	32	0.67	11.7	5.1	4.493	1.11	0.17
Pakistan	29.6	10.6	32	0.5	19	4.8	1.437	0.41	0.17
Peru	41.6	2.3	36	0.5	28.8	3.4	6.955	1.23	0.09
Philippines	42.3	2.4	34	0.42	37.1	2.2	3.413	0.55	0.14
Poland	28.8	2.2	58	0.58	13.3	3.3	15.699	1.04	0.19
Romania	34.8	3.8	44	0.58	15.2	3.9	12.958	1.21	0.15
Russia	37.7	4.5	28	0.5	2.6	4.5	11.536	1.17	0.16
Serbia	34.5	1.8	39	0.61	15.2	10.4	7.417	1.19	0.17
Slovakia	23.2	2.7	50	0.67	19	5.8	19.383	1.48	0.24
South Africa	63	4.1	44	0.33	47.5	25.5	6.688	4.61	0.05
Thailand	34.9	0.7	36	0.42	31.7	0.7	7.63	1.6	0.13
Tunisia	32.8	6.7	43	0.83	26.7	15.1	3.477	0.48	0.16
Turkiye	41.9	15.2	39	0.5	18.5	13.7	9.103	1.13	0.14

Table 3. Criteria weights

Criteria	Code	Weights (wj) Subjective
Gini	C1	0.2
Inflation rate	C2	0.05
Corruption perception index	C3	0.15
Rule of law	C4	0.1
Taxes on income. profits and capital gains	C5	0.05
Unemployment rate	C6	0.05
GDP_per capita	C7	0.15
Social assistance exp.	C8	0.05
Bottom_%50	C9	0.2

FUTURE DIRECTIONS FOR RESEARCH

It is very difficult to set a standard for the data of developing and poor countries on this issue and to collect the data completely. If these problems can be overcome in future studies, it may be possible to obtain more detailed results. Addressing issues such as gender inequalities, inequalities in education and health in developing countries in empirical studies can add a different dimension to income inequalities.

CONCLUSION

Despite the increasing material wealth around the world, the gap between the rich and the poor is increasing day by day. Today, the richest 10% have 40% of global income, while the poorest 10% have 2-7% of global income. Rising income inequality threatens social cohesion, slows economic growth and nullifies efforts to eradicate poverty. In countries where there is a high degree of inequality, the economy cannot function efficiently. In principle, having natural resources is very valuable for financing social expenditures and public investments in the fields of health and education. However, among the countries with the highest inequality rates are countries rich in natural resources. The best examples of these are the countries of Latin America and the Middle East. This problem is called the "curse of natural resources". The reason why these countries are unsuccessful is that natural resource management is difficult and resources cannot be used effectively and efficiently (Stiglitz, 2015: 91). The future of global income inequality will likely be shaped by rapid growth and rates of intra-country inequality in developing countries. But it is extremely difficult to predictwhich of these forces will dominate or whether high income inequalities are sustainable. However, if domestic inequalities continue to rise, it is estimated that global income inequalities will increase (Alverado et al., 2018: 250).

The important point that draws attention among the selected developing countries and related criteria in this study is that European countries are extremely successful in variables such as corruption, per capita income, and Rule of Law. Among the selected developing countries, the most successful ones in terms of income justice also have the highest per capita incomes, which brings to mind the inverted

Table 4. ARAS method findings

Country	Si	Ki	Rank
Albania	0.027	0.465	14
Argentina	0.023	0.405	23
Bangladesh	0.021	0.369	31
Belarus	0.030	0.520	9
Bolivia	0.021	0.358	32
Brazil	0.020	0.354	34
Bulgaria	0.026	0.446	16
Chile	0.030	0.516	10
China	0.025	0.438	18
Colombia	0.020	0.353	35
Czechcia	0.042	0.725	1
Dominikan Republic	0.023	0.401	24
Egypt	0.024	0.410	22
Estonia	0.038	0.662	2
Hungary	0.034	0.594	5
India	0.024	0.423	20
Indonesia	0.023	0.393	26
Kazakhstan	0.028	0.487	12
Latvia	0.032	0.558	8
Lithuania	0.030	0.515	11
Malaysia	0.034	0.586	6
Mexico	0.021	0.356	33
Moldova	0.025	0.441	17
Pakistan	0.022	0.380	29
Peru	0.023	0.392	27
Philippines	0.023	0.399	25
Poland	0.034	0.583	7
Romania	0.028	0.482	13
Russia	0.024	0.419	21
Serbia	0.026	0.453	15
Slovakia	0.038	0.660	3
South Africa	0.021	0.370	30
Thailand	0.035	0.599	4
Tunisia	0.024	0.424	19
Turkiye	0.023	0.391	28

U relationship between inequality and development. The low values of corruption and Rule of Law variables in a significant part of selected developing countries are an indication that administrative and systemic problems continue in these countries. This situation is one of the important reasons for the high income inequality in these countries. However inequalities are not inevitable. A more efficient and more equal distribution of income can be created by changing policies. But it is difficult to change the political processes that shape policies. Any form of mismanagement at the macro level can be a significant source of inequality.

In this study, the issue of income inequalities in selected developing countries has been discussed. For this purpose, the 2019 data compiled for the selected countries were analyzed using the ARAS method. A total of nine criteria thought to affect income inequalities were included in the analysis. Gini index, bottom 50% income share, corruption perception index and GDP per capita were determined as the most important criteria in the study in which the subjective weighting method was used.

From the findings of the ARAS method, which was carried out using the aforementioned weighting approach, it was determined that the countries with the best performance in terms of income justice were Chechia, Estonia, Slovakia, Thailand and Hungary. The results of the analysis showed that Colombia, Brazil Mexico, Bolivia and Bangladesh were the countries with the highest income inequality. The ARAS findings used in the study are theoretically and expectedly satisfactory. It has been determined that the countries that perform well in terms of fair income distribution are also in good condition in terms of criteria such as Gini index, bottom 50% income share, corruption perception index. The effect of the weighting method used in the ranking made as a result of the analysis is very important.

REFERENCES

Alverado, F., Chancel, L., Piketty, T., Saez, E., & Zucman, G. (2018). *World Inequality Report 2018.* World Inequality Lab. https://wir2018.wid.world/files/download/wir2018-full-report-english.pdf

Andres, A. R., & Carlyn, R.-D. (2011). Is Corruption Really Bad for Inequality? Evidence from Latin America. *The Journal of Development Studies, 47*(7), 959–976. doi:10.1080/00220388.2010.509784

Ayçin, E. (2019). *Çok Kriterli Karar Verme.* Nobel Akademik Yayıncılık.

Barro, R. J. (2000). Inequality and Growth in a Panel of Countries. *Journal of Economic Growth, 5*(1), 5–32. doi:10.1023/A:1009850119329

Bartak, J., Lukasz, J., & Tomkiewicz, J. (2022). Does income inequality explain public debt change in OECD countries? *International Review of Economics & Finance, 80*, 211–224. doi:10.1016/j.iref.2022.02.045

Binder, B., & Haupt, A. (2022). The fundamental role of tax systems in the relationship between workfare and inequality in the lower half of the income distribution. *Research in Social Stratification and Mobility, 80*, 100712. doi:10.1016/j.rssm.2022.100712

Birdsall, N. (2007). *Income Distribution: Effects on Growth and Development.* Center for Global Development Working Paper, No: 118.

Chancel, L., Piketty, T., Saez, E., & Zucman, G. (2022). *World Inequality Report 2022.* World Inequality Lab wir2022.wid.world

Clark, G. (2013). *Fukaralığa Veda Dünyanın Kısa İktisadi Tarihi.* Bilgi Üniversitesi Yayınları.

Cook, P., & Uchida, Y. (2008). Structural Change, Competition And Income Distribution. *The Quarterly Review of Economics and Finance*, *48*(2), 274–286. doi:10.1016/j.qref.2006.12.017

Dawson, P. J. (1997). On Testing Kuznets' Economic Growth Hypothesis. *Applied Economics Letters*, *4*(7), 409–410. doi:10.1080/135048597355159

Derviş, K., & Qureshi, Z. (2016). *Income distribution within countries: Rising inequality, Global Economy and Development at Brooking*. https://www.brookings.edu/wp-content/uploads/2017/12/income-inequality-within-countries_august-2016.pdf

Deutsch, J., & Silber, J. (2004). Measuring the impact of various income sources on the link between inequality and development: Implications for Kuznet Curve. *Review of Development Economics*, *8*(1), 110–127. doi:10.1111/j.1467-9361.2004.00223.x

Deyshappriya, N. P. R. (2017). *Impact of Macroeconomic Factors on Income Inequality and Income Distribution in Asian Countries*. ADBI Working Paper (696), Asian Development Bank Institute. https://www.adb.org/publications/impact-macroeconomic-factor s-income-inequality-distribution

Dincer, O. C., & Gunalp, B. (2012). Corruptıon And Income Inequalıty In The Unıted States. *Contemporary Economic Policy*, *30*(2), 283–292. doi:10.1111/j.1465-7287.2011.00262.x

Duncan, D., & Peter, K. S. (2016). Unequal inequalities: Do progressive taxes reduce income inequality? *International Tax and Public Finance*, *23*(4), 762–783. doi:10.100710797-016-9412-5

Engel, E. M. R. A., Galetovic, A., & Raddatz, C. E. (1999). Taxes and income distribution in Chile: Some unpleasant redistributive arithmetic. *Journal of Development Economics*, *59*(1), 155–192. doi:10.1016/S0304-3878(99)00009-7

Eurostat. (2017). *Sustainable Development in the European Union 2017*. European Union Publishing.

Güder, F. (2019). Yüksek Gelirli Ülkelerde Gelir Dağılımını Etkileyen Faktörler. *Fiscaoeconomia*, *3*(2), 198–216.

Gupta, S., Davoodi, H., & Terme, R. A. (2002). Does corruption affect income inequality and poverty? *Economics of Governance*, *3*(1), 23–45. doi:10.1007101010100039

Gyimah-Brempong, K. (2002). Corruption, economic growth, and income inequality in Africa. *Economics of Governance*, *3*(3), 183–209. doi:10.1007101010200045

Haidich, A. B., & Ioannidis, J. P. A. (2004). The Gini coefficient as a measure for understanding accrual inequalities in multicentes clinical studies. *Journal of Clinical Epidemiology*, *57*(4), 341–348. doi:10.1016/j.jclinepi.2003.09.011 PMID:15135834

Inam, B., Guzel, S., & Murat, D. (2019). The Correlation Between Corruption and Socioeconomic Development: An Application For OECD Countries. *Hacettepe University Journal of Economics and Administrative Sciences*, *37*(2), 325–339. doi:10.17065/huniibf.373711

Joumard, I., Pisu, M., & Debbie, B. (2012). Tackling income inequality: The role of taxes and transfers. *OECD Journal: Economic Studies*, *2012*(1), 37–70. doi:10.1787/eco_studies-2012-5k95xd6l65lt

Kaasa, A. (2005). *Factors Of Income Inequality And Their Influence Mechanisms: A Theoretical Overview*. University of Tartu Faculty of Economics and Business Administration Working Paper(No. 40).

Karacan, R. (2014). *Kapitalist Ekonomide Gelir Dağılımı ve Yoksulluk*. Yalın Yayıncılık.

Larch, M. (2012). Fiscal Performance and Income Inequality: Are Unequal Societies More Deficit-Prone? Some Cross-Country Evidence. *Kyklos*, *65*(1), 53–80. doi:10.1111/j.1467-6435.2011.00527.x

Lee, C. C., & Lee, C. C. (2018). The Impact of Country Risk on Income Inequality: A Multilevel Analysis. *Social Indicators Research*, *136*(1), 139–162. doi:10.100711205-016-1534-8

Li, H., Xu, L. C., & Zou, H.-F. (2000). Corruption, Income Distribution, and Growth. *Economics and Politics*, *12*(2), 155–182. doi:10.1111/1468-0343.00073

List, J. A., & Gallet, C. A. (1999). The Kuznets Curve: What Happens After the Inverted-U? *Review of Development Economics*, *3*(2), 200–206. doi:10.1111/1467-9361.00061

Malla, M. H., & Pathranarakul, P. (2022). Fiscal Policy and Income Inequality: The Critical Role of Institutional Capacity. *Economies*, *10*(5), 115. doi:10.3390/economies10050115

Namini, S. S., & Hudson, D. (2019). Inflation and income inequality in developed and developing countries. *Journal of Economic Studies (Glasgow, Scotland)*, *46*(3), 611–632. doi:10.1108/JES-02-2018-0045

Nantob, N. (2015). Income Inequality and Inflation in Developing Countries: An Empirical Investigation'. *Economic Bulletin*, *35*(4), 2888–2902.

Özbek, A. (2017). *Çok Kriterli Karar Verme Yöntemleri*. Seçkin Yayıncılık.

Öztürk, N. (2009). *İktisatta Bölüşüm*. Palme Yayıncılık.

Piketty, T. (2014). *Yirmi Birinci Yüzyılda KAPİTAL*. Türkiye İş Bankası Kültür Yayınları.

Policardoa, L., Edgar, J., Sanchez, C., & Risso, W. A. (2019). Causality between income inequality and corruption in OECD countries. *World Development Perspectives*, *14*, 100102. doi:10.1016/j.wdp.2019.02.013

Ravallion, M., & Chen, S. (2022). Is that really a Kuznets curve? Turning points for income inequality in China. *The Journal of Economic Inequality*, *20*(4), 749–776. doi:10.100710888-022-09541-x

Sliogeriene, J., Turskis, Z., & Streimikiene, D. (2013). Analysis and Choice of Generation Technologies: The Multiple Criteria Assessment on The Case Study of Energy Lithuania. *Energy Procedia*, *32*, 11–20. doi:10.1016/j.egypro.2013.05.003

Stiglitz, J. E. (2015). *Eşitsizliğin Bedeli. Bugünün Bölünmüş Toplumu Geleceğimizi Nasıl Tehlikeye Atıyor?* İletişim Yayınları.

Thalassinos, E., Uğurlu, E., & Muratoğlu, Y. (2012). Income Inequality and Inflation in the EU. *European Research Studies*, *15*(1), 127–140. doi:10.35808/ersj/347

Topuz, S. G., & Dağdemir, Ö. (2020). Analysis of the relationship between trade openness, structural change, and income inequality under Kuznets curve hypothesis: The case of Turkey. *The Journal of International Trade & Economic Development*, *29*(6), 647–664. doi:10.1080/09638199.2019.1711146

Tsakloglou, P. (1988). Development and Inequality Revisited. *Applied Economics*, *20*(4), 509–531. doi:10.1080/00036848800000061

Türk, İ. (1979). *Maliye Politikası Amaçlar- Araçlar ve Çağdaş Bütçe Teorileri*. Sevinç Matbaası.

Van Zanden, J. (Eds.). (2014). *How Was Life?: Global Well-being since 1820*. OECD Publishing. doi:10.1787/9789264214262-en

Wu, W., Wang, L., Erzurumlu, Y. Ö., Gozgor, G., & Yang, G. (2022). Effects of Country and Geopolitical Risks on Income Inequality: Evidence from Emerging Economies. *Emerging Markets Finance & Trade*, *58*(15), 4218–4230. doi:10.1080/1540496X.2022.2070002

Wu, Y., & Yao, H. (2015). Income Inequality, State Ownership, and the Pattern of Economic Growth – A Tale of the Kuznets Curve for China since 1978. *Atlantic Economic Journal*, *43*(2), 165–180. doi:10.100711293-015-9451-9

Zandi, G., Rehan, R., Hye, Q., Mubeen, S., & Abbas, S. (2022). Do Corruption, Inflation and Unemployment Influence the Income Inequality of Developing Asian Countries? *International Journal of Applied Economics. Finance and Accounting*, *14*(2), 118–128.

Zavadskas, E., & Turskis, Z. (2010). A New Additive Ratio Assessment (ARAS) Method in Multicriteria Decision-Making. *Technological and Economic Development of Economy*, *16*(2), 159–172. doi:10.3846/tede.2010.10

Zavadskas, E. K., Turskis, Z., & Vilutiene, T. (2010). Multiple Criteria Analysis of Foundation Instalment Alternatives by Applying Additive Ratio Assessment (ARAS) method. *Archives of Civil and Mechanical Engineering*, *X*(3), 123–141. doi:10.1016/S1644-9665(12)60141-1

ADDITIONAL READING

Becker, R. A. (2013). *The Economic Theory of Income Inequality*. Edward Elgar Publishing. doi:10.4337/9781784710392

Dadelo, S., Turskis, Z., Zavadskas, E. K., & Dadeliene, R. (2012). Multiple Criteria Assessment of Elite Security Personal on the Basis of ARAS and Expert Methods. *Economic Computation and Economic Cybernetics Studies and Research*, *46*(4), 65–87.

Pressman, S. (2015). *Understanding Piketty's Capital in the Twenty First Century*. Taylor Francis Publishing. doi:10.4324/9781315674728

Sliogeriene, J., Turskis, Z., & Streimikiene, D. (2013). Analysis and Choice of Generation Technologies: The Multiple Criteria Assessment on The Case Study of Energy Lithuania. *Energy Procedia*, *32*, 11–20. doi:10.1016/j.egypro.2013.05.003

Zavadskas, E. K., Turskis, Z., & Vilutiene, T. (2010). Multiple Criteria Analysis of Foundation Instalment Alternatives by Applying Additive Ratio Assessment (ARAS) method. *Archives of Civil and Mechanical Engineering*, *X*(3), 123–141. doi:10.1016/S1644-9665(12)60141-1

Zavadskas, E. K., Vainiunas, P., Turskis, Z., & Tamosaitiene, J. (2012). Multiple Criteria Decision Support System for Assessment of Projects Managers in Construction. *International Journal of Information Technology & Decision Making*, *11*(2), 501–520. doi:10.1142/S0219622012400135

KEY TERMS AND DEFINITIONS

Developed Country: The countries with high development levels.

Developing Country: Those other than the developed countries.

Income Inequality: Unequal distribution of income.

Inflation: A sustained increase in the general level of prices for goods and services.

Performance: A country's level of success in any subject.

Poverty: Not having enough income.

Tax: It is the monetary values that the state receives from individuals and institutions based on laws for the purpose of financing public services.

Unemployment: Inability to find a job despite the desire for employment.

Chapter 9
The Role of Development Banks in Green Finance and Sustainability

Hazik Mohamed
https://orcid.org/0000-0001-8322-2714
Stellar Consulting Group, Singapore

ABSTRACT

The development banks (DBs) contribute to a broader aspect of the financial system, rather than private banks that serve more specific areas in retail, wholesale, and investment needs. In this chapter, the author discusses how DBs work to support the implementation of the United Nations Sustainable Development Goals (SDGs) by providing financing for sustainable infrastructure, renewable energy, climate change adaptation and mitigation, and biodiversity conservation. They also help countries to build resilience to the impacts of climate change and environmental degradation. It is very critical to support sustainable economic development in various parts of the world, especially advanced and developed economies who are the major polluters. Therefore, development banks perform an important role in the contribution and achievement of public policy objectives through green and sustainable finance. The author concludes with his thoughts on existing regulations, programs, and incentives and further recommendations to support and build a more sustainable future.

1. INTRODUCTION

Promoting green finance (WEF, 2020) and sustainability requires the involvement of central banks and development banks through a variety of mechanisms, such as incentivizing the use of renewable energy and implementing policies to encourage sustainable banking practices. While central banks play key roles in ensuring financial stability and in shaping the regulatory landscape of financial services, development banks are a major promoter of economic development. DBs are important players in promoting sustainable finance and helping to mobilize private sector investment towards sustainable development

DOI: 10.4018/978-1-6684-8903-1.ch009

goals. Along with the need to support sustainable economic development in many parts of the world, green and sustainable finance are closely related to public policy objectives for both types of banks.

2. THE ROLE OF DEVELOPMENT BANKS

Development banks are public financial institutions tasked (usually) with promoting socio-economic development in a country, region or worldwide. Both developed and developing countries benefit from development banks' efforts to promote economic development by providing financing and advisory services and capacity-building programs to clients and sectors where commercial banks and local capital markets do not adequately meet their financial needs. Clients typically include SMEs, large private corporations and public bodies.

Development banks vary widely in scale and can take a number of different forms:

- **Multilateral Development Banks (MDBs)**

These institutions are owned by sovereign states, who are their shareholders. They often include developing countries in their remits, reflecting the development and cooperation policies established by these states. Among the MDBs are the World Bank, the International Finance Corporation (IFC), the Asian Development Bank (ADB), the African Development Bank (AfDB), the Inter American Development Bank (IDB), the European Bank for Reconstruction and Development (EBRD), the European Investment Bank (EIB) and the Asian Infrastructure Investment Bank (AIIB).

- **National Development Banks (NDBs)**

National Development Banks (NDBs) are financial institutions that are owned and controlled by the government. Their primary objective is to offer financing for the economic growth of the country, particularly for projects that promote industrialization, infrastructure development, and social welfare. NDBs often focus on providing funding to SMEs, as well as to projects in underdeveloped regions of the country. Some national development banks also provide financing for international development. NDBs tend to have in-depth local knowledge, relationships with, and understanding of, domestic policy and markets. Examples of NDBs include the China Development Bank, European Investment Bank, the Scottish National Investment Bank (SNIB) and the German KfW.

- **International Organizations**

There are international organizations that support the green movement such as the Global Green Growth Institute (GGGI). The GGGI is a global intergovernmental organization that supports and promotes robust, inclusive, sustainable growth. For example, in 2021, the Republic of Korea (ROK) established the Brunei Darussalam-Indonesia-Malaysia-Philippines East ASEAN Growth Area (BIMP-EAGA) within the GGGI, which includes Brunei Darussalam, Indonesia, Malaysia, and the Philippines. The aim of this partnership is to promote inclusive and balanced growth in the Southeast Asia region and promote ASEAN connectivity by enhancing partnerships between the BIMP-EAGA and the Republic of Korea.

Figure 1. Total climate finance by region
Source: 2020 Joint Report on Multilateral Development Banks' Climate Finance.

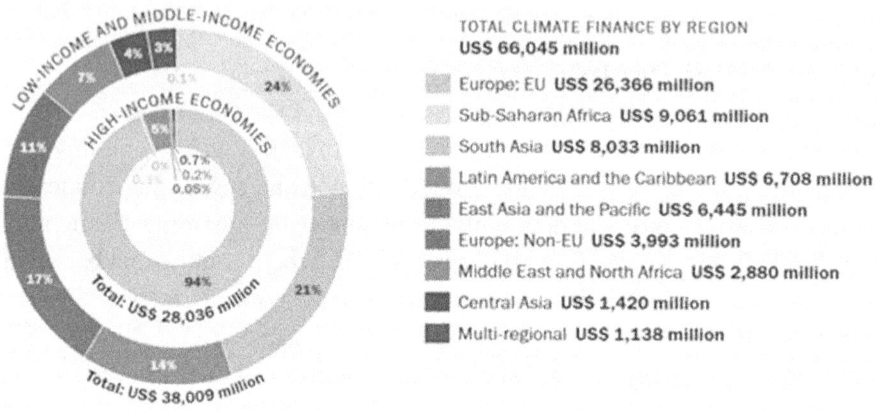

Focusing on industries that adopt clean and green technologies, the fund works with governments to support the development of SMEs.

- **Green Development Banks (GDBs)**

Green banks came onto the scene over a decade ago and have been established primarily to facilitate private investment in low-carbon, climate-resilient infrastructure in the domestic market, as well as other eco-friendly sectors, such as water and waste management (Böttcher, 2020). Green Banks were established in countries where there were financing gaps that did not exist in public or private institutions to support clean energy projects and enterprises. Also, there were policy mandates to scale up investment cost-effectively to meet climate imperatives as well as (in some cases) broader economic development goals. Despite the fact that the size, governance structure, missions, and tools of Green Banks differ from one another (e.g., certain Green Banks function within larger institutions as divisions), they all have certain common functions and characteristics that are essential for increasing green infrastructure investment.

Essentially, a Green Bank is a separate, dedicated fund or, an investment professional group with a dedicated pool of green capital. It is this model which has proven successful in creating new markets and enabling risk-mitigating interventions in Green Banks currently in operation.

2.1. Multilateral Development Banks and Sustainable Finance

Multilateral development banks (MDBs) in particular have played and contribute to the progress and development of the market for green and sustainable finance. There are many companies that have activities for mitigating and adapting to climate change, as key policy objectives, with the importance of this compared with other objectives (e.g. economic development) growing over the past decade.

- **European Investment Bank (EIB)**

Since 1958, the European Investment Bank (EIB) has promoted economic development and social progress in its member states within the European Union. A wide variety of green finance products are offered by the European Investment Bank (EIB), for example, including loans and equity investments. By the end of 2020, the EIB had issued green bonds totalling nearly €34 billion in 17 countries, including in 2018 the first 'Sustainability Awareness Bond', with proceeds earmarked for projects supporting the UN Sustainable Development Goals.

As part of its efforts to promote sustainable finance, the EIB has undertaken a number of initiatives, including:

i. The EIB has established a Climate Action and Resource Efficiency department to help member states in developing and realizing climate friendly and resource efficiency projects.
ii. It launched the European Fund for Strategic Investments (EFSI) to aid EU countries in the development and implementation of sustainable infrastructure, such as energy efficacy and sustainability projects.
iii. The EIB has also established the InnovFin Energy Demonstration Project (EDP) to support member countries in developing and implementing innovative clean energy projects.
iv. The EIB has also launched the European Green Bond Fund to support member countries in developing and implementing sustainable projects through the origination of green bonds.
v. In addition to its Green Financing strategy, the EIB develops sustainable finance products and services to mobilise private capital for sustainable infrastructure projects.
vi. EIB also has a dedicated lending arm for the private sector, EIB Invest, which focuses on providing finance to SMEs and mid-caps companies in Europe, with a focus on sustainable and innovative projects.

In November 2020, the EIB made a major strategic commitment to aligning its activities with green and sustainable finance and supporting the EU's European Green Deal and other sustainable finance activities with the publication of the Climate Bank Roadmap in November 2020. This set out the EIB's plans that by 2025 and beyond, climate action and environmental sustainability borrowers would represent more than 50% of the EIB's overall lending activities

In practice, the latter commitment meant the EIB would end financing of all oil, gas and coal projects, with the bank stating that it would do so by the end of 2021.

To date, the European Bank for Reconstruction and Development (EBRD) has financed some 2,000 green projects totalling €36 billion, which are estimated to have reduced annual greenhouse gas emissions by approximately 104 million tonnes CO_2e. By 2025, it intends to increase its green financing to over 50% of its total annual financing under its "Green Economy Transition" strategy. The EBRD's strategy focuses on five key themes: energy and resource efficiency, renewable energy, climate resilience, the just transition, and the circular economy.

The EBRD is also an important issuer of green bonds, referred to as "Environmental Sustainability Bonds". The EBRD issued its first such bond in 2010 and, as of the end of 2019, had issued 92 Environmental Sustainability Bonds totalling € 5.2 billion, supporting more than 350 sustainability projects.

- **Asian Development Bank (ADB)**

In 1966, the Asian Development Bank (ADB) was established with the aim of promoting economic advancement and community development in Asia Pacific. The ADB has been actively involved in promoting sustainable finance through a number of initiatives, including:

i. The ADB has established a Sustainable Infrastructure and Climate Change Department to help member states in developing and effecting sustainable infrastructure and climate change strategies.
ii. The ADB has also launched the Climate Change Fund to support member nations in developing and incorporating sustainability projects, as well as building climate-resilient infrastructure.
iii. The ADB created the Clean Energy Financing Partnership Facility (CEFPF) to support member countries in developing and implementing clean energy projects.
iv. The ADB also launched the Urban Climate Change Resilience Trust Fund (UCCRTF) to support member countries in developing and implementing climate-resilient urban infrastructure projects.
v. ADB launched the Private Sector Operations Department (PSOD) to promote sustainable and inclusive economic growth in member countries.
vi. The ADB has several policies and guidelines in place to ensure that the projects it finances align with sustainable finance principles, such as environmental and social assessments.
vii. ADB also has a Green Finance program that aims to mobilize private capital for sustainable infrastructure and other projects and works to develop sustainable finance products and services in the region.

The Asian Development Bank (ADB) provided more than US$40 billion of climate finance between 2011 and 2020, with a focus on cleaner infrastructure and technologies, conservation and forest management, environmental adaptation and making communities more robust.

As part of its commitment to mitigate climate change and disaster resilience (EESI, 2021), and adapt to environmental sustainability, the ADB committed to funding at least 75% of its activities by 2030 as part of the bank's "Strategy 2030" operational priorities. One year ahead of its 2020 target, the ADB announced in 2019 that it had doubled its climate investments from US$3 billion to US$6 billion since 2014.

- **African Development Bank (AfDB)**

Founded in 1964, the African Development Bank (AfDB) promotes economic development and social progress across the continent. Climate change affects many communities across Africa, even though Africa does not emit a great deal of greenhouse gases. As a result of global warming, sea levels will rise, large tracts of land will become uninhabitable, and extreme weather events such as droughts will be more frequent and severe. The AfDB has been actively involved in promoting sustainable finance through a number of initiatives, including:

i. The AfDB has established a Climate Change and Green Growth Department to aid member nations in developing and fulfilling climate change and green growth strategies. For instance, AfDB has a target of 40% of its overall portfolio supporting climate finance by 2021 and manages the Africa Climate Change Fund that is attuned to climate resilience and gender equality.
ii. The AfDB has also launched a Climate Investment Fund to support member countries in ensuring that sustainability and greening projects continue to be developed and implemented.

iii. The AfDB has also established the Africa Renewable Energy Initiative (AREI) to support member countries in developing renewable energy projects.
iv. The AfDB has also launched a Green Agriculture Transformation Program to support member countries in developing sustainable and climate-resilient agricultural practices.
v. The AfDB has also established the Sustainable Energy Fund for Africa (SEFA) to support member countries in developing and implementing sustainability and green energy projects.
vi. The AfDB has also launched the Sustainable Energy Inclusion Facility (SEIF) to support member countries in developing sustainable energy projects that have a positive impact on low-income communities.
vii. The AfDB also has several policies and guidelines in place to ensure that the projects it finances align with sustainable finance principles, such as environmental and social assessments, and aligning with the SDGs of the United Nations, the company has pledged to align its operations with those of the Paris Agreement.

The AfDB performs a steering function in developing the capacity of other institutions in Africa to embed sustainability into their activities, including central and national development banks, and in particular stimulating the climate-related and sustainability-linked debt market in Africa both through its own bond issuances and in helping to bring other issuers to market (e.g. the first Nigerian green bonds).

- **Inter-American Development Bank (IDB)**

While smaller than many of its peers, the IDB has a pivotal function in the financing of climate sustainability (and broader aspects of sustainability, such as social inclusion) in the Caribbean, Latin and South America.

The IDB has been actively involved in promoting sustainable finance through a number of initiatives, including:

i. The IDB has established a Climate Change and Sustainable Development Department to help member states in developing and achieving sustainability and climate change development plans.
ii. The IDB has also launched the Climate Change and Sustainability Fund to finance member nations in developing and executing sustainability and climate change projects.
iii. The IDB has also established the Sustainable Energy for All (SE4ALL) initiative to support member countries in developing and implementing sustainable energy projects.
iv. The IDB has also launched the Sustainable Transport Initiative (STI) to support member countries in developing sustainable transport systems that reduce emissions and promote social inclusion.
v. The IDB has also established the Sustainable Cities Initiative (SCI) to support member countries in developing sustainable and resilient cities.
vi. IDB also has a Sustainable Business Unit that works to promote sustainable business practices among its private sector clients and works to identify and finance sustainable projects.

The total amount of financing provided by the IDB in the period 2015-2020 was approximately US$1.5 billion, mainly focused on conservation and forest management; environmental management and governance; and climate resilience and disaster recovery. As well as financing and co-financing sustainability and disaster mitigation projects, a key focus for the IDB is capacity building, working with the region's public sector institutions, particularly finance and planning ministries, to help them develop relevant expertise to lead national climate change and resilience activities (EESI, 2021), and unlock investment to support these priorities.

- **Islamic Development Bank (IsDB)**

Founded in 1975, the Islamic Development Bank (IsDB) promotes economic growth and social development in its member countries, which are primarily Muslim-majority countries. The IsDB has been actively involved in promoting sustainable finance through a number of initiatives, including:

i. The IsDB has established a Sustainable Energy Financing Framework to support member countries in developing renewable energy and energy efficiency projects.
ii. The IsDB has also launched a Green Infrastructure Financing Facility to support member countries in developing environmentally friendly infrastructure projects.
iii. It has also established the Islamic Corporation for the Development of the Private Sector (ICD) to deliver financial and technical support for private sector projects in member countries with a focus on inclusive and sustainable growth.
iv. The IsDB has also published several guidance documents and regulations on sustainable finance to assist its member countries in developing environmentally friendly and socially responsible projects.
v. The IsDB has also launched several initiatives to support products and services for sustainable finance in its member nations, including the launch of the Sustainable Finance Platform, which intends to encourage products and services for green finance in the IsDB's member countries.
   - **World Bank Group**

Five international organizations comprise the World Bank Group [the International Bank for Reconstruction and Development (IBRD), the International Development Association (IDA), the International Finance Corporation (IFC), the Multilateral Investment Guarantee Agency (MIGA), and the International Centre for Settlement of Investment Disputes (ICSID)], which work concurrently to support developing nations in their economic and social improvement efforts. Globally, the World Bank Group, comprising the World Bank, the IFC, and IDA, provides the bulk of climate financing in developing countries. It coordinates a global response to climate change with other MDBs, governments, and other institutions.

The World Bank Group has been actively involved in promoting sustainable finance through a number of initiatives, including:

i. The World Bank has established a Climate Change and Carbon Finance department to aid member nations in developing and executing climate change and carbon finance projects.
ii. Global development and investment are supported by Climate Business, a department of the IFC that lends to the private sector, with a focus on sustainable and climate-resilient projects.
iii. The IFC has also launched the Global Infrastructure Facility (GIF) to support member countries in developing and implementing sustainable infrastructure projects.
iv. The IFC has also established the Sustainable Banking Network[1] (SBN) to support member countries in developing sustainable banking practices.

v. For political risk insurance to members in developing and implementing sustainable projects, the Multilateral Investment Guarantee Agency (MIGA) has launched the Climate and Development Guarantee Facility (CDGF).
vi. The World Bank also has a dedicated finance program for sustainable energy and energy efficiency program for assisting developing countries with sustainable energy development and energy efficiency improvements, called the Energy Sector Management Assistance Program (ESMAP), which gives diagnostic and practical support.

The Bank's 2016 Climate Change Action Plan set out an objective of increasing the proportion of climate finance in the Group's overall financing activities from 21% to 28%, a target exceeded in 2018. Developing nations received over US$83 billion in climate finance from the World Bank Group by the end of 2020, including US$21.4 billion just in 2020. The Bank continues its commitment to increasing this proportion to 35% of overall financing, in its second Climate Change Action Plan, covering the period 2021-2025, with half of the World Bank's climate finance earmarked to support adaptation and resilience measures – giving this equal weighting to investments to reduce emissions.

Other priorities for the World Bank to 2025 include:

- Making intelligent investments in key emission-reducing and climate-vulnerable systems, such as energy, food production, manufacturing and transportation; and
- Helping countries and regions successfully transition from coal power to more sustainable sources of energy.

As multilateral development banks (MDBs) increase their climate finance for mitigation and adaptation activities, the World Bank Group is also collaborating with them to develop common approaches to track and monitor their climate finance flows. MDBs align their financial flows to help countries comply with the Paris Agreement, implement NDCs, and facilitate activities that move development away from greenhouse gas emissions and toward climate resilience (Datta & Krishnamoorti, 2022).

In addition to climate finance, the Bank also develops innovative approaches to combating climate change, facilitating the sharing of best practice and implementing joint projects by bringing together the scientific, finance, policy and other communities. The Bank has also helped to establish many of the international frameworks, organisations and networks supporting the transition to a low-carbon world, helps its client countries develop and implement their National Determined Contributions, and has developed and published a wide range of tools and reports to assist organisations and policymakers with climate change and climate finance, such as the Climate & Disaster Risk Screening Tools, and Climate Adaptation Country Profiles.

2.2. National Development Banks in Climate Change Mitigation

A national development bank (NDB) is a government-owned financial institution that provides funding and financing for economic development and infrastructure projects within a country. The mandates of some NDBs also include providing financing and funding for green projects to mitigate climate adversity. The agencies can also assist with developing these projects with technical assistance, capacity building, and mobilizing private sector investment.

Also, the UN's Sustainable Development Goals (SDGs) can be accomplished with the help of NDBs, which provide funding and financing for sustainable agriculture, sustainable urban development, and other projects.

Brazil's National Economic and Social Development Bank (BNDES), Japan's Development Bank (DBJ), China's Development Bank (CDB), and Greece's National Investment Bank (ETBA) are among the NDBs responsible for supporting climate change mitigation. Sustainable and clean energy projects are specifically funded by these institutions through specific departments and initiatives.

2.3. Green Development Banks and Financing the SDGs

Besides MDBs and NDBs, there is a rapidly growing number of dedicated 'Green Development Banks' (GDBs) – sometimes simply referred to as 'Green Banks' – specialized financial institutions that provide funding and financing for environmentally-friendly and sustainable projects, including climate-resilient development, typically at a national or more local basis. Most of these entities are public-owned and may be set up on a national scale, state scale, or even a county or city scale (for example, Masdar, United Arab Emirates).

GDBs finance the SDGs in several ways. For example, they can provide financing for renewable energy projects, such as solar or wind farms, which contribute to SDG 7 (Affordable and Clean Energy). GDBs can also finance sustainable infrastructure projects, such as public transportation systems or water treatment plants, which contribute to SDG 9 (Industry, Innovation, and Infrastructure) and SDG 6 (Clean Water and Sanitation), respectively.

In addition, GDBs provide financing for projects that support climate adaptation and resilience, such as flood control systems or drought-resistant crops, which contribute to SDG 13 (Climate Action). GDBs can also support sustainable agriculture projects that promote food security and contribute to SDG 2 (Zero Hunger).

In the period 2012-2019, GDBs had committed a total of US$24.5 billion of their own capital and had unlocked an additional US$45.5 billion of co-investment from the private sector. As with MDBs and NDBs, a variety of financing mechanisms, including long-term loans (usually on more favourable terms than available from the private sector), equity investments, grants and guarantees, are deployed to stimulate investment in environmentally sustainable projects and activities.

Compared with the financing activities of MDBs and NDBs, the capital deployed and co-financed by GDBs is relatively small: in 2020 alone the German KfW provided funds totalling some €45 billion for climate finance and environmental protection, for example, substantially more than the total capital deployed by GDBs since 2012. The key role of many GDBs is less in the provision of finance and more in addressing perceived market failures (e.g. the failure to appropriately price climate risks and opportunities) and stimulate investment in new sustainable technologies, sectors and firms (NGFS, 2019).

2.4. Products in Mobilising Green Finance to Support Sustainability

There are several products (UNCTAD, 2021) that can be used to mobilize green finance to support sustainability. Some examples include:

a. **Climate Bond Funds**: These are investment funds that are focused on investing in green bonds and other sustainable financial products. They allow investors to easily diversify their investments across a range of sustainable projects and can help to increase the availability of capital for sustainable projects.

b. **Concessionary Loans**: Concessionary loans are provided at more favourable conditions than those offered by private financial institutions and can be in the form of zero or lower than market interest rates, lower collateral requirements, longer loan tenors and extended repayment schedules. The degree of concessions can be adjusted to the needs of a particular project, from highly concessional to just below market terms, depending on the balance between commercial and impact returns sought by the lender(s). As a result of their high cost associated with early market entry, concessionary loans can be used to develop new markets or achieve policy goals.

c. **First-Loss Provisions**: When there is a financial loss of security, first loss provisions protect investors from losing their capital first. Development banks may invest first-loss capital into a project or fund to help shield investors from a defined initial amount of losses, thereby reducing risk and improving the credit profile of the investment. One example is the Global Energy Efficiency and Renewable Energy Fund (GEEREF), established by the European Commission in 2008, that is used in conjunction with other structures as a first loss provision, which includes a first-loss provision financed by the original funders (the EU, Germany and Norway) to attract private sector investment by reducing the investment risk for such investors.

d. **Grants**: An effective way to reduce the overall costs of a project is to use grants to cover specific parts of it. Grants give projects a kick-start, used to accelerate projects, or as a means of reducing the cost of the project over its lifetime and, especially in the case of green and sustainable finance, support the development, proto-typing and proof of concept of new technologies or approaches supporting climate change mitigation and adaptation objectives (Rizello, 2022). For this latter reason in particular, grants can be crucial for pilot projects with high risks and uncertain returns.

e. **Green Bonds**: In this type of bond, capital is raised for all sorts of sustainable projects, such as agroforestry, energy efficiency, green buildings, transport and waste management. A green bond can be issued by a government, company, or another entity, and traded on a financial exchange.

f. **Green Revolving Funds**: These funds provide low-cost, long-term financing to organizations that invest in energy efficiency, renewable energy, and other sustainability projects. The savings generated by the projects are then used to pay back the loan, and the funds are then recycled to finance new projects.

g. **Partial Risk and Credit Guarantees**: When a loan default occurs, or another event triggers such a guarantee, one party commits to being liable for the debt in full or in part. Guarantees enable the risk to be shared between a private sector lender unable or unwilling to bear it all, with another that can, a development bank such as the Asian Development Bank – often, in the case of climate and sustainable finance. By reducing the risk to private sector lenders and investors, guarantees can support the growth of green and sustainable finance by improving a project's credit profile and enabling private finance to achieve the risk/return profile needed to justify investment (NGFS, 2019). This can be particularly important in countries where political instability and/or the lack of stable institutions and legal certainty significantly increases investment risks. Typically, guarantees cover only a portion of the amount borrowed, meaning that they do not cover the entire amount borrowed. Due to the guarantee not covering the full amount, it does not create moral hazard and ensures the lender still has an incentive to conduct due diligence on the borrower's viability and use of resources.

h. **Sustainable Equity Funds**: These are investment funds that are focused on investing in companies that are engaged in sustainable activities such as clean energy, energy efficiency and sustainable transportation, and promote sustainable development by supporting sustainable agriculture, sustainable urban development, and other projects that reinforce the UN SDGs.

i. **Sustainable Infrastructure Funds**: These are investment funds that are focused on investing in sustainable infrastructure projects. They allow investors to easily diversify their investments across a range of sustainable projects and can help to increase the availability of capital for sustainable projects.

j. **Sustainability-Linked Loans**: Such bespoke loans have similar features to commercial sustainability linked loans but also includes additional concessionary features that would not be viable in the private sector. An NDB can support borrowers in setting environmental and other sustainability-related performance targets (SPTs) and reporting publicly on achievement. Government policy and development banks' alignment in some cases has led to a powerful synergy between financing, regulation and policy. A combination of new government policies and new financing instruments is helping to effectively transmit policy objectives.

These are some of the products that can be used to mobilize green finance to support sustainability and can be combined to create a diverse portfolio of sustainable investments.

3. PUBLIC POLICY THROUGH DEVELOPMENTAL GREEN AND SUSTAINABLE FINANCE

Development banks (DBs) help public policy by supporting green initiatives in developing countries, and directly by investing in sizeable projects that may trickle down to MSMEs in its value chain. Through blended finance and credit enhancement mechanisms, DBs also support developing countries, to reduce risk exposure, and increase investor incentives to mobilize capital. To help companies – including start-ups – seeking funding build investor confidence and attract investors, the World Bank, Asian Infrastructure Investment Bank (AIIB), International Finance Corporation (IFC), and Asian Development Bank (ADB) have made private placements or become anchor investors in debt issuances and IPOs.

Medium-sized businesses also benefit from DB support through green bond issuances and green loans that help fund large green projects, such as those under the ASEAN Catalytic Green Finance Facility (Lau et al, 2022). MSMEs indirectly benefit from such issuances as larger corporations trickle down the products and services such as partnering with many suppliers and experts who can deliver reliable green and sustainable equipment and professionally install them for production needs that will be more sustainable, energy-efficient with lower carbon emissions. MSMEs will benefit from bio-diesel, EV battery and charging expertise, biomass gasifiers, boilers, energy efficient lighting, motors, air compression and air conditioning and ventilation, advanced energy storage, solar expertise, and waste water treatment plants. In the long-term, MSMEs can develop their own expertise in the maintenance, repair or installation of these greener equipment and low emission systems.

3.1. Financing Green-Focused Projects

Development banks can provide financing for projects that promote environmental sustainability, such as renewable energy, energy efficiency, sustainable agriculture, and sustainable forestry. By financing these projects, development banks can help reduce greenhouse gas emissions, improve resource efficiency, and promote sustainable development. Focused Finance Facilities that facilitates the development of a project pipeline between government, the private sector, and communities for green bond issuances. To improve the bankability of projects, capital is channelled into the pipeline using a blended finance approach, incorporating coverage for risks and enhancement of credit.

Some examples are the European Investment Bank's (EIB) Natural Capital Financing Facility (NCFF), Indonesia's Tropical Landscapes Finance Facility (TLFF) and the Credit Guarantee Investment Facility (CGIF) which utilizes the blended finance approach which facilitates funding access for bankable projects by providing technical support and technical assistance.

- **Credit Guarantee Investment Facility (CGIF)**

Green infrastructure investments can be supported by regional facilities such as the CGIF. This multilateral facility was established in 2010 by ASEAN+3 (China, Japan, and South Korea) and the ADB, and is headquartered in Hong Kong.

The CGIF's primary objective is to promote the development of local currency bond markets in the region by increasing investor confidence and facilitating access to long-term funding for infrastructure development and other priority sectors. The facility provides guarantees on local currency-denominated bonds issued by eligible entities, such as banks, corporations, and sovereigns, thereby reducing the credit risk associated with such bonds and making them more attractive to investors.

The CGIF's guarantee coverage ranges from 50% to 80% of the principal amount of the bonds, depending on the creditworthiness of the issuer and other factors. The facility also provides technical assistance to help issuers improve their creditworthiness and prepare for bond issuance. By providing guarantees, issuers in the region are able to obtain funding for longer-term debt and reduce currency and maturity mismatches in their local capital markets. Thus, the region's market can grow and remain stable.

- **European Investment Bank's (EIB) Natural Capital Financing Facility (NCFF)**

The NCFF was launched in 2015 and is managed by the EIB in partnership with the European Commission. The facility has a total budget of €1.2 billion and provides funding to projects in the European Union and beyond. The NCFF offers a range of financing instruments, including loans, guarantees, and equity investments, to support a wide range of natural capital projects through loans and other forms of financing to private sector companies and public sector organizations for projects that have a positive impact on natural capital and biodiversity, such as reforestation, habitat restoration, and sustainable agriculture.

In addition to providing financing, the NCFF also offers technical assistance and advice to help project developers prepare and implement their projects. This includes support with project design, stakeholder engagement, and monitoring and evaluation.

- **Tropical Landscapes Finance Facility (TLFF)**

This initiative was launched in 2016 by the Government of Indonesia in partnership with the United Nations Environment Programme, World Agroforestry Centre, ADM Capital, and BNP Paribas. It aims to invest in commercial projects with public capital to stimulate private investments which benefit the environment and society, namely sustainable agriculture, biodiversity preservation, forest management, and renewable energy. These kind of financing facilities affect multiple enterprises, including MSMEs, which benefit directly and indirectly from such large investments.

It delivered its first green bond in February 2018 as part of a US$350m project with a US$95m multi-tranche sustainability bond. Michelin of France and Barito Group of Indonesia formed a joint venture to arrange the financing, which was issued by TLFF I Pte Ltd. and arranged by BNP Paribas. With the proceeds from this project, Indonesian rubber plantations will be established on lands in Jambi and East Kalimantan that have been severely degraded. Farmers and agricultural MSMEs benefit from the improved forest management and biodiversity preservation which translates to more pliable land for work and income for them. To protect investors from losses greater than 50% of the principal, USAID provided a partial credit guarantee of US$70 million.

3.2. Dedicated Investment Funds

Another important green financing vehicle for public policy objectives are Dedicated Investment Funds, which raise money for the capitalization of businesses and/or projects that are considered eco-friendly (UNCTAD, 2021). Development banks can establish green investment funds that focus on financing green and sustainable projects. These funds can attract private sector investment and help to scale up sustainable finance. The following are some examples of regional funds that support infrastructure developments and can be leveraged to fund green projects.

- **ASEAN Infrastructure Fund (AIF)**

The AIF was launched in 2012 with an initial capitalization of US$485 million and is managed by the ASEAN Infrastructure Fund Limited (AIFL), a company registered in Malaysia. The AIFL is responsible for the implementation of the AIF's investment activities, including project identification, evaluation, and monitoring.

The AIF provides financing for infrastructure projects in ASEAN member countries in the areas of transportation, energy, water supply, and sanitation. The AIF aims to promote sustainable infrastructure development and enhance regional connectivity and economic growth. It offers loans, guarantees, and equity investments to support infrastructure projects in the region. The AIF also collaborates with other development partners, including multilateral development banks, to leverage additional financing and technical expertise.

To finance infrastructure projects in the ASEAN region, the AIF mobilizes regional savings, including foreign exchange reserves, as part of ADB and ASEAN's collaborative effort. In its first lending transaction, the fund invested US$25 million in the Java-Bali 500-kV Power Transmission Crossing Project. Recently, the AIF has approved the creation of a 'green window' for the financing of green infrastructure in ASEAN.

- **Currency Exchange Fund (TCX)**

As part of its mission to help developing and frontier markets mitigate currency risk, TCX was set up by 22 development finance institutions and microfinance investment vehicles in 2007 and is based in Amsterdam, Netherlands.

TCX offers innovative hedging solutions to its clients, such as forward contracts, currency swaps, and options. These solutions allow clients to manage currency risk in a cost-effective way and protect themselves against unexpected currency movements. One of the unique features of TCX is that it provides hedging solutions for local currencies in emerging and frontier markets, which are often illiquid and difficult to hedge through traditional financial instruments. TCX achieves this by entering into currency swap agreements with local banks in these markets, allowing clients to hedge their exposure to local currencies.

In some cases, no long-term hedging products exist for currencies for which there is no market at all. Emerging market bond issuance can be hampered by currency risk. Using hedging solutions, such as those offered by development finance institutions or TCX, can assist international investors in committing capital to local currency transactions. Also, it can reduce reliance on foreign currency for funding by growing a domestic, local currency bond market. In 2017-18, TCX was able to provide hedging facilities for the issuance of local currency bonds in Myanmar (TCX, 2018). Through the TCX hedging service, investors were able to lend in Myanmar's local currency (kyat). In order to subsidize these local currency loans, LIFT (a consortium of international donors) made funds available to bring the interest rates down to 13%, which is the interest rate cap set by the Central Bank. As a result, foreign investors and MFIs became more comfortable lending in kyat. More than USD 80 million in new investments were catalyzed by the initial US$10 million in Myanmar microfinance.

- **Green Climate Fund (GCF)**

The Green Climate Fund (GCF) is a financial mechanism established by the United Nations Framework Convention on Climate Change (UNFCCC) to support developing countries in their efforts to mitigate and adapt to climate change. It was established in 2010 and became fully operational in 2015. The GCF is headquartered in Songdo, South Korea.

The main objective of the GCF is to help developing countries reduce their greenhouse gas emissions and enhance their resilience to the impacts of climate change (EESI, 2021). It provides funding for projects and programs in areas such as renewable energy, energy efficiency, sustainable agriculture, forestry, and climate-resilient infrastructure. The fund aims to promote a paradigm shift towards low-emission and climate-resilient development pathways in developing countries.

The GCF is financed by contributions from developed countries, as well as from private sector entities, and it is governed by a Board of 24 members, with equal representation from developed and developing countries. The fund has an initial resource mobilization target of US$100 billion per year by 2020.

The GCF has a strong focus on ensuring that its investments promote gender equality and social inclusion, as well as environmental sustainability. It also aims to strengthen the capacity of developing countries to access and manage climate finance effectively.

- **Leading Asia's Private Sector Infrastructure Fund (LEAP)**

LEAP[2] is an ADB-managed fund capitalized with funding from the Japan International Cooperation Agency. Companies, projects, and financial intermediaries (e.g., holding companies and local currency vehicles) involved in infrastructure are supported by LEAP, and other private finance initiative projects, PPPs, joint ventures, and privatizations are sponsored. Project eligibility includes energy, including renewable energy generation, energy efficiency, and conservation; water and other urban infrastructure and services, including wastewater and solid waste management; transport (road, rail, air) and logistics; information and communications technology; and health.

LEAP's investment approach is to partner with reputable private sector investors and developers to finance infrastructure projects that are financially sustainable, socially responsible, and environmentally sound. LEAP provides long-term capital to support these projects, often taking significant minority stakes in project companies. It requires all its investments to comply with the ADB's environmental and social safeguards, which are designed to ensure that infrastructure projects are developed in an environmentally and socially responsible manner.

LEAP has made several investments since its launch, including investments in renewable energy projects in India and the Philippines, a water supply project in Myanmar, and a transport project in Bangladesh.

3.3. Capacity-Building and Technical Assistance

The ecosystem will ultimately be defined by investments in both core and emerging technologies, talent development, capacity building and enhancing policy environment for innovative start-ups driven towards the ESG agenda. Organizations can boost existing efforts or shore up weak areas and deficiency by establishing partnerships with a variety of organizations and stakeholders in the green ecosystem. Development banks can provide technical assistance to help companies and governments develop sustainable business models and adopt sustainable practices. This assistance can include training on sustainable finance, environmental and social risk management, and green project development.

Technical assistance and other advisory services are frequently provided by MDBs and their partners as part of a package of investment that can help to improve project preparation, planning and management, as well as improve the prospect of achieving the desired project outcomes. By providing assistance and expertise, an investment can be strengthened economically and technically, catalyzing private sector participation and funding. Furthermore, it can help build expertise and know-how that can be used to support future projects designed to promote climate change mitigation and adaptation.

In addition, supporting complex projects with specific technical assistance and building market awareness can facilitate the development of enabling environments for such complexity, and support the successful development of future projects. Technical assistance facilitates knowledge sharing and dissemination of experience and good practice, but it should be ensured that there is a transfer of knowledge and experience to local professionals to enhance the capacity and capability of national capital markets and institutions in respect of green and sustainable finance, rather than simply a demonstration effect that has no lasting impact.

3.4. Supporting Policy Reforms

Development banks can support policy reforms that promote sustainable finance, such as establishing regulations that require companies to report on their environmental and social performance, or implementing policies that incentivize investment in green projects. These banks can use their position and influence to engage with governments, civil society organizations, and other stakeholders to promote policy reforms.

Development banks can also share best practices and lessons learned from their own experiences in promoting sustainable finance. This can include sharing case studies, reports, and other resources that can help governments to develop effective policies and programs.

By collaborating with other stakeholders, such as civil society organizations, academic institutions, and private sector actors, development banks can collaborate to promote policy reforms related to sustainable finance. By working together, these stakeholders can leverage their collective resources and expertise to drive meaningful change.

4. CONCLUSION

In recent years, international organizations and development banks have increasingly focused on sustainability with renewed vigour to uphold ESG requirements, SDG targets and extenuation of environmental risks. These institutions have a unique ability to influence and shape the financial system through supporting public policies, and by leveraging capital towards green finance, they can help to drive the transition to a more sustainable economy. The financial system needs to be aligned fully with sustainability goals despite recent progress. The supervision of global systemically important banks requires collaboration between authorities within a jurisdiction and home-host coordination across jurisdictions. By coordinating public policy actions across regions, multilateral institutions could provide system-wide and cross-border information. It is important to set goals, assess the risks associated with climate change, collect data on whether the risk is occurring, and calibrate capital requirements over longer time frames as part of the many actions policymakers and banks can take to increase their capacity to manage climate-related financial risks.

REFERENCES

Datta, A., & Krishnamoorti, R. (2022). Understanding the Greenhouse Gas Impact of Deforestation Fires in Indonesia and Brazil in 2019 and 2020. *Frontiers in Climate*, *4*, 799632. doi:10.3389/fclim.2022.799632

EESI. (2021). *Fact Sheet: Strengthening Financial Resilience to Climate Change*. EESI.

Lau, H. C., Zhang, K., Bokka, H. K., & Ramakrishna, S. (2022). A Review of the Status of Fossil and Renewable Energies in Southeast Asia and Its Implications on the Decarbonization of ASEAN. *Energies*, *15*(6), 2152. doi:10.3390/en15062152

Network for Greening the Financial System (NGFS). (2019). *A Call for Action. Climate Change as a Source of Financial Risk*. Network for Greening the Financial System.

Rizzello, A. (2022). What's in a Name? Mapping the Galaxy of Green Finance. In *Green Investing*. Palgrave Studies in Impact Finance. Palgrave Macmillan. doi:10.1007/978-3-031-08031-9_2

The Currency Exchange Fund N.V. (2018). *Blended finance in Myanmar: TCX's role in realizing financial inclusion through innovative partnerships in Myanmar*. https://www.tcxfund.com/wp-content/uploads/2018/02/TCX-Myanmar-case-study.pdf

UNCTAD. (2021). *The Rise of the Sustainable Fund Market and its Role in Financing Sustainable Development*. United Nations. https://unctad.org/system/files/official-document/diae2021d1_en.pdf

World Economic Forum. (2020). *What is green finance and why is it important?* https://www.weforum.org/agenda/2020/11/what-is-green-finance/

ENDNOTES

1 Sustainable Banking Network and IFC, 2021. Sustainable Banking Network (SBN) Overview. https://www.ifc.org/wps/wcm/connect/98ed795e-559a-496c-b76d-b89ddb8c2716/SBN_Brief+20210511.pdf?MOD=AJPERES&CVID=nBpj8ZX

2 ADB. Leading Asia's Private Infrastructure (LEAP). https://www.adb.org/sites/default/files/page/631456/leap-brochure.pdf

Chapter 10
Constructing an Integrated Sustainable Halal Policy (ISHP) in Brunei Darussalam:
Refiguring the Domains of Conventional Policy Multiverses

Izni Azrein Noor Azalie
https://orcid.org/0000-0003-0616-3241
Universiti Brunei Darussalam, Brunei

ABSTRACT

This chapter aims to revisit some of the foundational questions that help create the domains often treated in exclusion or in silos, particularly those involving public, industrial, and economic policies, and proposed a new framework of which how the three could be integrated and synchronized by using experiences from the Brunei halal industry as a case study. This chapter is timely as the food industry is seen as one of the five main sectors aimed at diversifying the Bruneian economy and development envisioned in the Brunei Vision 2035, in tandem with some of the Sustainable Development Goals (SDG). The study is based on the experiences of Brunei's food industry players. Adapting it to the principles of Islamic governance not only puts into context the logic of why such an integrated halal policy is crucial for the alleviation of poverty (SDG1) and the development of sustainable cities and communities (SDG 8) alike but also answers the calls towards responsible production and consumption (SDG 12) whilst supporting the decent work and economic growth promotion (SDG 11).

BRUNEI'S PROGRESS IN THE SUSTAINABLE DEVELOPMENT GOAL (SDG)

The Brundtland Commission (1987) defined the concept of sustainable development as developing or progressing without jeopardizing the needs of the future generation. Fast forward to 25 years since its inception, numerous studies and research managed to highlight the complexities and multidimensionality

DOI: 10.4018/978-1-6684-8903-1.ch010

of diverse issues on people, environment, and development. The growing sentiments and acknowledgements on the role of civil society and governance in upholding the principles of sustainability, issues surrounding poverty, socio-economic inequalities, social and environmental justice, and climate change, to name a few, remained in existence with limited progress despite major changes brought about by technological development and globalisation. The 2030 Agenda for Sustainable Development adopted in 2015 resulted in the introduction of 17 Sustainable Development Goals (henceforth SDGs), calling for active participation and actions of all countries towards peace and prosperity for the people and the planet, at present and in the future.

Brunei Darussalam embraced SDG 17 and has been committed to pursuing and improving nine core areas of the SDG that the country view as important, under the auspice of the Secretariat to the Special National Coordination Committee on SDG (SSNCC), Brunei Prime Minister's Office. The nine core areas as reported by the SSNCC in their 2021 Annual Report on SDG are SDG 1 on zero poverty, SDG 2 on zero hunger, SDG 3 on good health and well-being, SDG 8 on decent work and economic growth, SDG 10 on reduced inequalities, SDG 12 on responsible consumption and production, SDG 13 on Climate Action, SDG 16 on peace, justice, and strong institutions as well as SDG 17 on strong partnerships (SSNCC, 2021). Brunei was ranked 84th in 2021 and 93rd in 2022 respectively concerning the progress made on their SDG commitments. Despite such a drop in ranking, the SDG pursuit was further enhanced by continuously working on its Brunei Vision 2035 through its Whole of Nation Approach. The Whole of Nation approach calls for the cooperation, collaboration and integration of the State's governing apparatuses and its citizens to materialise the national vision while at the same time, adhering to the Malay Islamic Monarchy (MIB) principles. Interestingly, the three main components of the Brunei Vision 2035 launched in 2007 were already in line or embedded with the SDGs 2030 Agenda as the vision aspires to produce educated, highly skilled and accomplished individuals measured by the highest international standards, to have a society which enjoys a high quality of life within the top 10 measurements of the United Nation's Human Development Index and a dynamic and sustainable economy (Secretariat of Brunei Vision 2035, n.d.).

Despite the effort in promoting and integrating the SDGs goals into the existing Vision 2035 framework, certain flaws do exist particularly relating to the definition and interpretation of these goals. Another flaw is also linked to the incongruency between the United Nation's (UN) assessment criteria of 'progress' in SDGs implementation in contrast to the national government's self-assessment. An example of this can be found with SDG 1 on zero poverty where the UN SDG reported its absence due to data unavailability, despite, the existence of poverty-related research being published (see Hassan et al, 2022; Gweshengwe and Hassan, 2019, 2020). The existence of Brunei's National Poverty Eradication Action Plan 2020-2024 as reported in the SSNC annual report (SSNC, 2021) but remained undetected by the UN's SDG reporting also highlighted the challenges in the use of the UN's conventional poverty line indicator against the actual national expected standard of living (Gweshengwe and Hassan, 2020). These discrepancies in the multi-scalar reporting on the SGDs' goal achievements point to the problems of contextualisation and issues in the use of indices or numerals for such reporting especially when it deals with people's experiences of poverty. Such check listings and indexing also indirectly veils poverty, making it less visible to the public. It is beyond the scope of this paper to address these discrepancies in detail. However, such an example is a reflection on how a seemingly globalised universal definition may not necessarily fit the local context in terms of its occurrences and how it is operationalised.

Within the economic sphere, the identification of halal food as a key driver of its economic diversification programme generates interest and warrants further investigation, particularly from the sustainability lens. This is because the Islamic economy and its activities have been seen as an alternative model of development, stemming from the strong commitment towards fairness and justice and mainly due to the belief that this is all part of good deeds or *ibadah*. Hence, analysis of the current halal policy and its subsequent effects from an adaptive, Islamic governance version of the SDG allows for the construction of an integrated sustainable halal policy. To do this, a conceptual deconstruction of current policy approaches is needed to help contextualise this chapter.

A Conceptual Deconstruction of the State and Policy

Although the term multiverses as a buzzword owed much to the hype surrounding Hollywood's popular culture, the hypothesis on the existence of multiverses though had been around since pre-Socratic times. Within contemporary quantum physics and astronomy, the word itself was often used as an alternative way of seeing humans' existence concerning their cosmos, to the many worlds that may have existed out there, waiting only to be discovered. Within the lens of this chapter, however, the word multiverse is used to frame the multiplicity and multidimensionality of explanans and explanandum relating to policy logic and the processes developed to implement it. This is a move away from the attempts of providing a unilinear, totalising way of framing policy and understanding its processes which usually, is void of contextualisation and criticality of the universality of a policy in general. The word multiverse automatically also suggested that any processes that occur within these realities are governed by a diverse set of logic and orders which runs in parallels within different timelines, not necessarily a continuation of any historical construction, but also as outcomes of discontinuities. So, the realities, in the context of this chapter, refer to the diverse aspects of life, the set of logic and orders on the other, can be linked to the different policy mechanisms, structures and agents involved in that particular moment in time whilst the parallels here refer to the operationalisation of all these processes running concurrently within different domains towards a common goal. This marked a divergence from current ways of defining reality and the policy used to 'police' or monitor it as derivatives of the past, requiring similar logic of regulation and approaches known to the policymakers. Only by taking this detachment approach can the reconceptualization of the State and its relation to policy be made. These newly emerging realities require new policy directions and approaches, forcing thinkers and policymakers to invent new policies and mechanisms that go beyond just tweaking and revisions.

Corpora of literature linking to public policy and the domains of which there were formulated have often been approached from either the dualistic structure-agency dichotomy or solely from the much more popular governance approach, notwithstanding the criticisms or contentions of which how both were being constructed or implemented thus far. Whilst policies were often seen as a mechanism or a tool to either achieve the intended goals of its user (Weimer and Vining, 1999; Weiss, 1998) as well as a guiding tool which provides information or knowledge on policy-related matters with potentially positive or detrimental outcomes towards those users namely the public (Weimer, 1998), it could be surmised that policy in its universality, is a product of modernity. Modernity in its diverse forms, old and new, served to fulfil the agenda brought about by the agenda-setters such as political scientists, politicians, policymakers, or decision-makers to name a few, in the name of progress and often, such progress is measured using a selection of criteria deemed useful and sensible to those who utilized it.

Despite such an approach, however, there is still room unexplored theoretically which requires revisiting particularly across domains in which public policy converges with industrial and economic policies. Often the causes of such lack of courage to define and redefine the theoretical aspects of the policy domains stem from the treatment of some practices which became irrelevant or obsolete over time as in the case of jumping into the 'governance' bandwagon and trends, the lack of coherency or incongruency that plagued policy-making concerning its intended use and end-user (James and Jorgensen, 2009) or the simplistic and mechanistic approach taken procedurally due to lack of or too much knowledge and depth on the subject required 'policing', resulting in fragmentation of the policy systems (Baumgartner and Jones, 2005). Some scholars even further highlighted the outcomes that multiple cultural and institutional factors could have on an already fragmented policy-governing system (May et al, 2006). Questions surrounding whose policy knowledge shall be selected or used, the degree of influence that one's positionality - both ontological and epistemological - and the invisible power dynamics may have towards these selections, the applicability of the grand narratives that policy practitioners embraced as well as the unintended, accidental but 'trendy' policy issues they aimed at solving, adds further complexities to an already tangled affair.

Interestingly, the use of policy as a tool or mechanism to achieve a particular end goal has not been limited to economists or industrialists per se, but it has also been used fundamentally by the State as a tool towards governing. Questions surrounding how a State should govern, the typology of policies that it needs to govern its citizens and the effects that it hopes to achieve as well as the direction in which its governance takes shape are therefore highly contextualized. Hence to understand how policies are being rationalised and later utilised, it is fruitful to address the kind of State that it is linked to. Government regimes which are highly authoritative and centralized often utilized the top-down approach, with the government at the helm of any development projects and initiatives. The Development State Model is an example of this where States' roles are not only limited to commanding and controlling the governing of State affairs but often, they are also in charge of enabling and facilitating change and development (Chang, 2002). This usually involves activities such as the removal of barriers, picking the winners and mobilization of resources to support the champions in the field (Chang, 2002; Aoki et al, 1997). Policies and other governing mechanisms introduced often protect the interests of these fledglings but the highly productive impresario by creating supportive industrial ecosystems that facilitate their growth potential (Eisinger, 1988). The main goal of the State in this instance is also to prevent systemic market failure through efficient and effective allocation of resources marked by sectoral resource transfer, investments, technological innovation and constructing advantage (Aoki et al, 1997; Chang, 2002) via clustering (Fujita et al, 1999).

For the Entrepreneurial States whose logic of governing follows one of entrepreneurialism and on the centrality of competition and the market in self-organising the economy, policies are often generated to allow for anticipating and creating demand whilst stabilising supplies through the creation of new markets and safeguarding economic development (Mazzucato, 2015). In this sense, the State not only acts as the regulator but also functions as an entrepreneur, in charge of creating opportunities, innovating the market, and accumulating wealth as the industry expands. Mazzucato (2015) argued that in the new innovation economies, 'big' thinking states are needed where there need to be mission-oriented, confident in enterprising, able to strategise and adjust based on their current advantage as well as have firms who are willing to invest in the long- term. In her definition of being entrepreneurial, the state is seen as an institution willing to take on "early, capital intensive, high-risk areas that private sector tend to fear. [...] able and willing to invest in areas of extreme uncertainty, courageously envisioning the *direction* of change across public agencies and departments". Yu (2001) argued that for the state to be able to achieve such a cognitive state of planning and strategising, the public agents involved should have the ability to learn and experiment based on previous successes and failures of intervention to be winners and eliminate errors through current information by being economically competitive. Such ability allows the state agents to be more flexible, decisive and highly alert or cautious in their venture. Being entrepreneurial is not only to identify where the opportunity lies but also to get things done (Schumpeter, 1934)(Cited in Yu, 2001). One of the roles of the state in this sense is to be the enabler of the development of which relationship between public-private is one of interdependence (Weiss, 1988). Patient capital investment as Mazzucato coined it, should look beyond merely jumpstarting innovation but the state should also look at "new directions and do things, which currently are not done at all" (Keynes, 1926) (cited in Mazzucato, 2015). Mathews (2006) and Lazzarini (2015) point out the need for the state to create a sustainable competitive advantage for firms through the use of industrial policy mechanisms as economic conditions are constantly changing, resonating closely with Mazzucato's interpretation of the entrepreneurial state. The policy mechanisms here may range from the social policy that allows for social capabilities and capacity building to setting up of focus economic vision or agenda, which should incorporate an emphasis on life, long learning, and human resources development (Karlsson and Karlsson, 2002) as well as through institutional relations i.e. network effects, nationally, regionally (regionalism) and/ or at international level (Karlsson and Karlsson, 2002).

Whilst these two models were not meant to be exhaustive, the characteristics of both models showed the centrality of the state in managing the industries through diverse actions and policies by coordinating actions aimed at minimising the potential of unexpected systemic market risks and failures. The state's drive towards fostering competition and innovation among industrial players dominates the industrial and business policy realms. Inter-organisational coordination, resulting from the interaction and network effects organisations of policymakers from different strands, sectors, or spheres, was hence the defining character of the state in these models. It also highlighted the structure and agency dynamics where coordination and organisation exist both vertically between the State and the governed i.e., industries, businesses, and the public as well as horizontally in the forms of inter-agencies, inter-businesses, and inter-public relationships (Peters, 1998; Cohen, 2006). Bornemann (2007) argued that such coordination aims at preventing emerging policies contradiction and calls for policy integration became more apparent when integration across trans-domain policies was seen as a panacea to current policy problems. Moreover, such focus towards industrial and business policies tends to marginalise the derivative socioeconomic cost incurred by the public and its effects on the living. Interestingly, recent scholarly work on China's adaptation of the capitalist model shows the combination of both models because of the identification of challenges brought about by State-led development initiatives (see Zhang 2006, 2013) leading to the coining of the term State Entrepreneurialism, a model where the State not only leads and regulates development practices but also functions similarly to an entrepreneur (see Wu, 2023; Yi et al, 2023).

Critiques on the overemphasis on the role of the state on development, the end of the Washington Consensus particularly with scholarly development in Europe on State, policymaking and strategic planning, the emerging realities on the increasing role of civil society as shapers and shakers of society resulted in the construction of new fields of development within the academia. This led to the rise of the governance model, having a major impetus towards the relationship between policy formulation, planning and governing.

Within development studies, the notion of Public-Private Partnership (PPP) towards governing, and the inclusion of the fourth 'P' (people) dimension into PPP is evident from current models of environmental governance (see Ahmed and Ali, 2006; Ng et al, 2013; Kumaraswamy et al, 2015) resulted in the expansion of the term whilst loosening further the scope or dimensions of which it was supposed to consolidate. Deconstruction of the relationship between the State and the people reveals that those agents or players such as industrialists, businesses and policymakers are mere actors within this whole political and economic system, objects of government that require policing. What is missing from the first two models discussed is the importance of agency, the whole notion of power, social empowerment, enrichment, social enterprising, and the enabling aspects of the people have over government. Owing to the works by Amartya Sen (1988, 1999, 2009) on the need to embrace ethical economics, protect the welfare of communities and expands individual freedom inclusive of capacity and competency development, as well as those geographers such as David Harvey's Social Justice and the City (1973), the role of human agency becomes more prominent and helped shaped the field of governance within development studies. Mobilisation of civil society and understanding their role towards agenda setting (Birkland, 1998; Sen, 2009), a strong emphasis on the role of reformers in fostering collaboration and cooperation rather than simply ousting the State's centrality and its status quo maintenance (Stone, 2006; Hogl, et al, 2016) and utilisation of targeted programs to foster economic development and ends socio-economic inequalities (Sachs, 2006; Acemoglu and Robinson, 2012) had been at the centre governance and societal empowerment debates. Such emergence of capillary power as Jessop (1998) calls it acts as the key towards the formulation of a more inclusive form of governing and policymaking which should be celebrated. Other major works from management and policy studies on collaborative governance, policy coordination and strategic planning (see Ansell and Gash, 2008; Bryson, 1998, 2018; Cosby and Bryson, 2005) as well as analysis on policy, governmental performances and inter-governmental relations (see Radin, 1997, 2013; Considine, 1999, 2005; Considine et al, 2018) mainly touched on the importance of positionality of the government as they managed State affairs either by promoting innovative management practices or by understanding the importance of networking and coordinating relations to achieve management goals.

Despite such advances in government management and administration research, there is still a need to highlight that government is not an institution or structure that is void of *realpolitik*. The dynamics of power relations and the effects of power towards the governed are real and it usually comes in the forms of higher socioeconomic and societal costs. Stone (2006) argued that even with the transfer of power to grassroots movements that may help in increasing the amount of work done, understanding the differences between the concept of 'power to' and 'power over' is a game changer. She argued that most NGOs are the harbingers of change that calls for a total overhaul of either existing policies or the system which also further demonstrates the problems associated with the 'power over' concept, deemed as unsustainable in the long run. The treatment of businesses or industrialists within the development literature, in general, was impartial or negative at its best due to the intergenerational problems brought about by Structural Adjustments Policies that benefitted the 'capitalist' (Booth et al, 2020; Vilas, 1995) the notion of capitalist greed, poverty and power inequalities as highlighted in the works by Moore and Schmitz (1995) and recently by Piketty (2014). This has also been mentioned in the works of Sen previously mentioned. In other words, the centrality of the State is not enough or sufficient in managing the industries or the economy regardless of the principles of governing that it follows particularly if such governing contributed towards non-intentional social costs, an outcome that social policy should address or prevent in the first place. A cautionary principle, however, shall also be practised when addressing any development-related questions as local contextualization is highly paramount and influential in determining any outcomes. Whilst the European experiences on the State-Policy-People relations have been fruitful in providing insights into the dynamism of the three components, there is a need to avoid embracing its universalistic tendencies as the human societal experiences across diverse geographical domains remained diverse and highly varied. Hence what kind of policy expectations and characteristics shall we see within Brunei's Integrated Sustainable Halal Policy (ISHP) model then?

Since the research dealt with the halal industry, a cultural industry based on religion, it is logical to deconstruct the relationship between the State and the policy it introduced from the lens of Islamic governance. Contemporary Islamic scholars often associated the application of Islamic governance and the principles surrounding it as not a 'new emergent' within the Islamic circle per se. This is due to empirical evidence based on historical events such as the election of the Rashidin Caliphs leading to the formation of the *shuratic* councils as well as the present ritualistic and living practices of Muslims daily based on Allah's commandments. It also highlights the close relationship between theology, its application and practicality stemming from the Quran, the Hadith, *Usul Fiqh, or* the *Ahkam*. However, its revival within Islamic scholarships and the increase in the use of the word 'Islamic governance' within the English-speaking world, have much closer relationships to the development in Europe and elsewhere around the world, particularly within the writings on postcolonial geographies. The problems associated with capitalism and the rise of material culture, the incongruency and disconnect between planning, policies and societal outcomes, and the emergence of critically aware masses or the 'woke' generation, have inadvertently required revisiting or rereading of the current approach towards Islamic governance. Hence, what is Islamic governance?

The work on Islamic governance derived from the seminal work of Ibn Khaldun (1406), particularly about the positionality of individuals within Islamic cosmology and earlier by Al-Mawardi (1058) concerning leadership, government, acts of governing and territoriality. Under the concept of *Maqasid Al-Sharia*, Ibn Khaldun attempted to describe and explain, scientifically, the relationship and interdependence between five main spheres, which in a nutshell, are vital in ensuring the protection of the welfare and well-being of individuals and the collective (*Ummah*). Governing of these core areas such as the Intellect *('Aql)*, Faith *(Din)*, Self *(Nafs)*, Posterity *(Nasl)* and Wealth *(Mal)*, within individuals and members of society require not only collective role of institutions where power resides (Chapra et al, 2008), but it also calls for the need for deeper understanding of individual roles and those of power *(Amir)* concerning the concept of viceregents *or Khalifa* on earth (Al-Mawardi, 1058; Asad and Grunebaum, 1961; Deuraseh, 2019). Within the *Maqasid,* the interdependence between the State as institutions of leaders *(Amir)*, formulators of policies in charge of decision-making, policing, and governors of the *Ummah* and the population should be seen as mutually self-reinforcing and self-reforming too since there exists some sense of self-purification due to the realisations of their responsibility and accountability in the eyes of God. This is because the role of the state as viceregents are not symbolic but rather practical, supporting the end goal of development through the provisions of safeguards vital for societal function and growth. Governing is both means and an end among individuals and the State, both inter and intra, and as a form of accumulation of good deeds *(Ibadah)*, a bridge that connects the worldly affair towards the hereafter. Hence, any governing policies and mechanisms introduced should weigh their effects towards the five core areas. The role of the State in providing effective checks and balances on the State, through the *shura* (parliaments, councils or the *majlis*), honest judiciary, properly conceived laws, and regulations, as well as a clear sense of direction, allows for the development to takes place by removal of uncertainties (Ogunbado, 2019). It functions as both a reflexive and a self-cleansing mechanism created to prevent or avoid conflict. Proper upbringing and having communities with strong volition in the implementation of Islamic values are important. Curtailment on the accumulation of wealth would affect the posterity of *Ummah* but too much wealth could also affect the human self out of greed or by refusal in contributing parts of wealth as alms or *zakah.* A lesser emphasis on faith *(Din)* would result in a situation depicted in the parable *'Like the blind leading the blind'* which eventually will negatively affect the self and society. While the Quran and the Hadith play central roles in guiding believers from going astray, the role of intellectuals and enrichment of individual intellects coupled with the knowledge generated from it should help or assist individuals in performing their role as the servant of God. A sense of balance within these 5 core areas is henceforth needed to achieve the enrichment and sustainability of individuals and the general population. It is beyond the scope of this chapter to discuss the multidimensional aspects of the Islamic governance concept. However, the point to take from the summary later is to explore how the 5 key themes can be applied to the SDG.

Concerning policy, the concept of the *Maqasid* viewed governing as a combination of the dynamism between the vertical and horizontal modes of governance through the utilisation of diverse policies, institutional mechanisms, and civic involvement. Whilst the top-down emphasises the centrality of the State in 'stewarding' its government and citizens (see Davis et al, 1997) by adhering to the accepted religious moral-political governing standard, the State also plays a role in integrating and absorbing feedback generated temporally at the point of governing through 'stakeholder' consultations (see Freeman et al, 2010). It is only by identification of where and how these dynamisms take place and by looking into the effects on communities that the practical establishment of ISHP is possible. By connecting the dots and filling in any gaps found through such stewardship governing and stakeholder consultation exercises, it offers the first step towards the generation of an integrated policy mechanism. Hence, unlike the two main references of policy as comprising of detailed guidelines and information towards goal achievements as well as knowledge generator for its designated end-user, the policy itself can function as an objective, an end on its own term.

Habermas's Communicative Rationality and Sustainable Policy Planning as a Third Space

Habermas's work on Communicative Rationality (CR) opens new avenues in addressing the problems constantly associated with policy planning, formulation, implementation, and development. Within the geographical concept of space, public space, follows a certain kind of order, discourses that are considered culturally/ socially acceptable by the mainstream cultures, time-sensitive and bound to change because of major paradigm shifts and development. Public spaces, in general, are governed by public institutions under the State as well as the populace that forms most of the given geographical space/ place. Private spaces, on the other hand, were often linked to geographical domains with strong bottom-up governance concepts as they centred on the grassroots, individuals, the 'private' component of the populace, linked closely to the exercise of their rights on spaces which were deemed public. Policy planning and formulation, when viewed from both spatial dynamism of public and private, hence, involved either the centralisation prowess of the 'public' state in deciding the best outcomes for its citizens or decentralised, capillary power situated within individuals that can shape changes. Whilst Habermas claimed that a morally acceptable, consensual approach to planning stems from the effective communication of visions or missions of the policymakers among them and the public via an agreed mechanism, one could not simply ignore the presence of 'white noises' that use emerging conflict as opportunities towards problem resolution.

The problems associated with this approach, however, are diverse and multi-faceted. Apart from grievances surrounding the prolonged conflict or escalation of distrust among conflicting parties in their search for common grounds and instability, it creates the overarching or universalistic tendencies that CR employed by ignoring the context of which things developed or are framed and how it can cause fractal policy planning. Buzzwords such as governance, competitiveness, empowerment, and enrichment, to common words such as industrial, business or even public with social policy tend to

Figure 1. Summary of major governing models, their characteristics and approaches towards policymaking

Model	Main characteristics	State and Citizen Relations	Policy Approach(es)
Developmental State	Authoritative and Centralised Regime Command and Control Facilitate Change i.e. Removal of Barriers, Picking the Winners, Resources and Supports for Champions, Subsidies etc Prevention of Systemic Market Failure Construct Advantage and Increase Competitiveness of Champions, Minimal Risk-Taker	Stewardship (Sociopolitical and Economic-centric)	(Divergence) Top-down
Entrepreneurial State	Market-Led and Mission-Oriented State Strategise and Adapts to Market Conditions Regulator cum Entrepreneur Demand Creator and Supply Provider Collaborate with Firms in the long-term, Invest 'Long' in Uncertainities, Huge Risk-Taker, Early Capital Intensive, Highly Flexible State Learning from Experiences of Successes and Failures Information Key to Strategic Positioning Enable, Facilitate and Empower Businesses and Industries	Stewardship and Stakeholder Coordinations (Economic-centric)	(Convergence) Top-down and Bottom-Up
Governance (Conventional)	Civil Society Led and Highly Dynamic Democratic, Protection of Civil Liberties, Individual Rights and Freedom Governing through Checks and Balances Conflict/ Dispute Settlement and Resolution through Collaboration and Reforms Highly Inclusive, Accountable, Ethical and Empowering Supports end to discrimination and inequalities	Stewardship and Stakeholder Coordinations (Political and Social-centric)	(Convergence) Top-down and Bottom-Up
Governance (Islamic)	Governors or *Amr* at the centre with advisories from councils Democratic, Protection of Civil Liberties, Individual Rights and Freedom as long as it follows God's Commandments and not at the expense of the public Governing through Checks and Balances Conflict/ Dispute Settlement and Resolution through Collaboration and Reforms but conflict avoidance/ prevention is preferable Highly Inclusive, Accountable, Ethical and Empowering with fairness and justice at the core Follows the Quran and Hadith (Maqasid Al-Sharia)	Stewardship and Stakeholder Coordinations (Political, Religious and Social-centric)	(Convergence) Top-down and Bottom-Up

have different meanings based on geographical locations. Its application to small economies like Brunei Darussalam requires one to not solely frame its definitive characteristics based on European experiences but also understand its adaptive rationale and relevance to the current national policy setting. Brunei's food industries are only sizable of which most can be categorised as Micro-Small Medium Enterprises

Figure 2. Habermas's communicative rationality (CR) and third space dynamics with public and private spaces in relation to sustainable policymaking

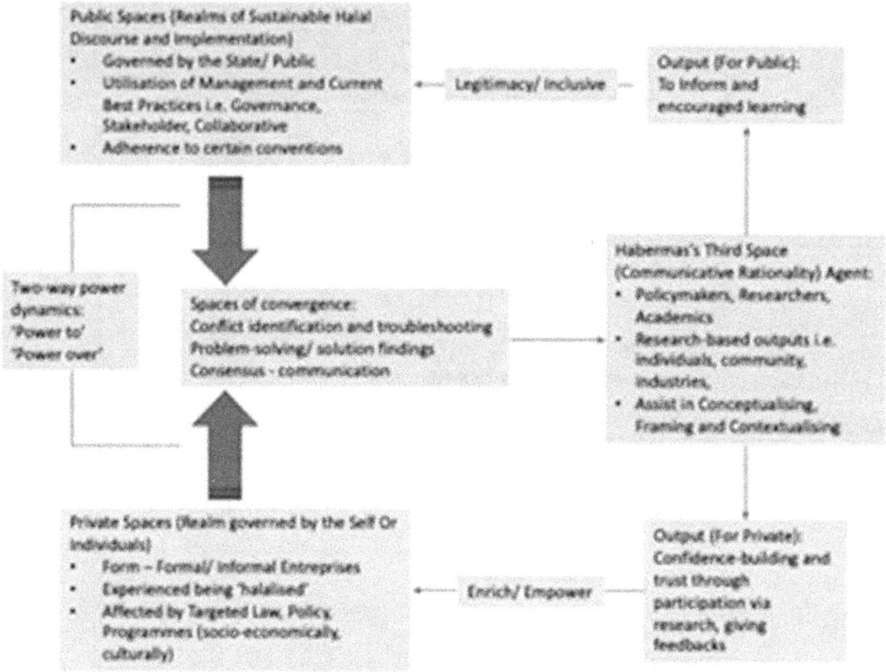

(MSMEs), a huge amount of it being informal i.e., home-based, or online and operated just for familial sustenance. The use of such huge concepts, unfortunately, may not be fruitful in sustaining its existence or growth in the long run. Treating industrial and business policies as belonging to separate domains from social policy whilst at the same time applying these bigger concepts without analysing the question of operationalisation and context will result in disconnects, unintended or unforeseen due to the two mis isms – misconceptualisation and miscontextualisation. Hence, halal policy formulation and its eventual review in Brunei should be reconceptualised by understanding the effects current halal policy has towards the industrial and business environment categorised above. In other words, policymaking and formulation would have to take place in the third space, not solely situated in the structures (macro) nor in the socio-private and public domains (micro), but rather at the middle level (meso) where the macro-micro levels converge. Therefore, businesses should not be treated as mere numbers for statistical or reporting purposes, but rather, as part of the public or society whose welfare needs to be safeguarded and protected. They are undoubtedly also part of the *Ummah* that is both directly and indirectly affected by changes within these policy domains. The diagram (Figure 2) best summarises the use of Habermas's CR in sustainable policymaking within the third space domains:

Halal Industrial Development in Brunei

In the case of the halal food industries, the exponential growth of its activities, feeding on the insatiable appetite of the ever-growing halal consumer markets has resulted in the development of halal industrial production. The halal economy has undergone rapid transformation, from one niche to mainstream and global. Due to these changes, different approaches are required in our attempt to understand the dynamism within these diverse halal industries concerning governing institutions. This is particularly pressing in the realms of both halal economic and industrial policies which if remained unchecked, could result in unwarranted socio-economic costs affecting the public.

Brunei Darussalam, being a small economy relative to its Southeast Asian neighbours, was the first to suggest the establishment of a global halal brand (Ayan, 2013) and a global standard with the establishment of the premium Brunei Halal Food Brand in 2008. This is part of its national attempt to develop its halal economy and its economic diversification strategy, under the auspicious banner known as Brunei Vision 2035. To date, only two countries developed state-backed halal standardisation and certification programmes namely Brunei and Malaysia. Similarly, its halal food policy was also one which was subject to adaption and co-optation from other existing policies of other Islamic nations, contextualised locally to fit into existing halal governing activities. Whilst contextualisation has been carried out, there seem to be no real questions raised surrounding the rationality of the policy adaptation and its implementations as well as on the outcomes of such activities at the ground level. Terminologies or academic jargon surrounding the policy domains such as governance, civil society, stakeholder consultations and stewardship, to name a few, were widely used within its industrial governing but its theoretical logic and its applicability to small national economies like Brunei have never been put to the test. Hence this chapter aimed to disentangle the current policy logic while refiguring and redefining the multiverses of policy domains by integrating it with the introduction of an Integrated, Sustainable Halal Policy (ISHP).

Halal Policy, Governing, and Sustainable Development: Current Approach

In the last 10 years, numerous studies have been done concerning Brunei's halal industry. Though new, halal studies relating to sustainability are mostly geared towards the competitive aspect of industries and businesses, particularly those along the lines of supply or value chains and sectoral studies other than on halal certification, quality assurances and quality credence. However, the critical review or assessment of Brunei's halal policies and governing, at present, remained superficial, descriptive or fractal at best as viewed in the works by Ibrahim (2022), Raffi (2019) and Sulaiman (2020). Whilst these works provide insights into the role of agencies, halal laws and regulations as well as strategic plans and roadmaps currently in place, it remains incoherent or lacks the required synergies to propel the industry forward. The inclusion of the 'sustainability' component into the current halal governing framework laid bare or exposed these weaknesses further as evidenced by the findings from the multiple research projects undertaken between 2016 to 2022.

The current halal policy and its halal-related mechanisms operating in Brunei can be found in Figure 1 below. Since halal and the concept governing halal have gone beyond concerns over the halal status of meat, the incorporation of the *tayyiban* principle helps in widening the scope of halal by acknowledging the importance of personal as well as hygienic processes that occur along the value chains. Unlike previous research that treats halal policy and the ensuing mechanism to be championed solely by the Brunei Halal Food Control Division of the Ministry of Religious Affairs (MORA), the researcher suggested the need to incorporate the standards such as the PBD 25:2016 on mass catering practices as well as PBD 30: 2016 concerning the production of finished fish and shellfish products as part of the *halalan tayyiban* mechanism as well. This is imperative since these standards were generics adopted and revised from 1) ASEAN's General Principles of Food Hygiene, 2) CAC/ RCP 39- 1993's Code of Hygienic

Figure 3. List of halal and halal-related acts, regulations, and guidelines used in governing the halal food industry accompanied by the targeted regulatory/policy end user

No.	Established & Redacted Acts/ Regulations/ Standard in Brunei	Regulatory Bodies/ Regimes	Targeted End User
1	Miscellaneous Licenses Act, Chapter 127, 1984 (Redacted)	Brunei Municipal Board & Committee, Ministry of Home Affairs	Businesses/ Commercial (Within Municipality)
2	Halal Meat Act, Chapter 183, 1998, Amended 2014	Halal Food Control Division, Ministry of Religious Affairs	Businesses/ Commercial
3	Brunei Certification Guideline 1 - Guideline for Halal Certification		Businesses/ Commercial
4	Brunei Certification Guideline 2 - Guideline for Halal Compliance Audit		Businesses/ Commercial
5	Brunei Certification Guideline 3 - Guideline for Halal Compliance Auditor		Quality Assurers/ Auditors
6	Brunei Certification Guideline 4 - Guideline for Halal Surveillance Audit		Quality Assurers/ Auditors
7	Piawai Brunei Darussalam (PBD) 24: 2007 - Brunei Darussalam Standard for Halal Food		Businesses/ Commercial
8	Halal Certificate and Halal Label Order 2008, Amendments 2012, 2016 and 2017		Enforcement/ Quality Assurers/ Auditors/ Businesses/ Commercial
9	Wholesome Meat Order 2011	Brunei Department of Agriculture and Agrifood (currently under Brunei Darussalam Food Authority)	Businesses/ Commercial (local and abroad)
10	Public Health (Food) Act, Chapter 182, 1998, Amended 2012	Food Safety and Quality Control Division and Public Health Services, Ministry of Health	Businesses/ Commercial
11	Public Health (Food) Regulations, 2001, Amended 2013		Businesses/ Commercial
12	Piawai Brunei Darussalam (PBD) 25: 2016 - Code of Hygienic Practice for Pre-Cooked and Cooked Foods for Masss Catering	Department of Energy, Prime Minister's Office and Food Safety and Quality Control Division and Public Health Services, Ministry of Health	Businesses/ Commercial
13	Piawai Brunei Darussalam (PBD) 30: 2016 - Standard for Crackers from Marine and Freshwater Fish, Crustacean and Molluscan Shellfish	Department of Energy, Prime Minister's Office, Department of Fisheries, Ministry of Primary Resources and Tourism and Food Safety and Quality Contoil Division and Public Health Services, Ministry of Health	Businesses/ Commercial

Practice for Precooked and Cooked Foods and Mass Catering, 3) PBD 12: 2014 building Guideline and Requirements and 4) CODEX STAN 222-2001 International Codex Standard for Crackers from Marine and Freshwater Fish, Crustacean and Molluscan Shellfish. Before the development of the comprehensive Brunei Halal Certification Guidelines (BCG 1-4) and subsequent Halal Certificate and Halal Label Order of 2005 amended in 2012, 2016 and 2017, the Public Health (Food) Act, Chapter 182, 1998, the Halal Meat Act, Chapter 183, 1998 and the now redacted Miscellaneous Act, Chapter 127, 1984 were used to govern halal-related activities.

Based on the figure above, it can be seen how, despite the current Whole of Nations Approach adopted by the Brunei government, the existing halal regulatory framework is still operating in silos. Whilst the Brunei Halal Food Control Division (HFCD) seems to possess numerous policy and regulatory mechanisms in governing halal, there also exist overlapping industrial standards or code of practice that governs domestic food production activities, situated within diverse agencies or governmental departments. The recently established Brunei Darussalam Food Authority (BDFA), for instance, has one legal law or order that dictates its overall functionality within the food industry, whilst the Ministry of Health have control over a few acts, both directly and indirectly, especially those involving public food health and safety. This ranges from those that deal with microbial culture, and chemical contaminations to the quality maintenance and securing of the content of products and raw materials used for industrial production activities. Inputs from the four projects carried out between 2014 to 2022 also showed the existence of some cooperation from inter-related government agencies in the execution or implementation of the various food acts. For instance, HFCD functions as the secretariat that feeds technical audits and reports to the final halal certificate and permit issuer, the Brunei Islamic Religious Council (MUIB). As part of its regulatory mandate, a few technical and working committees from various ministries are appointed in providing technical input to be used in informing MUIB's final decision-making. In the case of standards such as PBD 25: 2016 and PBD 30: 2016, there have also been instances where compliance with these standards does not warrant automated approvals of halal certificates and permit issuance as experienced by businesses. This was partly due to the centrality of MUIB as the sole bearer and authority that controls halal certification and permits. Interestingly, further investigation of the standards and other policy documents also suggests the existence of collaboration and cooperation between the diverse arms of the State spanning multiple agencies with prominent formal businesses towards the formulation of these standards. From these findings, it can be hypothesised that the dynamics between the State and the formulation of halal policy in Brunei follow two pathways, one of which the State functions as the steward that guide or determines the desired outcomes it envisioned and secondly, as the seekers of support, information, and knowledge through its stakeholders despite the centrality of power that lies within the State agencies and mechanisms of governing. The existing policy patchworks, though multifaceted and complex, still work wonders but effective and efficient operationalisation requires carefully crafted governing with agents requiring not only the capacity and competency but also capabilities to monitor and ensure smooth running.

Similarly, there have also been numerous initiatives taken by the State to assist the food industry and businesses, in general, to maximise their potential through the direct design of short to medium-strategic plans via agencies such as the Department of Agriculture and Agri-food (DAA) as well as using Government-Linked Companies (GLCs) such as Ghanim International and PDS Abattoir direct involvement in the halal food industry. DAA, had in the past, published two short-to-medium strategic plans, one for the periods between 2008-2013 and another for the years 2016-2020. Analyses of the two showed the first focus solely on developing the key infrastructure needed for the establishment of the Brunei halal food brand, leveraging from the Halal Certificate and Halal Label Order (HCHLO) of 2008. The second strategic plan was more targeted with an emphasis on government investments towards the improvement of the value chains and the whole value ecosystem of the halal food industry. These include investments in new technology and capabilities development in livestock and agriculture, the establishment of integrated food production facilities as well as enticing foreign investors in establishing joint ventures with local food companies and start-ups. All these initiatives are aimed at increasing the productivity and output of local halal production as part of increasing their competitiveness. As in the case of Ghanim International's Brunei halal foods brand, analysis of their strategies since their inception in 2008 shows interesting dynamics where the company evolved from trying to play catch up through product rebranding or repackaging to partnerships with local MSMEs and later through the construction of its production facilities.

If we are to deconstruct the diverse halal policies and laws and thematise them, the halal policy mechanisms in Brunei are segregated into industrial halal which focused on halal industrial development as part of national economic diversification strategies, followed by halal businesses growth, quality conformance and credence using certifications and permits issuance. Thirdly, on establishing and consolidating halal law and order through the development of regulatory action regimes. Fourthly is on halal and public health surveillance and management via disease detection, control, and safe consumption of food. Finally, to a certain extent, grassroots halal focused on business and consumer reporting as part of collective action. How integrated are these policy domains? How does it fair in relation to small informal businesses? What effects are we seeing as these policies are implemented?

It has been reported by various local studies (see Ibrahim, 2022; Sulaiman, 2020; Raffi, 2019) that the effects of the halal certification had been positive and sustainable thus far. However, further scrutiny of their studies highlighted the lack of substance to support these claims particularly when the concept of business competitiveness and individual business experiences were considered. The studies either highlighted the business communities' perceptions and opinions regarding the implementation of compulsory halal certification since 2016 or provides some descriptions of halal agencies' general roles or functionalities. Opinionated or perception-based studies, whilst useful in gauging the levels of awareness and views of businesses affected, it is deemed not beneficial to be used in policy formulation. Policy formulation requires hard, empirical evidence that revolves around the material and real-world effects towards the end-users. Extensive coverage concerning this has been made in the researcher's doctoral thesis, though still pending examination. But the combination of some studies carried out by the researcher between 2017 and 2023 on GLCs and MSMEs firm-to-firm dynamics, the investigation on the potential of halal packaging development in Brunei, the study on Brunei's tea and coffee sector (see Azalie and Kamarulzaman, 2023), as well as the global production network of Brunei halal food domestic firms (see Azalie and Samad, 2022), offer certain insights on the effects of halalisation on these businesses. Plus, the airing of business grievances over the amendments made to the HCHLO of 2016 which subsequently led to its revision in 2017 over general halal certification application cost, highlighted the caveats that current policy mechanisms failed to address. How does it affect small-time, informal businesses? Thus far, there has been no comprehensive study that investigates such details. Snippets from the researcher's doctoral thesis showed detrimental effects towards MSMEs, both formal and informal, related to an increase in costs of operations and productions as they undergo halal certification. In the study on power dynamics between the GLCs and their local 'partners', it was found that not only there exist one-sided partnerships and Non-Disclosures Agreements (NDAs) of which the MSMEs became embroiled in subjectification and indirect exploitation. But the rebranding or collaborations also increased the cost of operations, affecting their competitiveness as the MSMEs also have their own brand name products competing in the same market as their 'rebranded' or repackaged products. With business communities which are dwarfed by any international or regional standard but still sizeable ratio-wise when compared to the total population, there is a need for further redefinition or refinement of who they are. This is not limited to their size only but also due to the informal, home-based, or merely sustenance nature of their activities, in contrast to the standardised, industrial definitions which often aimed towards much larger firms involved in sizeable wealth creation, accumulation and expansion. Due to this, it begs the question of whether the former shall be treated similarly to how businesses were treated in other parts of the world, following approaches or models of the same vein, or does the current characteristics of these groups warrant a differential in treatments, hence, a different or totally new approach? Current halal policies, regardless of their focus be it on industrial, formal businesses (production-related) or consumer-centric approaches, omitted the protection of the welfare of the micro or home-based businesses. This is on top of the fact that its operationalisation is still in silos with limited levels of integration. Using Jurgen Habermas's Theory of Communicative Rationality and his idea of the 'third space', combined with the Principles of the Sharia envisioned by Ibn Khaldun, the following model is developed to aid the creation of a sustainable halal development policy, rooted in the principle of inclusivity, informed via the output of years of research, from the lenses of experts i.e., the Third Space, who study the dynamics between the halal food industry and governmental policy.

Towards an Integrated, Sustainable Halal Policy (ISHP) in the Context of SDG and Islamic Governance

The ISHP model proposed is aimed at not only integrating the multiverse policy domains, known to be fractal, period centric and works in binaries i.e., either top-down or bottom-up, making it difficult to create the required synergy. Whilst the various national governments be it in the developed or developing world managed to develop their research arms situated within government agencies and departments, questions surrounding the influence of power and the invisible power dynamics, the role of decision-makers in dictating decisions or outcomes of research need to be considered. This is to ensure that any policies or decisions made are not biased or are carried out only to whitewash or veiled the actual conditions experienced by the State and its citizens. Within development studies and even more so in the studies on sustainable development, these issues have long plagued the real world as social inequalities, from poverty to unequal income distribution to environmental resource utilisations still in place, widening at some, deepening further in some parts of the world.

It is due to this that a new model is required to better serve, protect, and safeguard the dignity, welfare, and survival of the people of the *Ummah*. Borrowing some of the themes of SDG 17 and adapting it in the context of the five components of the *Maqasid Al-Sharia*, the ISHP is designed by identifying the domains that require governmental-societal actions, improvements as well as refiguration as industrial halal takes off. It also tries to highlight the key spheres of life of the *Maqasid* likely affected as halalisation processes take place at the multilevel of industrial governance. In other words, the ISHP combines the Islamic governance dimensions with industrial and business components of halal policy linked to competitiveness, sustainability and growth adapted from the SDGs and projects the domains likely affected by halal development. At the heart of the domains mainly affected by such transformations are individuals and the family as an institution, whilst at the same time, acknowledging that any changes deemed to be detrimental to these two spheres would affect society in general as well. This may also include the State and the territories in which it governs.

It should be noted that these ISHP model needs to be framed within the context of halal certification and halal industrial development in general. Research writings on halal for the past decade or so have been focusing more on the halal maintenance of the religious dietary requirement relating to food production and consumption, its quality credence with recent alignment in relation to the environment and industrial sustainability. There has also been development in relation to the protection of animal welfare before their food conversion that reiterates the concept of *ihsaan*. *Ihsaan* investigates the need to carry out one's creed and has it reflected towards one's societal actions and obligations. In the case of halal, it is reflected in industrialists' and governors' corporate social responsibility (CSR) towards living beings, neither humans nor animals or the environment that they serviced. For halal producers, this comes in the form of halal food production. Despite such convictions, however, the focus on how it affects the five components of the *Maqasid* and its relation to sustainability have not been linked thoroughly. Hence, the proposed ISHP model that connotates these linkages, inter-relationships, or the point of intersection that each *Maqasid* component have is tabulated in Figure 4 to make sense of the final ISHP diagram (Figure 5) soon to follow.

Figure 4. Matrix showing the inter and intra-relationship or linkages of the five components of Maqasid (top) and relevant SDGs concerning halal industrial development (bottom)

Maqasid Components	Posterity (Nasl)	Intellect ('Aql)	Faith (Ad-Din)	Human-self (Nafs)	Wealth (Mal)
Posterity (Nasl)			x	x	x
Intellect ('Aql)			x	x	x
Faith (Ad-Din)	x	x		x	x
Human-self (Nafs)	x	x	x		
Wealth (Mal)	x	x	x		

	Sustainable Development Goals Relevant to ISHP on Halal Development						
Maqasid Components	SDG 1	SDG 3	SDG 8	SDG 10	SDG 11	SDG 12	SDG 13
Posterity (Nasl)		x			x	x	x
Intellect ('Aql)		x					
Faith (Ad-Din)					x	x	
Human-self (Nafs)		x	x				
Wealth (Mal)	x		x	x	x		

Based on Figure 3 above, the *Maqasid* component on Posterity *(Nasl)* when applied to halal development and the SDGs shows that for a sustainable halal to develop, there is a need to look at how it affects the individual as a person and the family as an institution. The need to aid or assist individuals or families to grow and reproduce by allowing them to enrich themselves through health protection, the ability to use resources responsibly and through the removals or freedom from debt-servicing burden will help peace to be maintained and conflict to be avoided. To be industrious and contribute towards societal benefits, is in line with the multiple components envisioned in the SDGs such as SDG 3 on good health and well-being, SDG 11 on development of sustainable communities and cities, SDG 12 on responsible production and consumption and SDG 13 on climate action. Halal policies that not only protect the consumers and the environment but are also inclusive of the producers themselves should allow them to have these safeguards as the industry reorganizes itself as halalisation takes place.

To be able to create and accumulate wealth *(Mal)* as a community halalised industrially helps strengthen further the foundation of the family as an institution as well as individuals. Wealth generation and accumulation allow for poverty reduction, avoidance, and alleviation, ensuring current end-users involved in any halalisation processes can ensure business survivability daily, increase positive-sum competition, reduce cost-related issues as well as share part of their wealth with those who belong to the poor or destitute. The sharing of wealth usually comes in the form of giving out of alms or the *sadaqah*, religious tithe or *zakah*. In the proposed ISHP, policies linked to halalisation should allow for business competitiveness and transactions to intensify, encouraging the diversity in halal productions and products to be offered to increase. The domains that this scope of the *Maqasid* tied together halal businesses and industrial performances whilst at the same time protecting the welfare of those involved in the activities. Programs such as certification procedures or processes, and their actual implementation as well as fairness in decision-making should allow for wealth creation to grow or develop. This is particularly the case if the current communities are regulated and comprised of MSMEs or small home-based, informal businesses. This sharia component complements the components of the SDGs relating to zero poverty (SDG 1), decent work and economic growth (SDG 8), reduction of inequalities (SDG 10) and the development of sustainable communities (SDG 11). Through the incorporation of the principles of justice and ethically responsible development, the removal of monopoly and encouragement in the forms of fairness in the competition will undoubtedly promote the growth of the MSMEs, with a strong sense of trust at its core. This differs from the notion of competitiveness presented by Porter (1998, 2008) whose focus is particularly on the centrality of profit maximization and high productivity at the expense of businesses' welfare and human well-being.

Linked to these two components *(Nasl* and *Mal)* is the need to safeguard the intellect *('Aql).* The creation of wealth and the ability to assist individuals to reproduce, enrich and enjoy a healthy and good quality of life, helps to safeguard the stability of an individual's mental health. Allowing people to disregard worrisome thoughts that any industrial activities carry, especially when one's business activity relies on debt services or reduction in uncertainties created by ineffective policies, allows for self-growth, learning and knowledge acquisition to be possible. This in turn helps them to innovate or construct advantages in the industry that they are involved in, in this case, the halal industry regardless of which sector it is. One of the main criteria of this shared knowledge should be its ability to be transferred or transmitted to halal businesses. It must be easily codified and easy to understand. This complements the third SDG (SDG 3) on the promotion of good health and well-being. Support services rendered to individuals as halal industrialisation takes place will help reduce the socioeconomic costs and burden broken communities bring, helping them towards enrichment and empowerment. Before the introduction of any related policies, a focus on this domain is imperative. Policymakers need to ensure that any introduction of new policies would not strain the end-users to the extent that it led to paralysis communally and individually in both plans and implementation. Hence, any mechanisms that will be introduced, be it an integration of the socio-health and guided industrial and social policies, need to be enabling, empowering and inclusive in the long run both for individuals as well as communities. Both studies on broken communities, the evaluation of the success of its mechanisms as well as the challenges policy and decision-makers faced in integrating the multifaceted aspect of the problems have been touched on in some of these studies by Kromer (2010), Welsh et al (2015) and Weisburd et al (2015). It reflects immaculately the strong relationship between the improvement in care, protection of the well-being of communities marginalised and alienated by the American economic system and their positive contribution socially as a result of their empowerment.

The establishment and growth of the halal industry thus far have been associated closely with the economic components only. How the development affects the personal and spirituality of those involved i.e., the human self *(Nafs)* is yet to be studied or considered. Whilst halal production and products were geared for the consumption of the *Ummah*, its contribution towards the sense of fulfilment of needs, individual's sense of obligation towards the common good and upholding of individual's dignity i.e., in terms of the rights to live and exercise their will, need to be considered as well. Policies that allow for the co-creation and sharing of knowledge whilst supporting an individual's usefulness and benefits to others are important, considering how the Muslims treated the *Ummah* as one collective. Meeting daily necessities such as the ability to be employed or work, to provide sustenance and sustain livelihood in the long run, and to be able to conduct or operate businesses as deemed fit so long as it does not cause harm towards others are policy criteria needed towards halalisation. Knowledge type here refers to both acceptable industrial knowledge required towards halalisation generated from adaptation, as seen from the Brunei halal standard as well as those that create certainties and confidence within the business communities. Some of the main concerns in all the halal research thus far relate to the difficulty in understanding the technicalities of the halal requirements which differs from the known halal knowledge learned in religious schools. For this to be possible, integration of the human self *(Nafs)* with the other three domains of the *Maqasid*, namely the Posterity *(Nasl)*, the Intellect *('Aql)* and Faith *(Ad-Din)* is needed. About the SDGs, SDG 3 and SDG 8 are closely linked themes that investigate the human-self aspect. The role of educational institutions and the early socialisation processes within the family are fundamental in shaping these aspects.

Undoubtedly, the processes towards halalisation and development of the halal industry are aimed at developing an alternative economic development model in contrast to the current capitalistic economy, whilst maintaining its adherence to Islamic teaching. Irresponsible exploitation of resources at the expense of humans, the environment and the rest of the Creations and the denial of individuals' ability to live in dignity due to lack of fairness or injustices need to be denounced and corrected. On top of protecting the religious dietary requirements of the collective as part of conformance and good deeds, maintenance of good relationships between the governor and the governed and adherence to Allah's commandments as a form of submission to His will are part of the final creed of the Islamic governance on Faith or *Ad-Din*. Living Islamically based on the *Ahkam*, the fear that any policy or decision will incur the wrath of Allah in the hereafter should deter unsustainable and irresponsible governing practices. Based on Figure 2 and the analysis of the policy components relating to SDGs thus far, the *Ad-Din* component proves to be the core that ties all components neatly. It is through the trust in Allah's commandments and the ability to exercise justice as envisioned in the Holy Quran and Prophetic sayings that the sustainable communities and cities development of the SDG (SDG 11) and Responsible Production and Consumption (SDG 12) linked to halal can be achieved.

Figure 5. Proposed integrated sustainable Halal policy framework linked to Islamic governance and SDG 17

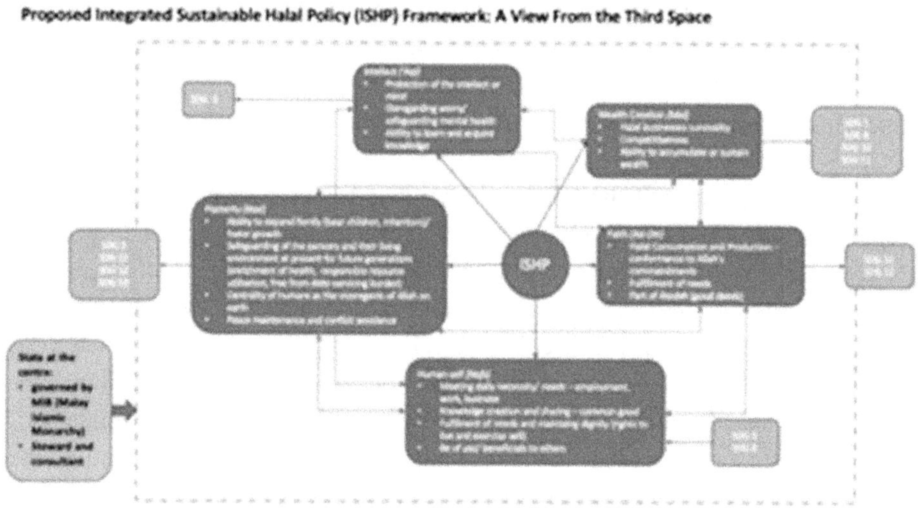

CONCLUDING REMARKS

Operationalisation of all these components synergistically resulted in the production of the model above to assist policymakers develop a sustainable but integrated halal policy (ISHP) by linking it to policy domains likely affected in this pursuit of policy multiverses integration. The State as it governed, both as a steward as well as a consultant for the halal industry plays a fundamental role in influencing growth. Ethical responsibilities of those halal agents or actors as they industrialise and embrace the *Maqasid* components provide not only grounds for checks and balances as they were governed. But it also allows policymakers and the mechanisms they introduced to enable the enrichment and empowerment of the communities, be they consumers or producers alike as they strive towards living a life blessed by Allah. The feedback gathered from industries and players provides useful materials to re-align policy goals and visions, as part of learning that act as determinants towards improvement. Integration of cost-efficiency and effectiveness principles in governing, acknowledgement of the current competitive climate of the industry as well as capabilities to analyse outcomes of governing and policy mechanisms towards the players makes ISHP more beneficial. Responsible halal governing and decision-making, thus, should be continued, if practised, or highlighted further as a function of sustainable halal governing. The point of convergence between the State as they governed (from top to bottom) and the Islamic community's reaction to their government (bottom-up) coupled with research on the businesses, industry, and governing policies as well as their effects on social institutions such as the family and individuals allows for integration to be possible. Structurally, establishing Brunei Darussalam's Food Authority (BDFA) can be the starting point for integration. However, in trying to act as a one-stop agency that both manages and governs the halal industry, there is a need to integrate the diverse agencies and governing functions that have overlapping jurisdictions over halal, from certification to permit issuance, from business and industrial development to its socioeconomic implications on the public. The utilisation of halal project-based initiatives between agencies, and the experiential learning gained from each project will allow these agencies to identify problems, understand the depth of work and foster integration among agencies required. This is vital to ensure any introduction of new legal acts, revisions and redaction of old acts and legislations provide clarity in governing and overcoming governing in silos highlighted earlier in the chapter. Not only political will is necessary, but capacity, competency and capabilities development are imperative for such refiguration of sustainable halal policy integrations to occur. Its establishment will be in line with the Brunei Vision 2035 and the SDG 17s goals. Being a small country does not require grand policy narratives but rather a patchwork of policies that can work by considering the country's context.

REFERENCES

Acemoglu, D., & Robinson, J. (2012). *Why Nations Fail: The Origins of Power, Prosperity, and Poverty*. Currency.

Ahmed, S., & Ali, S. M. (2006). People as partners: Facilitating people's participation in public-private partnerships for solid waste management. *Habitat International*, *30*(4), 781–796. doi:10.1016/j.habitatint.2005.09.004

Al-Mawardi, A. H. (2000). The Ordinances of Government: Al-Ahkam Al-Sultaniyya W'al-Wilayat Al-Diniyya. Garnet Publishing.

Ansell, C., & Gash, A. (2007). Collaborative governance in theory and practice. *Journal of Public Administration: Research and Theory*, *18*(4), 543–571. doi:10.1093/jopart/mum032

Aoki, M., Kim, H., & Okuno-Fujiwara, M. (1997). *The role of Government in East Asian Economic Development: Comparative Institutional Analysis*. Clarendon Press.

Asad, M., & Grunebaum, G. (1961). *The Principles of State and Government in Islam*. University of California Press. doi:10.1525/9780520313460

Ayan, A. (2013). *Accessing the Global Halal Market*. Createspace Publishing Ltd.

Azalie, I. A. & Kamarulzaman, N. (2023). Development linkages of Brunei Darussalam's coffee and tea sector: Global and regional value chain perspectives. *Journal of Business and Economic Analysis*, 1- 25. doi:10.1142/S2737566822500074

Azalie, I. A., & Samad, N. (2022). Brunei as a global halal hub: Production network and strategic relations in halal food production. *Journal of Contemporary Islamic Studies*, *8*(3), 1–22. doi:10.24191/jcis.v8i3.1

Baumgartner, F., & Jones, D. (2005). *The politics of attention: how government prioritizes problem*. The Chicago University Press Ltd.

Birkland, T. (1998). Focusing events, mobilization, and agenda setting. *Journal of Public Policy*, *18*(1), 53–74. doi:10.1017/S0143814X98000038

Booth, J., Wade, C., & Walker, T. (2020). *Understanding Central America: Global Forces and Political Change* (7th ed.). Routledge. doi:10.4324/9780429344282

Bornemann, B. (2007). Sustainable development and policy integration – some conceptual clarifications [Paper presentation]. The Marie Curie Summer School on Earth System Governance, Amsterdam, The Netherlands.

Brundtland, G. H. (1987). Our common future- Call for action. *Environmental Conservation*, *14*(4), 291–294. doi:10.1017/S0376892900016805

Bryson, J. (1988). A strategic planning process for public and non-profit organizations. *Long Range Planning*, *21*(1), 73–81. doi:10.1016/0024-6301(88)90061-1

Bryson, J. (2018). *Strategic planning for public and nonprofit organizations: A guide to strengthening and sustaining organizational achievement* (5th ed.). John Wiley & Sons Inc.

Chang, H. (2002). *Kicking Away the Ladder: Development Strategy in Historical Perspective*. Anthem Press Ltd.

Chapra, M., Khan, S., & Al Shaikh-Ali, A. (2006). *The Islamic Vision of Development in the Light of Maqasid Al-Shariah* (Vol. 15). International Institute of Islamic Thought.

Cohen, E. (2006). Theoretical foundations of industrial policy. *EIB Papers*, *11*(1), 84–106.

Considine, M. (2005). *Making Public Policy: Institutions, Actors and Strategies*. Polity Press.

Considine, M., & Lewis, J. M. (1999). Governance and ground level: The frontline bureaucrat in the age of markets and networks. *Public Administration Review*, *59*(6), 467–480. doi:10.2307/3110295

Considine, M., O'Sullivan, S., & Nguyen, P. (2018). The policymaker's dilemma: The risks and benefits of a 'black box' approach to commissioning active labour market programmes. *Social Policy and Administration*, *52*(1), 229–251. doi:10.1111pol.12309

Cosby, B., & Bryson, J. (2005). *Leadership for the common good: Tackling public problems in a shared-power world* (2nd ed.). Jossey-Bass.

Davis, J., Schoorman, D., & Donaldson, L. (1997). Davis, Schoorman and Donaldson reply: The distinctiveness of agency theory and stewardship theory. *Academy of Management Review*, *22*(3), 611–613.

Deuraseh, N. (2019). *Shariah and Life: Halalan Tayyiban Perspective*. UNISSA Press.

Eisinger, P. (1988). *The Rise of the Entrepreneurial State: State and Local Economic Development Policy in the United States*. Wisconsin University Press.

Freeman, R., Harrison, J., Wicks, A., Parmar, B., & De Colle, S. (2010). *Stakeholder theory: the state of the art*. Cambridge University Press. doi:10.1017/CBO9780511815768

Fujita, M., Krugman, P., & Venables, A. (1999). *The Spatial Economy: Cities, Regions and International Trade*. MIT Press. doi:10.7551/mitpress/6389.001.0001

Gweshengwe, B., & Hassan, N. H. (2019). Knowledge to policy: Understanding poverty to create policies that facilitate zero poverty in Brunei Darussalam. *Southeast Asia: A Multidisciplinary Journal, 19*, 95-104.

Gweshengwe, B., & Hassan, N. H. (2020). Defining the characteristics of poverty and their implications for poverty analysis. *Cogent Social Sciences*, *6*(1), 1768669. doi:10.1080/23311886.2020.1768669

Hassan, N. H., Rigg, J., Azalie, I. A., Yong, G., Zainuddin, N. H., & Muhammad Shamsul, M. A. S. (2022). Making do and staying poor: The poverty context of Urban Brunei. *Geoforum*, *136*, 132–141. doi:10.1016/j.geoforum.2022.09.012

Hogl, K., Kleinschmit, D., & Rayner, J. (2016). Achieving policy integration across fragmented policy domains: Forests, agriculture, climate and energy. *Environment and Planning. C, Government & Policy*, *34*(3), 399–414. doi:10.1177/0263774X16644815

Ibn Khaldun. (2004). The Muqaddimah: An Introduction to History. Princeton University Press.

Ibrahim, N. (2022). Halal policy in Brunei Darussalam. *Journal of Halal Science and Technology*, *1*(1), 86–91. doi:10.59202/jhst.v1i1.458

James, T., & Jorgensen, P. (2009). Policy knowledge, policy formulation and change: Revisiting a foundational question. *Policy Studies Journal: the Journal of the Policy Studies Organization*, *37*(1), 141–162. doi:10.1111/j.1541-0072.2008.00300.x

Jessop, B. (1998). The rise of governance and the risk of failure: The case of economic development. *International Social Science Journal*, *155*(155), 29–45. doi:10.1111/1468-2451.00107

Karlsson, C., & Karlsson, M. (2002). Economic policy, institutions and entrepreneurship. *Small Business Economics*, *19*(2), 163–182. doi:10.1023/A:1016259104162

Kromer, J. (2010). *Fixing Broken Cities: The Implementation of Urban Development Strategies*. Routledge.

Kumaraswamy, M., Zou, W., & Zhang, J. (2015). Reinforcing relationships for resilience – by embedding end-user 'people' in public-private partnerships. Civil Engineering and Environmental Systems, 32(1-2), 119-129. doi:10.1080/10286608.2015.1022727

Lazzarini, S. (2015). Strategizing by the government can industrial policy create firm-level competitive advantage? *Strategic Management Journal, 36*(1), 97–112. doi:10.1002mj.2204

Mathews, J. (2006). Catch-up strategies and the latecomer effect in industrial development. *New Political Economy, 11*(3), 313–355. doi:10.1080/13563460600840142

May, P., Sapotichne, J., & Workman, S. (2006). Policy coherence and policy domains. *Policy Studies Journal: the Journal of the Policy Studies Organization, 34*(3), 381–403. doi:10.1111/j.1541-0072.2006.00178.x

Mazzucato, M. (2015). *Building the entrepreneurial state: a new framework for envisioning and evaluating a mission-oriented public sector.* Working Paper No. 824, Levy Economics Institute.

Mohd Raffi, R. (2019). *Halal industry: an overview of Brunei Darussalam* [Paper presentation]. ICIEHI 2019, July 30-31, Malang, Indonesia.

Moore, D., & Schmitz, G. (1995). *Debating Development Discourse: Institutional and Popular Perspectives*. Palgrave MacMillan. doi:10.1007/978-1-349-24199-6

Ng, S., Wong, J., & Wong, K. (2013). A public-private people partnerships (P4) process framework for infrastructure development in Hong Kong. *Cities (London, England), 31*, 370–381. doi:10.1016/j.cities.2012.12.002

Ogunbado, A. (2019). *Leadership in Islam: Ibn Khaldun's Perspective*. UNISSA Press.

Peters, B. (1998). Managing horizontal government: The politics of co-ordination. *Public Administration, 76*(2), 295–311. doi:10.1111/1467-9299.00102

Piketty, T. (2014). *Capital in the Twenty-First Century*. Harvard University Press. doi:10.4159/9780674369542

Porter, M. (1998). Clusters and the new economics of competition. *Harvard Business Review*, (November-December), 77–90. PMID:10187248

Porter, M. (2008). The five competitive forces that shape strategy. *Harvard Business Review*, (January), 79–93. PMID:18271320

Radin, B. (1997). The evolution of the policy analysis field: From conversation to conversations. *Journal of Policy Analysis and Management, 16*(2), 204–218. doi:10.1002/(SICI)1520-6688(199721)16:2<204::AID-PAM1>3.0.CO;2-M

Radin, B. (2013). *Beyond Machiavelli: Policy analysis comes of Age*. Georgetown University Press.

Sachs, J. (2006). *The End of Poverty: Economic Possibilities for Our Time*. Penguin Books.

Secretariat of the Brunei Vision 2035. (n.d.). *Wawasan Brunei 2035: How to "Wawasan"*. Bandar Seri Begawan: Prime Minister's Office.

Sen, A. (1988). *On Ethics and Economics*. Blackwell Publishing Ltd.

Sen, A. (2000). *Development as Freedom*. Anchor Books.

Sen, A. (2009). *The Idea of Justice*. Belknap Press.

Special National Coordination Committee on SDGs Brunei Darussalam Secretariat. (2021). *Brunei Darussalam Sustainable Development Goals Annual Report 2021*. Prime Minister's Office.

Stone, C. (2006). Power, reform, and urban regime analysis. *City & Community*, *5*(1), 23–38. doi:10.1111/j.1540-6040.2006.00151.x

Sulaiman, N. S. (2020). Halal Sustainability: A Strategic Roadmapping for Brunei Darussalam. *Proceedings on 4th International Seminar on Halalan Thayyiban Products and Services,* 286-302.

Vilas, C. (1995). *Between Earthquakes and Volcanoes: Markets, State, And the Revolutions in Central America*. Monthly Review Press.

Weimer, D., & Vining, A. (1999). *Policy Analysis: Concepts and Practice*. Prentice Hall.

Weisburd, D., Hinkle, J., Braga, A., & Wooditch, A. (2015). Understanding the mechanisms of underlying broken windows policing: The need for evaluation evidence. *Journal of Research in Crime and Delinquency*, *52*(4), 589–608. doi:10.1177/0022427815577837

Weiss, C. H. (1998). *Evaluation*. Prentice Hall.

Welsh, B., Braga, A., & Bruinsma, G. (2015). Reimagining broken windows: From theory to policy. *Journal of Research in Crime and Delinquency*, *52*(4), 447–463. doi:10.1177/0022427815581399

Wu, F. (2023). Theorising urban development in China: 'State entrepreneurialism' from the ground up. *Dialogues in Human Geography*, *0*(0), 1–5. doi:10.1177/20438206231174638

Yi, L., Chen, W., & Wu, F. (2023). Building Chinese city regions under state entrepreneurialism. *Territory, Politics, Governance*, 1–18. Advance online publication. doi:10.1080/21622671.2023.2206430

Yu, T. (2001). Towards the theory of the entrepreneurial state. *International Journal of Social Economics*, *28*(9), 752–766. doi:10.1108/EUM0000000005692

Zhang, L. (2006). Market socialism revisited: The case of Chinese state-owned enterprises. *Issues & Studies*, *42*(3), 1–46.

Zhang, L. (2013). Dynamics and constraints of State-led global city formation in emerging economies: The case of Shanghai. *Urban Studies (Edinburgh, Scotland)*, *51*(6), 1162–1178. doi:10.1177/0042098013495577

Chapter 11
Education Reform to Attain SDG4:
A Broad Overview

Hamizah Haidi
https://orcid.org/0000-0002-3252-2052
Universiti Brunei Darussalam, Brunei

Jainatul Halida Jaidin
Universiti Brunei Darussalam, Brunei

ABSTRACT

This chapter explores a small country's efforts to achieve the fourth United Nations Sustainable Development Goal (SDG4). Many nations, including Brunei, strive to offer high-quality education. In doing so, policies and strategies have been introduced and put into effect in order to accomplish SDG4 targets. By thematically analysing educational policies and mapping them to all SDG4 targets, the current study sheds light on Brunei's progress toward SDG4. Overall, the findings indicate that Brunei is making steady strides toward providing high-quality education. It is also interesting to note that Brunei advanced despite the COVID-19 outbreak by implementing policies that ensure equitable access. In conclusion, through initiatives and ongoing partnerships, the Ministry of Education will work methodically and thoroughly to meet SDG4 targets by 2030, which calls for high-quality education as the basis of sustainable development and better living conditions. The discussion of findings in this chapter may assist policymakers identify policies that can close gaps in meeting SDG4 targets.

INTRODUCTION

The provision of quality education for all has become a priority for many countries. Quality education offers positive yields for the nation, and is a basic human right. Yet, this basic human right remains unattainable by many around the world due to various reasons caused by crises such as poverty. Such issues, worsened by the Covid-19 pandemic, have led to the widening economic and educational gap

DOI: 10.4018/978-1-6684-8903-1.ch011

between the rich and the poor (Deaton, 2021; United Nations Development Programs, n.d.). This issue has prompted intra-national bodies such as the United Nations and individual countries to act on addressing these gaps through formulating education policies and enacting formal education reforms.

Brunei is no exception. Despite contemporary Brunei's relatively young age, having only attained its 39th year of independence from British Protectorate Status, a number of education policies and education reforms have taken place (Mail et al, 2022). The latest education policy introduced is the New Education System for the 21st Century, or *Sistem Pendidikan Negara Abad ke-21* (hereby SPN21) in 2008, and education for the gifted/talented students in 2009.

In Brunei, the right to quality education is not merely a basic human right. It is highly regarded as a necessity to achieve two of Al-Ghazali's Maqasid of the Sharia, which are the preservation and promotion of intellect and wealth. Brunei provides a unique context to study. It is a small nation that practices a national ideology called *Melayu Islam Beraja*, or Malay Islamic Monarchy (Sharbawi & Mabud, 2021), with Al-Ghazali's Maqasid of the Sharia - preservation and promotion of faith, life, intellect, progeny, and wealth (Abdul Aziz, 2019) as reference.

Quality education is explicitly stated in the vision and mission of Brunei's Ministry of Education. The Ministry envisions to provide equitable quality education to Brunei's future generation, guided by the values of Malay Islamic Monarchy, equipping them with knowledge and 21st century skills to be future ready citizens. This is consistent with the main aim of SDG4, that is, "to ensure inclusive and equitable quality education and promote lifelong learning opportunities for all." (UNESCO, n.d.). In addition, Brunei is a supporter of the Paris Declaration (Global call to invest in the futures of education, n.d.).

This study investigates how far Brunei's educational reforms and policies have progressed in attaining SDG4 goals. The main objective is to examine Brunei's efforts to meet the SDG4 targets. "How significantly do educational policies and initiatives in Brunei contribute to the achievement of SDG4 goals?" is the primary research question that guides the paper's overall direction. To establish the context for the current paper, a brief review of Brunei's most recent educational policy, the SDG4 targets, and the Global Education Agenda will now be discussed.

LITERATURE REVIEW

Provision of Quality Education in Brunei Darussalam

Quality education has always been Brunei's priority and this is shown through the execution of three major educational policies (Mundia, 2010) over the past twenty-five years (1997-2022). The implementation of SPN21 brought substantial changes to educational practices throughout Brunei, aimed at achieving the Brunei Vision 2035 (*Wawasan Brunei* 2035). Three (3) strategic objectives were listed by Brunei's Ministry of Education 'to deliver holistic education to achieve fullest potential for all' (Ministry of Education, Brunei Darussalam, 2018, p. 9):

A. Transform our organisation human resource towards a performance-driven culture
B. Provide equal and equitable access to quality education
C. Enhance shared accountability with stakeholders in the development of teaching and learning

The second strategic objective is directly linked to SDG4. The main strategy is to systematically improve access to quality education and learning, giving priority to universal and inclusive education. This strategy has been translated into several initiatives, including promoting quality early childhood education; strengthening the delivery of basic education; improving the quality and access to post-secondary education; improving the inclusion of students at risk and disadvantage at all levels of education; and finally improving opportunities for life-long learning. (Ministry of Education, Brunei Darussalam, 2018, p. 27).

Sustainable Development Goal 4 (SDG4)

SDG4 comprises ten targets and twelve indicators (Goal 4, n.d.). The principal goal of SDG4 is 'to ensure inclusive and equitable quality education and promote lifelong learning opportunities for all' (SDG4, n.d.). All SDG4 targets highlight the importance of providing access to quality education for all, starting as early as preschool up to tertiary education. Each target goes together with a set of indicators, as listed in Table 1:

Global Education Agenda

UNESCO introduced a mechanism to co-ordinate the work towards achieving the ten goals of SDG4. This began in 2015 when global leaders signed the 2030 Agenda for Sustainable Development in Education, which is a structured way forward to making education accessible to all, and providing a basis for sustainable development and peace. The mechanism operates using the 2030 Education Action Plan as a road map for partnership, policy guidance, capacity-building, monitoring, and advocacy.

METHODOLOGY

The current study employs a qualitative inquiry to address the overarching research question. Reliable and available documents on educational policies were used to examine Brunei's efforts in realising quality education for all. To provide more information, members of the Ministry of Education were also interviewed.

Data Sources

Data for the study came from the following sources: a) published documents retrieved from the official Brunei's Ministry of Education website, as listed in Table 2, and; b) interviews with representatives of the Department of Policy, Planning, and Research in Brunei's Ministry of Education.

Data Analysis

The current study used document analysis, a standard qualitative research technique, to analyse the data. Document analysis is a process in which the researcher interprets materials to give context and meaning to a topic under review (Bowen, 2009). Documents are practical and valuable resources, but they can also be managed, making document analysis an effective technique for gathering data.

Table 1. SDG4 targets and indicators

No.	Targets	Indicators
4.1.	Ensure that all children complete at least nine to twelve compulsory years of free, equitable and quality primary and secondary education leading to relevant and effective learning outcomes by 2030	4.1.1. Proportion of children and young people (a) in Year 2/3 (aged between 7 and 8); (b) at the end of primary; and (c) at the end of lower secondary achieving at least a minimum proficiency level in (i) reading and (ii) mathematics, by sex 4.1.2. Completion rate (primary education, lower secondary education, upper secondary education)
4.2.	Ensure that quality early childhood development, care and pre-primary education; delivered by well-trained educators, are accessible for all children by 2030	4.2.1. Proportion of children aged 24–59 months, by sex, on a developmental path in health, learning and mental and social well-being 4.2.2. The participation rate in organised learning (one year before the official primary enrollment age), by sex
4.3.	Ensure that every adult person have equal access to affordable and quality technical, vocational and tertiary education by 2030, including provision of lifelong learning opportunities. Current international agreements highlight the need for free access to tertiary education	4.3.1. The proportion of young people and adults who have participated in formal and non-formal education and training over the last 12 months, by sex
4.4.	Increase the number of skilled youth and adults for financial success by 2030, through provision to develop high-level cognitive and non-cognitive/transferable skills that are useful for a wide range of occupational fields, as well as specialised skills for employment and entrepreneurship	4.4.1. The proportion of young people and adults with information and communication technology (ICT) skills, by type of skills
4.5.	Eliminate all discrimination in education by 2030, through ensuring equal access to all levels of education and vocational training, irrespective of sex, age, race, colour, ethnicity, language, religion, political or other opinion, national or social origin, property or birth, as well as people with disabilities, indigenous people and children in vulnerable situations	4.5.1. The parity indexes (female/male, rural/urban, lower/higher, disabilities status, indigenous and conflict-affected, and other information, as available) for all education indicators in this list that can be disaggregated
4.6.	Ensure that all young people and adults achieve a level of appropriate and recognised competence in functional literacy and numeracy skills equivalent to the level achieved at the successful completion of basic education by 2030	4.6.1. Proportion of population in a given age group achieving at least a fixed level of proficiency in functional (a) literacy and (b) numeracy skills
4.7.	Ensure that all learners acquire the knowledge and skills needed to promote sustainable development, through education for sustainable development and lifestyles, human rights, gender equality, promote a culture of peace and nonviolence, global citizenship and appreciation of cultural diversity and of culture's contribution to sustainable development by 2030	4.7.1. In terms of mainstreaming (i) global citizenship education and (ii) sustainable development education (a) in national education policy; (b) in curriculum; (c) in teacher education; and (d) in student assessment
4.a.	Build and upgrade education facilities that can accommodate safe, non-violent, inclusive and effective learning environment for all	4.a.1. The proportion of schools providing basic services by service type
4.b.	Expand higher education scholarships to developing countries	4.b.1. Volume of official development assistance flows for scholarships by sector and type of study
4.c.	Increase qualified teacher supply in developing countries by 2030	4.c.1. The proportion of teachers with minimum qualifications according to the level of education

All available data mentioned in Table 2 were examined and organised according to the following themes:

Table 2. Data source type and data source

Data Source Type	Data Source
Document Analysis	A. Brunei Darussalam Education Act 2010 B. Brunei Darussalam Compulsory Education Act Chapter 211 C. Brunei Darussalam Education Act (Supplementary) 2010 D. Brunei Darussalam Education Statistics 2010 E. Ministry of Education Strategic Plan F. PISA 2018 results (OECD, 2018)
Semi-Structured Interview	Representatives from the Department of Policy, Planning and Research, Ministry of Education. The following inquiries were posed to the representatives for more information: A. What proportion of young people, broken down by sex, complete secondary school, elementary school, and lower secondary school with at least a basic command of reading and mathematics? B. By sex, what percentage of children between the ages of 24 and 59 months have healthy, academic, and psychosocial well-being development that is on track? C. What are the trends in young people's engagement in formal (and informal) education over the past 12 months, by sex? The primary goal of the semi-structured interview was to get detailed information that was not provided in published documents.

A. Free Primary and Secondary Education
B. Equal Access to Quality Pre-Primary Education
C. Equal Access to Affordable Technical, Vocational, and Higher Education
D. Increase the Number of People with Relevant Skills for Financial Success
E. Eliminate All Discrimination in Education
F. Universal Literacy and Numeracy
G. Education for Sustainable Development and Global Citizenship
H. Build and Upgrade Inclusive and Safe Schools
I. Expand Higher Education Scholarships for Developing Countries
J. Increase the Supply of Qualified Teachers in Developing Countries

The SDG4 targets have been used, as was already stated, to establish the themes in this study.

Limitations

The results of the present study, however, are limited to statistics on education that are officially published by governmental and private organisations in Brunei. Discussions of the findings are then presented using the data that is currently available.

FINDINGS AND DISCUSSION

With regard to reaching SDG4, Brunei has made considerable progresses since 2015. (Othman, 2022). Brunei reported a favourable development during a meeting in Bangkok, Thailand, in 2018, which was intended to update national status of SDG4 achievements at a regional level. A Pre-Asia-Pacific Meeting on Education (APMED) Survey 2018 on the implementation and status of countries' most recent accomplishments against SDG4 indicators provided evidence of this. The purpose of the meeting was to examine if the suggested approaches could be implemented successfully and to identify the necessary support fields using monitoring indicators.

In a more recent development, the Brunei SDG key indicators will be included to the SDG tracker data repository system. This is in collaboration with the United Nations Economic and Social Commission for Asia and the Pacific (UNESCAP), aimed at enhancing monitoring capabilities and strengthening data capacities (Kon, 2022). The SDG4 targets are now explored in light of Brunei's accomplishments to date.

Free Primary and Secondary Education

According to the Brunei Darussalam Compulsory Education Act Chapter 211, parents are required to ensure that their children receive at least nine to twelve years of free, high-quality education (AGC, 2011). The Compulsory Education Act defined 'child of compulsory school age' as a child over the age of 6 who has not yet turned 15 and who satisfies such conditions for receiving primary and lower secondary education as the Permanent Secretary may determine. It also stated that 'child of compulsory school age' means a child who meets the requirements for receiving primary and lower secondary education as determined by the Permanent Secretary. In essence, the Act declares that failing to send a child of obligatory school age to school on a regular basis constitutes an offense against the parent:

Where a child of compulsory school age fails to attend regularly as a pupil at a Government school as required by subsection (1), each parent of that child is guilty of an offence. (Chapter 211 Section 3 (2), 2011, p.4)

The Compulsory Education Act, Section 9 (1) also states that parents must pay a fine if their children are not attending school:

Any person guilty of an offence under section 3(2) is liable on conviction to a fine not exceeding $5,000, imprisonment for a term not exceeding one year or both.

According to Section 16 of Chapter 210 of the National Education Policy (AGC, 2010), the Minister of Education:

Shall ensure that a child of school-going age is given the opportunity to attend primary and secondary school and complete the course of study provided therein.

Primary and Secondary Education provision is within the duty of the Minister of Education, according to Section 25 and 26 of the Education Act (Education Act, 2010, p.21-22):

Primary Education

25. (1) It shall be the Minister's duty to provide primary education in government schools.

(2) The Minister may, subject to the provisions of this Act, establish government primary schools and shall maintain such schools.

Secondary Education

26. (1) It shall be the duty of the Minister to provide secondary education in the following government secondary schools —

(a) academic secondary schools;

(b) secondary schools of such other description as the Minister may determine.

(2) The Minister may establish and maintain any such schools as described in subsection (1) subject to the provisions of this Act.

However, information on the indicators of equal access to primary and secondary education, is not available. That said, free primary and secondary education was made available online between 2020 and 2021 during Covid-19 lockdowns (Shahrill et al., 2021; Haidi & Hamdan, 2022). According to Haidi and Hamdan (2022), there were existing policies in place for online learning before the pandemic, and the reason for the digital divide was more related to parental financial means than to access.

Equal Access to Quality Pre-Primary Education

The Brunei Darussalam Compulsory Education Act does not apply to children under the age of six. The absence of inclusion of young children under the age of six does not, however, preclude them from having equitable access to high-quality pre-primary education.

The Brunei government's commitment to pre-primary education is reflected in the National Education System's inclusion of pre-primary education as one of the levels of study, as highlighted in Chapter 210, Section 17 (1), Page 20 (AGC, 2011).

Pre-school education and curriculum regulation is included under Sections 22, 23 and 24 in the Brunei Darussalam Education Act Chapter 210 (Chapter 210, p.21), as stated below:

Pre-School Education

22. The Minister may, subject to the provisions of this Act, establish and maintain kindergartens and pre-school classes.

Pre-School Curriculum

23. The programmes and activities of every kindergarten shall be based on the curriculum approved by the Minister.

The proportion of children aged 24-59 months who are developmentally on track in health, learning, and psychosocial well-being, by sex, as well as the participation rate in organised learning (one year before the official primary entry age), are the indicators of this target, but data for these indicators are unfortunately not available.

Equal Access to Affordable Technical, Vocational, and Higher Education

Technical, vocational and higher education is included in the National Education System (Chapter 210, p.20). Section 28 (2) stated that 'the Minister shall be responsible for the general direction of technical and vocational education' (Chapter 210, p.23). Section 28 (3) and Section 28 (4) then outlines the following:

(3) The Minister may provide technical and vocational education in —

(a) skills training centres or similar institutions;

(b) vocational schools;

(c) technical colleges;

(d) nursing colleges;

(e) technological institutions; and

(f) such other educational institutions as he may determine.

(4) The Minister may establish and maintain educational institutions to provide for the matters mentioned in subsection (3).

Provision of higher education is elucidated in Section 35 of the Education Act, as follows:

(1) The Minister may provide higher education in an educational institution in accordance with the provisions of this Act or any other written law relating to higher education and shall be responsible for the general direction thereof.

(2) The Minister may establish and maintain higher educational institutions and provide higher education within such institutions.

Women are more prominent in Brunei's higher education sector as a result of equal access to higher education. In 2010, there were 3726 women enrolled in Higher Education out of 5903 students (Brunei Darussalam Education Statistics, 2010). By 2018, 6705 out of 11046 students (Brunei Darussalam Education Statistics, 2018) were women, indicating that from 2010 to 2018, women made up 3 out of every 5 Higher Education students in Brunei.

Increase the Number of People with Relevant Skills for Financial Success

A variety of abilities are necessary for financial success, including language proficiency, communication, ICT, creativity and problem-solving, social, and lifelong learning. Section 19 (medium of instruction) of the Brunei Darussalam Education Act implicitly recognises multilingual language proficiency when it states explicitly the following:

19. (1) The Malay language shall be the main medium of instruction in all educational institutions.

(2) The English language may also be used as the medium of instruction, together with the Malay language, in all educational institutions.

(3) The Arabic language may be used as a medium of instruction in Arabic or other schools but in these schools the Malay language and the English language must be taught as compulsory subjects.

While it is not explicitly stated, SPN21 is a means for the country to realise its Brunei Vision 2035 (Wawasan 2035, n.d.), that is, for Brunei to have (i) citizens who are highly educated, highly skilled as measured according to the international standards; (ii) high quality of life according to United Nations Human Development Index; and (iii) a dynamic and sustainable economy. As a result, the goals of Brunei Vision 2035, including increasing the number of people with essential skills for financial success, are reflected in the SPN21 curriculum and also other kinds of skills it will instil in pupils. Moreover, SPN21 is designed to help students in developing the following core skills: a) religious skills; b) communication skills; c) numeracy skills; d) info communication and technology (hereby ICT) skills; e) thinking and problem-solving skills; f) study and work skills; g) social skills; h) physical skills; and i) aesthetics skills (SPN21, 2013). SPN21 also emphasise the development of high-level cognitive and non-cognitive/ transferable skills that can be applied to a variety of occupational fields, as well as specialised skills for employment and entrepreneurship.

Brunei has the highest rate of internet usage (95% in 2020 according to CIA n.d.) in Southeast Asia and the most Instagram users worldwide per capita (Othman, 2022). These figures demonstrated the growth of ICT skills in the Bruneian population, as well as the presence of a digital society (Anshari, Hamdan & Haidi, 2023) and a digital Islamic society (Haidi, 2023).

Eliminate All Discrimination in Education

The Compulsory Education Act of 2011 ensured that all children in Brunei, regardless of citizenship status, received an education (Compulsory Education Act, 2011, p.4):

3. (1) A child of compulsory school age who is —

(a) born on or after 1st January, 2002;

(b) a citizen of Brunei Darussalam; and

(c) residing in Brunei Darussalam

Basic education is provided for students with disabilities through the Special Education Unit (MOE website, n.d.). The unit is in charge of special education programmes and related services for children with special needs throughout Brunei, was formally established in 1994 (Abdul Latif, 2021).

The Education Act also makes reference to special education provisions in Chapter 210, Section 30 (Education Act, 2010, p.24):

30. (1) The Minister shall provide special education in such government primary or secondary schools as he thinks fit and in any special school established by the Minister.

(2) The Minister may, with the approval of His Majesty the Sultan and Yang Di-Pertuan, by regulations prescribe —

(a) the duration of primary and secondary education suitable to the needs of a pupil in receipt of special education;

(b) the curriculum to be used in respect of special education;

(c) the categories of pupils requiring special education and the methods appropriate for the education of pupils in each category of special schools;

It is worth noting that children attending schools with a high average socioeconomic status achieve better academic results than those attending schools with a lower average peer socioeconomic level. For example, according to the PISA 2018 results, socioeconomically advantaged pupils in Brunei achieved 103 points better in reading than students from disadvantaged backgrounds. Nevertheless, 9% of Brunei's disadvantaged pupils were able to achieve reading proficiency levels in the top quarter, demonstrating that disadvantage is not a given (OECD, 2018).

Universal Literacy and Numeracy

One of the skill sets taught in the SPN21 curriculum is literacy and numeracy (SPN21, 2013). The Literacy and Numeracy Coaching Programme (LNCP) was suitably introduced by Brunei's Ministry of Education in partnership with Education Development Trust (EDT, also branded as CfBT Brunei) to achieve universal literacy and numeracy.

Education for Sustainable Development and Global Citizenship

Environmental education is a component of education for sustainable development (hereafter, ESD), which also addresses socio-political issues such as equity, poverty, democracy, and quality of life (Venkataraman, 2010). The United Nations stated,

ESD gives learners of all ages the knowledge, skills, values and agency to address interconnected global challenges including climate change, loss of biodiversity, unsustainable use of resources, and inequality. It empowers learners of all ages to make informed decisions and take individual and collective action to change society and care for the planet. ESD is a lifelong learning process and an integral part of quality education. It enhances the cognitive, socio-emotional and behavioural dimensions of learning and encompasses learning content and outcomes, pedagogy and the learning environment itself. (United Nations, n.d.)

ESD is incorporated into the curriculum of SPN21. Students are encouraged to explore and appreciate the natural environment starting in preschool. It is anticipated that by the time students are between the ages of 9 and 12, they would have developed positive attitudes and values, as well as a caring attitude towards society and the environment (MOE, 2013). ESD, on the other hand, is made up of four thrusts (Wals & Kieft, 2010): a) improving access to quality basic education, b) reorienting existing education to address sustainability, c) increasing public understanding and awareness of sustainability, and d) providing training for all sectors of the economy.

Consequently, one could argue that Brunei's education reform has partially met the four thrusts by ensuring equal access to quality basic education through the Compulsory Education Act (AGC, 2011). Likewise, the existence of environmental NGOs like Green Brunei (Green Brunei, n.d.) stands in contrast to the absence of statistics as it is challenging to ascertain whether the current educational system is being reoriented to address sustainability or whether public comprehension and awareness of sustainability have increased.

As for global citizenship education, it "aims to empower learners of all ages to assume active roles, both locally and globally, in building more peaceful, tolerant, inclusive and secure societies." (United Nations, n.d.). Global citizenship education (hereby GCE) is framed differently in different parts of the world (Goren & Yemini, 2017). Goren and Yemini (2017) noted that the European framing of GCE focuses on social cohesion and acceptance of minorities and immigrants, the Asia-Pacific framing of GCE, on the other hand, focuses more on understanding how states can influence one another and how their students can learn skills that enables them to have a competitive edge in a global economy. One skill mentioned in Goren and Yemini (2017) that is part of the Asia-Pacific framing of GCE is knowledge of the English language, given its status as a global language. An example of such framing is a paper by Lim (2008) who discussed a study on Singaporean students learning Mathematics, English and Science as global citizens.

Given Brunei's geographical and political location within the Asia-Pacific region, this paper analyses the Bruneian response to GCE using an Asia-Pacific frame, where GCE is focused on developing students' ability to function in a globally connected society. Even though GCE is not expressly mentioned in any of the official publications, it is incorporated in some way in the Brunei educational system. The improvement of English language skills is one of these components.

In Brunei, the Education Act (AGC, 2011) states that the English language must be taught as a compulsory subject in schools (Education Act, 2010). The English language is already part of the primary and secondary school curriculum, as stated in both the Education (National Curriculum) Regulations (Education (National Curriculum) Regulations, 2004) and SPN21 (SPN21, 2013). Furthermore, the pre-school curriculum also makes reference to the English language:

The Malay language shall be the main medium of instruction but English may be used wherever appropriate. (Education (National Curriculum) Regulations. 2004, p. 7)

Critical thinking, cooperation, and conflict resolution are some of the core components of Oxfam's global citizenship curriculum, which is included in the SPN21 curriculum as well as other skills including problem-solving and communication skills (SPN21, 2013; Oxfam, 1997). All facets of educational governance, such as the national education policy, curriculum, teacher preparation, and assessment, already include these skills.

Build and Upgrade Inclusive and Safe Schools

Schools in Brunei are regulated by the government through the Education Act 2010 (AGC, 2010). The Education Act stated that the Minister is responsible to establish and maintain government-funded primary schools (Section 25(2)), secondary schools (Section 26(2)), post-secondary schools (Section 27(2)), and technical and vocational schools (Section 27(4)), (Education Act, 2010, p.21-23). Every school possess basic facilities required for students to learn comfortably, including access to electricity, clean water, classrooms, and other facilities.

Expand Higher Education Scholarships for Developing Countries

The Brunei Darussalam Government Scholarship (hereby BDGS) is a scholarship program sponsored by the government of Brunei to residents of other developing nations (MFA, n.d.). In addition, the Universiti Brunei Darussalam (hereafter UBD) offers international students the UBD Graduate Scholarship and UBD Graduate Research Scholarship. Many of these scholarships' beneficiaries are nationals of developing nations.

Increase the Supply of Qualified Teachers in Developing Countries

Teacher Education in Brunei is mentioned on Page 25 the Education Act (AGC, 2010):

31. (1) The Minister shall issue general directions in respect of teacher `education.

(2) No person shall establish or maintain an institution that provides teacher education except with the approval of the Minister.

(3) Subject to subsection (2), all teacher education institutions shall be registered under this Act.

(4) The courses of study and training programmes in teacher education institutions may only be conducted upon receiving approval from the Minister for such courses and programmes, subject to such conditions as the Minister may think fit to impose.

(5) A teacher education institution established under this Act may award a certificate, diploma or such other qualification as may be prescribed.

(6) The Minister may establish and maintain teacher education institution and provide teacher education within such institutions.

(7) The Minister may, with the approval of His Majesty the Sultan and Yang Di-Pertuan, make regulations for giving effect to and carrying out the provisions of this section in respect of institutions providing teacher education.

Typically, the number of teachers produced is determined by demand, which is based on needs in specific subject areas at various levels. Two institutions provide teacher education in Brunei: a) the

Sultan Hassanal Bolkiah Institute of Education, Universiti Brunei Darussalam (henceforth SHBIE); and b) the Kolej Universiti Perguruan Ugama Seri Begawan (hereby KUPUSB). The latter offers teacher preparation programmes for religious teachers, whereas the former is for teachers in general education.

SHBIE collaborates with the Ministry of Education to ensure quality in teacher preparation programs. The teacher preparation program includes Technology, Pedagogy, and Content Knowledge, or TPCK, as one of its core modules. This module introduces teacher candidates to a variety of online pedagogies that were immensely beneficial during the pandemic.

CONCLUSION

SDG4 in Brunei ensures that everyone has access to a high-quality education. The Ministry of Education has demonstrated a strong commitment to achieving all SDG4 targets and has recognised the need to develop an SDG4 framework. This was also demonstrated during the pandemic, when, while many countries around the world suffered educational and SDG4 setbacks as a result of Covid-19 (Bloom, 2022; Chabbot & Sinclair, 2020), Brunei's early preparedness (particularly by the Ministry of Education and teacher training institutions) allowed the country to remain on track with SDG4 despite the pandemic.

Hereafter, the establishment and coordination of program monitoring policies, the provision of technical and financial assistance to member countries in the capacity-building and expertise in the fields required by SDG4, the regulation of global, regional, and national level coordination systems, and stakeholder partnerships are all necessary in addition to this framework in order to deliver SDG4 impacts over the long term.

In sum, this study only provided a broad overview of SDG4 in Brunei. Building on this research, the researchers will look at how, despite equal access to education, women outnumber men in Brunei's higher education scene. More research will be required to determine how Brunei's curriculum has enabled GCE to function in the Asia-Pacific context.

REFERENCES

Abdul Aziz, A. (2019). Special Forward: Islamic Governance and the Articulation of Maqāṣid al-Sharī'ah in Brunei Darussalam. In R. Yunos (Ed.), *Maqāṣid Al-Sharī'ah in the Brunei Civil Service: Civil Servant's Perspectives*. Qasrun Nafis Publishing House.

Anshari, M., Hamdan, M., & Haidi, H. (2023) Gearing Towards A Stronger Digital Society. In A. Ananta, C.Y. Hoon & M. Hamdan (Eds.) Stability, Growth and Sustainability: Catalysts for Socio-economic Development in Brunei Darussalam (pp. 136-158). ISEAS: Yusof Ishak Institute.

Bloom, D. (2022). *Here's how COVID-19 impacted education – and what we need to do to get children's learning back on track*. World Economic Forum. Retrieved 13 December 2022, from https://www.weforum.org/agenda/2022/11/covid19-education-impact-legacy/

Brunei Darussalam | NON-STATE ACTORS IN EDUCATION | Education Profiles. (n.d.). Retrieved 6 September 2022, from https://education-profiles.org/eastern-and-south-eastern-asia/brunei-darussalam/~non-state-actors-in-education

Brunei Darussalam Compulsory Education Act 2011, (testimony of AGC).

Brunei Darussalam Education Act 2010, (testimony of AGC).

Brunei Darussalam Education (National Curriculum) Regulations, no. 2004. AGC.

Chabbott, C., & Sinclair, M. (2020). SDG 4 and the COVID-19 emergency: Textbooks, tutoring, and teachers. *Prospects*, *49*(1–2), 51–57. doi:10.100711125-020-09485-y PMID:32836424

CIA. (2022). Brunei. In *The World Factbook*. Central Intelligence Agency. https://www.cia.gov/the-world-factbook/countries/brunei

Deaton, A. (2021). COVID-19 and Global Income Inequality. *LSE Public Policy Review*, *1*(4), 1. doi:10.31389/lseppr.26 PMID:34308354

Global call to invest in the futures of education: Support the Paris Declaration | Education within the 2030 Agenda for Sustainable Development. (n.d.). Retrieved 6 September 2022, from https://www.sdg4education2030.org/global-call-invest-futures-education-support-paris-declaration

Goal 4 | Department of Economic and Social Affairs. (n.d.). Retrieved 6 September 2022, from https://sdgs.un.org/goals/goal4

Goren, H., & Yemini, M. (2017). Global citizenship education redefined – A systematic review of empirical studies on global citizenship education. *International Journal of Educational Research*, *82*, 170–183. doi:10.1016/j.ijer.2017.02.004

Green Brunei. (n.d.). *Green Brunei – Youth-led platform for environmental sustainability*. Retrieved 13 December 2022, from https://green-brunei.com/

Haidi, H., & Hamdan, M. (2022). Analysis of the home-based online teaching and learning policy during the COVID-19 second wave in Brunei: A joint parent/teacher perception. *Asia Pacific Education Review*. Advance online publication. doi:10.100712564-022-09798-x

Haidi, H. (2023). A Digital Ethnographic Account of a Digital Islamic Society During COVID-19: An Islamic Governance Perspective. In M. Anshari, A. Razzaq, M. Fithriyah, & A. Kamal (Eds.), *Digital Psychology's Impact on Business and Society* (pp. 150–178). IGI Global., doi:10.4018/978-1-6684-6108-2.ch007

Ibrahim, T. (2005). Global citizenship education: Mainstreaming the curriculum? *Cambridge Journal of Education*, *35*(2), 177–194. doi:10.1080/03057640500146823

Kon, J. (2022, November 1). Sultanate gets on SDG tracker » Borneo Bulletin Online. *Sultanate Gets on SDG Tracker*. https://borneobulletin.com.bn/sultanate-gets-on-sdg-tracker/

Lim, C. P. (2008). Global citizenship education, school curriculum and games: Learning Mathematics, English and Science as a global citizen. *Computers & Education*, *51*(3), 1073–1093. doi:10.1016/j.compedu.2007.10.005

Mail, A., Ampuan Tengah, A. B., Makmun, R., Abu Bakar, N. S., Pg Hj Besar, P. H. S. N., Tarasat, S., & Abu Bakar, T. (2022). Brunei Darussalam: Educational Policies in Six Decades. Brunei Historical Society/Persatuan Sejarah Brunei.

MFA. (n.d.). *Brunei Darussalam Government Scholarship (BDGS)*. Retrieved 17 November 2022, from https://www.mfa.gov.bn/Pages/bdgs/bdgs2022.aspx

MOE. (2010). *Brunei Darussalam Education Statistics 2010*. MOE.

MOE. (2013). *Sistem Pendidikan Negara Abad ke-21 (SPN-21)*. https://www.moe.gov.bn/spn21dl/SPN21%20Booklet%20FINAL%202013.pdf

MOE. (2018). *Brunei Darussalam Education Statistics 2014-2018*. MOE.

MOE. (2018). *Ministry of Education Strategic Plan (2018-2022)*. Retrieved 17 November 2022, from https://www.moe.gov.bn/DocumentDownloads/Strategic%20Plan%20Book%202018-2022/Strategic%20plan%202018-2022.pdf

MOE. (n.d.). *Ministry of Education, Brunei Darussalam—Special Education Unit*. Retrieved 16 November 2022, from https://www.moe.gov.bn/sites/bdta/SitePages/Special%20Education%20Unit.aspx

Mundia, L. (2010). Implementation of SPN21 Curriculum in Brunei Darussalam: A Review of Selected Implications on School Assessment Reforms. *International Education Studies*, *3*(2), 119–129. doi:10.5539/ies.v3n2p119

OECD. (n.d.). *PISA 2018 Brunei Darussalam*. Retrieved 17 November 2022, from https://www.oecd.org/pisa/publications/PISA2018_CN_BRN.pdf

Othman, A. (2022a, January 31). Brunei on right track towards achieving SDGs Borneo Bulletin Online. *Brunei on Right Track towards Achieving SDGs*. https://borneobulletin.com.bn/brunei-on-right-track-towards-achieving-sdgs/

Othman, A. (2022b, February 14). Instagram remains Brunei's most popular social media platform » Borneo Bulletin Online. *Instagram Remains Brunei's Most Popular Social Media Platform*. https://borneobulletin.com.bn/instagram-remains-bruneis-most-popular-social-media-platform-2/

Oxfam. (1997). *A curriculum for global citizenship*. Oxfam's Development Education Programme.

Shahrill, M., Noorashid, N., & Keasberry, C. (2021). COVID-19: Educational Practices and Responses in Brunei Darussalam. In P. Le Ha, A. Kumpoh, K. Wood, R. Jawawi, & H. Said (Eds.), *Globalisation, Education, and Reform in Brunei Darussalam* (pp. 325–354). Springer International Publishing. doi:10.1007/978-3-030-77119-5_16

Sharbawi, S., & Mabud, S. A. (2021). Malay, Muslim and Monarchy: An Introduction to Brunei Darussalam and Its National Identity. In P. Le Ha, A. Kumpoh, K. Wood, R. Jawawi, & H. Said (Eds.), *Globalisation, Education, and Reform in Brunei Darussalam* (pp. 45–66). Springer International Publishing. doi:10.1007/978-3-030-77119-5_3

Sustainable Development Goal 4 (SDG 4) | Education within the 2030 Agenda for Sustainable Development. (n.d.). Retrieved 5 September 2022, from https://www.sdg4education2030.org/the-goal

UNESCO. (2018, January 9). *What is global citizenship education?* UNESCO. https://en.unesco.org/themes/gced/definition

UNESCO. (n.d.). *What you need to know about education for sustainable development | UNESCO.* Retrieved 16 November 2022, from https://www.unesco.org/en/education/sustainable-development/need-know

United Nations Development Program. (2020). *Coronavirus vs. inequality.* Available from: https://feature.undp.org/coronavirus-vs-inequality/

Universiti Brunei Darussalam Graduate Admissions. (n.d.). Retrieved 17 November 2022, from https://ubd.edu.bn/admission/graduate/fees-and-funding(graduate)/ugrs.html

Universiti Brunei Darussalam Scholarships. (n.d.). Retrieved 17 November 2022, from https://ubd.edu.bn/admission/scholarships.html

Venkataraman, B. (2009). Education for Sustainable Development. *Environment, 51*(2), 8–10. doi:10.3200/ENVT.51.2.08-10

Wals, A. E. J., & Kieft, G. (2010). *Education for Sustainable Development.* Academic Press.

Wawasan 2035. (n.d.). *Wawasan Brunei 2035—Our Vision For 2035.* Retrieved 17 November 2022, from https://www.wawasanbrunei.gov.bn/SitePages/Our%20Vision%20For%202035.aspx

Chapter 12
Equity and Excellence in Education:
SDG 4 of the 2030 Agenda in the Italian Context – Public Education Policies and Their Impact

Valerio Ferrero
University of Turin, Italy

ABSTRACT

This chapter focuses on the policy commitment enshrined in 2030 Agenda with respect to schooling's role for social justice and equity as a horizon of pedagogical meaning for educational action. The reflection unfolds in three steps: (1) construction of a theoretical-conceptual framework on social justice and equity, with attention to classical and non-traditional factors of inequality; (2) analysis of the idea of equity promoted by 2030 Agenda, with particular reference to Goal 4 on quality education placed in relation to Goals 5, 10, and 16; (3) focus on the Italian context through a thematic analysis of public education policies developed to achieve Goal 4 and a literature review to understand their effect, with ameliorative proposals to increase equity in the school system. This chapter delves into 2030 Agenda's strategies for equity; the focus on the Italian context may also prove useful for those school systems with similar characteristics and issues.

INTRODUCTION

The 2030 Agenda (UN, 2015) is an indispensable reference for the 193 UN members who have signed it, committing themselves to building a more just and inclusive society in terms of sustainability, well-being and prosperity, with reference to people and the entire planet. It takes the form of a political responsibility to develop policies that move in the direction indicated by the document. Specifically, in this chapter we focus on the fourth goal of the 2030 Agenda, related to the need to ensure quality education for all.

DOI: 10.4018/978-1-6684-8903-1.ch012

Firstly, we will construct a theoretical-conceptual framework useful for guiding the actions of policymakers, school leaders and teachers under the banner of equity. Starting from the indispensable role of schools in achieving an ever-higher degree of social justice (Ferrero, 2023a; Hardiman et al., 2007; Hytten & Bettez, 2011), we will orient ourselves among the different strands of equity to position ourselves among those most consistent with this ideal. In this sense, we will be careful not to give in to interpretations that risk opening to social reproduction dynamics because they do not take into account how different starting conditions reverberate on educational pathways and to a compensatory pedagogy according to which there is a norm to strive for, with the commitment to equity being activated only as a result of a worsening of the *status quo*. However, reflection on social justice and equity in school systems cannot disregard a serious analysis of what can generate inequities in pupils' educational pathways: alongside the socio-economic and socio-cultural *background* of pupils (classical causes of inequality), non-traditional factors of inequality emerge (Ferrer-Esteban, 2011; Ferrero, 2022; 2023b Granata & Ferrero, 2022), i.e., inequalities originated by school systems themselves due to their organizational culture and operating choices. The use of this interpretative category is crucial for at least two reasons: (1) in order to understand how schools provoke inequality dynamics for the educational action of teachers (*micro*), for the organization of individual institutions (*meso*) especially in contexts of school autonomy, for education policies (*macro*); (2) in order to investigate the school and intervene in the dynamics that generate inequalities.

Secondly, we will concentrate on the fourth goal of the 2030 Agenda by analyzing what urgency determined its origin and what is planned for its realization. In general, in several areas of the world, many children do not access primary education and a considerable amount of young people lack basic skills in reading, writing and mathematics, with a slight majority in the female population (OECD, 2022; UNICEF, 2021). It is precisely for this reason that the fourth goal aims to ensure that every person has access to primary and secondary education and the achievement of adequate and concrete learning outcomes, with the possibility for all to access tertiary education (Agbedahin, 2019; Gabay & Ilcan, 2018); the goals also concern the achievement of gender equality in terms of the skills and competences acquired for the exercise of citizenship and the leading of a fulfilling life. Public educational and social policies on school building and curricula, financial support for schooling and teacher education are indispensable actions for the realization of this goal. Given the interconnectedness of the goals of the 2030 Agenda, it is useful to see the interrelationships with Goals 5, 10 and 16: the issue of equity in education is absolutely connected with gender equality throughout society, with the reduction of inequalities and with the institutional organization of school systems. The analysis will be careful to capture the *micro*, *meso* and *macro* aspects related to the realization of the goal (Boeren, 2019).

Thirdly, we will propose a focus on the Italian school context in order to understand how the commitment to equity enshrined in 2030 Agenda is being implemented. After an *excursus* on the history of the Italian education system and its indispensable role in the realization of the democratic project enshrined in the Constitution of the Republic (Cartabia & Lupo, 2022; Ferrari et al., 2019), we will propose a thematic analysis (Braun & Clarke, 2006; 2019; Peterson, 2017; Riger & Sigurvinsdottir, 2016; Terry et al., 2017) of the main public education policies developed in Italy to improve the equity of the education system since the signing of the 2030 Agenda. Precisely through the theoretical lenses described above, we will analyze the effects of Italian public educational policies with respect to equity in the education system thanks to a traditional literature review (Li & Wang, 2018; Rozas & Klein, 2010; Snyder, 2019): the strength of non-traditional factors of inequality in curbing the impact of educational policies in terms of equity will be noted.

Figure 1. Chapter structure
Source: Author's elaboration

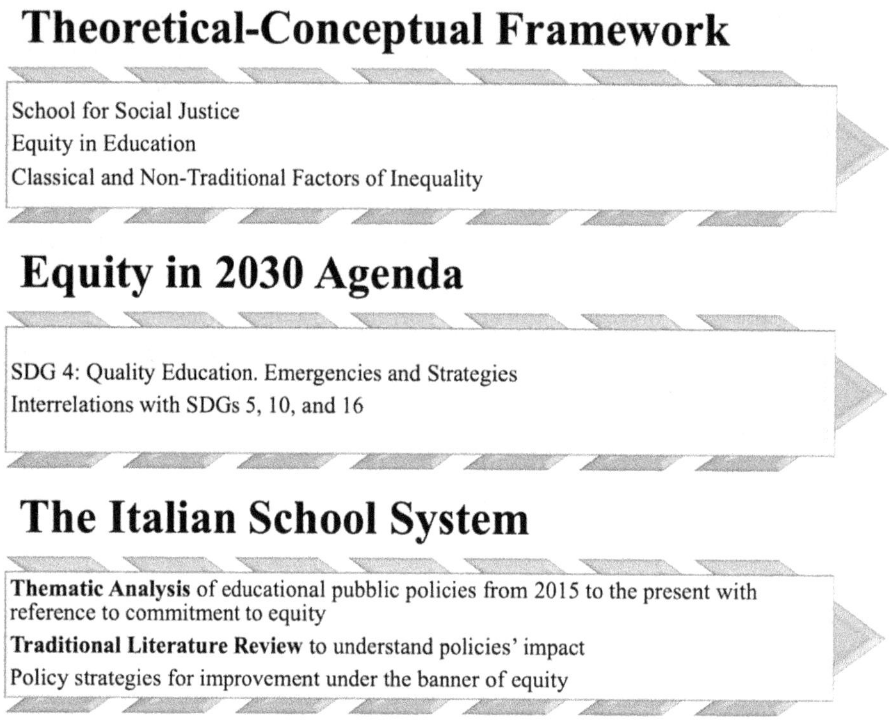

The contribution is conceptual in nature. The thematic analysis of public education policies and the subsequent traditional literature review to understand their impact are useful to take a snapshot of how far Italy is going in the direction set by 2030 Agenda with reference to Goal 4. The analysis referring to the Italian context can also be an opportunity for reflection for those school systems with similar characteristics and problems. In fact, the chapter concludes with some notes on the results of the thematic analysis and the traditional literature review, indicating some possible strategies for the improvement of the Italian education system in terms of educational policies, in coherence with Goal 4 of 2030 Agenda.

The 2030 Agenda and, in particular, Goal 4 assume crucial importance so that equity in education does not remain a chimera. The reflection conducted in this chapter is intended to be a contribution to pedagogical reflection to operationalize the 2030 Agenda political project, in the Italian context but not only.

SOCIAL JUSTICE, EQUITY, AND INEQUALITIES AT SCHOOL: A THEORETICAL-CONCEPTUAL FRAMEWORK

Schools play a crucial role in ensuring the achievement of an ever-higher degree of social justice (Adams, 2007; Buettner-Schmidt & Lobo, 2012; Griffiths, 2003): in fact, through excellent education for all it is possible to shape a more democratic, cohesive and inclusive society. Ensuring that everyone can realize their aspirations and reducing inequalities between citizens is internationally considered a categorical

Figure 2. School's commitment to social justice through the assumption of equity as a horizon of meaning
Source: Author's elaboration

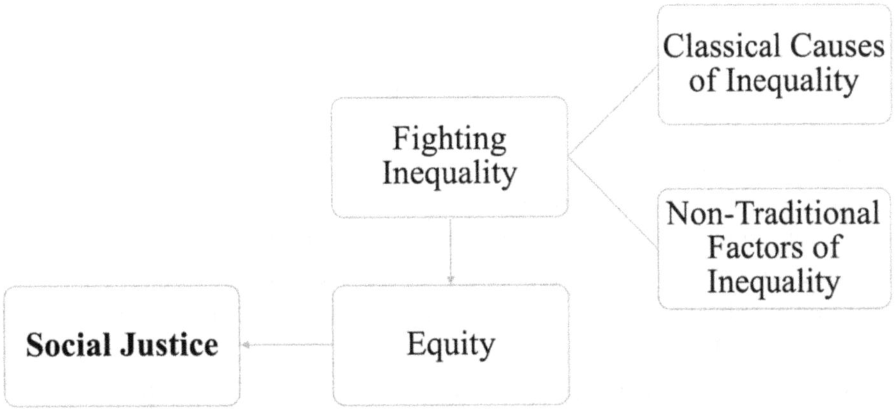

imperative: therefore, school systems must act under the banner of equity (Ainscow, 2020a; 2020b; Alcott et al., 2018; Jurado de Los Santos et al., 2020; Hippe et al., 2016; Schleicher, 2009), which becomes an indispensable horizon of meaning to be conceptually clarified given its multifaceted nature. Thus, the reference to social justice becomes essential to discern between the various interpretations and position oneself among those most consistent with this ideal.

This operation of terminological discernment and subsequent positioning represents a delicate step, also because it provides the interpretative lenses to read the dynamics of inequality that pose a threat to equity. In this sense, here we use two interpretative categories that allow us to understand how inequity does not depend so much on the starting conditions of the children but rather on the action of the school: in fact, it exacerbates and gives rise to distorting dynamics in terms of equity (Mayabi, 2015; Thompson, 2019). Indeed, the ethnography of education has long emphasized the distorting effects in terms of equity of school culture (Gobbo, 2011; Goldring, 2002). Thus, to understand what the obstacles to equity are, we use the category of classical causes of inequality to refer to families' socio-economic and socio-cultural status and the one of non-traditional factors of inequality to refer to the action of the school and education system in producing inequality among pupils.

A School for Social Justice: Equity as an Imperative Educational Criterion

Focusing on social justice, it appears as an ideal that has never been fully realized (Bauman & Tester, 2001), which requires constant commitment so that each person is included in democratic participatory processes (Gerwitz, 2006) and exercises self-determination despite the interdependence that binds human beings (Bell, 2007). The access to knowledge and the acquisition of skills to critically analyze what is happening are essential elements for being actors in history, identifying and opposing forms of injustice and oppression (Hackman, 2005).

The school's commitment to social justice becomes concrete only if it assumes equity as a horizon of meaning (Hess et al., 2007; Rudling et al., 2023; Shaeffer, 2019): the polysemy of the construct requires terminological discernment and subsequent positioning. The interpretations that are too oriented towards meritocracy (Nagel, 1991; Savidan, 2007) and negative freedom (Colombo, 2012; Van Hees, 1998) risk opening up to social reproduction dynamics, as they do not take into account how the different starting conditions reverberate on school paths. These two strands consider the results achieved without giving importance to the processes and pathways that determine them; moreover, they often do not consider the school's responsibility for the results achieved by the students, with the risk of indicating those who do not achieve specific results as disadvantaged, listless, unprepared. The other three strands, i.e., equality of opportunity (Bourdieu, 1966; Rawls, 1971; Roemer, 2000), capabilities (Nussbaum, 2013; Sen, 2009) and social inclusion (Kanor, 2021; Taket et al, 2013), make it possible not to give in to a compensatory pedagogy according to which there is a norm to strive for and not to activate the commitment to equity only as a result of a worsening of the *status quo*. Thus, pluralism is understood as an everyday experience and the urgency of breaking the interdependence between pupils' *backgrounds* and educational pathways is affirmed, emphasizing the role of schools so that everyone realizes their aspirations having acquired the capabilities to lead a fulfilling life.

Positioning within the last three interpretations is a choice with a strong ethical value (Hytten, 2015; Peters, 2015; Unterhalter, 2009) that allows for the development of a theoretical-practical definition of equity that intertwines the intercultural perspective (Abdallah-Pretceille, 2008; Akkari & Radhouane, 2022; Bhatti et al, 2007; Holmes & Corbett, 2022; Mincu, 2013; Woodrow et al., 2019) with developments in *post-colonial studies* (Aman, 2017; Ashcroft et al., 2013; Young, 2020) and intersectional theory (Crenshaw, 2017; Hill Collins, 2019). There is a need to ensure excellent education for all in terms of efficiency and effectiveness, aimed at acquiring the capabilities to exercise citizenship understood as active participation in social, political, cultural, economic life on the local and global levels. Diversity must not turn into inequality: there is no norm to adhere to and pluralism is an opportunity to enhance people's strengths, without differences being seen as factors of disadvantage.

Classical and Non-Traditional Factors of Inequality at School

Although the commitment to equitable and quality education for all has long been internationally shared (OECD, 2012; UN, 2015; UNICEF, 2013), ensuring an excellent school experience for all in terms of efficiency and effectiveness remains a chimera in most cases (UNICEF, 2018; OECD, 2022), with the pandemic and the economic crisis resulting from the war conflict in Ukraine worsening an already critical situation. However, it is important to shed light on the reasons that make equity a chimera: schools fail to be a *great equalizer* (Bernardi & Ballarino, 2016) not only because of the different starting situations of the children, but especially because of their own organizational and operating culture.

In fact, the dynamics of social reproduction, already denounced in the 1960s (Bourdieu, 1966; Bourdieu & Passeron, 1964; Don Milani, 1967), are still active (Eurydice, 2022; OECD, 2002; UNESCO, 2021): children replicate their parents' school and life trajectories. Socio-economic and socio-cultural *status* represent classical causes of inequality, but today new factors of inequality emerge: they are defined as non-traditional because it is the school itself that creates them due to its organizational choices and its functioning (Ferrer-Esteban, 2011; Ferrero, 2022; 2023a; 2023b; Granata & Ferrero, 2022): everyday educational practice, organizational aspects at school level and national education policies generate inequality dynamics. In fact, these non-traditional factors are numerous, act under the radar and are difficult to detect: their diversity from one context to another requires lenses of investigation and specific actions to overcome them. Classical and non-traditional factors combine, giving rise to unprecedented forms of injustice that affect all pupils and bend their schooling in a direction of inequity (OECD, 2022).

Figure 3. Unfairness pyramid
Source: Author's elaboration

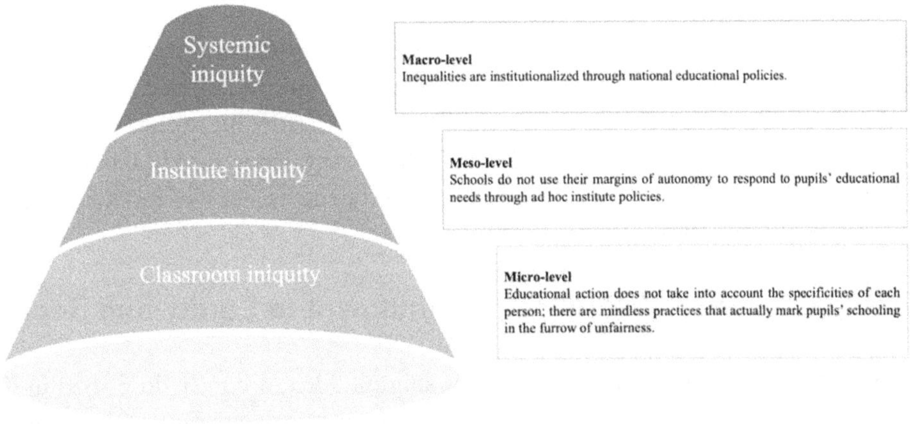

Schools cease to be engines of social justice because they fail to act in the name of equity, reducing inequalities. Indeed, the power of non-traditional factors of inequality is evident: Brofenbrenner's (2009) ecological model is useful in explaining the different level of origin of these dynamics and the responsibility of school systems in producing inequality. The classical causes are not school-dependent; in any case, it is not so much the starting conditions that determine the maintenance of the *status quo* in terms of social justice, but it is the non-traditional factors of inequality that cause first- and second-class schooling, exacerbating or creating inequality.

The dynamics of inequity can originate at different levels (Boeren, 2016); reading the interrelationships between them is crucial to understanding the effect of non-traditional factors of inequality on pupils' educational pathways (Giddens, 1984). At the micro-level we find inequality dynamics taking shape in the classroom, i.e., in the environment frequented by the student. Then, at the meso-level we have inequalities that originate in the organization of the school whose the student is a member: this category includes all those dynamics that involve the student's areas of life, such as the family or the territory. Finally, at the macro-level we have inequalities created by the socio-political and cultural system in which the student lives, thanks to educational policies that are not really oriented towards equity.

It is therefore urgent to bring back to the forefront the reflection on the role of the school for social justice: thematizing the issue is a precise ethical commitment, even more so in a historical moment in which various emergencies intersect, exacerbating social inequalities (UN, 2023). It is not just a matter of transmitting to the younger generations technical skills that they will be able to spend in an increasingly competitive labour market. Conversely, it is crucial to see school as a laboratory of citizenship: all students must acquire those fundamental skills to lead a life in which their voice can be heard, so that they can be free from ideological conditioning and possess the cultural tools that represent a common heritage that each person can interpret and help to make grow.

EQUITABLE AND EXCELLENT EDUCATION FOR ALL: 2030 AGENDA AS A POLITICAL COMMITMENT

There can be no sustainability without equity: this is the big educational message from the 2030 Agenda: an ever-higher level of social justice and well-being can only be achieved by making opportunities available to all people through appropriate policy actions (Deacon, 2016). Education is crucial in this project: indeed, Goal 4 emphasizes the need for an excellent school experience for all. Goals 5, 10 and 16 are somewhat related to this instance, advocating gender equality, the urgency of reducing inequalities and having strong educational institutions.

SDG 4: Quality Education. A Political Commitment to Equity and Social Justice

The fourth goal of the 2030 Agenda is aimed at realizing the idea of equity described in the previous paragraph: in fact, it aims to "provide quality, equitable and inclusive education and learning opportunities for all" (UN, 2015, p. 19). The schooling experience is understood as a tool to improve people's lives and achieve sustainable development (González García et al., 2020): this is why it becomes crucial to eliminate disparities in school completion, increasing children's acquisition of specific capabilities and ensuring that everyone completes primary and secondary education and has access to tertiary education (Ferguson & Roofe, 2020). Specific attention is paid to the inclusion of people with special educational needs and to the gender dimension: in fact, the goal enshrines the urgency of ensuring equal access to educational opportunities and equal opportunities to acquire capabilities and competences to live a fulfilling life and be sensitive to sustainability issues (Shulla et al., 2020).

This goal of the 2030 Agenda has a crucial importance. The access to educational opportunities is unequal in the World: in fact, in the poorest countries, one child in four does not have access to primary education. Moreover, across the planet, 58 million children do not have access to primary education, 129 million girls do not attend school (32 million from primary school, 30 million from middle school and 67 million from high school); then, 617 million boys do not reach adequate levels of competence (UNICEF, 2021). Indeed, the pandemic has aggravated an already precarious situation by excluding more pupils from the school experience. These data should certainly be studied in depth, but they paint a complex picture that needs urgent solutions. In this sense, as we have seen before, on the one hand family starting conditions affect children's access to education and their careers, on the other hand the school systems themselves produce dynamics of inequality: in a continuous cross-reference between local and global, it is necessary to consider convergences and divergences between educational systems (Bray et al., 2014), paying attention to the specificities of each context.

Obviously, the issue is to reduce the inequalities that characterize pupils' educational pathways, thereby concretizing every child's right to a quality education through which they can realize their aspirations (McGrath & Nolan, 2016). This is a precise political commitment that needs to be operationalized in each specific context (Sachs-Israel, 2016): in fact, each territory has different and particular dynamics that need specific improvement strategies adhering to the needs that emerge. Indeed, the 2030 Agenda qualifies as a policy document on a global scale, but in order for its goals to be realized, it is necessary to bring commitments back to the local dimension (Bonsu et al., 2020). In this sense, Goal 4 must also be the subject of analytical work to identify the educational needs and urgencies of each context.

In addition to this localization work, in developing strategies to overcome inequalities in education it is crucial to consider that there are different levels of action (micro, meso and macro) involving different

Figure 4. SDG 4: Quality education
Source: UN (2015)

actors and structures (Boeren, 2019), as we also pointed out in the previous section about non-traditional factors of inequality. At the micro-level we find pupils, teachers and families: acting from the perspective of educational co-responsibility guarantees greater chances of success at school since people become more aware of the functioning of the educational system by participating in the definition of its rules and organizational culture. At the meso-level we have the organization of schools, which must respect the specific needs of the student population in terms of space, school time and educational choices. At the macro-level we find the system of laws in which schools are embedded and must manage their autonomy (Blossfeld et al., 2014): a serious commitment is needed from political leaders so that equity in education does not remain an unfulfilled intention but becomes a project to be pursued with concrete proposals.

The action of the individual teacher is certainly important to guarantee every student an excellent schooling, but it is indispensable an equity-oriented policy action that supports the professional action of education professionals (Sayed & Moriarty, 2020): in fact, it is important to remember that the 2030 Agenda calls for a commitment on the part of political actors to improve school systems in terms of efficiency and effectiveness. In fact, the courses of action that are suggested (UN, 2015; UNESCO, 2019) open the way for educational reforms that affect the micro-level through actions aimed at the meso- and macro-levels. Several lines of action are suggested, i.e., (1) interventions on school curricula, to update them with respect to the needs of our times and make them more inclusive, (2) the increase of resources

Figure 5. SDGs 5, 10, and 16
Source: UN (2015)

allocated to education with more investments in school buildings, safety of environments, (3) the presence of learning technologies and materials, and (4) more scholarships to support the right to education of children with poorer socio-economic backgrounds, as well as emphasizing the crucial importance of teacher education.

The goals of the 2030 Agenda are interconnected, acting mutually as a lever for the realization of the overall project (Anderson et al., 2022). Therefore, it is absolutely useful to see the relationships of the fourth goal, in particular, with the fifth (Gender Equality), the tenth (Reduced Inequalities) and the sixteenth (Peace, Justice and Strong Institutions): in this way, we emphasize that the commitment to equity in education does not end with the school experience, but impacts the whole of society and takes the form of social justice work (Fonseca et al., 2020; Pham-Truffert et al., 2020).

SDGs 5, 10, and 16 and Equity in Education

Gender equality is a primary issue in terms of social justice. Goal 5 of the 2030 Agenda aims precisely at this, proposing to overcome gender segregation, differential access to educational opportunities, forms of discrimination and violence (Eden & Wagstaff, 2021; Koehler, 2016; Razavi, 2016). This is a fundamental dimension of equity in education (Esteves, 2018; Psaki et al., 2018; Subrahmanian, 2005): in fact, school systems must strive to eliminate inequalities related to schooling, acquisition of specific capabilities, attainment of a level of education that depends on gender or sexual orientation. This action is imperative and paves the way for equality throughout society, with the extension of rights to all people and the reduction of forms of violence and subordination.

Turning to Goal 10, we have already seen that reducing inequalities is an essential dimension of the commitment to equity in education. The 2030 Agenda examines the various dimensions of inequalities, in order to eliminate the social, economic and political obstacles that produce them makes them grow instead of reducing them (Apel, 2020; Saiz & Donald, 2017). Goal 10 urges action to reduce inequalities within and between countries (Cojocaru et al., 2020; Kuhn, 2020): only local action can lead to global improvements. Obviously, education plays a key role in ensuring that all people acquire those capabilities that are indispensable for active participation in political, economic, social and cultural life locally and globally: in this sense, it is essential that school systems themselves do not become producers of inequalities but drivers of equity.

Thus, the link with goal 16 seems obvious (Leininger et al., 2019): having educational institutions that identify with democratic ideals and are prepared to analyze their own functioning from a perspective of improving development is essential to reduce inequalities and so that equity does not remain a chimera (Malone, 2018). Therefore, political commitment is needed to make schools efficient and effective institutions, providing them with the right autonomy to better respond to the needs of their student population, obviously consistent with the goals set at the national and global level (Breuer et al., 2019; Ivanovic et al., 2018). Indeed, as we mentioned earlier, the commitment to equity and the reduction of inequalities is not the responsibility of the individual teacher, but must become an institutional imperative to be responded to with synergetic and systematized actions.

SDG4 IN ITALY: EDUCATIONAL POLICIES AND THEIR IMPACT FROM 2015 TO TODAY

In Italy, school is seen as the key instrument for the development of the country and the exercise of citizenship by all. In fact, the Constitution of the Italian Republic dedicates a considerable emphasis to it, enshrining the principles of substantial equality (Art. 3) and democratic education (Art. 34): together with freedom of teaching (Art. 33) and the right to education of every child (Art. 30), they are cornerstones of the Italian educational system and of the legislative production that regulates its functioning (Cartabia & Lupo, 2022; Ferrari et al., 2019). Creating a more inclusive and fairer society and realizing the democratic project is a task to which schools must contribute as a priority. The Italian education system is organized according to the principles of subsidiarity and autonomy of individual educational institutions (Barberis, 1998; Bracci, 2009): in the 1990s and early 2000s, Law 59/1997, Presidential Decree 275/1999 and Constitutional Law 3/2001 gave legal personality to school institutions, endowing them with organizational, management, financial, teaching and research autonomy; some 15 years later, Law 107/2015 reinforced this arrangement.

The State has exclusive legislative competence for the general rules on education and in determining the parameters that school services must ensure throughout the national territory. In addition, the State defines the fundamental principles that the regions must respect when they exercise their specific competences. The regions have concurrent legislative competence in the field of education (e.g., they can define the regional school calendar, deciding the beginning and end of lessons, the days of suspension of teaching activities) and exclusive competence in the field of education and vocational training (i.e., they can autonomously define the training plan of these courses). In this way, educational institutions make autonomous choices based on the training needs of their student population.

A specific focus deserves the School Council, the collegiate body in charge of formulating school policies and chaired by a parent, as provided for by Legislative Decree 297/1994: this is a non-causal detail, that indicates the need for close collaboration between the two educational agencies in the wake of a dialogue that is expressed not only in the relationship between parents and teachers, but also at a more apex level of governance. Indeed, it is necessary for all the actors involved in the life of the school to participate in the organizational choices: only in this way is it possible to develop solutions that take into account the different points of view and are truly oriented towards democratic governance.

The Italian education system is divided into different segments, as established by Law 53/2003. The first one corresponds to the integrated zero-six system and lasts six years: the educational services accommodate children from three months to three years, while kindergarten are open to children from three to six years. Then, compulsory schooling begins, from 6 to 16 years, and is divided into two different cycles. The first one is for pupils aged 6 to 14 years and includes primary school (6 to 11 years) and middle school (11 to 14 years). Then, there is the second cycle of education, which bifurcates into two different paths. Finally, there is the tertiary education offered by universities, High Artistic and Musical Education and Higher Technical Institutes. Families can freely decide which school to enroll their children in. However, at the end of compulsory schooling, there is compulsory education up to the age of 18: this is a right/duty that guarantees children the acquisition of a post-middle school diploma.

As far as equity in education is concerned, Italy's signing of the 2030 Agenda confirms a commitment that has long characterized the country. The thematic analysis of the educational policies enacted after the signing of the 2030 Agenda will illustrate the areas of intervention through which there has been an attempt to achieve Goal 4; the subsequent literature review with respect to the effects of these policies and, in general, to the level of equity in the Italian educational system will show how old and new inequalities persist and have effects on the students' educational paths.

SDG 4: Thematic Analysis of Italian Educational Policies from 2015 to Today

The thematic analysis of Italian public education policies addresses the regulations enacted from 2015 to the present to achieve Goal 4 of 2030 Agenda and thus to increase the level of equity in education. They are brought back into five categories that allow us to understand the scope of intervention and the desired impact in terms of equity (Braun & Clarke, 2006; 2019; Peterson, 2017). This analysis allows us to identify links between the various regulations and to understand whether the idea of education expressed in them is consistent with what is stated by Goal 4 of 2030 Agenda and functional from an equity perspective (Riger & Sigurvinsdottir, 2016; Terry et al., 2017).

Thus, in our case the thematic analysis allows us to clarify on which dimensions of the education system Italy has acted to achieve the goals set out in 2030 Agenda (Alhojailan & Ibrahim, 2012; Vaismoradi et al., 2013). The strands into which public education policies are traced are the following: (1) governance of individual educational institutions, (2) teacher education and recruitment, (3) inclusion, (4) school curricula, and (5) early childhood education and care. For each category, the regulations developed and their aims in terms of equity in education will be indicated.

Governance of Individual School Institutions

As we said before, in Italy schools are autonomous institutions. The aim is to improve the equity of the national education system by acting at the local level; however, it has often been questioned whether Italian school autonomy was formal or effective, also due to margins of manoeuvre for individual schools considered insufficient (Agasisti et al., 2013). This is precisely why Law 107 was enacted in 2015 (Domenici, 2015; Taglietti, 2016): increasing the autonomous choice of individual schools is considered a powerful tool for equity.

In fact, this law has further strengthened the school autonomy of institutions, with school leaders who must guide schools in organizational, economic, and institutional terms. They can expand the educational offer with a view to the diversification, flexibility, efficiency and effectiveness of the school service, using funds provided centrally by state and local institutions and funding from private entities or liberal donations from families. Moving between pedagogical vision and educational management,

Figure 6. Thematic analysis: Categories and regulations analysed
Source: Author's elaboration

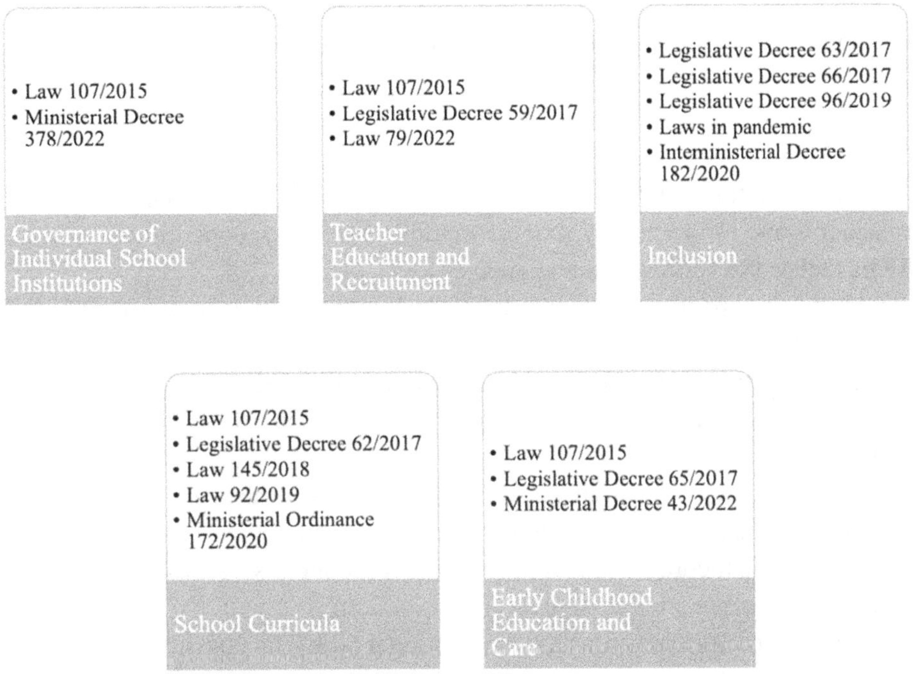

they must have a sensitivity in identifying and responding to the needs of a specific context. Therefore, leaders play a key role in translating the idea of democratic schooling into institute educational policies that integrate organizational and economic aspects. Schools must draw up a Three-Year Educational Offer Plan (PTOF): it is a document in which the school's educational policies are made explicit in terms of planning, strategies, programming. Together with the Self-Assessment Report (RAV) and the Improvement Plan (PdM), it contributes to planning useful actions to make the educational experience of all pupils excellent, oriented to the quantitative and qualitative growth of skills and useful in a lifelong and lifewide learning perspective. These documents emphasize the need for educational institutions to engage in accountability activities: increasingly, schools must communicate their management choices in the financial, organizational and educational spheres to the citizens.

Through school autonomy, schools develop educational policies that integrate the various actors who take part in the life of the school and the territory. It is a matter of building a participatory community in which each person has specific competences and tasks, also in the light of the legislation on collegiate bodies (Legislative Decree 297/1994) that sees leaders, teachers, parents and, in high schools, students acting together, according to a governance model that provides for middle management and distributed leadership (Pirola, 2015), in order to define the school's identity on an educational and management level.

Ministerial Decree 378/2022 provides autonomous school institutions with an additional tool: specifically, each high school will have at its disposal some tutor teachers who will have to support pupils through orientation activities after a training. These are professional resources that each school will be able to use according to a specific plan to accompany pupils in the transition between secondary and tertiary education and towards their first professional experiences.

Teacher Education and Recruitment

Teacher education and teacher recruitment are fundamental aspects for the quality of education systems. These are issues that have been at the centre of numerous reforms in Italy (Magni, 2020): Law 107/2015, later amended and supplemented by Legislative Decree 59/2017 and Law 79/2022, establishes the training pathways for future teachers and the modalities for fixed-term and permanent recruitment.

- Initial teacher education courses are distinguished for the 0-3 age group, for kindergartens and primary schools and for secondary schools (middle and high schools); there is a specific course for activities related to special educational needs.
    - For the 0-3 age group, a three-year degree in Education Science is required.
    - For kindergartens and primary schools there is a qualifying master's degree in Primary Education Sciences, with theoretical courses, workshops and internships in which to acquire pedagogical and teaching skills. Admission to the degree course takes place after passing an admission test.
    - For secondary schools (middle and high schools) there is the acquisition of a master's degree in a specific discipline followed by a university habilitation pathway equivalent to 60 ECTS divided between theoretical courses, workshops and internships. Admission to the qualifying pathway takes place after passing an admission test.
    - For special needs teachers, there is an additional 60 ECTS course to acquire the specialization to carry out this professional activity. Each school segment has a specific course, which is accessed after passing an admission test.
- Permanent recruitment takes place after passing a public competition based on qualifications and examinations, while the assignments of fixed-term employment is done through specific lists.

It should be specified that the law that established the degree course in Primary Education predates the signing of 2030 Agenda. In any case, the laws analyzed here have confirmed this set-up and improved the initial training of educators in the 0-3 bracket and of middle and high school teachers. This was certainly an intervention aimed at improving the education system in terms of quality, effectiveness and excellence through greater professionalization and training of the people daily involved in the professional contexts.

Inclusion

The special teacher education represents an improving intervention for inclusion. With reference to this area, several regulatory measures have followed since 2015 (Law 107/2015; Legislative Decrees 66/2017, 96/2019, the laws during the pandemic, the Interministerial Decree 182/2020 and various notes). They have strengthened the interventions for the inclusion (Canevaro et al., 2021), in a perspective of self-determination of the person for the best possible quality of life: the need for teamwork between all the actors involved in the life project of the student is emphasized, also in connection with the territory, and the modalities and configuration of the documentation that follows students in their school career are updated. A national Individualized Educational Plan model (a document that teachers must write if in their class there is a student with disabilities) based on the ICF is also constructed: it is useful to enhance the abilities of children from a biopsychosocial point of view, without it being bent on difficulties and absent abilities.

These interventions confirm the Italian vanguard in the field of the inclusion of pupils with disabilities at school (Maleduca, 2010), with concrete interventions to support a non-welfarist and non-compensatory vision of the educational paths of students with special educational needs. This commitment is certainly consistent with the idea of equity in education that we advocate here and with Goal 4 of 2030 Agenda.

School Curricula

Since 2015, several laws have insisted on the need to renew school curricula, which are also understood as an expression of school autonomy. Law 107/2015 and Legislative Decree 62/2017 introduce the "school curriculum" as a tool through which each school specifies its own didactic, educational and evaluative choices, with a view to verticality between school segments and competence-based teaching (Johnstone et al., 2014). Assessment takes on crucial importance: in addition to the disciplines, at the end of each school cycle the pupils' level of expertise is assessed for each key European citizenship competence. Then, the Ministerial Ordinance 172/2020 revolutionizes assessment in primary schools: it overcomes the measuring logic process with a sharp bend in the direction of authenticity and support for learning thanks to descriptive and no longer numerical judgements.

Law 92/2019 introduced the teaching of civic education, with schools committed to drawing up a curriculum relating to this discipline that would emphasize interdisciplinary links with the others, according to ministerial indications. Law 145/2018 also supplemented the curricula of high schools: pathways for transversal skills and orientation (PCTO) for students in their third and fourth year of high school were introduced, i.e., curricular projects that allow pupils to supplement traditional classroom experience with training periods in companies or private or public institutions that have an agreement with the school, but also in the school's laboratories or in simulation environments.

While these regulations do not completely change the structure of the school system, they are aimed at improving the educational experience of pupils through interventions in curricula and teaching and assessment methods. Thus, they can be seen as an attempt to give substance to Goal 4 of 2030 Agenda.

Early Childhood Education and Care

With reference to Goal 4 of the 2030 Agenda, it is crucial to reflect on early childhood education and care: in fact, the first part of pre-school education (0-3 years) is run independently by local authorities (municipalities, cities and regions), while for the 3-6 years age group there are numerous state-run kindergartens. They are part of the organizational framework of comprehensive institutes, i.e., facilities that also include primary and middle schools, representing a crucial junction for access to compulsory schooling.

Indeed, given the European recommendations (EU Commission, 2014; 2017) and studies on the importance of pre-school educational experiences (Melhuish, 2014; Ulferts et al., 2019; van Belle, 2016), also Italy has focused its attention on pre-school education, especially with reference to the 0-3 group. Law 107/2015, Legislative Decree 65/2017 and Ministerial Decree 43/2022 confirm the strategic role of kindergartens and establish the integrated 0-6 system: it aims to guarantee all children equal opportunities to develop their relational, autonomy, creativity and learning potential. The measures gave rise to documents of a pedagogical and organizational nature that defined the principles for an action that is not merely assistance but strongly characterized in an educational sense. The focus is on spreading early childhood education opportunities evenly throughout the country, encouraging the presence of public crèches, improving staff training and overcoming territorial inequalities that are too marked.

The Effects of Public Education Policies in Terms of Equity

The public policies analyzed above were aimed at improving the Italian education system in the direction indicated by 2030 Agenda. A traditional literature review (Li & Wang, 2018; Rozas & Klein, 2010; Snyder, 2019) can be useful to photograph their effect and understand what the emergencies of Italian schools are in terms of equity.

In general, the daily experience of students remains plagued by old and new inequalities (Gavosto, 2022). The socio-economic and socio-cultural background of pupils still weighs on their educational pathways, with children replicating their parents' school and life trajectories, as emerges from the scientific literature (Gentili & Pignataro, 2020; Giancola & Salmieri, 2020) and from documents of national and international research bodies and organizations (Eurydice, 2022; INVALSI, 2022; OECD, 2022). The incidence of background is so strong due to numerous non-traditional factors of inequality that exacerbate inequity and produce new disparities (Ferrero, 2023b).

At a micro-level we have almost unconscious actions that take shape in classroom life creating inequality:

- teachers' pedagogical ideals have effects on educational and teaching practices in terms of inclusion of diversities and assessment (Ciani & Vannini, 2017; Mincu & Granata, 2021; Pescarmona, 2012);
- Teachers' stereotypes and prejudices reverberate on assessment, with students with a migrant background (first and second generations) assessed less generously than classmates with Italian parents (Triventi, 2019; Triventi et al., 2021) or learning outcomes that differ according to gender, according to misconceptions that, for example, girls are less inclined towards mathematics and boys have no interest in reading or art (INVALSI, 2022; OECD, 2022);
- families play an important role in ensuring students' learning, but not all of them have the necessary skills to support their children in school activities, e.g., in assigned homework (Cordini & De Angelis, 2021; Grasso, 2015; Pastori et al., 2021).

Then, at a meso-level, there are institute policies that, while not contradicting the legislation, create inequalities and should be reformulated:

- requesting a financial contribution from families for the expansion of educational offerings is a rather widespread practice that risks diversifying learning opportunities according to parents' financial capabilities (Granata & Ferrero, 2022; Granello, 2010);
- The dynamics of school segregation, including internal segregation, create plexuses or classes of students with similar characteristics within the same institution, with reference to socioeconomic and sociocultural backgrounds, causing the loss of mixité and heterogeneity as indispensable educational resources to learn thanks to others and to understand the value of learning built together (Cardone et al., 2015; Oberti, 2007; Pacchi & Ranci, 2017);
- Extra staff assigned to school to strengthen the educational offer is often used in ways that are not consistent with the purposes for which they have been assigned to the school, being used for impromptu replacements of absent staff and not for specific educational planning (Cocconi, 2015);

- the management of the admission tests to "musical" middle school, which should be aptitude tests but often have a high level of selectivity, and its organization on the educational and didactic level lead to the formation of an elite section that precludes an important educational opportunity for some (Rizzo & De Angelis, 2019).

Finally, at a macro level we see national education policies that do not realize the commitment to equity:

- Given the heterogeneity of the national territory, schooling and financial policies at the central level not infrequently generate inequalities in individual contexts (Caloia, 2016; Sibiano & Agasisti, 2013);
- public spending on education is not sufficient to guarantee quality education for all (OECD, 2022);
- teacher education generates inequalities both within the same school segment and between different school orders (Eurydice, 2022);
- the recruitment system encourages precariousness, not allowing all students to be able to count on educational continuity (Ferrer-Esteban, 2011).

These dynamics make Goal 4 of 2030 Agenda still difficult to achieve. As a matter of fact, the public education policies presented in the previous paragraph have not had the expected improving impact.

1. As far as school autonomy is concerned, Italian schools continue to maintain a centralized structure (Schizzerotto & Barone, 2006) and what is planned in the Three-Year Educational Offer Plan (PTOF) often struggles to be translated into practice (Mincu, 2020); even the introduction of school evaluation, with the drawing up of the Self-Assessment Report (RAV) and the Improvement Plan (PdM), runs the risk of remaining a mere bureaucratic fulfilment if there is a lack of consolidated practices of peer review among teachers, continuous training, a shared idea of school and a virtuous circle between self-evaluation, improvement, external evaluation and social reporting (Cerini, 2016; Romano, 2016). Indeed, only in a few cases is school autonomy used creatively as a tool for equity (Gavosto, 2022).
2. Teacher education is a critical issue in Italy (Eurydice, 2022). Now the rules of access to the profession are clear and well defined even for middle and high schools (in any case, the application of Law 79/2022 has yet to become effective), but in previous years there was no specific initial training for these two segments and the only way to qualify for the profession was to pass a competition to be hired on a permanent basis. In fact, people without specific qualifications to practice the profession are often hired for fixed-term positions. In all school segments, it is common practice to give fixed-term assignments to people from other professional fields due to staff shortages. The situation is even more serious about special needs teachers (Ferrero, 2023c): more than half do not have the required specialization qualification.
3. The Italian law on inclusion is certainly in the vanguard, but its implementation is often difficult (Martinelli, 2015). Also due to the staff training problems highlighted above, we still witness separation and exclusion dynamics, as well as practices more aimed at welfarism than education (Ianes, 2023). Often, the drafting of project documents to support the educational pathway of pupils with special educational needs turns out to be a mere bureaucratic act without representing a moment of shared reflection between pupils, professionals and families; despite the new documentation push-

ing to work on people's strengths, there is difficulty in adhering to this biopsychosocial perspective on the part of professionals (Ravazzani et al., 2021).

4. The work on the school curriculum proved to be a useful moment of reflection on professional practice for teachers, but there was often difficulty in translating the design and assessment methods put on paper into practice (Castoldi, 2021). The same difficulty also affected the new primary school assessment (Scipione et al., 2022; Vegliante et al., 2022), with teachers sometimes engaged in clumsy attempts to restore numerical grades with specific descriptive expressions. The reintroduction of civic education also proved problematic: there was often a transmigration of content from one discipline to another, without the interdisciplinary character enshrined in the legislation being respected (Colombo, 2017).
5. The implementation of the integrated 0-6 system for the full realization of early childhood education and care is proving problematic (Silva et al., 2018). On the one hand, services, especially those for the 0-3 group, are unevenly present on the Italian territory; on the other hand, their quality also varies greatly, as sometimes the care character prevails over pedagogical planning (Sannipoli & Falcinelli, 2022). A further difficulty is determined by the different organization of the services for the 3-6 and 0-3 age group: the former are in the hands of the State, the latter depend on local authorities with wide margins for private initiative given the scarcity of public proposals, an aspect that makes the latter difficult to access for all (Eurydice, 2019).

The impact of Italian public education policies still proves to be insufficient for the realization of Goal 4 of the 2030 Agenda, as the UNESCO reports (2023; 2022) also underline in reference to the specific target. Interestingly, the regulations have not been transposed as real structural reforms to increase equity in the Italian education system, so that there are few studies monitoring their effects.

SOLUTIONS AND RECOMMENDATIONS

The analysis carried out in the previous paragraph shows that the Italian education system needs improvement interventions that can improve its equity and configure it as an instrument of social justice. Taking up the threads of the thematic analysis, we can indicate five areas of intervention.

1. It is necessary to support schools in the creative and original use of school autonomy, guiding them in the process of drawing up institute educational policies based on the needs of the target student population. In fact, in Italy school autonomy is not yet used to its full potential: training courses for teachers and school leaders and research-action paths that involve individual institutes could be useful in this sense.
2. Teacher education paths for future middle and high school teachers could be modelled on that of kindergarten and primary school teachers, with qualifying degree courses that include specific examinations in pedagogical, psychological and didactic subjects: this would ensure continuity in teacher education courses.
3. The issue of inclusion is crucial: it would be good to include training for support teachers in the initial training courses, so that it does not represent an extra cost for future teachers and so that the number of professionals trained on this issue is broadened. This would make inclusion effective,

since all teachers would have shared ideals on this dimension and would be able to create educational pathways based on the pupils' strengths.

4. In terms of the curriculum, descriptive assessment should also be extended to middle school and high school, so that assessment practice can take the form of feedback for students and families and not a mere certifying act. Then, a serious rethinking of school curricula from an inclusive, interdisciplinary and competence-based teaching perspective would be useful.
5. As we have said, the discourse on early childhood education and care is rather complex. In this sense, it would be necessary to invest more economic resources in the integrated 0-6 system to increase the spread of services (especially those aimed at the 0-3 age group) and their quality, with greater controls also on the personnel employed.

The improvement strategies hypothesized here are based on the studies consulted for the previous thematic analysis and could make a significant contribution to achieving Goal 4 of 2030 Agenda and, more generally, to raising the level of equity in the Italian education system. In the following lines, we delve into the effects that "Italia Domani" could have on schools: it is the National Recovery and Resilience Plan (NRP), which is expected to provide the school system and individual schools with additional resources to combat inequalities.

PNRR: An Opportunity not to Be Missed

A separate discourse deserves "Italia Domani", the National Recovery and Resilience Plan (PNRR) with which the Next Generation EU has been transposed and declined. Mission 4 of the plan is dedicated precisely to Education and Research, with the aim of creating a new, stronger education system that guarantees the right to study and consolidates digital skills. 30.88 billion, corresponding to 16,12% of the total amount of the PNRR, has been dedicated to this Mission, in order to build, upgrade and secure schools and to improve the educational offer from early childhood onwards and improve the teacher education.

Here, however, the investment "Scuola 4.0" gains particular relevance. In fact, Ministerial Decree 170/2022 has financed 500 million euro to combat school drop-out: it identifies as goals (1) the strengthening of basic skills starting from the first cycle, with a special focus on pupils with learning weaknesses according to a preventive approach to school failure, (2) combating school drop-out through a global and integrated approach that enhances the motivation and talents of each learner inside and outside the school in connection with local resources, (3) improving the inclusive approach of curricular and extracurricular teaching of educational institutions with a view to personalizing learning (Benadusi & Campione, 2022).

Due to their autonomy, individual institutions have had to elaborate their own projects and submit them to the Ministry of Education; once they have passed the assessment phase, these projects will become fully functioning starting from the 2023/2024 school year. Three lines of action are outlined, which in a synergic manner will be able to innovate teaching and prevent school drop-out by reducing the gap and ensuring greater equity: they concern innovative learning environments, training for digital professions, and specific interventions against school drop-out (Bianchi, 2022).

FUTURE RESEARCH DIRECTIONS

As we have seen, Goal 4 of 2030 Agenda has not yet been realized in Italy. A work of monitoring and pedagogical reflection on the issues of equity and inequalities in education is crucial to give a theoretical-conceptual framework to political commitment. However, support work is also needed for the development of equity-oriented public education policies specifically aimed at the realization of goal 4. Precisely by exploiting the potential of school autonomy, it is important to guide schools in action-research paths for the development of school-based education policies that improve the school experience of a specific student population. Through serious research and monitoring work, it would be appropriate to collect data and systematize good practices to institutionalize them according to a bottom-up logic and turn them into public educational policies.

Italy shares somewhat the same problems faced by countries characterised by the so-called governance of Southern Europe (Ferrera, 1996; Mincu, 2020). These are countries where there is strong teacher autonomy but weak autonomy at school level: thus, the quality of the educational experience is left to the individual teacher and there is no systemic reflection on equity. This conceptual work on the Italian case in relation to public education policies for the realization of Goal 4 of the 2030 Agenda is useful as a tool of analysis for school systems with similar characteristics: the theoretical framework developed can serve as a model and tool to put school systems and individual schools under investigation and understand what creates inequalities and hinders equity.

CONCLUSION

In this chapter we have delved into the meaning of Goal 4 of the 2030 Agenda, providing as a key to interpretation a theoretical-conceptual framework on equity in education and the dynamics of inequality that characterize educational systems: alongside the classic causes of inequality (census and family educational level), there are non-traditional ones that originate from the organizational culture of schools themselves. Then, we placed the focus on the Italian context, with a thematic analysis of public education policies developed in coherence with Goal 4 and a traditional literature review to understand their impact. The Italian education system is still far from a full realisation of Goal 4, even though its commitment to equity and social justice has characterised it since its inception.

Although the chapter focused on the Italian context, we are convinced that the reflections elaborated can serve as a trigger to open reflections in contexts that share similar problems and similar organization models. In fact, the 2030 Agenda represents a political commitment on a global scale: all countries must work to achieve an ever-higher degree of social justice involving all people and the planet.

REFERENCES

Abdallah-Pretceille, C. (2008). *Former et éduquer en contexte hétérogène*. Anthropos.

Adams, M. (2007). Pedagogical frameworks for social justice education. In M. Adams & L. A. Bell (Eds.), *Teaching for diversity and social justice* (pp. 39–58). Routledge. doi:10.4324/9780203940822-10

Agasisti, T., Catalano, G., & Sibiano, P. (2013). Can schools be autonomous in a centralised educational system? On formal and actual school autonomy in the Italian context. *International Journal of Educational Management, 27*(3), 292–310. doi:10.1108/09513541311306495

Agbedahin, A. V. (2019). Sustainable development, Education for Sustainable Development, and the 2030 Agenda for Sustainable Development: Emergence, efficacy, eminence, and future. *Sustainable Development (Bradford), 27*(4), 669–680. doi:10.1002d.1931

Ainscow, M. (2020b). Inclusion and equity in education: Making sense of global challenges. *Prospects, 49*(3-4), 123–134. doi:10.100711125-020-09506-w

Ainscow, M. (2020b). Promoting inclusion and equity in education: Lessons from international experiences. *Nordic Journal of Studies in Educational Policy, 6*(1), 7–16. doi:10.1080/20020317.2020.1729587

Akkari, A., & Radhouane, M. (2022). *Intercultural Approaches to Education. From Theory to Practice.* Springer. doi:10.1007/978-3-030-70825-2

Alcott, B., Rose, P., Sabates, R., & Torres, R. (2018). *Handbook on Measuring Equity in Education.* UNESCO Institute for Statistics.

Alhojailan, M.I., & Ibrahim, M. (2012). Thematic analysis: A critical review of its process and evaluation. *West East Journal of Social Sciences, 1*(1), 39-47.

Aman, R. (2017). *Decolinising Intercultural Education. Colonial differences, the geopolitics of knowledge, and interepistemic dialogue.* Routledge. doi:10.4324/9781315616681

Anderson, C. C., Denich, M., Warchold, A., Kropp, J. P., & Pradhan, P. (2022). A systems model of SDG target influence on the 2030 Agenda for Sustainable Development. *Sustainability Science, 17*(4), 1459–1472. doi:10.100711625-021-01040-8 PMID:34659581

Apel, H. (2020). Inequality in development: The 2030 Agenda, SDG 10 and the role of redistribution. *Real-World Economics Review, 21*(92), 228–237.

Ashcroft, B., Griffiths, G., & Tiffin, H. (2013). *Postcolonial studies. The key concepts.* Routledge. doi:10.4324/978023777855

Barberis, P. (1998). The New Public Management and a new accountability. *Public Administration, 76*(3), 451–470. doi:10.1111/1467-9299.00111

Bauman, Z., & Tester, K. (2001). *Conversations with Zygmunt Bauman.* Polity Press.

Bell, L. A. (2007). Theoretical foundations for social justice education. In M. Adams, L. A. Bell, & P. Griffin (Eds.), *Teaching for diversity and social justice* (pp. 1–14). Routledge.

Benadusi, L., & Campione, V. (2022). Parliamo di scuola. *Scuola Democratica, 13*(3), 551–560.

Bernardi, F., & Ballarino, G. (2016). Education as the great equalizer: a theoretical framework. In F. Bernardi & G. Ballarino (Eds.), *Education, Occupation and Social Origin. A Comparative Analysis of the Transmission of Socio-Economic Inequalities* (pp. 1–16). Edward Elgar. doi:10.4337/9781785360459.00006

Bhatti, G., Gaine, C., Gobbo, F., & Leeman, Y. (2007). *Social Justice and Intercultural Education.* Sterling: Trentham Books.

Bianchi, P. (2022). PNRR, istruzione e scuola. In L. Paganetto (Ed.), *Il piano italiano di ripresa e resilienza. Una sfida da vincere* (pp. 299–303). Eurilink University Press.

Blossfeld, H. P., Kilpi-Jakonen, E., Vono de Vilhena, D., & Buchholz, S. (Eds.). (2014). *Adult learning in modern societies: An international comparison from a life-course perspective.* Edward Elgar. doi:10.4337/9781783475186

Boeren, E. (2016). *Lifelong learning participation in a changing policy context: An interdisciplinary theory.* Palgrave-Macmillan. doi:10.1057/9781137441836

Boeren, E. (2019). Understanding Sustainable Development Goal (SDG) 4 on "quality education" from micro, meso and macro perspectives. *International Review of Education, 65*(2), 277–294. doi:10.100711159-019-09772-7

Bonsu, N. O., TyreeHageman, J., & Kele, J. (2020). Beyond 2030 Agenda: Future-oriented mechanisms in localising the sustainable development goals (SDGs). *Sustainability (Basel), 12*(23), 9797. doi:10.3390u12239797

Bourdieu, P. (1966). L'école conservatrice. L'inégalité sociale devant l'école et devant la culture. *Revue Française de Sociologie, 7*(3), 325–347. doi:10.2307/3319132

Bourdieu, P., & Passeron, J.C. (1964). *Les Héritiers. Les étudiants et la culture*. Parigi: Les éditions de Minuit.

Bracci, E. (2009). Autonomy, responsibility and accountability in the Italian school system. *Critical Perspectives on Accounting, 20*(3), 293–312. doi:10.1016/j.cpa.2008.09.001

Braun, V., & Clarke, V. (2006). Using thematic analysis in psychology. *Qualitative Research in Psychology, 3*(2), 77–101. doi:10.1191/1478088706qp063oa

Braun, V., & Clarke, V. (2019). Reflecting on reflexive thematic analysis. *Qualitative Research in Sport, Exercise and Health, 11*(4), 589–597. doi:10.1080/2159676X.2019.1628806

Bray, M., Adamson, B., & Mason, M. (Eds.). (2014). Comparative Education Research. Approaches and Method. Tin Wan: Hong Kong University Press. doi:10.1007/978-3-319-05594-7

Breuer, A., Janetschek, H., & Malerba, D. (2019). Translating sustainable development goal (SDG) interdependencies into policy advice. *Sustainability (Basel), 11*(7), 2092. doi:10.3390u11072092

Brofenbrenner, U. (2009). The Ecology of Human Development. Experiments by nature and design. Harvard University Press.

Buettner-Schmidt, K., & Lobo, M. L. (2012). Social justice: A concept analysis. *Journal of Advanced Nursing, 68*(4), 948–958. doi:10.1111/j.1365-2648.2011.05856.x PMID:22032609

Caloia, A. (2016). Disuguaglianze: la responsabilità delle scelte governative pubbliche. *Quaderni di economia del lavoro, 106*(2), 141-165.

Cardone, M., Falzetti, P., & Severoni, A. (2015). *Equità o segregazione scolastica? L'effetto della composizione delle classi sull'apprendimento degli studenti.* Working Paper n. 25. Roma: INVALSI.

Cartabia, M., & Lupo, N. (2022). *The Italian Constitution. A Contextual Analysis*. Hart Pub Ltd.

Castoldi, M. (2021). *Costruire il curricolo di istituto*. Carocci.

Cerini, G. (2016). Valutazione interna ed esterna. Attori e prospettive per il miglioramento della qualità dell'istruzione. *Scuola Democratica. Learning for Democracy*, *4*(2), 397–414.

Ciani, A., Ferrari, L., & Vannini, I. (2020). *Progettare e valutare per l'equità e la qualità nella didattica. Aspetti teorici e indicazioni metodologiche*. Franco Angeli.

Cocconi, M. (2015). Gli ingredienti necessari per una "buona" autonomia scolastica. *Istituzioni del Federalismo. Rivista di studi giuridici e politici, 19*(3), 647-675.

Cojocaru, T. M., Ionescu, G. H., Firoiu, D., Cismaş, L. M., Oţil, M. D., & Toma, O. (2022). Reducing inequalities within and among EU Countries—Assessing the achievement of the 2030 agenda for sustainable development targets (SDG 10). *Sustainability (Basel)*, *14*(13), 7706. doi:10.3390u14137706

Colombo, D. (2012). *Welfare mix* e neoliberismo: Un falso antagonismo. *Quaderni di Sociologia*, *20*(59), 167–177. doi:10.4000/qds.575

Colombo, E. (2017). The Contradictory Place of Civic Education in the Italian Education System. In C. Broom (Ed.), *Youth Civic Engagement in a Globalized World Citizenship Education in Comparative Perspective* (pp. 103–125). Palgrave-MacMilan. doi:10.1057/978-1-137-56533-4_6

Commission, E. U. (2014). *Proposal for Key Principles of a Quality Framework for Early Childhood Education and Care*. EU Commission.

Commission, E. U. (2017). *Taking Stock of the 2013 Recommendation on "Investing in Children: Breaking the Cycle of Disadvantage"*. EU Commission.

Cordini, M., & De Angelis, G. (2021). Families between care, education and work: The effects of the pandemic on educational inequalities in Italy and Milan. *European Journal of Education*, *56*(4), 578–594. doi:10.1111/ejed.12483 PMID:34898740

Crenshaw, K. (2017). *On Intersectionality. Essential Writings*. New Press.

Deacon, B. (2016). SDGs, Agenda 2030 and the prospects for transformative social policy and social development. *Journal of International and Comparative Social Policy*, *32*(2), 79–82. doi:10.1080/21699763.2016.1200112

Domenici, G. (2015). An Italian Paradox and an Important School System Reform. *Journal of Educational. Cultural and Psychological Studies*, *1*(12), 11–20.

Eden, L., & Wagstaff, M. F. (2021). Evidence-based policymaking and the wicked problem of SDG 5 Gender Equality. *Journal of International Business Policy*, *4*(1), 28–57. doi:10.105742214-020-00054-w

Esteves, M. (2018). Gender Equality in Education: A challenge for policy makers. *The International Journal of Social Sciences (Islamabad)*, *4*(2), 893–905.

Eurydice. (2019). *Key Data on Early Childhood Education and Care in Europe*. Luxembourg: Publications Office of the European Union.

Eurydice. (2022). *Structural Indicators for monitoring Education and Training System in Europe 2022. Overview of major reforms since 2015*. Luxembourg: Publications Office of the European Union.

Ferguson, T., & Roofe, C. G. (2020). SDG 4 in higher education: Challenges and opportunities. *International Journal of Sustainability in Higher Education*, *21*(5), 959–975. doi:10.1108/IJSHE-12-2019-0353

Ferrari, M., Matucci, G., & Morandi, M. (2019). *La scuola inclusiva dalla Costituzione a oggi. Riflessioni tra pedagogia e diritto*. FrancoAngeli.

Ferrer-Esteban, G. (2011). Beyond the Traditional Territorial Divide in the Italian Education System. Aspects of System Management Factors on Performance in Lower Secondary Education. *FGA Working Paper, 42*(12). Torino: Fondazione Giovanni Agnelli.

Ferrera, M. (1996). The "Southern model" of welfare in social Europe. *Journal of European Social Policy*, *6*(1), 17–37. doi:10.1177/095892879600600102

Ferrero, V. (2022). La scuola media unica nel primo ciclo di istruzione. Una riflessione tra equità e autonomia scolastica. *Dirigenti Scuola*, *41*(1), 41–55.

Ferrero, V. (2023a). Una scuola per la giustizia sociale. Riflessioni pedagogiche sull'equità in educazione in prospettiva gramsciana. *QTimes. Journal of Education. Technology and Social Study*, *15*(1-2), 97–108.

Ferrero, V. (2023b). School Between Equity and Inequalities: A Pedagogical Reflection on the Italian Context. In H. Vah Seliskar (Ed.), *Restorative Justice and Practices in the 21st Century* (pp. 175–204). IGI Global. doi:10.4018/978-1-6684-6145-7.ch008

Ferrero, V. (2023c). Inclusione: una questione di formazione? Formazione degli insegnanti di sostegno e modalità di reclutamento come fattori non tradizionali di disuguaglianza. *Annali online della Didattica e della Formazione Docente, 15*(25), 252-272.

Fonseca, L. M., Domingues, J. P., & Dima, A. M. (2020). Mapping the sustainable development goals relationships. *Sustainability (Basel)*, *12*(8), 3359. doi:10.3390u12083359

Gabay, C., & Ilcan, S. (2018). *The Politics Destination in the 2030 Sustainable Development Goals. Leaving No-One Behind*. Routledge. doi:10.4324/9780429490507

Gavosto, A. (2022). *La scuola bloccata*. Laterza.

Gentili, A., & Pignataro, G. (2020). *Disuguaglianze e istruzione in Italia. Dalla scuola primaria all'università*. Carocci.

Gerwitz, S. (2006). Towards a Contextualized Analysis of Social Justice in Education. *Educational Philosophy and Theory*, *38*(1), 69–81. doi:10.1111/j.1469-5812.2006.00175.x

Giancola, O., & Salmieri, L. (2020). *Sociologia delle disuguaglianze. Teorie, metodi, ambiti*. Carocci.

Giddens, A. (1984). *The constitution of society: Outline of the theory of structuration*. Blackwell/Polity Press.

Gobbo, F. (2011). Ethnographic research in multicultural educational contexts as a contribution to intercultural dialogue. *Policy Futures in Education*, *9*(1), 35–42. doi:10.2304/pfie.2011.9.1.35

Goldring, L. (2002). The power of school culture. *Leadership*, *32*(2), 32–35.

González García, E., Colomo Magaña, E., & Cívico Ariza, A. (2020). Quality education as a sustainable development goal in the context of 2030 agenda: Bibliometric approach. *Sustainability (Basel)*, *12*(15), 5884. doi:10.3390u12155884

Granata, A., & Ferrero, V. (2022). Nelle tasche della scuola. Coinvolgimento finanziario-organizzativo delle famiglie come fattore non tradizionale di disuguaglianza scolastica. *Scuola Democratica*, *10*(2), 363–384.

Grasso, M. (2015). Il successo scolastico dei giovani figli dell'immigrazione: Il ruolo della famiglia come capitale sociale. *Rivista Italiana Di Educazione Familiare*, *10*(1), 201–216.

Griffiths, M. (2003). *Action for social justice in education*. Open University Press.

Hackman, H. W. (2005). Five Essential Components for Social Justice Education. *Equity & Excellence in Education*, *38*(2), 103–109. doi:10.1080/10665680590935034

Hardiman, R., & Jackson, B. W. (1997). Conceptual foundations for social justice courses. In M. Adams, L. A. Bell, & P. Griffin (Eds.), *Teaching for diversity and social justice: A sourcebook* (pp. 16–29). Routledge.

Hess, D. J., Lanig, H., & Vaughan, W. (2007). Educating for equity and social justice: A conceptual model for cultural engagement. *Multicultural Perspectives*, *9*(1), 32–39. doi:10.1080/15210960701334037

Hill Collins, P. (2019). Intersectionality as critical social theory. Duke University Press.

Hippe, R., Araújo, L., & da Costa, P. D. (2016). *Equity in education in Europe*. Publications Office of the European Union.

Holmes, P., & Corbett, J. (Eds.). (2022). *Critical Intercultural Pedagogy for Difficult Times. Conflict, Crisis and Creativity*. Routledge. doi:10.4324/9781003150756

Hytten, K. (2015). Ethics in teaching for democracy and social justice. *Democracy & Education*, *23*(2), 1–10.

Hytten, K., & Bettez, S. C. (2011). Understanding education for social justice. *Educational Foundations*, *25*(1-2), 7–24.

Ianes, D. (2023). *Evolvere il sostegno si può (e si deve): Alcuni contributi di ricerca in Pedagogia e Didattica speciale al dibattito sulla Legge 107*. Erickson.

INVALSI. (2022). *Rapporto INVALSI 2022*. INVALSI.

Ivanovic, A., Cooper, H., & Nguyen, A. M. (2018). Institutionalisation of SDG 16: More a trickle than a cascade? *Social Alternatives*, *37*(1), 49–57.

Johnstone, S. M., & Soares, L. (2014). Principles for developing competency-based education programs. *Change*, *46*(2), 12–19. doi:10.1080/00091383.2014.896705

Jurado de Los Santos, P., Moreno-Guerrero, A. J., Marín-Marín, J. A., & Soler Costa, R. (2020). The term equity in education: A literature review with scientific mapping in Web of Science. *International Journal of Environmental Research and Public Health, 17*(10), 3526. doi:10.3390/ijerph17103526 PMID:32443493

Kanor, K. (2021). *L'inclusion sociale. Une utopie réalisable*. Paris: L'Harmanattan.

Koehler, G. (2016). Tapping the Sustainable Development Goals for progressive gender equity and equality policy? *Gender and Development, 24*(1), 53–68. doi:10.1080/13552074.2016.1142217

Kuhn, H. (2020). Reducing inequality within and among countries: Realizing SDG 10—A developmental perspective. *Sustainable Development Goals and Human Rights, 5*, 137-153.

Leininger, J., Lührmann, A., & Sigman, R. (2019). *The Relevance of Social Policies for Democracy. Preventing Autocratisation through Synergies between SDG 10 and SDG 16*. Bonn: Deutsches Institut für Entwicklungspolitik gGmbH.

Li, S., & Wang, H. (2018). Traditional literature review and research synthesis. In A. Phakiti, P. De Costa, L. Plonsky, & S. Starfield (Eds.), *The Palgrave handbook of applied linguistics research methodology* (pp. 123–144). Palgrave MacMillan. doi:10.1057/978-1-137-59900-1_6

Magni, F. (2020). *Formazione iniziale e reclutamento degli insegnanti in Italia. Percorso storico e prospettive pedagogiche*. Studium.

Maleduca, M. (2010). Inclusive Education in Italy: An Overview. In V. Timmons & P. Noonan-Walsh (Eds.), A long Walk to School. Global Perspectives on Inclusive Education (pp. 115-135). Paderbon: Brill.

Malone, D. M. (2018). On SDG 16: Peace, justice, and strong institutions. *Freedom from Fear, 2018*(14), 174–179. doi:10.18356/0f6c0938-en

Martinelli, M. (2015). *Didattica speciale. Insegnare a persone con disabilità, difficoltà e svantaggi*. Mondadori Università.

Mayabi, C. (2015). *The Role of Education in Fighting Inequality*. GRIN.

McGrath, S., & Nolan, A. (2016). SDG 4 and the Child's Right to Education. *Norrag News, 54*, 122–123.

Melhuish, E. (2014). The impact of early childhood education and care on improved wellbeing. In British Academy (Eds.), If you could do one thing... Nine local actions to reduce health inequalities (pp. 33-43). London: British Academy.

Milani, L., & Scuola di Barbiana. (1967). *Lettera a una professoressa*. Firenze: LEF.

Mincu, M. E. (2013). Balancing Citizenship and Interculturalism: A Comparison of Two European Policy Context. *Intercultural Education, 24*(6), 521–531. doi:10.1080/14675986.2013.864872

Mincu, M. E. (2020). *Sistemi scolastici nel mondo globale. Educazione comparata e politiche educative*. Mondadori Università.

Mincu, M. E., & Granata, A. (2021). Teachers' informal leadership for equity in France and Italy during the first wave of education emergency. *Teachers and Teaching*, 1–22. doi:10.1080/13540602.2021.1986695

Nagel, T. (1991). *Equality and Partiality*. Oxford University Press.

Nussbaum, M. (2013). Creating Capabilities: The Human Development Approach. Harvard University Press. doi:10.2307/j.ctt2jbt31

Oberti, M. (2007). *L'école dans la ville. Ségrégation – mixité – carte scolaire*. Parigi: Les Presses de Sciences Po.

OECD. (2012). *Equity and Quality in Education. Supporting Disadvantaged Students and Schools*. OECD Publishing.

OECD. (2022). *Education at a Glance 2022: OECD Indicators*. OECD Publishing.

Pacchi, C., & Ranci, C. (Eds.). (2017). White flight a Milano: La segregazione sociale ed etnica nelle scuole dell'obbligo. Milano: Franco Angeli.

Pastori, G., Pagani, V., Mangiatordi, A., & Pepe, A. (2021). Parents' view on distance learning during lockdown. A national survey. *Rivista Italiana Di Educazione Familiare*, *18*(1), 61–96. doi:10.36253/rief-10256

Pescarmona, I. (2012). *Innovazione educativa tra entusiasmo e fatica*. CISU.

Peters, R. S. (2015). *Ethics and Education*. Routledge.

Peterson, B. L. (2017). Thematic analysis/interpretive thematic analysis. In J. Matthes (Ed.), *The international encyclopedia of communication research methods* (pp. 1–9). John Wiley & Sons. doi:10.1002/9781118901731.iecrm0249

Pham-Truffert, M., Metz, F., Fischer, M., Rueff, H., & Messerli, P. (2020). Interactions among Sustainable Development Goals: Knowledge for identifying multipliers and virtuous cycles. *Sustainable Development (Bradford)*, *28*(5), 1236–1250. doi:10.1002d.2073

Pirola, L. (2015). Middle Management and School Autonomy in Italy: The Case of Teachers as "Instrumental Functions". *Educational. Cultural and Psychological Studies*, *6*(11), 89–101. doi:10.7358/ecps-2015-011-piro

Psaki, S. R., McCarthy, K. J., & Mensch, B. S. (2018). Measuring gender equality in education: Lessons from trends in 43 countries. *Population and Development Review*, *44*(1), 117–142. doi:10.1111/padr.12121

Ravazzani, S., Mazzei, A., Fisichella, C., & Butera, A. (2021). Diversity and inclusion management: An analysis of practice developments in Italy. *Sinergie Italian Journal of Management*, *39*(3), 213–229. doi:10.7433116.2021.11

Rawls, J. (1971). A Theory of Justice. Belknap Press. doi:10.4159/9780674042605

Razavi, S. (2016). The 2030 Agenda: Challenges of implementation to attain gender equality and women's rights. *Gender and Development*, *24*(1), 25–41. doi:10.1080/13552074.2016.1142229

Riger, S., & Sigurvinsdottir, R. (2016). Thematic analysis. In L. A. Jason & D. S. Glenwick (Eds.), *Handbook of methodological approaches to community-based research: Qualitative, quantitative, and mixed methods* (pp. 33–41). Oxford University Press.

Rizzo, A. L., & De Angelis, B. (2019). La progettualità inclusiva nel PTOF: il ruolo della dimensione ludico-musicale. In G. Elia, S. Polenghi, & V. Rossini (Eds.), *La scuola tra saperi e valori etico-sociali. Politiche culturali e pratiche educative* (pp. 625–636). Pensa Multimedia.

Roemer, J. K. (2000). Equality of Opportunity. In K. Arrow, S. Bowles, & S. N. Durlauf (Eds.), *Meritocracy and Economic Inequality* (pp. 17–32). Princeton University Press. doi:10.1515/9780691190334-004

Romano, B. (2016). L'utilizzo dei test standardizzati. Identificare le scuole in difficoltà e stabilire priorità nelle azioni di miglioramento. *Scuola Democratica. Learning for Democracy*, *5*(2), 309–330.

Rozas, L. W., & Klein, W. C. (2010). The value and purpose of the traditional qualitative literature review. *Journal of Evidence-Based Social Work*, *7*(5), 387–399. doi:10.1080/15433710903344116 PMID:21082469

Rudling, E. S., Emery, S., Shelley, B., te Riele, K., Woodroffe, J., & Brown, N. (Eds.). (2023). *Education and Equity in Times of Crisis: Learning, Engagement and Support.* Springer International Publishing. doi:10.1007/978-3-031-18671-4

Sachs-Israel, M. (2016). The SDG 4-education 2030 agenda and its framework for action–the process of its development and first steps in taking it forward. *Bildung und Erziehung*, *69*(3), 269–290. doi:10.7788/bue-2016-0303

Saiz, I., & Donald, K. (2017). Tackling inequality through the Sustainable Development Goals: Human rights in practice. *International Journal of Human Rights*, *21*(8), 1029–1049. doi:10.1080/13642987.2017.1348696

Sannipoli, M., & Falcinelli, F. (Eds.). (2022). *Il sistema integrato 0-6. Riflessioni e buone pratiche*. Carocci.

Savidan, P. (2007). *Repenser l'égalité des chances.* Grasset.

Sayed, Y., & Moriarty, K. (2020). SDG 4 and the "education quality turn": Prospects, possibilities, and problems. In A. Wulff (Ed.), Grading goal four. Tensions, Threats, and Opportunities in the Sustainable Development Goal on Quality Education (pp. 194-213). Leida: Brill.

Schizzerotto, A., & Barone, C. (2006). *Sociologia dell'istruzione.* Il Mulino.

Schleicher, A. (2009). Securing quality and equity in education: Lessons from PISA. *Prospects*, *39*(3), 251–263. doi:10.100711125-009-9126-x

Scipione, L., Bertolini, C., & Vezzani, A. (2022). La valutazione come problema. La scuola primaria e la sfida del cambiamento. In A. La Marca & A. Marzano (Eds.), *Ricerca didattica e formazione degli insegnanti per lo sviluppo delle Soft Skills* (pp. 734–746). Pensa MultiMedia.

Sen, A. (2009). *The idea of Justice*. Penguin Books.

Shaeffer, S. (2019). Inclusive education: A prerequisite for equity and social justice. *Asia Pacific Education Review*, *20*(2), 181–192. doi:10.100712564-019-09598-w

Shulla, K., Filho, W. L., Lardjane, S., Sommer, J. H., & Borgemeister, C. (2020). Sustainable development education in the context of the 2030 Agenda for sustainable development. *International Journal of Sustainable Development and World Ecology*, *27*(5), 458–468. doi:10.1080/13504509.2020.1721378

Sibiano, P., & Agasisti, T. (2013). Efficiency and heterogeneity of public spending in education among Italian regions. *Journal of Public Affairs, 13*(1), 12–22. doi:10.1002/pa.1404

Silva, C., Freschib, E., & Casellic, P. (2018). ECEC in the European Union: analysis and governance of ECEC systems of four Member States L'ECEC nell'Unione Europea: analisi e governance dei sistemi di educazione e cura dell'infanzia di quattro Paesi membri. *Form@ re-Open Journal per la formazione in rete, 18*(1), 234-247.

Snyder, H. (2019). Literature review as a research methodology: An overview and guidelines. *Journal of Business Research, 104*, 333–339. doi:10.1016/j.jbusres.2019.07.039

Subrahmanian, R. (2005). Gender equality in education: Definitions and measurements. *International Journal of Educational Development, 25*(4), 395–407. doi:10.1016/j.ijedudev.2005.04.003

Taglietti, D. (2016). An archaeological analysis of the last Italian education reform policy. *Italian Journal of Sociology of Education, 8*(3), 195–221.

Taket, A., Crisp, B. R., Graham, M., Hanna, L., Goldingay, S., & Wilson, L. (2013). *Practising Social Inclusion*. Routledge. doi:10.4324/9780203766798

Terry, G., Hayfield, N., Clarke, V., & Braun, V. (2017). Thematic analysis. In C. Willig & W. Staiton-Roger (Eds.), *The SAGE handbook of qualitative research in psychology* (pp. 17–37). Sage. doi:10.4135/9781526405555.n2

Thompson, R. (2019). *Education, Inequality and Social Class*. Routledge. doi:10.4324/9781315141749

Triventi, M. (2019). Are children of immigrants graded less Generously by their teachers than natives, and why? Evidence from student population data in Italy. *The International Migration Review, 54*(3), 765–795. doi:10.1177/0197918319878104

Triventi, M., Vlach, E., & Pini, E. (2022). Understanding why immigrant children underperform: Evidence from Italian compulsory education. *Journal of Ethnic and Migration Studies, 48*(10), 2324–2346. doi:10.1080/1369183X.2021.1935656

Ulferts, H., Wolf, K. M., & Anders, Y. (2019). Impact of process quality in early childhood education and care on academic outcomes: Longitudinal meta-analysis. *Child Development, 90*(5), 1474–1489. doi:10.1111/cdev.13296 PMID:31407322

UN. (2015). *Transforming Our World: The 2030 Agenda for Sustainable Development*. New York: UN.

UN. (2023). *Leaving No One Behind in an Ageing World. World Social Report 2023*. New York: UN.

UNESCO. (2019). *Incheon Declaration and Framework for Action for the implementation of Sustainable Development Goal 4*. UNESCO.

UNESCO. (2021). *The State of Global Education Crisis. A joint UNESCO, UNICEF, and World Bank Report*. UNESCO.

UNESCO. (2022). *Setting commitments: national SDG 4 benchmarks to transform education*. UNESCO.

UNESCO. (2023). *SDG4 scorecard progress report on national benchmarks: focus on early childhood*. UNESCO.

UNICEF. (2013). *Leave No Child Behind. Building Equity for Children*. UNICEF.

UNICEF. (2018). *An Unfair Start. Inequality in Children's Education in Rich Countries*. UNICEF.

UNICEF. (2021). *Every Child Learns*. UNICEF.

Unterhalter, E. (2009). What is equity in education? Reflections from the capability approach. *Studies in Philosophy and Education*, *28*(1), 415–424. doi:10.100711217-009-9125-7

Vaismoradi, M., Turunen, H., & Bondas, T. (2013). Content analysis and thematic analysis: Implications for conducting a qualitative descriptive study. *Nursing & Health Sciences*, *15*(3), 398–405. doi:10.1111/nhs.12048 PMID:23480423

van Belle, J. (2016). *Early Childhood Education and Care (ECEC) and its long-term effects on educational and labour market outcomes*. Rand Europe. doi:10.7249/RR1667

Van Hees, M. (1998). On the Analysis of Negative Freedom. *Theory and Decision*, *45*(3), 175–197. doi:10.1023/A:1004938512267

Vegliante, R., Miranda, S., & Santonicola, M. (2022). Le declinazioni pratico-operative della valutazione nella scuola primaria. In A. La Marca & A. Marzano (Eds.), *Ricerca didattica e formazione degli insegnanti per lo sviluppo delle Soft Skills* (pp. 685–696). Pensa MultiMedia.

Woodrow, D., Verma, G. K., Rocha-Trindade, M. B., Campani, G., & Bagley, C. (Eds.). (2019). *Intercultural Education: Theories, Policies and Practice*. Routledge. doi:10.4324/9780429024047

Young, R. J. C. (2020). *Postcolonialism. A very short introduction*. Oxford University Press. doi:10.1093/actrade/9780198856832.001.0001

KEY TERMS AND DEFINITIONS

2030 Agenda: Document promulgated by the UN and signed by 193 countries that takes the form of a political commitment to a more just and inclusive society from the perspective of sustainability, well-being and prosperity, with reference to people and the entire planet.

Education: Discipline studying educational processes and school systems.

Education Policies: Regulations concerning schools and education, defining their pedagogical principles, aims, organisation and operation.

Equity: Need to ensure excellence in education for all in terms of effectiveness and efficiency, equipping everyone with the skills necessary to exercise citizenship in terms of participation in political, social, cultural, economic life on a local and global level and maintaining that pluralism is the norm and there is no canon to adhere to.

Italian Educational System: Set of all state educational structures organised according to the principles of subsidiarity and autonomy.

Non-Traditional Factors of Inequality: Inequalities created by schools due to their organisational culture and operating choices; they are very specific and differ from school to school and make the school experience unfair for students.

Schools: Institution aimed at the education and training of children and young people according to principles of equity, social justice, and democracy.

Social Justice: An ideal that has never been fully realised, according to which all people must be actors in history and exercise their own self-determination despite the interdependence that binds all human beings.

Chapter 13
Impact of Audio-Visual Resources on Student Performance in Higher Education in Support of SDG 4

Mohamed Mohi El-Din Ahmed
https://orcid.org/0000-0002-1352-6277
Universiti Brunei Darussalam, Brunei

ABSTRACT

The Sustainable Development Goal (SDG) 4 emphasizes the importance of quality education for all, aiming to provide inclusive, equitable, and lifelong learning opportunities. In line with this goal, higher institutions have embraced technological advancements, particularly the integration of audiovisual resources, to enhance the learning experience for students. This research explores the impact of audio-visual resources on student achievement in higher institutions and its contribution to advancing SDG 4. Students in higher institutions have widely adopted mobile technologies in their academic pursuits, presenting an opportunity to leverage these technologies for educational purposes. Specifically, the study focuses on the use of audiovisual resources to teach Arabic language skills to non-native speakers at Universiti Brunei Darussalam. A semi-experimental approach was employed, and a randomly selected sample of Arabic language students participated in the study.

INTRODUCTION

Students at the Universiti Brunei Darussalam have mobile technologies such as smartphones, laptops and smart boards that use the Internet. Students have free internet access within the university and use mobile technologies in everyday life and matters related to academic study. The university's "canvas" program encourages the use of modern technologies in the development of learning processes in and out of the classroom (Hasmawati et al., 2020; Anshari & Lim, 2017). E-learning has been shown to help develop speech and listening skills (Guangying, 2014), giving students repeated training opportunities

DOI: 10.4018/978-1-6684-8903-1.ch013

and continuous learning that is not limited by place and time. This helps increase students' motivation towards self-learning leading to the development of their language skills (Ahad & Anshari, 2017; Anshari et al., 2016a).

The European Union has recommended the use of a Common Language Framework of Reference for Languages (Council of Europe, 2001) (abbreviated as CEFR or CEF) as a system aimed at verifying the linguistic competence of language learners. The CEFR framework should be the focus of the educational process, especially in university education (Wright, Gloria Brown, 2011). Many researches have been conducted on the effectiveness of e-learning in increasing the efficiency of learning, and the importance of advanced techniques to achieve better and faster learning (Mulyani et al., 2019a; Anshari et al., 2022b). This type of learning takes into account individual differences and allows learners to progress according to their individual pace (Collis et al., 2005). There are statistically significant differences between students who utilised computerised learning and traditional methods respectively in problem-solving skills (Taradi et al., 2005; Anshari et al., 2022a).

Studies have shown that the combination of traditional methods and modern methods are more useful (Corina Constanta Sirbu, & Others, 2014). The provision of e-learning syllabus leads to increased student participation in the learning process and provides new educational opportunities where the syllabuses are available online, (Learning Technology Center 2010). In this way, the student is connected to online syllabuses that improve the students' language skills (Hamdan et al., 2020). There are a number of potential advantages to blended learning that are emerging, of which revolves around accessibility, pedagogical effectiveness, and course interaction. Students requiring more repetition and exercises can have that opportunity without taking face-to-face class time away from those who might not need the extra reinforcement. (Strambi, A. & Bouvet, E. 2003; Anshari et al., 2015). To maximize the benefit of individualizing instruction through blending, provided redundancy to students in the form of audio, video, and textual versions of modules and increased the variety of ways students could engage the material. Without the bounds of in-class time, students can spend as much time as necessary to master the material. Through utilizing blended learning, accreditation and high standards can be maintained while providing the additional flexibility that students require. (Dziuban, et al. 2004: 3-6; Anshari et al., 2016b)

This study uses mobile technologies to train Arabic language skills by converting level 1 syllabus content into a computerised electronic program that uses video, audio, image, songs, games, exercises and electronic tests. The program supports blended learning comprising traditional (classroom) and e-learning (both within and outside the classroom), as in Figure 1. The program supports Arabic language skills and components in an integrated manner, and the four basic language skills: listening, speaking, reading and writing as well as linguistic elements: sound, vocabulary and grammatical structures (www.arabic-teacher.com).

To identify the effectiveness of the use of audiovisual resources on the level of achievement of Arabic language students at Universiti Brunei Darussalam. This study attempts to answer the following questions: Does the use of audiovisual resources in teaching Arabic language skills to students in the experimental group improve their scores in their post-test compared to their grades in the pre-test? Are there statistically significant differences between the mean level of achievement of the experimental and control groups in the post-test application for the experimental group?

Figure 1. Concept of integrated education

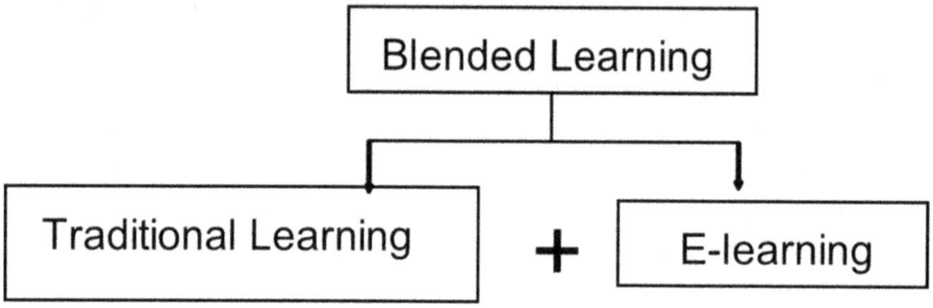

Literature Review

In today's rapidly changing educational environment, technology has become an integral component of higher education instruction and learning (Anshari & Hamdan, 2022; Ahad et al., 2017). The incorporation of audiovisual resources, such as multimedia content, educational videos, and online lectures, has garnered popularity as an efficient means of enhancing the learning experience and fostering student achievement. This literature review seeks to investigate the existing research and studies on the effect of audiovisual resources on student learning outcomes and their alignment with Sustainable Development Goal 4 (SDG 4) - Quality Education (Anshari et al., 2023).

Numerous studies have examined the function of audiovisual resources in contexts of higher education. Clark and Mayer's (2016) research demonstrates that well-designed multimedia content can enhance learning outcomes by fostering cognitive processes such as dual coding, where visual and auditory information is processed simultaneously. This cognitive synergy improves students' retention and comprehension of information.

In addition, Misseyanni et al., (2018) emphasise that the use of audiovisual resources promotes active learning, student engagement, and motivation. Quizzes, animations, and simulations are examples of interactive elements that encourage student participation and generate a dynamic learning environment.

Engagement is essential to the learning process. Sablić et al., (2021) investigated the relationship between video-based learning and student participation in online courses. Students who engaged with video content demonstrated higher participation and completion rates than those who did not interact with the videos, according to the study (Mulyani et al., 2019b).

The incorporation of audiovisual resources is consistent with the goals of SDG 4, as it facilitates the delivery of quality education and inclusive learning opportunities. According to research conducted by White and Mitchelmore (2010), technology-enhanced learning can promote equity and accessibility, thereby addressing the diverse learning requirements of students.

In addition, Voogt et al. (2018) discuss the significance of educational technology in promoting lifelong learning in their study. By promoting self-directed learning through audiovisual resources, higher education institutions contribute to the achievement of SDG 4 by fostering a culture of continuous learning among students.

In addition, a study conducted by Klobas and McGill (2010) highlighted the significance of video lectures in enhancing student engagement and interest in course material. The findings revealed that video lectures enabled flexible learning by allowing students to review difficult concepts at their own time (Mulyani et al., 2021).

Methodology

This study is a semi-experimental study in which the effect of the independent variable on the outcome (dependent variable) can be used to verify the effect of the use of audiovisual resources on the development of the language skills of the students. The experimental group is exposed to the use of audiovisual resources while isolating them from the control group. Thus, the independent variable is the use of audiovisual resources. The dependent variable is the development of language skills (listening, speaking, reading, and writing).

Experiment variables: Independent experimental variable: the use of audiovisual resources to determine their effectiveness in the development of Arabic language skills.

1. Dependent variable: the achievement level of students
2. Intermediate variables: It is between the independent variable and the dependent variable and requires a homogeneity between them in the two groups, i.e. controls these variables so as not to interfere in the impact on the dependent variable, including the age, gender, and the level of achievement.

Experimental design: The experiment comprises students of the optional Arabic language module at the Universiti Brunei Darussalam, one of the many languages offered by the University's Language Centre. The Arabic language module is divided into levels. The first group is the experimental group and the second group is the control group.

Table 1. Design of the experiment

Groups	Pre-test	Independent Variables (Audiovisual Resources)	Post-Test	Dependent Variables (The Achievement Level of Students)
Experimental	Test 1	Used	Test 2	Test 1-Test 2
Control	Test 1	Not used	Test 2	Test 1-Test 2

The study requested the teacher to teach the experimental and control groups so that the control group is instructed using the traditional method, while the audiovisual resources are used with the experimental group, and the results are compared. This experiment was conducted in a real study environment. To achieve the objectives of the study, the duration of the educational process was approximately two months (nine weeks), at the rate of four hours per week for both experimental and control groups.

Experimental group: The sample of the experiment was randomly selected from the university students who study the Arabic language optionally. The study population is limited to students of both groups.

Sample selection: The sample of the experiment consists of the university students who submitted and were accepted to study the Arabic language, so that the two groups, experimental and control, are equal in terms of age, study level, school environment and social environment. They are aged 17 and 18 years and have obtained similar scores for their final secondary school exams. They study the applied sciences and have no background in the Arabic language. The study population consists of 30 students, 14 male and 16 first-year female students at the Universiti Brunei Darussalam. Both the experimental and the control group consisted of seven male and eight female students

Students in the experimental group are not aware that they are subject to experimentation and are unaware that there is a control group. This is also the case for the control group. This group does not know that there is a pilot group, so as to reduce the probability of communication between both experimental and control groups regarding their educational processes which would impact the outcome of the experiment.

Experiment tools: The test for this study was conducted before and after the experiment to measure the linguistic levels of the students in question. To verify the veracity of the test, they were presented to a number of specialists in the methods of teaching Arabic to non-native speakers from Mansoura University in Egypt, Sultan Al-Sharif Ali Islamic University in Brunei, Sultan Idriss University in Malaysia, Teachers' University in Bandar Seri Begawan and others. They discussed the pre- and post-tests.

Steps and Procedures for Implementing the Experiment

1. The two groups included in the experiment were randomly selected.
2. The preparation of audiovisual resources and equipment for training Arabic language skills.
3. The pre-test was conducted on the experimental and control groups, corrected the answer sheets and monitored the grades of the students, in order to determine their level of language and collection before the experiment.
4. The teacher was trained to use audiovisual resources and instructed on the teaching method of the experimental group. This study asked him to conceal the audiovisual resources from the control group that used the book only. Hence, the independent variable was used: using audiovisual resources with the experimental group.
5. The trial took about two months (nine weeks), at a rate of four hours per week for both experimental and control groups.
6. The post-test was conducted on the experimental and control groups, correcting the answer sheets and monitoring the grades of the students in order to determine their linguistic and statistical level after the experiment.
7. The results of the tests (tribal and remote) were compared to the results of the use of audiovisual resources in the teaching of Arabic language on the achievement and linguistic level of the experimental group compared with the achievement level and language of the control group.
8. The results of the experiment were processed using statistical methods such as arithmetic averages, standard deviation, correlation coefficient, and t-test for the independent samples.
9. Interpretation of information in the light of the questions and hypotheses of the experiment.
10. Presentation of the summary of the experiment and the most important results and recommendations.

Statistical analyses: SPSS statistical packages will be adopted in the calculation of the statistical operations.

Building and Controlling the Achievement Test (Pre- and Post-Tests)

The students underwent many various tests. The tests are especially important in teaching foreign languages, including the teaching of the Arabic language to non-native speakers. The language tests are the only means to evaluate the learner's competence and achievement. Tests are intended to measure what a learner has achieved in a particular program or level, measure its general adequacy in language, or measure its linguistic readiness. It consists of a set of questions that the student answers in order to measure his or her level of a particular language skill, to indicate the extent of his or her progress and compare it with his peers. The tests are taught in the second or foreign language about questions related to the elements of the language: vocabulary, grammar, and the four skills of listening, speech, reading and writing.

A test is a measurement tool comprising systematic steps to produce desirable characteristics in order to provide quantitative data to serve the purposes of the research. It is concerned with the validity and consistency of the test.

The objective of testing: This test aims to measure the level of linguistic achievement expressed by the language skills included in the program that were taught to the students of the experimental group.

Formulation and timing of the test: This study is designed to measure the extent of students' achievement in the skills they have learned during this level. The skills are distributed approximately as follows: listening 30%, speech 30%, reading 20%, writing 20%. Question 1: Listening, Question 2: Listening, Question 3: Listening, Question 4: Reading and Comprehension, Question 5: Writing, Question 6: Reading and Comprehension, Question 7: Writing, Question 8: Reading and Speaking - Writing - Grammar, Question 9: Reading and Comprehension - Writing - Grammar, Question 10: Reading and Comprehension - Writing - Grammar. The last three questions refer to oral conversation and speech 30%

In order to calculate the test time, this study recorded the time taken by all the students in the survey. The test was applied to 30 students. The total number of students (30) was calculated by dividing it with the total time (1824). The test time is 60.8 minutes; approximately one hour.

External validity of the test: The research methods in education include some of the criteria taken by the students for accurate and objective research. This includes valid measures which are defined as an instrument that measures the intended measure. The results were submitted to a panel of experts in the teaching of the Arabic language who evaluated the validity of the tools in terms of the relevance of the questions to the age of students, the comprehensiveness, adequacy and integration of the elements, the clarity of the wording, consistency, accuracy of the test instructions, the appropriate grades for each question, and any amendments the experts consider necessary for more effective measurements. Following their feedback, adjustments were made and the test is finalised. Upon acting on their feedback, the test was finalised.

Reliability: Reliability refers to the ability of the construct to produce the same results in similar conditions. This study repeated the test to verify its reliability. This helps ensure that the ranking of the individual for their respective group does not change substantially if the test is re-applied under the same conditions. Further, by repeating the test, we are able to obtain stable results. In such cases, reliability is expressed by the coefficient of correlation between the grades the individuals obtained when initially sitting for the test and the grades obtained when re-sitting the test.

After 15 days, the test will be re-applied to the same group. The test will then be marked, and the results will be monitored. The results of the first test will be met with the results of the second test. The correlation coefficient will then be calculated to confirm the reliability of the test.

Table 2. Distribution of the test

Group	No. of Male Students	No. of Female Students	Total
Experimental	7	8	15
Control	7	8	15
			Total: 30

Applying the Test

After this study confirmed the reliability and validity of the test, it is then administered. Table (2) shows the distribution of the test.

The study attempted to have the experimental and control groups equal in terms of age, scientific level, school environment and social environment. The respondents were aged between 17 and 18 and scored similar results for their final secondary exams. Moreover, they were all studying the applied sciences and had no background in the Arabic language.

Analysis

The experimental group consisted of seven males and eight female students. The pre and post-test were conducted on this group. The lowest score for the pre-test was 51%, and the highest was 91%. The lowest score for the post-test was 66%, and the highest was 100%.

The correlation coefficient was 0.90, and this value gives a good indication of the reliability of the test scores and their validity to achieve the intended purposes.

Table 3. The statistical result of the pre- and post-test scores of the experimental group

Statistical Result	Pre-Test	Post-Test	Mean-Difference
Arithmetic mean (Q)	71.93	86.47	14.54
Standard deviation (p)	14.18	10.70	
Number (n)	15	15	
Coefficient of correlation	0.90		There is a strong correlation
The value of t	3.1701		Have no statistical significance
Significance level	0.05		

Table (3) shows the statistical result of the pre-test and post-test scores of the experimental group. We note that the mean of the students' grades in the pre-test is 71.93, while the average of the post-test is 86.47. The difference between the two tests is 14.54 (86.47-71.93 = 14.54).

The control group consisted of seven male and eight female students. The pre-test and post-test were conducted on this group. For the pre-test, the lowest score was 56%, and the highest was 81%. For the post-test, the lowest score was 63%, and the highest was 83%.

Table 4. The statistical result of the pre- and post-test scores of the control group

Statistical Result	Pre-Test	Post test	Mean-Difference
Arithmetic mean (Q)	68.20	71.60	3.40
Standard deviation (p)	5.39	6.39	
Number (n)	15	15	
Coefficient of correlation	0.87		There is a strong correlation
Values	1.5752		Have no statistical significance
Significance level	0.05		

The correlation coefficient was 0.87. This value gives a good indication of the correlation between the value of the test scores and their validity.

Table (4) shows the statistical result of the pre-test and post-test scores of the control group. We note that the average of the students' scores in the pre-test is 68.20, while the average of the post-test is 71.60. The differences in mean between both tests are 4.3 (71.60- 68.20 = 3.40).

The result obtained from the t-test for the independent samples indicate that these two groups differ in terms of the change in the achievement level. The change in achievement scores is due to the use of audiovisual resources in teaching Arabic.

DISCUSSION

This study attempts to ascertain the validity of the hypotheses of the experiment and answer the following questions:

Question 1: Does the use of audiovisual resources in the teaching of Arabic to students in the experimental group improve their scores in the post-test compared to their grades in the pre-test?

Table (3) shows the statistical results of the pre-test and post-test scores of the experimental group. We note that the mean of the students' grades in the pre-test is 71.93 while the average of the post-test is 86.47. The difference in mean for the experimental group between both tests in 14.54 (86.47-71.93 = 14.54).

From the previous statistical result, we conclude that the use of audiovisual resources for the students of the experimental group leads to an improvement in their grades in the post-test compared to their grades in the pre-test. In other words, audiovisual resources increase the students' level of achievement, and the relationship between them is statistically significant.

Table (4) shows the statistical result of the pre-test and post-test scores of the control group. We note that the mean of the pre-test is 68.20, and 71.60 for the post-test. The difference in mean scores is 4.3 (71.60- 68.20 = 3.40).

This indicates that those who did not use audiovisual resources did not improve their results and recorded only marginal improvement between the pre- and post-tests.

The results support a statistically significant difference between the average achievement of the students of the experimental group who used audiovisual resources in teaching Arabic and the students of the control group who did not use audiovisual resources. In addition, the result obtained from the t-test for the independent samples means that these two groups are different in terms of the change in their achievement level. The change in achievement scores is due to the use of audiovisual resources in teaching Arabic.

This study supports the results of Alejandro Spiegela & Georgina Rodrígueza (2016) where students prefer to use their mobile devices despite the absence of instruction from their teachers and that students prefer audio and visual language in academic university study. Further, Joy (2000) concluded that the use of computers in education leads students to acquire accurate difference understandings rapidly. Grgurovic (2011) found that the combination of e-learning and traditional teaching aids in improving speech and pronunciation skills. Further, Guangying (2014) emphasised that integrated education improves speech and listening skills.

CONCLUSION

This study concludes that students who use audiovisual resources increase their language skills as they are trained to self-study and study outside the classroom before and after the lesson. The results emphasize the importance of blended learning - the combination of e-learning and traditional education. Education using audiovisual resources helps reduce/tackle boredom sourced from the traditional classroom process. In addition, it creates a good environment for teaching Arabic language skills, and creates a supportive environment for self-guided learning while encouraging the use of mobile technologies outside the classroom.

REFERENCES

Ahad, A. D., & Anshari, M. (2017). Smartphone habits among youth: Uses and gratification theory. *International Journal of Cyber Behavior, Psychology and Learning*, *7*(1), 65–75. doi:10.4018/IJCBPL.2017010105

Ahad, A. D., Anshari, M., & Razzaq, A. (2017). Domestication of smartphones among adolescents in Brunei darussalam. *International Journal of Cyber Behavior, Psychology and Learning*, *7*(4), 26–39. doi:10.4018/IJCBPL.2017100103

Anshari, M., Alas, Y., & Guan, L. S. (2016b). Developing online learning resources: Big data, social networks, and cloud computing to support pervasive knowledge. *Education and Information Technologies*, *21*(6), 1663–1677. doi:10.100710639-015-9407-3

Anshari, M., Alas, Y., Sabtu, N. P. H., & Hamid, M. S. A. (2016a). Online Learning: Trends, issues and challenges in the Big Data Era. *Journal of E-learning and Knowledge Society*, *12*(1).

Anshari, M., Alas, Y., Yunus, N., Sabtu, N. I., & Hamid, M. H. (2015). Social customer relationship management and student empowerment in online learning systems. *International Journal of Electronic Customer Relationship Management*, *9*(2-3), 104–121. doi:10.1504/IJECRM.2015.071711

Anshari, M., Almunawar, M. N., & Masri, M. (2022a). Digital twin: Financial technology's next frontier of robo-advisor. *Journal of Risk and Financial Management, 15*(4), 163.

Anshari, M., & Hamdan, M. (2022). Enhancing e-government with a digital twin for innovation management. *Journal of Science and Technology Policy Management.*

Anshari, M., & Lim, S. A. (2017). E-government with big data enabled through smartphone for public services: Possibilities and challenges. *International Journal of Public Administration, 40*(13), 1143–1158. doi:10.1080/01900692.2016.1242619

Anshari, M., Syafrudin, M., & Fitriyani, N. L. (2022b). Fourth industrial revolution between knowledge management and digital humanities. *Information (Basel), 13*(6), 292. doi:10.3390/info13060292

Anshari, M., Syafrudin, M., Tan, A., Fitriyani, N. L., & Alas, Y. (2023). Optimisation of Knowledge Management (KM) with Machine Learning (ML) Enabled. *Information (Basel), 14*(1), 35. doi:10.3390/info14010035

Clark, R. C., & Mayer, R. E. (2016). *E-learning and the science of instruction: Proven guidelines for consumers and designers of multimedia learning*. John Wiley & Sons.

Collis, B. (2005). Multiple Perspectives on Blended Learning Design. *Journal of Learning Design*, 12–21.

Corina Constanta Sirbu. (2014). Aspects concerning the usage of modern methods for teaching – learning – evaluation in universities. *Procedia - Social and Behavioral Sciences, 182* . doi:10.1016/j.sbspro.2015.04.777

Council of Europe. (2001). *Common European Framework of Reference for languages: Learning, teaching, assessment.* Cambridge University Press. https://www.coe.int/t/dg4/linguistic/Source/Framework_EN.pdf

Dzuiban, C., Hartman, J., & Moskal, P. (2004). *Blended Learning Educat Use Center For Applied Research (ECAR), No. 7.* www.educause.edu.ecar

Grgurovic, M. (2011). Blended learning in an ESL class: A case study. *CALICO Journal, 29*(1), 100–117. doi:10.11139/cj.29.1.100-117

Guangying, C. (2014). An experimental research on blended learning in the development of listening and speaking skills in China. *Southern African Linguistics and Applied Language Studies, 32*(4), 447–460. doi:10.2989/16073614.2014.999989

Hamdan, M., Jaidin, J. H., Fithriyah, M., & Anshari, M. (2020, December). E-learning in time of COVID-19 pandemic: Challenges & experiences. In *2020 sixth international conference on e-learning (econf)* (pp. 12-16). IEEE.

Hasmawati, F., Samiha, Y. T., Razzaq, A., & Anshari, M. (2020). Understanding nomophobia among digital natives: Characteristics and challenges. *Journal of Critical Reviews, 7*(13), 122–131.

Joy, F. (2000). *Integrating Technology into Instruction in an Inclusive Classroom for Diverse Learners.* Rowan University.

Klobas, J. E., & McGill, T. J. (2010). The role of involvement in learning management system success. *Journal of Computing in Higher Education, 22*(2), 114–134. doi:10.100712528-010-9032-5

Learning Technology Center. (2010). *Hybrid Courses.* www.uwm.edu/1tc/hybrid/faculty/....//tips.cfm

Misseyanni, A., Lytras, M. D., Papadopoulou, P., & Marouli, C. (Eds.). (2018). *Active learning strategies in higher education: Teaching for leadership, innovation, and creativity*. Emerald Publishing Limited. doi:10.1108/9781787144873

Mulyani, M. A., Razzaq, A., Ridho, S. L. Z., & Anshari, M. (2019b, October). Smartphone and Mobile Learning to Support Experiential Learning. In *2019 International Conference on Electrical Engineering and Computer Science (ICECOS)* (pp. 6-9). IEEE. 10.1109/ICECOS47637.2019.8984501

Mulyani, M. A., Razzaq, A., Sumardi, W. H., & Anshari, M. (2019a, August). Smartphone adoption in mobile learning scenario. In *2019 International Conference on Information Management and Technology (ICIMTech)* (Vol. 1, pp. 208-211). IEEE. 10.1109/ICIMTech.2019.8843755

Mulyani, M. A., Yusuf, S., Siregar, P., Nurihsan, J., Razzaq, A., & Anshari, M. (2021, August). Fourth industrial revolution and educational challenges. In *2021 International Conference on Information Management and Technology (ICIMTech)* (Vol. 1, pp. 245-249). IEEE. 10.1109/ICIMTech53080.2021.9535057

Razzaq, A., Samiha, Y. T., & Anshari, M. (2018). Smartphone habits and behaviors in supporting students self-efficacy. *International Journal of Emerging Technologies in Learning*, *13*(2), 94. doi:10.3991/ijet.v13i02.7685

Sablić, M., Mirosavljević, A., & Škugor, A. (2021). Video-based learning (VBL)—past, present and future: An overview of the research published from 2008 to 2019. Technology. *Knowledge and Learning*, *26*(4), 1061–1077. doi:10.100710758-020-09455-5

Spiegela, A., & Rodrígueza, G. (2016). Students at university have mobile technologies. Do they do m-learning? *Procedia: Social and Behavioral Sciences*, *217*, 846–850. doi:10.1016/j.sbspro.2016.02.006

Strambi, A., & Bouvet, E. (2003). Flexibility and interaction at a distance: A mixed-mode environment for language learning. *Language Learning & Technology*, *7*(3), 81–102.

Taradi, K. (2005). Blended Problem-Based Learning Outcomes in Acid-Base Physiology. https://advan.physiology.org/cgi/cotent/abstract/29/1/35

Voogt, J. M., Pieters, J. M., & Handelzalts, A. (2018). Teacher collaboration in curriculum design teams: Effects, mechanisms, and conditions. In *Teacher Learning Through Teacher Teams* (pp. 7–26). Routledge. doi:10.4324/9781315123431-2

White, P., & Mitchelmore, M. C. (2010). Teaching for abstraction: A model. *Mathematical Thinking and Learning*, *12*(3), 205–226. doi:10.1080/10986061003717476

Wright, G. B. (2011). Student-Centered Learning in Higher Education. *International Journal on Teaching and Learning in Higher Education*, *23*(3), 93–94. www.arabic-teacher.com

Chapter 14
Public Policy and Sustainable Waste Management:
The Concept of Waste in Islam in Relation to Sustainability

Fathin Awang Mat Japar
https://orcid.org/0009-0009-6392-8459
Universiti Brunei Darussalam, Brunei

Emil Ali
Universiti Brunei Darussalam, Brunei

Hamizah Haidi
Universiti Brunei Darussalam, Brunei

ABSTRACT

Public policy has an effect on diverse aspects of the public domain, including the domain of waste management, which falls under SDG12: sustainable consumption and production. This chapter discovers and discusses the definition of the waste management concept derived from the Qur'ān and Sunnah (Prophetic traditions) from the ground up, beginning with the concept of waste itself. It is found that the concept of waste in Islam comprises an interdisciplinary approach, thus leading to the understanding of the concept of waste management in Islam that incorporates sustainability elements and integration of multiple dimensions.

1. INTRODUCTION

Waste management studies serve as an imperative source for the latest data, framework models and actionable strategies for achieving sustainable development goals. The reasons behind the need and rise of these studies are also significant in terms of how the research will unfold and provide emergent solutions for the ubiquitous impacts of excessive waste generation and mismanagement to the respective domains

DOI: 10.4018/978-1-6684-8903-1.ch014

of priority particularly the sustainable development goals and the environmental health missions pursued by a diverse demographic of stakeholders and affected groups. The different objectives underlying different worldviews have an influence on the research outcomes, such that scientists that are after the sustaining of human development on this planet would have a different set of focus compared to scholars who are pursuing the higher divine objectives with matters of the hereafter in mind when dealing with waste management research. There is a substantial number of research studies being conducted on the management of waste in broad, but not as many of these studies on waste management are premised on the worldview of the Islamic faith. Oftentimes, there is a paradigm contradiction occurring in the studies where the supposed Islamic take on waste management still approaches the concept of waste and its management based on non-Islamic worldviews. While it is logical and necessary to establish the concept of waste on the tangible lived reality, an understanding derived from Islamic teaching on the concept of waste would be a significant contribution to the research if one claims that a waste management framework is founded upon a true Islamic worldview.

2. LITERATURE REVIEW

This section reviews existing literature surrounding the conventional understanding of sustainability, waste management and governance of waste management. There exist the memorable definitions of sustainability throughout many disciplines that are somewhat similar yet distinct, and there are also the other less popular yet significant definitions of sustainability derived from other paradigms of knowledge. Among the most prominent definitions of sustainability found in literature searches are those pertaining to health and medical disciplines, such as the sustainability of health interventions; sustainable growth in the world of entrepreneurship; and the field of sustainable development, which is the scope of this chapter. Inconsistencies in the sustainability definition may endure even within a discipline (Moore et al., 2017). On the other hand, the definition reflected in the 1987 Brundtland Report was more frequently cited in publications on sustainable development (Johnston et al., 2007). This definition was revised in 2006 to add comprehensive coverage in its specifications, particularly as "a long-term vision for sustainability in which economic growth, social cohesion and environmental protection go hand in hand and are mutually supporting" (EUR-Lex Glossary of Summaries, n.d.). The three pillars of sustainability (or more specifically, of sustainable development), namely the environmental, economic, and social aspects, appear to be the focus of the definitions given. Other similar definitions of sustainability are mentioned in the works of many (Morse et al., 2013; Office of Sustainability, n.d.), and these popular 'definitions' are construed in the sense that they are in the form of envisioned goals or anticipated outcomes of sustainability rather than definitions of sustainability in terms of its fundamental actuality. Meanwhile, there are many who reject the search for an objective and conceptual definition of sustainability in favour of a more Panglossian approach that suggests development in the absence of a universal definition (Owens, 2003).

Another interesting take on the sustainability definition is that of Tainter (vlada, 2012) which is "an active condition of problem-solving." This is further defined in detail in one of his lectures as follows: "maintaining something at a desired condition, usually what's valued in people's life; it is sustaining something that people value." (Ibid.) He emphasised that the act of sustaining or maintaining something was undertaken in order to achieve a certain condition that is valued from a human perspective, arguably regardless of the utter and total value outside of our restricted human understanding. His critical assessment of 'sustainability' stands on a more realistic foundation as his view of sustainability also focuses on the idea that it is a dynamic process that persists over time rather than a static state. Finally, a definition of sustainability that was inspired by Tainter's is one which incorporates a systems-thinking approach to the idea of Symbiosis in Development (SiD) (Symbiosis in Development, n.d.). This emphasis stems from the fact that sustainability is a multidisciplinary endeavour that struggles to find a unifying perspective, leading to the presence of variations like the circular economy and the thriving planet theory (also known as the Gaia hypothesis), among others. In SiD, sustainability is defined as a 'state' of a multifaceted, fluid system that continues to thrive robustly, harmoniously, and without needing input from beyond its system parameters. It is declared as a holistic framework that integrates the indicators of resilience, autonomy, and harmony as well as specific tools as a means of monitoring the system sustainability and identifying interconnections, feedback mechanisms, and orientations in attaining sustainable systems regardless of the activity domains.

Within the discourse of sustainability, waste management is one of the many significant domains that have a direct impact on sustainable development. In this context, waste refers to refuse generated by anthropogenic activities, especially that of domestic and municipal solid waste. The management of these generated wastes is crucial for human progress on all levels, including the national, regional and international levels ("Why is waste management important?",n.d.; Adefolu, n.d.). There is a demand for an increase in studies on strategies that are more integrated and holistic rather than solely focused on disposal (Concari et al., 2020). The control and direction of waste management operations normally require some kind of authority or governance. Waste management typically involves a variety of governance models, such as individual self-governance, municipal solid waste management, and transnational initiatives to stop the migration of waste across international borders (Vallero, 2019). In this instance, waste governance could be characterised as the principles, policies, laws, and values developed within a specific socio-political environment with the intention of assisting all stakeholders involved in waste management through achieving the goals of sustainable waste management. Waste governance is unquestionably crucial to the implementation of any waste management strategies for a socio-political organisation, such as a nation or locality. This version of waste governance is derived from the concept of governance that aligns with that of an Islamic governance paradigm (Amin, 2021).

There is a growing number of literatures surrounding the Islamic aspect of the concept of waste in relation to sustainability, although still in paucity. This chapter will acknowledge and discuss only a select number due to relevance and limited space. For instance, Ansari et al.'s (2012) work on the Islamic dimension of sustainable development aims to pursue an expositional study to show how Islamic rulings incorporate the need for sustainable development. This might mean that the study aims to represent Islam pursuant to the contemporary 'sustainable development' as we know it today, which in this context, refers to effective resource utilisation without compromising the future needs of the planet. This definition is premised on the Brundtland definition of sustainability by which human beings are at the centre, implying an issue of possible contradiction between the paradigms of realities involved. However, the study supports the fact that the imperatives of sustainable development – in its literal definition – are readily contained within Islamic teachings. The authors also provide insightful frameworks that depict the connectedness of sustainable development with Islam's holistic approach to a sustainable society, including the environmental, social and economic pillars of sustainability. Their take on waste management in Islam revolves around the Islamic principle of avoiding waste, including resource-sharing and recycling as part of Islam's sharī'ah-oriented policies of protecting the environment.

Another instance of the Islamic approach to waste management in relation to sustainability is Omar et al.'s (2018) focus on Islamic ethics pertaining to waste management. In addition to similar principles conveyed by the previous authors, this study also highlights the Islamic ethics of cleanliness and moderate consumption as being core to waste management. Similarly, Abdelhamid's (2021) approach to Islamic waste management puts an emphasis on waste minimisation, focusing on the harm of excess due to gluttony and conspicuous spending as well as the need for self-governance on one own's waste minimisation as the individual's responsibility. These studies albeit lacking in a framework that allows for strategising operations for waste management from the Islamic paradigm, do provide the foundational principles and ethics toward designing a more sustainable waste management framework rooted in Islamic epistemology.

3. METHODOLOGICAL APPROACH

This study is premised on the worldview as per guided by the divine source of the Islamic faith. Research is considered insufficient in the field of Islamic studies if it is only grounded in common sense without the support of the Qur'an and Hadith (Akram, 2018). Primarily, there are three main themes underpinning the Islamic worldview, namely the ontology, epistemology and the axiological aspect of the worldview. However, this chapter will only highlight the first two principles and the several elements embedded within the metaphysical paradigm as understood from a worldview of Islamic scholarship due to scope and word count limitation. To recap, ontology can be simplified as the study of 'what reality is' based on the researcher's perspective whilst epistemology is the study of how to verify this knowledge of reality. On the higher level of the worldview, the ontology of Islam is understood as that of a realist approach, whereby there is an independent existence of reality regardless of one's awareness of it (The Qur'ān, Al-Baqarah: 31-32). Specifically, the Islamic worldview recognises that God is the ultimate source, originator, creator and architect of reality whether or not this reality is known to human knowledge (Lantong, 2018). However, there is also room for the subjectivist outlook on the lower levels of knowledge as the Creator has given His human subjects the ability to learn and construct their own reality (The Qur'ān, An-Nahl: 80). A believer of the Islamic faith thus derives their knowledge of reality by referring to the epistemology of Almighty God, also known as Islamic epistemology.

Based on Islamic epistemology, knowledge regarding reality holds the objectivist perspective in which Absolute Truth is set by the Almighty God (The Qur'ān, Yunus: 35), with subjectivist tendencies on certain matters interpretative by context. Therefore, this knowledge is derived from the principal sources of the Islamic faith, namely the Noble Qur'ān and its manifestations in the form of the messenger Muhammad ﷺ's Sunnah, particularly his teachings, sayings, deeds and tacit approvals. Inferring to these sources, knowledge is primarily categorised into two classifications, namely revealed knowledge and acquired knowledge (Lantong, 2018), where revealed knowledge refers to divine knowledge delivered by messengers and acquired knowledge refers to knowledge derived from observations and scientific methods. In the context of this study, the concept of waste in relation to sustainability is explored by the means of Conceptual Analysis of the Qur'ān and Sunnah (Prophetic traditions), i.e. revealed knowledge, including from the linguistic dimension, relevant elements such as universal laws, principles and values, and finally the emergence of the whole framework. The findings discovered from this method would serve as additional support for the pool of literature, present and future, on the acquired knowledge of the concept of waste and waste management from the Islamic perspective, inshā Allah.

Embedded within this methodology is the belief that reality appears like that of a web or tapestry of truths, rudiments, and profundity of the interconnectedness of elements, including integration that creates a sense of wholism and thus leads to an emergence of complex meanings of the interconnected-

Figure 1. Diagram of the conceptual framework of the study

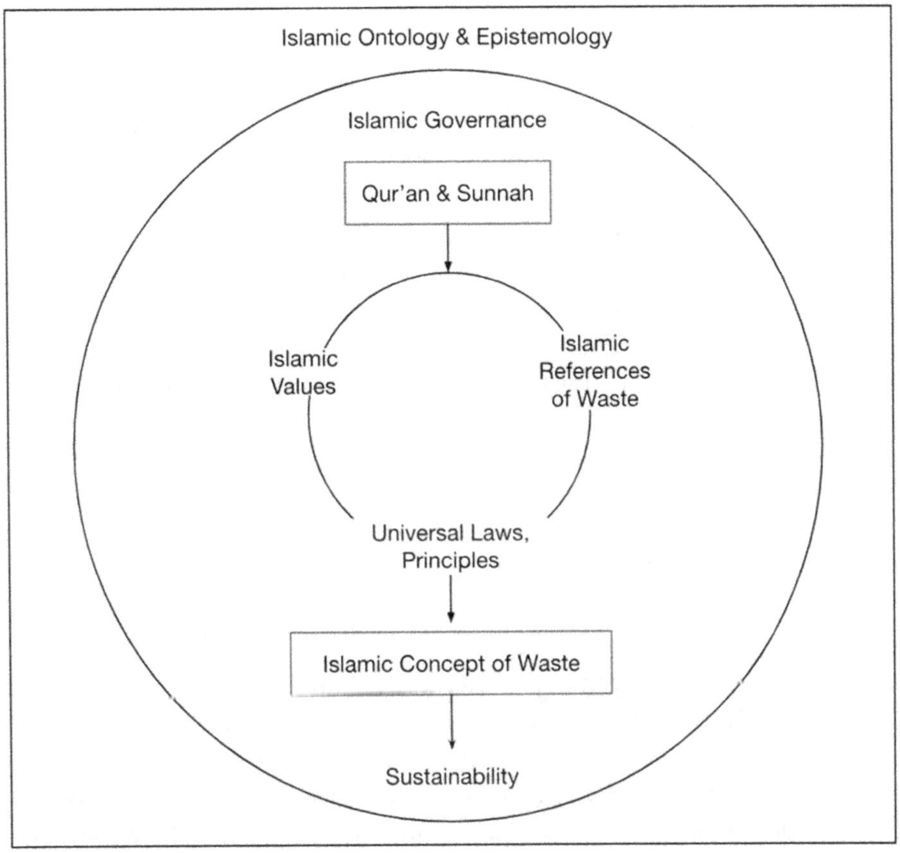

ness between the elements. A fundamental constituent to this wholistic meaning is the objectives at a higher level of integration and awareness. This is proved by the methodological analysis of the Qur'ān and the Sunnah, an instance being that a complex human emerges as a whole from the constituents of their parts and proportions, of bones, flesh and veins (The Qur'ān, Al-Infitar: 8; Al-Mu'minun: 14). On the creation of humans, The Creator also elucidates on the higher objectives of this complex creation, which is for the humankind to know Him, worship Him, to remedy and refine earth and preserve life, and to connect what is commanded to be connected (Auda, 2022). From this understanding, this research proceeds in such a way that not only the content and linguistic dimensions from the Qur'ān and Sunnah on the concept of waste are looked at, but the relevant elements surrounding the methodology, as well as the concept of waste, such as the universal laws, principles and values, are also taken into account when discovering the concept of waste in relation to sustainability as it emerges in the Islamic faith through the interconnectedness of the elements.

4. CONCEPTUAL FRAMEWORK

The diagram above illustrates the framework of concepts involved in this study and their interconnections with one another. First of all, it has to be noted that the whole of this study is premised on the Islamic ontological and epistemological approach that envelopes the rest of the research components. Within this methodological approach, the study thus sets the context for the discussion of the concept of waste in Islam in relation to sustainability to be situated within the Islamic system of governance. As is with this methodology, the source of knowledge is primarily from the Qur'ān, which is manifested in the Sunnah of the Messenger Muhammad ﷺ. Within these principal sources are references to the concept of waste, Islamic values, as well as mentions of relevant universal laws and principles. These elements are interconnected with one another within the tapestry of reality. Through the process of conceptual analysis, an emergence of a framework for the Islamic Concept of Waste (ICW) from which there will be elements of sustainability to be discussed. The ICW framework is part of the bigger research this study is a part of, and may not be illustrated in this chapter as a model nor explained in detail. Instead, only the discussion on sustainability and a number of other relevant elements pertaining to the concept of waste in Islam will be elucidated in order to respect the scope of this book chapter.

5. THE CONCEPT OF WASTE IN ISLAM

5.1. Linguistic Dimension of Waste in Islam

The importance and peculiarities of the language of delivery cannot be ignored in the process of understanding waste from an Islamic perspective, particularly the Arabic language with which Al-Qur'ān has been conveyed. Since the Qur'ānic teachings are manifested by the Prophet Muhammad ﷺ, it could be understood that the prophetic traditions or *sunnah* also revolve around this same language and its surrounding cultural values. Therefore, when looking at the concept of waste as perceived by the Islamic worldview, it is imperative that we look as well at the linguistic dimension of the concept of waste as is found in the sources of Islamic faith, namely the noble Qur'ān and the *sunnah* of Prophet Muhammad ﷺ. In order to comprehend the Qur'ānic teachings extensively, one must possess a certain level of knowledge, understanding and skills pertaining to the Arabic language (Baharun, 2020). On top of that, in light of the fact that spoken Arabic differs from the classical Arabic in which the Qur'ān was revealed, studying the teachings of the Qur'ān would necessitate the use of particular terminology, grammatical conventions, and rhetorical devices, among other things (Ibid.). The Qur'ān has been translated into many different languages, yet these translations frequently do not convey the same sense as the original text. Additionally, a lack of context awareness would seriously impair comprehension, which would lead to a misinterpretation of the Qur'anic meaning. Therefore, this study will supplement the linguistic analysis of the concept of waste in Islam from the interpretations of scholars of tafsīr (Qur'ānic interpretations) where available and relevant.

Both the Qur'ān and the Sunnah contain several references to waste. This section will first identify the notion of waste as it appears in the Qur'ān, then explain the meanings of the many names for waste as they relate to Arabic language. This will then be followed by a similar analysis to the references to waste documented from the Sunnah. Understanding the various ways in which these phrases are used has consequences for comprehending how Islam views the concept of waste. Prior to the analysis process, a select number of the references to waste are tabulated below, both in its English translation and original Arabic text:-

As can be seen in items numbered one and two (1-2) from the above table, the latter verse shows that the Arabic term for wasteful people is *mubadzirīn*, which is derived from *tabdzīr*, which means "in

Table 1. Compilation of selected references to waste in the Qur'ān

No.	English Translation	Arabic Text
1	"Give to close relatives their due, as well as the poor and ˹needy˺ travellers. And do not <u>spend wastefully</u>." (The Qur'ān, Al-Isra: 26)	رۡذَبُت الَو ِليِبَّسلٱ َنۡبٱو َنيِكۡسِمۡلٱو ُهَّقَح ٰىَبۡرُقۡلٱ اَذ ِتاَءَو .اري ذۡبَت
2	"Surely the <u>wasteful</u> are ˹like˺ brothers to the devils. And the Devil is ever ungrateful to his Lord." (The Qur'ān, Al-Isra: 27)	ۦِهِّبَرِل ُنَٰطۡيَّشلٱ َناَكَو ۖ ِنيِطَٰيَّشلٱ َنَٰوۡخِإ ْآوُناَك َنيِرِّذَبُمۡلٱ َّنِإ .اروُفَك
3	"And He it is who causes gardens to grow, [both] trellised and untrellised, and palm trees and crops of different [kinds of] food and olives and pomegranates, similar and dissimilar. Eat of [each of] its fruit when it yields and give its due [zakah] on the day of its harvest. And be not <u>excessive</u>. Indeed, He does not like <u>those who commit excess</u>." (The Qur'ān, Al-An'am: 141)	َعۡرَّزلٱو َلۡخَّنلٱو ٖتَٰشوُرۡعَم َرۡيَغَو ٖتَٰشوُرۡعَّم ٖتَّٰنَج َأَشنَأ ٓيِذَّلٱ َوُهَو نم اوُلُك ۚ ٖهِبَٰشَتُم َرۡيَغَو اٗهِبَٰشَتُم َناَّمُّرلٱو َنوُتۡيَّزلٱو ُهُلُكُأ اًفِلَتۡخُم ُّبِحُي اَل ُهَّنِإ ۚ ْآوُفِرۡسُت اَلَو ۖۦِهِداَصَح َمۡوَي ُهَّقَح ْاوُتاَءَو َرَمۡثَأ ٓاَذِإ ٓۦِهِرَمَث .َنيِفِرۡسُمۡلٱ
4	"O believers! Do not forbid the good things which Allah has made lawful for you, and do not <u>transgress</u>. Indeed, Allah does not like <u>transgressors</u>." (The Qur'ān, Al-Ma'idah: 87)	ْۚاوُدَتۡعَت اَلَو ۡمُكَل ُهَّللٱ َّلَحَأ اَم ِتَٰبِّيَط ْاوُمِّرَحُت اَل ْاوُنَماَء َنيِذَّلٱ اَهُّيَأٓـَٰي .َنيِدَتۡعُمۡلٱ ُّبِحُي اَل َهَّللٱ َّنِإ
5	"O Children of Adam! Dress properly whenever you are at worship. Eat and drink, but do not <u>waste</u>. Surely He does not like <u>the wasteful</u>." (The Qur'ān, Al-'Araf: 31)	اَلَو ْاوُبَرۡشٱو ْاوُلُكَو ٖدِجۡسَم ِّلُك َدنِع ۡمُكَتَنيِز ْاوُذُخ َمَداَء ٓيِنَبَٰي ۞ ْۚآوُفِرۡسُت .َنيِفِرۡسُمۡلٱ ُّبِحُي اَل ُهَّنِإ
6	˹saying,˺ "Eat from the good things We have provided for you, but do not <u>transgress</u> in them, or My wrath will befall you. And whoever My wrath befalls is certainly doomed." (The Qur'ān, Taha: 81)	ۡمُكۡيَلَع َّلِحَيَف ِهيِف ْاۡوَغۡطَت اَلَو ۡمُكَٰنۡقَزَر اَم ِتَٰبِّيَط نِم ْاوُلُك ٰىَبَضَغ ۖ ۥِهۡيَلَع ۡلِلۡحَي نَمَو ٰىَوَه ۡدَقَف .يِبَضَغ
7	"˹They are˺ those who spend neither <u>wastefully</u> nor stingily, but moderately in between." (The Qur'ān, Al-Furqan: 67)	.اٗمَاوَق َكِلَٰذ َنۡيَب َناَكَو ْاوُرُتۡقَي ۡمَلَو ْاوُفِرۡسُي ۡمَل ْاوُقَفنَأ ٓاَذِإ َنيِذَّلٱو
8	"And We certainly delivered the Children of Israel from the humiliating torment. of Pharaoh. He was truly a tyrant, <u>a transgressor.</u>" (The Qur'ān, Ad-Dukhan: 30-31)	َناَك ُهَّنِإ ۚ َنۡوَعۡرِف نِم .ِنيِهُمۡلٱ ِباَذَعۡلٱ َنِم َليِٓءَٰرۡسِإ ٓيِنَب اَنۡيَّجَن ۡدَقَلَو .َنيِفِرۡسُمۡلٱ َنِّم اٗيِلاَع

a wasteful manner." The underlying word (*budzûr*) literally means "spreading and dispersing," and it refers to the scattering and dispersion of objects such as seeds (Sahabuddin, 2007; Bidabad and Sherafati, 2017). In this context, the term "*tabdzīr*" can be translated as "overconsumption," which refers to spending when it is not necessary, and which is a form of waste. The term referring to waste used in the passage specifically refers to the overconsumption or over-expenditure of wealth, property and materials such as food instead of the wider meaning of waste (Bidabad and Sherafati, 2017). *Tabdzīr*, as an act of overconsumption, is also applicable depending on the individual's level of affluence. For instance, consumption is not considered to be excessive for a wealthy person when buying a property that is regarded as a moderate expense and investment according to their current savings. However, the same property may affect a significant part of another person's life savings to the point of causing excessive debt and compromising their means for basic life sustenance, and this is considered as *tabdzīr* to the latter individual.

Waste, according to Al-Qur'an scholar Abdullah ibn Abbas, is everything that is used improperly (Yasin, 2018). A scholar of *tafsīr* (Qur'ānic Interpretation), Mujahid, posited that the whole of wealth spent in the way of truth has not been wasted, whilst even the slightest of wealth spent for improper avenues subscribe to waste (Ibid.). Yasin (2018) thus deduced that 'waste' is determined by where and how the expenditure or consumption is conducted over its quantity. Another scholar of *tafsīr*, Qatadah, prepended on Mujahid's interpretation of waste as any spending or consumption of wealth or materials that is not lawful; that leads to harm; and that leads to insubordination to God (Ibid.). In these verses, God commands His servants to be modest in the giving of wealth to those who are entitled to it. People are not to be unduly frugal nor extravagant to the point where one's generosity causes harm to themselves and/or others. Waste occurs when either the withholding or the donating part of one's bestowed possessions arrives beyond the point of moderation in accordance with Islamic teachings.

On the other hand, item number three (3) shows a verse which has another version of the translation that defines the underlined words as "extravagant" and "the extravagant" instead of the terms in the above table. Therefore word for waste in this verse may be defined in a broad sense based on the varying adjectives that are used to allude to waste in this verse (e.g. wasteful, excessive). The specific term used to describe waste in this context is *israaf*, which also means to be excessive in the sense of going beyond the bounds of something, which could be from an array of matters (IslamQuest, n.d.). In order to clarify this further, the term *israaf* refers to having an excessive amount of both tangible and intangible things, such as passions, attitudes, behaviours, lifestyles, ideologies, norms, and social virtues, irrespective of their quantity or quality. The verses described above serve as some illustrations of how the terminology used to describe waste differs. Items numbered four to eight (4-8) in the table further illustrate the references made to the concept of waste in the Qur'ān. Due to the word count limit, only a summary of the conceptual analysis will be included here: *Ta'tadû* and *tatghaw* are two other words from the aforementioned verses that likewise allude to extravagance or waste.

The term *ta'tadû* comes from the Arabic root word *adâ*, from which many morphologies ultimately lead to the word *zhulm* (Sahabuddin, 2007), which is characterised as straying off course or beyond the bounds of truth, whether it be less than or greater than the stance within the boundaries of truth as laid out by the omnipotent source. In simpler terms, it means breaking the law in a number of different ways. It is frequently used in the context of noncompliance, unfairness, tyranny, imperiousness, and violence; nevertheless, it is also occasionally used to allude to recklessness, excess, and wastage. The last word is derived from the verbs in its root words, *thaghâ-yathghû*, which express "exceeding the provision or defined bounds" (Sahabuddin, 2007). Both of these concepts are less restricted to transgressing in terms of excess or wastefulness, whether it be on material or immaterial aspects, and are more broad and flexible in their definitions of what constitutes going beyond the limits set by law. The different allusions to waste and terminology related to waste that can be found in the Qur'ān have been expressed above. In summary, the concept of waste in Islam is primarily distinguished between the two Arabic words, *tabdzīr* and *israaf*, according to various publicly available texts. Although both terms refer to waste, a closer look at respective definitions reveals that they do not mean the same thing. Despite the fact that *tabdzīr* (wasteful spending) is one of the many types of *israaf* (extravagance), this is not true otherwise, yet extravagance still points to being wasteful. In addition to the two dominant words for waste stated in the Qur'ān, there are other terms that infer waste but utilise language that is more general in the perception of transgression.

In this context, the Sunnah pertains to the Prophet's ﷺ divinely decreed conduct and speech, which manifest both on the individual and community levels. It is crucial to keep in mind that the sunnah is prevalently cited as the contextual premise or rationale for the transmission of specific Qur'ānic verses. The following table will compile a select number of *ahadīth* (collection of *hadīth*) corresponding to their respective summary of the conceptualisation of its substance in relation to the concept of waste:-

Table 2. Conceptualisation of selected references to waste in the Sunnah

No.	English Translation	Conceptual Analysis
1	Abu Huraira reported Allah's Messenger (ﷺ) as saying: *"Verily Allah likes three things for you and He disapproves three things for you. He is pleased with you that you worship Him and associate nor anything with Him, that you hold fast the rope of Allah, and be not scattered; and He disapproves for you irrelevant talk, persistent questioning and the wasting of wealth."* (Sunnah, Sahih Muslim: 1715a)	The Arabic term for wasting in this narration is ÅöÖóÇÚóÉ which means the act or instance of wasting. The Arabic term of 'wealth' ÇáúãóÇá commonly means 'money' but also means possessions, property or the supply of any desirable things such as food, clothes, tools and other everyday items. Conceptually, generating waste on purpose is a prohibited act that is to be prevented.
2	Narrated `Aisha: Allah's Messenger (ﷺ) said, *"When a woman gives in charity from her husband's meals without wasting the property of her husband, she will get a reward for it, and her husband too will get a reward for what he earned and the storekeeper will have the reward likewise."* (Sunnah, Sahih al-Bukhari: 1437)	Although there is mention of waste in this narration, the limelight of this hadith is on the concept of charity. Since waste is mentioned nonetheless, it is noted with a degree of importance. Conceptually, Islam teaches the notion of not wasting even in permissible and/or preferred matters (e.g. charity, consumption of resources, manufacturing of goods).
3	Usaid narrated: On the day of Badr, Allah's Messenger (ﷺ) said to us, *"When the enemy comes near to you, shoot at them but use your arrows sparingly (so that your arrows should not be wasted)."* (Sunnah, Sahih al-Bukhari: 3984)	The context of this narration occurred during one of the wars at the battlefield of Badr, specifically during the times of conflict.The fact that the Prophet ﷺ asked the trained archers to avoid wasting the arrows by using them infrequently alludes to the concept of strategising the quantities of resources to be utilised as to avoid the act of wasting and wasted resources (i.e. resource optimisation).
4	Al-A'mash reported God's messenger ﷺ as saying, *"The calamity which affects knowledge is forgetfulness, and wasting it is to convey it to those who are unworthy of it."* (Sunnah, Mishkat al-Masabih: 265)	Remarkably, the concept of waste in Islam is so broad that it includes the concept of waste in the sphere of knowledge. Conceptually, it is deemed wasteful to transmit knowledge to persons who are unworthy of or unreceptive to knowledge or matters with immaterial value.
5	In Al-Bukhari's report, narrated Abu Hurairah (RA): The Prophet (ﷺ) said: *"Whoever accepts other people's wealth intending to pay it back, Allah will pay it back for him. And whoever accepts it intending to waste it, Allah, the Most High, will waste (destroy) him."* (Sunnah, Sahih Bukhari: 2387)	There is a strong warning in this narration about the act of waste when it comes to borrowing resources from other sources. It is implied here that the intent and conduct of waste in terms of loans, whether in cash or in-kind or even in other material resources, would lead to harm and destruction.
6	Ibn 'Abbas said that he said that *"the squanderers" were those who wasted money incorrectly."* (Sunnah, Al-Adab Al-Mufrad: 445)	Those who administer and redistribute wealth or money without acquiring and exercising proper money management skills and knowledge are regarded to be unwise and wasteful. As a conclusion, fortune and asset mismanagement can be characterised as an act of waste in Islam.
7	Narrated Al-Mughira bin Shu`ba: The Prophet (ﷺ) said, *"Allah has forbidden for you, (1) to be undutiful to your mothers, (2) to bury your daughters alive, (3) to not to pay the rights of the others (e.g. charity, etc.) and (4) to beg of men (begging). And Allah has hated for you (1) vain, useless talk, or that you talk too much about others, (2) to ask too many questions, (in disputed religious matters) and (3) to waste the wealth (by extravagance)."* (Sunnah, Sahih al-Bukhari: 2408)	Among other activities stated as forbidden and despised by God, recklessness in the expenditure of resources is labelled as a wasteful deed that is disapproved of in Islam. To analyse this text, the concept of waste in Islam includes economic factors such as fiscal and property management.

5.2. Relevant Universal Laws, Principles, and Values

The Qur'ān and Sunnah provide holistic guidance and are replete with values to be internalised and practised upon, thus isolating the references to waste in the Qur'ān and Sunnah from the relevancy of Islamic principles, universal laws and values may lead to an incomplete picture of how one should approach waste, among other matters in life. Therefore, this section offers a compilation of elements whether they be universal laws, principles or values discovered thus far related to the concept of waste in Islam. One of the universal laws relevant in this discussion is the 'law of circularity'. Law of circularity is mentioned in the Qur'ān several times (The Qur'ān, At-Tariq: 11; Az-Zumar: 21; Al-Baqarah: 222). For instance, the Qur'ān mentions the hydrological process among other circular natural cycles. According to Javaid (2022), the teachings of Islam inspire the establishment of a social order that enables circularisation. Another universal law worthy of mention is that of 'harmony'. This universal law is indicated in various places within the Qur'ān as well as in the Sunnah (The Qur'ān, Al-An'am: 38; Sunnah, At-Tirmidhi: 2515; Sahih Muslim: 1553a). The Qur'ān and Sunnah also contain references to universal laws of Autonomy (The Qur'ān, Ar-Ra'd: 11) as well as Resilience (Sunnah, Sahih Bukhari: 1471; Al-Albani: 480) which are interrelated in the approach to waste management.

Besides universal laws, references to principles and values beneficial to approach the concept of waste management are also prominent in the Qur'ān and Sunnah, such as self-governance (The Qur'ān, Al-Fatir: 18), social responsibility (The Qur'ān, Al-Jathiyah: 28), self-sufficiency (The Qur'ān, Az-Zumar: 21) and the concept of stewardship: An article by GreenIftar (n.d.) emphasises that through the responsibility of stewardship, Allah both bestows honour upon and tests humankind. While humans are granted the privilege of utilising nature, they are also accountable for its balanced and sustainable utilisation. Ultimately, nothing belongs to humans; rather, they are tasked with governing the entrusted resources that Allah has made available to them (The Qur'ān, Yunus: 14). Some instances of Islamic values surrounding the management of waste are moderation (The Qur'ān, Al-Maidah: 77), humility (The Qur'ān, Al-Isra: 37) to Allah's commands and towards other creations of Allah such as the varying species and biomes; responsibility (The Qur'ān, Al-Isra: 84; Yunus: 41; Al-An'am: 104); patience (The Qur'ān, Al-Anfal: 46; An-Nahl: 127; Hud: 115) in regards to upholding Islamic values and in executing sustainable waste management strategies; compassion (The Qur'ān, Ghafir: 7; Al-Anbiya: 107) towards other organisms and the earth; integrity / Amanah (The Qur'ān, Al-Baqarah: 30; Al-Ahzab: 72; Sunnah, Sahih Bukhari: 7138) in maintaining a sustainable waste management system; and justice (The Qur'ān, Al-Maidah: 8; Ar-Rahman: 7-10) and fairness in placing importance to other living things as to not disregard the environment and social harmony when disposing and managing waste generated.

5.3. Islamic Concept of Waste: Islamic Waste Management and Sustainability

From the process of conceptual analysis in previous sections, the primary author has simplified the Islamic Concept of Waste (ICW) as: "the outcome and action of deliberate mismanagement or recklessness of transactions from what is permissible and especially non-permissible, whether abstract or tangible, in excess or unworthy causes that eventually leads to harm and destruction as revealed in the Qur'ān and Sunnah." In light of this, therefore Islamic Waste Management (IWM) is perceived as "the practice of strategic resource and process optimisation in all permissible matters, whether abstract or tangible, in moderate and worthy causes and hence preventing waste while adhering to the principles and values derived from the Qur'ān and Sunnah in order to fulfil the higher divine objectives." It has also been discovered the concept of waste and its management in Islam embeds relevant universal laws, principles and values; and requires a wholistic approach to the integration of different dimensions and stakeholders, including the notion of circularity into management systems and strategies. This finding demonstrates that the concept of waste in Islam and its management share similar elements with the contemporary circular model of sustainability (SiD). Therefore, this study conveys the potential to contribute insights to contemporary sustainability discourses such as the concept of waste and waste management for future projects.

In relation to sustainability, it can be seen from the literature review that the SiD concept of sustainability shares a number of similarities to the principles, universal laws and values derived from the Qur'ān and Sunnah. For instance, principles of Resilience, Autonomy and Harmony are taught in Islamic sources of knowledge and at the same time are SiD indicators of sustainability that could perhaps be utilised in the formulation of strategies, policies and practical implementation of future sustainability projects. To be more specific, the SiD sustainability indicators along with their respective parameters could be incorporated into the formulation of operational waste governance inspired by Amin's (2021) definition of governance mentioned at the beginning of this chapter. With a framework that serves as an analytical tool and offers practicality, an amalgamation of the Islamic-oriented indicators of sustainability would be beneficial for the advancement of sustainable waste management moving forward. Furthermore, the definition of sustainability embedded within the concept of waste in Islam is not merely oriented towards the expected outcome of being able to maintain future needs, but ICW considers the Islamic principles and values that support sustainable development and its concomitant IWM concept highlights the actual levels of sustainability that can be monitored through its indicators and parameters that are aligned with Islamic teachings.

6. CHALLENGES AND CONCLUSION

Although presenting potential for further research, the concept of waste in Islam discovered during this study is not free from its own challenges and limitations. Any kind of concept, system or framework can be proficiently developed while incorporating some promising elements and methods. However, the system is ineffectual if there are no operators to direct it or if the operators are incompetent at doing so. Human agency consisting of experts and specialists as well as assistance from governing authorities are therefore crucial in the attempt to actualise these ideas. For instance, the contribution from knowledge specialists in the fields of circular economy, industrial ecology and sustainable manufacturing might be required during the formulation of facilitation strategies and policies to produce efficient and zero-waste manufacturing practices as part of the Islamic Waste Management concept (IWM) derived from the Islamic concept of waste (ICW). Another limitation to this ICW is that not all relevant Qur'ānic verses or *hadith* may have been accounted for yet. Hence, there is a need for additional reflection for a more holistic coverage, thus the plausible need to employ a comprehensive Qur'ānic methodology for future studies, such as the Maqasid Methodology (Auda, 2022). Furthermore, more practical strategies need to be developed throughout all levels of governance (individual, society, governance) according to priority levels and leverage points and the conceptual framework previously illustrated does not suffice in explicating this notion.

In this chapter, the concept of waste in Islam has been explored and it has been discovered that the Islamic Concept of Waste (ICW) and its concomitant Islamic Waste Management (IWM) concept encompass an interdisciplinary perspective, resulting in a comprehensive understanding of waste management that integrates sustainability principles and incorporates various dimensions. This chapter has introduced readers to the various definitions of sustainability and in accordance with the methodology adopted, clarified that sustainability should be defined as more than its expected outcomes in the three pillars of sustainable development, but rather defined in its actuality of a dynamic system with indicators that monitor the balance of resilience, autonomy and harmony of a sustainable waste management system, by which indicators and their respective parameters are aligned with the principles and values derived from the authentic sources of Islamic knowledge. This discovery may serve as the foundational conceptualisation for the development of a more robust and comprehensive framework for sustainable waste management that could further support sustainable development goals.

ACKNOWLEDGEMENT

This chapter was part of a research thesis submitted in partial fulfilment of the requirements for the degree of Master in Islamic Governance (By Research) at the Institute of Policy Studies, Universiti Brunei Darussalam.

REFERENCES

Abdelhamid, A. (2018). Islamic Principles on Waste Minimization. *Ecomena*. https://www.ecomena.org/waste-minimization-islam/

Adefolu, B. (n.d.). *Towards sustainable waste management in Lagos State: Possible adoptions from Finland*. Bitstream. https://www.theseus.fi/bitstream/handle/10024/95996/OjuriBabakolade_Thesis%20new.pdf?sequence=1&isAllowed=y

Akram Hassan, S. (2018). Reasoning Method: An Analysis from the Islamic Perspective. *International Journal of Academic Research in Business & Social Sciences*, *8*(11), 965–972. doi:10.6007/IJARBSS/v8-i11/4974

Al-Jayyousi, O. (2018). How Islam can represent a model for environmental stewardship. *United Nations Environment Programme*. https://www.unep.org/news-and-stories/story/how-islam-can-represent-model-environmental-stewardship

Amin. (2021). *KP5117: Madīnian Polity: Visions of Islamic Governance: Discussion 3: The Concept of State [PDF]*. Institute of Policy Studies, Universiti Brunei Darussalam.

Ansari, A. H., Jamal, P., & Oseni, U. A. (2012). Sustainable development: Islamic dimension with special reference to conservation of the environment. *Advances in Natural and Applied Sciences*, *6*(5), 607–619.

Auda, J. (2022). *Re-envisioning Islamic scholarship: Maqasid methodology as a new approach*. Claritas Books.

Baharun, H., Abd Rahman, S., Ahmad, H., & Saazai Mat Saad, N. (2020). Quranic Understanding among Non-Native Speaker of Arabic: Malaysian Experts' Perspectives. *Journal of Language Studies*, *20*(2), 154–169. doi:10.17576/gema-2020-2002-12

Bidabad, B., & Sherafati, M. (2017). Sustainable financing and anti-squandering measures in Rastin banking. *International Journal of Law and Management*, *59*(6), 939–949. doi:10.1108/IJLMA-04-2016-0037

Concari, A., Kok, G., & Martens, P. (2020). A systematic literature review of concepts and factors related to pro-environmental consumer behaviour in relation to waste management through an interdisciplinary approach. *Sustainability: Science. Sustainability (Basel)*, *12*(11), 4452. doi:10.3390u12114452

EUR-Lex Glossary of Summaries. (n.d.). *Sustainable development.* EUR-Lex. https://eur-lex.europa.eu/summary/glossary/sustainable_development.html

GreenIftar. (n.d.). Islam and sustainability. *Green Iftar.* https://www.greeniftar.com/en/islam-and-sustainability/

IslamQuest. (n.d.). What is the Quran's perspective on waste and extravagance? *Islam Quest.* https://www.islamquest.net/en/archive/fa21210

Javaid. (2022). View of The Principles of a Circular Economy in the Light of Islamic Values and Beliefs. *Journal of Islamic Thought and Civilization*, 212–230. https://journals.umt.edu.pk/index.php/JITC/article/view/2113/996

Johnston, P., Everard, M., Santillo, D., & Robèrt, K.-H. (2007). Reclaiming the definition of sustainability. *Environmental Science and Pollution Research International*, *14*(1), 60–66. doi:10.1065/espr2007.01.375 PMID:17352129

Lantong, A. M. (2018). The Islamic Epistemology and its Implications for Education of Muslims in the Philippines. *Journal of Education and Practice*, *9*(15), 68–73.

Moore, J. E., Mascarenhas, A., Bain, J., & Straus, S. E. (2017). Developing a comprehensive definition of sustainability. *Implementation Science : IS*, *12*(1), 110. doi:10.118613012-017-0637-1 PMID:28865479

Morse, S., & McNamara, N. (2013). *Sustainable livelihood approach: A critique of theory and practice.* Springer Science & Business Media. doi:10.1007/978-94-007-6268-8

Office of Sustainability, University of Alberta. (n.d.). *What is sustainability?* McGill. https://www.mcgill.ca/sustainability/files/sustainability/what-is-sustainability.pdf

Owens, S. (2003). Is there a meaningful definition of sustainability? *Plant Genetic Resources*, *1*(1), 5–9. doi:10.1079/PGR20034

Sahabuddin. (2007). *Ensiklopedia Al-Qur'an : Kajian Kosakata* [Trans] Lentera Hati. Sunnah. https://sunnah.com

Vallero, D. A. (2019). Waste governance. In *Waste* (pp. 651–671). Elsevier. doi:10.1016/B978-0-12-815060-3.00033-5

Vlada. (2012, August 6). *Collapse of complex societies by Dr. Joseph Tainter* [Video]. YouTube. https://www.youtube.com/watch?v=G0R09YzyuCI

Why is waste management important? (2019). *Science Park.* https://sciencepark.com.ph/blog/waste-management-important/

Yasin, A. (2018). *Tafsir Surah Al-Isra': Ayat 26-30* [Video]. YouTube. https://www.youtube.com/watch?v=A4aPvT-MikA&t=513s

Chapter 15
Radiological Detector Aircraft for Marine Life's Sustainability in Supporting Sustainable Development Goals (SDGs)

Aldi Alauddin Pattiroei
Universiti Brunei Darussalam, Brunei

Muhammad Anshari
https://orcid.org/0000-0002-8160-6682
Universiti Brunei Darussalam, Brunei

Mahani Hamdan
Universiti Brunei Darussalam, Brunei

Emil Ali
Universiti Brunei Darussalam, Brunei

ABSTRACT

Sustainable development goals (SDGs) aim to protect oceans by ensuring their sustainable use. This includes safeguarding marine and coastal habitats, reducing marine pollution, and minimising ocean acidification. This chapter seeks to promote the implementation of SDGs by evaluating the capability of Indonesia's marine patrols, as the world maritime axis, to address the issues presented by the use of nuclear energy as an alternative source of energy for maritime patrol. Data was gathered using the qualitative method from nuclear specialists and maritime patrol officers. After data collection reached saturation, data were codified and analysed. The Ishikawa Model is also deployed to portray stakeholder analysis structure. The research revealed the significance of Indonesia's ability to identify nuclear material as a part of the world maritime axis. The risk of failure or leakage in the water is a challenge of marine life's resilience. The research is expected to contribute to the body of knowledge by addressing how nuclear energy can be used to enhance maritime patrol capabilities.

DOI: 10.4018/978-1-6684-8903-1.ch015

1. INTRODUCTION

The world is rapidly becoming a global community due to the increasing daily energy needs of all populations. In order to satisfy human social and economic development, like welfare and healthcare, the need for energy consumption is increasing significantly worldwide and its connected services are growing (Anshari et al., 2019). There are many studies confirming that energy consumption affects economic growth, financial development, industrialization, and urbanization in the global context (Anshari, 2020). In fact, energy consumption exhibits long-term bidirectional causal relationships with financial development as well as industrialization (Shahbaz & Lean, 2012; Anshari et al., 2020). The statistic shows that the world's total energy supply from 1990 to 2018 grew by 65.6% and reached 594 EJ. Asia was the main reason for this growth; Asia was responsible for 82.1% of the world's growth during this time. It increased by more than four times in China alone, making up more than a fifth of the world in 2018. From 35.2% of the world in 1990 to 18.4% in 2018, Europe has lost 17.1 EJ of its share of the world. The United States' share of the world market has decreased by 6.7 percentage points, to 15.7% in 2018 since 1990. However, the country's total output has increased by 13.1 EJ during this time. In 2018, international bunkers were equal to 17.3 EJ, or 2.9% of the world's total (UN, 2021). In addition, the International Maritime Organization (IMO) has adopted key short-term measures to reduce the carbon intensity of all ships by at least 40% by 2030 (IMO, 2021).

Due to this requirement, it requires energy sources that are already available that use the majority of utilised fuels, which impacts combustion residues that affect global temperatures. As global temperatures continue to increase, there are significant consequences for human health and wellbeing, as well as for the land, air, and water that sustain people (Anshari et al., 2022; Samiha et al., 2021). Carbon dioxide and other greenhouse gases (GHG) are emitted when fossil fuels are burned. The presence of these gases in the atmosphere contributes to global warming. Excess heat on land, in the ocean, and in the atmosphere exacerbates extreme weather (Energyfactsaustralia, 2018). The use of energy also includes transportation, which is utilized to support the expansion of the world's economy in line with its development. Water transportation contributes to around 3% of worldwide greenhouse gas emissions. If nothing is done to prevent it, it is expected that the amount of greenhouse gas emissions caused by shipping would increase by 2050 to a level that is twice as high as it is today (SIA, 2018). If this is not dealt with in a prompt and comprehensive manner by lowering emissions of greenhouse gases, then additional negative and potentially cataclysmic impacts will be inflicted upon humanity.

The use of fossil fuels to generate electricity is one of the primary contributors to climate change. Switching to renewable energy sources is one of the most effective ways to reduce this type of pollution. Recent national policies, strategies, and development plans of many countries have placed sustainable development at the center (Anshari & Almunawar, 2022). At the United Nations headquarters in New York, the Open Working Group presented a proposal to the United Nations General Assembly for a set of global SDGs. These SDGs included 169 targets and 17 goals. In addition, a preliminary set of 330 indicators was presented in March 2015 after being developed. In comparison to the Millennium Development Goals (MDGs), the SDGs place a higher priority and higher standard on the research community (Anshari et al., 2021). In order to address climate change, the provision of renewable energy, food, health care, and water requires coordinated worldwide monitoring and modelling of numerous elements that are directed socially, economically, and environmentally (Abbott et al., 2022).

Nuclear energy is an alternative energy source that is becoming more popular at the moment (Rhodes, 2020). There is the possibility of utilising nuclear power as a transportation energy source, particularly for marine shipping. In addition to lowering greenhouse gas emissions, the use of nuclear energy will improve financial efficiency. The advantage of nuclear energy is also the speed with which the ship may be built, and, of course, there is no need to reload for up to 25 or even 50 years (Smith, 2021). Despite the benefits of nuclear energy, there are risks, particularly to the environment and humanity, in the event of an accident or leakage.

The growth of nuclear-powered marine transportation, in particular on ships and submarines, is a significant risk that every government, including Indonesia, which is an archipelagic country, needs to take into consideration because of the possibilities that it poses. As an archipelagic nation, Indonesia relies heavily on the use of ships, as do international trade vessels. In addition, Indonesia's vision as the world's maritime axis is very concerned about the sustainability of marine ecology. There is a risk that the marine ecology would not be able to sustain itself if there is a likelihood of failure and leaking of nuclear material. In light of the fact that pollution is occurring at sea, the purpose of this paper is to discuss the significance of increasing maritime patrols that are uniformly diffused across the entirety of Indonesian waters. This is especially important in light of the fact that the development of nuclear power across Indonesian waters is currently in the planning stages.

The novelty of the radiological detector aircraft for marine life's sustainability lies in its potential to detect and map radiation levels in marine environments from an aerial perspective, which is not currently available through existing detection methods. The use of an aircraft-mounted detector to detect and monitor radiation levels in the ocean is a relatively new concept, and the development of such technology could potentially have significant implications for marine conservation efforts. Radiological detectors on planes can help reach several Sustainable Development Goals (SDGs), including SDG 14 (Life Below Water). The research could focus on developing and testing new radiological detector technologies that are suitable for use on ship patrols as well as exploring how these technologies can be integrated into existing marine patrol operations.

This paper is expected to assist in the formation of policies, especially those related to Indonesia's vision as the world's maritime axis. In addition, this article will be followed by a literature review in the second section, a methodology section in the third section, research findings as well as analysis and discussion in the fourth section, and a conclusion section in the fifth section. The final section will consist of some recommendations and some conclusions.

2. LITERATURE REVIEW

2.1 The Global Economic Need for Ships

The development of world trade affects the development of the number of goods transported by sea transportation. It was noted that in 2010, the total amount of cargo transported was 1.2 billion tonnes and grew to 1.85 billion tonnes in 2020 (Statista, 2022). In 2020, developments in Asia recorded 509 million containers, which is 62% of all container traffic in the world. To fulfil this, the number of ships needed for world trade has also grown from year to year. As analysed by the United Nations Conference on Trade and Development (UNCTAD), from 2020 to 2026, there will be an increase in the number of fleets at sea for trade needs of 2.4% per year (UNCTAD, 2021). Until now, the sea route has been the first choice to meet the world's needs because it is the cheapest for financing. Therefore, 80% of the world's needs still use the sea route. And it is estimated that by 2050, it will reach a significant increase of two times compared to 2010 (SIA, 2018).

2.2 Indonesia as an Archipelago Country

Indonesia is the biggest archipelago country in the world. The number of islands officially reported is 16,771 islands (Buntoro, 2015). It has 2.8 million square kilometres of water, including 92,877 square kilometres of inland waters and 1.82 million square kilometres of land. If Indonesia's exclusive economic zone (EEZ), which goes beyond the archipelago, is included, Indonesia's sea area grows to 7.9 million square kilometres (Cribb, n.d.).

The archipelagic nature of Indonesia creates two different but related governance issues. First, by dividing Indonesia's landmass into islands, the water presents unique communication, coordination, and identification issues. The presence of the sea makes it more challenging to govern the land. The waters surrounding and between these islands must also be managed. Even though regulating the maritime zone is hard to do in practice, these oceans are very important strategic, economic, and cultural resource for Indonesia that cannot be ignored (Cribb, n.d.).

The vast marine region that encompasses and surrounds the Indonesian archipelago is vital to the Indonesian government for a variety of reasons. The water facilitates transportation and communication. It connects the islands of Indonesia to each other and to the rest of the world, transporting the imports and exports that maintain the economy (Cribb, n.d.). As part of international relations and to provide access to international transportation, Indonesia has three Indonesian Archipelago Channels (ALKI), namely ALKI I, ALKI II, and ALKI III (Nainggolan, 2015). ALKI I is extremely lengthy and winding, passing through a collection of large and small islands that present a variety of issues and potential threats. ALKI II is a channel for international shipping and flights that can be utilised normally and peacefully by foreign ships and aircraft in waters under the control of the Indonesian government. ALKI III is accessible to all foreign ships and aircrafts whose goal is to regularly transit the territorial waters of the Indonesian Archipelago in accordance with the Law of the Sea Convention (LOSC) from one portion of the Exclusive Economic Zone (EEZ) to another (Buntoro, 2015).

Indonesia as the World Maritime Axis

Indonesia has great maritime potential as the world's biggest archipelago, where two-thirds of its area is water and it has the second-longest coastline in the world. In addition, Indonesia's location between two continents, Asia and Australia, and two oceans, the Pacific and the Indian, places it at a key crossroads of sea lanes connecting the eastern and western continents. With this position, 40% of the approximately 90% of global trade that is moved by sea flows via Indonesian waterways (Setneg, 2021).

The World Maritime Axis is a vision of Indonesia to make Indonesia a sovereign, advanced, independent, strong and capable maritime nation. In accordance with national interests, Indonesia makes a positive contribution to the security and defence as well as peace of the region and the world. The Vision of the World Maritime Axis, which was introduced in 2014, has 7 pillars in its application, namely first, Marine Resource Management and Human Resource Development. Second, defence, security, law enforcement, and safety at sea. Third, Marine Governance and Institutions. Fourth, the economy and marine infrastructure and the improvement of welfare. Fifth, there are marine spatial management and marine environmental protection; sixth, there is maritime culture; and finally, there is maritime diplomacy (Ardi et al., 2020). Then, this policy is built on six policy principles, namely Archipelago Insight, Sustainable Development, Blue Economy, Integrated and Transparent Management, Participation, and Equality (Ardi et al., 2020).

Ship Routes in Indonesia

As archipelagic country, Indonesia has an important shipping lane in world trade. The development of sea traffic in Indonesia is quite significant. When compared from 2016 to 2020, the number of ship voyages in Indonesia has increased from 19,109 to 27,236 voyages. Meanwhile, the number of sailing ships increased by 25% (UNCTAD, 2021). This will continue to grow as long as Indonesia's "Global Maritime Axis" policy is in place. This policy affects the growth of Indonesia's marine transportation infrastructure. Indonesia wants to become a maritime power because it has almost 95,000 km of coastline. President Joko Widodo's plans to improve Indonesia's infrastructure and way of life in order to make it more competitive within ASEAN and around the world have put a lot of attention on the country's maritime infrastructure. Widodo wants to improve ports, make connections between islands as good as possible, and make Indonesia a "Global Maritime Axis." The government also wants to rebuild Indonesia's maritime culture and build up its navy. This is possible because the military budget is going up from less than 1% to 1.5% of the country's total budget (Austrade, 2015). It also wants to improve Indonesia's ports and other shipping infrastructure in a big way so that the country can do more business between the Indian and Pacific oceans. This will improve logistics and help Indonesia make better use of the fact that it is made up of many islands.

2.3 Nuclear Development for Ships

Utilizing nuclear power will enhance the performance and resistance of ships at sea. By utilising nuclear power, ships gain increased speed and power. Nuclear power is ideally suited for ships that must remain at sea for extended periods without refuelling and for submarines with tremendous propulsion. In the 1950s, work started on making merchant ships that run on nuclear power, but they have not been very successful in the business world. The 22,000-ton NS Savannah was built in the US and put into service in 1962. It was taken out of service eight years later (World-Nuclear, 2021). However, with the growth and consumption of energy that releases gas emissions that cause global temperature increases, alternative energy, including nuclear, is increasingly being targeted for use on ships. If ships use nuclear power and there are no accidents, they will not put out any SOx, NOx, CO2, or particulates because there are not any. In fact, nuclear power is millions of times more powerful than fossil fuels and popular alternative fuels like methanol, ammonia, and hydrogen. Without a doubt, nuclear power can help shipping meet the IMO's goal of reducing greenhouse gases (GHG) by 2050 (Safety4sea, 2021). Ships that run on nuclear power use about half as much fuel as ships of the same size that run on oil. For the shipping business, the higher number of trips and higher profits seem to more than make up for the higher costs of running nuclear power plants (Dade, 2017). Shipowners will have difficult decisions in the future when deciding on their new development strategy. Committing to zero-carbon fuel now carries the very real danger that future bunkering infrastructure will be inadequate where ships will trade. However, with nuclear-powered ships not requiring refuelling for 25 years or perhaps 50 years and still being able to travel at higher service speeds, this could be a potential option for merchant ships (Smith, 2021).

The Dangers of Nuclear Waste for the Environment

For a generation, nuclear power has produced reliable electric power around the world but has also attracted bad press regarding concerns about safety and nuclear waste handling. Nuclear energy has long been regarded as an important alternative for guaranteeing global energy security, and it is now being marketed as a solution for climate change mitigation. Nuclear power, on the other hand, remains highly controversial due to the risks involved with it—nuclear accidents and troublesome radioactive waste disposal. Nuclear power plants are associated with radioactive risk, either in the context of previous nuclear accidents or of vast amounts of long-lived nuclear waste that have been increasing for decades and pose a substantial environmental concern (Pravalie et al., 2018). However, because these wastes can harm human health and the environment, their safe disposal has received a lot of attention around the world (Rahman, 2021). Nuclear technology, both military and commercial, offers serious environmental challenges in terms of current and future threats to humans and the environment. These risks, as proved by nuclear testing and nuclear reactor accidents, extend beyond national boundaries, can continue for thousands of years, and can have multigenerational health consequences (Kyne & Bob, 2016). There is a significant uncertainty in the United States about the health consequences of nuclear power plants for the more than 87 million people who live within a 50-mile radius of commercial reactors (Kyne & Bob, 2016). Various nuclear reactor dangers and contamination have been demonstrated in Chornobyl in Russia (1986), Three Mile Island (TMI) in the United States (1979), and, most recently, Fukushima in Japan (2011). Indeed, on the 30th anniversary of the Chornobyl tragedy in 2016, no technology was available to deal with the 2000-tonne radioactive core that melted from a failing reactor, a core that would be lethal to people for thousands of years (Schofield, 2016). In a recent development, hundreds of US sailors who participated in the Fukushima disaster rescue operations have experienced rare cancers, blindness, birth deformities, and two fatalities, prompting lawsuits against Japanese nuclear power firms (CBS, 2014).

Marine Pollution by Nuclear

Nuclear energy continues to have its pros and cons. The use of energy sources is an option to deal with the threat of climate change because it is considered environmentally friendly. But on the other hand, the failure and leakage of this material can be a source of environmental pollution that can damage ecosystems in the ocean. There are three possible sources for this radioactive pollution: the release of radioactive liquid from the damaged site, the fall of radioactive particles from the atmosphere to the ocean's surface, and the transfer of radioactive pollution by leaching via contaminated soil (IRSN, 2011).

Furthermore, the oceans can also be polluted with nuclear waste due to illegal dumping, atomic bomb testing (for example, by France in 1995 in the South Pacific), or accidents involving nuclear-powered ships or nuclear reactor sites near the coastline. Even though the environment is "non-ideal" because of this nuclear waste pollution, the damage caused by radioactive spills at sea will be less than if they occur on land. But even so, as with the oil spill, nuclear waste affects marine life in the area affected by nuclear waste pollution (Rubin, 2022).

Figure 1 shows a bibliographic analysis of previous publications using the search keywords "marine," "nuclear," and "detection." From this figure, you can see the research trend for this topic domain by year. Colors with red clusters indicate current research topics that talk a lot about water pollutants, detection methods and procedures, nuclear power plants, marine environments, marine biology, fish, and radioactivity. From the results of this bibliographic analysis, not many have studied the need for a

Figure 1. Bibliographic analysis of marine AND nuclear AND detection
Source: Authors' Compilation, 2022

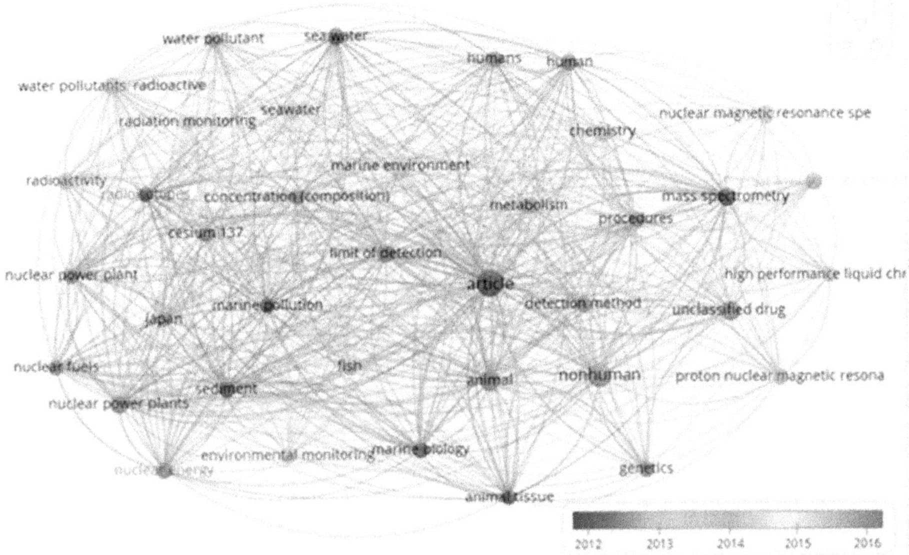

radiological detector aircraft, especially for large ocean areas such as the one in Indonesia. Therefore, this research will contribute to the body of knowledge, especially marine sustainability.

2.4 Maritime Patrol in Indonesia

For decades, maritime law enforcement and the Indonesian navy did not have sufficient resources to carry out maritime patrols and combat unlawful behavior. However, Indonesia has made some real efforts in order to overcome various threats originating from the maritime domain in recent years. This effort involves several related parties. First, the President of the Republic of Indonesia, as the executive, has issued policies, such as the World Maritime Axis, which restores Indonesia's maritime spirit and begins with increasing security and trade in sea lanes. Second, Indonesia formed a coordinating ministry to support the maritime sector as well as special task forces, such as the Indonesian Maritime Security Agency (BAKAMLA) and the Indonesian President's Task Force to Combat Illegal Fishing (SATGAS 115). And finally, in 2017, Indonesia started investing in infrastructure and capability development in order to maintain maritime security (Morris, 2022).

2.5 Ishikawa Model Analysis

This study uses the Ishikawa model as an analytical tool to identify the root cause of the problem. The Ishikawa Model diagram as an analysis tool becomes one alternative to assist in determining the underlying reasons or causes of this study. Ishikawa model diagrams are also known as Cause-and-Effect Diagrams, Fishbone Diagrams, and Herringbone Diagrams (Mind Tool, n.d). Cause and Effect Analysis was developed in the 1960s by Kaoru Ishikawa, a quality management pioneer. After that, he published the approach in his 1990 book, "Introduction to Quality Control". This model diagram supports in

Figure 2. Qualitative design based participant selection for study
Source: Author's Compilation, 2022

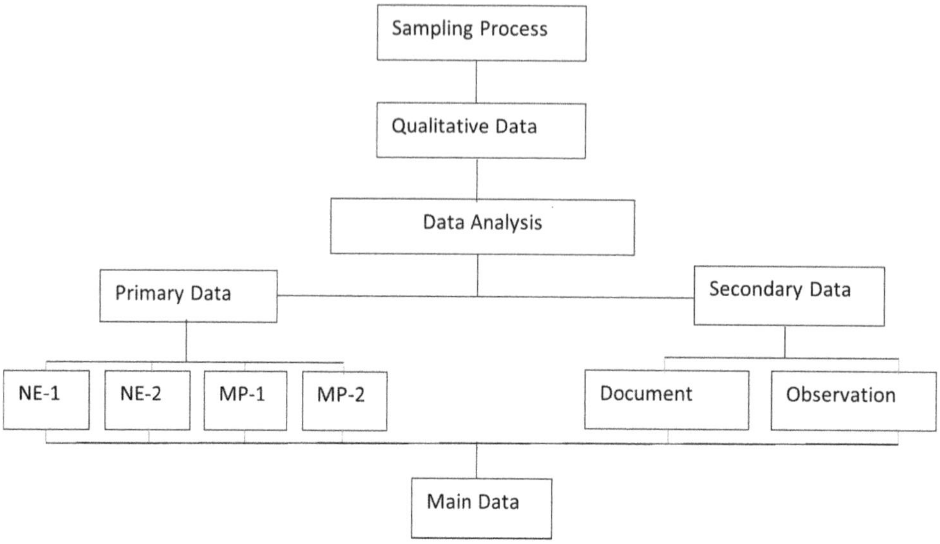

determining the source of an issue, analyzing to identify the problem and determining the location and cause of a process's failure (Mind Tool, n.d). This model guides the definition of the root of the problem by identifying several factors that have a relation to the problem (API, n.d.).

3. RESEARCH METHODOLOGY

3.1 Research Design

This paper was conducted using a qualitative approach, with interviews as the primary data collection method. Figure 2 shows the details of the research design. The study is expected to achieve comprehensive findings about the problem statements highlighted in the previous sections. All the interview results were coded to understand the patterns and alternative solutions for the theme. This study investigated, from the perspective of an aircrew patrol aircraft in Indonesia, the possibility of developing water transportation using nuclear power in order to understand its potential and challenges. The themes focused on three main dimensions: the possibility of developing nuclear-powered ships in the future, the possibility of nuclear failure, and the security readiness for radioactive pollution. The study also used secondary data collection to figure out what questions to ask in interviews and to reach its goals.

3.2 Participant

The objective of this paper is to figure out how ready Indonesia's maritime patrol unit is for the possible use of nuclear energy in shipping. There were two nuclear experts interviewed for this study, which is then coded as NE-1 and NE-2 in subsequent reports. The NE's perspective was critical to examining the research gaps on the future of nuclear energy in sea transportation and its usage in Indonesia. The next two respondents were two pilots of the patrol aircraft, which are then coded as MP-1 and MP-2. The data collection from MP represents the expert's perspective of the crew from the maritime patrol unit, who have extensive experience in this field, especially maritime security, focusing on nuclear energy in sea transportation.

3.3 Data Collection

Based on the literature analysis, interview questions were developed, encompassing all the factors in the theme of the research. Conducting a pilot test involves testing the interview questions with a small sample of participants to check if the questions are clear, relevant, and appropriate and to identify any potential problems or issues. Revise the interview questions and make any necessary changes or improvements based on the feedback from the pilot test. Schedule and conduct the online interviews. Then, record and transcribe the interviews. This involved recording the interviews with the consent of the participants and transcribing them into text format for analysis. Analyse and interpret the data from the interviews by coding, categorising, and summarising the data from the interviews and identifying themes, patterns, and insights that answer your research question.

Finally, report and present the findings from the interviews by presenting, summarising, and discussing the findings from the interviews and relating them to your research objectives and literature. The time to complete the interview for each source was 40 minutes.

The data validation was conducted by assessing the expertise of the interviewer and the interviewees. Before the interviewees were chosen, their educational background, time of service, and responses to the interview questions were all validated.

3.4 Data Analysis

Qualitative analysis in this study uses interviews with experts in nuclear power and also pilots for maritime patrol. In the data analysis process, steps were taken to identify the main themes that emerged from the experts' responses by looking for recurring ideas, phrases, or concepts that appeared throughout the interview. Then, categorise the experts' responses into different groups based on those themes. After categorising the responses, find patterns or trends that emerge within each group. Are there particular concerns or issues that multiple experts have mentioned? Are there any areas where the experts seemed to disagree or have different perspectives? Once we have identified the main themes and patterns, we can analyse the data to draw conclusions and gain insights. Consider the implications of the experts' responses for the design, development, and deployment of the radiological detector aircraft. Finally, report your findings in a clear and concise manner by including recommendations for how the radiological detector aircraft can be improved based on the insights you gained from the experts' responses.

4. RESULT

4.1 The Possibility of Developing Nuclear-Powered Ships in the Future

The first topic discussed the potential of nuclear development for marine transportation in the global and Indonesian contexts. The finding was that there was the possibility of using nuclear energy for ships. The following was a statement from sources:

Indonesia is one of the countries that ratified an international treaty called the Nuclear Non-Proliferation Treaty (NPT), which is an agreement not to manufacture and deploy nuclear weapons. As for nuclear power plants, there is no limit because it is for peaceful purposes. So if it is for ships, then there is also no limit. There is a very high possibility of making or developing ships with nuclear power. (NE-1)

This possibility does not just happen. The problem of global warming, which is of concern to the world, directs all industries to look for environmentally friendly energy sources (Asif & Muneer, 2007). This includes the ship industry. Nuclear energy is an alternative that provides this possibility. In addition, this nuclear energy will reduce the cost of the fuel used. This is also explained by the source in the interview as below.

It consumes less than a gram of fuel to produce 24 Megawatt-hours (MWh) of 100% clean energy. This means a Capesize bulk carrier would use less than 200 kg of fuel in 25 years, with zero emissions and making little waste.(NE-2)

With this data, the role of sea transportation will be significant in reducing emissions in the world and will play a role in reducing global temperatures significantly. The possibility of nuclear energy is indeed very possible. Attention to environmental sustainability, especially with the existence of the UN program, namely the Sustainability Development Program, will strengthen alternative nuclear energy that will expand to large transportation, one of which is the sea transportation industry. Nuclear energy as an alternative energy source and clean energy was repeatedly mentioned in this discussion, especially discussions with nuclear experts. As noted by one participant as explained below;

Indeed, it is now a hot issue. Because actually, nuclear power is clean energy. (NE-1)

This statement was reinforced by statements from other participants.

That means the ship provides the benefit of 100% clean power in port and then departs leaving no environmental footprint. Advanced nuclear power is best suited to the energy demands of the largest, ocean-going ships. The Fourth IMO GHG Study (2020) identifies over 12,500 ships (container, tanker, bulk carrier, cruise, and reefer) where the case could be made for using nuclear power. The expanding that to the 12,500 largest ships will effectively cut 70% of all airborne emissions from ocean transportation, which would be transformational to the shipping and wider industries. (NE-2)

4.2 The Possibility of Radioactive Failure

The collection of data on this theme begins with the question of the possible failure of a nuclear reactor and its impact on the environment and humans. The discussion was quite interesting because the participants were nuclear experts with more than 40 years of experience and followed developments in the use of nuclear energy in Indonesia and around the world. From these questions, this study obtained provides an interesting data. Nuclear energy is a very clean energy source and has the highest safety value in the world. As stated by one of the participants as the primary data source in this study,

However, the safety value of this type of nuclear power plant is the highest. Usually, nuclear power plants are analysed by probabilistic risk assessment (PRA) or probabilistic safety assessment (PSA). There are requirements before a nuclear power plant operates. For example, you must have a PSA of 10^{-6}. And every single parameter must be measured by being measured by several different measuring instruments. (NE-1)

At first, the answer indicated that the security level is very safe. However, further data analysis indicated that the highest level of safety can have a potential of a high level of danger. Therefore, high risk must be balanced with a high level of safety. This data was gathered from the statement of one of the participants in this study.

Radiation from radioactive is indeed dangerous. But like a double-edged knife, it can be very dangerous if it is not used according to applicable procedures and regulations. This radiation can kill cells in the form of alpha, beta, gamma rays, protons, neutrons, and these rays have duality as particles. And when exposed to amounts above the limit, it will damage cells. So it's very dangerous. Because the level of danger is very high, the safety level of nuclear energy must be high. (NE-1)

Therefore, nuclear material, which emits radioactivity, will also be dangerous for the environment. Furthermore, the findings also indicated that the possibility for failure is also considered high, just like any other energy usage. The obvious examples were Chernobyl or the incident in Japan where operator error was the cause of the accident. This was conveyed by one participant (NE-1) below.

It is very possible for it to happen, even if the ship uses a special design. It will definitely be shock-resistant, impact-resistant, and so on. But accidents can still happen. There are some cases where that happens, but again, most of them are human errors. Human error causes the most accidents in nuclear. There were also accidents before Chernobyl, at Three Mile Island in America in 1977. accidents that were quite serious but not as bad as those at Chernobyl and Fukushima. The incident at Three Mile Island was also due to human error. Therefore, it is very possible that there is the possibility of accidents, because no technology is free from accidents. (NE-1)

In light of this, the utilization of nuclear energy is in potential with risk due to human error linked to the risks posed by radioactive compounds that are polluting the water (see Figure 3). A review of the relevant literature and data collected from interviews found that radioactive waste can also get into the water through illegal dumping, atomic bomb tests (like the ones France did in 1995 in the South Pacific), or accidents involving nuclear-powered ships or nuclear reactors near the shore (Rubin, 2022).

Figure 3. Ishikawa model for marine pollution by nuclear
(Source: Author's Compilation, 2022).

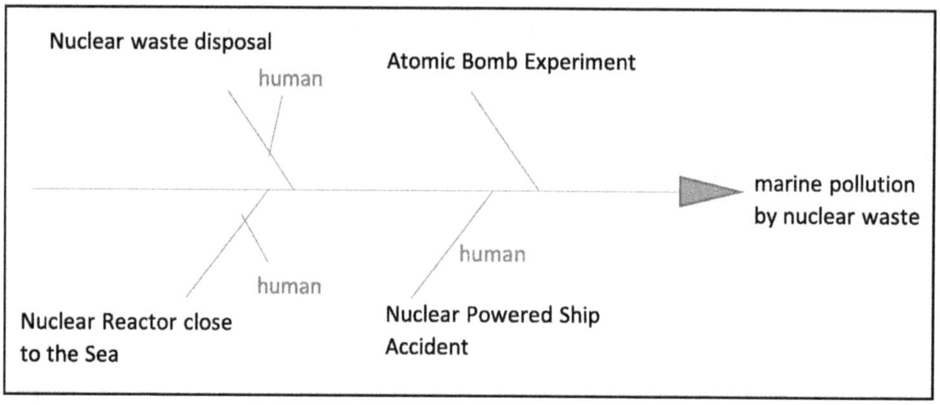

Figure 3 shows the Ishikawa model of analysis to explain the challenges of using nuclear power as an energy alternative that potentially affects marine pollution and human factors are the causes that need to be considered.

4.3 The Readiness of Indonesian Maritime Patrol for Radioactive Pollution

The discussion began by discussing violations that often occur in Indonesian waters. Marine pollution is one of the violations that have been found several times.

During my experience from 2019, the violations that were often found were illegal fishing, illegal logging, and, most recently, marine pollution. This finding was obtained from the results of routine observation missions throughout the year in ALKI I, which we reported and ordered to observe the impact of sea water pollution. (MP-1)

The problem of environmental pollution has become a concern for patrols in Indonesia, especially by patrol aircraft units, which are participants in this research. As stated by a participant who monitors seawater pollution. Patrols are tasked with finding the impact of marine pollution on the environment affected by oil leaks.

From the results of observing the photos and videos that we got, the pollution was caused by the leakage of fuel in the form of diesel, and the impact was damaging the area around the polluted sea in the form of ecosystem damage and fish deaths. (MP-1)

These observations were obtained from visualization data either directly or using visual aids, as noted by the participant.

If we look at the current patrol force, 70% rely on visual observations, including existing tools as well as visual tools. (MP-2)

The nature of the radioactive substance will be a challenge for Indonesian water patrol units. Because visual aids will not be able to detect nuclear material which is colourless and odourless, such as data obtained from one participant.

Radioactive substances are colourless and odourless. The distance must be close and not be far away. At this time, remote mapping can be carried out with drones (NE-1).

5. ANALYSIS AND RECOMMENDATION

The world's economy is still very dependent on sea transportation. Efforts to move these goods, of course, also require costs for operations. Therefore, the fuel used will be a consideration to reduce costs incurred for sea transportation business owners. Nuclear energy, which is renewable energy, can go without refuelling for 25 to 50 years. With this, the possibility of the use of nuclear material will occur.

Furthermore, apart from being a renewable energy source, nuclear energy is a clean energy source. The use of nuclear energy does not emit emissions that can contribute to the increase in global temperatures. Moreover, marine transportation currently plays a part in the production of emissions that increase global temperatures. In the future, nuclear power is likely to be the main alternative to fossil fuels.

However, the use of nuclear energy has a very high risk. Therefore, the level of assessment on the use of nuclear energy is the highest compared to other energy uses. As with other energy uses, nuclear energy also has the risk of an accident, as was the case in three major nuclear reactor accidents: Chernobyl, Fukushima, and Three Mile Island. A high level of security also has a risk of failure. So, while nuclear energy on ships is a good alternative, it poses a significant environmental risk in the form of radioactive pollution in the ocean.

The possible risk of this pollution will be a challenge for Indonesia, which is an archipelagic country. The Vision of the World Maritime Axis faces challenges in the use of nuclear energy as an alternative energy source for sea transportation. Regulations as well as maritime security guarantees are pillars of the vision of the World Maritime Axis. In addition, in this vision, Indonesia also emphasises increasing welfare through marine resources. So, radioactive contamination will be a problem for both the safety of the ocean and the long-term use of its resources.

Indonesian maritime security is aimed at both domestic and international users of Indonesian sea lanes. The ship makes sure that everyone on the water is safe, but it can also be a source of rules being broken and pollution. Indonesian air patrol units keep an eye out for ships that break the rules while passing through Indonesia. This includes monitoring of marine pollution as a result of fuel leakage, which has a negative impact on the marine environment. This can also happen on ships that use nuclear energy. Radioactive material leaks are very likely to occur.

Thus, marine pollution from radioactive substances will become a target area for marine security. However, challenges will be faced because radioactive substances are colourless and odourless. This will be an obstacle for maritime patrol units in Indonesia because of the limitations of radioactive substance detection equipment. In addition, it can endanger the safety of the crew of the patrol unit if they unknowingly enter an area exposed to radioactive substances. Thus, Indonesian maritime patrols must be prepared, and their capabilities must be improved, namely the ability to detect the use of nuclear fuel in the ocean and also the ability to detect radioactive substances. Therefore, Indonesia will be better prepared for maritime security activities in the future if it has this ability.

In conclusion, the use of nuclear energy as a source of clean and affordable energy can contribute to the achievement of SDG Goal 7, which is to ensure access to clean and affordable energy. Nuclear energy is a low-carbon energy source that can provide a reliable and stable electricity supply, which is essential for economic development and poverty reduction in many countries around the globe. However, it is important to note that nuclear energy comes with a number of risks and issues, such as the possibility of accidents, the need to store radioactive waste for an extended period of time, and the possibility that nuclear weapons could fall into the wrong hands. The use of nuclear energy must therefore be carefully weighed against the need to ensure safety and security.

Recommendation

If Indonesian maritime patrol equipment can find radioactive materials, it will be in better shape. The use of nuclear energy for sea transportation should be faced with a good security system, with all the potential dangers that it will be faced with. Thus, equipping maritime patrol equipment in Indonesia with radioactive detection equipment is a step that needs to be considered. Currently available detection tools include detection tools and visual detection aids. Therefore, special detection devices for odourless and colourless radioactive substances need to be installed on maritime patrol equipment.

Furthermore, the speed of ships that use nuclear energy will increase. This is a challenge for maritime patrols in Indonesia. Moreover, Indonesia has a very wide sea area. Therefore, a maritime patrol tool is needed that has speed and also has a wide range. Maritime patrol equipment that can be used as the main alternative for developing radioactive detection capabilities for the initial stage is maritime patrol aircraft. The development of radioactive substance detection technology can be carried out for aircraft, or a plan to buy an aircraft that can detect radioactive substances can be put into action.

Currently, the only aircraft with this capability is the Boeing WC-135 Constant Phoenix. This aircraft has the ability to detect radioactive substances by collecting particles and waste gases around the nuclear test area. The Constant Phoenix aircraft can be deployed to monitor nuclear weapons testing, search for radioactive leaks, and track other nuclear disasters. Since its introduction in the 1960s, the WC-135 fleet has developed a reputation for itself by monitoring high-profile nuclear catastrophes during historic missions. In 1986, WC-135s were used to assess the Chernobyl nuclear power plant disaster and to monitor the air quality after the explosion. In 2011, the final remaining WC-135W was sent from Offutt Air Force Base in Nebraska to detect hazardous elements in the atmosphere above Japan following the magnitude 9.0 earthquake that devastated the Fukushima nuclear power plant (Giangreco, 2016).

Alternatively, detecting tools could be developed independently or in partnership with friendly nations. South Korea, for instance, has created radioactive detecting equipment with a 1-kilometre range (3000 feet), using electromagnetic waves. With these capabilities, it is suitable for conducting horizontal and vertical radioactive detection air patrols. So that it can provide an early warning before approaching a radioactively contaminated area. Accordingly, the development of this equipment will be better than the air sampling system on the WC-135 Constant Phoenix.

Diplomatic cooperation in the fields of science and defence be carried out to participate in developing this technology (Colglazier, 2018). In partnership with the Indonesian Institute of Science (LIPI), this technology can be used to the maritime patrol aircraft to create a new platform or variation in the form of a maritime patrol aircraft with radioactive detecting capabilities.

6. LIMITATION AND FUTURE DIRECTION

This research has a number of limitations. The study relied on qualitative interviews with nuclear experts and maritime patrol officers as sources. The data could be strengthened by collecting more data from other stakeholders, such as policymakers in energy security. Finally, this research is confined to Indonesia due to its unique qualities as an archipelagic nation with a vast water area; thus, it is applicable only to Indonesia and other nations with similar characteristics. So, more research needs to be done so that the results can be more objective and useful for everyone. Nuclear energy has great potential as an alternative to fossil fuels. Thus, to achieve the objectivity of this research, data on the use of nuclear energy in existing marine transportation, such as aircraft carriers and submarines, is needed. Further research will be more useful and wider, not only for Indonesia, because the whole world needs sustainability in marine life, which faces challenges in the use of nuclear energy in the sea. Despite the fact that there are technologies that hold promise for safe nuclear energy, there are still challenges to be addressed, including cost, scalability, and waste management. Future studies ought to examine whether the use of more nuclear energy is safe if the appropriate steps are taken to prevent accidents and manage nuclear waste.

7. CONCLUSION

Since nuclear energy is both clean and renewable, it promises to be a cost-effective replacement for fossil fuels in maritime transportation. As a result of nuclear energy's high level of safety, the risk of accidents and leaks poses a high level of danger. Therefore, Indonesia, which has a vision for the world maritime axis, must strengthen and prepare maritime patrols capable of addressing the use of nuclear energy in maritime transportation. This is because Indonesia has archipelagic maritime routes and waterways that are used by both domestic and foreign ships. Consequently, the likelihood of accidents and pollution by nuclear materials and radioactive compounds in Indonesian waters is high. As a recommendation, in order to meet future challenges, maritime patrol aircraft is the most efficient and effective alternative as maritime patrol equipment. Purchasing the WC-135 Constant Phoenix aircraft will provide the ability to identify radioactive substances. However, the development of electromagnetic-wave-based long-range radioactive detection technology is an alternative that could be considered. In addition, this development may lead to the domestic production of aircraft that is capable of detecting radioactive substances. As a result, the development of radiological detection aircraft will aid and strengthen Indonesia's vision of becoming the world's maritime axis.

REFERENCES

Abbott, J. K., Lew, D. K., Whitehead, J. C., & Woodward, R. T. (2022). The future of fishing for fun: The economics and sustainable management of recreational fisheries. *Review of Environmental Economics and Policy*, *16*(2), 262–281. doi:10.1086/720987

Anshari, M. (2020, March). Workforce mapping of fourth industrial revolution: Optimization to identity. [). IOP Publishing.]. *Journal of Physics: Conference Series*, *1477*(7), 072023. doi:10.1088/1742-6596/1477/7/072023

Anshari, M., & Almunawar, M. N. (2022). Adopting open innovation for SMEs and industrial revolution 4.0. *Journal of Science and Technology Policy Management, 13*(2), 405–427. doi:10.1108/JSTPM-03-2020-0061

Anshari, M., Almunawar, M. N., & Masri, M. (2020). Financial technology and disruptive innovation in business: Concept and application. [IJABIM]. *International Journal of Asian Business and Information Management, 11*(4), 29–43. doi:10.4018/IJABIM.2020100103

Anshari, M., Almunawar, M. N., Masri, M., & Hamdan, M. (2019). Digital marketplace and FinTech to support agriculture sustainability. *Energy Procedia, 156*, 234–238. doi:10.1016/j.egypro.2018.11.134

Anshari, M., Almunawar, M. N., Masri, M., Hamdan, M., Fithriyah, M., & Fitri, A. (2021, November). Digital wallet in supporting green FinTech sustainability. In *2021 Third International Sustainability and Resilience Conference: Climate Change* (pp. 352-357). IEEE. 10.1109/IEEECONF53624.2021.9667957

Anshari, M., Syafrudin, M., Fitriyani, N. L., & Razzaq, A. (2022). Ethical Responsibility and Sustainability (ERS) Development in a Metaverse Business Model. *Sustainability (Basel), 14*(23), 15805. doi:10.3390u142315805

API. (n.d). *How to Use the Fishbone Tool for Root Cause Analysis*. API.

Ardi, M. R., Subianto, A., & Sudirman, S. (2020, April 20). IMPLEMENTATION OF INDONESIA'S MARINE POLICY A CASE STUDY:(Implementation of Presidential Regulation No. 16 of 2017 Concerning Indonesian Maritime Policy, Specifically Maritime Diplomacy in Papua). *JOURNAL ASRO., 11*(2), 1–7. doi:10.37875/asro.v11i2.263

Asif M, Muneer T. (2007). Energy supply, its demand and security issues for developed and emerging economies. *Renewable and sustainable energy reviews, 11*(7), 1388-413.

Austrade.gov. (2015). Export Markets- Indonesia. Austrade. https://www.austrade.gov.au/australian/export/export-markets/countries-and-economies/indonesia/industries/maritime-to-indonesia.

CBS. (2014). *U.S. Navy Sailors Sue Japan Power Co. for Radiation Exposure during 2011 Quake, Tsunami Rescue*. CBS.

Colglazier EW. (2018). Science diplomacy and future worlds. *Science & Diplomacy, 7*(3), 1-20.

Cribb, R., & Ford, M. (n.d.). *(n.d). "Indonesia as an Archipelago: Managing Island*. Managing The Sea.

Dade, T., & Witzig, W. (2017). Container Ships: Oil Fueled versus Nuclear Powered. *Nuclear Technology*, 196.

Energyfactsaustralia. (2018). *Energy and Climate Change*. Energy Facts Australia. https://www.energyfactsaustralia.org.au/key-issues/energy-and-climate-change/

Giangreco L. (2016). Small UAVs would rapidly collect nuclear information along with WC-135. *Inside the Air Force, 27*(24), 1-1.

IMO. (2021). *Cutting GHG emissions from shipping - 10 years of mandatory rules*. IMO. https://www.imo.org/en/MediaCentre/PressBriefings/pages/DecadeOfGHGAction.aspx

IRSN. (2011). *Impact on the marine environment of radioactive releases following the nuclear accident at Fukushima Daiichi*. IRSN.

Kyne, D. & Bolin, B. (2016). Emerging Environmental Justice Issues in Nuclear Power and Radioactive Contamination. *Environmental Research and Public Health, 700.*

Rahman, R. A. O, & Hung, Y. T. (2011). Liquid Radioactive Wastes Treatment. *Water (Basel)*, 551.

Ministry of State Secretariat of the Republic of. Indonesia. (2021). *Indonesia jasi poror martim dunia perlu peran semua pihak*. Setneg. https://www.setneg.go.id/baca/index/wujudkan_indonesia_jadi_poros_maritim_dunia_perlu_peran_semua_pihak

Morris, L. (2018). *CSIS*. AMTI. https://amti.csis.org/assessing-recent-developments-in-indonesian-maritime-security/

Nainggolan, P. P. (2015). Security Threats to Indonesia's Sea Lanes. *Center for Research, Data and Information Processing, DPR RI, 2015*, 5.

Pravalie, R., & Bandoc, G. (2018). Nuclear energy: Between global electricity demand, worldwide decarbonisation imperativeness, and planetary environmental implications. *Journal of Environmental Management*, *209*, 81–92. doi:10.1016/j.jenvman.2017.12.043 PMID:29287177

Rhodes, R., & Beller, D. (2020). The need For Nuclear Power. IAEA, 43.

Rubin, K. (2022). *Department of Geology and Geophysics University of Hawaii*. SOEST. https://www.soest.hawaii.edu/GG/ASK/waterpol2.html

Safety4sea. (2021). *Is Nuclear Power the future of shipping*. safety4sea. https://safety4sea.com/cm-is-nuclear-power-the-future-of-shipping/

Samiha, Y. T., Handayani, T., Razzaq, A., Fitri, A., Fithriyah, M., & Anshari, M. (2021, November). Sustainability of Excellence in Education 4.0. In *2021 Sustainable Leadership and Academic Excellence International Conference (SLAE)* (pp. 1-5). IEEE. 10.1109/SLAE54202.2021.9788095

Schofield. (2016). *Ruined Chernobyl Nuclear Plant will Remain a Threat for 3000 Years*. Schofield.

Shahbaz, M., & Lean, H. H. (2012). Does financial development increase energy consumption? The role of industrialization and urbanization in Tunisia. *Energy Policy*, *40*, 473–479. doi:10.1016/j.enpol.2011.10.050

Sia-Partners. (2018). *Towards cleaner and more sustainable shipping: the required actions*. SIA. https://www.sia-partners.com/en/news-and-publications/from-our-experts/towards-cleaner-and-more-sustainable-shipping-required (accessed August 3, 2022).

Smith, M. (2021). *Shipping to go nuclear on climate change*. Nepia. https://www.nepia.com/articles/shipping-to-go-nuclear-on-cli
mate-change/

Statista. (2022). *International seaborne trade carried by containers.* Statista. https://www.statista.com/statistics/253987/international-seaborne-trade-carried-by-containers/

Tool, M. MInd Tool. (n.d). https://www.mindtools.com/pages/article/newTMC_03.htm

UN. (2021). *Energy Statistic Pocket Book.* New York: UN-Departement of Economics and Social Affair.

UNCTAD. (2021). *Maritime Transport Review*. UNCTAD. https://hbs.unctad.org/maritime-transport-indicators/

World-Nuclear.org. (2021). *Nuclear Powered Ships/* World-Nuclear.org. https://world-nuclear.org/information-library/non-power-nuclear-applications/transport/nuclear-powered-ships.aspx (accessed August 3, 2022).

Chapter 16
The Use of Benefits Management in E-Government Projects

Teresa Matos Fernandes
Portuguese Administration, Portugal

Jorge Vareda Gomes
https://orcid.org/0000-0003-0656-9284
Universidade Lusófona, Lisboa, Portugal

Mario Romão
https://orcid.org/0000-0003-4564-1883
ISEG, Universidade de Lisboa, Portugal

ABSTRACT

The expenses in information systems and information technology (IS/IT) represent a substantial share in organizations' budgets. However, IS/IT investment projects seem to continue to show reduced success rates. The benefits management (BM) has gained relevance as a way, not only to understand these failures, but also as a tool available to organizations to improve the success of IS/TI investments. The objective of this article is to understand how BM can be applied in IS/IT investments in the public administration (PA) and help to leverage the benefits of these investments. A case study was conducted using an e-Government project in the Portuguese PA. The study showed how a BM approach can be applied in this environment and also identified some difficulties that must be considered. Several benefits, which were not foreseen, were identified and evaluated, or proposed some criteria for their evaluation, highlighting, this way, the true contribution of IS/IT investments in delivering services to citizens and increasing public organizations performance.

DOI: 10.4018/978-1-6684-8903-1.ch016

INTRODUCTION

All organizations strive for sustainability, whether they are organizations in the public sector seeking to maximize their effectiveness or private firms looking to maximize their shareholder value. IS/IT has become instrumental in ensuring profitability and sustainability (Askedal, 2019). However, such implementation is far from straightforward, and many organizations struggle to realize the intended benefits of ICT investments (Doherty et al., 2012).

Investments in IS/IT continue to have significant and growing importance in organizations' budgets, with the average organization spending around 3.4% of its revenues (Gartner, 2015).

These investments have provided significant transformations in business and productivity gains but continue to fall short of expectations (Lin & Pervan, 2003). Almost 30 years later, the claim of the Nobel laureate in economics, Solow (1987), over the business value of IS/IT investments, what became known as the Productivity Paradox, seems to remain valid. Academics and practitioners argue that projects are a structured way to implement business change. It is thus vital that organizations ensure the success of their projects and, in this way, the success of the implementation of their strategy (Serra & Kunc, 2015). Most researchers and organizations involved in project management continue to use the *iron triangle criterion* to evaluate project success (Atkinson, 1999). These are execution and delivery criteria, but the post-delivery phase should also be considered and two additional success criteria must be added, such as the quality of the delivered product, and the benefits to key to stakeholders (Atkinson, 1999). DeLone & McLean (2003) redefined their initial framework to evaluate the success of an IS/IT project (DeLone & McLean, 1992) to include the *net benefits* as one of the six dimensions to consider in evaluating success.

According to Ward & Daniel (2006), IS/IT projects have a poor reputation in many organizations, because often these investments fail to deliver the expected benefits: 70 to 85% of IS/IT investments fail to realize the promised benefits (Ward & Daniel, 2013). The idea that technology alone would bring competitive advantages to organizations has led many of them to spend more on technology (Carr, 2003) than would be desirable, or, at least, to do so in a non-selective way (Serrano & Caldeira, 2002). Managers have felt increasing difficulty in approving their investments in IS/IT (Lin & Pervan, 2003) and also a pressure to justify and measure the contribution of these investments to the organization's performance (Lin et al., 2005). Considerable resources are wasted on projects that deliver few or no benefits (Holgeid & Jørgensen, 2020). Benefits management is a management philosophy that puts the benefits in the central point for all actors' activities in organizational change (Badewi & Shehab, 2016). According to Ward et al., (1996) the benefits management model, benefits management goes through six processes: Benefits identification, planning, implementation, execution, reviewing and exploitation. Realizing the benefits of IS/IT investments must consider the organization's strategic objectives. This means that, on the one hand, investments in modern and efficient information technology must be an integral part of the company's strategy and, on the other hand, information technology must help the company to achieve its strategic goals/objectives (Koi-Akrofi, 2020). Research has demonstrated that many programs and related projects do not achieve their potential benefits mainly because they are not aligned with organisational strategy (Badewi, 2016). Organizations can derive more benefits from IT projects when benefits are stipulated up front and are managed throughout the project's life cycle (Marnewick, 2016).

The main objective of this study is to analyse how Benefit Management (BM) in IS/IT investments, in particular in e-Government projects, can help to leverage the benefits of these investments and thus contribute to the value creation for organizations, citizens and companies.

This study is intended to answer to the following questions: (1) How can a BM approach be applied to e-Government projects? (2) What are the main difficulties and constraints to its application? (3) What are the main advantages or benefits of its application?

For this purpose, a case study was developed involving a e-Government initiative.

BACKGROUND

Introduction

The 2030 Agenda for Sustainable Development, adopted by all United Nations Member States in 2015, provides a shared vision for peace and prosperity for people and the planet. A set of 17 Sustainable Development Goals make an urgent call to action for all countries in a global partnership. They identify the need to end poverty and other deprivations, in addition to recognizing the need for strategies that improve health and education, reduce inequality and stimulate economic growth, while combating climate change and working to preserve our oceans and forests.

IS/IT Investments

While IS/IT serve as critical enablers of business processes in organizations, there is no obvious positive relation between IS/IT investments and business performance (Shichor & Zviran, 2016). For decades, practitioners and researchers have been seeking to find ways to improve the return from IS/IT investments and efficient and effective ways of carrying out post-IT project activities such as maintenance and operations. Much research has focused on improving outcome of IS/IT projects, while less research appears to also consider value that comes from maintenance activities (Holgeid et al., 2022). IS/IT investments are inevitable in today's business world, as IS/IT plays a key role in shaping all forms of business to ensure productivity and efficiency (Lin, 2007). IS/IT investments are typically managed through projects and project portfolios. The evaluation methods and criteria used for decision support naturally have an impact on which projects are implemented and to what extent (Schnabl & Grechenig, 2020). The business value of IS/IT, and thus IS/IT projects, comprises cost reduction, revenue growth and securing of revenue (Afflerbach, 2015). The analysis of value contributions of IT investments is fairly complex and is mostly associated with a high ex-ante estimation inaccuracy and an inconsistent ex-post review probability (Afflerbach, 2015). Revenue effects are more difficult to quantify than the effects on costs. Quantification of strategic value includes even more uncertainty (Martinsuo & Killen, 2014).

Benefits Management

Benefit driven approaches are based on the premise that, given IT has no inherent value, benefits will only arise as and when IT enables people to do things differently (Ward & Daniel, 2012). For this reason, the starting point of any benefit-driven approach is to consider the impacted stakeholders, what they are going to do differently in the context of new investment and how this is of benefit to them (Wijesinghe, Scheepers & Mcloughlin, 2015).

BM was initially developed in the 1980s and 1990s (Breese, 2012) by several authors (e.g. Ward et al., 1996; Remenyi & Smith, 1998; Atkinson, 1999; Farbey et al., 1999) with the focus to justify the significant investments in IS/IT, to which the application of valuation methodologies based on purely financial criteria did not seem to be satisfactory (Ward et al., 1996). Although it is an area of study that has received increasing interest from academics and professionals, it is still a young discipline with a limited number of models and tools that need to be tested (Doherty, 2014). BM can be defined as a process that includes the identification, planning, measurement and follow-up of the benefits of a program or project (Serra & Kunc, 2015).

Organizations aim to create value for their stakeholders. The creation of value is based on the delivery of benefits, whether these are translated into financial return or the provision of public services (ISACA, 2012). The strategic planning of IS/IT aims to align these investments with the business strategy, with the focus on obtaining competitive advantages and thus maximize the benefits that will be obtained through these investments (Ward et al., 1996). It is also recognized that IS/IT alone does not bring value to the business. Without business and organizational changes, that implement them, there are no benefits and, therefore, change management is also a relevant area that must be considered (Ward & Daniel, 2013). Our study adopted the Cranfield School Approach, developed by Ward, Taylor and Bond (1996), that deals with investments in IS/IT as business projects in which both business and IS/IT stakeholders plan and manage the availability of technology, business and organizational changes that will enable the benefits achievement (Ward & Elvin, 1999).

The reasons for the adoption of this approach were mainly because this tool is a decision-making framework that promotes the maximization of benefits delivery of investments (Gomes & Romão, 2012). It is also one of the most tested approaches in real situations and in several sectors of activity, namely in the public sector, where it proved to be successfully applied (Ward & Daniel, 2006). The adopted approach is widely documented in the literature, which is an adoption facilitating factor. This approach implements a five stages BM process that has is roots on the management model of strategic change developed by Pettigrew and Whipp (1991) that recognizes that the process by which a major change is managed needs to be relevant to the content of the change involved both internal and external. This is an iterative process that covers the entire life cycle of IS/IT investments and not just the prior appraisal of the benefits (investment appraisal). Throughout the investment life cycle, active management is focused on the realization of the benefits. In a post-project phase, a critical evaluation of the achievement of the objectives and the expected benefits (investment evaluation) is carried out, which in addition to the *lessons learned*, allows evaluating the possibility of additional benefits (Ward et al., 1996). The key tool of this approach is Benefits Dependency Network (BDN). BDN is a cause-and-effect network that reflects how improvements can be achieved by combining changes and business and technological facilitators. This network provides a robust business case for investments, enhancing the reliability of delivery of intended benefits (Gomes & Romão, 2015). The BDN construction begins with the answer to the following questions: (1) Why is the investment being made, that is, why we want to change or improve? (2) What kind of benefits do you want to get? (3) How will these benefits be obtained? (4) Who is responsible for the benefits management process? The analysis of these answers allows the definition of the investment objectives, which should address some of the *concerns* maintained by top managers, regarding what is important for the business or for the organization in each period, i.e., the organizational and business drivers. It also identifies the *owner* of each benefit and who will be accountable for their delivery, as well as the *owner* of each change.

Table 1. Measure 6: Evaluation of IS/IT projects and expenses (GPTIC, 2012)

Dimension	*Description*
Economic value of the investment	Return of the investment in a cost-effective perspective, considering the total cost of ownership of the projects against the expected benefits;
Alignment with IS/IT policies	Alignment between the project objectives, the agency's strategic objectives, the Ministry and/or the Public Administration;
Risk investment	Risk associated with project implementation and alignment with information and technology architectures of reference

IS/IT Investments in Public Administration

Following a commitment of the Portuguese Government with the European Community, the International Monetary Fund and the European Central Bank, a strategic IS/IT plan was developed in the Portuguese Public Administration (GPTIC, 2012; AMA, 2013). This plan was developed by a working group and includes 25 integrated measures in five fundamental axes, one of which includes the *Measure 6 - Evaluation of IS/IT Projects and Expenses*, abbreviated as *M6* (Table 1).

E-Government

A commonly accepted definition is the one proposed by the United Nations (UN) in its electronic page, which defines e-Government as the "use of information and communication technologies to provide citizens and businesses with more efficient and effective public services" (UN, 2016). The Organisation for Economic Co-operation and Development (OECD) definition puts emphasis in the use of the Internet when defines e-Government as the "use of information and communication technologies, especially the Internet, as a tool for better governance" (OECD, 2003). Defining e-Government is linked to a process of transformation in governments and governance, politics and public management directly associated with the growth of the Internet from the mid to late 1990s (Curtin, 2007). E-Government is a natural extension of the technological revolution that has led to the information society, adding new concepts such as transparency, accountability and citizen participation in the evaluation of governments (Almarabeh & AbuAli, 2010). Today, new opportunities arising from the latest technological developments, such as Big Data, Business Analytics, Social Networking, Mobile Apps, Cloud Computing and the Internet of Things are widening the way we view e-Government (UN, 2014). In this way, e-Government is a multidisciplinary and interdisciplinary concept, ranging from computer science and engineering to political

Table 2. Interaction levels

Designation		*Description*
G2G	Government-to-Government	Provision of services to other public entities
G2C	Government-to-Citizens	Provision of services to citizens
G2B	Government-to-Business	Provision of services to companies
G2E	Government-to-Employees	Provision of services to (public) employees.

science, public management, marketing and communication, and a special reference to legal sciences (Curtin, 2007) which develop the necessary legal frameworks for the development of e-Government.

According to the recipients of the electronic services four levels of interaction are defined (Gupta et al., 2008; Esteves & Joseph, 2008; Löstedt 2005) (Table 2).

The G2G level is materialized in the integration of the back offices of various governmental entities, enabling the provision of optimized services to citizens and companies. An example of this type of service is the so-called *one-stop-shop* (UN, 2016), where single portals provide the various services geared to the needs of citizens, without multiple interactions, and providing the service or information in a single access point. The services on these portals are organized, preferably, by *life events,* such as, *search for new employment* (UN, 2016, Silcock, 2001; Veenstra et al., 2011).

e-Government cannot be seen as a one-time process or through a single project: it is an evolutionary process that involves several stages of growth. The development of capacity maturity models has been a trend in many technological and organizational areas, as they prove to be of added value to organizations by typically describing best practices related to their scope and providing frameworks of improvement (Concha et al., 2012). Since 2003, the UN has made available the *E-Government Survey* which, in addition to the dissemination of good practices, includes the *E-Government Development Index* (EGDI). This indicator is calculated for all 193 member countries, based on three factors: (1) online services; (2) communications and other infrastructures; and (3) population literacy. According to the respective EGDI each country is classified as having an EGDI from *very high* to *low*. Portugal in 2016, was in the group of high EGDI, ranked in the 38th overall position, being the first position occupied by the United Kingdom (UN, 2016). Usually, higher levels of e-Government development: are associated to higher levels of economic development. In 2016, 29 of the 32 countries with the lowest levels of e-Government (EGDI <0.25) were least developed countries (UN, 2016).

RESEARCH METHODOLOGY

Methodological Approach

The case study was considered the most appropriate methodological research approach to answer the research questions. The case study should be adopted when the focus is an in-depth study of a contemporary phenomenon, in a real context, without the researcher's influence (Yin, 2009). Yin (2009) proposes six sources for data collection: archival logging, documentation, interviews, direct observation, participant observation, and physical artefacts. It also states that the use of multiple sources of information allows the researcher to cover a wider range of subjects and to develop convergent lines of research through the triangulation process. The present study applied the BM's principles to an e-Government project, allowing an empirical answer to be given to the stated research questions.

PEPAC Program

The analysis unit is the PEPAC Program (Professional Training Program in the Central Public Administration) that includes the development and implementation of IS and supporting technological infrastructure. The PEPAC Program was created in 2010, and it was proposed to be an annual program of professional internship placements for unemployed, or looking for the first job, young graduates (less

Table 3. List of interviewed

Code	*Profile*	*Function*
PME1	Program Management Entity	Business manager
PME 2	Program Management Entity	Business manager
PME 3	Program Management Entity	Business manager
PME 4	Program Management Entity	Technical business staff
PE1	Promotion Entity	Business manager
PE2	Promotion Entity	RH Manager
PE3	Promotion Entity	Technical RH staff
IS/TIS	IS/IT Implementation unit	IS/TI specialist

than 35 years). The PEPAC Program has the following objectives: (1) Facilitate the access of young graduates into the labour market; (2) Promote training and new professional skills that can boost the modernization of public services; (3) Guarantee the beginning of a process of acquisition of professional experience in contact and learning with the rules, good practices and sense of public service; (4) Encourage the contact of young people with other workers and activities, avoiding the risk of their isolation, demotivation and marginalization.

Data Collection

The study collected data from the following sources:

- **Direct observation:** knowledge and information obtained by direct contact with the project.
- **Documentation:** several project documents were consulted, such as requirements documents, implementation plans, technical manuals and training contents among others.
- **Data queries to database:** several queries on the IS's database were also elaborated to characterize the case under study, as well as to obtain quantitative data to evaluate benefits arising from the project.
- **Interviews:** some of the main stakeholders were interviewed, especially those related to the business, some of whom with responsibility in the project implementation. The purpose of the interviews was essentially to gather information that would allow to identify objectives in the origin of the PEPAC Program, to structure benefits deriving from its implementation and other relevant information for the construction of the BDN. All the interviewees with responsibility in the PEPAC Program, reported that they were not aware of any study at the base of the Program, which could provide some information for the development of this work. These interviews were of the semi-structured type, with the previous preparation of interview scripts concerning the interviewee's profile. The interviews were conducted and assigned a code to each interviewee to guarantee the confidentiality of the responses (Table 3).
- **Electronic survey:** it was applied to candidates and trainees. The objective was to validate with the main recipients of the benefits about their actual realization. For the construction of the ques-

tionnaire, the information collected through various other sources was considered. The invitation was sent by email with the provision of a link that allowed access to the form without identifying the respondent. It was explained, in the questionnaire, the purpose of the investigation and guaranteed the confidentiality of the information. The questionnaire was previously validated with other potential respondents, who were excluded from the universe of analysis. For each subject, open questions, scale-type questions (Likert 5 points) and specific questions for trainees were addressed.

Data Analysis

Data analysis involves triangulation from different sources and different collection methods. To help with the qualitative analysis, data was grouped by question and interviewed, to facilitate the comparison of the same topic and to extract the necessary information. The study used the MAXQDA software to analyse the answers to open questions with their categorization. For the quantitative analysis, the IBM SPSS software was used.

THE CASE STUDY

Business Drivers

Portugal as well as the rest of Europe in 2010 was under a strong global economic crisis. Although youth unemployment rates are traditionally higher than those of the general population, the 2008 economic crisis has strongly penalized young people (Eurostat, 2010). According to the statistics provided by Eurostat (2010), the unemployment rate for young people (aged under 25 years) reached 27.5% in Portugal in the first quarter of 2010, against the 21.4% of the EU. Portugal was ranked in seventh place of the highest young unemployment rates. Thus, the main driver of Portuguese governmental program was *boosting growth and promoting employment* (GOP, 2010-2013).

To overcome the global crisis, it was developed the *European Economic Recovery Plan* (EURCOM, 2008). According with this, policies to stimulate economic activity and employment were implemented in Portugal and other member states of EU. Because of this expansionary policy, as well as the contagion of the *subprime crisis* to the European financial sector, the clear majority of EU countries fell into a strong public budget imbalance, which in turn led to the European Commission's opening of excessive deficit procedures to some countries, including Portugal. In this way, budget policy for 2010, along with the objective of supporting the recovery of the economy and employment, was characterized by the guarantee of the sustainability of economic growth through concrete measures of consolidation of public accounts with medium and long-term implications (Portuguese Government, 2009).

According to Ward & Daniel (2006) the drivers in PA tend to be imposed and are derived from the public policies. In this sense, measures of a strong budget reduction were taken, namely in terms of personnel expenses, wage containment and reinforcement of restrictions on new admissions to PA. Regarding the driver's identification, several public access documents were consulted, such as legislation, reports of activities of the organizations and political-economic and social guidelines

Figure 1. Linking investment objectives to business drivers

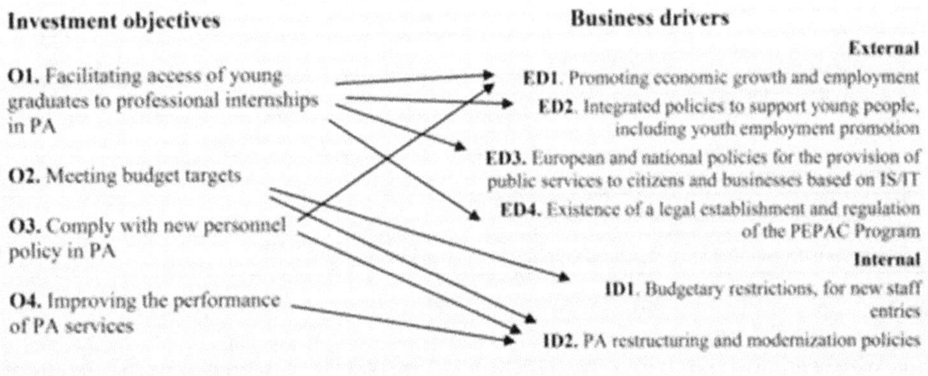

Investment Objectives

The investment objectives should address at least one business driver, without which it would not be possible to justify the project (Ward & Daniel, 2006). The Figure 1 explains these connections in the case of the present case study.

Changes and Changes Enablers

To implement a centralized solution, it was necessary to define and standardize processes. The following processes were modified, standardized and implemented in the IS/IT: (1) Survey of training needs; (2) Applications; (3) Evaluation and selection of candidates; (3) Candidates notification; (4) Candidates placement; (5) User support. To facilitate the changes, were carried out sessions with the main stakeholders for presentation of the Program (PME1).

Structuring Investment Benefits

Candidates and trainees are the main beneficiaries of the Program (PME1, PME2, PME3), so their perspective on the benefits achieved is of particular relevance, which can be obtained analysing the questionnaire results. The macro benefits (Table 4) measured by the questionnaire are MB1 and MB2. The main recipients of these macro benefits are the candidates. The survey also allows MB4 to be measured. MB4 translates in benefits for trainees by increasing the number of vacancies filled and also by a suitable allocation of internships to trainees' qualifications, increasing trainees' employability. MB4, on the other hand, has an impact on MB5, because the increase in the placement rate and the suitability of the placements enhances the transmission of skills and the adoption of new processes in public services. This relationship is represented in the BDN.

All the respondents claimed to prefer an application process such as that made available by PEPAC Program, i.e., based on a website made available on the Internet. When asked to justify this preference, by responding to an open question, the ease and convenience of use, the speed of the process and the economic factor were the main reasons for this appreciation.

Table 4. Macro benefits

Id	Macro Benefits
MB1	Quality improvement of services provided
MB2	Reduced costs for applicants
MB3	Reduced costs for PA
MB4	Increased Program effectiveness
MB5	Increased effectiveness of public services
MB6	Increased decision-making capacity for policy makers and managers

The results were categorized, using the MAXQDA. In fact, it was precisely the group of questions related to the application process that was the most highly rated by the respondents, with a score of 4.34. The notification process, which used the sending of SMS and e-mails, was the second most well-ranked group (3.89) followed by the quality of the IS used to support the Program (3.86). These three groups of questions were evaluated above the general average of responses to all groups, which stood at 3.83, showing moderate satisfaction with the Program (Table 5).

Table 5. Results by groups of questions

Item	*Group of Questions*	*Value*
3.1	Application process	4,34
3.2	Selection and placement process	3,60
3.3	Notification procedure	3,89
3.4	User support process	3,66
3.5	Application process	4,34
5.1	Suitableness of the attended stage	3,77
6.1	IS quality	3,86
6.2	IS user support	3,68

It was found that the results obtained by the analysis of the answers to the open questions were consistent with those obtained in the answers to the scale questions, which gives some consistency and reliability to the results of the survey. Additionally, the Cronbach's alpha value obtained for the whole questionnaire presents values much higher than those considered acceptable in this type of studies (α=0.92 to 21 items) (Maroco & Garcia-Marques 2006).

The benefits to the sponsor were mainly related with the redesign and normalization of processes and the introducing of some automatic methods to support its implementation. The centralization allowed the rationalization of processes, namely avoiding the multiplication of applications and their evaluation by several public entities, as was the case in the previous program. Public entities that previously consumed many resources, the human resources, with the operationalization of all the processes leading to the recruitment of their trainees, are now free of most of these tasks.

Regarding the increase in the effectiveness of the public services (MB5), it can be mentioned that there was a high level of receptivity by the promotion entities that received the trainees, and for many of them it was the first renewal of their human resources, since long time (PE2). It meant a rejuvenation of services and a real advantage enabling the introduction of new ways of work (PE2). It also served to fill shortages of staff with higher education in some public entities (PE2) as well as in specific knowledge areas (EGP4). From the point of view of benefits to PA and policy makers, the option for centralization has brought great advantages, since information became available faster, and new information was obtained and with higher quality (PME1). The information, that first was dispersed by the various entities and not always in the electronic format, now resides in a single database to support the PEPAC Program. It was also possible to obtain updated and consolidated information relevant to the orientation of studies and the decision-making. The access and exploitation of the information has been affected in a more adequate way in function of the intended objective, either through the implementation of pre-defined reports or *ad hoc* research on the BI component. The Annex 1 (Table 6) presents the PEPAC Program benefits structure, including information that leads to the evaluation of each benefit and the stakeholder (s) that are the beneficiaries of the benefit. The primary sources of information (in addition to the direct observation) used to the identification of the benefit, are also indicated.

Benefits Dependency Network

The information obtained in this case study can be consolidated in the benefits dependency network (BDN) where is stressed the relationship of cause-effect between its components. To illustrate this dependency chain, we start by selecting a benefit, for example MB1. The quality improvement of services provided is obtained by the realisation of the Objective 1, facilitating young people's access to professional internships in PA. However, without the implementation of the new organizational processes supported in the IS (OBC2) it will not be possible to deliver this macro benefit. Additionally, organizational processes defined by law is an enabling change factor (EC2). The availability of new SI PEPAC (T1), including the BI component (T5) and the discontinuation of the previous solution, PEPAP (T2) are the technological components that will support the new business processes. The *benefit stream* described is represented in the BDN (marked by the arrow and shaded in yellow) of PEPAC represented in Figure 2.

CONCLUSION

The realization of benefits through IS/IT investments that results in organizational change and development is one of the most frequent and critical business and policy issues being discussed and researched in the domain of information systems (Ward & Daniel, 2012). The continued failure of registered IS/IT projects globally poses significant challenges for organizations to properly execute their IS/IT-driven change projects in order to achieve the expected business benefits (Gingnell et al., 2014). The realization of benefits from projects is a growing concern for organizations that rely on projects for innovation, change and value creation. The need for organizations to successfully execute strategy, realize business objectives and deliver benefits through their projects has been highlighted in professional reports (PMI, 2016) and academic studies (Badewi, 2016; Laursen & Svejvig, 2016; Serra & Kunc, 2015; Winter et al., 2006).

Figure 2. Benefits dependency network

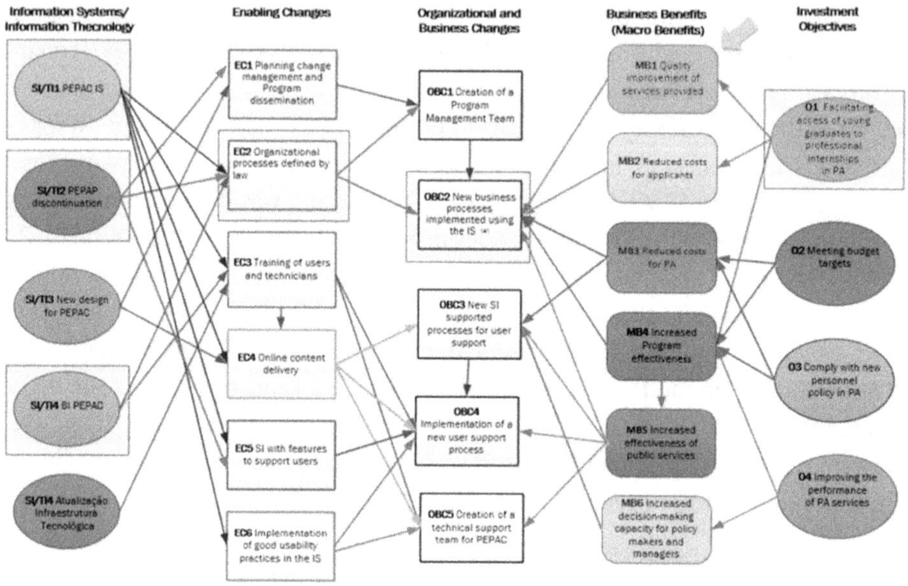

It was possible to exemplify through the presented case study how BM can successfully be applied in e-Government projects, in line with the results already achieved by other authors. However, some difficulties have been identified in its application. The main difficulty arises when collecting data to evaluate the benefits. The unit of analysis of the case study is a project already completed, so it was not possible to plan *a priori* the collecting of those data. Often benefits are evaluated by the difference between pre-investment and post-investment organizational performance. This leads to the need to plan the collecting of data to evaluate benefits, namely business performance before project implementation.

It was possible to identify some benefits that were not included in the list of desired benefits when the Program was proposed. These are not only financial benefits, such as cost reductions, but also include many intangible benefits such as increased decision-making capacity for policy makers and managers, increased transparency of public processes and greater satisfaction of service recipients. When presenting these results, we are first demonstrating the true contribution of IS/IT to the performance of organizations and to the all country, as is the case in e-Government projects. On the other hand, in times of increasing scarcity of resources, it is of crucial importance its allocation. The present approach shows, *a priori*, what objectives will be achieved and what benefits will be obtained in alternative investments, enabling organizations to choose those that best suit the needs of companies, public organizations or citizens.

If *a priori* appraisal of investments is important, its *ex-post* evaluation allows measuring the effectiveness of policies to conduct eventual corrective measures and to draw lessons for the future. Many organizations, not only in the public sector, tend not to carry out this type of analysis, even when conducting *a priori* review of benefits. In the case of the Portuguese PA, in which there is *a priori* evaluation of investments required by law, recommended through the M6, it is not implemented the *ex-post* evaluation, although it is planned in M6. In this study, when we carried out this evaluation, it was possible to identify that one of the main benefits of the project, the increased employability of young graduates, may not be providing the desired results. This assumption was obtained by analysing the results of the survey of trainees. However, it would require complementary analysis to assess this result and identify possible causes in its origin and, if necessary, to implement corrective or complementary measures. The present study shows that the application of a BM approach in e-Government projects remains relevant, despite the drivers of these projects being imposed.

REFERENCES

Afflerbach, P. (2015). The Business Value of IT in Light of Prospect Theory. *Business & Information Systems Engineering*, *57*(5), 299–310. doi:10.100712599-015-0400-6

Almarabeh, T., & AbuAli, A. (2010). A General Framework for E-Government: Definition Maturity Challenges, Opportunities, and Success. *European Journal of Scientific Research*, *39*(1), 29–42.

AMA. (2013). Definição e Implementação de Metodologia, Modelo e Ferramentas para Avaliação de Projetos e Despesas TIC - Overview do Processo de Avaliação de Projetos e Despesas TIC. Available at: https://m6.ama.pt/docs/AMA-20130925-AP-Overview do Processo v8.pdf

Askedal, K. (2019). *Understanding the Complexity of Benefits Management in an Interorganizational eHealth Effort*. In the *52nd Hawaii International Conference on System Sciences*, Maui, Hawaii, USA. 10.24251/HICSS.2019.484

Atkinson, R. (1999). Project management: Cost, time and quality, two best guesses and a phenomenon, it's time to accept other success criteria. *International Journal of Project Management*, *17*(6), 337–342. doi:10.1016/S0263-7863(98)00069-6

Badewi, A. (2016). The impact of project management (PM) and benefits management (BM) practices on project success: Towards developing a project benefits governance framework. *International Journal of Project Management*, *34*(4), 761–778. doi:10.1016/j.ijproman.2015.05.005

Badewi, A., & Shehab, E. (2016). The impact of organizational project benefits management governance on ERP project success: Neo-institutional theory perspective. *International Journal of Project Management*, *34*(3), 412–428. doi:10.1016/j.ijproman.2015.12.002

Breese, R. (2012). Benefits realisation management: Panacea or false dawn? *International Journal of Project Management*, *30*(3), 341–351. doi:10.1016/j.ijproman.2011.08.007

Carr, N. G. (2003). IT Doesn't Matter. *Harvard Business Review*, *81*(5), 41–49. PMID:12747161

Concha, G., Astudillo, H., Porrúa, M., & Pimenta, C. (2012). E-Government procurement observatory, maturity model and early measurements. *Government Information Quarterly*, *29*, S43–S50. doi:10.1016/j.giq.2011.08.005

Curtin, G. G. (2007). E-Government. In L. L. Kaid & C. Holtz-Bacha (Eds.), *Encyclopedia of Political Communications*. SAGE Publications, Inc.

DeLone, W. H., & McLean, E. R. (1992). Information Systems Success: The Quest for the Dependent Variable. *Information Systems Research*, *3*(1), 60–95. doi:10.1287/isre.3.1.60

DeLone, W. H., & Mclean, E.R. (2003). The DeLone and McLean Model of Information Systems Success: A Ten-Year Update. *Journal of Management Information Systems, 19*(4), 9–30.

Doherty, N. F. (2014). The role of socio-technical principles in leveraging meaningful benefits from IT investments. *Applied Ergonomics, 45*(2, 2A), 181–187. doi:10.1016/j.apergo.2012.11.012 PMID:23305923

Doherty, N. F., Ashurst, C., & Peppard, J. (2012). Factors Affecting the Successful Realisation of Benefits from Systems Development Projects: Findings from Three Case Studies. *Journal of Information Technology, 27*(1), 1–16. doi:10.1057/jit.2011.8

Esteves, J., & Joseph, R. C. (2008). A comprehensive framework for the assessment of eGovernment projects. *Government Information Quarterly, 25*(1), 118–132. doi:10.1016/j.giq.2007.04.009

EURCOM. (2008). *The Commission launches a major Recovery Plan for growth and jobs, to boost demand and restore confidence in the European economy*. Europa. https://europa.eu/rapid/press-release_IP-08-1771_en.htm

Eurostat. (2010). *Unemployment statistics*. Europa. http://ec.europa.eu/eurostat/statistics-explained/index.php/Unemployment_statistics#Unemployment_trends

Farbey, B., Land, F., & Targett, D. (1999). Moving IS evaluation forward: Learning themes and research issues. *The Journal of Strategic Information Systems, 8*(2), 189–207. doi:10.1016/S0963-8687(99)00021-9

Gartner. (2015). *IT Key Metrics Data 2015: Executive Summary*. Gartner. https://www.gartner.com/doc/2939218/it-key-metrics-data

Gingnell, L., Franke, U., Lagerström, R., Ericsson, E., & Lilliesköld, J. (2014). Quantifying Success Factors for IT Projects—An Expert-Based Bayesian Model. *Information Systems Management, 31*(1), 21–36. doi:10.1080/10580530.2014.854033

Gomes, J., & Romão, M. (2012). Seleção de uma abordagem de gestão de investimentos em Sistemas e Tecnologias da Informação. *RISTI (Porto), 0*(10), 35–49. doi:10.4304/risti.10.35-50

Gomes, J., & Romão, M. (2015). Enhancing Organizational Maturity with Benefits Management. *International Journal of Information Technology Project Management, 6*(4), 34–47. doi:10.4018/IJITPM.2015100103

Portuguese parliament. (2010). *Grandes Opções do Plano 2010-2013*. Portuguese parliament. https://www.parlamento.pt/orcamentoestado/documents/gop/gop_2010-2013_vf.pdf

GPTIC. (2012). *Plano global estratégico de racionalização e redução de custos nas TIC*. Administração Pública Horizonte. https://tic.gov.pt/pgetic/PGETIC_v1.0.pdf

Gupta, B., Dasgupta, S., & Gupta, A. (2008). Adoption of ICT in a government organization in a developing country: An empirical study. *The Journal of Strategic Information Systems, 17*(2), 140–154. doi:10.1016/j.jsis.2007.12.004

Holgeid, K., & Jørgensen, M. (2020). Benefits management and agile practices in software projects: how perceived benefits are impacted. In proceedings of the *2020 IEEE 22nd Conference on Business Informatics (CBI),* Antwerp, Belgium, 48-56. 10.1109/CBI49978.2020.10057

Holgeid, K., Krogstie, J., Patrick, M., Saur, E., & Sjøberg, D. (2022). Benefits management and Information Technology work distribution. *IET Software, 16*(4), 438–454. doi:10.1049fw2.12062

ISACA. (2012). *Cobit 5 - Business Framework for the Governance and Management of Enterprise IT.* ISACA.

Koi-Akrofi, G. (2020). Justification of, and Benefits Realization Beyond IT Investments: Analysis from Literature. *International Journal of Managing Value and Supply Chains, 11*(3), 1–16. doi:10.5121/ijmvsc.2020.11301

Laursen, M., & Svejvig, P. (2016). Taking stock of project value creation: A structured literature review with future directions for research and practice. *International Journal of Project Management, 34*(4), 736–747. doi:10.1016/j.ijproman.2015.06.007

Lin, B.-W. (2007). Information technology capability and value creation: Evidence from the US banking industry. *Technology in Society, 29*(1), 93–106. doi:10.1016/j.techsoc.2006.10.003

Lin, C., & Pervan, G. (2003). The practice of IS/IT benefits management in large Australian organizations. *Information & Management, 41*(1), 13–24. doi:10.1016/S0378-7206(03)00002-8

Lin, C., & Pervan, G. (2005). IS/IT Investment Evaluation and Benefit Realization Practices in Taiwanese SMEs. *Journal of Research and Practice in Information Technology, 37*(3), 235–251.

Löfstedt, U. (2005). E-Government: Assessment of Current Research and some Proposals for Future Directions. *International Journal of Public Information Systems, 1*, 39–52.

Marnewick, C. (2016). Benefits of information system projects: The tale of two countries. *International Journal of Project Management, 34*(4), 748–760. doi:10.1016/j.ijproman.2015.03.016

Maroco, J., & Garcia-Marques, T. (2006). Qual a fiabilidade do alfa de Cronbach? Questões antigas e soluções modernas. *Laboratório de Psicologia, 4*(1), 65–90.

Martinsuo, M., & Killen, C. (2014). Value Management in Project Portfolios: Identifying and Assessing Strategic Value. *Project Management Journal, 45*(5), 45. doi:10.1002/pmj.21452

OCDE. (2003). The Case for E-Government: Excerpts from the OECD Report "The E-Government Imperative". *OECD Journal on Budgeting, 3*(1), 1987–1996.

Pettigrew, A., & Whipp, R. (1991). *Managing change for competitive success.* Blackwell Publishers.

PMI. (2016). *The Strategic Impact of Projects: Identify Benefits to Drive Business Results.* Project Management Institute.

Portuguese Government. (2009). Programa do XVIII Governo Constitucional para 2009 - 2013, 2009. Programa do XVIII Governo Constitucional.p.129. Portuguese parliament. https://www.parlamento.pt/orcamentoestado/documents/gop/gop_2010-2013_vf.pdf

Remenyi, D., & Sherwood-Smith, M. (1998). Business benefits from information systems through an active benefits realisation programme. *International Journal of Project Management, 16*(2), 81–98. doi:10.1016/S0263-7863(97)00024-0

Schnabl, A., & Grechenig, T. (2020). Benefit Evaluation in IT Project Portfolio Management at Austrian Financial Service Providers. In proceedings of the *3rd International Conference on Computers in Management and Business* (ICCMB '20), (pp. 290–295). ACM. 10.1145/3383845.3383889

Serra, C., & Kunc, M. (2015). Benefits Realisation Management and its influence on project success and on the execution of business strategies. *International Journal of Project Management, 33*(1), 53–66. doi:10.1016/j.ijproman.2014.03.011

Serrano, A., & Caldeira, M. M. (2002, January-March). Um Modelo para a Gestão de Investimentos em Sistemas e Tecnologias de Informação. *Revista Portuguesa de Gestão, 17*(1), 14–23.

Shichor, Y., & Zviran, M. (2016). Factors Influencing Perceived Benefits and User Satisfaction in Knowledge Management Systems. *Information Systems Management, 33*(1), 55–73. doi:10.1080/10580530.2016.1117873

Silcock, R. (2001). What is e-Government? *Parliamentary Affairs, 54*(1), 88–101. doi:10.1093/pa/54.1.88

Solow, R. (1987). We'd better watch out. *New York Times.*

UN. (2014). *United Nations E-Government Survey 2014: E-Government for the Future We Want.* New York: UN.

UN (2016). *E-Government Survey 2016: E-Government in Support of Sustainable Development.* New York: UN.

Ward, J., & Daniel, E. (2012). Benefits Management: How to increase the Business Value of Your IT Projects. John Wiley and Sons. doi:10.1002/9781119208242

Ward, J., & Daniel, E. (2013). How to deliver more business benefits from IT investments. *The European Financial Review.* http://www.europeanfinancialreview.com/?p=1033

Ward, J., & Elvin, R. (1999). A new framework for managing IT-enabled business change. *Information Systems Journal, 9*(3), 197–221. doi:10.1046/j.1365-2575.1999.00059.x

Ward, J., Taylor, P., & Bond, P. (1996). Evaluation and realisation of IS/IT benefits: An empirical study of current practice. *European Journal of Information Systems, 4*(4), 214–225. doi:10.1057/ejis.1996.3

Wijesinghe, R., Scheepers, H., & Mcloughlin, S. (2015). *Defining the optimal level of business benefits within IS/IT projects: Insights from benefit identification practices adopted in an IT Service Management (ITSM) project.* In the 6th Australasian Conference on Information Systems, Adelaide, Australia.

Winter, M., Smith, C., Morris, P., & Cicmil, S. (2006). Directions for future research in project management: The main findings of a UK government-funded research network. *International Journal of Project Management, 24*(8), 638–649. doi:10.1016/j.ijproman.2006.08.009

Yin, R. K. (2009). Case Study Research: Design and Methods, Cap 4- 6, (4th Ed.) Thousand Oaks: Sage.

APPENDIX 1

Table 6. Identifying and structuring benefits

ID	Benefit Description	MB	Metric	Value before PEPAC	Value after PEPAC	Type (a)	Source (b)	Benefit recipient Stakeholder(c)		Impact
								Main	Secondary	
B1.1	Faster application process	MB1	Average time to apply for the Program by one candidate (may include the application to several internships)	High	Low	M	CTSurv [1.b)]; PME4	Candidates	PME; PE	Very significant
B1.2	Faster selection and placement process	MB1	Interval of time from the end of the application deadline to the completion of all placements; Candidates/Trainees' satisfaction level	6 months Not available	3 months; Medium (3,45)	M	PME4; PME1; CTSurv [3.2 a)]	Candidates	PME; PE	Important
B1.3	More convenient and easier application process	MB1	Candidates' satisfaction level	Not available	High (4,37)	M	CTSurv [3.2 a)]	Candidates	PME; PE	Very significant
B1.4	Improved quality of user support	MB1	Average response time to a support request; Number of reopened support requests; Candidates/Trainees' satisfaction level	Not available	High (3,68)	M	PME3 CTSurv [Average of 3.4 a) b) c) 6.2c)]	Candidates	PME; PE	Important
B1.5	Increased reliability of services provided	MB1	Percentage of complaints	Not available	Near 0	Q	PME1	Candidates	PME; PE	Significant
B1.6	Greater transparency of processes	MB1	Number of standard processes for public access; Internet publication of the results of the placements for consultation; Candidates' satisfaction level	0 (d); No; Not available	5 (d); Yes; High (3,65)	Q	PME1; PME2; PME4; CTSurv [3.2 b)]	Candidates	Citizens; PA; Sponsor	Important
B1.7	Greater availability and easier access to information	MB1	Candidates and Trainee' satisfaction level	Not available	Very high (4,85)	Q	CTSurv [Average of 6.1 a) b)];	Candidates	PME; PE	Important
B2.1	Reduction of costs with Program applications	MB2	Cost per candidate = Σ for all candidacies of the candidate of: cost of obtaining application documents + shipping costs; Candidates' Satisfaction Level	High; Not available	Almost zero; Very high (4,52)	F	PME4; CTSurv [3.1 b)]	Candidates	Citizens; PA	Very significant
B2.2	Elimination of travel costs for candidates to submit to selection methods	MB2	Cost per candidate = Σ for all candidacies of the candidate of: Travel cost for submission to selection methods	Significant	Zero	M	CTSurv [1.b)]; PME1; PME4	Candidates	PME; PE	Very significant
B3.1	Reduction of personnel costs in the implementation of the Program	MB3	Σ for all PEs of the effort to implement the Program	3 m.h x 6 m x 210 (e)	3 m.h x 3 m (e)	F	Estimated by the author	Citizens; Sponsor; PME	PA; Sponsor; Citizens	Very significant
B3.2	Elimination of communication costs to contact candidates	MB3	Σ for all PEs of communication costs	Not available	Not available	F	PME1; PME4	PE	Sponsor; Citizens	Significant
B3.3	Elimination of other costs with program implementation.	MB3	Σ para todas as PE de outros custos para implementação Programa	Not available	Not available	F	PME1; PME4; PE2	PE	Sponsor; Citizens	Significant
B4.1	Increase in % of vacancies filled	MB4	(Number of vacancies filled / Total number of vacancies) x 100	71%	57,1%	M	PME (f); BD	Candidates	PE; PME; Sponsor	Not verified
B4.2	Greater adequacy of traineeships to trainees' qualifications	MB4	Result of survey or evaluation of workers and managers	Not available	Hight (4,1)	O	CTSurv [5.1 a)]; PME2	Candidates	PE; PME; Sponsor	No significant change
B4.3	Increased professional expertise and employability of trainees	MB4	Result of the survey of trainees	Not available	Satisfactory (3,12)	M	CTSurv [5.1 c)]	Candidates	PE; PME; Sponsor	Needs additional research
B5.1	Increased skills of PE workers	MB5	Result of survey or evaluation of workers and managers	Not available	Verified	O	PE2	PE; PME; Sponsor	PA; Citizens	Verified
B5.2	Introduction of new work processes	MB5	Result of survey or evaluation of workers and managers	Not available	Verified	O	PE2	PE; PME; Sponsor	PA; Citizens	Not verified
B6.1	Increased information available to managers and sponsor	MB6	Number of information entities available for consulting in the IS	3 (g)	6 (g)	M	PME2	PME; Sponsor	PE; Citizens	Important
B6.2	Search flexibility	MB6	Availability of *ad hoc* queries on the information provided	No	Yes	M	PME1; PME2	PME; Sponsor	PE; Citizens	Little impact

(a) F-Financial; Q-Quantifiable; M-Measurable; O-Observable. (b) DB=Data Base; CTSurv= Survey carried out, in the context of this case study, to candidates and trainees (CE); Interviewees: cf. List of Interviewees. (c) According to the analysis of stakeholders and main interests in the project. (d) Processes: Before PEPAC: Application (partially), Application Form / With PEPAC: Application, Evaluation and Selection, Notification, Placing, User Support. (e) m.h. = man hours; 210 = Number of PE in the PEPAC. (f) (DGAEP (2010c)).
(g) Information entities and attributes available: Before PEPAC: Trainees (identification), Traineeship, PE/ With PEPAC: Candidates (identification, academic qualifications, other competences); Candidate Evaluation, Trainees (identification, academic qualifications, other competences), Traineeship, Relationship between Trainees and Traineeships.

Chapter 17
Rethinking Anti-Corruption Efforts in Algeria:
The Role of Civil Society

Abderrahmane Benlahcene
https://orcid.org/0000-0003-1743-5679
Universiti Utara Malaysia, Malaysia

Hapini Awang
Universiti Utara Malaysia, Malaysia

Nurul Izaah Mohamad Ghozali
Universiti Utara Malaysia, Malaysia

ABSTRACT

The main purpose of this chapter is to scrutinize the role of civil society in curbing corruption in Algeria. This chapter argues that the active engagement of civil society actors in the fight against corruption is likely to promote a better balance between prevention and enforcement measures in addressing the ill-effects of corruption. Moreover, effective and engaged civil society is key to the realization of the United Nations 2030 Agenda for sustainable development SDGs. The conclusions drawn from this chapter will generate valuable insights into the issues of anti-corruption and civil society involvement in sustainable development in Algeria and other countries of similar social and cultural settings. Also, the chapter attempts to draw the attention of researchers, policy-makers, and anti-corruption professionals to the significant role of civil society in the collective efforts of combating corruption and strengthening institutional accountability in the country.

1. BACKGROUND

According to the World Bank, the problem of corruption has been one of the greatest obstacles to socio-economic development which does not merely lead to a maldistribution of resources but also, the loss of

DOI: 10.4018/978-1-6684-8903-1.ch017

lives and properties. Corruption undermines development by destabilizing the economic foundations of institutions and weakening the rule of law (Owusu, Chan, & Darko, 2019). Moreover, corruption corrodes the fabric of society by generating environments that foster the violation of human rights (Luna-Pla & Nicolás-Carlock, 2020). Corruption also has a direct effects on human development by negatively influencing its dimensions (health, education, and poverty) and indirectly affecting the determinants of these dimensions such as investments and economic growth (Fhima, Nouira, & Sekkat, 2023). The global cost of this phenomenon is estimated to run up to 2.6 trillion a year, which represents 5 percent of the global gross domestic product (Bautista-Beauchesne & Garzon, 2019; Fayed, 2018).

The issue of corruption has been a major issue in previous literature, political and social discourses, law and public policy, religious and philosophical texts (Wedel, 2012). Studies on the phenomenon of corruption are dispersed and variegated across a wide range of scholarly disciplines (H. Alatas, 1990; Ceschel, Hinna, & Homberg, 2022; Enste & Heldman, 2017; Mungiu-Pippidi, 2013). The previous bulk of research has established the detrimental consequences of corruption on the development process in many countries (Lambsdorff, 2006; Murshed & Mredula, 2018). Corruption weakens economic growth, equality, increases government debt, and hinders the struggle against poverty (Cardona, Ortiz, & Vázquez, 2018). It also threatens the stability of institutions, erodes trust among the different socio-economic actors, and damages the social fabric of any society (Fhima et al., 2023). Given the grave consequences of corruption on the development and stability of social, economic, and political entities especially in developing countries, the study of mechanisms and tools by which the phenomenon of corruption, in all its manifestations, can be controlled and fought against is very important. In line with this, Ipadeola (2016) argued that any discourse on the phenomenon of corruption within developing nations in the current era is not to establish its existence, as this is well established. Rather, it is needed in order to discern the various proportions, manifestations, and patterns of corruption. Particularly, to ascertain means by which we can curb its prevalent threat to the process of development (Ipadeola, 2016).

In Algeria, the widespread corruption has resulted in delaying the process of development and led to social and political unrest (Haykal, 2017; Sissani, 2016). In line with this, Limam (2012) stated that corruption has become so prevalent that it has gone from what Algerians once called the "sport of the elite" to being the "national sport". Also, corruption not only infiltrated epidemic proportions at all levels but also it has become a culture in itself (Limam, 2012). Corruption is the utmost challenge for companies intending or operating in Algeria. A large range of corrupt practices are criminalized in the legal framework in the country but means of enforcement remain a challenge and government officials engage in corruption with impunity (Integrity, 2016). Although, during the past six decades of independence, many political and social efforts have been made to make the country more immune to the problem of corruption. These efforts have proven to be futile in curbing the widespread corruption at all levels (Marwane, 2019). Syed Hussein Alatas, one of the pioneering scholars on the phenomenon of corruption in developing countries mentioned that the "determination to root out corruption is one thing and to find the means to do so another" (S. H. Alatas, 2015).

In light of the above, the argument in this chapter is that civil society in Algeria could play a significant role in combating corruption and contributing to the realization of a concrete process of sustainable development as set by the United Nations, especially SDG 16 which focuses on promoting inclusive and peaceful societies for sustainable development, build accountable and effective government institutions at all levels, and establish accessible ways to justice for all. However, civil society actors have been alienated in the process and implementation of anti-corruption efforts in the country (Guemar, 2021). Achy (2013) noted that Algerians frequently encounter political exclusion, and the country is deficient in open politi-

Table 1. Trends of corruption in Algeria (2008-2022)

Years	Ranking
2008	92/180
2009	111/180
2010	105/178
2011	112/182
2012	105/174
2013	94/177
2014	100/174
2015	88/168
2016	108/176
2017	112/180
2018	105/180
2019	106/180
2020	104/179
2021	117/180
2022	116/180

Source: Transparency International

cal systems or functional civil society organizations that can address people's grievances (Achy, 2013). The process of designing, implementing, and monitoring any anti-corruption strategy needs among other factors, a deeper understanding of the socio-economic, political, and cultural contexts. It also requires the presence of strong political will and an inclusive involvement from other non-governmental actors.

The development of strategic partnership between civil society and the state is very crucial in establishing a long-term effect of anti-corruption efforts. Also, the presence of an active and strong civil society is greatly recommended in the current anti-corruption agendas (Neshkova & Rosenbaum, 2015). Civil society is an important ally to the efforts of the state in curbing corruption and minimizing its spread within the society. Accordingly, the main objective of this chapter is to examine the role of civil society actors in curbing corruption in Algeria. In doing so, this chapter approached the problem of corruption in Algeria from two perspectives; the human rights-based approach which depicts corruption as a violation of human rights. The chapter will also look at the issue through the lenses of the collective action perspective which advocates for widespread behavior of involvement and engagement in formal or informal actions against corruption and the establishment of a society free of corruption at all levels. This chapter argues that civil society in Algeria should serve as a crucial preventive and corrective measure against corrupt activities within the country, acting as an external tool to help control corruption.

2. THEORETICAL APPROACHES

2.1 Human Rights-Based Approach

While there is no universally agreed upon human rights-based approach (HRBA), a consensus is emerging on its basic elements, including express linkages to rights, accountability, empowerment, participation, non-discrimination, and attention to vulnerable groups (Pilapitaya, 2005). This approach can be a powerful weapon in the battle against corruption, as it is centered around the victim and empowers individuals in the fight against corruption. It can also promote a bottom-up approach to combating corruption and increase the social stigma of corrupt behavior (Institute, 2017). This perspective implies that rights-holders within the civil society both have a right and an interest in keeping public sector officials, as duty-bearer, accountable for the use of public resources. Therefore, there is both an expectation and a democratic imperative that civil society plays its role as the ultimate controller of the public purse (Disch, Vigeland, Sundet, & Gibson, 2009). Investigating the socio-legal values underlying a human rights-based strategy against corruption could assist in establishing the significance of humanizing anti-corruption initiatives, going beyond punitive measures to address the root causes of corruption. Recognizing that corruption is inextricably intertwined with human rights violations, this approach advocates for a thorough grasp of corruption's social, economic, and political components.

As Cornwall (2002) argued, this approach gives a very different perspective to development; instead of talking about "beneficiaries with needs" or "consumers with choices" the human rights approach speaks of "citizens with rights." Citizens are active subjects in the political sphere, not objects of intervention by government programs or passive choosers in the marketplace (Ackerman, 2014). Moreover, John C. Mubangizi and Sewpersadh (2017) describe HRBA as an approach that enables people to know and claim their rights, as well as strengthening the ability and accountability of individuals and institutions responsible for respecting, defending, and fulfilling rights. This entails offering people more opportunities to influence decisions that affect their human rights. It also entails improving the ability of individuals charged with fulfilling rights to understand and respect those rights, as well as ensuring that they can be held accountable (John C. Mubangizi & Sewpersadh, 2017). Furthermore, exploring the phenomenon of corruption through the lenses of human rights steers our attention to the accountability and obligations of the state to facilitate the establishment and maintenance of a society in which human dignity is promoted and human rights are respected. To a certain degree this means examining the existing discourses of the features that are considered to be significant for the idea of a good society and the consequences of corruption on these features. Also, it involves scrutiny of ideas of development, democracy, accountability of power, the rule of law (Pearson, 1999).

A human rights-based approach ensures that citizens can hold public officials and representatives accountable for their actions, by demanding responsibility and transparency (John C Mubangizi, 2020). Additionally, Pearson (1999) stated that investigating an issue through a human rights perspective implies an emphasis on the consequences that a practice or a policy has on the fundamental rights of people. It includes acknowledgement that people have inherent rights, the protection of which must have recognition in the practices and policies of the state. It also includes examining these practices and policies to determine their effectiveness or otherwise in preserving human rights (Pearson, 1999). Given that human rights are defined as those rights that are inherent to being human, corruption poses a significant threat to these rights. This is because it undermines accountability, violates numerous international human rights agreements, and contradicts fundamental principles such as human dignity, equality, social justice, and non-discrimination (John C. Mubangizi & Sewpersadh, 2017).

There are two elements to the relationship between human rights and corruption. First, corruption can have a detrimental impact on human rights realization, and second, corruption can directly or indirectly violate a specific human rights or norms. This perspective offers a foundation for the most vulnerable to hold governments legally accountable for their failings and subsequent violations of human rights. This, in turn, can have an effect on their general human well-being. According to the United Nations Convention Against Corruption, "a comprehensive and multidisciplinary approach is required to effectively prevent and combat corruption." As a result, it is believed that an adoption of HRBA in conjunction with the traditional means of controlling corruption will result in a more effective strategy to address the problem (de Man, 2022). The human rights-based approach provides a valuable perspective for examining and addressing corruption in both developed and developing countries. By recognizing citizens as rights-holders, this approach offers a more comprehensive understanding of the far-reaching effects of corruption, which not only impact financial and economic development but also other crucial aspects of societal development in communities affected by systemic corruption.

2.2 Collective Action Approach

A growing number of authors argue that the wide-scale failure of anti-corruption efforts stems from the flawed theoretical foundations that underpin their design. Anti-corruption programs are largely based on principal-agent theory, which portrays corruption as occurring when public officials with discretion over public services lack accountability. This approach focuses on the rational decision-making that drives individual acts of corruption and assumes that corruption can be addressed through policies that alter these calculations. However, critics contend that these assumptions are flawed, particularly in contexts where corruption is systemic and best understood as a collective action problem (Heather Marquette & Peiffer, 2015). Collective action theories challenge the assumption that every society has a group of actors willing to act as "principals" and enforce monitoring and punishment regimes, as proposed by the principal-agent framework. Instead, they question the relevance of such regimes because they assume that all actors, including rulers, bureaucrats, and citizens, are self-interested maximizers. However, this does not mean that all actors are necessarily corrupt. Instead, collective action theory recognizes that rationality is bounded and dependent on shared expectations about how others will behave (Mugellini, Della Bella, Colagrossi, Isenring, & Killias, 2021; Persson, Rothstein, & Teorell, 2010).

According to (Mungiu-Pippidi, 2013), the collective action viewpoint provides a framework for understanding how individuals, communities, and organizations may effectively collaborate to restrict corruption. The theory of collective action was brought to prominence by Olson (1965), who explored the challenges associated with the production of public goods by groups. Since then, Olson's thesis on collective action has been applied to a wide range of other goods as well as other disciplines. Collective action theory can also be applied to the case of corruption, where corruption is seen as a manifestation of the free-riding phenomenon. This is due to the belief that corruption involves putting one's personal interests ahead of the collective interest, with the collective interest in this case being either quite abstract or concrete. In an abstract sense, a group may want no corruption so that they can live under an impartial public administration or government, while in a concrete sense, corruption can visibly reduce resources earmarked for public use, such as funds required for the delivery of public services, which can be depleted by corruption (Marczell, 2018; Heather Marquette, Pavarala, & Malik, 2014; Heather Marquette & Peiffer, 2015).

Researchers have extensively studied the factors that influence an individual's decision to contribute to collective action, and among these factors, the understanding of trust within the group appears to be the most important. This emphasizes the collective aspect of corruption rather than conceptualizing it as an individual behavior. In other words, corruption arises from mutual distrust in society and the norms that emerge end up solidifying systemic corruption. This is because a lack of trust in others means that the rational choice for an individual is to be corrupt, and so it is the larger group that must instill the foundations for non-corrupt behavior. Therefore, according to the collective action theory, trust or perception towards other members in the group is critical for overcoming corruption (Marczell, 2018). Collective action theory highlights the significance of intra-group trust in shaping individual decisions, but it has further contributions to offer. When applied to corruption, this theory emphasizes that individual decisions about engaging in corruption are not made in isolation, but rather within the context of wider society and the behavior of others. Therefore, factors such as monitoring, transparency, and sanctions, which influence an individual's decision to engage in corruption, must also take into account the potential impact of group dynamics, which may encourage free riding (Heather Marquette & Peiffer, 2015; Perumal, 2023). Coordination of efforts among many anti-corruption players, as well as the conundrum of free riding, in which individuals or organizations are hesitant to actively participate owing to fear of punishment or the belief that others would act on their behalf, can stymie development. To overcome these problems, trust must be built, incentives must be created, and effective leadership and coordination must be ensured (Mungiu-Pippidi, 2013). Building trust among stakeholders promotes collaboration, while awarding incentives or recognition for anti-corruption efforts might stimulate active participation. Effective coordination procedures and strong leadership are also required for the successful implementation of collective anti-corruption activities.

In this chapter, we argue that corruption in Algeria must be perceived as a collective problem and the eradication of it as a collective responsibility that requires the involvement of all members of society, including government officials, civil society organizations, and communities. Only by working together can we challenge the current state of affairs and promote integrity for lasting change (Khair, 2018). The reframing of systemic corruption as a collective action rather than a principal-agent problem has significant policy implications. In particular, curbing corruption requires altering the beliefs of actors about the behavior of other actors regarding corrupt practices, so that most actors trust most other actors to act fairly (Bauhr, 2017; Persson et al., 2010). Moreover, in contexts where corruption is prevalent it is unlikely that the use of punishment regimes and monitoring devices will be effective, given the fact that there will be one willing to impose accountability on corrupt public officials (Peiffer & Walton, 2022; Persson et al., 2010). More specifically, as stated by Persson, Rothstein, and Teorell (2013), In thoroughly corrupt settings, corruption more closely resembles a collective action problem, which can lead to the failure of anti-corruption reforms that are based on the principal-agent framework. This is because such reforms assume the existence of non-corruptible 'principals,' which may not be true in corrupt settings (Persson et al., 2013). Thus, measures for monitoring and punishment should also be backed by methods that can foster intra-group trust, which will help align the efforts of society members towards eradicating corruption. Civil society actors in Algeria must recognize that bringing about change requires more than just enacting new laws or establishing new anti-corruption agencies.

3. THE NEXUS BETWEEN SUSTAINABLE DEVELOPMENT, CIVIL SOCIETY, AND ANTI-CORRUPTION

The pursuit of sustainable development goals is a global commitment to address the pressing challenges facing humanity, including environmental conservation, poverty eradication, and equitable development. The achievement of SDGs depends in part on the role of civil society, which encompasses a diverse array of non-governmental organizations, community groups, and activists advocating for social change. One of the key obstacles in realizing SDGs is corruption, which impedes progress, erodes public trust, and diverts resources away from development initiatives. Civil society plays a crucial role in advancing sustainable development by mobilizing grassroots movements, raising awareness, and holding governments and corporations accountable. As the voice of marginalized communities, civil society actors foster inclusivity and ensure that development efforts are responsive to the needs and concerns of all citizens. Furthermore, Civil society organizations act as conduits for citizen participation, encouraging active involvement in decision-making processes, and thereby empowering communities to become stakeholders in the pursuit of sustainable development.

The United Nations' Sustainable Development Goals (SDGs) agenda, which was initially embraced by the 193 member states, is now being increasingly adopted by non-governmental organizations, public policy bodies, and private sector organizations beyond the UN's scope. Corruption can be seen to be a salient threat to achieving universal improvement in economy, society and environment across the globe. The United Nations SDGs, a set of 17 high-level goals and 169 corresponding targets, which all United Nations Member States adopted in 2015, articulate a ubiquitous plan towards such an improved future. The complexity of corruption, its scale of impact, and potential threat to the achievement of the SDGs, that makes it particularly worthy of study as a serious problem (Hunter, Uwaydah Mardini, El-Seblani, & Elsayed, 2020; Muurlink & Macht, 2020). The pervasiveness of corruption in Africa and other developing countries impedes development progress and exacerbates poverty, depriving marginalized populations of equitable access to crucial public goods and services required for sustainable development. Consequently, tackling corruption is crucial for achieving the SDGs, and addressing the root of the problem has become a top policy priority for development institutions and an increasing number of countries. In that respect, SDG 16 aims "*to promote peaceful and inclusive societies for sustainable development, provide access to justice for all and build effective, accountable and inclusive institutions at all levels*". Among its targets (Target 16.5) is "*to substantially reduce corruption and bribery in all their forms" (Emara, 2020; Hope, 2022).*

The detrimental effects of corruption on the economy, society, and politics have been comprehensively documented, which has prompted significant organizations to accentuate the significance of decreasing corruption. This includes, but is not limited to, the United Nations' Sustainable Development Goals, where fighting corruption is not only an explicit objective but also widely recognized as a crucial prerequisite for the successful execution of other SDGs geared towards poverty alleviation, healthcare improvement, and educational advancement (Gans-Morse et al., 2018). The attainment of sustainable development is hindered where corruption and bribery are rampant. In fact, corruption creates more "sand than grease" in the wheels of development. Consequently, persistent corruption impedes sustainable development, making it imperative to address corruption in order to advance development (Hope, 2022). Therefore, African countries should, as a matter of urgency, establish a functional institutional framework that will help to eradicate corruption, which is undermining the continent and obstructing the attainment of national goals such as the Sustainable Development Goals (Ahmed & Anifowose, 2023).

Understanding the broader impact of civil society engagement in supporting accountable and transparent governance systems requires understanding the link between civil society's role in combating corruption and Sustainable Development Goal 16 (SDG 16). Laberge and Touihri (2019) suggest that civil society organizations can help hold governments responsible and advocate for evidence-based anti-corruption policies by monitoring and analyzing SDG 16 indicators relating to corruption, access to justice, and transparency. Civil society's active participation in utilizing SDG 16 data enables them to advocate for policy changes, enhance anti-corruption measures, and create an enabling climate for sustainable development. Civil society organizations are uniquely positioned to monitor government institutions, raise awareness about corruption dangers, and push for effective anti-corruption policies (Radin, 2019).

Civil society organizations can help to promote open, accountable, and efficient public institutions by aligning their work with the values of sustainable development goals. This, in turn, promotes sustainable development by assuring equitable resource allocation, decreasing corruption risks, and increasing citizen service delivery. The active participation of civil society in anti-corruption measures extends beyond basic data monitoring. Their participation entails encouraging citizen participation, promoting openness, and lobbying for policy changes. Civil society organizations can empower individuals and communities to actively participate in decision-making processes and demand greater responsibility from public institutions through awareness campaigns, public consultations, and grassroots mobilization. Civil society contributes to the attainment of SDG 16's objectives and the larger sustainable development strategy by amplifying the voices of marginalized groups and encouraging inclusivity. To fully realize the potential of civil society in combating corruption and achieving SDG 16, it is critical to strengthen their capacities, provide resources, and create an enabling environment for their operations (Laberge & Touihri, 2019). This involves ensuring their freedom of expression, improving access to information, and involving them in policy-making processes. In addition, increasing collaboration and knowledge-sharing across civil society organizations at various levels can increase their overall influence and contribute to more effective anti-corruption efforts (Radin, 2019).

Finally, the literature emphasizes the critical link between civil society', combating corruption, and SDG 16. Civil society organizations function as change agents, actively monitoring, advocating, and mobilizing grassroots support to promote transparency, accountability, and inclusive governance. Civil society organizations contribute to the accomplishment of sustainable development goals and build a culture of integrity and good governance by aligning their actions and those of the government with the ideals of SDGs. Policymakers and stakeholders must recognize and support civil society's critical role in anti-corruption initiatives, as they are significant partners in establishing a more just, peaceful, and sustainable future. Taking into account that corruption impedes development objectives, and one of the fundamental steps in establishing a lasting solution to corruption is by recognizing corrupt practices as symptoms of a deeper issue in the relationship between the state and society in general, and in the functioning of democracy in particular (Ackerman, 2014). It is imperative that civil society organizations be included in the development process and in any genuine efforts to curb corruption.

The interdependent relationship between Sustainable Development, civil society, and anti-corruption efforts is clear in their reciprocal support towards a shared objective – a fair, just, and sustainable world. The active involvement of civil society is crucial in promoting transparency, accountability, and civic participation, thereby minimizing corruption's impact and advancing sustainable development in Algeria. The Algerian government must acknowledge the indispensable role of civil society in shaping policy, implementing anti-corruption measures, and driving transformative change. Only by fostering strong partnerships and collaborative efforts can we envision a future where sustainable development and a corruption-free country become a reality.

4. DISCUSSION

In the last two decades, countries with widespread corruption, primarily located in developing regions of the world, have implemented anti-corruption reforms with international support. However, the success of these efforts has been limited, and many of these countries remain as corrupt as before. As a result, little progress has been made in reducing corruption in these countries (Dikmen & Çiçek, 2023; Persson et al., 2013). Algeria experiences grand corruption, where high-ranking public officials, top leaders, and managers of state-owned companies exploit their power for personal gain at the expense of the public good. Additionally, the country faces petty corruption, involving everyday abuse of power by low and mid-level bureaucrats, both in local authorities and the central administration (Achy, 2013; Saha & Ali, 2017). According to the 2022 Corruption Index released by Transparency International, Algeria's position on a global scale is indicative of high levels of corruption within the country, as it ranked 116 out of 180 nations. Despite the pervasive corruption in Algeria (Josua, 2017) and the threat it poses to the country's socio-economic development, the government's efforts to address the issue over the years have been insufficiently grounded in a comprehensive understanding of the underlying causes of corruption and the essential elements required for effective anti-corruption policies.

The implementation of anti-corruption measures should be tailored to the specific context and inclusive of various civil society actors in the country. The fight against corruption, which is a complex and deeply ingrained problem, requires the participation of society as a whole in order to achieve positive results. In Algeria, the credibility of political authorities in their anti-corruption efforts is being called into question by the public, who are frustrated with the lack of concrete action resulting from past campaigns (Hadjadj, 2007). Taking into account the protests against the former President Abdelaziz Bouteflika and the leading figures of the Algerian government, it can be inferred that these demonstrations were primarily motivated by economic stagnation and widespread corruption that affected most political, economic, and social sectors (Wolf, 2019), it is vital for both researchers and policymakers to conduct a more comprehensive analysis of the issues surrounding corruption and institutional accountability from multiple viewpoints in order to devise and implement effective anti-corruption strategies that can support sustainable development. Algeria ratified the United Nations Convention Against Corruption in 2004 and enacted a corruption prevention law in 2006. Subsequently, in 2006, the National Commission for the Prevention and Combating of Corruption was established. However, the president did not appoint the commission's seven members until 2010, and it has yet to produce any tangible outcomes. Despite the government's repeated anti-corruption pledges, most have been largely symbolic (Achy, 2013).

Corruption is a pervasive issue that transcends time, place, and cultural differences, affecting society regardless of political regime, social norms, or economic conditions. It can occur in various sectors, from government to businesses, law enforcement, and judiciary, and have a profound impact on the most vulnerable members of society. Regardless of its scope, corruption undermines trust in institutions and hinders economic development (Fayed, 2018; Serrat, 2017). Therefore, anti-corruption measures should be developed with a comprehensive understanding of the relevant contextual factors. In this chapter, we contend that civil society is a crucial player in the fight against corruption, as it can help galvanize anti-corruption efforts, foster trust among various stakeholders, and supplement existing measures implemented by the state. Moreover, in order to comprehend the deficiencies of the existing measures taken to eliminate corruption in Algeria, it is crucial to ask the right questions in relation to the ongoing battle against corruption. According to Rothstein (2011), a society that aims to address systemic corruption and establish 'good governance' needs to ask itself two crucial questions. Firstly, what types of structural reforms are required to reduce corruption? Some suggestions include creating new or modifying existing legal institutions to alter the incentive structures for bribes. Secondly, what types of processes are likely to be effective in implementing these reforms? Although research on corruption has primarily focused on the first question, the second question about the change of processes, strategies, and agents' cognition has been largely overlooked (Rothstein, 2011).

Elsayed (2021) claims that the permanent state of emergency and unstable political environment in Algeria are significant contributors to corruption. Which has resulted in the president, ruling party, and military having robust control over the country and its political and economic activities. As a result, the lack of respect for the rule of law and growing income inequality among the population are considered the primary causes of corruption in Algeria (Elsayed, 2021). While these certainly play a role in the ongoing problem of corruption in the country and are reasons why previous anti-corruption measures have failed, we believe that the roots of corruption are much more complex and deeply ingrained. Additionally, portraying the formal authorities as the sole perpetrator is oversimplifying the issue and does not effectively address the causes of corruption in Algeria. According to Ackerman (2014), reformers and researchers should not be tempted to depict the problem of corruption in developing countries as the result of a bureaucratic breakdown or of fragile rule of law. These approaches restrict policy options to a series of superficial choices which generally do not generate long-term outcomes.

The pervasiveness of corruption in Algeria is not solely attributed to the actions of official institutions, but rather it is exacerbated by a culture of acceptance and tolerance among many stakeholders in the country. However, the absence of a vibrant civil society, which can act as a watchdog by monitoring government actions and corporate practices, has exacerbated the problem. Prabowo, Sriyana, and Syamsudin (2018) argued that with corruption being deeply ingrained in the culture and system of many countries, it is imperative for successful anti-corruption measures to be implemented for economic growth and development to occur. Additionally, according to Limam (2012), effective corruption control measures in Algeria require a comprehensive national policy of reforms that address the country's political, economic, social, and cultural structures (Limam, 2012).

An active and dynamic civil society is a crucial factor in the success of anti-corruption efforts in Algeria (Haykal, 2017) and the partnership between the state and civil society is a sine qua non condition to effective anti-corruption initiatives. However, civil society organizations in Algeria encounter numerous challenges in executing their oversight role effectively and have been sidelined in anti-corruption initiatives in the country (Jasmin & Bunk, 2017). In addition, By the early 2000s, Algeria had approximately 66,000 civil society organizations, with over 900 operating on a national scale. However, these organizations faced limitations in their ability to maneuver, as they were subject to political pressures through biased funding, intimidation, and a lack of autonomy. Furthermore, civil society associations were weak and unable to impact decision-making processes (Achy, 2013; Muradova, 2016; Thieux, 2019). Currently, it is challenging to secure a comprehensive understanding of the Algerian civil society. The number of active civil society organizations is estimated to be over 100,000, but a considerable portion of these organizations are dormant in practice (Jasmin & Bunk, 2017). Moreover, these organizations have no effective communication or collaboration among them. This situation has led to a state of confusion pertaining the exact number of existing bodies, which has served the state well in justifying operations of "cleansing" and imposing further restriction on the activities of civil society in the country (Bessadi, 2019).

In a state with widespread corruption, it is simpler for critics to be silenced, human rights to be violated, and justice to be subverted. When corruption is rampant, basic freedoms and human rights are endangered, and social and economic interactions become unpredictable (Pilapitaya, 2005). The effectiveness of civil society organizations in engaging in their role depends on the political space available, which is often restricted in more authoritarian states where rent exaction is a crucial aspect of the power structure, leading to systematic constraints on their activities (Disch et al., 2009). In the Algerian case, it should be noted that political parties and civil society associations that came into existence in the absence of transparency have been influenced by this dysfunctional environment at all levels (Limam, 2012). While the Algerian government has made some efforts to tackle the problem of corruption throughout the past years. Yet, the role of civil society has been overlooked in anti-corruption initiatives in the country (Benlahcene & Abdullah, 2021). This chapter highlights the potential for Algerian civil society organizations to contribute to anti-corruption efforts, provided they have the necessary conditions to collaborate effectively with the government. In the same line, Dixit (2018) asserted that corruption is a composite and multi-dimensional problem which requires multi-directional anti-corruption efforts (Dixit, 2018).

There is a growing body of scholarly research that recognizes the importance of civil society in curbing corruption (Grimes, 2008; Kumari, 2013). Civil society organizations are an important component of anti-corruption policies in both developed and developing countries (Themudo, 2013). However, Limam (2012) argued that civil society organizations in Algeria have contributed in facilitating ways of corruption. He also suggested that one of the main causes of corruption in Algeria is the state of civil society. Additionally, the Algerian civil society has been considered by many to lack any genuineness, and can be depicted as merely a facade presented by the Algerian government in an attempt to appear to liberalize (Butcher, 2014). Nonetheless, the problems, challenges, and circumstances surrounding the activities of civil society in Algeria are unclear and lack a proper examination which can assist in understanding the current situation and help in placing this sector in the right track in order to maximize its contribution to the anti-corruption efforts. It is crucial to understand the role of civil society in the fight against corruption in Algeria, including its efforts and the challenges it faces, in order to gain insights that can help address existing problems and improve the current situation.

Civil society organizations play an important role in mobilizing collective actions against corruption by raising awareness, encouraging citizen participation, and putting pressure on government institutions to enact anti-corruption policies (H Marquette & Peiffer, 2014). These organizations are seen as important participants in the battle against corruption because they raise public awareness of the negative consequences of corruption and empower individuals to act. Civil society organizations provide a platform for citizens to express their concerns and demand change through campaigns, marches, and advocacy projects (H Marquette & Peiffer, 2014). To ensure the success of anti-corruption measures, it is critical to establish collaborative networks that include multiple stakeholders such as government agencies, non-governmental organizations (NGOs), the media, and foreign organizations. (Martín, 2014) emphasizes the importance of developing these networks because they bring varied ideas and resources together and work to improve transparency, accountability, and integrity in the fight against corruption.

In this chapter, we contend that Algerian civil society actors should assume a critical role in raising social and cultural awareness about the consequences of corruption by acting as a potent catalyst for change. Through various public awareness campaigns, advocacy initiatives, community engagement programs, and by highlighting the adverse impacts of corruption on all stakeholders. Civil society organizations in Algeria should promote a culture of accountability and transparency, encouraging citizens to actively participate in anti-corruption efforts and demand greater integrity from public officials and institutions. By empowering communities with knowledge and fostering collective action, civil society can help in building intra-group trust and galvanize collective forces to combat corruption and cultivate a society committed to upholding ethical principles. Heather Marquette and Peiffer (2015) emphasized the importance of tailoring anti-corruption efforts to the specific context, which requires a deep understanding of contextual factors. This is not a new idea, but it cannot be overstated. The context should drive anti-corruption efforts, rather than theory or models, regardless of the inspiration for interventions, whether they are based on principal-agent or collective action theories, or something else entirely (Heather Marquette & Peiffer, 2015). Likewise, there is a need for anti-corruption agendas, policies, and initiatives that are tailored to the current situation in Algeria.

5. CONCLUSION

While the issue of corruption in Algeria is well acknowledged, there is a lack of understanding regarding the root causes of the problem, the role of civil society in addressing its effects, and its impact on the country development. Further empirical analysis is needed to explore these uncharted territories. To date, the topic received scant attention in the previous body of literature and most studies on the problem of corruption are conceptual in nature. Although, some studies have attempted to explore the phenomenon of corruption and its causes and ramifications, there is very few empirical studies that covered the role of civil society in curbing corruption in Algeria. This calls for sound investigation in order to shed lights on the important role of civil society in the fight against corruption and its implications.

With growing understanding of the damaging impact of corruption on development, formulating effective anti-corruption measures is now a paramount concern in policy-making circles. It is important to understand the ill-effects of corruption on human rights, its role in eroding trust within society, and impeding socio-economic development in Algeria. Likewise, establishing the significance of collective actions against corruption by various formal and informal institutions in the country is crucial to the development of effective anti-corruption measures. Particularly, there is a need for fostering the involvement of civil society in combatting corruption and attaining sustainable development goals in Algeria. Civil society organizations must be strengthened, and collaborative networks that foster stakeholders' cooperation must be established. By doing so, public institutions can get closer to being more transparent, accountable, and corrupt-free. More research should be done to investigate the impact and effectiveness of collective action projects in the Algerian context. Such research efforts would provide useful insights into how to improve their impact on the ongoing battle against corruption. Also, understanding the sociopolitical processes and cultural aspects that motivate collective action in Algeria is critical for fostering lasting social change.

The chapter is expected to ignite new interest in the examination of the role of civil society actors in Algeria in combating corruption. This will help in enriching the discussion on issues relevant to the role of civil society in Algeria and the Arab region. Further analysis of different aspects of anti-corruption efforts in Algeria will generate theoretical and practical insights into the study of civil society and anti-corruption efforts not just in Algeria but also other Arab states of similar political, social, and cultural settings. Practically, the issues brought to light in this chapter will be important in pushing for more sound examination of the role of various actors of civil society in their efforts to curb corruption. This deeper understanding which will be generated through empirical analysis will help researchers, policy-makers, and anti-corruption activists in establishing their efforts and agendas on a better understanding of the issue. Theoretically, various theories and methods have been employed in combating corruption across countries and regions. However, no single approach or method has gained universal acceptance as the most appropriate for all contexts and circumstances, owing to the unique social, cultural, and institutional characteristics of each state and society. We argue that part of an explanation to why anti-corruption reforms in Algeria plagued failed is that they are based on a theoretical mischaracterization and lack of sound understanding of the various causes of the problem. This chapter lays the groundwork for future research that should focus on exploring a range of issues and aspects related to anti-corruption efforts in Algeria. Such research will help optimize the collective efforts of anti-corruption in Algeria.

6. REFERENCES

Achy, L. (2013). *The price of stability in Algeria* (Vol. 25). Carnegie Endowment for International Peace.

Ackerman, J. M. (2014). Rethinking the International Anti-corruption Agenda: Civil Society, Human Rights and Democracy. *American University International Law Review*, *29*(2), 2.

Ahmed, A., & Anifowose, M. (2023). Corruption, corporate governance, and sustainable development goals in Africa. *Corporate Governance: The International Journal of Business in Society*.

Alatas, H. (1990). *Corruption: Its nature, causes, and functions*. Avebury.

Alatas, S. H. (2015). *The problem of corruption*. The Other Press.

Bauhr, M. (2017). Need or greed? Conditions for collective action against corruption. *Governance: An International Journal of Policy, Administration and Institutions*, *30*(4), 561–581. doi:10.1111/gove.12232

Bautista-Beauchesne, N., & Garzon, C. J. (2019). *Conceptualizing corruption prevention: a systematic literature review*. Research Gate.

Benlahcene, A., & Abdullah, N. S. B. (2021). *Anti-corruption Efforts in Algeria: Prevention Through Non-State Actors*. Paper presented at the Proceedings of the 2nd International Conference on Government and Public Affairs 2021 (ICOGPA2021), Malaysia.

Bessadi, N. (2019). *Algerian activists demand a place at the table*. Qantara. https://en.qantara.de/content/civil-society-and-democratic-transition-in-algeria-algerian-activists-demand-a-place-at-the

Butcher, C. (2014). Can oil-reliant countries democratize? An assessment of the role of civil society in Algeria. *Democratization*, *21*(4), 722–742. doi:10.1080/13510347.2013.769959

Cardona, L. A., Ortiz, H., & Vázquez, D. J. H. R. Q. (2018). Corruption and Human Rights. *Possible Relations.*, *40*(2), 317–341.

Ceschel, F., Hinna, A., & Homberg, F. (2022). Public Sector Strategies in Curbing Corruption: A Review of the Literature. *Public Organization Review*, *22*(3), 571–591. doi:10.100711115-022-00639-4

Cornwall, A. (2002). *Beneficiary consumer citizen: perspectives on participation for poverty reduction* (Vol. 2). Swedish International Development Cooperation Agency.

de Man, A. (2022). Reconsidering corruption as a violation of the rights to equality and non-discrimination based on poverty in South Africa. *Journal for Juridical Science*, *47*(1), 52–76. doi:10.18820/24150517/JJS47.i1.3

Dikmen, S., & Çiçek, H. G. (2023). Fighting against corruption and bribery in public procurements during the Covid-19 pandemic. In The Ethics of Bribery: Theoretical and Empirical Studies (pp. 309-328): Springer. doi:10.1007/978-3-031-17707-1_18

Disch, A., Vigeland, E., Sundet, G., & Gibson, S. (2009). Anti-corruption approaches: A literature review. Retrieved from Dixit, A. (2018). Anti-corruption institutions: Some history and theory. In Institutions, Governance and the Control of Corruption (pp. 15-49): Springer.

Elsayed, D. (2021). Corruption in North Africa: Monopoly of Power and Widespread Ignorance. In P. M. H. Dan Hough (Ed.), *Corruption in the MENA Region: Beyond Uprisings* (pp. 165–234). Palgrave Macmillan. doi:10.1007/978-3-030-55314-2_7

Emara, A. M. (2020). The impact of corruption on human development in egypt. *Asian Economic and Financial Review*, *10*(5), 574–589. doi:10.18488/journal.aefr.2020.105.574.589

Enste, D., & Heldman, C. (2017). *Causes and consequences of corruption: An overview of empirical results*. Retrieved from Fayed, A. A. (2018). Researching corruption: understanding its key concepts. *Rule of Law and Anti-corruption Center Journal*, *2018*(2), 11.

Fhima, F., Nouira, R., & Sekkat, K. (2023). How does corruption affect sustainable development? A threshold non-linear analysis. *Economic Analysis and Policy*, *78*, 505–523. doi:10.1016/j.eap.2023.03.020

Gans-Morse, J., Borges, M., Makarin, A., Mannah-Blankson, T., Nickow, A., & Zhang, D. (2018). Reducing bureaucratic corruption: Interdisciplinary perspectives on what works. *World Development*, *105*, 171–188. doi:10.1016/j.worlddev.2017.12.015

Grimes, M. J. Q. (2008). *The conditions of successful civil society involvement in combating corruption: A survey of case study evidence*. Research Gate.

Guemar, K. (2021). Prevention of institutional corruption and mechanisms to combat it (Constituents and constraints). مجلة الأبحاث القانونية والسياسية.

Hadjadj, D. J. M. P. (2007). Algeria: A Future Hijacked by Corruption. *PERSPECTIVE*, *12*(2), 263–277.

Haykal, S. H. (2017). Fighting Corruption in MENA Region: Towards a Conceptual Framework. *Middle East Review of Public Administration*, *3*(2), 1833.

Hope, S. Sr. (2022). Reducing corruption and bribery in Africa as a target of the sustainable development goals: Applying indicators for assessing performance. *Journal of Money Laundering Control*, *25*(2), 313–329. doi:10.1108/JMLC-03-2021-0018

Hunter, M., Uwaydah Mardini, R., El-Seblani, A., & Elsayed, S. (2020). Anti-corruption, transparency and accountability: case study of healthcare in the Arab countries. *Global Health Action*, *13*(sup1), 1704529.

RW Institute. (2017). *Anti-corruption and Human Rights: How to become mutually reinforcing?* RW Institute. https://rwi.lu.se/publications/anti-corruption-human-rights-become-mutually-reinforcing/

Gan Integrity. (2016). *Algeria: Country Profile.* Gan Integrity. https://www.ganintegrity.com/portal/country-profiles/algeria/

Ipadeola, O. (2016). Qualitative study on the patterns, experiences and manifestations of corruption in Nigeria. In Jasmin, L., & Bunk, B. (2017). *Using civil society as an authoritarian legitimation strategy: Algeria and Mozambique in comparative perspective. Democratization, 24*(6), 987–1005.

Josua, M. (2017). Legitimation towards whom? Managing the legitimacy crisis in Algeria during the Arab Uprisings. *Political Behavior, 11*(2), 301–324.

Khair, S. (2018). UNCAC and civil society activism against corruption in Bangladesh. In Asian Yearbook of International Law, 20, 115-162. doi:10.1163/9789004379770_005

Kumari, R. (2013). Role of civil society for combating corruption in India. *International Journal of Innovative Research and Development, 2*(3), 34–50.

Laberge, M., & Touihri, N. (2019). Can SDG 16 data drive national accountability? A cautiously optimistic view. *Global Policy, 10*(S1), 153–156. doi:10.1111/1758-5899.12607

Lambsdorff, J. G. (2006). Causes and consequences of corruption: What do we know from a cross-section of countries. *RePEc Econpapers, 1*, 3-51.

Limam, M. H. (2012). Detailed analysis of the phenomenon of political corruption in Algeria: Causes, repercussions and reform. *Contemporary Arab Affairs, 5*(2), 252–278. doi:10.1080/17550912.2012.671999

Luna-Pla, I., & Nicolás-Carlock, J. R. (2020). Corruption and complexity: A scientific framework for the analysis of corruption networks. *Applied Network Science, 5*(1), 1–18. doi:10.100741109-020-00258-2

Marczell, Z. (2018). *The Effect of Civil Society Organizations on Corruption Perception: The Case of EU28.* (M.Sc. Public Policy and Human Development). Maastricht University, .

Marquette, H., Pavarala, V., & Malik, K. K. (2014). Religion and attitudes towards corruption in India: A collective action problem? *Development in Practice, 24*(7), 854–866.

Marquette, H., & Peiffer, C. (2014). Corruption and collective action: Shifting the equilibrium. *Research Paper,* (32).

Marquette, H., & Peiffer, C. (2015). *Collective action and systemic corruption.* Paper presented at the ECPR Joint Sessions of Workshops, University of Warsaw.

Martín, A. N. (2014). Internal Investigations, Whistle-Blowing, and Cooperation: The Struggle for Information in the Criminal Process. *Preventing Corporate Corruption: The Anti-Bribery Compliance Model*, 69-92.

Marwane, A. (2019). The Uncertain Future of Algeria's Anti-corruption Battles. *FIKRA Forum*. https://www.washingtoninstitute.org/fikraforum/view/the-uncertain-future-of-algerias-anti-corruption-battles

Mubangizi, J. C. (2020). A human rights based approach to fighting corruption in Uganda and South Africa: Shared perspectives and comparative lessons. *Law. Democracy & Development*, *24*(1), 225–247. doi:10.17159/2077-4907/2020/ldd.v24.10

Mubangizi, J. C., & Sewpersadh, P. (2017). A Human Rights-based Approach to Combating Public Procurement Corruption in Africa. *African Journal of Legal Studies*, *10*(1), 66–90. doi:10.1163/17087384-12340015

Mugellini, G., Della Bella, S., Colagrossi, M., Isenring, G. L., & Killias, M. (2021). Public sector reforms and their impact on the level of corruption: A systematic review. *Campbell Systematic Reviews*, *17*(2), e1173. doi:10.1002/cl2.1173 PMID:37131927

Mungiu-Pippidi, A. (2013). Controlling corruption through collective action. *Journal of Democracy*, *24*(1), 101–115. doi:10.1353/jod.2013.0020

Muradova, L. (2016). Oil wealth and authoritarianism: Algeria in the Arab Spring. *Revista Española de Ciencia Política*, *40*, 63–89.

Murshed, M., & Mredula, F. (2018). Impacts of corruption on sustainable development: A simultaneous equations model estimation approach. *Journal of Accounting. Finance and Economics*, *8*(1), 109–133.

Muurlink, O., & Macht, S. A. (2020). Managing (out) corruption in NGOs: A case study from the Bangladesh delta. *Journal of Management & Organization*, *26*(6), 1014–1029. doi:10.1017/jmo.2020.17

Neshkova, M. I., & Rosenbaum, A. (2015). Advancing good government through fighting corruption. In Handbook of Public Administration.

Owusu, E. K., Chan, A. P., & Darko, A. (2019). Thematic overview of corruption in infrastructure procurement process. *Journal of Infrastructure Systems*, *25*(2), 02519001. doi:10.1061/(ASCE)IS.1943-555X.0000484

Pearson, Z. (1999). *An international human rights approach to corruption*. JSTOR.

Peiffer, C., & Walton, G. W. (2022). Getting the (right) message across: How to encourage citizens to report corruption. *Development Policy Review*, *40*(5), e12621. doi:10.1111/dpr.12621

Persson, A., Rothstein, B., & Teorell, J. (2010). *The failure of anti-corruption policies: a theoretical mischaracterization of the problem*. GU SE.

Persson, A., Rothstein, B., & Teorell, J. (2013). Why anti-corruption reforms fail—Systemic corruption as a collective action problem. *Governance: An International Journal of Policy, Administration and Institutions*, *26*(3), 449–471. doi:10.1111/j.1468-0491.2012.01604.x

Perumal, K. (2023). Rethinking global anti-corruption campaign. *Journal of Social and Economic Development*, 1–15.

Pilapitaya, T. (2005). *The impact of corruption on the human rights based approach to development.* SSRN.

Prabowo, H. Y., Sriyana, J., & Syamsudin, M. J. (2018). *Forgetting corruption: unlearning the knowledge of corruption in the Indonesian public sector.* UII.

Radin, D. (2019). Sustainable Development Goal 16: Focus on public institutions, World Public Sector Report 2019. *Public Sector Economics, 43*(4), 477–483. doi:10.3326/pse.43.4.8

Rothstein, B. (2011). Anti-corruption: The indirect 'big bang' approach. *Review of International Political Economy, 18*(2), 228–250. doi:10.1080/09692291003607834

Saha, S., & Ali, M. S. B. (2017). Corruption and economic development: New evidence from the Middle Eastern and North African countries. *Economic Analysis and Policy, 54*, 83–95. doi:10.1016/j.eap.2017.02.001

Serrat, O. (2017). Fighting Corruption with ICT: Strengthening Civil Society's Role. In Knowledge Solutions (pp. 797-811): Springer.

Sissani, M. (2016). The algerian economy governed by black corruption: an empirical study from 2002 to 2015. *Studies and Scientific Researches, Economics Edition* (24).

Themudo, N. S. (2013). Reassessing the impact of civil society: Nonprofit sector, press freedom, and corruption. *Governance: An International Journal of Policy, Administration and Institutions, 26*(1), 63–89. doi:10.1111/j.1468-0491.2012.01602.x

Thieux, L. (2019). Algerian youth and the political struggle for dignity: Evolution, trends and new forms of mobilisation. *Journal of North African Studies*, 1–17.

Wedel, J. R. (2012). Rethinking corruption in an age of ambiguity. *Annual Review of Law and Social Science, 8*(1), 453–498. doi:10.1146/annurev.lawsocsci.093008.131558

Wolf, A. (2019). The myth of stability in Algeria. *Journal of North African Studies, 24*(5), 707–712. doi:10.1080/13629387.2019.1647899

Compilation of References

't Hart, P. (1997). Preparing policy makers for crisis management: The role of simulations. *Journal of Contingencies and Crisis Management*, *5*(4), 207–215. doi:10.1111/1468-5973.00058

Abbott, J. K., Lew, D. K., Whitehead, J. C., & Woodward, R. T. (2022). The future of fishing for fun: The economics and sustainable management of recreational fisheries. *Review of Environmental Economics and Policy*, *16*(2), 262–281. doi:10.1086/720987

Abdallah-Pretceille, C. (2008). *Former et éduquer en contexte hétérogène*. Anthropos.

Abdelgafar, B. I. (2018). *Public policy: Beyond traditional jurisprudence: A Maqasid approach*. International Institute of Islamic Thought (IIIT).

Abdelhamid, A. (2018). Islamic Principles on Waste Minimization. *Ecomena*. https://www.ecomena.org/waste-minimization-islam/

Abdul Aziz, A. (2019). Special Forward: Islamic Governance and the Articulation of Maqāṣid al-Sharī'ah in Brunei Darussalam. In R. Yunos (Ed.), *Maqāṣid Al-Sharī'ah in the Brunei Civil Service: Civil Servant's Perspectives*. Qasrun Nafis Publishing House.

Acemoglu, D., & Robinson, J. (2012). *Why Nations Fail: The Origins of Power, Prosperity, and Poverty*. Currency.

Achy, L. (2013). *The price of stability in Algeria* (Vol. 25). Carnegie Endowment for International Peace.

Ackerman, J. M. (2014). Rethinking the International Anti-corruption Agenda: Civil Society, Human Rights and Democracy. *American University International Law Review*, *29*(2), 2.

Acuto, M. (2018). *Engaging with global urban governance. In Doing Global Urban Research*. Sage.

Acuto, M., & Rayner, S. (2016). City networks: Breaking gridlocks or forging (new) lock-ins? *International Affairs*, *92*(5), 1147–1166. doi:10.1111/1468-2346.12700

Adagunodo, M. (2022). The Effect of Oil Receipts and Fuel Subsidy Payment on the Current Account Deficit in Nigeria and Venezuela. Annals of Spiru Haret University. *Economic Series*, *22*(1), 137–152.

Adams, M. (2007). Pedagogical frameworks for social justice education. In M. Adams & L. A. Bell (Eds.), *Teaching for diversity and social justice* (pp. 39–58). Routledge. doi:10.4324/9780203940822-10

Adanan Abdul Latiff. (2016). Corak dan Seni Bina Rumah Melayu Brunei Tinjauan Ringkas. Dewan Bahasa dan Pustaka, Bandar Seri Begawan.

Adefolu, B. (n.d.). *Towards sustainable waste management in Lagos State: Possible adoptions from Finland*. Bitstream. https://www.theseus.fi/bitstream/handle/10024/95996/OjuriBabakolade_Thesis%20new.pdf?sequence=1&isAllowed=y

Adekunle, I. A., & Oseni, I. O. (2021). Fuel subsidies and carbon emission: Evidence from asymmetric modelling. *Environmental Science and Pollution Research International, 28*(18), 22729–22741. doi:10.100711356-021-12384-0 PMID:33423202

Afflerbach, P. (2015). The Business Value of IT in Light of Prospect Theory. *Business & Information Systems Engineering, 57*(5), 299–310. doi:10.100712599-015-0400-6

Agasisti, T., Catalano, G., & Sibiano, P. (2013). Can schools be autonomous in a centralised educational system? On formal and actual school autonomy in the Italian context. *International Journal of Educational Management, 27*(3), 292–310. doi:10.1108/09513541311306495

Agbedahin, A. V. (2019). Sustainable development, Education for Sustainable Development, and the 2030 Agenda for Sustainable Development: Emergence, efficacy, eminence, and future. *Sustainable Development (Bradford), 27*(4), 669–680. doi:10.1002d.1931

Ahad, A. D., & Anshari, M. (2017). Smartphone habits among youth: Uses and gratification theory. *International Journal of Cyber Behavior, Psychology and Learning, 7*(1), 65–75. doi:10.4018/IJCBPL.2017010105

Ahad, A. D., Anshari, M., & Razzaq, A. (2017). Domestication of smartphones among adolescents in Brunei darussalam. *International Journal of Cyber Behavior, Psychology and Learning, 7*(4), 26–39. doi:10.4018/IJCBPL.2017100103

Ahmed, A., & Anifowose, M. (2023). Corruption, corporate governance, and sustainable development goals in Africa. *Corporate Governance: The International Journal of Business in Society.*

Ahmed, S., & Ali, S. M. (2006). People as partners: Facilitating people's participation in public-private partnerships for solid waste management. *Habitat International, 30*(4), 781–796. doi:10.1016/j.habitatint.2005.09.004

Ahyani, H., Slamet, M., &Mutmainah, N. (2021). The Contribution of the Western World to the Islamic Economy in Indonesia. *Al-Amwal: Jurnal Ekonomi dan PerbankanSyari'ah, 13*(2), 153-170.

Ainscow, M. (2020b). Inclusion and equity in education: Making sense of global challenges. *Prospects, 49*(3-4), 123–134. doi:10.100711125-020-09506-w

Ainscow, M. (2020b). Promoting inclusion and equity in education: Lessons from international experiences. *Nordic Journal of Studies in Educational Policy, 6*(1), 7–16. doi:10.1080/20020317.2020.1729587

Akanle, O., & Omobowale, A. O. (2022). Contemporary Issues in Public Policy. In *Public Policy and Research in Africa* (pp. 123–158). Springer International Publishing.

Akinola, A. O. (2018). Oil subsidy administration in Nigeria. *Globalization, Democracy and Oil Sector Reform in Nigeria*, 231-265.

Akkari, A., & Radhouane, M. (2022). *Intercultural Approaches to Education. From Theory to Practice*. Springer. doi:10.1007/978-3-030-70825-2

Akram Hassan, S. (2018). Reasoning Method: An Analysis from the Islamic Perspective. *International Journal of Academic Research in Business & Social Sciences, 8*(11), 965–972. doi:10.6007/IJARBSS/v8-i11/4974

Al-Amidi, A.M (d. 631/1233). Al-Ihkam fi Usul al-Ahkam. Dar Al-kitab AL-Araby.

Alatas, H. (1990). *Corruption: Its nature, causes, and functions*. Avebury.

Alatas, S. H. (2015). *The problem of corruption*. The Other Press.

Alba, D., & Frenkel, S. (2020). Medical Expert Who Corrects Trump Is Now a Target of the Far Right. *The New York Times*. https://www.nytimes.com/2020/03/28/technology/coronavirus-fauci-trump-conspiracy-target.html

Alcott, B., Rose, P., Sabates, R., & Torres, R. (2018). *Handbook on Measuring Equity in Education*. UNESCO Institute for Statistics.

Alden Wily, L. (2011). *Customary Land Tenure in the Modern World Rights to Resources in Crisis: Reviewing the Fate of Customary Tenure in Africa*. Brief #1 of 5. https://dlc.dlib.indiana.edu/dlc/bitstream/handle/10535/7713/customary%20land%20tenure%20in%20the%20modern%20world.pdf?sequence=1

Al-Ghazali, M. (d.505 AH/1111 CE). Al-Mustasfa

Alhojailan, M.I., & Ibrahim, M. (2012). Thematic analysis: A critical review of its process and evaluation. *West East Journal of Social Sciences, 1*(1), 39-47.

Al-Jayyousi, O. (2018). How Islam can represent a model for environmental stewardship. *United Nations Environment Programme*. https://www.unep.org/news-and-stories/story/how-islam-can-represent-model-environmental-stewardship

Al-Kabeesy, B. M.L. (2006). Al-Maqasid al-Shar'iyyahwakayfiyyatut-Ta'mulma'hah 'indat-ta'arud. *Journal of kuliyyah al-Imam al-A'zam,* 1.

All Answers Ltd. (2022). Right to Environment of Human Right. *Lawteacher.net*. https://www.lawteacher.net/free-law-essays/human-rights/right-to-environment-of-human-right.php?vref=1

Allen, C., Metternicht, G., & Wiedmann, T. (2018). Initial progress in implementing the Sustainable Development Goals (SDGs). A review of evidence from countries. *Sustainability Science, 13*(5), 1453–1467. doi:10.100711625-018-0572-3

Almarabeh, T., & AbuAli, A. (2010). A General Framework for E-Government: Definition Maturity Challenges, Opportunities, and Success. *European Journal of Scientific Research, 39*(1), 29–42.

Al-Mawardi, A. H. (2000). The Ordinances of Government: Al-Ahkam Al-Sultaniyya W'al-Wilayat Al-Diniyya. Garnet Publishing.

Al-Shatibi,I. (d. 790 AH/1388 CE) al-Muwafaqat fi Usul al-Shari'ah al-Islamiyyah.

Alverado, F., Chancel, L., Piketty, T., Saez, E., & Zucman, G. (2018). *World Inequality Report 2018*. World Inequality Lab. https://wir2018.wid.world/files/download/wir2018-full-report-english.pdf

AMA. (2013). Definição e Implementação de Metodologia, Modelo e Ferramentas para Avaliação de Projetos e Despesas TIC - Overview do Processo de Avaliação de Projetos e Despesas TIC. Available at: https://m6.ama.pt/docs/AMA-20130925-AP-Overview do Processo v8.pdf

Aman, R. (2017). *Decolinising Intercultural Education. Colonial differences, the geopolitics of knowledge, and interepistemic dialogue*. Routledge. doi:10.4324/9781315616681

Amin. (2021). *KP5117: Madīnian Polity: Visions of Islamic Governance: Discussion 3: The Concept of State [PDF]*. Institute of Policy Studies, Universiti Brunei Darussalam.

Amir Singh, J. (2020). COVID-19: Science and global health governance under attack. *SAMJ: South African Medical Journal, 110*(6), 1–2. PMID:32880545

Anderson, C. C., Denich, M., Warchold, A., Kropp, J. P., & Pradhan, P. (2022). A systems model of SDG target influence on the 2030 Agenda for Sustainable Development. *Sustainability Science, 17*(4), 1459–1472. doi:10.100711625-021-01040-8 PMID:34659581

Andres, A. R., & Carlyn, R.-D. (2011). Is Corruption Really Bad for Inequality? Evidence from Latin America. *The Journal of Development Studies*, *47*(7), 959–976. doi:10.1080/00220388.2010.509784

Ankersmit, L. (2012). The diversion of the Acheloos river under EU environmental law. *European Law Blog*. https://europeanlawblog.eu/2012/09/26/the-diversion-of-the-acheloos-river-under-eu-environmental-law/

Ansari, A. H., Jamal, P., & Oseni, U. A. (2012). Sustainable development: Islamic dimension with special reference to conservation of the environment. *Advances in Natural and Applied Sciences*, *6*(5), 607–619.

Ansell, C., Boin, A., & Keller, A. (2010). Managing transboundary crises: Identifying the building blocks of an effective response system. *Journal of Contingencies and Crisis Management*, *18*(4), 195–207. doi:10.1111/j.1468-5973.2010.00620.x

Ansell, C., & Gash, A. (2007). Collaborative governance in theory and practice. *Journal of Public Administration: Research and Theory*, *18*(4), 543–571. doi:10.1093/jopart/mum032

Anshari, M., & Hamdan, M. (2022). Enhancing e-government with a digital twin for innovation management. *Journal of Science and Technology Policy Management*.

Anshari, M., Almunawar, M. N., & Masri, M. (2022a). Digital twin: Financial technology's next frontier of robo-advisor. *Journal of Risk and Financial Management, 15*(4), 163.

Anshari, M., Hamdan, M., & Haidi, H. (2023) Gearing Towards A Stronger Digital Society. In A. Ananta, C.Y. Hoon & M. Hamdan (Eds.) Stability, Growth and Sustainability: Catalysts for Socio-economic Development in Brunei Darussalam (pp. 136-158). ISEAS: Yusof Ishak Institute.

Anshari, M. (2020, March). Workforce mapping of fourth industrial revolution: Optimization to identity. [). IOP Publishing.]. *Journal of Physics: Conference Series*, *1477*(7), 072023. doi:10.1088/1742-6596/1477/7/072023

Anshari, M., Alas, Y., & Guan, L. S. (2016b). Developing online learning resources: Big data, social networks, and cloud computing to support pervasive knowledge. *Education and Information Technologies*, *21*(6), 1663–1677. doi:10.100710639-015-9407-3

Anshari, M., Alas, Y., Sabtu, N. P. H., & Hamid, M. S. A. (2016a). Online Learning: Trends, issues and challenges in the Big Data Era. *Journal of E-learning and Knowledge Society*, *12*(1).

Anshari, M., Alas, Y., Yunus, N., Sabtu, N. I., & Hamid, M. H. (2015). Social customer relationship management and student empowerment in online learning systems. *International Journal of Electronic Customer Relationship Management*, *9*(2-3), 104–121. doi:10.1504/IJECRM.2015.071711

Anshari, M., & Almunawar, M. N. (2022). Adopting open innovation for SMEs and industrial revolution 4.0. *Journal of Science and Technology Policy Management*, *13*(2), 405–427. doi:10.1108/JSTPM-03-2020-0061

Anshari, M., Almunawar, M. N., & Masri, M. (2020). Financial technology and disruptive innovation in business: Concept and application. [IJABIM]. *International Journal of Asian Business and Information Management*, *11*(4), 29–43. doi:10.4018/IJABIM.2020100103

Anshari, M., Almunawar, M. N., Masri, M., & Hamdan, M. (2019). Digital marketplace and FinTech to support agriculture sustainability. *Energy Procedia*, *156*, 234–238. doi:10.1016/j.egypro.2018.11.134

Anshari, M., Almunawar, M. N., Masri, M., Hamdan, M., Fithriyah, M., & Fitri, A. (2021, November). Digital wallet in supporting green FinTech sustainability. In *2021 Third International Sustainability and Resilience Conference: Climate Change* (pp. 352-357). IEEE. 10.1109/IEEECONF53624.2021.9667957

Anshari, M., & Lim, S. A. (2017). E-government with big data enabled through smartphone for public services: Possibilities and challenges. *International Journal of Public Administration, 40*(13), 1143–1158. doi:10.1080/01900692.2016.1242619

Anshari, M., Syafrudin, M., & Fitriyani, N. L. (2022b). Fourth industrial revolution between knowledge management and digital humanities. *Information (Basel), 13*(6), 292. doi:10.3390/info13060292

Anshari, M., Syafrudin, M., Fitriyani, N. L., & Razzaq, A. (2022). Ethical Responsibility and Sustainability (ERS) Development in a Metaverse Business Model. *Sustainability (Basel), 14*(23), 15805. doi:10.3390u142315805

Anshari, M., Syafrudin, M., Tan, A., Fitriyani, N. L., & Alas, Y. (2023). Optimisation of Knowledge Management (KM) with Machine Learning (ML) Enabled. *Information (Basel), 14*(1), 35. doi:10.3390/info14010035

Antimiani, A., Costantini, V., & Paglialunga, E. (2023). Fossil fuels subsidy removal and the EU carbon neutrality policy. *Energy Economics, 119*, 106524. doi:10.1016/j.eneco.2023.106524

Aoki, M., Kim, H., & Okuno-Fujiwara, M. (1997). *The role of Government in East Asian Economic Development: Comparative Institutional Analysis*. Clarendon Press.

Apel, H. (2020). Inequality in development: The 2030 Agenda, SDG 10 and the role of redistribution. *Real-World Economics Review, 21*(92), 228–237.

API. (n.d). *How to Use the Fishbone Tool for Root Cause Analysis*. API.

Ardi, M. R., Subianto, A., & Sudirman, S. (2020, April 20). IMPLEMENTATION OF INDONESIA'S MARINE POLICY A CASE STUDY:(Implementation of Presidential Regulation No. 16 of 2017 Concerning Indonesian Maritime Policy, Specifically Maritime Diplomacy in Papua). *JOURNAL ASRO., 11*(2), 1–7. doi:10.37875/asro.v11i2.263

Asad, M., & Grunebaum, G. (1961). *The Principles of State and Government in Islam*. University of California Press. doi:10.1525/9780520313460

Asare, J., Reguant, M., Saab, M., & Sacchetto, C. (2020). Low oil prices during COVID-19 and the case for removing fuel subsidies. *Internation Growth Centre*, (August), 1–15.

Asfaw, A. (2011). *Assessment of the monitoring and evaluation processes and challenges: the case of integrated family service organization, sustainable development for children project* [Doctoral dissertation]. St. Mary's University.

Ashcroft, B., Griffiths, G., & Tiffin, H. (2013). *Postcolonial studies. The key concepts*. Routledge. doi:10.4324/978023777855

Asif M, Muneer T. (2007). Energy supply, its demand and security issues for developed and emerging economies. *Renewable and sustainable energy reviews, 11*(7), 1388-413.

Askedal, K. (2019). *Understanding the Complexity of Benefits Management in an Interorganizational eHealth Effort*. In the *52nd Hawaii International Conference on System Sciences*, Maui, Hawaii, USA. 10.24251/HICSS.2019.484

Atkinson, R. (1999). Project management: Cost, time and quality, two best guesses and a phenomenon, it's time to accept other success criteria. *International Journal of Project Management, 17*(6), 337–342. doi:10.1016/S0263-7863(98)00069-6

Auda, J. (2008). Maqasid al-Shariah: An introductory guide. Herndon: International Institute of Islamic Thought.

Auda, J. (2022). *Re-envisioning Islamic scholarship: Maqasid methodology as a new approach*. Claritas Books.

Austrade.gov. (2015). Export Markets- Indonesia. Austrade. https://www.austrade.gov.au/australian/export/export-markets/countries-and-economies/indonesia/industries/maritime-to-indonesia.

Ayan, A. (2013). *Accessing the Global Halal Market*. Createspace Publishing Ltd.

Ayçin, E. (2019). *Çok Kriterli Karar Verme*. Nobel Akademik Yayıncılık.

Azalie, I. A. & Kamarulzaman, N. (2023). Development linkages of Brunei Darussalam's coffee and tea sector: Global and regional value chain perspectives. *Journal of Business and Economic Analysis,* 1- 25. doi:10.1142/S2737566822500074

Azalie, I. A., & Samad, N. (2022). Brunei as a global halal hub: Production network and strategic relations in halal food production. *Journal of Contemporary Islamic Studies*, *8*(3), 1–22. doi:10.24191/jcis.v8i3.1

Aziz, A. (2019). Islamic governance and the articulation of Maqasid al-Shariah in Brunei Darussalam. In *Maqasid al-Shari'ah in the Brunei Civil Service: Civil Servants' Perspectives.* Bandar Seri Begawan: QasrunNafis Publishing House. Available online also at: https://www. academia. edu/41888816/MAQ% C4

Badewi, A. (2016). The impact of project management (PM) and benefits management (BM) practices on project success: Towards developing a project benefits governance framework. *International Journal of Project Management*, *34*(4), 761–778. doi:10.1016/j.ijproman.2015.05.005

Badewi, A., & Shehab, E. (2016). The impact of organizational project benefits management governance on ERP project success: Neo-institutional theory perspective. *International Journal of Project Management*, *34*(3), 412–428. doi:10.1016/j.ijproman.2015.12.002

Bagirov, M., & Mateus, C. (2019). Oil prices, stock markets and firm performance: Evidence from Europe. *International Review of Economics & Finance*, *61*, 270–288. doi:10.1016/j.iref.2019.02.007

Baharun, H., Abd Rahman, S., Ahmad, H., & Saazai Mat Saad, N. (2020). Quranic Understanding among Non-Native Speaker of Arabic: Malaysian Experts' Perspectives. *Journal of Language Studies*, *20*(2), 154–169. doi:10.17576/gema-2020-2002-12

Bakar, R. H. A. (2021). Gov't studying viability of new public housing in Kampong Ayer. *The Scoop*. https://thescoop.co/2021/03/20/ moha-reconsiders-building-new-public-housing-in-kg-ayer/

Baltaci, A., & Balcı, A. (2017). Complexity leadership: A theorical perspective. *International Journal of Educational Leadership and Management*, *5*(1), 30–58. doi:10.17583/ijelm.2017.2435

Barberis, P. (1998). The New Public Management and a new accountability. *Public Administration*, *76*(3), 451–470. doi:10.1111/1467-9299.00111

Barro, R. J. (2000). Inequality and Growth in a Panel of Countries. *Journal of Economic Growth*, *5*(1), 5–32. doi:10.1023/A:1009850119329

Bartak, J., Lukasz, J., & Tomkiewicz, J. (2022). Does income inequality explain public debt change in OECD countries? *International Review of Economics & Finance*, *80*, 211–224. doi:10.1016/j.iref.2022.02.045

Batchabi, D. (2022). *World social protection report 2020-22*. Regional companion report for Africa.

Bauhr, M. (2017). Need or greed? Conditions for collective action against corruption. *Governance: An International Journal of Policy, Administration and Institutions*, *30*(4), 561–581. doi:10.1111/gove.12232

Bauman, Z., & Tester, K. (2001). *Conversations with Zygmunt Bauman*. Polity Press.

Baumgartner, F., & Jones, D. (2005). *The politics of attention: how government prioritizes problem*. The Chicago University Press Ltd.

Bautista-Beauchesne, N., & Garzon, C. J. (2019). *Conceptualizing corruption prevention: a systematic literature review*. Research Gate.

Bazilian, M., & Onyeji, I. (2012). Fossil fuel subsidy removal and inadequate public power supply: Implications for businesses. *Energy Policy*, *45*, 1–5. doi:10.1016/j.enpol.2012.02.057

Beer, A., McKenzie, F., Blažek, J., Sotarauta, M., & Ayres, S. (2020). *Every place matters: towards effective place-based policy*. Routledge. doi:10.4324/9781003110118

Behdad, S., & Nomani, F. (Eds.). (2006). *Islam and the everyday world: Public policy dilemmas*. Routledge. doi:10.4324/9780203028032

Bell, L. A. (2007). Theoretical foundations for social justice education. In M. Adams, L. A. Bell, & P. Griffin (Eds.), *Teaching for diversity and social justice* (pp. 1–14). Routledge.

Bello, H. S., Ahmad, N., & Galadima, I. S. (2018). Islamic economy as an alternative solution to managing economic crisis: Some fashionable case studies of Iran, Malaysia Saudi Arabia. Academic Press.

Benadusi, L., & Campione, V. (2022). Parliamo di scuola. *Scuola Democratica*, *13*(3), 551–560.

Bendana, C. (2022). Uganda takes to the courts to stop land grabs and protect forests. *farmlandgrab.org*. https://www.farmlandgrab.org/post/view/31319

Benlahcene, A., & Abdullah, N. S. B. (2021). *Anti-corruption Efforts in Algeria: Prevention Through Non-State Actors*. Paper presented at the Proceedings of the 2nd International Conference on Government and Public Affairs 2021 (ICOGPA2021), Malaysia.

Bernardi, F., & Ballarino, G. (2016). Education as the great equalizer: a theoretical framework. In F. Bernardi & G. Ballarino (Eds.), *Education, Occupation and Social Origin. A Comparative Analysis of the Transmission of Socio-Economic Inequalities* (pp. 1–16). Edward Elgar. doi:10.4337/9781785360459.00006

Bessadi, N. (2019). *Algerian activists demand a place at the table*. Qantara. https://en.qantara.de/content/civil-society-and-democratic-transition-in-algeria-algerian-activists-demand-a-place-at-the

Beyerlin, U., & Grote Stoutenburg, J. (2010). *Environment, International Protection*. Max Planck Encyclopedia of Public International Law.

Beyerlin, U., & Marauhn, T. (2011). *International Environmental Law*. Hart Publishing. doi:10.5771/9783845265582

Bhatti, G., Gaine, C., Gobbo, F., & Leeman, Y. (2007). *Social Justice and Intercultural Education*. Sterling: Trentham Books.

Bianchi, P. (2022). PNRR, istruzione e scuola. In L. Paganetto (Ed.), *Il piano italiano di ripresa e resilienza. Una sfida da vincere* (pp. 299–303). Eurilink University Press.

Biancone, P. P., &Shakhatreh, M. Z. (2015). Using Islamic Finance for infrastructure Projects in non-Muslim countries. *European Journal of Islamic Finance*, (2).

Bidabad, B., & Sherafati, M. (2017). Sustainable financing and anti-squandering measures in Rastin banking. *International Journal of Law and Management*, *59*(6), 939–949. doi:10.1108/IJLMA-04-2016-0037

Binder, B., & Haupt, A. (2022). The fundamental role of tax systems in the relationship between workfare and inequality in the lower half of the income distribution. *Research in Social Stratification and Mobility*, *80*, 100712. doi:10.1016/j.rssm.2022.100712

Birdsall, N. (2007). *Income Distribution: Effects on Growth and Development*. Center for Global Development Working Paper, No: 118.

Birkland, T. (1998). Focusing events, mobilization, and agenda setting. *Journal of Public Policy, 18*(1), 53–74. doi:10.1017/S0143814X98000038

Birnie, P., Boyle, A., & Redgwell, C. (2009). *International Law and the Environment*. Oxford University Press.

Bitabarova, A. G. (2018). Unpacking Sino-Central Asian engagement along the new silk road: A case study of Kazakhstan. *Journal of Contemporary East Asia Studies, 7*(2), 149–173. doi:10.1080/24761028.2018.1553226

Bloom, D. (2022). *Here's how COVID-19 impacted education – and what we need to do to get children's learning back on track*. World Economic Forum. Retrieved 13 December 2022, from https://www.weforum.org/agenda/2022/11/covid19-education-impact-legacy/

Blossfeld, H. P., Kilpi-Jakonen, E., Vono de Vilhena, D., & Buchholz, S. (Eds.). (2014). *Adult learning in modern societies: An international comparison from a life-course perspective*. Edward Elgar. doi:10.4337/9781783475186

Boeren, E. (2016). *Lifelong learning participation in a changing policy context: An interdisciplinary theory*. Palgrave-Macmillan. doi:10.1057/9781137441836

Boeren, E. (2019). Understanding Sustainable Development Goal (SDG) 4 on "quality education" from micro, meso and macro perspectives. *International Review of Education, 65*(2), 277–294. doi:10.100711159-019-09772-7

Bogojević, S., & Zou, M. (2021). Making Infrastructure 'Visible'in Environmental Law: The Belt and Road Initiative and Climate Change Friction. *Transnational Environmental Law, 10*(1), 35–56. doi:10.1017/S2047102520000278

Boin, A., Hart, P., Stern, E., & Sundelius, B. (2005). *The politics of crisis management: Understanding public leadership when it matters most*. Academic Press.

Boin, A. (2009). The new world of crises and crisis management: Implications for policymaking and research. *The Review of Policy Research, 26*(4), 367–377. doi:10.1111/j.1541-1338.2009.00389.x

Boin, A., Hart, P. T., McConnell, A., & Preston, T. (2010). Leadership style, crisis response and blame management: The case of Hurricane Katrina. *Public Administration, 88*(3), 706–723. doi:10.1111/j.1467-9299.2010.01836.x

Boin, A., Stern, E., & Sundelius, B. (2016). *The politics of crisis management: Public leadership under pressure*. Cambridge University Press. doi:10.1017/9781316339756

Bonsu, N. O., TyreeHageman, J., & Kele, J. (2020). Beyond 2030 Agenda: Future-oriented mechanisms in localising the sustainable development goals (SDGs). *Sustainability (Basel), 12*(23), 9797. doi:10.3390u12239797

Booth, J., Wade, C., & Walker, T. (2020). *Understanding Central America: Global Forces and Political Change* (7th ed.). Routledge. doi:10.4324/9780429344282

Bornemann, B. (2007). Sustainable development and policy integration – some conceptual clarifications [Paper presentation]. The Marie Curie Summer School on Earth System Governance, Amsterdam, The Netherlands.

Bourdieu, P., & Passeron, J.C. (1964). *Les Héritiers. Les étudiants et la culture*. Parigi: Les éditions de Minuit.

Bourdieu, P. (1966). L'école conservatrice. L'inégalité sociale devant l'école et devant la culture. *Revue Française de Sociologie, 7*(3), 325–347. doi:10.2307/3319132

Boyd, N. M., & Martin, E. C. (2020). Sense of community responsibility at the forefront of crisis management. *Administrative Theory & Praxis*, 1–13.

Bracci, E. (2009). Autonomy, responsibility and accountability in the Italian school system. *Critical Perspectives on Accounting, 20*(3), 293–312. doi:10.1016/j.cpa.2008.09.001

Braun, V., & Clarke, V. (2006). Using thematic analysis in psychology. *Qualitative Research in Psychology, 3*(2), 77–101. doi:10.1191/1478088706qp063oa

Braun, V., & Clarke, V. (2019). Reflecting on reflexive thematic analysis. *Qualitative Research in Sport, Exercise and Health, 11*(4), 589–597. doi:10.1080/2159676X.2019.1628806

Bray, M., Adamson, B., & Mason, M. (Eds.). (2014). Comparative Education Research. Approaches and Method. Tin Wan: Hong Kong University Press. doi:10.1007/978-3-319-05594-7

Breese, R. (2012). Benefits realisation management: Panacea or false dawn? *International Journal of Project Management, 30*(3), 341–351. doi:10.1016/j.ijproman.2011.08.007

Breuer, A., Janetschek, H., & Malerba, D. (2019). Translating sustainable development goal (SDG) interdependencies into policy advice. *Sustainability (Basel), 11*(7), 2092. doi:10.3390u11072092

Bridges, T., & Eubank, D. (2020). *Leading Sustainably: The Path to Sustainable Business and how the SDGs Changed Everything*. Routledge. doi:10.4324/9780367855468

Brofenbrenner, U. (2009). The Ecology of Human Development. Experiments by nature and design. Harvard University Press.

Brown, J. D., & Brown, J. D. (2019). Ideologies, worldviews, and personalities. Reflective Practice of Counseling and Psychotherapy in a Diverse Society, 33-52.

Brundtland, G. H. (1987). Our common future- Call for action. *Environmental Conservation, 14*(4), 291–294. doi:10.1017/S0376892900016805

Brunei Darussalam | NON-STATE ACTORS IN EDUCATION | Education Profiles. (n.d.). Retrieved 6 September 2022, from https://education-profiles.org/eastern-and-south-eastern-asia/brunei-darussalam/~non-state-actors-in-education

Brunei Darussalam Climate Change Secretariat. (2023). *About Brunei Climate Change Secretariat*. http://www.climatechange.gov.bn/SitePages/Pages/about-bccs.aspx

Brunei Darussalam Compulsory Education Act 2011, (testimony of AGC).

Brunei Darussalam Education (National Curriculum) Regulations, no. 2004. AGC.

Brunei Darussalam Education Act 2010, (testimony of AGC).

Bryson, J. (1988). A strategic planning process for public and non-profit organizations. *Long Range Planning, 21*(1), 73–81. doi:10.1016/0024-6301(88)90061-1

Bryson, J. (2018). *Strategic planning for public and nonprofit organizations: A guide to strengthening and sustaining organizational achievement* (5th ed.). John Wiley & Sons Inc.

Buck, S. J. (1992). Governing the Commons: The Evolution of Institutions for Collective Action by Elinor Ostrom. *Natural Resources Journal, 32*(2), 415–417. https://www.jstor.org/stable/24884388

Buettner-Schmidt, K., & Lobo, M. L. (2012). Social justice: A concept analysis. *Journal of Advanced Nursing, 68*(4), 948–958. doi:10.1111/j.1365-2648.2011.05856.x PMID:22032609

Burkart, K. (2022). Indigenous land rights take center stage in a new global framework for biodiversity conservation (commentary). *Mongabay*. https://news.mongabay.com/2022/03/indigenous-land-rights-take-center-stage-in-a-new-global-framework-for-biodiversity-conservation/

Burrows, T., Goldman, S., Pursey, K., & Lim, R. (2017). Is there an association between dietary intake and academic achievement: A systematic review. *Journal of Human Nutrition and Dietetics, 30*(2), 117–140. doi:10.1111/jhn.12407 PMID:27599886

Butcher, C. (2014). Can oil-reliant countries democratize? An assessment of the role of civil society in Algeria. *Democratization, 21*(4), 722–742. doi:10.1080/13510347.2013.769959

Butler, M. J., & Allen, P. M. (2008). Understanding policy implementation processes as self-organizing systems. *Public Management Review, 10*(3), 421–440. doi:10.1080/14719030802002923

Caiado, R. G. G., Leal Filho, W., Quelhas, O. L. G., de Mattos Nascimento, D. L., & Ávila, L. V. (2018). A literature-based review on potentials and constraints in the implementation of the sustainable development goals. *Journal of Cleaner Production, 198*, 1276–1288. doi:10.1016/j.jclepro.2018.07.102

Cairney, P. (2012). Complexity theory in political science and public policy. *Political Studies Review, 10*(3), 346–358. doi:10.1111/j.1478-9302.2012.00270.x

Caloia, A. (2016). Disuguaglianze: la responsabilità delle scelte governative pubbliche. *Quaderni di economia del lavoro, 106*(2), 141-165.

Cardona, L. A., Ortiz, H., & Vázquez, D. J. H. R. Q. (2018). Corruption and Human Rights. *Possible Relations., 40*(2), 317–341.

Cardone, M., Falzetti, P., & Severoni, A. (2015). *Equità o segregazione scolastica? L'effetto della composizione delle classi sull'apprendimento degli studenti.* Working Paper n. 25. Roma: INVALSI.

Carey, G., Malbon, E., Carey, N., Joyce, A., Crammond, B., & Carey, A. (2015). Systems science and systems thinking for public health: A systematic review of the field. *BMJ Open, 5*(12), e009002. doi:10.1136/bmjopen-2015-009002 PMID:26719314

Carr, N. G. (2003). IT Doesn't Matter. *Harvard Business Review, 81*(5), 41–49. PMID:12747161

Cartabia, M., & Lupo, N. (2022). *The Italian Constitution. A Contextual Analysis*. Hart Pub Ltd.

Castoldi, M. (2021). *Costruire il curricolo di istituto*. Carocci.

CBS. (2014). *U.S. Navy Sailors Sue Japan Power Co. for Radiation Exposure during 2011 Quake, Tsunami Rescue*. CBS.

CDC. (2012). *Program Evaluation for Public Health Programs: A Self-Study Guide*. Retrieved from https://www.cdc.gov/eval/guide/step1/

Cerini, G. (2016). Valutazione interna ed esterna. Attori e prospettive per il miglioramento della qualità dell'istruzione. *Scuola Democratica. Learning for Democracy, 4*(2), 397–414.

Ceschel, F., Hinna, A., & Homberg, F. (2022). Public Sector Strategies in Curbing Corruption: A Review of the Literature. *Public Organization Review, 22*(3), 571–591. doi:10.100711115-022-00639-4

Chabbott, C., & Sinclair, M. (2020). SDG 4 and the COVID-19 emergency: Textbooks, tutoring, and teachers. *Prospects, 49*(1–2), 51–57. doi:10.100711125-020-09485-y PMID:32836424

Chancel, L., Piketty, T., Saez, E., & Zucman, G. (2022). *World Inequality Report 2022.* World Inequality Lab wir2022.wid.world

Chang, H. (2002). *Kicking Away the Ladder: Development Strategy in Historical Perspective.* Anthem Press Ltd.

Chapra, M. U. (2011). *The Economic Problem: Can Islam Play an Effective Role in Solving it Efficiently as well as Equitably?* Working Papers 2011-1, The Islamic Research and Teaching Institute (IRTI).

Chapra, M., Khan, S., & Al Shaikh-Ali, A. (2006). *The Islamic Vision of Development in the Light of Maqasid Al-Shariah* (Vol. 15). International Institute of Islamic Thought.

Chatri, F. (2014). Economy-Wide Effects of Fuel Subsidy Removals in Malaysia. *Proceedings of the 9th Malaysian National Economic Conference.*

Checkland, P. B. (1989). Soft systems methodology. *Human Systems Management*, *8*(4), 273–289. doi:10.3233/HSM-1989-8405

Checkland, P., & Poulter, J. (2010). Soft systems methodology. In *Systems approaches to managing change: A practical guide* (pp. 191–242). Springer. doi:10.1007/978-1-84882-809-4_5

Chelminski, K. (2018). Fossil fuel subsidy reform in Indonesia. *The politics of fossil fuel subsidies and their reform*, 193-211.

Chibonore, W. C. (2016). *Monitoring and evaluation practices in selected non governmental organisations* [Doctoral dissertation].

Chimwendo. (2004). *Designing Monitoring and Evaluation Systems for NEPAD Projects.* UNECA.

Chung, H., & Thewissen, S. (2011). Falling back on old habits? A comparison of the social and unemployment crisis reactive policy strategies in Germany, the UK and Sweden. *Social Policy and Administration*, *45*(4), 354–370. doi:10.1111/j.1467-9515.2011.00779.x

CIA. (2022). Brunei. In *The World Factbook.* Central Intelligence Agency. https://www.cia.gov/the-world-factbook/countries/brunei

Ciani, A., Ferrari, L., & Vannini, I. (2020). *Progettare e valutare per l'equità e la qualità nella didattica. Aspetti teorici e indicazioni metodologiche.* Franco Angeli.

Clark, R. C., & Mayer, R. E. (2016). *E-learning and the science of instruction: Proven guidelines for consumers and designers of multimedia learning.* John Wiley & Sons.

Clark, G. (2013). *Fukaralığa Veda Dünyanın Kısa İktisadi Tarihi.* Bilgi Üniversitesi Yayınları.

Cleland, D. I. (1998). Stakeholder management. In J. Pinto (Ed.), *Project management handbook.* Jossey-Bass.

Client Earth. (2020). *Enforcing the Habitats Directive in national courts.* https://www.clientearth.org/media/pb5g0lpe/webinar-8-enforcing-the-habitats-directive-in-national-courts.pdf

Cocconi, M. (2015). Gli ingredienti necessari per una "buona" autonomia scolastica. *Istituzioni del Federalismo. Rivista di studi giuridici e politici, 19*(3), 647-675.

Cohen, E. (2006). Theoretical foundations of industrial policy. *EIB Papers*, *11*(1), 84–106.

Cojocaru, T. M., Ionescu, G. H., Firoiu, D., Cismaş, L. M., Oţil, M. D., & Toma, O. (2022). Reducing inequalities within and among EU Countries—Assessing the achievement of the 2030 agenda for sustainable development targets (SDG 10). *Sustainability (Basel)*, *14*(13), 7706. doi:10.3390u14137706

Colglazier EW. (2018). Science diplomacy and future worlds. *Science & Diplomacy, 7*(3), 1-20.

Collis, B. (2005). Multiple Perspectives on Blended Learning Design. *Journal of Learning Design*, 12–21.

Colombo, D. (2012). *Welfare mix* e neoliberismo: Un falso antagonismo. *Quaderni di Sociologia, 20*(59), 167–177. doi:10.4000/qds.575

Colombo, E. (2017). The Contradictory Place of Civic Education in the Italian Education System. In C. Broom (Ed.), *Youth Civic Engagement in a Globalized World Citizenship Education in Comparative Perspective* (pp. 103–125). Palgrave-MacMilan. doi:10.1057/978-1-137-56533-4_6

Commission, E. U. (2014). *Proposal for Key Principles of a Quality Framework for Early Childhood Education and Care*. EU Commission.

Commission, E. U. (2017). *Taking Stock of the 2013 Recommendation on "Investing in Children: Breaking the Cycle of Disadvantage"*. EU Commission.

Concari, A., Kok, G., & Martens, P. (2020). A systematic literature review of concepts and factors related to pro-environmental consumer behaviour in relation to waste management through an interdisciplinary approach. *Sustainability: Science. Sustainability (Basel), 12*(11), 4452. doi:10.3390u12114452

Concha, G., Astudillo, H., Porrúa, M., & Pimenta, C. (2012). E-Government procurement observatory, maturity model and early measurements. *Government Information Quarterly, 29*, S43–S50. doi:10.1016/j.giq.2011.08.005

Considine, M. (2005). *Making Public Policy: Institutions, Actors and Strategies*. Polity Press.

Considine, M., & Lewis, J. M. (1999). Governance and ground level: The frontline bureaucrat in the age of markets and networks. *Public Administration Review, 59*(6), 467–480. doi:10.2307/3110295

Considine, M., O'Sullivan, S., & Nguyen, P. (2018). The policymaker's dilemma: The risks and benefits of a 'black box' approach to commissioning active labour market programmes. *Social Policy and Administration, 52*(1), 229–251. doi:10.1111pol.12309

Cook, P., & Uchida, Y. (2008). Structural Change, Competition And Income Distribution. *The Quarterly Review of Economics and Finance, 48*(2), 274–286. doi:10.1016/j.qref.2006.12.017

Cooper, R. (1992). Forecasting and Understanding Local Weather in Brunei Darussalam. *Brunei Museum Journal, 7*(4), 88–98.

Cordini, M., & De Angelis, G. (2021). Families between care, education and work: The effects of the pandemic on educational inequalities in Italy and Milan. *European Journal of Education, 56*(4), 578–594. doi:10.1111/ejed.12483 PMID:34898740

Corina Constanta Sirbu. (2014). Aspects concerning the usage of modern methods for teaching – learning – evaluation in universities. *Procedia - Social and Behavioral Sciences, 182* . doi:10.1016/j.sbspro.2015.04.777

Cornwall, A. (2002). *Beneficiary consumer citizen: perspectives on participation for poverty reduction* (Vol. 2). Swedish International Development Cooperation Agency.

Cosby, B., & Bryson, J. (2005). *Leadership for the common good: Tackling public problems in a shared-power world* (2nd ed.). Jossey-Bass.

Couharde, C., & Mouhoud, S. (2020). Fossil fuel subsidies, income inequality, and poverty: Evidence from developing countries. *Journal of Economic Surveys, 34*(5), 981–1006. doi:10.1111/joes.12384

Council of Europe. (2001). *Common European Framework of Reference for languages: Learning, teaching, assessment.* Cambridge University Press. https://www.coe.int/t/dg4/linguistic/Source/Framework_EN.pdf

Council of the European Unition (2022). *Proposal for a Directive of the European Parliament and the Council on the protection of the environment through criminal law*. Author.

Coveney, P., & Highfield, R. (1995). *Frontiers of complexity: The search for order in a chaotic world*. Fawcett Columbine.

Crenshaw, K. (2017). *On Intersectionality. Essential Writings*. New Press.

Cribb, R., & Ford, M. (n.d.). *(n.d). "Indonesia as an Archipelago: Managing Island*. Managing The Sea.

Crown. (2021). *The Economics of Biodiversity: The Dasgupta Review*. https://assets.publishing.service.gov.uk/government/uploads/system/uploads/attachment_data/file/962785/The_Economics_of_Biodiversity_The_Dasgupta_Review_Full_Report.pdf

Curlee, W., & Gordon, R. L. (2013). *Successful program management: Complexity theory, communication, and leadership*. CRC Press. doi:10.1201/b15925

Curtin, G. G. (2007). E-Government. In L. L. Kaid & C. Holtz-Bacha (Eds.), *Encyclopedia of Political Communications*. SAGE Publications, Inc.

Dade, T., & Witzig, W. (2017). Container Ships: Oil Fueled versus Nuclear Powered. *Nuclear Technology*, 196.

Damit, D. H. D. A., Harun, A., Martin, D., Othman, B., & Ahmad, H. (2019). What makes a non-Muslim purchase halal food in a Muslim country? An application of theory of planned behaviour. *Management Science Letters*, *9*(12), 2029–2038. doi:10.5267/j.msl.2019.7.003

Dartanto, T. (2013). Reducing fuel subsidies and the implication on fiscal balance and poverty in Indonesia: A simulation analysis. *Energy Policy*, *58*, 117–134. doi:10.1016/j.enpol.2013.02.040

Datta, A., & Krishnamoorti, R. (2022). Understanding the Greenhouse Gas Impact of Deforestation Fires in Indonesia and Brazil in 2019 and 2020. *Frontiers in Climate*, *4*, 799632. doi:10.3389/fclim.2022.799632

Davis, J., Schoorman, D., & Donaldson, L. (1997). Davis, Schoorman and Donaldson reply: The distinctiveness of agency theory and stewardship theory. *Academy of Management Review*, *22*(3), 611–613.

Dawson, P. J. (1997). On Testing Kuznets' Economic Growth Hypothesis. *Applied Economics Letters*, *4*(7), 409–410. doi:10.1080/135048597355159

de Man, A. (2022). Reconsidering corruption as a violation of the rights to equality and non-discrimination based on poverty in South Africa. *Journal for Juridical Science*, *47*(1), 52–76. doi:10.18820/24150517/JJS47.i1.3

de Oliveira, C. M., Viater Tureck, L., Alvares, D., Liu, C., Horimoto, A. R. V. R., Balcells, M., de Oliveira Alvim, R., Krieger, J. E., & Pereira, A. C. (2020). Relationship between marital status and incidence of type 2 diabetes mellitus in a Brazilian rural population: The Baependi Heart Study. *PLoS One*, *15*(8), e0236869. doi:10.1371/journal.pone.0236869 PMID:32745127

Deacon, B. (2016). SDGs, Agenda 2030 and the prospects for transformative social policy and social development. *Journal of International and Comparative Social Policy*, *32*(2), 79–82. doi:10.1080/21699763.2016.1200112

Deaton, A. (2021). COVID-19 and Global Income Inequality. *LSE Public Policy Review*, *1*(4), 1. doi:10.31389/lseppr.26 PMID:34308354

DeLone, W. H., & Mclean, E.R. (2003). The DeLone and McLean Model of Information Systems Success: A Ten-Year Update. *Journal of Management Information Systems*, *19*(4), 9–30.

DeLone, W. H., & McLean, E. R. (1992). Information Systems Success: The Quest for the Dependent Variable. *Information Systems Research*, *3*(1), 60–95. doi:10.1287/isre.3.1.60

Department of Statistics. (2023). *National Accounts*. Bandar Seri Begawan: Department of Economic Planning and Statistics. Ministry of Finance and Economy, Brunei Darussalam. https://deps.mofe.gov.bn/SitePages/National%20Accounts.aspx

Derviş, K., & Qureshi, Z. (2016). *Income distribution within countries: Rising inequality, Global Economy and Development at Brooking*. https://www.brookings.edu/wp-content/uploads/2017/12/income-inequality-within-countries_august-2016.pdf

Deuraseh, N. (2019). *Shariah and Life: Halalan Tayyiban Perspective*. UNISSA Press.

Deutsch, J., & Silber, J. (2004). Measuring the impact of various income sources on the link between inequality and development: Implications for Kuznet Curve. *Review of Development Economics*, *8*(1), 110–127. doi:10.1111/j.1467-9361.2004.00223.x

Deyshappriya, N. P. R. (2017). *Impact of Macroeconomic Factors on Income Inequality and Income Distribution in Asian Countries*. ADBI Working Paper (696), Asian Development Bank Institute. https://www.adb.org/publications/impact-macroeconomic-factors-income-inequality-distribution

Dikmen, S., & Çiçek, H. G. (2023). Fighting against corruption and bribery in public procurements during the Covid-19 pandemic. In The Ethics of Bribery: Theoretical and Empirical Studies (pp. 309-328): Springer. doi:10.1007/978-3-031-17707-1_18

Dincer, O. C., & Gunalp, B. (2012). Corruptıon And Income Inequalıty In The Unıted States. *Contemporary Economic Policy*, *30*(2), 283–292. doi:10.1111/j.1465-7287.2011.00262.x

Disch, A., Vigeland, E., Sundet, G., & Gibson, S. (2009). Anti-corruption approaches: A literature review. Retrieved from Dixit, A. (2018). Anti-corruption institutions: Some history and theory. In Institutions, Governance and the Control of Corruption (pp. 15-49): Springer.

Djafri, F., Laldin, M. A., & Laallam, A. (2021). The global perspective of Islamic finance and the potential for China to tap into the Islamic finance market. *Journal of Islamic Business and Management*, *11*(1), 14–28.

Doherty, N. F. (2014). The role of socio-technical principles in leveraging meaningful benefits from IT investments. *Applied Ergonomics*, *45*(2, 2A), 181–187. doi:10.1016/j.apergo.2012.11.012 PMID:23305923

Doherty, N. F., Ashurst, C., & Peppard, J. (2012). Factors Affecting the Successful Realisation of Benefits from Systems Development Projects: Findings from Three Case Studies. *Journal of Information Technology*, *27*(1), 1–16. doi:10.1057/jit.2011.8

Domenici, G. (2015). An Italian Paradox and an Important School System Reform. *Journal of Educational. Cultural and Psychological Studies*, *1*(12), 11–20.

Dotinga, H. (2022). *Overriding Public Interest' to speed up permitting procedures for RES and grids? A legal perspective on the application of 'Imperative Reasons of overriding Public Interest' (IROPI) – and related risks under the EU Nature Directive*. RGI. https://renewables-grid.eu/fileadmin/user_upload/Files_RGI/Event_material/RGI_IROPI_Webinar_120522_HD_text_and_maps_only.pdf

Drexhage, J., & Murphy, D. (2010). *Sustainable Development: From Brundtland to Rio 2012*. UN.

Duncan, D., & Peter, K. S. (2016). Unequal inequalities: Do progressive taxes reduce income inequality? *International Tax and Public Finance*, *23*(4), 762–783. doi:10.100710797-016-9412-5

Dusuki, A. W. (2009). *Challenges of Realizing Maqasid Al-shari'ah (objectives of Shari'ah) in the Islamic Capital Market: Special Focus on Equaty-based Sukuk Structures.* International Shari'ah Research Acedemy for Islamic Finance (ISRA).

Dzuiban, C., Hartman, J., & Moskal, P. (2004). *Blended Learning Educat Use Center For Applied Resarch (ECAR), No. 7.* www.educause.edu.ecar

Eden, L., & Wagstaff, M. F. (2021). Evidence-based policymaking and the wicked problem of SDG 5 Gender Equality. *Journal of International Business Policy*, *4*(1), 28–57. doi:10.105742214-020-00054-w

Edmondson, C. (2020). Trump's Response to Protests Draws Bipartisan Rebuke in Congress. *The New York Times.* https://www.nytimes.com/2020/06/02/us/politics/trump-congress-protesters-tear-gas.html

EESI. (2021). *Fact Sheet: Strengthening Financial Resilience to Climate Change.* EESI.

Eisinger, P. (1988). *The Rise of the Entrepreneurial State: State and Local Economic Development Policy in the United States.* Wisconsin University Press.

Elliott, L., & Carrington, D. (2021, February 2). Economics' failure over destruction of nature presents 'extreme risks'. *The Guardian.* https://www.theguardian.com/environment/2021/feb/02/economics-failure-over-destruction-of-nature-presents-extreme-risk

Elsayed, D. (2021). Corruption in North Africa: Monopoly of Power and Widespread Ignorance. In P. M. H. Dan Hough (Ed.), *Corruption in the MENA Region: Beyond Uprisings* (pp. 165–234). Palgrave Macmillan. doi:10.1007/978-3-030-55314-2_7

Emara, A. M. (2020). The impact of corruption on human development in egypt. *Asian Economic and Financial Review*, *10*(5), 574–589. doi:10.18488/journal.aefr.2020.105.574.589

Energyfactsaustralia. (2018). *Energy and Climate Change.* Energy Facts Australia. https://www.energyfactsaustralia.org.au/key-issues/energy-and-climate-change/

Engel, E. M. R. A., Galetovic, A., & Raddatz, C. E. (1999). Taxes and income distribution in Chile: Some unpleasant redistributive arithmetic. *Journal of Development Economics*, *59*(1), 155–192. doi:10.1016/S0304-3878(99)00009-7

Enste, D., & Heldman, C. (2017). *Causes and consequences of corruption: An overview of empirical results.* Retrieved from Fayed, A. A. (2018). Researching corruption: understanding its key concepts. *Rule of Law and Anti-corruption Center Journal*, *2018*(2), 11.

Eppel, E. A., & Rhodes, M. L. (2018). Complexity theory and public management: A 'becoming' field. *Public Management Review*, *20*(7), 949–959. doi:10.1080/14719037.2017.1364414

Equality and Human Rights Commission. (2021). *What is the Charter of Fundamental Rights of the European Union?* https://www.equalityhumanrights.com/en/what-are-human-rights/how-are-your-rights-protected/what-charter-fundamental-rights-european-union

Erickson, P., Down, A., Lazarus, M., & Koplow, D. (2017). Effect of subsidies to fossil fuel companies on United States crude oil production. *Nature Energy*, *2*(11), 891–898. doi:10.103841560-017-0009-8

Esteves, J., & Joseph, R. C. (2008). A comprehensive framework for the assessment of eGovernment projects. *Government Information Quarterly*, *25*(1), 118–132. doi:10.1016/j.giq.2007.04.009

Esteves, M. (2018). Gender Equality in Education: A challenge for policy makers. *The International Journal of Social Sciences (Islamabad)*, *4*(2), 893–905.

EURCOM. (2008). *The Commission launches a major Recovery Plan for growth and jobs, to boost demand and restore confidence in the European economy*. Europa. https://europa.eu/rapid/press-release_IP-08-1771_en.htm

EUR-Lex Glossary of Summaries. (n.d.). *Sustainable development.* EUR-Lex. https://eur-lex.europa.eu/summary/glossary/sustainable_development.html

European Commission (2016). Commission Staff Working Document Fitness Check of the EU Nature Legislation (Birds and Habitats Directives) Directive 2009/147/EC of the European Parliament and of the Council of 30 November 2009 on the conservation of wild birds and Council Directive 92/43/EEC of 21 May 1992 on the conservation of natural habitats and of wild fauna and flora.

European Commission (2016). Fitness Check of the EU Nature Legislation (Birds and Habitats Directives) Directive 2009/147/EC of the European Parliament and of the Council of 30 November 2009 on the conservation of wild birds and Council Directive 92/43/EEC of 21 May 1992 on the conservation of natural habitats and of wild fauna and flora. *Commission Staff Working Document.*

European Commission (2021). EU Biodiversity Strategy for 2020. Bringing Nature Back into our lives. *Communication from the Commission to the European Parliament, the Council, the European Economic and Social Committee and the Committee of the Regions.*

European Commission. (1990). *ESDP European Spatial Development Perspective*. Towards Balanced and Sustainable Development of the Territory of the European Union.

European Commission. (2006). *Nature and Biodiversity Cases Ruling of the European Court of Justice*. Author.

European Commission. (2007). *Guidance document on Article 6(4) of the 'Habitats Directive' 92/43/EEC*. Author.

European Commission. (2013). *Guidelines on Wilderness in Natura 2000*. Author.

European Commission. (2017). *Natura 2000 and spatial planning*. Author.

European Commission. (2019). *Air Quality and Noise Legislation, Module 4: Principles for Directives 2008/50/EC and 2002/49/EC*. https://ec.europa.eu/environment/legal/law/5/e_learning/module_4_7.htm

European Commission. (2022). *Commission Staff Working Document Criteria and guidance for protected areas designations*. https://environment.ec.europa.eu/system/files/2022-01/SWD_guidance_protected_areas.pdf

European Commission. (2022). *Proposal for a Regulation of the European Parliament and of the Council on nature restoration*. Author.

European Commission. (2022). *Statement by President von der Leyen on the Kunming-Montreal biodiversity agreement*. https://ec.europa.eu/commission/presscorner/detail/en/statement_22_7827

European Commission. (n.d.). *Public consultations and other consultation activities*. https://ec.europa.eu/social/main.jsp?catId=333&langId=en

European Environment Agency. (2012). *Protected areas in Europe — an overview*. Author.

European Environment Agency. (2012). *Workshop on EU legislation, Principles of EU Environmental Law, the Polluter Pays Principle*. Author.

European Environment Agency. (2020a). *An introduction to Europe's Protected Areas 2020*. Author.

European Environment Agency. (2020b). *Building a coherent Trans European Nature Network*. Author.

European Environment Agency. (2022). *EU27 - Birds and Habitats Directives*. https://www.eea.europa.eu/data-and-maps/figures/natura-2000-birds-and-habitat-directives-12/eu27-birds-and-habitats-directives

European Parliament. (2013). *Semi-Subsistence Farming: Value and Directions of Development*. Author.

European Union. (2022). *Sustainable development in the European Union, Monitoring report on progress towards the SDGs in an EU context, 2022 edition*. Author.

Eurostat. (2010). *Unemployment statistics*. Europa. http://ec.europa.eu/eurostat/statistics-explained/index.php/Unemployment_statistics#Unemployment_trends

Eurostat. (2017). *Sustainable Development in the European Union 2017*. European Union Publishing.

Eurydice. (2019). *Key Data on Early Childhood Education and Care in Europe*. Luxembourg: Publications Office of the European Union.

Eurydice. (2022). *Structural Indicators for monitoring Education and Training System in Europe 2022. Overview of major reforms since 2015*. Luxembourg: Publications Office of the European Union.

Evans, K. (2020, March 20). In 2017, New Zealand granted legal personhood to the Whanganui River. Since then, other nations have followed suit in an effort to protect the environment. *BBC*.

Ezeh, P. C., & Nkamnebe, A. D. (2022). Determinants of Islamic banking adoption among non-Muslim customers in a Muslim zone. *Journal of Islamic Accounting and Business Research*, *13*(4), 666–683. doi:10.1108/JIABR-10-2021-0280

Farazmand, A. (2007). Learning from the Katrina crisis: A global and international perspective with implications for future crisis management. *Public Administration Review*, *67*, 149–159. doi:10.1111/j.1540-6210.2007.00824.x

Farbey, B., Land, F., & Targett, D. (1999). Moving IS evaluation forward: Learning themes and research issues. *The Journal of Strategic Information Systems*, *8*(2), 189–207. doi:10.1016/S0963-8687(99)00021-9

Farrell, G. M. (2009). *Results-based monitoring and evaluation at the Commonwealth of Learning. Commonwealth of Learning*. COL.

Fathurrahman, F., Kat, B., & Soytaş, U. (2017). Simulating Indonesian fuel subsidy reform: A social accounting matrix analysis. *Annals of Operations Research*, *255*(1-2), 591–615. doi:10.100710479-015-1954-x

Ferguson, T., & Roofe, C. G. (2020). SDG 4 in higher education: Challenges and opportunities. *International Journal of Sustainability in Higher Education*, *21*(5), 959–975. doi:10.1108/IJSHE-12-2019-0353

Ferrari, M., Matucci, G., & Morandi, M. (2019). *La scuola inclusiva dalla Costituzione a oggi. Riflessioni tra pedagogia e diritto*. FrancoAngeli.

Ferrera, M. (1996). The "Southern model" of welfare in social Europe. *Journal of European Social Policy*, *6*(1), 17–37. doi:10.1177/095892879600600102

Ferrer-Esteban, G. (2011). Beyond the Traditional Territorial Divide in the Italian Education System. Aspects of System Management Factors on Performance in Lower Secondary Education. *FGA Working Paper, 42*(12). Torino: Fondazione Giovanni Agnelli.

Ferrero, V. (2023c). Inclusione: una questione di formazione? Formazione degli insegnanti di sostegno e modalità di reclutamento come fattori non tradizionali di disuguaglianza. *Annali online della Didattica e della Formazione Docente, 15*(25), 252-272.

Ferrero, V. (2022). La scuola media unica nel primo ciclo di istruzione. Una riflessione tra equità e autonomia scolastica. *Dirigenti Scuola*, *41*(1), 41–55.

Ferrero, V. (2023a). Una scuola per la giustizia sociale. Riflessioni pedagogiche sull'equità in educazione in prospettiva gramsciana. *QTimes. Journal of Education. Technology and Social Study*, *15*(1-2), 97–108.

Ferrero, V. (2023b). School Between Equity and Inequalities: A Pedagogical Reflection on the Italian Context. In H. Vah Seliskar (Ed.), *Restorative Justice and Practices in the 21st Century* (pp. 175–204). IGI Global. doi:10.4018/978-1-6684-6145-7.ch008

Fhima, F., Nouira, R., & Sekkat, K. (2023). How does corruption affect sustainable development? A threshold non-linear analysis. *Economic Analysis and Policy*, *78*, 505–523. doi:10.1016/j.eap.2023.03.020

Fischer, F. (2020). Post-truth politics and climate denial: Further reflections. *Critical Policy Studies*, *14*(1), 124–130. doi:10.1080/19460171.2020.1734846

Fischer, F. (2021). *Truth and Post-Truth in Public Policy*. Cambridge University Press. doi:10.1017/9781108854344

Folke, O., & Rickne, J. (2020). All the single ladies: Job promotions and the durability of marriage. *American Economic Journal. Applied Economics*, *12*(1), 260–287. doi:10.1257/app.20180435

Fonseca, L. M., Domingues, J. P., & Dima, A. M. (2020). Mapping the sustainable development goals relationships. *Sustainability (Basel)*, *12*(8), 3359. doi:10.3390u12083359

Fraser, B. (2022, January 24). Is a river a person? Advocates for the legal rights of nature say yes. *Earthbeat*.

Freeman, R., Harrison, J., Wicks, A., Parmar, B., & De Colle, S. (2010). *Stakeholder theory: the state of the art*. Cambridge University Press. doi:10.1017/CBO9780511815768

Fujita, M., Krugman, P., & Venables, A. (1999). *The Spatial Economy: Cities, Regions and International Trade*. MIT Press. doi:10.7551/mitpress/6389.001.0001

Fuller, R., Landrigan, P. J., Balakrishnan, K., Bathan, G., Bose-O'Reilly, S., Brauer, M., Caravanos, J., Chiles, T., Cohen, A., Corra, L., Cropper, M., Ferraro, G., Hanna, J., Hanrahan, D., Hu, H., Hunter, D., Janata, G., Kupka, R., Lanphear, B., ... Yan, C. (2022). Pollution and health: A progress update. *The Lancet. Planetary Health*, *6*(6), e535–e547. doi:10.1016/S2542-5196(22)00090-0 PMID:35594895

Fu, Y., Zhou, X., Zhou, D., Sun, W., & Jiang, C. (2019). Sea Level Trend and Variability in the South China Sea. *ISPRS Annals of the Photogrammetry, Remote Sensing and Spatial Information Sciences*, *IV-2*(W5), 589–593. doi:10.5194/isprs-annals-IV-2-W5-589-2019

Gabay, C., & Ilcan, S. (2018). *The Politics Destination in the 2030 Sustainable Development Goals. Leaving No-One Behind*. Routledge. doi:10.4324/9780429490507

Gan Integrity. (2016). *Algeria: Country Profile*. Gan Integrity. https://www.ganintegrity.com/portal/country-profiles/algeria/

Gans-Morse, J., Borges, M., Makarin, A., Mannah-Blankson, T., Nickow, A., & Zhang, D. (2018). Reducing bureaucratic corruption: Interdisciplinary perspectives on what works. *World Development*, *105*, 171–188. doi:10.1016/j.worlddev.2017.12.015

Gartner. (2015). *IT Key Metrics Data 2015: Executive Summary*. Gartner. https://www.gartner.com/doc/2939218/it-key-metrics-data

Gavosto, A. (2022). *La scuola bloccata*. Laterza.

Gentili, A., & Pignataro, G. (2020). *Disuguaglianze e istruzione in Italia. Dalla scuola primaria all'università*. Carocci.

Gerwitz, S. (2006). Towards a Contextualized Analysis of Social Justice in Education. *Educational Philosophy and Theory, 38*(1), 69–81. doi:10.1111/j.1469-5812.2006.00175.x

Geyer, R., & Rihani, S. (2010). *Complexity and public policy: a new approach to twenty-first century politics, policy and society*. Routledge Press.

Giancola, O., & Salmieri, L. (2020). *Sociologia delle disuguaglianze. Teorie, metodi, ambiti*. Carocci.

Giangreco L. (2016). Small UAVs would rapidly collect nuclear information along with WC-135. *Inside the Air Force, 27*(24), 1-1.

Giddens, A. (1984). *The constitution of society: Outline of the theory of structuration*. Blackwell/Polity Press.

Gidigbi, M. O., & Bello, K. M. (2020). Petroleum Subsidy Reduction and Poverty in Nigeria: A Choice between Maintaining the Subsidy or Providing Infrastructural Services Equivalent to the Deadweight Loss. *Asian Development Perspectives, 11*(1), 70–81.

Gingnell, L., Franke, U., Lagerström, R., Ericsson, E., & Lilliesköld, J. (2014). Quantifying Success Factors for IT Projects—An Expert-Based Bayesian Model. *Information Systems Management, 31*(1), 21–36. doi:10.1080/10580530.2014.854033

Global call to invest in the futures of education: Support the Paris Declaration | Education within the 2030 Agenda for Sustainable Development. (n.d.). Retrieved 6 September 2022, from https://www.sdg4education2030.org/global-call-invest-futures-education-support-paris-declaration

Goal 4 | Department of Economic and Social Affairs. (n.d.). Retrieved 6 September 2022, from https://sdgs.un.org/goals/goal4

Gobbo, F. (2011). Ethnographic research in multicultural educational contexts as a contribution to intercultural dialogue. *Policy Futures in Education, 9*(1), 35–42. doi:10.2304/pfie.2011.9.1.35

Goldring, L. (2002). The power of school culture. *Leadership, 32*(2), 32–35.

Gomes, J., & Romão, M. (2012). Seleção de uma abordagem de gestão de investimentos em Sistemas e Tecnologias da Informação. *RISTI (Porto), 0*(10), 35–49. doi:10.4304/risti.10.35-50

Gomes, J., & Romão, M. (2015). Enhancing Organizational Maturity with Benefits Management. *International Journal of Information Technology Project Management, 6*(4), 34–47. doi:10.4018/IJITPM.2015100103

González García, E., Colomo Magaña, E., & Cívico Ariza, A. (2020). Quality education as a sustainable development goal in the context of 2030 agenda: Bibliometric approach. *Sustainability (Basel), 12*(15), 5884. doi:10.3390u12155884

Gordon, D. J., & Johnson, C. A. (2018). City-networks, global climate governance, and the road to 1.5 C. *Current Opinion in Environmental Sustainability, 30*, 35–41. doi:10.1016/j.cosust.2018.02.011

Goren, H., & Yemini, M. (2017). Global citizenship education redefined – A systematic review of empirical studies on global citizenship education. *International Journal of Educational Research, 82*, 170–183. doi:10.1016/j.ijer.2017.02.004

Gosling, L., & Edwards, M. (2003). *Toolkits: A practical guide to planning, monitoring, evaluation and impact assessment*. Save the Children UK.

GOV.UK. (2021). *European Convention on Human Rights protocol comes into force*. https://www.gov.uk/government/news/european-convention-on-human-rights-protocol-comes-into-force

GPTIC. (2012). *Plano global estratégico de racionalização e redução de custos nas TIC*. Administração Pública Horizonte. https://tic.gov.pt/pgetic/PGETIC_v1.0.pdf

Granata, A., & Ferrero, V. (2022). Nelle tasche della scuola. Coinvolgimento finanziario-organizzativo delle famiglie come fattore non tradizionale di disuguaglianza scolastica. *Scuola Democratica*, *10*(2), 363–384.

Grasso, M. (2015). Il successo scolastico dei giovani figli dell'immigrazione: Il ruolo della famiglia come capitale sociale. *Rivista Italiana Di Educazione Familiare*, *10*(1), 201–216.

Green Brunei. (n.d.). *Green Brunei – Youth-led platform for environmental sustainability*. Retrieved 13 December 2022, from https://green-brunei.com/

GreenIftar. (n.d.). Islam and sustainability. *Green Iftar.* https://www.greeniftar.com/en/islam-and-sustainability/

Grgurovic, M. (2011). Blended learning in an ESL class: A case study. *CALICO Journal*, *29*(1), 100–117. doi:10.11139/cj.29.1.100-117

Griffiths, M. (2003). *Action for social justice in education*. Open University Press.

Grimes, M. J. Q. (2008). *The conditions of successful civil society involvement in combating corruption: A survey of case study evidence*. Research Gate.

Grossman, P. Z. (2019). Utilizing Ostrom's institutional analysis and development framework toward an understanding of crisis-driven policy. *Policy Sciences*, *52*(1), 3–20. doi:10.100711077-018-9331-7

Guangying, C. (2014). An experimental research on blended learning in the development of listening and speaking skills in China. *Southern African Linguistics and Applied Language Studies*, *32*(4), 447–460. doi:10.2989/16073614.2014.999989

Güder, F. (2019). Yüksek Gelirli Ülkelerde Gelir Dağılımını Etkileyen Faktörler. *Fiscaoeconomia*, *3*(2), 198–216.

Guemar, K. (2021). Prevention of institutional corruption and mechanisms to combat it (Constituents and constraints). مجلة الأبحاث القانونية والسياسي.

Guerrero, O. A., & Castañeda, G. (2020). Policy priority inference: A computational framework to analyze the allocation of resources for the sustainable development goals. *Data & Policy*, *2*, e17. doi:10.1017/dap.2020.18

Guntzburger, Y., & Pauchant, T. C. (2014). Complexity and ethical crisis management: A systemic analysis of the Fukushima Daiichi nuclear disaster. *Journal of Organizational Effectiveness: People and Performance*, *1*(4), 378–401. doi:10.1108/JOEPP-09-2014-0060

Gupta, B., Dasgupta, S., & Gupta, A. (2008). Adoption of ICT in a government organization in a developing country: An empirical study. *The Journal of Strategic Information Systems*, *17*(2), 140–154. doi:10.1016/j.jsis.2007.12.004

Gupta, S., Davoodi, H., & Terme, R. A. (2002). Does corruption affect income inequality and poverty? *Economics of Governance*, *3*(1), 23–45. doi:10.1007101010100039

Gweshengwe, B. & Hassan, N.H. (2019). Knowledge to Policy: Understanding Poverty to Create Policies that Facilitate Zero Poverty in Brunei Darussalam. Southeast Asia: A Multidisciplinary Journal, 19, 95-104.

Gweshengwe, B., & Hassan, N. H. (2019). Knowledge to policy: Understanding poverty to create policies that facilitate zero poverty in Brunei Darussalam. *Southeast Asia: A Multidisciplinary Journal, 19*, 95-104.

Gweshengwe, B., & Hassan, N.H. (2020). Defining the characteristics of poverty and their implications for poverty analysis. *Cogent Soc. Sci.*, *6*(1). https://www.tandfonline.com/doi/epub/10.1080/23311886.2020.1768669?needAccess=true

Gweshengwe, B., & Hassan, N. H. (2020). Defining the characteristics of poverty and their implications for poverty analysis. *Cogent Social Sciences*, *6*(1), 1768669. doi:10.1080/23311886.2020.1768669

Gweshengwe, B., Hassan, N. H., & Ali Maricar, H. (2020). Perceptions of the Language and Meaning of Poverty in Brunei Darussalam. *Journal of Asian and African Studies*, *55*(7), 929–946. doi:10.1177/0021909619900218

Gyimah-Brempong, K. (2002). Corruption, economic growth, and income inequality in Africa. *Economics of Governance*, *3*(3), 183–209. doi:10.1007101010200045

Hackman, H. W. (2005). Five Essential Components for Social Justice Education. *Equity & Excellence in Education*, *38*(2), 103–109. doi:10.1080/10665680590935034

Hadjadj, D. J. M. P. (2007). Algeria: A Future Hijacked by Corruption. *PERSPECTIVE*, *12*(2), 263–277.

Haidich, A. B., & Ioannidis, J. P. A. (2004). The Gini coefficient as a measure for understanding accrual inequalities in multicentes clinical studies. *Journal of Clinical Epidemiology*, *57*(4), 341–348. doi:10.1016/j.jclinepi.2003.09.011 PMID:15135834

Haidi, H. (2023). A Digital Ethnographic Account of a Digital Islamic Society During COVID-19: An Islamic Governance Perspective. In M. Anshari, A. Razzaq, M. Fithriyah, & A. Kamal (Eds.), *Digital Psychology's Impact on Business and Society* (pp. 150–178). IGI Global., doi:10.4018/978-1-6684-6108-2.ch007

Haidi, H., & Hamdan, M. (2022). Analysis of the home-based online teaching and learning policy during the COVID-19 second wave in Brunei: A joint parent/teacher perception. *Asia Pacific Education Review*. Advance online publication. doi:10.100712564-022-09798-x

Hamdan, M., Jaidin, J. H., Fithriyah, M., & Anshari, M. (2020, December). E-learning in time of COVID-19 pandemic: Challenges & experiences. In *2020 sixth international conference on e-learning (econf)* (pp. 12-16). IEEE.

Hamdi, M. F. Z., Abdullah, N., Diyana, H., & Carnegie, P. J. (2023). Belonging and unbelonging in Kampong Ayer, Brunei Darussalam. In *(Re)presenting Brunei Darussalam: A Sociology of the Everyday*. Springer Nature Singapore. . doi:10.1007/978-981-19-6059-8

Hamlett, C. (2021, October 18). Could Property Law Help Achieve 'Rights of Nature' for Wild Animals? *The Revelator.*

Hannah, A., & Baekkeskov, E. (2020). The promises and pitfalls of polysemic ideas: 'One Health' and antimicrobial resistance policy in Australia and the UK. *Policy Sciences*, *53*(3), 437–452. doi:10.100711077-020-09390-3 PMID:32836405

Hardiman, R., & Jackson, B. W. (1997). Conceptual foundations for social justice courses. In M. Adams, L. A. Bell, & P. Griffin (Eds.), *Teaching for diversity and social justice: A sourcebook* (pp. 16–29). Routledge.

Harring, N., Jönsson, E., Matti, S., Mundaca, G., & Jagers, S. C. (2023). Cross-national analysis of attitudes towards fossil fuel subsidy removal. *Nature Climate Change*, *13*(3), 244–249. doi:10.103841558-023-01597-5

Hartley, K. (2015). *Can Government Think? Flexible economic opportunism and the pursuit of global competitiveness*. Routledge Press. doi:10.4324/9781315744674

Hartley, K., & Bales, S. (2020). COVID-19 response in Vietnam: Coordination and capacity in the new developmentalist paradigm. *Policy Design and Practice*.

Hartley, K., Kuecker, G., & Woo, J. J. (2019). Practicing public policy in an age of disruption. *Policy Design and Practice*, *2*(2), 163–181. doi:10.1080/25741292.2019.1622276

Hartley, K., Leischow, G., Waschak, M., Woo, J. J., & Phua, C. (2020). Conclusion: The future of Asian cities in an age of disruption. In K. Hartley, G. Kuecker, M. Waschak, J. J. Woo, & C. C. R. Phua (Eds.), *Governing cities: Asia's urban transformation* (pp. 270–275). Routledge. doi:10.4324/9780429439940-20

Harun, M., Mat, S. H. C., Fadzim, W. R., Khan, S. J. M., & Noor, M. S. Z. (2018). The effects of fuel subsidy removal on input costs of productions: Leontief input-output price model. *International Journal of Supply Chain Management, 7*(5), 529–534.

Hasan, N. N. B. A., Noor, K. B. M., Malik, A. A., & Ghani, Z. A. (2018). *The proposed model of the integration of the principle of Maqasid Al-Shariah in managerial decision-making process in shariah-compliant securities. Journal of Islamic, Social, Economics and Development.*

Hasmawati, F., Samiha, Y. T., Razzaq, A., & Anshari, M. (2020). Understanding nomophobia among digital natives: Characteristics and challenges. *Journal of Critical Reviews, 7*(13), 122–131.

Hassan, M. K., Saraç, M., & Khan, A. (2021). *Islamic finance and sustainable development.* Springer International Publishing. doi:10.1007/978-3-030-76016-8

Hassan, N. H., Rigg, J., Azalie, I. A., Yong, G. Y. V., Nurul, H. H. Z., & Shamsul, M. A. S. M. (2022). Making do and staying poor: The poverty context of Urban Brunei. *Geoforum, 136*, 132–141. doi:10.1016/j.geoforum.2022.09.012

Hattingh, S. (2018). Preparing the workforce for the Fourth Industrial Revolution. *Skills at Work: Theory and Practice Journal, 9*(1), 6–18.

Haykal, S. H. (2017). Fighting Corruption in MENA Region: Towards a Conceptual Framework. *Middle East Review of Public Administration, 3*(2), 1833.

Head, B. W. (2019). Forty years of wicked problems literature: Forging closer links to policy studies. *Policy and Society, 38*(2), 180–197. doi:10.1080/14494035.2018.1488797

Heikkilä, J., & Laukkanen, I. (2022). Gender-specific call of duty: A note on the neglect of conscription in gender equality indices. *Defence and Peace Economics, 33*(5), 603–615. doi:10.1080/10242694.2020.1844400

Hermann, C. F. (1963). Some consequences of crisis which limit the viability of organizations. *Administrative Science Quarterly, 8*(1), 61–82. doi:10.2307/2390887

Hermann, M. G. (2001). How decision units shape foreign policy: A theoretical framework. *International Studies Review, 3*(2), 47–81. doi:10.1111/1521-9488.00234

Hermann, M. G., & Dayton, B. W. (2009). Transboundary crises through the eyes of policymakers: Sense making and crisis management. *Journal of Contingencies and Crisis Management, 17*(4), 233–241. doi:10.1111/j.1468-5973.2009.00590.x

Herweijer, C., Combes, B., Johnson, L., McCargow, R., Bhardwaj, S., Jackson, B., & Ramchandani, P. (2018). *Enabling a sustainable Fourth Industrial Revolution: How G20 countries can create the conditions for emerging technologies to benefit people and the planet (No. 2018-32).* Economics Discussion Papers.

Hess, D. J., Lanig, H., & Vaughan, W. (2007). Educating for equity and social justice: A conceptual model for cultural engagement. *Multicultural Perspectives, 9*(1), 32–39. doi:10.1080/15210960701334037

Heyneman, S. P. (Ed.). (2004). *Islam and social policy.* Vanderbilt University Press. doi:10.2307/j.ctv17vf6q5

Hildt, L. (2019). *Implementation of rulings for nature conservation Court of Justice of the European Union case studies.* EEB.

Hill Collins, P. (2019). Intersectionality as critical social theory. Duke University Press.

Hillix, W. A., & L'Abate, L. (2011). The role of paradigms in science and theory construction. In *Paradigms in theory construction* (pp. 3–17). Springer New York.

Hippe, R., Araújo, L., & da Costa, P. D. (2016). *Equity in education in Europe*. Publications Office of the European Union.

Hoffman, S. (2022). China's Tech-Enhanced Authoritarianism. *Journal of Democracy*, *33*(2), 76–89. doi:10.1353/jod.2022.0019

Hogl, K., Kleinschmit, D., & Rayner, J. (2016). Achieving policy integration across fragmented policy domains: Forests, agriculture, climate and energy. *Environment and Planning. C, Government & Policy*, *34*(3), 399–414. doi:10.1177/0263774X16644815

Holder, J. (1997). Case C-44/95, R. v. Secretary of State for the Environment, ex parte Royal Society for the Protection of Birds, Judgment of the Court of Justice 11 July 1996, [1996] ECR I-3805. *Common Market Law Review*, *34*(6), 1469–1480. doi:10.54648/148721

Holgeid, K., & Jørgensen, M. (2020). Benefits management and agile practices in software projects: how perceived benefits are impacted. In proceedings of the *2020 IEEE 22nd Conference on Business Informatics (CBI),* Antwerp, Belgium, 48-56. 10.1109/CBI49978.2020.10057

Holgeid, K., Krogstie, J., Patrick, M., Saur, E., & Sjøberg, D. (2022). Benefits management and Information Technology work distribution. *IET Software*, *16*(4), 438–454. doi:10.1049fw2.12062

Holmes, P., & Corbett, J. (Eds.). (2022). *Critical Intercultural Pedagogy for Difficult Times. Conflict, Crisis and Creativity*. Routledge. doi:10.4324/9781003150756

Homei, A. (2016). The science of population and birth control in post-war Japan. *Science, technology, and medicine in the modern Japanese empire.*

Homer-Dixon, T. (2011). Complexity science. *Oxford Leadership Journal*, *2*(1), 1–15.

Hope, S. Sr. (2022). Reducing corruption and bribery in Africa as a target of the sustainable development goals: Applying indicators for assessing performance. *Journal of Money Laundering Control*, *25*(2), 313–329. doi:10.1108/JMLC-03-2021-0018

Houeland, C. (2020). Contentious and institutional politics in a petro-state: Nigeria's 2012 fuel subsidy protests. *The Extractive Industries and Society*, *7*(4), 1230–1237. doi:10.1016/j.exis.2020.05.010

Houeland, C. (2022). The social contract and industrial citizenship: Nigerian trade unions' role in the recurring fuel subsidy protests. *Africa*, *92*(5), 860–879. doi:10.1017/S0001972022000523

Hunter, M., Uwaydah Mardini, R., El-Seblani, A., & Elsayed, S. (2020). Anti-corruption, transparency and accountability: case study of healthcare in the Arab countries. *Global Health Action, 13*(sup1), 1704529.

Hutchison, A. (2014). The Whanganui River as a Legal Person. *Alternative Law Journal*, *39*(3), 179–182. doi:10.1177/1037969X1403900309

Huxham, C., & Vangen, S. (2013). *Managing to collaborate: The theory and practice of collaborative advantage*. Routledge Press. doi:10.4324/9780203010167

Hynes, W. (2017). Introduction: a complexity approach to economic challenges. In *Debate the Issues: Complexity and policy making. OECD Insights*. OECD Publishing. doi:10.1787/9789264271531-

Hytten, K. (2015). Ethics in teaching for democracy and social justice. *Democracy & Education*, *23*(2), 1–10.

Hytten, K., & Bettez, S. C. (2011). Understanding education for social justice. *Educational Foundations, 25*(1-2), 7–24.

Ianes, D. (2023). *Evolvere il sostegno si può (e si deve): Alcuni contributi di ricerca in Pedagogia e Didattica speciale al dibattito sulla Legge 107*. Erickson.

Ibn Khaldun. (2004). The Muqaddimah: An Introduction to History. Princeton University Press.

Ibrahim, N. (2022). Halal policy in Brunei Darussalam. *Journal of Halal Science and Technology, 1*(1), 86–91. doi:10.59202/jhst.v1i1.458

Ibrahim, T. (2005). Global citizenship education: Mainstreaming the curriculum? *Cambridge Journal of Education, 35*(2), 177–194. doi:10.1080/03057640500146823

Idrisu, B. (2020). *Fossil fuel subsidy reform for sustainable development in Nigeria: the role of renewable energy diffusion*. University of Delaware.

Ike, M., Donovan, J. D., Topple, C., & Masli, E. K. (2019). The process of selecting and prioritising corporate sustainability issues: Insights for achieving the Sustainable Development Goals. *Journal of Cleaner Production, 236*, 117661. doi:10.1016/j.jclepro.2019.117661

ILO. (2022, September 29). *UN General Assembly recognizes human right to a clean, healthy, and sustainable environment*. https://www.ilo.org/global/about-the-ilo/newsroom/news/WCMS_857164/lang--en/index.htm#:~:text=This%20reality%20was%20recognized%20by,been%20a%20long%20time%20coming

Im, J. (2020). Earth observations and geographic information science for sustainable development goals. *GIScience & Remote Sensing, 57*(5), 591–592. doi:10.1080/15481603.2020.1763041

IMO. (2021). *Cutting GHG emissions from shipping - 10 years of mandatory rules*. IMO. https://www.imo.org/en/MediaCentre/PressBriefings/pages/DecadeOfGHGAction.aspx

Inam, B., Guzel, S., & Murat, D. (2019). The Correlation Between Corruption and Socioeconomic Development: An Application For OECD Countries. *Hacettepe University Journal of Economics and Administrative Sciences, 37*(2), 325–339. doi:10.17065/huniibf.373711

INVALSI. (2022). *Rapporto INVALSI 2022*. INVALSI.

Ipadeola, O. (2016). Qualitative study on the patterns, experiences and manifestations of corruption in Nigeria. In Jasmin, L., & Bunk, B. (2017). *Using civil society as an authoritarian legitimation strategy: Algeria and Mozambique in comparative perspective. Democratization*, *24*(6), 987–1005.

Irfan, M., Zhao, Z. Y., Ahmad, M., & Mukeshimana, M. C. (2019). Solar energy development in Pakistan: Barriers and policy recommendations. *Sustainability (Basel), 11*(4), 1206. doi:10.3390u11041206

IRSN. (2011). *Impact on the marine environment of radioactive releases following the nuclear accident at Fukushima Daiichi*. IRSN.

ISACA. (2012). *Cobit 5 - Business Framework for the Governance and Management of Enterprise IT*. ISACA.

IslamQuest. (n.d.). What is the Quran's perspective on waste and extravagance? *Islam Quest*. https://www.islamquest.net/en/archive/fa21210

Itumo, A., & Onyejiuba, E. I. (2019). Oil Subsidy And Development Of Local Refineries In Nigeria: A Critical Analysis. *African Journal of Politics and Administrative Studies, 12*, 1.

Ivanovic, A., Cooper, H., & Nguyen, A. M. (2018). Institutionalisation of SDG 16: More a trickle than a cascade? *Social Alternatives*, *37*(1), 49–57.

Izni Azrein Noor Azalie & Yong, G.Y.V. (2022). Heritage Industry as Conservation Strategy for Kampong Ayer (Brunei Darussalam). *The Brunei Museums J.*

Jabareen, Y. (2011). Teaching Sustainability: A Multidisciplinary Approach. *Scientific Research*, *2*(4), 388–392.

Jackson, A. P., & Meyers, J. (2016). The role of social support in reducing psychological distress among African American single mothers. *Journal of Family Issues*, *37*(10), 1428–1452.

Jacobs, M. (2020). *Beyond growth: towards a new economic approach*. OECD Publishing.

James, T., & Jorgensen, P. (2009). Policy knowledge, policy formulation and change: Revisiting a foundational question. *Policy Studies Journal: the Journal of the Policy Studies Organization*, *37*(1), 141–162. doi:10.1111/j.1541-0072.2008.00300.x

Javaid. (2022). View of The Principles of a Circular Economy in the Light of Islamic Values and Beliefs. *Journal of Islamic Thought and Civilization*, 212–230. https://journals.umt.edu.pk/index.php/JITC/article/view/2113/996

Jessop, B. (1998). The rise of governance and the risk of failure: The case of economic development. *International Social Science Journal*, *155*(155), 29–45. doi:10.1111/1468-2451.00107

Johal, S., Anthony, L., Dragicevic, N., Thirgood, J., & Dockree, T. (2022). *Navigating Complexity: Policy Making for an Evolving World*. Canadian Standards Association.

Johnstone, S. M., & Soares, L. (2014). Principles for developing competency-based education programs. *Change*, *46*(2), 12–19. doi:10.1080/00091383.2014.896705

Johnston, P., Everard, M., Santillo, D., & Robèrt, K.-H. (2007). Reclaiming the definition of sustainability. *Environmental Science and Pollution Research International*, *14*(1), 60–66. doi:10.1065/espr2007.01.375 PMID:17352129

Josua, M. (2017). Legitimation towards whom? Managing the legitimacy crisis in Algeria during the Arab Uprisings. *Political Behavior*, *11*(2), 301–324.

Joumard, I., Pisu, M., & Debbie, B. (2012). Tackling income inequality: The role of taxes and transfers. *OECD Journal: Economic Studies*, *2012*(1), 37–70. doi:10.1787/eco_studies-2012-5k95xd6l65lt

Joy, F. (2000). *Integrating Technology into Instruction in an Inclusive Classroom for Diverse Learners*. Rowan University.

Judiasih, S. D., Sudini, L. P., Rubiati, B., Yuanitasari, D., Kusmayanti, H., & Salim, E. F. (2019). Sustainable Development Goals and Elimination of Children's Marriage Practice in Indonesia. *JurnalNotariil*, *4*(1), 1–12.

Jurado de Los Santos, P., Moreno-Guerrero, A. J., Marín-Marín, J. A., & Soler Costa, R. (2020). The term equity in education: A literature review with scientific mapping in Web of Science. *International Journal of Environmental Research and Public Health*, *17*(10), 3526. doi:10.3390/ijerph17103526 PMID:32443493

Kaasa, A. (2005). *Factors Of Income Inequality And Their Influence Mechanisms: A Theoretical Overview*. University of Tartu Faculty of Economics and Business Administration Working Paper(No. 40).

Kahn, L. H. (2020). *Who's In charge? Leadership during epidemics, bioterror attacks, and other public health crises*. ABC-CLIO.

Kanor, K. (2021). *L'inclusion sociale. Une utopie réalisable*. Paris: L'Harmanattan.

Kapucu, N., Arslan, T., & Collins, M. L. (2010). Examining intergovernmental and interorganizational response to catastrophic disasters: Toward a network-centered approach. *Administration & Society, 42*(2), 222–247. doi:10.1177/0095399710362517

Karacan, R. (2014). *Kapitalist Ekonomide Gelir Dağılımı ve Yoksulluk*. Yalın Yayıncılık.

Karan, A., Negandhi, H., Hussain, S., Zapata, T., Mairembam, D., De Graeve, H., Buchan, J., & Zodpey, S. (2021). Size, composition and distribution of health workforce in India: Why, and where to invest? *Human Resources for Health, 19*(1), 1–14. doi:10.118612960-021-00575-2 PMID:33752675

Kariuki, P., & Reddy, P. (2017). Operationalising an effective monitoring and evaluation system for local government: Considerations for best practice. *African Evaluation Journal, 5*(2), 1–8. doi:10.4102/aej.v5i2.240

Karlsson, C., & Karlsson, M. (2002). Economic policy, institutions and entrepreneurship. *Small Business Economics, 19*(2), 163–182. doi:10.1023/A:1016259104162

Karraker, A., Latham, K., & Segrin, C. (2019). Divorce and health: Current trends and future directions. *Journal of Marriage and Family, 81*(4), 835–851.

Keiner, M., & Kim, A. (2007). Transnational city networks for sustainability. *European Planning Studies, 15*(10), 1369–1395. doi:10.1080/09654310701550843

Khair, S. (2018). UNCAC and civil society activism against corruption in Bangladesh. In Asian Yearbook of International Law, 20, 115-162. doi:10.1163/9789004379770_005

Khan, M. A. (1990). Elimination of poverty in the Islamic economic framework. *Islamic Studies, 29*(2), 143–162.

Khetran, M. S. B., & Khalid, M. H. (2019). The China-Pakistan Economic Corridor: Gateway to Central Asia. *China Quarterly of International Strategic Studies, 5*(03), 455–469. doi:10.1142/S2377740019500179

Kilonzo, S. M., & Ojebode, A. (2022). Research Methods for Public Policy. In *Public Policy and Research in Africa* (pp. 63–85). Springer International Publishing.

Klobas, J. E., & McGill, T. J. (2010). The role of involvement in learning management system success. *Journal of Computing in Higher Education, 22*(2), 114–134. doi:10.100712528-010-9032-5

Koball, H. L., Moiduddin, E., Henderson, J., Goesling, B., & Besculides, M. (2010). What Do We Know About the Link Between Marriage and Health? *Journal of Family Issues, 31*(8), 1019–1040. doi:10.1177/0192513X10365834

Koehler, G. (2016). Tapping the Sustainable Development Goals for progressive gender equity and equality policy? *Gender and Development, 24*(1), 53–68. doi:10.1080/13552074.2016.1142217

Koi-Akrofi, G. (2020). Justification of, and Benefits Realization Beyond IT Investments: Analysis from Literature. *International Journal of Managing Value and Supply Chains, 11*(3), 1–16. doi:10.5121/ijmvsc.2020.11301

Kon, J. (2022, November 1). Sultanate gets on SDG tracker » Borneo Bulletin Online. *Sultanate Gets on SDG Tracker*. https://borneobulletin.com.bn/sultanate-gets-on-sdg-tracker/

Kromer, J. (2010). *Fixing Broken Cities: The Implementation of Urban Development Strategies*. Routledge.

Kuecker, G. D., & Hartley, K. (2020a). How smart cities became the urban norm: Power and knowledge in New Songdo City. *Annals of the American Association of Geographers, 110*(2), 516–524. doi:10.1080/24694452.2019.1617102

Kuecker, G. D., & Hartley, K. (2020b Forthcoming). Disaster risk reduction and the development narrative: towards a new public policy epistemic. In A. Brik & L. Pal (Eds.), *The Future of the Policy Sciences*. Edward Elgar Publishing.

Kuhn, H. (2020). Reducing inequality within and among countries: Realizing SDG 10—A developmental perspective. *Sustainable Development Goals and Human Rights, 5*, 137-153.

Kuik, C. C. (2021). Laos's Enthusiastic Embrace of China's Belt and Road Initiative. *Asian Perspective, 45*(4), 735–759. doi:10.1353/apr.2021.0042

Kumaraswamy, M., Zou, W., & Zhang, J. (2015). Reinforcing relationships for resilience – by embedding end-user 'people' in public-private partnerships. Civil Engineering and Environmental Systems, 32(1-2), 119-129. doi:10.1080/10286608.2015.1022727

Kumari, R. (2013). Role of civil society for combating corruption in India. *International Journal of Innovative Research and Development, 2*(3), 34–50.

Kumar, P., Ahmed, F., Singh, R. K., & Sinha, P. (2018). Determination of hierarchical relationships among sustainable development goals using interpretive structural modeling. *Environment, Development and Sustainability, 20*(5), 2119–2137. doi:10.100710668-017-9981-1

Kyle, J. (2018). Local corruption and popular support for fuel subsidy reform in Indonesia. *Comparative Political Studies, 51*(11), 1472–1503. doi:10.1177/0010414018758755

Kyne, D. & Bolin, B. (2016). Emerging Environmental Justice Issues in Nuclear Power and Radioactive Contamination. *Environmental Research and Public Health, 700.*

Laberge, M., & Touihri, N. (2019). Can SDG 16 data drive national accountability? A cautiously optimistic view. *Global Policy, 10*(S1), 153–156. doi:10.1111/1758-5899.12607

Lai, K. P., Lin, S., & Sidaway, J. D. (2020). Financing the Belt and Road Initiative (BRI): Research agendas beyond the "debt-trap" discourse. *Eurasian Geography and Economics, 61*(2), 109–124. doi:10.1080/15387216.2020.1726787

Laldin, M. A., & Furqani, H. (2013). Developing Islamic finance in the framework of maqasid al-Shari'ah: Understanding the ends (maqasid) and the means (wasa'il). *International Journal of Islamic and Middle Eastern Finance and Management, 6*(4), 278–289. doi:10.1108/IMEFM-05-2013-0057

Lambsdorff, J. G. (2006). Causes and consequences of corruption: What do we know from a cross-section of countries. *RePEc Econpapers, 1*, 3-51.

Langridge, C. (2013). *Liberalism: Another Tool of Western Hegemony*. E-International Relations.

Lantong, A. M. (2018). The Islamic Epistemology and its Implications for Education of Muslims in the Philippines. *Journal of Education and Practice, 9*(15), 68–73.

Larch, M. (2012). Fiscal Performance and Income Inequality: Are Unequal Societies More Deficit-Prone? Some Cross-Country Evidence. *Kyklos, 65*(1), 53–80. doi:10.1111/j.1467-6435.2011.00527.x

Larson, E. W., & Gray, C. F. (2017). *Project Management: The Managerial Process* (7th ed.). McGraw-Hill Education.

Lau, H. C., Zhang, K., Bokka, H. K., & Ramakrishna, S. (2022). A Review of the Status of Fossil and Renewable Energies in Southeast Asia and Its Implications on the Decarbonization of ASEAN. *Energies, 15*(6), 2152. doi:10.3390/en15062152

Laursen, M., & Svejvig, P. (2016). Taking stock of project value creation: A structured literature review with future directions for research and practice. *International Journal of Project Management, 34*(4), 736–747. doi:10.1016/j.ijproman.2015.06.007

Law Insider. (2023). *Overriding reasons relating to the public interest definition*. https://www.lawinsider.com/dictionary/overriding-reasons-relating-to-the-public-interest

Law, S., Leung, A. W., & Xu, C. (2020). Severe acute respiratory syndrome (SARS) and coronavirus disease-2019 (COVID-19): From causes to preventions in Hong Kong. *International Journal of Infectious Diseases, 94*, 156–163. doi:10.1016/j.ijid.2020.03.059 PMID:32251790

Lazzarini, S. (2015). Strategizing by the government can industrial policy create firm-level competitive advantage? *Strategic Management Journal, 36*(1), 97–112. doi:10.1002mj.2204

Leal Filho, W., Tripathi, S. K., Andrade Guerra, J. B. S. O. D., Giné-Garriga, R., Orlovic Lovren, V., & Willats, J. (2019). Using the sustainable development goals towards a better understanding of sustainability challenges. *International Journal of Sustainable Development and World Ecology, 26*(2), 179–190. doi:10.1080/13504509.2018.1505674

Learning Technology Center. (2010). *Hybrid Courses*. www.uwm.edu/1tc/hybrid/faculty/....//tips.cfm

Lee, C. C., & Lee, C. C. (2018). The Impact of Country Risk on Income Inequality: A Multilevel Analysis. *Social Indicators Research, 136*(1), 139–162. doi:10.100711205-016-1534-8

Lee, H. L., & Shen, Z. J. M. (2020). Supply chain and logistics innovations with the Belt and Road Initiative. *Journal of Management Science and Engineering, 5*(2), 77–86. doi:10.1016/j.jmse.2020.05.001

Lee, M. (2008). Government Influence on the Formation of Nonprofits: A dual relationship between local government and local nonprofits. *International Review of Public Administration, 13*(2), 97–115. doi:10.1080/12294659.2008.10805124

Legutko, A. J. (2018). NGO in the Modern State. *Institutionalist Perspectives on Development: A Multidisciplinary Approach*, 59-74.

Leininger, J., Lührmann, A., & Sigman, R. (2019). *The Relevance of Social Policies for Democracy. Preventing Autocratisation through Synergies between SDG 10 and SDG 16*. Bonn: Deutsches Institut für Entwicklungspolitik gGmbH.

Leischow, S. J., Best, A., Trochim, W. M., Clark, P. I., Gallagher, R. S., Marcus, S. E., & Matthews, E. (2008). Systems thinking to improve the public's health. *American Journal of Preventive Medicine, 35*(2), S196–S203. doi:10.1016/j.amepre.2008.05.014 PMID:18619400

Lemke, A. A., & Harris-Wai, J. N. (2015). Stakeholder engagement in policy development: Challenges and opportunities for human genomics. *Genetics in Medicine, 17*(12), 949–957. doi:10.1038/gim.2015.8 PMID:25764215

Leonhardt, D. (2020). A Complete List of Trump's Attempts to Play Down Coronavirus. *The New York Times*. https://www.nytimes.com/2020/03/15/opinion/trump-coronavirus.html

Lewis, D. J., Yang, X., Moise, D., & Roddy, S. J. (2021). Dynamic synergies between China's belt and road initiative and the UN's sustainable development goals. *Journal of International Business Policy, 4*(1), 58–79. doi:10.105742214-020-00082-6

Li, G., Fang, C., Wang, S., & Sun, S. (2016). The effect of economic growth, urbanization, and industrialization on fine particulate matter (PM2. 5) concentrations in China. *Environmental Science & Technology, 50*(21), 11452–11459. doi:10.1021/acs.est.6b02562 PMID:27709931

Li, H., Xu, L. C., & Zou, H.-F. (2000). Corruption, Income Distribution, and Growth. *Economics and Politics, 12*(2), 155–182. doi:10.1111/1468-0343.00073

Li, L. (2021). Integrating climate change impact in new building design process: A review of building life cycle carbon emission assessment methodologies. *Cleaner Engineering and Technology, 5*, 100286. doi:10.1016/j.clet.2021.100286

Limam, M. H. (2012). Detailed analysis of the phenomenon of political corruption in Algeria: Causes, repercussions and reform. *Contemporary Arab Affairs, 5*(2), 252–278. doi:10.1080/17550912.2012.671999

Lim, C. P. (2008). Global citizenship education, school curriculum and games: Learning Mathematics, English and Science as a global citizen. *Computers & Education, 51*(3), 1073–1093. doi:10.1016/j.compedu.2007.10.005

Lin, B., & Li, A. (2012). Impacts of removing fossil fuel subsidies on China: How large and how to mitigate? *Energy, 44*(1), 741–749. doi:10.1016/j.energy.2012.05.018

Lin, B.-W. (2007). Information technology capability and value creation: Evidence from the US banking industry. *Technology in Society, 29*(1), 93–106. doi:10.1016/j.techsoc.2006.10.003

Lin, C., & Pervan, G. (2003). The practice of IS/IT benefits management in large Australian organizations. *Information & Management, 41*(1), 13–24. doi:10.1016/S0378-7206(03)00002-8

Lin, C., & Pervan, G. (2005). IS/IT Investment Evaluation and Benefit Realization Practices in Taiwanese SMEs. *Journal of Research and Practice in Information Technology, 37*(3), 235–251.

Lipton, E., Sanger, D., Haberman, M., Shear, M., Mazzetti, M., & Barnes, J. (2020). He Could Have Seen What Was Coming: Behind Trump's Failure on the Virus. *The New York Times*. https://www.nytimes.com/2020/04/11/us/politics/coronavirus-trump-response.html

Li, S., & Wang, H. (2018). Traditional literature review and research synthesis. In A. Phakiti, P. De Costa, L. Plonsky, & S. Starfield (Eds.), *The Palgrave handbook of applied linguistics research methodology* (pp. 123–144). Palgrave MacMillan. doi:10.1057/978-1-137-59900-1_6

List, J. A., & Gallet, C. A. (1999). The Kuznets Curve: What Happens After the Inverted-U? *Review of Development Economics, 3*(2), 200–206. doi:10.1111/1467-9361.00061

Liu, F., Li, L., Zhang, Y., Ngo, Q. T., & Iqbal, W. (2021). Role of education in poverty reduction: Macroeconomic and social determinants form developing economies. *Environmental Science and Pollution Research International, 28*(44), 63163–63177. doi:10.100711356-021-15252-z PMID:34226999

Liu, H., & Reczek, C. (2015). Cohabitation and US adult mortality: An examination by gender and race. *Journal of Health and Social Behavior, 56*(3), 405–422.

Li, Y., & Zhu, X. (2019). The 2030 agenda for sustainable development and China's belt and road initiative in Latin America and the Caribbean. *Sustainability (Basel), 11*(8), 2297. doi:10.3390u11082297

Lodhi, I. (2021). Globalisation and public policy: Bridging the disciplinary and epistemological boundaries. *Policy and Society, 40*(4), 522–544. doi:10.1080/14494035.2021.1987137

Löfstedt, U. (2005). E-Government: Assessment of Current Research and some Proposals for Future Directions. *International Journal of Public Information Systems, 1*, 39–52.

Low, J. (2016). Singapore's Whole-of-Government Approach in Crisis Management. *Ethos (Berkeley, Calif.)*, 16.

Luna-Pla, I., & Nicolás-Carlock, J. R. (2020). Corruption and complexity: A scientific framework for the analysis of corruption networks. *Applied Network Science, 5*(1), 1–18. doi:10.100741109-020-00258-2

Ly, B. (2020). Challenge and perspective for digital Silk road. *Cogent Business & Management, 7*(1), 1804180. doi:10.1080/23311975.2020.1804180

Magagula, B. S. (2019). *An evaluation of the implementation of monitoring and evaluation systems in the office of the Premier, Free State provincial government* [Doctoral dissertation]. Central University of Technology, Free State.

Magni, F. (2020). *Formazione iniziale e reclutamento degli insegnanti in Italia. Percorso storico e prospettive pedagogiche*. Studium.

Mahyudi, M. (2015). Reviving the Islamic economic system through shariah-based public policy. *Humanomics, 31*(4), 415–429. doi:10.1108/H-06-2015-0037

Mail, A., Ampuan Tengah, A. B., Makmun, R., Abu Bakar, N. S., Pg Hj Besar, P. H. S. N., Tarasat, S., & Abu Bakar, T. (2022). Brunei Darussalam: Educational Policies in Six Decades. Brunei Historical Society/Persatuan Sejarah Brunei.

Majekodunmi, A. (2013). The political economy of fuel subsidy removal in Nigeria. *International Journal of Management and Social Sciences Research, 2*(7), 76–81.

Maleduca, M. (2010). Inclusive Education in Italy: An Overview. In V. Timmons & P. Noonan-Walsh (Eds.), A long Walk to School. Global Perspectives on Inclusive Education (pp. 115-135). Paderbon: Brill.

Malhotra, N., & Kuo, A. G. (2008). Attributing blame: The public's response to Hurricane Katrina. *The Journal of Politics, 70*(1), 120–135. doi:10.1017/S0022381607080097

Malla, M. H., & Pathranarakul, P. (2022). Fiscal Policy and Income Inequality: The Critical Role of Institutional Capacity. *Economies, 10*(5), 115. doi:10.3390/economies10050115

Malone, D. M. (2018). On SDG 16: Peace, justice, and strong institutions. *Freedom from Fear, 2018*(14), 174–179. doi:10.18356/0f6c0938-en

Manson, S. M. (2001). Simplifying complexity: A review of complexity theory. *Geoforum, 32*(3), 405–414. doi:10.1016/S0016-7185(00)00035-X

Marczell, Z. (2018). *The Effect of Civil Society Organizations on Corruption Perception: The Case of EU28.* (M.Sc. Public Policy and Human Development). Maastricht University, .

Markiewicz, A., & Patrick, I. (2016). *Developing monitoring and evaluation frameworks (No. BOOK).* Sage Publications. doi:10.4135/9781071878774

Marnewick, C. (2016). Benefits of information system projects: The tale of two countries. *International Journal of Project Management, 34*(4), 748–760. doi:10.1016/j.ijproman.2015.03.016

Maroco, J., & Garcia-Marques, T. (2006). Qual a fiabilidade do alfa de Cronbach? Questões antigas e soluções modernas. *Laboratório de Psicologia, 4*(1), 65–90.

Marquette, H., & Peiffer, C. (2014). Corruption and collective action: Shifting the equilibrium. *Research Paper,* (32).

Marquette, H., & Peiffer, C. (2015). *Collective action and systemic corruption.* Paper presented at the ECPR Joint Sessions of Workshops, University of Warsaw.

Marquette, H., Pavarala, V., & Malik, K. K. (2014). Religion and attitudes towards corruption in India: A collective action problem? *Development in Practice, 24*(7), 854–866.

Martín, A. N. (2014). Internal Investigations, Whistle-Blowing, and Cooperation: The Struggle for Information in the Criminal Process. *Preventing Corporate Corruption: The Anti-Bribery Compliance Model*, 69-92.

Martinelli, M. (2015). *Didattica speciale. Insegnare a persone con disabilità, difficoltà e svantaggi.* Mondadori Università.

Martinsuo, M., & Killen, C. (2014). Value Management in Project Portfolios: Identifying and Assessing Strategic Value. *Project Management Journal, 45*(5), 45. doi:10.1002/pmj.21452

Marwane, A. (2019). The Uncertain Future of Algeria's Anti-corruption Battles. *FIKRA Forum.* https://www.washingtoninstitute.org/fikraforum/view/the-uncertain-future-of-algerias-anti-corruption-battles

Marzuki, S. Z., Zreik, M., Buyong, S. Z., Goyipnazarov, S., Mirzaliev, S., & Bakhramovna, I. A. (2023). An Importance Satisfaction Analysis of Hosting Events in Hangzhou, China: A Pilot Study. *Advances in Social Sciences Research Journal, 10*(6.2), 107–117. doi:10.14738/assrj.106.2.14996

Mathews, J. (2006). Catch-up strategies and the latecomer effect in industrial development. *New Political Economy, 11*(3), 313–355. doi:10.1080/13563460600840142

Mathew, V. N., Abdullah, A. M. R. A., & Ismail, S. N. M. (2014). Acceptance on halal food among non-Muslim consumers. *Procedia: Social and Behavioral Sciences, 121*, 262–271. doi:10.1016/j.sbspro.2014.01.1127

May, C. (2020). Should rivers have legal rights? *Melbourne Law School.* https://law.unimelb.edu.au/news/MLS/should-rivers-have-legal-rights

Mayabi, C. (2015). *The Role of Education in Fighting Inequality*. GRIN.

May, P., Sapotichne, J., & Workman, S. (2006). Policy coherence and policy domains. *Policy Studies Journal: the Journal of the Policy Studies Organization, 34*(3), 381–403. doi:10.1111/j.1541-0072.2006.00178.x

Mayya, S. (2015). Role of Non Governmental Organisation in Rural Development: A Study in Dakshina Kannada District. *Sumedha Journal of Management, 4*(4), 27–38.

Mazzucato, M. (2015). *Building the entrepreneurial state: a new framework for envisioning and evaluating a mission-oriented public sector.* Working Paper No. 824, Levy Economics Institute.

McArthur, J. W., & Rasmussen, K. (2018). Change of pace: Accelerations and advances during the Millennium Development Goal era. *World Development, 105*, 132–143. doi:10.1016/j.worlddev.2017.12.030

McCulloch, N., Moerenhout, T., & Yang, J. (2021). Fuel subsidy reform and the social contract in Nigeria: A micro-economic analysis. *Energy Policy, 156*, 112336. doi:10.1016/j.enpol.2021.112336 PMID:34483438

McGrath, S., & Nolan, A. (2016). SDG 4 and the Child's Right to Education. *Norrag News, 54*, 122–123.

McKay, V. (2018). Introducing a parallel curriculum to enhance social and environmental awareness in South African school workbooks. Balancing individualism and collectivism: Social and environmental justice, 97-122. doi:10.1007/978-3-319-58014-2_5

McKean, M., & Ostrom, E. (n.d.). *Common property regimes in the forest: Just a relic from the past?* Academic Press.

Meirison, M. (2017). The development of Islamic economics in various parts of the world. *JEBI (Jurnal Ekonomi dan Bisnis Islam), 2*(2), 197-206.

Melhuish, E. (2014). The impact of early childhood education and care on improved wellbeing. In British Academy (Eds.), If you could do one thing... Nine local actions to reduce health inequalities (pp. 33-43). London: British Academy.

MFA. (n.d.). *Brunei Darussalam Government Scholarship (BDGS)*. Retrieved 17 November 2022, from https://www.mfa.gov.bn/Pages/bdgs/bdgs2022.aspx

Milani, L., & Scuola di Barbiana. (1967). *Lettera a una professoressa*. Firenze: LEF.

Mincu, M. E. (2013). Balancing Citizenship and Interculturalism: A Comparison of Two European Policy Context. *Intercultural Education, 24*(6), 521–531. doi:10.1080/14675986.2013.864872

Mincu, M. E. (2020). *Sistemi scolastici nel mondo globale. Educazione comparata e politiche educative*. Mondadori Università.

Mincu, M. E., & Granata, A. (2021). Teachers' informal leadership for equity in France and Italy during the first wave of education emergency. *Teachers and Teaching*, 1–22. doi:10.1080/13540602.2021.1986695

Ministry of State Secretariat of the Republic of. Indonesia. (2021). *Indonesia jasi poror martim dunia perlu peran semua pihak*. Setneg. https://www.setneg.go.id/baca/index/wujudkan_indonesia_jadi_poros_maritim_dunia_perlu_peran_semua_pihak

Misseyanni, A., Lytras, M. D., Papadopoulou, P., & Marouli, C. (Eds.). (2018). *Active learning strategies in higher education: Teaching for leadership, innovation, and creativity*. Emerald Publishing Limited. doi:10.1108/9781787144873

Mocca, E. (2017). City networks for sustainability in Europe: An urban-level analysis. *Journal of Urban Affairs*, *39*(5), 691–710. doi:10.1080/07352166.2017.1282769

Möckel, S. (2017). The European ecological network "Natura 2000" and its derogation procedure to ensure compatibility with competing public interests. *Nature Conservation*, *23*, 87–116.

MOE. (2010). *Brunei Darussalam Education Statistics 2010*. MOE.

MOE. (2013). *Sistem Pendidikan Negara Abad ke-21 (SPN-21)*. https://www.moe.gov.bn/spn21dl/SPN21%20Booklet%20FINAL%202013.pdf

MOE. (2018). *Brunei Darussalam Education Statistics 2014-2018*. MOE.

MOE. (2018). *Ministry of Education Strategic Plan (2018-2022)*. Retrieved 17 November 2022, from https://www.moe.gov.bn/DocumentDownloads/Strategic%20Plan%20Book%202018-2022/Strategic%20plan%202018-2022.pdf

MOE. (n.d.). *Ministry of Education, Brunei Darussalam—Special Education Unit*. Retrieved 16 November 2022, from https://www.moe.gov.bn/sites/bdta/SitePages/Special%20Education%20Unit.aspx

Mohammed, A. B., Ahmed, F. F., & Adedeji, A. N. (2020). Assessment of Impact of Fuel Subsidy Removal on Socio-economic Characteristics: A Survey of Households in Maiduguri, Borno State, Nigeria. *Journal of Business and Economic Development*, *5*(1), 10. doi:10.11648/j.jbed.20200501.12

Mohd Raffi, R. (2019). *Halal industry: an overview of Brunei Darussalam* [Paper presentation]. ICIEHI 2019, July 30-31, Malang, Indonesia.

Moore, D., & Schmitz, G. (1995). *Debating Development Discourse: Institutional and Popular Perspectives*. Palgrave MacMillan. doi:10.1007/978-1-349-24199-6

Moore, J. E., Mascarenhas, A., Bain, J., & Straus, S. E. (2017). Developing a comprehensive definition of sustainability. *Implementation Science : IS*, *12*(1), 110. doi:10.118613012-017-0637-1 PMID:28865479

Morçöl, G. (2013). *A complexity theory for public policy*. Routledge Press. doi:10.4324/9780203112694

Morris, L. (2018). *CSIS*. AMTI. https://amti.csis.org/assessing-recent-developments-in-indonesian-maritime-security/

Morse, S., & McNamara, N. (2013). *Sustainable livelihood approach: A critique of theory and practice*. Springer Science & Business Media. doi:10.1007/978-94-007-6268-8

Mouritz, F. (2020). Implications of the COVID-19 pandemic on China's Belt and Road Initiative. *Connections*, *19*(2), 115–124. doi:10.11610/Connections.19.2.09

Moynihan, D. P. (2009). The network governance of crisis response: Case studies of incident command systems. *Journal of Public Administration: Research and Theory*, *19*(4), 895–915. doi:10.1093/jopart/mun033

Mubangizi, J. C. (2020). A human rights based approach to fighting corruption in Uganda and South Africa: Shared perspectives and comparative lessons. *Law. Democracy & Development*, *24*(1), 225–247. doi:10.17159/2077-4907/2020/ldd.v24.10

Mubangizi, J. C., & Sewpersadh, P. (2017). A Human Rights-based Approach to Combating Public Procurement Corruption in Africa. *African Journal of Legal Studies*, *10*(1), 66–90. doi:10.1163/17087384-12340015

Mugellini, G., Della Bella, S., Colagrossi, M., Isenring, G. L., & Killias, M. (2021). Public sector reforms and their impact on the level of corruption: A systematic review. *Campbell Systematic Reviews*, *17*(2), e1173. doi:10.1002/cl2.1173 PMID:37131927

Mulyani, M. A., Razzaq, A., Ridho, S. L. Z., & Anshari, M. (2019b, October). Smartphone and Mobile Learning to Support Experiential Learning. In *2019 International Conference on Electrical Engineering and Computer Science (ICECOS)* (pp. 6-9). IEEE. 10.1109/ICECOS47637.2019.8984501

Mulyani, M. A., Razzaq, A., Sumardi, W. H., & Anshari, M. (2019a, August). Smartphone adoption in mobile learning scenario. In *2019 International Conference on Information Management and Technology (ICIMTech)* (Vol. 1, pp. 208-211). IEEE. 10.1109/ICIMTech.2019.8843755

Mulyani, M. A., Yusuf, S., Siregar, P., Nurihsan, J., Razzaq, A., & Anshari, M. (2021, August). Fourth industrial revolution and educational challenges. In *2021 International Conference on Information Management and Technology (ICIMTech)* (Vol. 1, pp. 245-249). IEEE. 10.1109/ICIMTech53080.2021.9535057

Mundia, L. (2010). Implementation of SPN21 Curriculum in Brunei Darussalam: A Review of Selected Implications on School Assessment Reforms. *International Education Studies*, *3*(2), 119–129. doi:10.5539/ies.v3n2p119

Mungiu-Pippidi, A. (2013). Controlling corruption through collective action. *Journal of Democracy*, *24*(1), 101–115. doi:10.1353/jod.2013.0020

Muradova, L. (2016). Oil wealth and authoritarianism: Algeria in the Arab Spring. *Revista Española de Ciencia Política*, *40*, 63–89.

Murshed, M., & Mredula, F. (2018). Impacts of corruption on sustainable development: A simultaneous equations model estimation approach. *Journal of Accounting. Finance and Economics*, *8*(1), 109–133.

Muurlink, O., & Macht, S. A. (2020). Managing (out) corruption in NGOs: A case study from the Bangladesh delta. *Journal of Management & Organization*, *26*(6), 1014–1029. doi:10.1017/jmo.2020.17

Nagel, T. (1991). *Equality and Partiality*. Oxford University Press.

Nainggolan, P. P. (2015). Security Threats to Indonesia's Sea Lanes. *Center for Research, Data and Information Processing, DPR RI*, *2015*, 5.

Namini, S. S., & Hudson, D. (2019). Inflation and income inequality in developed and developing countries. *Journal of Economic Studies (Glasgow, Scotland)*, *46*(3), 611–632. doi:10.1108/JES-02-2018-0045

Nantob, N. (2015). Income Inequality and Inflation in Developing Countries: An Empirical Investigation'. *Economic Bulletin*, *35*(4), 2888–2902.

Neshkova, M. I., & Rosenbaum, A. (2015). Advancing good government through fighting corruption. In Handbook of Public Administration.

Network for Greening the Financial System (NGFS). (2019). *A Call for Action. Climate Change as a Source of Financial Risk*. Network for Greening the Financial System.

Ng, S., Wong, J., & Wong, K. (2013). A public-private people partnerships (P4) process framework for infrastructure development in Hong Kong. *Cities (London, England)*, *31*, 370–381. doi:10.1016/j.cities.2012.12.002

Nicklin, G. (2019). Dynamic narrative: A new framework for policy success. *International Review of Public Policy*, *1*(2), 173-193.

Niland, J. (1991). *The Appropriate Role of Property Rights in Environmental Protection*. doi:10.1177/103530469100200108

NOAA. (2008). *National Weather Services. Climate Prediction Centre*. https://www.cpc.ncep.noaa.gov/data/teledoc/teleintro.shtml

NOAA. (2022, August 23). *What's Behind Chinook and Chum Salmon Declines in Alaska?* https://www.fisheries.noaa.gov/feature-story/whats-behind-chinook-and-chum-salmon-declines-alaska

Noor Hasharina Hassan, & Rigg, J. (forthcoming). Borneo, Livelihoods and The Meantime: Learning from Brunei's Kampong Ayer. In Within Borneo, Beyond Borneo: Issues and Perspectives. Springer Nature Singapore.

Noor Hasharina Hassan, & Yong, G.Y.V. (2019). The Cultural Value of Bakuts in Kampong Ayer, Brunei Darussalam. *Southeast Asia: A Multidisciplinary J.*, *19*, 47–63.

Noor Hasharina Hassan, & Yong, G.Y.V. (2019a). The Cultural Value of Bakuts in Kampong Ayer, Brunei- Darussalam. Southeast Asia: A Multidisciplinary Journal,19, 47–63.

Noor Hasharina Hassan, & Yong, G.Y.V. (2019b). A Vision in Which Every Family Has Basic Shelter. In Sustainable Development Goals in Southeast Asia and ASEAN: National and Regional Approaches. Brill.

Nowag, J., Mundaca, L., & Åhman, M. (2021). Phasing out fossil fuel subsidies in the EU? Exploring the role of state aid rules. *Climate Policy*, *21*(8), 1037–1052. doi:10.1080/14693062.2021.1965523

Nurhayati, L., Mandey, S. L., Taroreh, R. N., Trang, I., & Djamali, R. (2021). Why Non-Muslims Become Customers of Islamic Banking? *Estudios de Economía Aplicada*, *39*(12). Advance online publication. doi:10.25115/eea.v39i12.6336

Nurul Hazirah Haji Zainuddin. (2021). Evolution of Stilts in Kampong Ayer. *Brunei Museum J.*

Nussbaum, M. (2013). Creating Capabilities: The Human Development Approach. Harvard University Press. doi:10.2307/j.ctt2jbt31

Oberti, M. (2007). *L'école dans la ville. Ségrégation – mixité – carte scolaire*. Parigi: Les Presses de Sciences Po.

OCDE. (2003). The Case for E-Government: Excerpts from the OECD Report "The E-Government Imperative". *OECD Journal on Budgeting*, *3*(1), 1987–1996.

OECD. (2012). *Equity and Quality in Education. Supporting Disadvantaged Students and Schools*. OECD Publishing.

OECD. (2022). *Education at a Glance 2022: OECD Indicators*. OECD Publishing.

OECD. (n.d.). *PISA 2018 Brunei Darussalam*. Retrieved 17 November 2022, from https://www.oecd.org/pisa/publications/PISA2018_CN_BRN.pdf

Office of Sustainability, University of Alberta. (n.d.). *What is sustainability?* McGill. https://www.mcgill.ca/sustainability/files/sustainability/what-is-sustainability.pdf

Ogunbado, A. (2019). *Leadership in Islam: Ibn Khaldun's Perspective*. UNISSA Press.

Ogunode, N. J., Ahmed, I., & Olugbenga, A. V. (2023). Application of Petrol Subsidy Funds to Address the Problems of Universal Basic Education for Sustainable Development in Nigeria. Web of Scholars. *Multidimensional Research Journal*, *2*(1), 1–9.

Okongwu, C. J., & Imoisi, S. E. (2022). Removal of Petrol Subsidy: Legal Implications for the Nigerian Economy. *Nnamdi Azikiwe University Journal of International Law and Jurisprudence*, *13*(2), 135–139.

Olujobi, O. J. (2021). Deregulation of the downstream petroleum industry: An overview of the legal quandaries and proposal for improvement in Nigeria. *Heliyon*, *7*(4), e06848. doi:10.1016/j.heliyon.2021.e06848 PMID:33997390

Omitogun, O., Longe, A. E., Muhammad, S., & Adekomi, I. J. (2021). Environmental Impact of Economic Growth and Fuel Subsidy in Nigeria. *Economic Insights - Trends and Challenges*, *2021*(1), 1. doi:10.51865/EITC.2021.01.03

Omotosho, B. S. (2020). Oil price shocks, fuel subsidies and macroeconomic (in) stability in Nigeria. *Fuel Subsidies and Macroeconomic (In) stability in Nigeria.*

Othman, A. (2022a, January 31). Brunei on right track towards achieving SDGs Borneo Bulletin Online. *Brunei on Right Track towards Achieving SDGs.* https://borneobulletin.com.bn/brunei-on-right-track-towards-achieving-sdgs/

Othman, A. (2022b, February 14). Instagram remains Brunei's most popular social media platform » Borneo Bulletin Online. *Instagram Remains Brunei's Most Popular Social Media Platform.* https://borneobulletin.com.bn/instagram-remains-bruneis-most-popular-social-media-platform-2/

Ouyang, X., & Lin, B. (2014). Impacts of increasing renewable energy subsidies and phasing out fossil fuel subsidies in China. *Renewable & Sustainable Energy Reviews*, *37*, 933–942. doi:10.1016/j.rser.2014.05.013

Ovaga, O. H., & Okechukwu, M. E. (2022). Subsidy in the downstream oil sector and the fate of the masses in Nigeria. *Kuwait Chapter of Arabian Journal of Business and Management Review*, *1*(6), 1–20.

Owens, S. (2003). Is there a meaningful definition of sustainability? *Plant Genetic Resources*, *1*(1), 5–9. doi:10.1079/PGR20034

Owusu, E. K., Chan, A. P., & Darko, A. (2019). Thematic overview of corruption in infrastructure procurement process. *Journal of Infrastructure Systems*, *25*(2), 02519001. doi:10.1061/(ASCE)IS.1943-555X.0000484

Oxfam. (1997). *A curriculum for global citizenship.* Oxfam's Development Education Programme.

Özbek, A. (2017). *Çok Kriterli Karar Verme Yöntemleri.* Seçkin Yayıncılık.

Ozili, P. (2022). COVID-19 in Africa: Socio-economic impact, policy response and opportunities. *The International Journal of Sociology and Social Policy*, *42*(3/4), 177–200. doi:10.1108/IJSSP-05-2020-0171

Ozili, P. K., & Arun, T. (2023). Spillover of COVID-19: impact on the Global Economy. In *Managing inflation and supply chain disruptions in the global economy* (pp. 41–61). IGI Global.

Ozili, P. K., & Ozen, E. (2021). Global energy crisis: impact on the global economy. In *Proceedings of IAC in Budapest 2021* (Vol. 1, pp. 85-89). Czech Institute of Academic Education.

Öztürk, N. (2009). *İktisatta Bölüşüm.* Palme Yayıncılık.

Pacchi, C., & Ranci, C. (Eds.). (2017). White flight a Milano: La segregazione sociale ed etnica nelle scuole dell'obbligo. Milano: Franco Angeli.

Page, E. C. (2016). What's methodology got to do with it? Public policy evaluations, observational analysis and RCTs. In *Handbook of Research Methods and Applications in Political Science* (pp. 483–496). Edward Elgar Publishing. doi:10.4337/9781784710828.00042

Parry, I., Black, M. S., & Vernon, N. (2021). *Still not getting energy prices right: a global and country update of fossil fuel subsidies*. International Monetary Fund.

Paru, B. (2019). *The role of monitoring and evaluation system in promoting performance of Non-Governmental Organizations in Juba County*.

Pastori, G., Pagani, V., Mangiatordi, A., & Pepe, A. (2021). Parents' view on distance learning during lockdown. A national survey. *Rivista Italiana Di Educazione Familiare*, *18*(1), 61–96. doi:10.36253/rief-10256

Paul, K. A. (2021). Collaborative Evaluation for Program Monitoring. In Total School Cluster Grouping & Differentiation (pp. 87-96). Routledge. doi:10.4324/9781003239239-7

Pearce, D., & Turner, R. K. (1990). *Economics of natural resources and the environment*. Johns Hopkins University Press.

Pearson, Z. (1999). *An international human rights approach to corruption*. JSTOR.

Peiffer, C., & Walton, G. W. (2022). Getting the (right) message across: How to encourage citizens to report corruption. *Development Policy Review*, *40*(5), e12621. doi:10.1111/dpr.12621

PeiS.KandulaS.ShamanJ. 2020. Differential Effects of Intervention Timing on COVID-19 Spread in the United States. medRxiv.

Permata, M. (2017). *Usaha Pelihara Kg. Ayer*. https://mediapermata.com.bn/usaha-pelihara-kg-ayer/.

Persson, A., Rothstein, B., & Teorell, J. (2010). *The failure of anti-corruption policies: a theoretical mischaracterization of the problem*. GU SE.

Persson, A., Rothstein, B., & Teorell, J. (2013). Why anti-corruption reforms fail—Systemic corruption as a collective action problem. *Governance: An International Journal of Policy, Administration and Institutions*, *26*(3), 449–471. doi:10.1111/j.1468-0491.2012.01604.x

Perumal, K. (2023). Rethinking global anti-corruption campaign. *Journal of Social and Economic Development*, 1–15.

Pescarmona, I. (2012). *Innovazione educativa tra entusiasmo e fatica*. CISU.

Peters, B. (1998). Managing horizontal government: The politics of co-ordination. *Public Administration*, *76*(2), 295–311. doi:10.1111/1467-9299.00102

Peters, B. G. (2017). What is so wicked about wicked problems? A conceptual analysis and a research program. *Policy and Society*, *36*(3), 385–396. doi:10.1080/14494035.2017.1361633

Peters, B. G., & Pierre, J. (2019). Populism and public administration: Confronting the administrative state. *Administration & Society*, *51*(10), 1521–1545. doi:10.1177/0095399719874749

Peterson, B. L. (2017). Thematic analysis/interpretive thematic analysis. In J. Matthes (Ed.), *The international encyclopedia of communication research methods* (pp. 1–9). John Wiley & Sons. doi:10.1002/9781118901731.iecrm0249

Peters, R. S. (2015). *Ethics and Education*. Routledge.

Pettigrew, A., & Whipp, R. (1991). *Managing change for competitive success*. Blackwell Publishers.

Pham-Truffert, M., Metz, F., Fischer, M., Rueff, H., & Messerli, P. (2020). Interactions among Sustainable Development Goals: Knowledge for identifying multipliers and virtuous cycles. *Sustainable Development (Bradford), 28*(5), 1236–1250. doi:10.1002d.2073

Phelan, S.E. (2001). What is complexity science, really? *Emergence, A Journal of Complexity Issues in Organizations and Management, 3*(1), 120-136.

Phelps, J. (2021). *Environmental liability litigation could remedy biodiversity loss*. Wiley. doi:10.1111/conl.12821

Piketty, T. (2014). *Capital in the Twenty-First Century*. Harvard University Press. doi:10.4159/9780674369542

Piketty, T. (2014). *Yirmi Birinci Yüzyılda KAPİTAL*. Türkiye İş Bankası Kültür Yayınları.

Pilapitaya, T. (2005). *The impact of corruption on the human rights based approach to development*. SSRN.

Pirola, L. (2015). Middle Management and School Autonomy in Italy: The Case of Teachers as "Instrumental Functions". *Educational. Cultural and Psychological Studies, 6*(11), 89–101. doi:10.7358/ecps-2015-011-piro

Platt, A., & Warwick, S. (1995). Review of soft systems methodology. *Industrial Management & Data Systems, 95*(4), 19–21. doi:10.1108/02635579510086698

PMI. (2016). *The Strategic Impact of Projects: Identify Benefits to Drive Business Results*. Project Management Institute.

Policardoa, L., Edgar, J., Sanchez, C., & Risso, W. A. (2019). Causality between income inequality and corruption in OECD countries. *World Development Perspectives, 14*, 100102. doi:10.1016/j.wdp.2019.02.013

POPT. (n.d.). *Benefits of Monitoring and Evaluation*. Retrieved from http://www.popstoolkit.com/riskmanagement/module/step5/benefits.aspx

Porter, M. (1998). Clusters and the new economics of competition. *Harvard Business Review*, (November-December), 77–90. PMID:10187248

Porter, M. (2008). The five competitive forces that shape strategy. *Harvard Business Review*, (January), 79–93. PMID:18271320

Portuguese Government. (2009). Programa do XVIII Governo Constitucional para 2009 - 2013, 2009. Programa do XVIII Governo Constitucional.p.129. Portuguese parliament. https://www.parlamento.pt/orcamentoestado/documents/gop/gop_2010-2013_vf.pdf

Portuguese parliament. (2010). *Grandes Opções do Plano 2010-2013*. Portuguese parliament. https://www.parlamento.pt/orcamentoestado/documents/gop/gop_2010-2013_vf.pdf

Prabowo, H. Y., Sriyana, J., & Syamsudin, M. J. (2018). *Forgetting corruption: unlearning the knowledge of corruption in the Indonesian public sector*. UII.

Practical Law. (2023). *Overriding interests*. https://uk.practicallaw.thomsonreuters.com/5-107-6954?transitionType=Default&contextData=(sc.Default)&firstPage=true

Pravalie, R., & Bandoc, G. (2018). Nuclear energy: Between global electricity demand, worldwide decarbonisation imperativeness, and planetary environmental implications. *Journal of Environmental Management, 209*, 81–92. doi:10.1016/j.jenvman.2017.12.043 PMID:29287177

Preskill, H., & Jones, N. (2009). *A practical guide for engaging stakeholders in developing evaluation questions*. Academic Press.

Psaki, S. R., McCarthy, K. J., & Mensch, B. S. (2018). Measuring gender equality in education: Lessons from trends in 43 countries. *Population and Development Review*, *44*(1), 117–142. doi:10.1111/padr.12121

Purtell, K. M., & Gershoff, E. T. (2015). Fast food consumption and academic growth in late childhood. *Clinical Pediatrics*, *54*(9), 871–877. doi:10.1177/0009922814561742 PMID:25480321

Raco, M., & Savini, F. (Eds.). (2019). *Planning and knowledge: How new forms of technocracy are shaping contemporary cities*. Policy Press.

Radin, B. (1997). The evolution of the policy analysis field: From conversation to conversations. *Journal of Policy Analysis and Management*, *16*(2), 204–218. doi:10.1002/(SICI)1520-6688(199721)16:2<204::AID-PAM1>3.0.CO;2-M

Radin, B. (2013). *Beyond Machiavelli: Policy analysis comes of Age*. Georgetown University Press.

Radin, D. (2019). Sustainable Development Goal 16: Focus on public institutions, World Public Sector Report 2019. *Public Sector Economics*, *43*(4), 477–483. doi:10.3326/pse.43.4.8

Rahman, R. A. O, & Hung, Y. T. (2011). Liquid Radioactive Wastes Treatment. *Water (Basel)*, 551.

Rahman, M. M., Rana, R., & Khanam, R. (2022). Determinants of life expectancy in most polluted countries: Exploring the effect of environmental degradation. *PLoS One*, *17*(1), e0262802. doi:10.1371/journal.pone.0262802 PMID:35061838

Raji, A. (2018). *Fuel subsidy removal and the lives of rural dwellers in Nigeria* [Doctoral dissertation]. Department of Sociology, Faculty of Social Sciences, University of Ilorin, Ilorin, Nigeria.

Ram, J., & Zhang, Z. (2020). Belt and road initiative (BRI) supply chain risks: Propositions and model development. *International Journal of Logistics Management*, *31*(4), 777–799. doi:10.1108/IJLM-12-2019-0366

Rana, P. B., & Ji, X. (2020). *China's Belt and Road Initiative*. Springer Singapore. doi:10.1007/978-981-15-5171-0

Ravallion, M., & Chen, S. (2022). Is that really a Kuznets curve? Turning points for income inequality in China. *The Journal of Economic Inequality*, *20*(4), 749–776. doi:10.100710888-022-09541-x

Ravazzani, S., Mazzei, A., Fisichella, C., & Butera, A. (2021). Diversity and inclusion management: An analysis of practice developments in Italy. *Sinergie Italian Journal of Management*, *39*(3), 213–229. doi:10.7433116.2021.11

Rawls, J. (1971). A Theory of Justice. Belknap Press. doi:10.4159/9780674042605

Razavi, S. (2016). The 2030 Agenda: Challenges of implementation to attain gender equality and women's rights. *Gender and Development*, *24*(1), 25–41. doi:10.1080/13552074.2016.1142229

Razzaq, A., Samiha, Y. T., & Anshari, M. (2018). Smartphone habits and behaviors in supporting students self-efficacy. *International Journal of Emerging Technologies in Learning*, *13*(2), 94. doi:10.3991/ijet.v13i02.7685

Reichert, G., Schwind, S., De Petris, A., Jousseaume, M. (2020, May 20). EU Communication, Biodiversity Strategy 2030. *cepPolicyBrief*.

Remenyi, D., & Sherwood-Smith, M. (1998). Business benefits from information systems through an active benefits realisation programme. *International Journal of Project Management*, *16*(2), 81–98. doi:10.1016/S0263-7863(97)00024-0

Renwick, N., Gu, J., & Gong, S. (2018). *The impact of BRI investment in infrastructure on achieving the Sustainable Development Goals. In K4D emerging issues report*. Institute of Development Studies.

Rhodes, R., & Beller, D. (2020). The need For Nuclear Power. IAEA, 43.

Riger, S., & Sigurvinsdottir, R. (2016). Thematic analysis. In L. A. Jason & D. S. Glenwick (Eds.), *Handbook of methodological approaches to community-based research: Qualitative, quantitative, and mixed methods* (pp. 33–41). Oxford University Press.

Rippa, A. (2020). Mapping the margins of China's global ambitions: Economic corridors, Silk Roads, and the end of proximity in the borderlands. *Eurasian Geography and Economics*, *61*(1), 55–76. doi:10.1080/15387216.2020.1717363

Rittel, H. W., & Webber, M. M. (1973). Dilemmas in a general theory of planning. *Policy Sciences*, *4*(2), 155–169. doi:10.1007/BF01405730

Rizzello, A. (2022). What's in a Name? Mapping the Galaxy of Green Finance. In *Green Investing*. Palgrave Studies in Impact Finance. Palgrave Macmillan. doi:10.1007/978-3-031-08031-9_2

Rizzo, A. L., & De Angelis, B. (2019). La progettualità inclusiva nel PTOF: il ruolo della dimensione ludico-musicale. In G. Elia, S. Polenghi, & V. Rossini (Eds.), *La scuola tra saperi e valori etico-sociali. Politiche culturali e pratiche educative* (pp. 625–636). Pensa Multimedia.

Roemer, J. K. (2000). Equality of Opportunity. In K. Arrow, S. Bowles, & S. N. Durlauf (Eds.), *Meritocracy and Economic Inequality* (pp. 17–32). Princeton University Press. doi:10.1515/9780691190334-004

Romano, B. (2016). L'utilizzo dei test standardizzati. Identificare le scuole in difficoltà e stabilire priorità nelle azioni di miglioramento. *Scuola Democratica. Learning for Democracy*, *5*(2), 309–330.

Rothstein, B. (2011). Anti-corruption: The indirect 'big bang'approach. *Review of International Political Economy*, *18*(2), 228–250. doi:10.1080/09692291003607834

Rozas, L. W., & Klein, W. C. (2010). The value and purpose of the traditional qualitative literature review. *Journal of Evidence-Based Social Work*, *7*(5), 387–399. doi:10.1080/15433710903344116 PMID:21082469

Rubin, K. (2022). *Department of Geology and Geophysics University of Hawaii*. SOEST. https://www.soest.hawaii.edu/GG/ASK/waterpol2.html

Rudling, E. S., Emery, S., Shelley, B., te Riele, K., Woodroffe, J., & Brown, N. (Eds.). (2023). *Education and Equity in Times of Crisis: Learning, Engagement and Support*. Springer International Publishing. doi:10.1007/978-3-031-18671-4

RW Institute. (2017). *Anti-corruption and Human Rights: How to become mutually reinforcing?* RW Institute. https://rwi.lu.se/publications/anti-corruption-human-rights-become-mutually-reinforcing/

Saadiah, D.D.W.W., & Haji, T. (2009). Kampong Ayer Brunei Darussalam: Meniti arus pembangunan. *Borneo Res. J.*, *3*, 209–219.

Sabatier, P. (2007). *Theories of the Policy Process*. Taylor & Francis.

Sablić, M., Mirosavljević, A., & Škugor, A. (2021). Video-based learning (VBL)—past, present and future: An overview of the research published from 2008 to 2019. Technology. *Knowledge and Learning*, *26*(4), 1061–1077. doi:10.100710758-020-09455-5

Sachs-Israel, M. (2016). The SDG 4-education 2030 agenda and its framework for action–the process of its development and first steps in taking it forward. *Bildung und Erziehung*, *69*(3), 269–290. doi:10.7788/bue-2016-0303

Sachs, J. (2006). *The End of Poverty: Economic Possibilities for Our Time*. Penguin Books.

Sachs, J. D., Schmidt-Traub, G., Mazzucato, M., Messner, D., Nakicenovic, N., & Rockström, J. (2019). Six transformations to achieve the sustainable development goals. *Nature Sustainability*, *2*(9), 805–814. doi:10.103841893-019-0352-9

Safety4sea. (2021). *Is Nuclear Power the future of shipping.* safety4sea. https://safety4sea.com/cm-is-nuclear-power-the-future-of-shipping/

Sahabuddin. (2007). *Ensiklopedia Al-Qur'an : Kajian Kosakata* [Trans] Lentera Hati. Sunnah. https://sunnah.com

Saha, S., & Ali, M. S. B. (2017). Corruption and economic development: New evidence from the Middle Eastern and North African countries. *Economic Analysis and Policy*, *54*, 83–95. doi:10.1016/j.eap.2017.02.001

Saiz, I., & Donald, K. (2017). Tackling inequality through the Sustainable Development Goals: Human rights in practice. *International Journal of Human Rights*, *21*(8), 1029–1049. doi:10.1080/13642987.2017.1348696

Samiha, Y. T., Handayani, T., Razzaq, A., Fitri, A., Fithriyah, M., & Anshari, M. (2021, November). Sustainability of Excellence in Education 4.0. In *2021 Sustainable Leadership and Academic Excellence International Conference (SLAE)* (pp. 1-5). IEEE. 10.1109/SLAE54202.2021.9788095

Sampedro, J., Arto, I., & González-Eguino, M. (2017). Implications of switching fossil fuel subsidies to solar: A case study for the European Union. *Sustainability, 10*(1), 50.

Sandström, G., & Stanfors, M. (2022). Socio-economic status and the rise of divorce in Sweden: The case of the 1880–1954 marriage cohorts in Västerbotten. *Population Studies*, 1–19. PMID:36603598

Sannipoli, M., & Falcinelli, F. (Eds.). (2022). *Il sistema integrato 0-6. Riflessioni e buone pratiche*. Carocci.

Sarif, S. M., Ismail, Y., & Azlan, Z. (2017). Effects of Maqasid Al-Shariah for ethical decision making among social entrepreneurs. *Journal of Islamic Management Studies*, *1*(1), 1–14.

Savidan, P. (2007). *Repenser l'égalité des chances*. Grasset.

Sayed, Y., & Moriarty, K. (2020). SDG 4 and the "education quality turn": Prospects, possibilities, and problems. In A. Wulff (Ed.), Grading goal four. Tensions, Threats, and Opportunities in the Sustainable Development Goal on Quality Education (pp. 194-213). Leida: Brill.

Schizzerotto, A., & Barone, C. (2006). *Sociologia dell'istruzione*. Il Mulino.

Schleicher, A. (2009). Securing quality and equity in education: Lessons from PISA. *Prospects*, *39*(3), 251–263. doi:10.100711125-009-9126-x

Schleicher, J., Schaafsma, M., & Vira, B. (2018). Will the Sustainable Development Goals address the links between poverty and the natural environment? *Current Opinion in Environmental Sustainability*, *34*, 43–47. doi:10.1016/j.cosust.2018.09.004

Schnabl, A., & Grechenig, T. (2020). Benefit Evaluation in IT Project Portfolio Management at Austrian Financial Service Providers. In proceedings of the *3rd International Conference on Computers in Management and Business* (ICCMB '20), (pp. 290–295). ACM. 10.1145/3383845.3383889

Schneider, S. K. (1995). *Flirting with disaster: Public management in crisis situations*. ME Sharpe.

Schofield. (2016). *Ruined Chernobyl Nuclear Plant will Remain a Threat for 3000 Years*. Schofield.

Schubert, J. N., Stewart, P. A., & Curran, M. A. (2002). A defining presidential moment: 9/11 and the rally effect. *Political Psychology*, *23*(3), 559–583. doi:10.1111/0162-895X.00298

Scipione, L., Bertolini, C., & Vezzani, A. (2022). La valutazione come problema. La scuola primaria e la sfida del cambiamento. In A. La Marca & A. Marzano (Eds.), *Ricerca didattica e formazione degli insegnanti per lo sviluppo delle Soft Skills* (pp. 734–746). Pensa MultiMedia.

Secretariat of the Brunei Vision 2035. (n.d.). *Wawasan Brunei 2035: How to "Wawasan"*. Bandar Seri Begawan: Prime Minister's Office.

Sen, A. (1988). *On Ethics and Economics*. Blackwell Publishing Ltd.

Sen, A. (2000). *Development as Freedom*. Anchor Books.

Sen, A. (2009). *The Idea of Justice*. Belknap Press.

Sen, A. (2009). *The idea of Justice*. Penguin Books.

SER. (2021). *Scientists in Support for an Ambitious EU Nature Restoration Law*. SER.

Serra, C., & Kunc, M. (2015). Benefits Realisation Management and its influence on project success and on the execution of business strategies. *International Journal of Project Management*, *33*(1), 53–66. doi:10.1016/j.ijproman.2014.03.011

Serrano Alvarez, J. A. (2014). When the enemy is the state: Common lands management in northwest Spain (1850–1936). *The International Journal of the Commons*, *8*(1), 107–133. doi:10.18352/ijc.389

Serrano, A., & Caldeira, M. M. (2002, January-March). Um Modelo para a Gestão de Investimentos em Sistemas e Tecnologias de Informação. *Revista Portuguesa de Gestão*, *17*(1), 14–23.

Serrat, O. (2017). Fighting Corruption with ICT: Strengthening Civil Society's Role. In Knowledge Solutions (pp. 797-811): Springer.

Sewerin, S., Cashore, B., & Howlett, M. (2022). New pathways to paradigm change in public policy: Combining insights from policy design, mix and feedback. *Policy and Politics*, *50*(3), 442–459. doi:10.1332/030557321X16528864819376

Shaeffer, S. (2019). Inclusive education: A prerequisite for equity and social justice. *Asia Pacific Education Review*, *20*(2), 181–192. doi:10.100712564-019-09598-w

Shagali, A. A., & Yusuf, R. (2022). Political economy of fuel subsidy removal in Nigeria: Issues, challenges and the way forward. *Zamfara Journal of Politics and Development*, *3*(3), 12–12.

Shahbaz, M., & Lean, H. H. (2012). Does financial development increase energy consumption? The role of industrialization and urbanization in Tunisia. *Energy Policy*, *40*, 473–479. doi:10.1016/j.enpol.2011.10.050

Shahrill, M., Noorashid, N., & Keasberry, C. (2021). COVID-19: Educational Practices and Responses in Brunei Darussalam. In P. Le Ha, A. Kumpoh, K. Wood, R. Jawawi, & H. Said (Eds.), *Globalisation, Education, and Reform in Brunei Darussalam* (pp. 325–354). Springer International Publishing. doi:10.1007/978-3-030-77119-5_16

Shakib, M., Yumei, H., Rauf, A., Alam, M., Murshed, M., & Mahmood, H. (2022). Revisiting the energy-economy-environment relationships for attaining environmental sustainability: Evidence from Belt and Road Initiative countries. *Environmental Science and Pollution Research International*, *29*(3), 3808–3825. doi:10.100711356-021-15860-9 PMID:34402005

Sharbawi, S., & Mabud, S. A. (2021). Malay, Muslim and Monarchy: An Introduction to Brunei Darussalam and Its National Identity. In P. Le Ha, A. Kumpoh, K. Wood, R. Jawawi, & H. Said (Eds.), *Globalisation, Education, and Reform in Brunei Darussalam* (pp. 45–66). Springer International Publishing. doi:10.1007/978-3-030-77119-5_3

Shear, M., & Rogers, K. (2020). Trump and Aides Try to Change the Narrative of the White House Protests. *The New York Times*.https://www.nytimes.com/2020/06/03/us/politics/trump-protests.html>

Sheyin, A. O. (2018). The Effects of Subsidy Removal on the Escalation of Political Corruption in Nigeria. *KIU Journal of Social Sciences*, *4*(3), 157–168.

Sheying, C. (2003). General Public Policy and Development Strategy. The Chinese state in perspective. *China perspectives, 2003*(48).

Shichor, Y., & Zviran, M. (2016). Factors Influencing Perceived Benefits and User Satisfaction in Knowledge Management Systems. *Information Systems Management, 33*(1), 55–73. doi:10.1080/10580530.2016.1117873

Shulla, K., Filho, W. L., Lardjane, S., Sommer, J. H., & Borgemeister, C. (2020). Sustainable development education in the context of the 2030 Agenda for sustainable development. *International Journal of Sustainable Development and World Ecology, 27*(5), 458–468. doi:10.1080/13504509.2020.1721378

Sia-Partners. (2018). *Towards cleaner and more sustainable shipping: the required actions.* SIA. https://www.sia-partners.com/en/news-and-publications/from-our-experts/towards-cleaner-and-more-sustainable-shipping-required (accessed August 3, 2022).

Sibiano, P., & Agasisti, T. (2013). Efficiency and heterogeneity of public spending in education among Italian regions. *Journal of Public Affairs, 13*(1), 12–22. doi:10.1002/pa.1404

Silcock, R. (2001). What is e-Government? *Parliamentary Affairs, 54*(1), 88–101. doi:10.1093/pa/54.1.88

Silva, C., Freschib, E., & Casellic, P. (2018). ECEC in the European Union: analysis and governance of ECEC systems of four Member States L'ECEC nell'Unione Europea: analisi e governance dei sistemi di educazione e cura dell'infanzia di quattro Paesi membri. *Form@ re-Open Journal per la formazione in rete, 18*(1), 234-247.

Sissani, M. (2016). The algerian economy governed by black corruption: an empirical study from 2002 to 2015. *Studies and Scientific Researches, Economics Edition* (24).

Sliogeriene, J., Turskis, Z., & Streimikiene, D. (2013). Analysis and Choice of Generation Technologies: The Multiple Criteria Assessment on The Case Study of Energy Lithuania. *Energy Procedia, 32*, 11–20. doi:10.1016/j.egypro.2013.05.003

Ślusarczyk, B. (2018). Industry 4.0: Are we ready? *Polish Journal of Management Studies*, 17.

Smith, M. (2021). *Shipping to go nuclear on climate change.* Nepia. https://www.nepia.com/articles/shipping-to-go-nuclear-on-climate-change/

Snyder, H. (2019). Literature review as a research methodology: An overview and guidelines. *Journal of Business Research, 104*, 333–339. doi:10.1016/j.jbusres.2019.07.039

Solow, R. (1987). We'd better watch out. *New York Times.*

Sommer, M., Torondel, B., Hennegan, J., Phillips-Howard, P. A., Mahon, T., Motivans, A., Zulaika, G., Gruer, C., Haver, J., & Caruso, B. A.Monitoring Menstrual Health and Hygiene Group. (2021). How addressing menstrual health and hygiene may enable progress across the Sustainable Development Goals. *Global Health Action, 14*(1), 1920315. doi:10.1080/16549716.2021.1920315 PMID:34190034

Soud, N. S., & Sayılır, Ö. (2017). Perceptions of Islamic banking among Muslim and Non-Muslim citizens in Tanzania. *International Journal of Islamic Economics and Finance Studies, 3*(3), 15–29.

Special National Coordination Committee on SDGs Brunei Darussalam Secretariat. (2021). *Brunei Darussalam Sustainable Development Goals Annual Report 2021.* Prime Minister's Office.

Spiegela, A., & Rodrígueza, G. (2016). Students at university have mobile technologies. Do they do m-learning? *Procedia: Social and Behavioral Sciences, 217*, 846–850. doi:10.1016/j.sbspro.2016.02.006

Spillane, J. P. (1999). External reform initiatives and teachers' efforts to reconstruct their practice: The mediating role of teachers' zones of enactment. *Journal of Curriculum Studies, 31*(2), 143–175. doi:10.1080/002202799183205

Statista. (2022). *International seaborne trade carried by containers.* Statista. https://www.statista.com/statistics/253987/international-seaborne-trade-carried-by-containers/

Stead, S. M. (2019). Using systems thinking and open innovation to strengthen aquaculture policy for the United Nations Sustainable Development Goals. *Journal of Fish Biology*, *94*(6), 837–844. doi:10.1111/jfb.13970 PMID:30887512

Stiglitz, J. E. (2015). *Eşitsizliğin Bedeli. Bugünün Bölünmüş Toplumu Geleceğimizi Nasıl Tehlikeye Atıyor?* İletişim Yayınları.

Stone, C. (2006). Power, reform, and urban regime analysis. *City & Community*, *5*(1), 23–38. doi:10.1111/j.1540-6040.2006.00151.x

Strambi, A., & Bouvet, E. (2003). Flexibility and interaction at a distance: A mixed-mode environment for language learning. *Language Learning & Technology*, *7*(3), 81–102.

Strona, G., & Bradshaw, C. J. A. (2022, December 16). Coextinctions dominate future vertebrate losses from climate and land use change. *Science Advances*, *8*(50), eabn4345. doi:10.1126ciadv.abn4345 PMID:36525487

Subrahmanian, R. (2005). Gender equality in education: Definitions and measurements. *International Journal of Educational Development*, *25*(4), 395–407. doi:10.1016/j.ijedudev.2005.04.003

Su, C. W., Qin, M., Tao, R., Moldovan, N. C., & Lobonţ, O. R. (2020). Factors driving oil price—From the perspective of United States. *Energy*, *197*, 117219. doi:10.1016/j.energy.2020.117219

Sulaiman, N. S. (2020). Halal Sustainability: A Strategic Roadmapping for Brunei Darussalam. *Proceedings on 4th International Seminar on Halalan Thayyiban Products and Services,* 286-302.

Sustainable Development Goal 4 (SDG 4) | Education within the 2030 Agenda for Sustainable Development. (n.d.). Retrieved 5 September 2022, from https://www.sdg4education2030.org/the-goal

Swain, R. B., & Ranganathan, S. (2021). Modeling interlinkages between sustainable development goals using network analysis. *World Development*, *138*, 105136. doi:10.1016/j.worlddev.2020.105136

Sweeney, S. (2020, January). Weaponizing the Numbers: The Hidden Agenda Behind Fossil-Fuel Subsidy Reform. *New Labor Forum*, *29*(1), 87–92. doi:10.1177/1095796019893317

Swinkels, M. (2020). How ideas matter in public policy: a review of concepts, mechanisms, and methods. *International Review of Public Policy, 2*(3), 281-316.

Sylves, R. T. (2006). President Bush and Hurricane Katrina: A presidential leadership study. *The Annals of the American Academy of Political and Social Science*, *604*(1), 26–56. doi:10.1177/0002716205286066

Taglietti, D. (2016). An archaeological analysis of the last Italian education reform policy. *Italian Journal of Sociology of Education*, *8*(3), 195–221.

Tajudeen, A. L.(2017). *Deficiencies and incompatibility of neither Qualitative nor Quantitative research paradigms with Islamic research: How could Grounded Theory methodology help*? An unpublished workshop presentation as part of mini-conference SPARC organized by Sultan Hassanal Bolkiah Institute of education, University of Brunei Darussalam.

Taket, A., Crisp, B. R., Graham, M., Hanna, L., Goldingay, S., & Wilson, L. (2013). *Practising Social Inclusion.* Routledge. doi:10.4324/9780203766798

Taradi, K. (2005). Blended Problem-Based Learning Outcomes in Acid-Base Physiology. https://advan.physiology.org/cgi/cotent/abstract/29/1/35

Terry, G., Hayfield, N., Clarke, V., & Braun, V. (2017). Thematic analysis. In C. Willig & W. Staiton-Roger (Eds.), *The SAGE handbook of qualitative research in psychology* (pp. 17–37). Sage. doi:10.4135/9781526405555.n2

Thalassinos, E., Uğurlu, E., & Muratoğlu, Y. (2012). Income Inequality and Inflation in the EU. *European Research Studies, 15*(1), 127–140. doi:10.35808/ersj/347

The Currency Exchange Fund N.V. (2018). *Blended finance in Myanmar: TCX's role in realizing financial inclusion through innovative partnerships in Myanmar.* https://www.tcxfund.com/wp-content/uploads/2018/02/TCX-Myanmar-case-study.pdf

The Lawyers and Jurists. (n.d.). *The Principle of Sustainable Development Means an Integration of Development and Environmental Imperatives.* https://www.lawyersnjurists.com/article/the-principle-of-sustainable-development-means-an-integration-of-development-and-environmental-imperatives/

The World Bank. (1993). *Housing Enabling Markets to Work.* World Bank Books.

Themudo, N. S. (2013). Reassessing the impact of civil society: Nonprofit sector, press freedom, and corruption. *Governance: An International Journal of Policy, Administration and Institutions, 26*(1), 63–89. doi:10.1111/j.1468-0491.2012.01602.x

Thieux, L. (2019). Algerian youth and the political struggle for dignity: Evolution, trends and new forms of mobilisation. *Journal of North African Studies*, 1–17.

Thompson, R. (2019). *Education, Inequality and Social Class.* Routledge. doi:10.4324/9781315141749

Tool, M. MInd Tool. (n.d). https://www.mindtools.com/pages/article/newTMC_03.htm

Topuz, S. G., & Dağdemir, Ö. (2020). Analysis of the relationship between trade openness, structural change, and income inequality under Kuznets curve hypothesis: The case of Turkey. *The Journal of International Trade & Economic Development, 29*(6), 647–664. doi:10.1080/09638199.2019.1711146

Trief, P. M., Wade, M. J., Britton, K. D., & Weinstock, R. S. (2002). A prospective analysis of marital relationship factors and quality of life in diabetes. *Diabetes Care, 25*(7), 1154–1158. doi:10.2337/diacare.25.7.1154 PMID:12087013

Triventi, M. (2019). Are children of immigrants graded less Generously by their teachers than natives, and why? Evidence from student population data in Italy. *The International Migration Review, 54*(3), 765–795. doi:10.1177/0197918319878104

Triventi, M., Vlach, E., & Pini, E. (2022). Understanding why immigrant children underperform: Evidence from Italian compulsory education. *Journal of Ethnic and Migration Studies, 48*(10), 2324–2346. doi:10.1080/1369183X.2021.1935656

Tsakloglou, P. (1988). Development and Inequality Revisited. *Applied Economics, 20*(4), 509–531. doi:10.1080/00036848800000061

Tsuya, N. O., Choe, M. K., & Wang, F. (2019). *Convergence to very low fertility in East Asia: Processes, causes, and implications.* Springer Japan. doi:10.1007/978-4-431-55781-4

Türk, İ. (1979). *Maliye Politikası Amaçlar- Araçlar ve Çağdaş Bütçe Teorileri.* Sevinç Matbaası.

Turner, J. R., & Baker, R. M. (2019). Complexity theory: An overview with potential applications for the social sciences. *Systems, 7*(1), 4. doi:10.3390ystems7010004

Uhl-Bien, M., Marion, R., & McKelvey, B. (2007). Complexity leadership theory: Shifting leadership from the industrial age to the knowledge era. *The Leadership Quarterly, 18*(4), 298–318. doi:10.1016/j.leaqua.2007.04.002

Ulferts, H., Wolf, K. M., & Anders, Y. (2019). Impact of process quality in early childhood education and care on academic outcomes: Longitudinal meta-analysis. *Child Development, 90*(5), 1474–1489. doi:10.1111/cdev.13296 PMID:31407322

Ullah, A., Pinglu, C., Ullah, S., Abbas, H. S. M., & Khan, S. (2021). The role of e-governance in combating COVID-19 and promoting sustainable development: A comparative study of China and Pakistan. *Chinese Political Science Review, 6*(1), 86–118. doi:10.100741111-020-00167-w

Umeji, G., & Eleanya, E. (2021). *Assessing the Impact of Fuel Subsidy Removal in Nigeria on the Poor in the COVID-19 Era.* SERBD-International Journal of Multidisciplinary Sciences.

Umweltbundesamt. (2019). *BD-R-2: Protected areas.* https://www.umweltbundesamt.de/en/topics/climate-energy/climate-impacts-adaptation/impacts-of-climate-change/monitoring-report-2019/indicators-of-climate-change-impacts-adaptation/cluster-biodiversity/bd-r-2-protected-areas#bd-r-2-protected-areas

UN (2016). *E-Government Survey 2016: E-Government in Support of Sustainable Development.* New York: UN.

UN Department of Economic and Social Affairs. (n.d.a). *Sustainable Development. The 17 Goals.* https://sdgs.un.org/goals

UN Department of Economic and Social Affairs. (n.d.b). *Sustainable Development. Goals 13. Take urgent action to combat climate change and its impacts.* https://sdgs.un.org/goals/goal13

UN General Assembly. (1992). *Rio Declaration on Environment and Development.* Author.

UN. (1987). 42/187 Report of the World Commission on Environment and Development. *General Assembly 42nd session.*

UN. (1987). *Our Common Future.* Report of the World Commission on Environment and Development.

UN. (2007). *Framing Sustainable Development The Brundtland Report – 20 Years On.* Sustainable Development in Action.

UN. (2014). *United Nations E-Government Survey 2014: E-Government for the Future We Want.* New York: UN.

UN. (2015). *Transforming Our World: The 2030 Agenda for Sustainable Development.* New York: UN.

UN. (2020). *Sustainable Development: From Brundtland to Rio 2012.* http://www.surdurulebilirkalkinma.gov.tr/wp-content/uploads/2016/06/Background_on_Sustainable_Development.pdf

UN. (2021). *Energy Statistic Pocket Book.* New York: UN-Departement of Economics and Social Affair.

UN. (2021). *The right to a healthy environment: 6 things you need to know.* UN News. https://news.un.org/en/story/2021/10/1103082

UN. (2022). *The Sustainable Development Goals Report 2022.* UN.

UN. (2023). *Leaving No One Behind in an Ageing World. World Social Report 2023.* New York: UN.

UN. (n.d.). *Transforming our world: the 2030 Agenda for Sustainable Development.* https://sdgs.un.org/2030agenda

UNCTAD. (2021). *Maritime Transport Review.* UNCTAD. https://hbs.unctad.org/maritime-transport-indicators/

UNCTAD. (2021). *The Rise of the Sustainable Fund Market and its Role in Financing Sustainable Development.* United Nations. https://unctad.org/system/files/official-document/diae2021d1_en.pdf

UNEP. (2022). *Convention on Biological Diversity, Kunming-Montreal Global biodiversity framework, Draft decision submitted by the President.* https://www.cbd.int/doc/c/e6d3/cd1d/daf663719a03902a9b116c34/cop-15-l-25-en.pdf?appLinkHandling=true

UNEP. (2022). *COP15 ends with landmark biodiversity agreement*. https://www.unep.org/news-and-stories/story/cop15-ends-landmark-biodiversity-agreement

UNESCO. (2018, January 9). *What is global citizenship education?* UNESCO. https://en.unesco.org/themes/gced/definition

UNESCO. (2019). *Incheon Declaration and Framework for Action for the implementation of Sustainable Development Goal 4*. UNESCO.

UNESCO. (2021). *The State of Global Education Crisis. A joint UNESCO, UNICEF, and World Bank Report*. UNESCO.

UNESCO. (2022). *Setting commitments: national SDG 4 benchmarks to transform education*. UNESCO.

UNESCO. (2023). *SDG4 scorecard progress report on national benchmarks: focus on early childhood*. UNESCO.

UNESCO. (n.d.). *What you need to know about education for sustainable development | UNESCO*. Retrieved 16 November 2022, from https://www.unesco.org/en/education/sustainable-development/need-know

UNICEF. (2013). *Leave No Child Behind. Building Equity for Children*. UNICEF.

UNICEF. (2018). *An Unfair Start. Inequality in Children's Education in Rich Countries*. UNICEF.

UNICEF. (2021). *Every Child Learns*. UNICEF.

United Nations (UN) Environment Programme. (n.d.). *Rio+20 outcome document "The Future We Want"*. https://www.unep.org/resources/report/rio20-outcome-document-future-we-want

United Nations Department of Economic and Social Affairs. (2017). *2016 Family Expert Group Meeting*. Accessed from https://www.un.org/esa/socdev/family/docs/egm16/summary.pdf

United Nations Development Program. (2020). *Coronavirus vs. inequality*. Available from: https://feature.undp.org/coronavirus-vs-inequality/

United Nations. (n.d.). *The 17 Goals*. Department of Economic and Social Affairs Sustainable Development. Retrieved from https://sdgs.un.org/goals

Universiti Brunei Darussalam Graduate Admissions. (n.d.). Retrieved 17 November 2022, from https://ubd.edu.bn/admission/graduate/fees-and-funding(graduate)/ugrs.html

Universiti Brunei Darussalam Scholarships. (n.d.). Retrieved 17 November 2022, from https://ubd.edu.bn/admission/scholarships.html

Unterhalter, E. (2009). What is equity in education? Reflections from the capability approach. *Studies in Philosophy and Education*, *28*(1), 415–424. doi:10.100711217-009-9125-7

Vaismoradi, M., Turunen, H., & Bondas, T. (2013). Content analysis and thematic analysis: Implications for conducting a qualitative descriptive study. *Nursing & Health Sciences*, *15*(3), 398–405. doi:10.1111/nhs.12048 PMID:23480423

Vallero, D. A. (2019). Waste governance. In *Waste* (pp. 651–671). Elsevier. doi:10.1016/B978-0-12-815060-3.00033-5

van Belle, J. (2016). *Early Childhood Education and Care (ECEC) and its long-term effects on educational and labour market outcomes*. Rand Europe. doi:10.7249/RR1667

Van Hees, M. (1998). On the Analysis of Negative Freedom. *Theory and Decision*, *45*(3), 175–197. doi:10.1023/A:1004938512267

Van Zanden, J. (Eds.). (2014). *How Was Life?: Global Well-being since 1820*. OECD Publishing. doi:10.1787/9789264214262-en

Varvasovszky, Z., & Brugha, R. (2000). A stakeholder analysis. *Health Policy and Planning, 15*(3), 338–345. doi:10.1093/heapol/15.3.338 PMID:11012410

Vegliante, R., Miranda, S., & Santonicola, M. (2022). Le declinazioni pratico-operative della valutazione nella scuola primaria. In A. La Marca & A. Marzano (Eds.), *Ricerca didattica e formazione degli insegnanti per lo sviluppo delle Soft Skills* (pp. 685–696). Pensa MultiMedia.

Venkataraman, B. (2009). Education for Sustainable Development. *Environment, 51*(2), 8–10. doi:10.3200/ENVT.51.2.08-10

Versluis, E., van Asselt, M., & Kim, J. (2019). The multilevel regulation of complex policy problems: Uncertainty and the swine flu pandemic. *European Policy Analysis, 5*(1), 80–98. doi:10.1002/epa2.1064 PMID:34616904

Vigoda, E. (2002). From responsiveness to collaboration: Governance, citizens, and the next generation of public administration. *Public Administration Review, 62*(5), 527–540. doi:10.1111/1540-6210.00235

Vilas, C. (1995). *Between Earthquakes and Volcanoes: Markets, State, And the Revolutions in Central America*. Monthly Review Press.

Vlada. (2012, August 6). *Collapse of complex societies by Dr. Joseph Tainter* [Video]. YouTube. https://www.youtube.com/watch?v=G0R09YzyuCI

Voogt, J. M., Pieters, J. M., & Handelzalts, A. (2018). Teacher collaboration in curriculum design teams: Effects, mechanisms, and conditions. In *Teacher Learning Through Teacher Teams* (pp. 7–26). Routledge. doi:10.4324/9781315123431-2

Wada, K. (2015). *The Economic Impact of Population Decline and Aging in Japan: The Post-demographic Transition Phase*. Springer.

Wals, A. E. J., & Kieft, G. (2010). *Education for Sustainable Development*. Academic Press.

Waltner-Toews, D., Kay, J., Kay, J. J., & Lister, N. M. E. (Eds.). (2008). *The ecosystem approach: complexity, uncertainty, and managing for sustainability*. Columbia University Press.

Wan Ahmad, W. M., Hisham Hanifa, M., & Hyo, K. C. (2019). Are non-Muslims willing to patronize Islamic financial services? *Journal of Islamic Marketing, 10*(3), 743–758. doi:10.1108/JIMA-01-2017-0007

Ward, J., & Daniel, E. (2012). Benefits Management: How to increase the Business Value of Your IT Projects. John Wiley and Sons. doi:10.1002/9781119208242

Ward, J., & Daniel, E. (2013). How to deliver more business benefits from IT investments. *The European Financial Review*. http://www.europeanfinancialreview.com/?p=1033

Ward, J., & Elvin, R. (1999). A new framework for managing IT-enabled business change. *Information Systems Journal, 9*(3), 197–221. doi:10.1046/j.1365-2575.1999.00059.x

Ward, J., Taylor, P., & Bond, P. (1996). Evaluation and realisation of IS/IT benefits: An empirical study of current practice. *European Journal of Information Systems, 4*(4), 214–225. doi:10.1057/ejis.1996.3

Waugh, W. L., & Streib, G. (2006). Collaboration and leadership for effective emergency management. *Public Administration Review, 66*(s1), 131–140. doi:10.1111/j.1540-6210.2006.00673.x

Wawasan 2035. (n.d.). *Wawasan Brunei 2035—Our Vision For 2035*. Retrieved 17 November 2022, from https://www.wawasanbrunei.gov.bn/SitePages/Our%20Vision%20For%202035.aspx

Wawasan Brunei. (2019). *Wawasan Brunei 2035*. https://www.wawasanbrunei.gov.bn/en/SitePages/wawasan-brunei-2035.aspx

Weber, E., & Khademian, A. M. (2008). Managing collaborative processes: Common practices, uncommon circumstances. *Administration & Society*, *40*(5), 431–464. doi:10.1177/0095399708320181

Wedel, J. R. (2012). Rethinking corruption in an age of ambiguity. *Annual Review of Law and Social Science*, *8*(1), 453–498. doi:10.1146/annurev.lawsocsci.093008.131558

Weimer, D., & Vining, A. (1999). *Policy Analysis: Concepts and Practice*. Prentice Hall.

Weisburd, D., Hinkle, J., Braga, A., & Wooditch, A. (2015). Understanding the mechanisms of underlying broken windows policing: The need for evaluation evidence. *Journal of Research in Crime and Delinquency*, *52*(4), 589–608. doi:10.1177/0022427815577837

Weiss, C. H. (1993). Where politics and evaluation research meet. *Evaluation Practice*, *14*(1), 93–106. doi:10.1177/109821409301400119

Weiss, C. H. (1998). *Evaluation*. Prentice Hall.

Welsh, B., Braga, A., & Bruinsma, G. (2015). Reimagining broken windows: From theory to policy. *Journal of Research in Crime and Delinquency*, *52*(4), 447–463. doi:10.1177/0022427815581399

Wenzelburger, G., König, P. D., & Wolf, F. (2019). Policy theories in hard times? Assessing the explanatory power of policy theories in the context of crisis. *Public Organization Review*, *19*(1), 97–118. doi:10.100711115-017-0387-1

Whisman, M. A., Li, A., Sbarra, D. A., & Raison, C. L. (2014). Marital quality and diabetes: Results from the Health and Retirement Study. *Health Psychology*, *33*(8), 832–840. doi:10.1037/hea0000064 PMID:25068454

White, P., & Mitchelmore, M. C. (2010). Teaching for abstraction: A model. *Mathematical Thinking and Learning*, *12*(3), 205–226. doi:10.1080/10986061003717476

Why is waste management important? (2019). *Science Park*. https://sciencepark.com.ph/blog/waste-management-important/

Wibowo, M. W., & Ahmad, F. S. (2016). Non-Muslim consumers' halal food product acceptance model. *Procedia Economics and Finance*, *37*, 276–283. doi:10.1016/S2212-5671(16)30125-3

Wijesinghe, R., Scheepers, H., & Mcloughlin, S. (2015). *Defining the optimal level of business benefits within IS/IT projects: Insights from benefit identification practices adopted in an IT Service Management (ITSM) project*. In the 6th Australasian Conference on Information Systems, Adelaide, Australia.

Wiktor-Mach, D. (2020). What role for culture in the age of sustainable development? UNESCO's advocacy in the 2030 Agenda negotiations. *International Journal of Cultural Policy*, *26*(3), 312–327. doi:10.1080/10286632.2018.1534841

Wilkins, S., Butt, M. M., Shams, F., & Pérez, A. (2019). The acceptance of halal food in non-Muslim countries: Effects of religious identity, national identification, consumer ethnocentrism and consumer cosmopolitanism. *Journal of Islamic Marketing*, *10*(4), 1308–1331. doi:10.1108/JIMA-11-2017-0132

Williams, J., Robinson, C., & Bouzarovski, S. (2020). China's Belt and Road Initiative and the emerging geographies of global urbanisation. *The Geographical Journal*, *186*(1), 128–140. doi:10.1111/geoj.12332

Williams, R., Karuranga, S., Malanda, B., Saeedi, P., Basit, A., Besançon, S., Bommer, C., Esteghamati, A., Ogurtsova, K., Zhang, P., & Colagiuri, S. (2020). Global and regional estimates and projections of diabetes-related health expenditure: Results from the International Diabetes Federation Diabetes Atlas. *Diabetes Research and Clinical Practice*, *162*, 108072. doi:10.1016/j.diabres.2020.108072 PMID:32061820

Winch, G. M. (2007). *Managing project stakeholders. The Wiley Guide to Project, Program, and Portfolio Management*. Wiley.

Winkler, K., Fuchs, R., Rounsevell, M., & Herold, M. (2022, May). Global land use changes are four times greater than previously estimated. *Nature Communications*. https://www.nature.com/articles/s41467-021-22702-2

Winter, M., Smith, C., Morris, P., & Cicmil, S. (2006). Directions for future research in project management: The main findings of a UK government-funded research network. *International Journal of Project Management*, *24*(8), 638–649. doi:10.1016/j.ijproman.2006.08.009

Wolf, A. (2019). The myth of stability in Algeria. *Journal of North African Studies*, *24*(5), 707–712. doi:10.1080/13629387.2019.1647899

Woodrow, D., Verma, G. K., Rocha-Trindade, M. B., Campani, G., & Bagley, C. (Eds.). (2019). *Intercultural Education: Theories, Policies and Practice*. Routledge. doi:10.4324/9780429024047

World Bank. (2022). *World Development Report 2022: Finance for an equitable recovery*. The World Bank.

World Commission for Environment and Development. (1987). *Our Common Future*. Oxford University Press.

World Economic Forum. (2020). *What is green finance and why is it important?* https://www.weforum.org/agenda/2020/11/what-is-green-finance/

World-Nuclear.org. (2021). *Nuclear Powered Ships/* World-Nuclear.org. https://world-nuclear.org/information-library/non-power-nuclear-applications/transport/nuclear-powered-ships.aspx (accessed August 3, 2022).

Wright, G. B. (2011). Student-Centered Learning in Higher Education. *International Journal on Teaching and Learning in Higher Education*, *23*(3), 93–94. www.arabic-teacher.com

Wu, F. (2023). Theorising urban development in China: 'State entrepreneurialism' from the ground up. *Dialogues in Human Geography*, *0*(0), 1–5. doi:10.1177/20438206231174638

Wu, W., Wang, L., Erzurumlu, Y. Ö., Gozgor, G., & Yang, G. (2022). Effects of Country and Geopolitical Risks on Income Inequality: Evidence from Emerging Economies. *Emerging Markets Finance & Trade*, *58*(15), 4218–4230. doi:10.1080/1540496X.2022.2070002

Wu, Y., & Yao, H. (2015). Income Inequality, State Ownership, and the Pattern of Economic Growth – A Tale of the Kuznets Curve for China since 1978. *Atlantic Economic Journal*, *43*(2), 165–180. doi:10.100711293-015-9451-9

Wyatt, D. (2020). *The Anaemic Existence of the Overriding Public Interest in Disclosure in the EU's Access to Documents Regime*. Cambridge University Press.

Yang, S., Zhao, W., Liu, Y., Cherubini, F., Fu, B., & Pereira, P. (2020). Prioritizing sustainable development goals and linking them to ecosystem services: A global expert's knowledge evaluation. *Geography and Sustainability*, *1*(4), 321–330. doi:10.1016/j.geosus.2020.09.004

Yaro, I., Arshad, R., & Salleh, D. (2017). Relevance of stakeholders in policy implementation. *Journal of Public Management Research*, *3*(1), 25–2. doi:10.5296/jpmr.v3i1.10632

Yasin, A. (2018). *Tafsir Surah Al-Isra': Ayat 26-30* [Video]. YouTube. https://www.youtube.com/watch?v=A4aPvT-MikA&t=513s

Ye, C., Li, S., Zhuang, L., & Zhu, X. (2020). A comparison and case analysis between domestic and overseas industrial parks of China since the Belt and Road Initiative. *Journal of Geographical Sciences*, *30*(8), 1266–1282. doi:10.100711442-020-1781-0

Yi, L., Chen, W., & Wu, F. (2023). Building Chinese city regions under state entrepreneurialism. *Territory, Politics, Governance*, 1–18. Advance online publication. doi:10.1080/21622671.2023.2206430

Yin, R. K. (2009). Case Study Research: Design and Methods, Cap 4- 6, (4th Ed.) Thousand Oaks: Sage.

Yin, W. (2019). Integrating sustainable development goals into the belt and road initiative: Would it be a new model for green and sustainable investment? *Sustainability (Basel)*, *11*(24), 6991. doi:10.3390u11246991

Yong, G. Y. V. (2010). Brunei (Negara Brunei Darussalam). In E. C. F. Bird (Ed.), *Encyclopedia of the World's Coastal Landforms* (pp. 1141–1144). Springer. doi:10.1007/978-1-4020-8639-7_211

Yong, G. Y. V. (2021). Identifying Cultural Traits of the Historic Kampong Ayer of Brunei Darussalam using Biomimetic Analysis. *International Journal of Environment, Architecture, and Societies*, *1*(2), 83–94. doi:10.26418/ijeas.2021.1.02.83-94

Yong, G. Y. V. (2022). Climate-Resilient Urban Design from Biomimicry-Arcology Perspective. *International Journal of Environment, Architecture, and Societies*, *2*(1), 1–15. doi:10.26418/ijeas.2022.2.01.1-15

Young, R. J. C. (2020). *Postcolonialism. A very short introduction*. Oxford University Press. doi:10.1093/actrade/9780198856832.001.0001

Yu, T. (2001). Towards the theory of the entrepreneurial state. *International Journal of Social Economics*, *28*(9), 752–766. doi:10.1108/EUM0000000005692

Zahariadis, N. (2007). The multiple streams framework: Structure, limitations, prospects. In P. A. Sabatier (Ed.), *Theories of the policy process*. Westview Press.

Zandi, G., Rehan, R., Hye, Q., Mubeen, S., & Abbas, S. (2022). Do Corruption, Inflation and Unemployment Influence the Income Inequality of Developing Asian Countries? *International Journal of Applied Economics. Finance and Accounting*, *14*(2), 118–128.

Zavadskas, E. K., Turskis, Z., & Vilutiene, T. (2010). Multiple Criteria Analysis of Foundation Instalment Alternatives by Applying Additive Ratio Assessment (ARAS) method. *Archives of Civil and Mechanical Engineering*, *X*(3), 123–141. doi:10.1016/S1644-9665(12)60141-1

Zavadskas, E., & Turskis, Z. (2010). A New Additive Ratio Assessment (ARAS) Method in Multicriteria Decision-Making. *Technological and Economic Development of Economy*, *16*(2), 159–172. doi:10.3846/tede.2010.10

Zguir, M. F., Dubis, S., & Koç, M. (2021). Embedding Education for Sustainable Development (ESD) and SDGs values in curriculum: A comparative review on Qatar, Singapore and New Zealand. *Journal of Cleaner Production*, *319*, 128534. doi:10.1016/j.jclepro.2021.128534

Zhang, F., Yu, M., Yu, J., & Jin, Y. (2017). The effect of RMB internationalization on belt and road initiative: Evidence from bilateral swap agreements. *Emerging Markets Finance & Trade*, *53*(12), 2845–2857. doi:10.1080/1540496X.2017.1382346

Zhang, L. (2006). Market socialism revisited: The case of Chinese state-owned enterprises. *Issues & Studies*, *42*(3), 1–46.

Zhang, L. (2013). Dynamics and constraints of State-led global city formation in emerging economies: The case of Shanghai. *Urban Studies (Edinburgh, Scotland)*, *51*(6), 1162–1178. doi:10.1177/0042098013495577

Zhuang, Y., Yang, S., Razzaq, A., & Khan, Z. (2022). Environmental impact of infrastructure-led Chinese outward FDI, tourism development and technology innovation: A regional country analysis. *Journal of Environmental Planning and Management*, *66*(2), 367–399. doi:10.1080/09640568.2021.1989672

Zreik, M. (2021a). The Potential of a Sino-Lebanese Partnership through the Belt and Road Initiative (BRI). *Contemporary Arab Affairs, 14*(3), 125–145. doi:10.1525/caa.2021.14.3.125

Zreik, M. (2021b). Academic Exchange Programs between China and the Arab Region: A Means of Cultural Harmony or Indirect Chinese Influence? *Arab Studies Quarterly, 43*(2). Advance online publication. doi:10.13169/arabstudquar.43.2.0172

Zreik, M. (2023). Analytical study on Foreign Direct Investment Divestment Inflows and Outflows in Developing Economies: Evidence of China. *Chinese Economy*, 1–16. doi:10.1080/10971475.2023.2193118

Zreik, M., Iqbal, B. A., & Rahman, M. N. (2022). Outward FDI: Determinants and Flows in Emerging Economies: Evidence from China. *China and WTO Review, 8*(2), 385–402. doi:10.14330/cwr.2022.8.2.07

Zulch, B. (2014). Leadership communication in project management. *Procedia: Social and Behavioral Sciences, 119*, 172–181. doi:10.1016/j.sbspro.2014.03.021

About the Contributors

Mahani Hamdan is Senior Assistant Professor in Accounting and Finance at UBD School of Business and Economics, and also serves as Director for the Institute of Policy Studies and Institute for Leadership, Innovation and Advancement, Universiti Brunei Darussalam (UBD). She obtained her first degree in Accounting and Financial Management from the University of Sheffield; a Master degree with distinction from the University of Leeds; and PhD from Queensland University of Technology in the field of organisational management and psychology. She learned about public policies, governance and politics during her post-doctoral period at Goldman School of Public Policy, University of California, Berkeley, through the Independent Leader Scholar Programme. Her current research interests are in the areas of accounting for non-public interest entities, operational excellence, leadership, public finance and governance. She is the co-author of Brunei Darussalam: Making Strides with a Renewed Focus on the Future for Southeast Asian Affairs 2019, and co-editor of Stability, Growth and Sustainability: Catalysts for Socio-economic Development in Brunei Darussalam in 2023 published by ISEAS-Yusof Ishak Institute. Besides teaching, research, and administrative services in UBD, she is also a member of Brunei Darussalam Accounting Standards Council and Income Tax Board of Review.

Muhammad Anshari has been named on the Stanford University List of Top 2% World Researchers in 2022 for the categories of ICT, Business & Management. Currently, he serves as Deputy Director Institute of Policy Studies and Academic Staff at School of Business & Economics, Universiti Brunei Darussalam. His professional experience started when he was IT Business Analyst at Astra International. Research Fellowship from The Government Republic of China (Taiwan) at National Taiwan University (Jan-Dec, 2014). Research Fellowship from King Saud University - the Kingdom of Saudi Arabia 2009. Senior Associate Researcher of Informatics Department, Universitas Islam Negeri Yogyakarta, Indonesia.

Emil Zahrin Haji Ali graduated from the University of Loughborough, United Kingdom with a BSc (Hons) in Business Economics and Finance (2006) and started his working career as an Education Officer. With a keen interest in doing research as well as teaching higher institutions, he moved to Universiti Brunei Darussalam as a Tutor in 2007. He went to study abroad that same year and completed his Master in Public Administration (MPA) with distinction from the University of York, United Kingdom. In June 2009, he was appointed as a Lecturer in the Universiti Brunei Darussalam School of Business and Economics (UBDSBE) where he teaches a range of modules including public organizations, public budgeting and finance, strategic public management, public management, public finance and the economic aspects of public policy. He is interested in the areas of public sector finance including (but not limited to) financing public goods and services, welfare spending, privatisation and public private partnership.

Norainie Ahmad works for the Institute of Policy Studies at the University of Brunei Darussalam. Her research areas include Social Policy; Family Demography; Women's Studies and Gender; Public Policy & Policy Analysis. She has been affiliated with St. Cross College, Oxford University, Oxford Institute of Population Ageing, and the Sociology Department at Oxford University.

Emil Ali is a lecturer and researcher at the Institute of Policy Studies (IPS), Universiti Brunei Darussalam. Prior to this, he started his career as an Education Officer working with the Ministry of Education. He obtained his first degree in Business Economics and Finance from the University of Loughborough; and his Master's degree in Public Administration (MPA) with distinction from the University of York, United Kingdom. His research interests are in the areas of public-sector finance with a special interest in Public-Private Partnerships. His recent publications include "Public Private Partnerships in Small States: The Case of Brunei Darussalam"; "COVID-19, Artificial Intelligence, Ethical Challenges and Policy Implications". AI & Soc. He currently works on his PhD research with a topic on "Evaluating Risk in the Management of UK Waste Public-Private Partnerships."

Hapini Awang possesses over a decade of experience across various educational roles, including as a school teacher and education officer. Currently focusing on Information Systems (IS), his research interests encompass e-learning, virtual learning environments, ICT in education, and instructional technology. He holds a Ph.D. in Information Systems from Universiti Utara Malaysia (2019) and has been recognized with awards such as Hadiah Latihan Persekutuan (HLP) in 2015 and Anugerah Perkhidmatan Cemerlang (APC) in 2012 from the Ministry of Education. As an active member of the Association of Information Systems, Malaysian Chapter (MyAIS), Hapini engages with the Pacific Asia Conference of Information Systems (PACIS) since 2017 and serves as a reviewer and editorial board member for several conferences and journals.

Fathin Awang Mat Japar is a graduate researcher at Universiti Brunei Darussalam. Fathin holds a Bachelor's degree in Environmental Studies from Universiti Brunei Darussalam and leverages her academic foundation to delve into the complexities of Waste Management. With a year of hands-on experience gained at a local recycling centre as a Project Officer, Fathin's research pursuits are driven by her desire to humbly contribute to the intricate Islamic system of Governance, focusing on sustainability elements and values derived from the Qur'ān and Sunnah pertaining to waste management. She is the appointed Youth Ambassador of Climate Change to TotalEnergies Brunei and a certified Climate Fresk facilitator.

Abderrahmane Benlahcene is a senior lecturer at the School of Government, Universiti Utara Malaysia. He obtained his bachelor's degree in Management Science from the University of Batna, Algeria, his Master's degree in Public Management from Universiti Utara Malaysia, and his PhD in the field of Public Management from School of Government, Universiti Utara Malaysia. His research interests are in the areas of organizational behaviour in public organisations with a special focus on unethical leadership behaviour. Other research interests include government-citizen communication and the role of civil society in anti-corruption efforts in developing countries.

Marisa Cleveland with more than two decades in the education and publishing industries, Dr. Marisa Cleveland is adamant about supporting efforts toward the betterment of the human condition. Cleveland is the executive director for The Seymour Agency, a trustee for Hodges University Board of Trustees, and co-author of the leadership book, There Is No Box. Cleveland holds an Ed.D. in Organizational Leadership from Northeastern University, and an M.A. in Educational Administration and a B.A. in Speech Communication from George Mason University.

Simon Cleveland is a professor of project management at Purdue University Global. Dr. Cleveland is a graduate of George Mason University and The George Washington University, with Bachelor of Science degree in Business and a Master of Science degree in Project Management respectively, and has a Ph.D. in Information Systems from Nova Southeastern University and an Ed.D. in Organizational Leadership from Northeastern University. He is also certified as a project management professional (PMP), Six Sigma Black Belt (SSBB) expert, and Information Technology Infrastructure Library (ITIL) foundations expert. Dr. Cleveland is the author of over 50 peer-reviewed publications in journals and conferences, and is a three-time recipient of the prestigious Dr. Harold Kerzner Scholarship which is awarded by the Project Management Institute Educational Foundation. Professionally, Dr. Cleveland has worked as both technology manager, program manager and PMO Director for organizations such as MD Anderson Cancer Center, Department of Homeland Security, NASA, Accenture, and AOL.

Teresa Fernandes works in the Portuguese Public Administration, where she has been developing her career in the implementation of IS/IT solutions. She holds a master degree in IS/IT Management from ISEG, University of Lisbon.

Valerio Ferrero is a PhD fellow in Education at University of Turin. He works on intercultural education. His research themes are equity in education and non-traditional factors of inequality, democratic schooling and education policy, Philosophy for Children. He is author of various essays on his research topics.

Nurul Izaah Ghozali Nurul's academic journey began with a Diploma in Syariah 2019, sparking her passion for Islamic studies. She also obtained a bachelor's degree in Islamic Studies in 2022 which deepened her understanding. She will complete a master's degree in Islamic Studies in 2023. She held different roles as a research assistant for SDGSJR and ERASMUS+, and collaborated with international scholars. She is currently a research assistant at the IASDO Universiti Utara Malaysia. Her future research interests are geared towards the field of Islamic studies and exploring innovative solutions to issues related to global Muslim communities.

Jorge Gomes is a researcher at ADVANCE, ISEG, School of Economics & Management of the Universidade de Lisboa. He holds a PhD in Management from ISEG and a Masters in Management Sciences from ISCTE-IUL, He also have a post-graduation in Project Management from INDEG/ISCTE, and a degree in Geographic Engineering from the Faculty of Sciences of the Universidade de Lisboa. During the past 30 years, he has worked as an engineer, project manager, quality auditor and consultant. Teaches Management at ULHT, Lisboa. His research interests include Benefits Management, Project Management, Project Success, Maturity Models, IS/IT Investments, IS/IT in Healthcare and IS/IT Management.

Noor Hasharina Hassan is a Senior Assistant Professor in the Geography, Environment & Development Programme at the Faculty of Arts and Social Sciences, Universiti Brunei Darussalam (UBD). She obtained her MA and Ph.D. in Geography from the University of Southampton specializing in Urban

Economy and Culture. Her research began with a focus on sustainable urban development particularly looking at the financial regulations, urban consumption, and social sustainability of the urban dwellers in Brunei. She has subsequently expanded her urban sustainability research into social welfare including poverty and housing. Her latest work focuses on the resiliency of vulnerable urban communities, their adaptation capabilities, and their relationship with their environment.

Antje Ilberg is an architect (MSc equiv.), urban planner (Doctorate and MA), and LLM in environmental law (EU, UK and International), providing advisory services to governments and institutions in policy and strategy development, urban governance, institution building, and policy and project implementation. Bridging from analysis to practical solutions, she is concerned with the mitigation of climate risks and vulnerabilities and of biodiversity decline.

Betül İnam is an Assistant Professor at Bilecik Seyh Edebali University. She got her Bachelor's degree in Public Finance from Bursa Uludag University, Faculty of Economics and Administrative Sciences in 2004. She had worked in the banking and finance sector between 2005-2009. Then in 2012 she started to work as a research assistant at Bursa Uludag University. She received a Ph.D. degree at the same university in 2019. She has several papers published in various academic journals in English and in Turkish on her primary research interests, which are including income inequalities, public expenditures, and tax policies.

Hazik Mohamed is a business strategist with substantial market research, operational management and start-up experience. He consults for MSMEs and MNCs on various business-related issues including market penetration, operational process trouble-shooting, investment management, and strategic execution. Specialized PhD in behavioral research and analysis using game theory in view of conventional and Islamic economics perspectives. Its applications include understanding consumer/user behavior and viral marketing strategies as well as policy formulation and regulatory implementation through effective low-cost behavioral interventions. Other interests include region-wide strategic planning as well as implementation of innovative, disruptive and scalable technologies.

Dilek Murat is an Associate Professor at Bursa Uludag University. She got her Bachelor's degree in Econometrics from Uludağ University, Faculty of Economics and Administrative Sciences in 2003. Then, her Ph.D. degree after finishing the Bursa Uludag University, Institute of Social Sciences, Program of Econometrics in 2013. She has several studies and papers published in various academic journals in English and in Turkish on her primary research interests, which are including multi criteria decision making, multivariate statistics, and design of experiments

Izni Azrein Noor Azalie is a human geographer who graduated with an MSc in Global Transformations from Loughborough University UK and is currently in the final stages of his PhD at University College London, researching halal industrial governing and its effects on Brunei agri-food producers. He did professional consultancies involving environmental and communal advisories relating to oil and gas explorations, environmental monitoring, and impact assessments on urban development projects and the socio-economic costs of industrial development for communities in Brunei Darussalam. His specialization covers industrial networks of production, urban economic growth, and industrial development, specifically, which falls under the general theme on Urban and Cultural Economy. He was involved in poverty and poverty alleviation studies in the former city centre of the Bruneian Sultanate, Kampong Ayer which concluded in 2022. His current research is on understanding the dynamics between a place's genus loci (both cultural and economic attributes/ networks) and urban plan construction for one of the earliest places to be urbanized in Brunei, the Menglait Gadong area. Between 2021 and the present, he is also involved in research involving Brunei's rising coffee and tea sector. He teaches modules under the Geography, Environment and Development (GED) Programme, mainly on urban/ cultural economy, industrial governing and development as well as people, places and cultures.

Peterson Ozili is an Economist.

Mário José Batista Romão is an Associate Professor of Information Systems at ISEG – University of Lisbon. He is Director of the Master's program in Computer Science and Management. He holds a PhD in Management Sciences by ISCTE-IUL and by Computer Integrated Manufacturing at Cranfield University (UK). He also holds a MsC in Telecommunications and Computer Science, at IST - Instituto Superior Técnico, University of Lisbon. He is Pos-Graduated in Project Management and holds the international certification Project Management Professional (PMP), by PMI – Project Management International. He has a degree in Electrotecnic Engineer by IST.

Ahmad-Labeeb Tajudeen is an Associate Professor of Islamic Studies at the College of Islamic Studies, Islamic University of Minnesota, Bloomington, USA. He is also an adjunct Associate Professor of Arabic Applied Linguistics and Arabic Grammer at the Faculty of Languages, Al-Madinah International University, Kuala Lumpur, Malaysia. He is a researcher (on contract) for the Saudi Ministry of Foreign Affairs through its Embassy in Bandar Seri Begawan, Brunei Darussalam.

Gabriel Yong has a BSc (hon) Geol. Geophysics, Reading UK, 1986 MSc Environmental Analysis & Dynamics, Hull UK, 1999 Lecturer at Universiti Brunei Darussalam since 1999. Area of specialisation: Environment of Brunei, Environmental Systems, EIA, Integrated Coastal Management, Biomimicry

Mohamad Zreik is a recognized scholar in International Relations, specializing in China's Arab-region foreign policy. His extensive knowledge spans Middle Eastern Studies, China-Arab relations, East Asian and Asian Affairs, Eurasian geopolitics, and Political Economy, providing him a unique viewpoint in his field. Dr. Zreik is a proud recipient of a PhD from Central China Normal University (Wuhan). He's written numerous acclaimed papers, many focusing on China's Belt and Road Initiative and its Arab-region impact. His groundbreaking research has established him as a leading expert in his field. His significant contributions make him a crucial figure in understanding contemporary international relations.

Index

www.ingramcontent.com/pod-product-compliance
Lightning Source LLC
LaVergne TN
LVHW081250011026
849162LV00006BA/1367